*The Way to*

# VOCABULARY POWER
# AND CULTURE

# The Way to

# VOCABULARY POWER
# AND CULTURE

*by*

WILFRED FUNK, Litt.D.

*Author of "The Merry-go-round Breaks Down," "So You Think It's New,"
and other books, and co-author of "Thirty Days to a
More Powerful Vocabulary"*

WILFRED FUNK, INC.

*Publishers*                                      *New York*

Published February, 1946
Second Printing, April, 1946
Third Printing, July, 1946
Fourth Printing, November, 1946
Fifth Printing, May, 1947
Sixth Printing, November, 1948

PRINTED IN THE UNITED STATES OF AMERICA
BY J. J. LITTLE & IVES COMPANY, NEW YORK

*To*

MY FRIEND AND ASSOCIATE

DOUGLAS E. LURTON

# ACKNOWLEDGMENTS

THE DEBT that an author owes to those who have helped him holds little interest for the public, but the author himself would be both ungracious and unhappy unless he made full acknowledgment of his obligations.

I must express my deepest gratitude first to Douglas E. Lurton for his many creative suggestions, for his continuing advice and for the professional editorial supervision that he gave to these pages: to Constance Stark who was at all times my right hand, and who contributed over a period of two years a vast amount of expert research to this volume: to Dr. Charles Earle Funk, the eminent lexicographer, who gave me his practiced and scholarly aid in pronunciations and definitions, and helped me with his critical judgment on other parts of the manuscript: to Dr. Robert H. Seashore of Northwestern University, upon whose able pioneer work I leaned so heavily in preparing the vocabulary tests: and to a host of associates and friends who have served as patient listeners and sacrificial guinea pigs.

I also want to thank Funk & Wagnalls Company who granted me permission to base such definitions as are given in this volume upon the copyrighted definitions that appear in the New Unabridged Standard Dictionary, 1940 Edition; and the Reader's Digest for permission to reprint several items.

# CONTENTS

# PRONUNCIATION KEY

ONLY THE chief differences in vowel sounds are indicated in this book, for the intent of this volume is simplicity and the aim has been to make all of the key words as nearly as possible self-pronouncing. In a few cases more than one pronunciation of a word is acceptable. The pronunciation that appears in this volume is usually the one favored by most of the leading dictionaries.

### ACCENTS

Primary accents are marked ′          Secondary accents are marked ″

### VOWELS

The long vowels, marked by a straight line (macron) above, have the same sound as the actual letter.

| | | | |
|---|---|---|---|
| ā, āy | sounded as in | | lāte, lāy |
| ē, ee | " | " " | ēve, bee |
| ī | " | " " | fīne |
| ō | " | " " | tōne |
| ū, yū | " | " " | pūre (or few) |
| o͞o | " | " " | fo͞od |

Vowels not marked at all are sounded like those usually taught in classes learning to read phonetically, as in hat, bed, did, lot, cut.

Short vowels are marked with a breve above to show that they are almost equivalent to an apostrophe.

| | | | |
|---|---|---|---|
| ă | sounded as in | | fī′năl |
| ĕ | " | " " | hov′ĕl |
| ĭ | " | " " | em′ĭ grănt |
| ŏ | " | " " | fŏr bid′ |
| ŭ | " | " " | mī′nŭs |

Other sounds indicated are:
*ah* for *a*, as in father (fah′ther)
*a(h)* for *a* whenever it occurs in words where usage permits it to be pro-
    nounced correctly in two ways. The word ask, for instance, will be
    respelled a(h)sk for purposes of pronunciation, since the *a* can be
    pronounced either as the *a* in hat, or the *a* in father.
*aw* for the sound of *a*, as in ball (bawl)
*uh* for an *a* that is so short that it is neutral, as in about (uh bout′)
*ow* or *ou* for *ou*, as in out (owt)
*o͞o* sounded as in fo͞ot is halfway between but and boot

## CONSONANTS

*hw* gives the sound for *wh*, as in when (hwen)

*kw* " " " " *qu*, as in quite (kwite)

*zh* " " " " *s* or *z* in such words as azure (azh′ur), treasure (trezh′ur)

*k* gives the hard sound of *ch*, as in chasm (kas″m), chorus (kō′rŭs)

*g* gives the hard sound of *g*, as in give

## FOREIGN WORDS

*n* in French words is almost like *ng* but the *g* is only half sounded.   This is indicated by a capital *N* in the pronunciation.

*oe* in French and *ö* in German resemble a very, very short *er*, or a short neutral *uh* sound.

*u* in French and *ü* in German are something like *ew* in few and sounded with the lips drawn together in a tiny circle.

*The Way to*

# VOCABULARY POWER
# AND CULTURE

# CHAPTER I

## WHAT A LARGER VOCABULARY WILL DO
## FOR YOU

A RICH VOCABULARY is the most common and invaluable possession of the leaders in every profession, in every commercial enterprise, and in every department of active living.

Repeated surveys have shown that the managing heads of successful organizations, whether of laundries, labor unions, or universities, as a rule possess superior vocabularies that are much larger than the average vocabularies of the assistants and clerks whom they supervise.

If we were to examine the men and the women who make up the personnel of any given business enterprise, we should find what all expert investigators have found: We should discover that, while these employees had a host of traits between them in common, they would differ radically in their knowledge of words, and the proportionate size of the vocabulary of each man and each woman would reflect, often with astonishing accuracy, the position that he or she held in the organization. Vocabulary is so intimately tied up with success that from now on we might as well talk of the two as though they were one and the same thing. It is hoped that this book may offer to the reader a pleasant and profitable plan for acquiring this all-important vocabulary of power, culture and high utility.

### HOW VOCABULARY BUILDING BRINGS GREATER SUCCESS

The close correlation between success and vocabulary is a new and startling discovery that offers to you an opportunity to gain more success and more influence for yourself in whatever field of activity you have chosen.

Of course, there should be no great mystery about the power and culture that attend a large vocabulary. You know how you

1

are influenced by the words of others and how you in turn can influence others with your own words. You know that you write with words; that you understand with them; that they are your communications system with the outside world. You realize that, when you are thinking, you are merely talking to yourself and that the words you happen to know are the instruments with which you reason. Each new word you learn represents a new angle to an idea, a particular facet. Therefore, the more words you know the more powerfully you can think and the more forcefully you can present your ideas. Conversely, the more words you *don't* know the more you are handicapped. *You can neither write, nor speak, nor even think with words you don't know.*

### HOW TO WIN YOUR WAY WITH WORDS

It is possible, for instance, that a man may develop an idea that could gain him advancement in his own career or that might even be worth a fortune, but unless he has the words, the tools of thought, with which to work the idea out in detail in his own mind, and unless he has the tools of speech or of writing to project it clearly and with little loss upon the minds of other men, he may never be able to sell his idea.

Your language—your vocabulary—is your projection lens, and, unless it is accurately ground and polished, the picture of your idea that you throw on the minds of others will be out of focus and wholly distorted. That is, your plan, no matter how worth while it is, may be a failure.

You have heard a person say: "I know exactly what I mean but I can't quite explain it to you." If he can't explain it to you, the idea in his own mind is still foggy. *He hasn't as yet been able even to explain it to himself.*

The able leaders in this world of ours never allow themselves to be held up by this stammering incompetence. They have developed a mastery of English that gives them the clarity of thought and the eloquence of expression that always go hand in hand with leadership.

There is one brilliant and historic example of this power that is still sharp in the memories of all living men. It was after the epic of Dunkirk, when England, disarmed and prostrate, was awaiting invasion. At that moment the only shield and the only weapons that democracy had against disaster were the words of Winston Churchill.

"The man," says the political writer, Dorothy Thompson, "the man with nothing but words—words gushing from the deepest springs of our glorious language, words of faith, fortitude, memory, hope, pride, humility, broke the frozen paralysis of a people and stood them on their feet, while the young, anonymous eagles of the air beat off the threat to civilization."

## WORDS WILL GIVE YOU POWER

Yes, words are mighty instruments of power. They are the greatest force put in the hands of man. They serve us in times of crisis. They can serve us, too, in the more humble processes of our daily life. They can be made your slaves. And mine. And while a study of them may not be the only way to open the door to opportunity, it is still the quickest and the easiest way.

At this point you might reasonably ask, "Are words themselves so important? Doesn't it depend largely on how you use them?"

You are partly right. If you can use these words aptly after you have learned them; if you are a phrase maker, that is, and can work them, like a Winston Churchill, into telling sentences, so much the better. But never forget this. It has been proved again and again that if you will merely add new words to your vocabulary, and do nothing else, this simple act in itself will enrich your mind, enlarge your intellectual capacity, increase your self-confidence, and will help you make more money, gain social acceptance and achieve greater influence and prominence in your own community.

Let us be sure that we are clear about this business of words and their peculiar importance to you.

Success in life is, of course, made up of many elements besides a knowledge of words. That is just common sense. The fact that you and the man working beside you may know the same number of words doesn't necessarily mean that he is as able as you are. You may have qualities of mind and character that he never will possess. Nevertheless, if you and he increase your arsenals of words, I can promise you with mathematical certainty that you will both go higher up whatever ladder you are trying to climb.

## ARE YOU A VOCABULARY CRIPPLE?

It is because vocabulary is such a good index of the mind that word tests are being used more and more in colleges, and also by the employment heads in industrial institutions as measures of ability and intelligence. And further than this, practical army officers tell me that they judge the officer capacity of a candidate largely by his vocabulary rating. I have before me, for example, a form letter from a major in aviation, who says, "After giving our mental screening test to hundreds of young men, both high school and college students, I find the greatest deficiency is a limited vocabulary and a lack of precision and exactitude in the use of words." And, as one educator comments, "If students do not know the meanings of words they cannot receive any further education conveyed in words. *If they cannot use words precisely, they cannot think precisely.*"

In an average and normal day, if you are an articulate person, you will talk an estimated 30,000 words, and these words will reveal *you* to your listener—your mental processes, your character, your ability, your personality. Then how important it is to be sure that your conversation is revealing the *real* you—the "you" that will gain the respect of others.

Like it or not, there is class distinction in language. As soon as we speak, strangers begin to classify us, and, if our vocabularies are hackneyed and humdrum they will receive the impression of colorless and commonplace personalities. If our vocabularies are poor, they may come to the conclusion that we are lacking in intelligence.

A man may be ever so well-groomed, be good looking, and have all the outward appearance of good breeding and fine intellect, but if he misuses words, if he misspells them, and if he is deficient in the fine art of pronunciation, he is advertising to all who hear him that his early education has been limited and that he is not accustomed to the society of cultured people. And he is also publishing abroad the fact that he has been too lazy or too careless to do anything about it.

It is so unnecessary to put oneself in this position, particularly now that modern methods have made it so simple and so easy to correct and to cure these faults.

### THE MAGIC KEY TO A MORE POWERFUL VOCABULARY

But remember that a powerful or a cultured vocabulary comes to you neither by invitation, by birth, nor by wishful thinking. In the middle twenties a person's word development has already virtually stopped growing, and from then on it is necessary to make a slight but conscious daily effort to improve it. If *you* will make this effort in your own behalf you will not only find your vocabulary expanding week by week, but you will also be on your way to revolutionizing every department of your life.

I sincerely hope that you will use this book as an instrument to gain these advantages for yourself. You can do it so easily. And the rewards that you are sure to receive will astonish you. But before you begin, I want to tell you why these pages were written.

For years I have given vocabulary tests to young men. I have found that those who had a high rating usually won executive positions in later life. Those who proved poor in words almost always had to resign themselves to mediocrity. I went beyond this and examined the vocabularies of older men who had won a measure of profit and prestige in the world. I discovered that even those who were without early education, former truck-drivers and stevedores and the like, had somehow gained for themselves an amazing vocabulary.

### HERE ARE YOUR WORDS OF POWER AND CULTURE

I began to watch the words that men and women of standing used; made lists of them; studied them. These magic words of culture and power had not been suddenly invented. They existed for all of us. Here was a secret of achievement that could be ferreted out and written down for the use of others. Such words as these, I felt, could be so presented to a reader that he could easily make them his own. The job was to search them out.

In building these lists I naturally skipped the "thes," "ands," "buts," "starts," "stops," and other simple words that should be known to all. I passed by, also, the highly specialized technical terms that could play no profitable part in your vocabulary or mine. I tried, rather, to select those words that are the prized possessions and the important verbal tools of the outstanding men and women of our day. Words that have helped our leaders, in every field of thought, of action, and of commerce, to have and to hold their leadership.

My early fear was that this selected vocabulary of power and culture and high utility would be so tremendous that it could not be listed in a popularly priced volume. This fear was a natural one, for I soon discovered that the vocabulary I was winnowing from the writings and speeches of successful men and women was going to include almost the entire living heart of the English language.

To my surprise, after repeated checks, the number of the most valuable words amounted to only some 5,600, and even with this small list I found myself including words which will be known to even the uneducated without the necessity of either definition or illustration.

The word treatment in this book follows a lifelong practice of my own that I now urge you to adopt. From childhood I have always looked up a word that was strange to me. I do this now. If it happens to be one that will serve no particular purpose, I forget it. If it seems to be a usable one, I write it down in a notebook, with its pronunciation, its most common meaning, *and a sentence in which it is used.*

This last is most important, as a word means little or nothing unless it is at work. From time to time I review these words and try to use them in a letter or in conversation.

I have incorporated my personal method into this present book. You are given the word, its spelling and pronunciation, a simple meaning and a sentence in which it has been used.

These sentences have been chosen carefully, after vast research, not from classical sources but rather from books and magazines, from radio addresses, and from interviews and speeches that have been printed in the daily press. They represent the living English of the men and the women of our modern days who have carved out lesser or greater careers for themselves. While these men and these women who are quoted in the following pages will not all be known to you, the overwhelming majority of them, nevertheless, have won places of distinction for themselves, and their reputations are assured in their own special circles. These words of theirs, that illustrate this book, are the words that they have used to think and talk and write their way to success.

Before you begin this word study program, may I suggest that you do not try to get word-rich too quickly. It will be far better to spend not more than fifteen or twenty minutes each and every day at this vocabulary building game, rather than to try a wholesale acquisition of words at irregular intervals. If you make this fascinating study a *daily* habit, these few minutes will in the end give you a mastery of the words in this volume. Once you gain this mastery you will have a grasp of the English language that is rare to find in the world, and you will be able, with full confidence, to talk to any individual or group on any subject of general interest.

### YOUR REWARD WILL BE GREAT

Why not become one of the millionaires of the language? The opportunity is great. Your competition will be slight. There are so few who have learned to speak and write well. Most people go along on a minimum number of words, and the greater part of English remains a foreign language to them. Yet we have a language so well worth learning and one that seems destined to encircle the entire earth.

It is a restless language of bravery and daring, blessed by an imagination and an inventiveness that has favored no other language in all history: a colorful speech that is often terse, vivid and bold. *To know it is the best badge of culture that a human being can possess. And it is power at your tongue's end.*

But, before you set out on this program, and in order to truly possess the words in this book, it will be necessary for you to do a very small amount of planning, else you may find yourself quitting before very long.

Perhaps it might be wise to take a personal inventory right now. What qualities have you to go on? Are you efficient? Eager? Ambitious? Have you kept and developed your intellectual curiosity? Have you made up your mind definitely as to what you want most of all out of life? Honestly, now, would you be considered a good business manager if you ran a firm as you run yourself? Perhaps you ought to fire yourself!

Why not make a definite plan now. Decide how many minutes you can give out of each twenty-four hours to the subject of words. Set a date for completing each chapter. Make it a generous date so that you won't get discouraged or fall behind in your schedule. *And then demand a daily performance of yourself.* It will soon become as much fun as a game.

One way to increase your vocabulary is by purposely increasing your interest in the life around you. If you become vividly interested in life, your vocabulary will grow. And conversely, if you build your vocabulary, you will automatically increase your interest in life. The two go together.

So cultivate enthusiasm. This *can* be done. Picture yourself in situations where you will be triumphant because of your new power. Then you are on the way to becoming that rarity, a willing and exuberant worker.

And here is the delightful part of this whole performance. You will not have to wait for months before you notice the profound benefits that you are destined to derive from your growing vocabulary. They will begin at once. The very first day will open your eyes to them.

# CHAPTER II

## A TEST TO MEASURE YOUR TOTAL VOCABULARY

WE WILL BEGIN your new career with a test that will present a challenge to you that you have probably never met in your life before, the challenge to measure the full extent of your present English vocabulary. Before you start learning new words it will be wise to discover how many words you know now.

There are, of course, a host of vocabulary tests in existence, but when you have finished taking them they merely show you that your vocabulary is large, small, or average as compared with the vocabularies of other people.

When you have completed the following 15-MINUTE TOTAL VOCABULARY TEST, you *will know for the first time the actual size of your basic vocabulary*. This is the first total English vocabulary test ever prepared that is so simple that it can be taken successfully without supervision.

You will probably be immensely surprised at the results. Most people discover that they know ten or more times as many words as they think they do.

It is my hope that the results of this test will be a challenge to everyone who takes it, and that it will inspire the reader with the determination to acquire a progressively larger and larger vocabulary.

On page 430 you will find, for your later reference, the story of this test, the general principles on which it is based, and, largely for the purposes of the record, the complete MASTER ENGLISH VOCABULARY TEST from which this 15-MINUTE TEST was derived.

DIRECTIONS FOR TAKING YOUR 15-MINUTE VOCABULARY TEST

(N.B.: *Before you begin your test it is highly important that you read the rules.*)

*First:* With a sheet of paper, cover up all the words on page 10, and following, except the numbered list of key-words running down the extreme left-hand side.

8

*Second:* Now begin with the first word. This will be "achromatic" in the short test you are now about to take ["aardvark" in the MASTER TEST that is printed at the end of this volume]. Are you fairly sure that you have seen or known the word before? If so, take your pencil and make a check mark in front of it. If, to the best of your knowledge, it is a complete stranger to you, don't check it. Simply pass it by. That word is no part of your vocabulary. Don't waste time trying to figure it out. You have either seen the word before or you haven't, and you will find in 98 per cent of the cases where you are in doubt that you still won't know the word when you remove the sheet of paper and read the rest of the test. If, however, there is a *reasonable* doubt in your mind, give yourself the benefit of the doubt and put a check mark in front of the word.

Follow this method with each of the words to the end of the test, always covering up all the words on each page except the left-hand list.

Don't worry, as you go along, if many of the words are completely unknown to you. Some of them would puzzle scholars and would be wholly useless to you. Several will not even appear in your abridged dictionary, and many of them are not included in this book. But in order to take a total vocabulary test, it is necessary to sample the *entire* Unabridged Dictionary.

When you have finished checking all of the words that you recognize, you are ready for the next step.

*Third:* Now go back to page 10 and run down the left-hand list until you come to the first word that you have checked. To the right of it you will find four numbered words or phrases. One of these is *nearer in meaning* to the key word than the other three. Underline the word or phrase that you believe is *nearest in meaning* to the key word on the left.

Let us make up an example so that the process will be perfectly clear.

Forest   a. an oasis   b. a desert   c. a valley   d. a large wood

In this case, of course, you would have checked "forest" when you first went over the list as a word you recognized, and on your second reading you would underline the phrase "a large wood," as being the nearest in meaning to "forest," of the four choices.

Now go right on to the end of your test, underlining in each case the word or phrase that you believe to be nearest in meaning to the key words you have checked. Move through your test with reasonable rapidity. Taking time for study will probably not add 2 per cent to your score.

Occasionally you will check a simple word in the key list and then you may discover that there is no word or phrase following it that seems to be near to it in meaning. In this case you will have to remember that such a simple word as "run" has at least ninety-two meanings and you naturally are not apt to know them all. Therefore, if any word has a meaning with which you are not familiar, don't count it. You are simply not familiar with that particular meaning of the word.

Pay no attention to the words you haven't checked. They are no part of your test.

Please don't guess. Be fair to yourself and don't be overconscientious, but leave pure guesswork out as this would render your results valueless. This is a scientific test and not a game. As you know, on the law of averages, with four choices available, you have a one-to-four chance of guessing each word correctly even though you have never seen it before, but by doing this you would be building up a vocabulary total that you just don't happen to have. One more warning. In two or three instances it might be possible to make the correct choice by elimination. That is, you may be able to determine that three of the four words are not similar in meaning to the key word, therefore, the remaining word must be the right one. This again is guesswork. *If at the end of your test you find that more than 3 per cent of your answers are wrong, it should raise a strong suspicion in your mind that you have been guessing.*

Of course, if you know your Greek and Latin roots, and if you recognize the meaning of a word because of this knowledge, that would not be considered guessing. That word could be counted, as you undoubtedly would recognize its meaning if you happened to be reading and saw it in a sentence.

*Fourth:* At the end of the test you will find the directions that will show you how to determine your total vocabulary, and you will then be able to give yourself a vocabulary rating.

## Your 15-Minute Total Vocabulary Test

1. achromatic      a. a musical scale   b. containing chromic acid   c. colorless   d. relating to time measurement

2. affection      a. the act of influencing   b. the consideration of disease   c. a pledge   d. an assertion

3. aldose      a. sugar   b. salt   c. a prescription   d. a certain amount

4. **ambulacrum**      **a.** a sacred vessel   **b.** part of a wing   **c.** sucker of a parasite   **d.** an echo

5. **Anhalonium**      **a.** a man's name   **b.** a town in Sicily   **c.** a genus of plants   **d.** a genus of snakes

6. **apishamore**      **a.** an Indian squaw   **b.** a saddle blanket   **c.** a song   **d.** a silly trick

7. **Argidae**      **a.** South American fish   **b.** herbs   **c.** Greek islands   **d.** a family of mites

8. **assurance**      **a.** a pledge   **b.** a bait   **c.** timidity   **d.** rancor

9. **auxiliary**      **a.** exaggeration   **b.** a bone   **c.** helper   **d.** deceiver

10. **baluster**      **a.** a tiny star   **b.** a small pillar   **c.** a great noise   **d.** a bright light

11. **battle**      **a.** concord   **b.** combat   **c.** tangerine   **d.** a fort

12. **beshrew**      **a.** consecrate   **b.** curse   **c.** scatter   **d.** honor

13. **blind**      **a.** to admire   **b.** beseech   **c.** to announce   **d.** to deprive of sight

14. **border**      **a.** a tool   **b.** an edge   **c.** a person who boards   **d.** a rustic dance

15. **Bridgnorth**      **a.** a prison   **b.** a title   **c.** a palace   **d.** a borough in England

16. **Burnet**      **a.** a jewel   **b.** a Scotch minister   **c.** a canal   **d.** an Indian

17. **Callista**      **a.** a composer   **b.** shrubs   **c.** a novel   **d.** an opera

18. **card**      **a.** a coal   **b.** a rifle   **c.** a blue monkey   **d.** a piece of cardboard

19. **Catostomi**      **a.** apples   **b.** fishes   **c.** love-birds   **d.** catkins

20. **chap**      **a.** a metal plate   **b.** a chapel   **c.** a fellow   **d.** a feud

21. **chloral**      **a.** a song   **b.** a cloak   **c.** an oily compound   **d.** a green bird

22. **claim**      **a.** demand   **b.** clog   **c.** clap   **d.** deny

23. **cockerel**      **a.** a young cock   **b.** a conceited person   **c.** a feather   **d.** a rosette

24. **Commiphora**      **a.** bandits   **b.** a town   **c.** a group of shrubs   **d.** a comedy

25. **connate**      **a.** wicked   **b.** dissipated   **c.** knowing   **d.** inborn

26. **cora**      **a.** a duplicate   **b.** an antelope   **c.** a subtraction   **d.** a glaze

27. **courtesy**      **a.** graciousness   **b.** fantasy   **c.** famine   **d.** hatred

28. **crossed**      **a.** mounted   **b.** marked crosswise   **c.** waked   **d.** waited

29. **cyclic**      **a.** mystic   **b.** of recent date   **c.** of recurring periods   **d.** corrosive

30. **decentralization**      **a.** solution   **b.** distribution   **c.** contribution   **d.** abolition

31. **depressor**      **a.** an impostor   **b.** a stimulant   **c.** a plaster   **d.** an oppressor

32. **die**      **a.** a jingle   **b.** a cooper   **c.** a cube   **d.** a musical instrument

33. dispensatory    a. of receiving   b. of dealing out   c. of forgiving d. of recovering

34. Douglas    a. an opera   b. a Scottish warrior   c. a county in New York State   d. an Irish critic

35. dye    a. an explosive   b. victuals   c. coloring-matter d. a support

36. eland    a. an antelope   b. a chick-beetle   c. an isle   d. a kite

37. endotheliolysin    a. a restorative   b. a sedative   c. an antitoxin d. a poison

38. erd    a. a mistake   b. earth   c. gloom   d. an ant

39. eventuation    a. calmness   b. issue   c. dislike   d. a contest

40. Ezzolied    a. an opera   b. a war song   c. a dirge   d. a life of Christ

41. felicitate    a. to disgust   b. to agitate   c. to congratulate d. to urge

42. Firenze    a. an opera   b. a girl's name   c. a province of Italy   d. a violinist

43. fly    a. decide   b. move in the air   c. torture   d. dawdle

44. Fox River    a. a glacier   b. a river in Wisconsin   c. a hunter d. a magician

45. gablock    a. magic   b. a hook   c. a buttress   d. a symbol

46. geochemical    a. of knees   b. of humor   c. of styles   d. of geology and chemistry

47. gnaw    a. grow angry   b. to drink   c. to bite persistently d. to gnash

48. graphite    a. a grain   b. a spear   c. a carbon   d. an anchor

49. guide    a. a surmise   b. a conductor   c. a cure   d. a reward

50. hand    a. a wish   b. an insect   c. a mouse   d. a part of a limb

51. heaven    a. something hoisted   b. tightness   c. supreme happiness   d. weight

52. hextetrahedron    a. of six atoms   b. a crystal form   c. a radical d. a tetrarch

53. homotaxis    a. namesakes   b. the same category   c. small taxis d. not taxable

54. hurry    a. haste   b. applause   c. a growl   d. a nook

55. ideally    a. substantially   b. organically   c. perfectly d. actually

56. Inca    a. a war-chief   b. a Japanese measure   c. an Arab tribe   d. a corporation

57. ingress    a. access   b. exit   c. discourtesy   d. attention

58. interruption    a. persistence   b. decay   c. a breaking in   d. a bursting forth

59. itzli    a. a bulb   b. a Mexican peasant   c. goats   d. volcanic rock

60. journal    a. a cape   b. an idol   c. a curtsy   d. a diary

61. kettle    a. a trumpet   b. a vessel   c. a fish-bowl   d. a cap

62. kriyasakti      a. minerals  b. a Hindu god  c. a stork  d. creative power
63. lapideon        a. a musical instrument  b. a lapel  c. a stonecutter  d. lava
64. legion          a. a plait  b. an army force  c. a barge  d. a myth
65. light-year      a. a depression  b. a unit  c. a science  d. intellect
66. Loco-foco       a. a writer  b. a political party  c. a Roman senator  d. a town
67. luster          a. the sundew  b. juiciness  c. furze  d. gloss
68. malacon         a. a gem  b. a Parsee  c. appetite  d. softness
69. Mars            a. god of war  b. a month  c. an Indian  d. a river
70. meet            a. abound  b. come together  c. eat  d. heat
71. meteorological  a. of meteors  b. of records  c. of dates  d. of weather changes
72. miraculous      a. desirous  b. supernatural  c. lucid  d. latent
73. monstrosity     a. a monster  b. uniformity  c. gravity  d. civility
74. murder          a. gloom  b. killing  c. silence  d. grumbling
75. naturalization  a. gluttony  b. death  c. admission to citizenship  d. haunch
76. niggard         a. nestled  b. negroid  c. ugly  d. stingy
77. nummulite       a. a coin  b. a count  c. an organism  d. a makeshift
78. old             a. recent  b. aged  c. scanty  d. frequent
79. organic         a. vital  b. visual  c. venial  d. vestal
80. ox              a. a gas  b. an animal  c. an introduction  d. a prickle
81. paposite        a. a salt  b. a papoose  c. an orangutan  d. a priest
82. patent          a. a sufferer  b. a disease  c. a sole right  d. a monk
83. pentosan        a. a compound  b. a traitor  c. a trough  d. a roof
84. pharmacopœia    a. a book of drugs  b. a mania  c. a chemist  d. a theory
85. pill            a. a vagrant  b. a shaft  c. a tiny ball  d. a spear
86. playable        a. quick  b. that may be played  c. peaceful  d. idle
87. political       a. of exhibits  b. farcical  c. daily  d. of public affairs
88. postmaster      a. a stamp  b. a carrier  c. a newsman  d. a public official
89. pressman        a. a nerve  b. one who prints  c. a whirlwind  d. a speed
90. prompt          a. puny  b. prolonged  c. prone  d. punctual
91. pudency         a. modesty  b. mischief  c. distemper  d. virginity
92. quartet         a. an altar  b. a prey  c. a jonquil  d. a composition
93. rape            a. a twig  b. grape juice  c. a rib  d. a seam

94. reflex — a. reformation  b. refreshment  c. regiment  d. reflection

95. responsory — a. a psalm  b. an absorbent  c. a balm  d. a sound

96. righteously — a. rudely  b. rightly  c. restlessly  d. ruefully

97. roulette — a. a game  b. a quail  c. a degenerate  d. a scoop

98. sage — a. an oil  b. a myth  c. a plant  d. an officer

99. Sault Sainte Marie — a. a church  b. two towns  c. a mountain  d. a cape

100. screw — a. an harangue  b. a grooved cylinder  c. a rake  d. a stamp-mill

101. send — a. to help  b. to dispatch  c. to begin  d. to receive

102. shears — a. sheep  b. an instrument  c. shad  d. shells

103. sierra — a. a short nap  b. a province  c. a yellow color  d. a mountain chain

104. slaughter — a. to massacre  b. to flap  c. to dabble  d. to salute

105. solar — a. of the sky  b. alone  c. of the sun  d. of the soil

106. speech — a. reason  b. rascal  c. dumbness  d. utterance

107. squeeze — a. to compress  b. to defeat  c. to comply  d. to delegate

108. stethoscope — a. a muscle  b. an apparatus  c. a spasm  d. an atom

109. strive — a. to endeavor  b. to vibrate  c. to lament  d. to inject

110. sunflower — a. an aperture  b. a crate  c. a stout herb  d. a ray

111. sycophant — a. to derive  b. to cringe  c. to multiply  d. to swoon

112. Tannhäuser — a. a river  b. a crusader  c. a poem  d. a castle

113. testamentary — a. variegated  b. bequeathed by  c. outside  d. of a loan

114. Thunbergia — a. a queen  b. climbing plants  c. sea fish  d. a State

115. tongue — a. a secret society  b. a fleshy organ  c. a junk  d. a light coat

116. trappoid — a. of a rock  b. of a harness  c. of a trail  d. of a snare

117. tryst — a. a commotion  b. a meeting-place  c. a sail  d. a pore

118. umbilical — a. central  b. yellow  c. clustered  d. shadowy

119. Ustilaginales — a. mosses  b. acids  c. hawks  d. fungi

120. ver sacrum — a. a dedication  b. free verse  c. a lobe  d. a contraction

121. vulgar — a. solemn  b. chaste  c. coarse  d. injurious

122. weave — a. to entwine  b. to shirk  c. to measure  d. to clothe

123. will        a. a device   b. stupidity   c. a ruse   d. self-determination

124. Wrangel      a. a phantom   b. an explorer   c. a county   d. a college

125. zooid        a. a polecat   b. an organism   c. a carving   d. a frieze

## HOW TO COMPUTE YOUR VOCABULARY

Now that you have completed your test, check the words that you have underlined against the answers which follow. Add up your *correct* answers, and multiply the total by 1,229. This result will give you your total basic vocabulary. Let us presume, as an example, that you had 60 correct answers. Sixty multiplied by the key number, 1,229, will give you 73,740, and this then would represent your total basic vocabulary.

When you have determined your total vocabulary, compare your results with the graded vocabularies given on page 16 and see how you stand.

### ANSWERS TO 15-MINUTE TOTAL VOCABULARY TEST

| | | | | |
|---|---|---|---|---|
| 1 — c | 6 — b | 11 — b | 16 — b | 21 — c |
| 2 — a | 7 — a | 12 — b | 17 — c | 22 — a |
| 3 — a | 8 — a | 13 — d | 18 — d | 23 — a |
| 4 — c | 9 — c | 14 — b | 19 — b | 24 — c |
| 5 — c | 10 — b | 15 — d | 20 — c | 25 — d |
| 26 — b | 31 — d | 36 — a | 41 — c | 46 — d |
| 27 — a | 32 — c | 37 — d | 42 — c | 47 — c |
| 28 — b | 33 — b | 38 — b | 43 — b | 48 — c |
| 29 — c | 34 — b | 39 — b | 44 — b | 49 — b |
| 30 — b | 35 — c | 40 — d | 45 — b | 50 — d |
| 51 — c | 56 — a | 61 — b | 66 — b | 71 — d |
| 52 — b | 57 — a | 62 — d | 67 — d | 72 — b |
| 53 — b | 58 — c | 63 — a | 68 — a | 73 — a |
| 54 — a | 59 — d | 64 — b | 69 — a | 74 — b |
| 55 — c | 60 — d | 65 — b | 70 — b | 75 — c |
| 76 — d | 81 — a | 86 — b | 91 — a | 96 — b |
| 77 — c | 82 — c | 87 — d | 92 — d | 97 — a |
| 78 — b | 83 — a | 88 — d | 93 — b | 98 — c |
| 79 — a | 84 — a | 89 — b | 94 — d | 99 — b |
| 80 — b | 85 — c | 90 — d | 95 — a | 100 — b |
| 101 — b | 106 — d | 111 — b | 116 — a | 121 — c |
| 102 — b | 107 — a | 112 — b | 117 — b | 122 — a |
| 103 — d | 108 — b | 113 — b | 118 — a | 123 — d |
| 104 — a | 109 — a | 114 — b | 119 — d | 124 — b |
| 105 — c | 110 — c | 115 — b | 120 — a | 125 — b |

## YOUR VOCABULARY RATING

The classifications given below are intended for adults, and a generous allowance would, of course, have to be made for children. These divisions are broad and, necessarily, somewhat arbitrary, but they will enable you to get a very helpful measure of your present vocabulary level. If your results are good, it should encourage you to work for further improvement. If your test has indicated any weaknesses, it should be a challenge to you that you should immediately accept.

130,000 words and up................extraordinary
110,000 to 130,000....................superior
90,000 to 110,000.....................excellent
80,000 to 90,000......................very good
70,000 to 80,000......................good
50,000 to 70,000......................fair
50,000 and under......................poor

# CHAPTER III

## YOUR VERBS OF POWER

WITH THE invaluable verbs that have been selected for this chapter we are dealing largely in words of motion, action and resolve. These are the dynamos that turn the wheels of our language. They are the powder charges that give force to our sentences. To speak or to write effectively, we should have not a few, but as many of them as possible at the tips of our mental fingers.

Simply repeat such words as these out loud:

*annihilate; devastate; torture; paralyze; repudiate; persecute*

You can feel their impact, and it is easy to understand how words such as these can convince, command, persuade and even terrify.

We can further dramatize this subject by choosing the simple verb "hate," where the meaning has been worn as thin as a much handled coin.

The poor in language are apt to say:

> I hate that man.
> I hate a liar.
> I hate snakes.
> I hate a coward.
> I hate an uncivil person.
> I hate those who cheat.
> I hate bribes.
> I hate crime.

With the inexhaustible treasury of language to draw upon, these various shades and degrees of hatred can be expressed more effectively as:

> I hate that man.
> I detest a liar.

I loathe snakes.
I despise a coward.
I dislike an uncivil person.
I scorn those who cheat.
I disdain bribes.
I abominate crime.

These verbs of power present different facets of the same idea. *Hatred*, for instance, is a feeling of aversion, plus ill-will, while *detest* implies a mixture of indignation and contempt. *Loathe* indicates an intense feeling of moral or physical disgust. When we *despise*, we are looking down on something we consider degraded. *Dislike* is a milder verb signifying our displeasure with something disagreeable. Haughty contempt goes with *disdain*. *Scorn* adds derision to contempt, while *abominate* is a combination of violent disgust, hatred, loathing and often horror.

There is a great beauty and utility in these words, and their meanings shade and grade into all the colors of the spectrum. They help give clear definition to an otherwise cloudy thought, and the use of one of them can turn a dull sentence into one electric with interest.

We will select and list a few living sentences from the pages that follow to illustrate the dynamic power that well chosen verbs can have. These quotations are from the writings and speeches of the leaders of America. After each verb we will put a substitute in parentheses. Reread the sentence with the substitute to note how measurably the power is weakened:

"Your inspiring words will be *emblazoned* (kept) always in my memory."—Douglas MacArthur.

"We see Democracy *jettisoned* (thrown away) in a feverish quest of national security."—James P. Warburg.

"It rides the radio waves, *spews* (pours) from the presses."—Harold L. Ickes.

"He had spent vast sums and *squandered* (wasted) youthful blood."—Bruce Barton.

"A man who allows his knowledge and skill to *stagnate* (lie idle) is of weak character."—Karl T. Compton.

Men such as these have long since recognized the supreme and practical importance of words and they have acquired the art of accurate and forceful expression.

Even simpler words than these just quoted can contain powder charges. A young friend of mine devised the phrase, "You *lend* your money; they *give* their lives," and in answer to this magic use of "lend" and "give" in government advertising millions of dollars worth of War Bonds were bought for World War II.

A large number of verbs in this chapter will be as old friends of yours as "lend" and "give." But some of them will surely be new to you, and I believe you will be surprised how many of even the most familiar ones you have forgotten to use, and have made no part of your working vocabulary.

It is not enough to be able to recognize a word and the meaning when you see it in print; that is, if you want to get full value received. If this is all you know about the word, you will then be able to use it merely as a part of your recognition vocabulary for reading and for understanding. It will only be running on two cylinders. How much better if you can recall and employ such a word at will and instantly.

Nothing makes a man feel more inferior than a faulty vocabulary. Supreme confidence will come with superior self-expression. So look over these lists of verbs that have been chosen from the vocabularies of the men and the women who are running our world. See whether your own supply of words is limited, and whether those that you have in stock are not somewhat battered, stale and trite.

## VERBS OF POWER

**ab jures'** (ab jŏŏrz'). Disclaims; refuses; renounces.—"One of the underlying causes of the tragedy is, that if a man *abjures* love, if he bases his career on hate, he can seize great power."—Deems Taylor.

**ac cen'tu ate** (ak sen'chŏŏ āte). Emphasize; place a stress on.—"Occasional tables and ornaments that *accentuate* the yellow, coral or blue are an addition."—Emily Post.

**ac claim'** (ă klaim'). To shout applause; to proclaim by acclamation. —"These are the very institutions whose excellence it continues to *acclaim*."—Nicholas Murray Butler.

**ac'er bat"ed** (ass'er bāte"id). Embittered; made sharp or bitter; irritated; exasperated.—"Though there have been differences of opinion between us, they have never been *acerbated* by hard words."—Neville Chamberlain.

**ac'ti vat"ed** (ak'ti vāte"id). Made active or set in motion.—"Every thought and deed of Napoleon was *activated* by a burning ambition."—Donald G. Cooley.

**ac'tu at"ed** (ak'chŏŏ āte"id). Incited to action; impelled; influenced.—"Men and women can work effectively together only if they are *actuated* by a desire to contribute to the common effort."—James F. Byrnes.

**ad jured** (ă jŏŏrd'). Earnestly entreated; appealed to; solemnly commanded; charged, as under some penalty.—"We are *adjured* not to call the piece whimsical or fantastic."—C. A. Lejeune.

**af front'** (ă frunt'). Offend purposely; insult openly; displease by word or action; offer an indignity.—"I would not *affront* you with generalities."—Winston Churchill.

**an ni'hi lat"ed** (ă nī'ĭ lāte"id). Reduced to nothing; abolished.—"Modern science has so *annihilated* distance that what affects one people must affect all other people."—Madame Chiang Kai-shek.

**an nun'ci at"ed** (ă nun'shi āte"id). Announced; proclaimed; made known as ready.—"The court listened gravely as the king *annunciated* his new program."—Donald G. Cooley.

**ap pro'pri ate** (ă prō'pri āte). Take for one's own use; take possession of.—"America did not *appropriate* even a square inch of territory."—Francis J. Spellman.

**as tound'** (ă stound': 'ou' as in 'out'). To overwhelm with wonder; to amaze; to surprise; to confound.— "Growth in the arts, sciences, business, commerce has been sufficient to *astound* the world."—George Matthew Adams.

**a venge'** (uh venje'). Take vengeance in behalf of; get revenge for; exact a penalty for an injury to; inflict retribution in behalf of.—"He was laying his plans and figuring out how he could best *avenge* himself."—Hendrik Willem Van Loon.

**a verred'** (uh vurd'). Declared positively; asserted formally; affirmed confidently, from positive knowledge. —"It is the very smallest in that exclusive quarter, its occupant always modestly *averred*." — Edith Wharton.

**badg'ered** (baj'erd). Baited as a badger; hence, pestered; annoyed; worried persistently.—"They are *badgered* by a subtle yet pervasive sense of futility."—Florence Haxton Bullock.

**balked** (bawkt). Rendered unsuccessful; thwarted; frustrated.—"Our every effort has been *balked* by clashing national interests."—John Cudahy.

**ban'ished** (ban'isht). Expelled from its place; driven out.—"There is a theory that private free enterprise should be *banished* in favor of government operation."—T. C. Hannah.

**barged** (barjd). Moved clumsily and slowly; lurched or thrust himself awkwardly forward.—"He *barged* into the room without so much as an apology."—Charles Henry Weston.

**bat'tened** (bat"nd). Prospered; flourished; thrived; grown fat or wealthy at another's expense.—"He was an overrated fraud who had *battened* on his acquaintance with the great figures of his time."—John P. Marquand.

**be rate'** (bē rāte'). Scold; chide severely; reprove; rail at.—"You cannot *berate* these countries without eventually involving the nation in war."—Robert E. Wood.

**be seech'** (bē seech'). Entreat urgently; supplicate; beg; ask earnestly; implore; plead.—"I do not merely ask, I *beseech*, your forgivnesss."—Douglas E. Lurton.

**bilk** (bilk). Defraud; cheat; deceive; take advantage of; swindle.—"It was the practice of the shore-front saloon to *bilk* the sailors on every occasion." —Donald G. Cooley.

**black'guard** (blag'ahrd). Revile or abuse, using coarse or obscene language.—"They *blackguard* us for our opposition."—Herbert Hoover.

**blared** (blaird). Made a loud, harsh sound, as a trumpet; gave forth a noisy, brazen sound.—"The music of the brass band *blared* forth from behind a clump of palms."—Pearl S. Buck.

**blight'ed** (blīte'id). Caused to decay; hence, ruined; frustrated; withered; impaired and destroyed.—"They were so badly nourished that both intelligence and energy were *blighted*."—Louis Bromfield.

**blurt'ed** (blurt'id). Uttered suddenly and impulsively; spoke abruptly; burst out with.—" 'I ran into some of the fellows down at the corner,' he *blurted* out."—Morley Callaghan.

**botched** (botcht). Performed in a bungling way; bungled; spoiled.— "Political pressure and indecision in high places have badly *botched* the administration of the Act."—Clare Boothe Luce.

**bran'dish** (bran'dish). Wave or shake in a threatening way; flourish defiantly or menacingly.—"That was in the days when the dictators would mouth their boasts and *brandish* their swords."—John J. Green.

**but'tressed** (but'rĕst). Sustained or upheld by some strengthening support; propped up, steadied, or strengthened.—"Precept, say the Chinese, must be *buttressed* by example."—Oren Root, Jr.

**ca lum'ni at"ed** (kuh lum'ni āte"id). Slandered; said false and harmful things about; accused falsely and maliciously; defamed.—"No President was ever more reviled and *calumniated* than Lincoln."—Donald G. Cooley.

**cap'ti vat"ed** (kap'tĭ vāte"id). Fascinated; charmed; allured; captured; won over.—"Many of us were *captivated* by the critical mood of the era."—Harold W. Dodds.

**ca reen'ing** (kuh reen'ing). Tipping or leaning to one side; tilting over; heeling over; swaying from side to side.—"The great unruly yaks were *careening* over rocks exactly like tanks."—Eleanor Lattimore.

**cash ier'** (kash eer'). Discharge; dismiss suddenly in disgrace; send away from service.—"They instantly decided to *cashier* the accountant."—George F. Gahagan.

**cav'il** (kav'il). To find fault with; to raise objections.—"He had always felt his own insignificance and imperfections and was not inclined to *cavil* at fate."—John Buchan.

**clam'or** (klam'er). To utter loud demands.—"It is bad to *clamor* for a thing when we do not know the details."—Eduard Beneš.

**clenched** (klencht). Closed tightly; clinched; closed in a tight and rigid grip.—"She began to weep aloud, her hand *clenched* and pressed against her mouth."—Pearl S. Buck.

**com man deered'** (kom ăn deerd'). Taken possession of for public use, as under military necessity.—"The material they have *commandeered* reaches staggering figures."—Madame Chiang Kai-shek.

**com mis'er ate** (kŏ miz'ur āte). Express sorrow for; feel compassion for; lament over something with someone. —"Through misuse, sympathy has come to be synonymous with pity. Instead of sympathizing, we *commiserate*."—Gelett Burgess.

**con found'ing** (kon found'ing: 'ou' as in 'out'). Overwhelming; discomforting; perplexing; throwing into confusion; defeating.—"By practicing what you preach you will be *confounding* the critics of free private enterprise."—H. W. Prentis, Jr.

**con fute'** (kŏn fūte'). To confound; to prove (a person) to be wrong; to refute (an argument) or prove it false.—"The everpresent eagerness to *confute* other critics is in the long run wearying."—Samuel C. Chew.

**con sumed'** (kŏn sūme'd'). Engrossed; so closely absorbed as to be oblivious of all else; had the whole attention centered on.—"I was at peace with myself but *consumed* with a desire to get to work."—Roy Chapman Andrews.

**con'sum mat"ed** (kŏn'suh māte"id). Completed; perfected or brought to completion by intercourse.—"Her hair was done in the style of a bride whose marriage has been *consummated*."—Roy Chapman Andrews.

**con temn'** (kŏn tem'). Treat with scorn; view with contempt; scornfully disregard; disdain.—"I despise the traitor and *contemn* his treachery." —Emory L. Fielding.

**con vuls'ing** (kŏn vulce'ing). Agitating violently; making a violent disturbance in.—"What is *convulsing* the world today?"—Harold L. Ickes.

**coun'te nance** (koun'tē nănce: 'ou' as in 'out'). Approve; support; encourage; sanction.—"We cannot *countenance* injustice, from whersoever it may come."—Franklin Delano Roosevelt.

**cov'ets** (kuv'ets). Has an inordinate desire for something belonging to someone else; craves; longs for.—"Our nation *covets* nothing for itself."—Franklin Delano Roosevelt.

**cru sad'ing** (kroō sāde'ing). Engaging in a vigorous enterprise to remedy some condition.—"I am *crusading* to make people conscience-stricken."—Eddie Rickenbacker.

**cul'mi nat"ed** (kul'mĭ nāte"id). Reached a final effect; attained the highest point or degree.—"His long series of bitter failures finally *culminated* in triumphant success."—Douglas Brewster.

**de barred'** (dē bahrd'). Prevented; prohibited; shut out; barred out; hindered; precluded.—"Severe inflammation of the eyes *debarred* him attempting to read or write."—Maud Diver.

**dec'i mat"ed** (dess'ĭ māte"id). One of every ten killed; a large proportion destroyed.—"The other peoples, however *decimated*, will survive."—Israel Goldstein.

**de lude'** (dē lūde'). To mislead the mind or judgment; to deceive.—"Not many of them would stoop to *delude* the ignorant with promises of impossible benefits."—John W. Davis.

**del'uged** (del'ūje'd). Inundated; submerged; overwhelmed; flooded.—"I have been *deluged* with telegrams and messages."—Albert W. Hawkes.

**de mol'ish** (dē mol'ish). To destroy by tearing down; to ruin.—"Fearing that our wealth could not otherwise be secured, they strove to *demolish* it."—Bernard A. Brown.

**de nounced'** (dē nounst': 'ou' as in 'out'). Attacked as deserving punishment or censure; accused; censured.—"He unsparingly *denounced* the government."—Carter Glass.

**de plore'** (dē plōre'). Regret deeply; express great sorrow for; feel very sorry about; lament.—"She cynically admitted the fact of a loss that she could not *deplore*."—Maud Diver.

**dep're cate** (dep'rē kāte). Express disapproval of or regret for.—"I *deprecate* the discussions of this matter."—Winston Churchill.

**de sist'** (dē zist'). Cease from action; stop.—"If Government will desist from costly experiments, there will be re-employment."—C. M. Chester.

**de ter'mines** (dē tur'minz). Gives a definite form to; decrees; decides.—"What we think about ourselves *determines* in the long run what we are and what we are capable of doing."—Francis Biddle.

**de test'ed** (dē test'ed). Hated; disliked intensely; abhorred; loathed.—"She got herself a job which she *detested*."—Rose Feld.

**dev'as tates** (dev'ăss tātes). Lays waste; destroys; ravages.—"This scourge *devastates* and depopulates the world."—Sumner Welles.

**de vot'ed** (dē vōte'id). Given or surrendered completely.—"I can think of nothing so unpleasant as a life *devoted* to nothing but pleasure."—John D. Rockefeller, Jr.

**dis dains'** (diss dainz'). Scorns; considers it unworthy of oneself; thinks it unsuitable and beneath one.—"You are shown everything with a grim objectivity which *disdains* to drape reality with pretty phrases."—Edmund Wilson.

**dis gorged'** (diss gorjd'). Threw out from within, as from a throat or stomach; gave up, as gains or booty; ejected violently.—"The railway *disgorged* machinery and building materials."—Sigrid Undset.

**dis mem'bered** (diss mem'berd). Tore limb from limb; hence, separated into parts; divided; cut off some parts or sections.—"She annexed one country and *dismembered* another."—Jules Romains.

**dis pels'** (diss pelz'). Drives away; dissipates; clears away.—"News *dispels* rumors."—Carl W. Ackerman.

**dis'si pat"ed** (diss'ĭ pāte"id). Dispersed or scattered utterly.—"The catastrophe must surely have *dissipated* such ideas."—Wendell L. Willkie.

**di vulge'** (dĭ vulje'). To tell, as a secret; to disclose; to impart.—"One of the missionaries was given the water cure to make him *divulge* information."—Joseph C. Grew.

**dom'i nate** (dom'ĭ nāte). Exercise control over; govern.—"I have already been at some pains to set forth the serious preoccupations which *dominate* us."—Winston Churchill.

**dumb"found'ed** (dum"found'ed: 'ou' as in 'out'). Amazed; struck dumb with surprise; confounded; confused and speechless.—"He was at once *dumbfounded* and very flattered."—Stephen Vincent Benét.

**ef faced'** (e fāyst'). Blotted out; made to remain unnoticed; eclipsed; kept from being noticed.—"They were talking about things beyond his range. He was *effaced*."—H. G. Wells.

**ef fec'tu ate** (e fek'choŏ āte). To carry through; to put into action.—

"Under the executive there must be an independent police to *effectuate* the legislative policy."—Owen J. Roberts.

**em bla′zoned** (em blāy′z′nd). Set off in resplendent colors; inscribed, as though with heraldic emblems; pictured prominently.—"Your inspiring words will be *emblazoned* always in my memory."—Douglas MacArthur.

**em broil′** (em broyl′). To involve in dissension or warfare; to entangle; to implicate.—"God never made a man wise enough to be entrusted with the power to *embroil* a great nation in the horrors of war."—Hugh S. Johnson.

**em pow′ered** (em pou′urd: 'ou' as in 'out'). Given the power; authorized; delegated authority; licensed.—"Upon arrival in New York he was *empowered* as sole agent."—Alexander Woollcott.

**en gen′dered** (en jen′durd). Brought forth; produced.—"Hate never *engendered* peace."—Pius XII.

**en join′** (en joyn′). Command as an admonition; lay an injunction upon; urge authoritatively; prescribe by order.—"I *enjoin* you not to speak of these things."—Charles Henry Crozier.

**e nun′ci at″ed** (ē nun′si āte″id). Stated with formal exactness.—"President Wilson first *enunciated* this definite statement."—Franklin Delano Roosevelt.

**e pit′o mize** (ē pit′ō mīze). To reduce to a concise summary; summarize.—"These plans *epitomize* all that we want."—Madame Chiang Kai-shek.

**e quiv′o cat″ed** (ē kwiv′ō kāte″id). Used ambiguous language with intent to deceive; said one thing but meant another.—"The priest had not lied, but he had *equivocated*."—John Buchan.

**e rad′i cates** (ē rad′′ī kātes). Uproots; extirpates; gets rid of altogether; destroys entirely; exterminates completely.—"Timid boys and girls, who may possess latent ability, often find that this work *eradicates* an inferiority complex."—Al Nelson.

**es chew′** (ess chōō′). Shun, as something unworthy or injurious.— 'For India he would *eschew* violence."—Edmund D. Lucas.

**e vict′ed** (ē vikt′ed). Turned out; expelled forcibly; dispossessed.—"The minister had been *evicted* from the parish."—Sigrid Undset.

**e vince′** (ē vince′). Show plainly; make evident.—"They do not *evince* much dissatisfaction with their wages."—William Beveridge.

**ex ac′er bate** (eg zass′er bāte). To aggravate; to make more bitter.— "They were bound to stir up a political tempest as well as to *exacerbate* still further our strained diplomatic relations."—Anne O'Hare McCormick.

**ex alt′ed** (eg zawl′ted). Raised to a state of delight or elation; filled with satisfaction and joy; elated; dignified or lifted up.—"He is *exalted* by his vision of love."—Edmund Wilson.

**ex celled′** (ek seld′). Surpassed in good qualities; gone beyond others; shown superiority; outdone others.— "Women have *excelled* in the field of historical fiction."—J. Donald Adams.

**ex cise′** (ek sīze′). To cut off; to remove; to extirpate; to erase or cancel.—"It is the task of organized labor to *excise* this threat of compromise and appeasement."—Philip Murray.

**ex′cul pat″ing** (eks′kul pāte″ing). Exonerating; freeing from alleged blame; absolving from a charge of guilt; attempting to vindicate or clear or excuse.—"I had some considerable difficulty in *exculpating* us both."—Christopher Morley.

**ex′e crat″ed** (ek′sē krāte″id). Cursed; detested; abhorred; denounced.— "Not since Abraham Lincoln, I suppose, has any President of the United States been so *execrated* and so glorified."—Eric Johnston.

**ex pa′ti ate** (eks pāy′shi āte). To discuss fully; to discourse widely upon. —"If divine authority be denied, it is an affront to reason for rulers to *expatiate* on the need of human authority."—Edmund A. Walsh.

**ex′pe dite** (eks′pē dīte). To hasten the movement or progress of; to speed up a process.—"Our maritime commission must *expedite* the sending of supplies."—James B. Conant.

**ex pos'tu lat"ed** (eks poss'choŏ lāte"-id). Remonstrated; protested; reasoned earnestly about an action.— " 'The child had no way of keeping the matter quiet,' he *expostulated*."—Lloyd C. Douglas.

**ex punge'** (eks punje'). Blot out; erase; wipe out; obliterate; efface.—"The more he drinks the more certain he is to remember the very things he hopes to *expunge* from his brain."—Edmund Wilson.

**ex'tir pate** (ek'stur pāte). To root out; to destroy wholly; to eradicate.— "The powers of the State cannot hope, unaided, to *extirpate* crime."—Edmund A. Walsh.

**ex tolled'** (eks toll'd'). Praised; admired; magnified; glorified; commended.—"We believed him when he *extolled* lies and false propaganda." —Maxim Litvinoff.

**ex'tri cat"ing** (eks'tri kāte"ing). Liberating from entanglement; setting free from a difficult position.—"It was my intention to slip across the river, thereby *extricating* my force from an almost impossible position."—Harold Alexander.

**ex ud'ed** (eks ūde'id). Discharged; cast out, as through the pores; sent out in drops, as sweat.—"His language is something that is exhaled like breath or *exuded* like perspiration."—Edmund Wilson.

**fam'ished** (fam'isht). Starved; made very hungry; feeling extreme hunger. —"Nobody had ever seen so much food before; there was everything the world was *famished* for."—Willa Cather.

**fas'ci nat"ed** (fass'ĭ nāte"id). Held spellbound, as by some charm; attracted; captivated; held or influenced irresistibly.—"The native chief was *fascinated* by our mode of arrival by parachute."—Eric Sevareid.

**fend'ed** (fend'ed). Kept off; warded off; kept away; guarded.—"He has been *fended* off from the full life he might have had."—H. G. Wells.

**fer'ret** (fer'et). To find by keen and persevering search; to hunt out; to search.—"There is but one thing left

—to *ferret* out and punish the criminals."—Wright Patman.

**filch'ing** (filch'ing). Stealing small things; pilfering; taking small amounts from someone slyly.—"An economic system that permits leaders to enrich their pockets by *filching* from the workers their hard-earned wages is not worth preserving."—Rt. Rev. Msgr. Fulton J. Sheen.

**flaunt'ed** (flawnt'ed). Displayed boastfully; paraded; made an ostentatious show of.—"The papers *flaunted* great black headlines."—Roy Chapman Andrews.

**flounc'ing** (floun'sing: 'ou' as in 'out'). Flinging around from side to side; jerking proudly; throwing one way and another.—"The small girl was *flouncing* her too short skirt with an unmistakable air of triumph."—Helen C. White.

**flout'ed** (flout'ed: 'ou' as in 'out'). Scoffed at; mocked; treated with contempt.—"Who could have imagined that this mandate would be ignored or *flouted*."—John Haynes Holmes.

**foist** (foyst). To thrust in slyly; to palm off.—"The combination tried to *foist* a bureaucratic control on the farmers."—Henry Breckinridge.

**fo ment'ed** (fō ment'ed). Stirred up to heat or violence; instigated.—"Disturbances have been *fomented* in that nation."—Winston Churchill.

**fore stall'** (fōre stawl'). To hinder or guard against by preparation.—"Our powers to combat or *forestall* such dangers are now greater."—Theodore S. Wilkinson.

**for swear'** (for swair'). Reject; renounce; give up; abandon; abjure.— "Fearing that liquor may turn him into a maniac, will he permanently *forswear* drink?"—Rose Feld.

**foun'dered** (foun'durd: 'ou' as in 'out'). Filled with water and sank.— "The boats *foundered* in many cases with their crews."—Winston Churchill.

**ful'mi nate** (ful'mĭ nāte). To cause to explode; to issue.—"You may as well argue with a cyclone as to expect to *fulminate* calm and order into a

world on the verge of starvation."—
Rufus M. Jones.

**fumed** (fūme'd). Complained very angrily; gave vent to furious anger; raved; showed great annoyance.— "The Emperor *fumed* and snuffled, but he hadn't the energy to sustain his varied indignations."—Lloyd C. Douglas.

**gal'va nize** (gal'vuh nīze). To arouse to action as if by an electric shock; to stimulate.—"Radio broadcasting will *galvanize* into action all the resources of international life."—Pedro de Alba.

**gar'ble** (gahr'b'l). To change injuriously; to pervert or mutilate.—"In these times human passions take occasion to *garble* words and facts."—Pius XII.

**ger'mi nate** (jur'mĭ nāte). Begin to develop or grow.—"As a soil in which ideas for machines or methods of economy can *germinate*, it has proved sterile ground."—Henry M. Wriston.

**ges tic'u lat"ing** (jess tik'ū lāte"ing). Making gestures or motions.—"All the time he was talking, laughing, *gesticulating*."—Leland Stowe.

**gloat'ing** (glōte'ing). Gazing with cruel satisfaction; exulting.—"*Gloating* over power and abusing it is the enemy within the gates and without." —Joseph Jastrow.

**glow'er ing** (glou'er ing: 'ou' as in 'out'). Staring with scowling faces; gazing angrily; watching in a threatening manner.—"The mob stood *glowering*, waiting for someone to rush me first."—Roy Chapman Andrews.

**glut'ted** (glut'ed). Filled to excess; oversupplied; satiated.—"We were so *glutted* with victory that in our folly we cast it away."—Winston Churchill.

**gnashed** (nasht). Struck together angrily; ground together in a rage; grated or snapped.—"In the final debacle the criminal leaders *gnashed* their teeth in rage."—Henry J. Powers.

**goad** (gōde). Drive on as with a spur; prick or urge to action; stimulate; incite.—"Handicaps and obstacles will *goad* many a man to success."— Douglas Brewster.

**gorged** (gorj'd). Ate greedily; fed in a gluttonous way; ate voraciously until full.—"The salmon *gorged* fat that summer on prawns and sand eels."— Brooke Dolan.

**goug'ing** (gou'jing: 'ou' as in 'out'). Scooping out, as with a chisel-like tool.—"The tiny welds from a hard metal tend to ride over the parent surface instead of *gouging* into it."— E. L. Hemingway.

**grill** (gril). To question persistently; to subject to a severe and detailed examination.—"He asked a few questions, but he had not the heart to *grill* the lad too long."—Douglas E. Lurton.

**grov'el ing** (grov'ĕl ing). Lying prone in an abject manner; crawling; floundering; lying face downward.— "The men crept forward, *groveling* in shallow pits."—Richard Llewellyn.

**har'ass** (har'uhss). Vex; worry by repeated attacks; persecute; ravage.— "They could *harass* and sink transports over the entire route."—Burton K. Wheeler.

**har'ry** (har'i). To pillage or plunder; to harass in any way.—"The cruisers are designed to patrol sea lanes to protect our shipping and *harry* the commerce of the enemy."—H. L. Roosevelt.

**hound** (hound: 'ou' as in 'out'). Hunt; pursue; chase; hence, persecute.— "The very same gossips who could *hound* a man to the point of desperation could also be ministering angels."—Don Marquis.

**hurled** (hurld). Threw with violence; hence, uttered vehemently; sent forth with great force.—"Sixty minutes after that stab in the back, he *hurled* this challenge at the foe."— Henry C. Wolfe.

**hur'tle** (hur't'l). Rush headlong; move rapidly.—"We *hurtle* through space at a rate that can be counted only in astronomical billions."—Fred A. Eldean.

**im brued'** (im brōō'd'). Drenched; stained; soaked through with blood.— "The fields of Europe were *imbrued* with blood."—Charles Henry Crozier.

**im bued'** (im būde'). Pervaded; permeated; saturated; hence, filled.—

"Both labor and capital are men—human beings *imbued* with the same weaknesses and virtues."—John D. Rockefeller, Jr.

**im mured'** (i mūre'd'). Shut up, as within walls.—"We were *immured* in that tub with a cargo of copra and salt fish."—Noel Coward.

**im paled'** (im pāle'd'). Pierced with a pointed stake; hence, tortured by being fixed to something from which it is almost impossible to escape.—"Humanitarians find themselves *impaled* on a soul-disturbing dilemma."—H. W. Prentis, Jr.

**im pends'** (im pendz'). Hangs over; threatens; is near and ready to happen.—"Can we avert the catastrophe which *impends?*"—Franklin Delano Roosevelt.

**im plore'** (im plōre'). Entreat; supplicate; plead; beseech; beg.—"I *implore* businessmen throughout the United States to think clearly."—Percy C. Magnus.

**im"por tuned'**    (im"por tūne'd'). Urged persistently; asked repeatedly; begged pertinaciously; troubled with frequent requests.—"If one wished to spend the night that was ten yen, but one was never *importuned*."—Roy Chapman Andrews.

**im pugn'** (im pūne'). Gainsay; call in question; deny as false.—"No one can *impugn* the high ideals of freedom in which this nation was conceived."—Adolphus Andrews.

**im put'ed** (im pūte'id). Attributed; charged; set to the account of.—"The offenses of the few are *imputed* to the profession as a whole."—William L. Ransom.

**in censed'** (in senst'). Incited to anger; exasperated; made very angry.—"Motorists are *incensed* by the failure of the administrative authorities to organize shipments."—William J. Gottlieb.

**in cit'ing** (in sīte'ing). Stirring up; instigating; arousing; stimulating.—"By *inciting* class hatred you do not further brotherhood."—Howard W. Jackson.

**in crim'i nat"ed**    (in krim'ĭ nāte"id). Connected with a crime; charged with the crime; fastened the crime

on; showed to be guilty.—"His work *incriminated* the mosquito as the carrier of malaria."—Raymond B. Fosdick.

**in fest'ing** (in fest'ing). Being present in annoying numbers; besetting.—"They attempted to drive out the oppressors who were *infesting* her soil."—Franklin Delano Roosevelt.

**in fil'trat"ed** (in fil'trāte"id). Penetrated or entered as through a filter; pierced through tiny openings.—"We are being *infiltrated* by alien philosophies."—C. M. Chester.

**in fur'i ate** (in fū'ri āte). Make furious; enrage; make very angry; madden.—"The book will *infuriate* you if you take the author's ideas seriously."—Allan Nevins.

**in grained'** (in grain'd') Indelibly impressed; deeply fixed.—"How *ingrained* in congregations is parochialism."—Henry Sloane Coffin.

**in hib'it** (in hib'it). Check or block mental or nervous activity by another opposed process; restrain; hinder by checking.—"An effort must be made to determine the motives that thwart and *inhibit* a child."—Samuel Z. Orgel.

**in spires'** (in spīre'z'). Animates; awakens the best instincts.—"The broad vision of unity of the Americas *inspires* all men of good will."—Henry A. Wallace.

**in'sti gate** (in'stĭ gāte). To goad to action; to spur on, or encourage.—"We should *instigate* community action on a school luncheon."—Elizabeth L. Kingsbury.

**in'su late** (in'sū lāte). Isolate; place in a detached state, so as to have no association with others.—"We can never so *insulate* ourselves as not to be vitally affected by philosophies that prevail elsewhere in the world."—W. W. Waymack.

**in tim'i date** (in tim'ĭ dāte). To cause to become frightened; to use violence to overawe; to frighten; to alarm.—"The mob was imported to *intimidate* the farmers."—Westbrook Pegler.

**in ured'** (in ūre'd'). Hardened or toughened by use; accustomed; habituated.—"The people of the north are *inured* to hardship and deeds of reckless daring."—Sigrid Undset.

**in val'i date** (in val'ĭ dāte). To destroy the value or power of; to weaken the force of; to nullify; to make void.—"A bill was introduced to *invalidate* the executive order.'—John H. Baker.

**in veighed'** (in vāde'). Censured vehemently; made violent verbal attacks; denounced severely.—"He *inveighed* against those who shout for free enterprise."—H. W. Prentis, Jr.

**jeop'ard ize** (jep'ur dīze). To expose to danger of loss or injury; to risk.— "Today, the cost of unemployment is tending to *jeopardize* the financial stability of our government."— Alfred P. Sloan.

**lac'er at"ed** (lass'ur āte"id). Torn; afflicted with grief; harrowed.—"The heart of the Mussulmans of India has become *lacerated*."—Mohandas K. Gandhi.

**lan'guish es** (lang'gwish iz). Loses strength or animation; becomes weak.—"Confidence *languishes* and cannot live without honesty and honor."—Franklin Delano Roosevelt.

**liq'ui dat"ed** (lik'wĭ dāte"id). Discharged or paid off, as debts; hence, disposed of, removed out of the way, as by imprisonment or death.— "Cicero was *liquidated* in a purge fomented by Mark Anthony."— H. W. Prentis, Jr.

**lux u'ri at"ed** (luks ū'ri āte"id). Took great delight; indulged freely; reveled.—"He *luxuriated* in the well-equipped baths."—Lloyd C. Douglas.

**mac'er at"ed** (mass'er āte"id). Reduced to a soft mass by soaking; separated and softened by steeping. —"It was not until A.D. 1150 that the art of forming thin sheets of paper from *macerated* fibers was finally introduced into Spain."— Dard Hunter.

**ma ligned'** (muh līne'd'). Defamed; slandered; held in contempt; falsely assailed.—"I explained that my friend who was being *maligned* suffers from a defect of vision known as farsightedness."—Burton Rascoe.

**ma nip'u lat"ed** (muh nip'ū lāte"id). Influenced artfully; tampered with; managed unfairly; changed to gain an advantage.—"Tariffs in subject areas must not be *manipulated* for the benefit of the ruling races."—Francis B. Sayre.

**ma raud'ing** (muh rawd'ing). Pillaging; plundering; robbing.—"We still remember the *marauding* raids."— John Curtin.

**marred** (mahrd). Spoiled; impaired; tainted.—"No hatred of men *marred* the Cardinal's utterances."—Richard Downey.

**mauled** (mawld). Bruised by blows; suffering from rough handling; damaged by pounding or beating; torn or mangled, as by a wild beast.— "They were all horribly *mauled* in the face and hands."—Axel Munthe.

**mill'ing** (mil'ing). Moving round and round in a circle, like cattle; moving about in a confused or riotous mass —"The people were *milling* about in the central plaza."—Lloyd C. Douglas.

**mit'i gat"ing** (mit'ĭ gāte"ing). Rendering less harsh or painful; making milder; softening.—"Preparations on an extensive scale are in progress for *mitigating* the inevitable severities of the winter."—Winston Churchill.

**mol'li fied** (mol'ĭ fīde). Softened; hence, appeased; pacified; calmed; allayed anger or irritation.—"I explained that I was only joking, and this *mollified* him."—Louis A. Stone.

**mo'ti vat"ed** (mō'tĭ vāte"id). Induced; prompted to action; impelled.— "Our actions are *motivated* by high hopes of accomplishment."—Herbert Hoover.

**mu'ti lat"ed** (mū'tĭ lāte"id). Deprived of a limb or essential part; disfigured; seriously injured.—"We see the old symbols of honesty, sincerity, and character *mutilated*."—H. W. Prentis, Jr.

**nul'li fy** (nul'ĭ fī). To deprive of effect; to destroy; to make useless.—"The creeping inflation must not be allowed to continue and to *nullify* all the progress we have made."— James F. Byrnes.

**ob sessed'** (ŏb sest'). Haunted; harassed; beset with the fixed idea.— "We are still *obsessed* by the idea of poverty in the midst of plenty."— Richard Law.

**ob trude′** (ŏb trōōd′). Push in where they are not welcome; thrust themselves into prominence.—"The stark facts of tragedy and evil suddenly *obtrude*, and we have to rethink."— James B. Conant.

**ob′vi ate** (ob′vi āte). Anticipate so as to remove; clear away, as a difficulty or obstruction; remove.—"The mere existence of such a force probably would *obviate* in large degree the necessity for its use."—Joseph H. Ball.

**of fend′** (ŏ fend′). Violate; transgress; displease; give offense to; affront.— "Some phases of modern art *offend* good taste."—Tom Pennell.

**per′jure** (pur′jur). Violate an oath; forswear; bear false witness.—"Some citizens will go on the witness stand and *perjure* themselves for someone they know to be guilty."—J. Edgar Hoover.

**per turbed′** (pur turb'd′). Thoroughly disquieted; greatly disturbed; agitated.—"We are very much *perturbed*, we are deeply alarmed by the disquieting circumstances that face us." —Clare Boothe Luce.

**pin′ioned** (pin′yŭnd). Bound; confined; shackled; restrained by binding or holding the arms, so as to make helpless.—"He must have stood for several minutes before he realized that his arms were no longer *pinioned*.—Helen C. White.

**pla′cat ed** (plā′kāte id). Pacified; appeased; turned from anger to friendliness.—"There was no gold-braided politician to be *placated*, but a man of action to be informed."—Alexander P. de Seversky.

**plagued** (plāyg'd). Tormented; harassed; vexed; annoyed; bothered.— "Legislators, *plagued* by greater and often more obvious problems, are sometimes misinformed about the alien question."—Louis Adamic.

**pol lute′** (pŏ lūte′). To contaminate, defile, or make corrupt.—"Contraband goods should not be allowed to *pollute* the channels of interstate trade."—Franklin Delano Roosevelt.

**pored** (pōrd). Read with great attention; studied long and earnestly;

pondered with close application.— "For days they *pored* over plans with an architect."—Roy Chapman Andrews.

**pre cip′i tate** (prē sip′ĭ tāte). To hasten; to urge forward rashly; to rush headlong; to cause to happen hurriedly.—"They are trying to *precipitate* disaster."—Dorothy Thompson.

**pre empts′** (prē empts′). Acquires or appropriates the right of preference beforehand; takes possession and excludes others.—"There are certain fields in which radio naturally *preempts*, but there are others in which newspapers have equally natural advantages."—Ralph M. Ingersoll.

**pre sage′** (prē sāje′). Foretell; portend; predict; give a warning of.—"They think the moaning winds that shake the giant trees *presage* disaster."— Christine von Hagen.

**pro faned′** (prō faind′). Desecrated; put to unworthy and degrading use; debased; defiled.—"This same multitude in the name of the liberty they professed and *profaned*, made the streets of Paris run red with blood." —George W. Maxey.

**pro hib′it ed** (prō hib′it ed). Forbidden by authority or legal enactment.—"Profiteering and exploitation must be *prohibited*."—William L. Green.

**pro mul′gat ed** (prō mul′gāte id). Officially announced to the public; widely published; proclaimed.— "This impression is skillfully *promulgated*."—Anne O'Hare McCormick.

**pro pelled′** (prō peld′). Pushed ahead; drove forward; urged on; forced onward.—"His voice trailed off as he *propelled* the confused landlady down the hall."—Gene Fowler.

**pro pi′ti ate** (prō pish′i āte). Appease; conciliate; win the favor of; pacify.— "They try everything to *propitiate* the gods, whom they fear."—Christine von Hagen.

**pro pound′** (prō pound′: 'ou' as in 'out'). To state formally for consideration; to propose; to put forward.— "He used this opportunity to *propound* his personal political philosophy."—L. J. Dickinson.

**pros'ti tute** (pross'tĭ tūte). To devote to base or wrong purposes; corrupt; put to wrong use.—"Pressure groups *prostitute* sincerity in politics."—Emil Schram.

**punc'tu at"ed** (pungk'chŏŏ āte"id). Broken up into intervals; emphasized by interruptions.—"Only a part of this revenue was wrung from Congress after months of delay, *punctuated* by vetoes."—Herbert Hoover.

**pur loined'** (pur loynd'). Carried away by theft; stole; filched.—"I *purloined* the sponge bag and filled it with frogs."—Thomas Barbour.

**railed** (rail'd). Scoffed; used insolent language; uttered loud complaints; gave vent to noisy reproach.—"He once *railed* publicly at a race track vendor who wanted to overcharge him."—Jay Nelson Tuck.

**ran'kled** (rang'k'ld). Caused irritation or sore feelings; caused bitterness; created a painful resentment.—"To be unbidden to the Opera on fashionable nights *rankled* more with her than with her daughters."—Edith Wharton.

**ran'sacked** (ran'sakt). Pillaged; searched through and looted; plundered.—"Under their rule your library would be *ransacked*."—Monroe E. Deutsch.

**rav'age** (rav'ij). Lay waste; rob; despoil; plunder.—"They attempted to *ravage* their neighbor's vineyard."—Winston Churchill.

**rav'ish ing** (rav'ish ing). Seizing by violence; violating; raping; dispossessing.—"In those days a ruthless military and air power was *ravishing* all Europe."—Yates Stirling, Jr.

**razed** (raizd). Leveled with the ground; demolished; utterly destroyed.—"Whole towns were *razed* by the hordes of Attila, the Hun."—Ainslee Mockridge.

**re but'** (rē but'). Overthrow by contrary evidence; disprove; refute.—"He undertook to *rebut* your testimony."—Walter P. Stacy.

**rec'ti fied** (rek'tĭ fīde). Made right; corrected; adjusted; put right.—"Fortunately the error was *rectified*."—Julia Elsen.

**reeks** (reeks). Smells badly; emits a very unpleasant odor; exudes fetid air; is permeated with.—"The view *reeks* with self-pity over a fate that threatens tough days ahead."—Harold W. Dodds.

**re fut'ed** (rē fūte'id). Disproved; proved false; confuted.—"The statement is completely *refuted* by the record."—Jesse H. Jones.

**re"ha bil'i tate** (rē"huh bil'ĭ tāte). To restore to a former better or higher state; restore to a good condition.—"Music should *rehabilitate* minds and souls."—Sergei Rachmaninoff.

**re mon'strat ed** (rē mon'strāte id). Spoke words of protest; expostulated; urged reasons against actions; declared objections.—"The kindly pastor *remonstrated* with the boys but the little curmudgeons paid no attention."—Douglas E. Lurton.

**rend** (rend). To tear apart violently; to split; to tear asunder; to wrench apart; hence, abuse unexpectedly.—"Most authors would be glad to *rend* critics from end to end."—Ellery Marsh Egan.

**rep'ri mand"ed** (rep'ri mand"ed). Reproved sharply or publicly; censured severely.—"A carpenter was *reprimanded* for taking too long over his cup of tea."—Edward R. Murrow.

**rep'ro bat"ed** (rep'rō bāte"id). Disapproved; condemned with great dislike; refused to sanction; censured.—"We have regretted and *reprobated* what they have done."—Carlton J. H. Hayes.

**re pu'di ate** (rē pū'di āte). Refuse to accept or have dealings with; reject; disclaim; renounce; disown.—"Sustain me now, or *repudiate* me."—John L. Lewis.

**re scind'** (rē sind'). Repeal; annul; cancel; abolish.—"Legislation was proposed to *rescind* the sections of the New York City charter."—I. Ogden Woodruff.

**re sus'ci tat"ed** (rē suss'ĭ tāte"id). Brought back to life; revivified; reanimated.—"This foul obsession has been *resuscitated* from the underworld of the past."—Jan Christiaan Smuts.

**re tal'i ate** (rē tal'i āte). Pay back like for like; repay or return evil for evil;

do an injury in return for an injury; requite an act with a similar act.— "If you are teased never get angry, never seek to *retaliate*."—Priscilla Wayne.

**re trieved'** (rē treevd'). Brought back from a state of loss to an improved condition; made good; remedied.— "Our self-respect has been *retrieved*." —Donald G. Cooley.

**re vi'tal ize** (rē vī'tăl īze). Give new life to; restore vitality to; revive; endow with fresh life and power.— "The challenge of failure can sometimes stimulate and *revitalize* a courageous man."—Donald G. Cooley.

**re viv'i fy** (rē viv'ĭ fī). Restore to life and activity; revive; give new spirit to; endue with new vigor.—"One new and brilliant playwright can sometimes vitalize and *revivify* the theater."—John J. Green.

**rile** (rīle). Vex; irritate; disturb; stir up anger or resentment in.—"She seemed a mild-mannered housewife with not a trait about her to *rile* the most irascible."—John J. Green.

**ri post'ed** (rē pōst'ed). Made a quick retort or reply; given a clever reply; made a sharp rejoinder.—"If he had been obliged to say something, he would have *riposted* with a snappy, 'No comment.' " — Horatio Winslow.

**riv'en** (riv'ĕn). Rent asunder; split; torn asunder.—"The tropical heavens were *riven* by a sudden lightning flash and an appalling cannonade of thunder."—Ellery Marsh Egan.

**roiled** (royl'd). Stirred up; disturbed; irritated; vexed; riled; ruffled.— "The shudder *roiled* the waters of the doctor's spirit."—Don Marquis.

**rous'ing** (rouz'ing: 'ou' as in 'out'). Waking from sleep or lethargy; exciting to vigorous action; stirring up; spurring to strong and active thought. —"He remembered his father's voice persuading the people to justice or *rousing* them to the love of state."— Caroline Dale Snedeker.

**rout** (rout: 'ou' as in 'out'). To drive forth; put out; force out; to uproot; to tear out by the roots.—"It was easy to *rout* Allah out of the Mosque, but Allah in a human heart was a different problem of eradication."— H. G. Wells.

**sa'ted** (sāy'ted). Supplied with more than enough; satiated; filled to satiety; surfeited; fed up to the full.— "In these books one was *sated* with the fetch-and-carry young men and rudeness to natives."—Maud Diver

**scoffed** (skoft). Derided; mocked; jeered; sneered; treated with scorn. —"The lust for power has exalted might and *scoffed* at right."—John D. Rockefeller, Jr.

**scout** (skout: 'ou' as in 'out'). Reject contemptuously; refuse to believe in; flout; scoff at; decline scornfully to accept.—"The eminent scientists *scout* the new theory as being unsound and absurd."—John J. Green.

**scur'ried** (skur'id). Moved hurriedly; scampered; hurried; ran quickly.— "The neighbors *scurried* about the house to get coverings for the babies." —Allan Roy Dafoe.

**seeth'ing** (seethe'ing: 'th' as in 'the'). Boiling; hence, moving in a state of agitation; bubbling over; giving vent to disturbances.—"All over the United States the 'color' problem is *seething* just below the surface."— John Chamberlain.

**se ques'tered** (sē kwess'turd). Separated from their fellows; removed from public life and society; taken into judicial custody.—"In country after country it was the intellectuals who were sequestered first."—Archibald MacLeish.

**slaugh'tered** (slaw'turd). Killed ruthlessly; destroyed in large numbers; murdered wantonly; hence, erased; wiped out.—"Our hearts break every night over the beautiful adjectives *slaughtered* by the copyreaders." —Emma Bugbee.

**smirch'ing** (smurch'ing). Sullying; soiling with disgrace or dishonor; hence, defaming; degrading; speaking ill of.—"He quoted the evil harpies of society who enjoy *smirching* a character."—Bradwell E. Tanis.

**sneered** (sneer'd). Laughed with contempt; smiled with scorn; scoffed; made a grimace of derision; jeered; taunted.—"I *sneered* at him, I reviled him."—Gene Fowler.

**so lid'i fy** (sō lid'ĭ fī). Make solid; bring to a solid state; hence, bring together in harmony or unity.—"It took that sharp and unfair challenge to *solidify* the opposition."—Donald G. Cooley.

**spews** (spūze). Pours forth; is forcibly ejected.—"It rides the radio waves, *spews* from the presses."—Harold L. Ickes.

**squan'dered** (skwon'durd). Spent wastefully; wasted.—"He had spent vast sums and *squandered* youthful blood."—Bruce Barton.

**stag'nate** (stag'nāte). Become dull or inert; become inactive and clogged from lack of use.—"A man who allows his knowledge and skill to *stagnate* is of weak character."—Karl T. Compton.

**sti'fling** (stī'fling). Stopping the action of; holding back; choking.—"This present price system is *stifling* farm production."—Herbert Hoover.

**stig'ma tize** (stig'muh tīze). Brand with a stigma or mark of disgrace; describe in opprobrious or scornful terms.—"He began to *stigmatize* the annual function as a one-horse show."—A. S. M. Hutchinson.

**sub or'di nat"ed** (sŭ bor'dĭ nāte"id). Made subject or subservient; made dependent on; made of less importance.—"Everything must be *subordinated* to this one great purpose."—William Green.

**sub stan'ti ate** (sŭb stan'shi āte). To establish, as a truth, by strong proof; to verify.—"Evidence to *substantiate* the belief is apparent in many committees."—Jesse H. Jones.

**sub vert'ed** (sub vurt'ed). Overturned; overthrown; hence, brought to ruin; undermined; corrupted.—"All political parties, including our own, have been *subverted* from time to time."—Wendell L. Willkie.

**suc cumbed'** (suh kumd'). Sank down as under a burden; died.—"The criminal pride of that empire *succumbed*, vanquished by free peoples."—William L. Shirer.

**sun'der** (sun'der). Separate; divide into parts.—"Some can talk to you of where the geographical boundaries which *sunder* nations ought to be."—George N. Shuster.

**sur charged'** (sur chahrjd'). Overcharged; overloaded; overburdened; containing an additional or excessive amount.—"Death, disease, sex are topics so *surcharged* with emotion that it is tactless to discuss them unless you are sure of your company."—Daniel P. Eginton.

**tes'ti fy** (tess'tĭ fī). To bear witness; to declare; to bear testimony; to state positively; to give evidence.—"I wish to *testify* to the fine and noble character of my old friend."—Charles Driscoll.

**throt'tling** (throt'ling). Obstructing; choking; shutting off; strangling.—"We are blocking the broad distribution of income and thereby *throttling* economic progress."—Harold G. Moulton.

**thwart** (thwawrt). To prevent someone from accomplishing something; to hinder by counter moves; to oppose.—"There is a group of men in Congress who are trying to *thwart* the will of the nation."—James P. Warburg.

**tol'er ate** (tol'ur āte). Endure with impunity; suffer to be done without active opposition; permit; allow.—"We cannot *tolerate* further increases in prices."—Franklin Delano Roosevelt.

**tra duced'** (truh dūce't). Wilfully misrepresented; held up to ridicule; defamed; slandered; reviled.—"In his lifetime Lincoln was maligned and *traduced*."—Stephen S. Wise.

**tram'pling** (tram'pling). Stepping heavily so as to bruise; encroaching ruthlessly; stamping upon.—"Time is short, and destiny is *trampling* upon our heels."—Watson Davis.

**tran scend'ed** (tran send'ed). Surpassed; exceeded; gone beyond; risen above in excellence.—"Human separatism has *transcended* every previous experiment of life in individuality."—Donald Culross Peattie.

**trans fix'** (trance fiks'). To pierce through or impale as though by a sharp point or weapon; hence, to hold a person to the spot as though rooted or paralyzed.—"She had a casual malice all her own and liked to stand in the gloom of the upper stair waiting for someone to *transfix*."—Christopher Morley.

**trun'cat ed** (trung'kāte id). Having had the top cut off; without a top or vertex; ending abruptly.—"What was left was a peakless pyramid, a *truncated* generation."—Sigmund Neumann.

**val'i date** (val'ĭ dāte). Prove the truth of; confirm; endorse; substantiate.— "He went to extraordinary lengths to *validate* the authentic record of that tragic figure."—Lewis Gannett.

**vil'i fy** (vil'i fī). Treat as base or vile; defame; malign; speak evil of.—"If an alien is poor we *vilify* him for causing us to support him."—Harold Fields.

**vin'di cat"ing** (vin'dĭ kāte"ing). Defending against attacks; justifying; maintaining; upholding.—"He met the corrupt demands of its government by *vindicating* the dignity of the republic."—James M. Beck.

**vi'o lat"ed** (vī'ō lāte"id). Broken; disregarded; set at naught; transgressed.—"Any law of Nature that is *violated* demands immediate, and heavy, payment."—George Matthew Adams.

**vi'tal iz"ing** (vī'tăl īze"ing). Endowing with life; animating; giving essential force to; imparting energy or power to; making vital or alive.—"The springs of laughter, essential for the *vitalizing* of the scene, refused to flow."—L. P. Jacks.

**vouch safed'** (vouch saift': 'ou' as in 'out'). Condescended to grant; deigned to give.—"The King *vouchsafed* his Prime Minister a share of the honors."—James L. Blackman.

**wran'gle** (ran'g'l). Argue or dispute noisily; debate angrily.—"Who in America would again *wrangle* with the Filipinos over marketing opportunities?"—H. A. Burgers.

**wrest'ed** (rest'ed). Snatched forcibly; wrenched or taken violently.—"It is our intention to make them pay dearly for every inch of ground they have *wrested* from us."—Madame Chiang Kai-shek.

**writhed** (rīthe'd: 'th' as in 'the'.) Twisted about; turned and twisted themselves into contorted or distorted shapes.—"We had to step with care over the roots that *writhed* and twisted among the rocks."— S. Dillon Ripley.

## ONE-MINUTE REFRESHER

Under this following list of words you will find nine sentences. Fill each blank space with that word from the list that most aptly fits the meaning. Just good practice—that's all:

a. obsessed      d. propitiate      g. delude
b. extirpate      e. extricating      h. inciting
c. gorged      f. galvanize      i. repudiate

1. I was _____ my men from this highly dangerous situation.
2. If you are _____ class hatred, you are inviting trouble.
3. The savages tried everything to _____ the gods whom they fear.
4. The lumberjacks _____ themselves with food.
5. Don't let them _____ you with attractive, but false, promises.
6. It was a challenge to _____ him into action.
7. His mind was _____ with the idea of revenge.
8. I _____ with disdain the charges of dishonesty that you make against me.
9. The powers of the state cannot hope, unaided, to _____ crime.

*Answers:* 1 — e; 2 — h; 3 — d; 4 — c; 5 — g; 6 — f; 7 — a; 8 — i; 9 — b.

# CHAPTER IV

## WORDS ABOUT YOU AND YOUR FRIENDS

MEN AND WOMEN have so many forms of conduct, so many mental quirks and moods, and such a multitude of varying characteristics and points of view that they have inspired thousands of words. These, most naturally, are intensely interesting words, warm and human, and they can be made to describe you and your fellow man most accurately.

(1) Do you happen to daydream a little too much? Do you indulge in wishful thinking? Are you apt to overdo the movies or the radio in order to avoid facing the hard facts of life? Then we call you an "escapist" and you are said to be practicing "escapism." This rather new psychological word comes, of course, from the English word "escape" and that word in turn traces its history to the Latin *ex* + *cappa* which literally means "out of your cape." When your enemy made a grab for you in the ancient Roman days and managed only to seize the cape you were wearing, you slid out of it and "escaped"!

(2) There are some people who are noisy and riotous wherever they go. At every social affair they are boisterous and clamorous and it is impossible to quiet them down. This certainly could not be said of you, but if you have a friend of that ilk you can properly call him "obstreperous." The Latins had a word for it: *ob*, "before," and *strepo*, "roar." An "obstreperous" man "roars before" the crowd and he is apt to be rambunctious if you attempt to silence him.

(3) You, no doubt, are of a quieter and more gentle disposition than the "obstreperous" type. We will say that you are easy to manage and easy to teach. In school or in after life, you paid attention to instructions and advice and tried to follow and not oppose them. If this is your bent you are "docile." A refractory child is difficult to handle and resists authority. A "docile" child listens and learns and is compliant, amenable, and tractable. Again we turn to a Latin word *docere*, which means "to teach."

34

(4) Do you try to avoid being rude? Do you practice courtesy? Are you obliging and soft spoken and do you observe all the proprieties of social intercourse? Then you are an extremely "civil" person. You always keep a "civil" tongue in your head and people comment on your "civility." It's strange how many of our English terms that mean "well-mannered" come from the ancient words that originally meant "city." If you are a "civil" or a "civilized" person you then have the smooth manners of the Roman *civis* (citizen). The "urbane" man, with his suave ways, traces his history to *urbs*, the Latin word for "city." And when you make a speech that is discreet and "polite" and people compliment you by telling you that your remarks were most "politic," they are indebted for the term "politic" to the Greek word *polis*, which again means "city."

(5) Now you may have two men friends among your wide circle whose predominant traits can be identified by two words. One of these acquaintances of yours is unmarried and women play no intimate part in his life whatsoever. He, then, like a monk or a priest, is a "celibate." *Caelibis* in Latin means "unmarried." Your other friend, however, is a playboy, amatory in his habits. Light ladies are his delight and sexual love is his weakness. His tendencies are properly called "erotic," for *Eros* was the Greek god of love.

These words that we have just discussed express certain ideas compactly, richly and effectively. It will be of great assistance to you in learning the rest of the words in this chapter if you will dramatize them in similar fashion by recalling or even by writing down the name of a friend or a public character who best personifies the word in question.

Harold Ickes, for instance, once called himself a "curmudgeon." As a result, hundreds of thousands of people now remember the word and its meaning.

Very well. As you read over the words in the pages just to come, pair each one off with an actor, a movie star, a radio broadcaster, a public character, or with a friend of yours. What critic, for example, could be called "captious"? What politician an "opportunist"? What labor leader "choleric"? What newspaper columnist "carping"?

This practice will greatly help your memory by associating a famous name or a friendly name with a specific word. You can't learn words in a vacuum.

Here is a safe rule in all vocabulary building. Make your new words bear some relationship to you, to your way of living and to the ways of life about you. Then you can the more easily make these words your own.

## Words About You and Your Friends

**ab stract′ed** (ab strakt′ed). Absent-minded; lost in reverie or thought; inattentive; preoccupied.—"His eyes caught an *abstracted* benevolence and he became more interested in the press cuttings."—H. G. Wells.

**ac″qui es′cence** (ak″wi ess′ĕnce). Passive consent; quiet agreement; tacit acceptance; submission to something that seems inevitable.—"He tested the willingness of the allied world to say him nay, and the record shows *acquiescence*."—David Lawrence.

**a dapt″a bil′i ty** (uh dap″tuh bil′ĭ ti). Ability to adjust oneself to circumstances or conditions; power to change in order to fit in with a different situation.—"I had the *adaptability* of youth."—Roy Chapman Andrews.

**ad″ap ta′tion** (ad″ap tā′shŭn). The process of adjusting to new conditions; the act of fitting into an environment.—"The age of high school graduates permits ready *adaptation* to most types of office work."—Frank L. Rowland.

**ad dress′** (ă dress′). Bearing; manner; deportment; manner of speaking.—"His clothes, his speech, his whole *address* persuaded us that he was a man of eminence."—Donald G. Cooley.

**af″fec ta′tion** (af″ek tā′shŭn). Insincerity; behavior that is unnatural and artificial; assumption of something that is imitated, not real; affectedness; pretense.—"The master unites the Gentleman with the Scholar, without *affectation* or pedantry."—André Maurois.

**ag grieved′** (ă greev′d′). Subjected to ill treatment; unjustly injured.—"International law leaves *aggrieved* states who cannot obtain redress by peaceful means to exact it by force."—Charles Evans Hughes.

**a gil′i ty** (uh jil′ĭ ti). Nimbleness; quickness and ease of movement; alert activity.—"Too many of us now lack *agility*, are without grace of body movement."—Edmund Ezra Day.

**a loof′** (uh lōōf′). Reserved; apart; distant; desiring to keep at a distance from others; unsympathetic and indifferent.—"He was somewhat *aloof* at first."—Henry James Forman.

**am″bi dex′trous ness** (am″bi dek′strŭss ness). Ability to use both right and left hands equally well; skill or dexterity.—"Business men have to develop *ambidextrousness* to enable them to direct energy to private pursuits and at the same time leave them free to exercise their abilities in the common good."—A. W. Robertson.

**a me′na ble** (uh mee′nuh b'l). Tractable; submissive; responsive; subject to authority.—"He's *amenable*. He's half with us."—H. G. Wells.

**a men′i ties** (uh men′ĭ tiz). Acts that express agreeableness and civility.—"After a brief exchange of social *amenities* I had a cup of tea in the outer office and went home."—Noel Coward.

**a″mi a bil′i ty** (āy″mi uh bil′ĭ ti). Charm; kindliness; friendliness; pleasing personality; good-natured, complaisant behavior; sweetness of disposition.—"She shows good manners of the kind which spring from genuine *amiability*."—Rebecca West.

**am′i ty** (am′ĭ ti). Mutual goodwill; friendship; peaceful relations.—"In the new democracy of nations, we hope to conduct with *amity* and good sense the common concerns of mankind."—Lord Keynes.

**a mor′al** (a mor′ăl). Outside the sphere of morals; unconcerned about morals; non-moral; making no distinction between right and wrong.—"It is doubtful whether he realized how ruthless and *amoral* the man had become."—George N. Shuster.

**an′i mate** (an′ĭ māte). Quicken and make more alive; inspire; give vigor to.—"It will take all our philosophy to carry on with the spirit that should *animate* our business."—Ralph Starr Butler.

**an tag″o nis′tic** (an tag″ō niss′tik). Hostile; opposed; conflicting; acting as a rival or adversary.—"He is unenthusiastic, if not critical and *antagonistic*."—Margaret Mead.

**ap″pa ri′tion** (ap″uh rish′ŭn). An appearance; something strange and ghostlike; the semblance of a specter; an unusual or unexpected sight or object.—"Her hair dishevelled, her clothes wet and torn she flung herself into the room—an appalling *apparition*."—L. P. Jacks.

**ap″pli ca′tion** (ap″li kā′shŭn). The act of close and continuous attention.—"Every American boy by strict *application* can master the technique of any business."—James A. Farrell.

**ap proach′a ble** (ă prōch′uh b'l). Easy to approach or draw nigh to; accessible; easy to come near to or to speak with; easy of access.—"Jesus was the most *approachable* of all men."—Bradwell E. Tanis.

**arch′ly** (ahrch′li). Roguishly; coyly; playfully; naïvely; slyly; mischievously.—" 'You will see him presently,' she replied, *archly*."—Lloyd C. Douglas.

**at″ti tu′di niz″ing** (at″ĭ tū′dĭ nīze″-ing). Striking an affected attitude or pose; posing for effect; assuming an attitude or posture.—"There were times when John Barrymore could not help *attitudinizing*."—Emory L. Fielding.

**a typ′i cal** (a tip′i kăl). Not typical; irregular; not according to type; not having the nature or characteristics of a type or pattern.—"We have cinema records of the behavior development of both normal and *atypical* infants."—Arnold Gesell.

**ba nal′i ty** (buh nal′ĭ ti). A commonplace gesture; a triteness; a triviality. —"His expression of gratification was not a mere *banality*, a platitude."—Lord Cecil.

**be nign′** (bē nīne′). Kindly; manifesting kindness and generosity.—"Philosophers asserted that the world was growing better by the inward necessity of its own *benign* forces."—H. W. Dodds.

**bland** (bland). Affable in manner; suave; neither irritating nor stimulating; soothing or cajoling.—"With *bland* and callow unconcern they sat smugly through the proceedings."—Alben W. Barkley.

**blear′y** (bleer′i). Blurred; made dim, as by tears or rheum; weak-sighted; blear-eyed; having sore or inflamed eyes.—"He looked at his *bleary* and bloated face in a mirror."—Channing Pollock.

**bon″ho mie′** (bon″ō mee′). Good nature; geniality; good-fellowship; an easy and genial manner.—"On account of his *bonhomie* he has been able to sell his tales to these periodicals."—Ludwig Lewisohn.

**boor′ish** (boor′ish). Like a boor or ill-bred person; rude; ill-mannered; awkward.—"It is common enough experience to sit next to a *boorish* bully of a financier, and then discover in the taxi-driver a sovereign gentleman."—Alexander Woollcott.

**bra va′do** (bruh vah′dō). Arrogant defiance; affectation of bravery.—"If you restrict young people too rigidly, they often show foolish *bravado* in their liberating gestures."—S. Bernard Wortis.

**brawn** (brawn). Firm muscle; strength. —"Something more than brains, *brawn*, machines and material is needed to bring peace to mankind." —Francis J. Spellman.

**brood′ed** (brōōd′ed). Meditated long and moodily; pondered.—"Even under less challenging conditions they *brooded* and labored over problems of security."—Arthur A. Ballantine.

**brusque′ly** (brŭsk′li). Bluntly; abruptly; in a curt, offhand way.— "He went out and *brusquely* told his men to go home to their farms."— Pearl S. Buck.

**bur′ly** (bur′li). Stout; sturdy; of heavy build; strong; lusty; bluff in manner.

—"He is now in his 60's, tall, *burly* and white-headed."—J. P. McEvoy.

**can'dor** (kan'dur). Frankness; freedom from prejudice; fairness.—"I cannot with *candor* tell you that general international relationships are improved."—Franklin Delano Roosevelt.

**can'ny** (kan'i). Wary; cautious; prudent; shrewd in affairs of the world; worldly-wise; knowing.—"*Canny* states, all! They must first see which way fate was like to leap before taking their stand."—Caroline Dale Snedeker.

**cap'tious** (kap'shŭs). Faultfinding; cross and critical; hard to please.— "He is *captious* if they hesitate to put his ideas into immediate use."— Colby M. Chester.

**ca ress'es** (kuh ress'ez). Loving touches; tender kisses; acts of fondling or embracing.—"She was apparently enjoying his *caresses*."—Roy Chapman Andrews.

**ca roused'** (kuh rouz'd': 'ou' as in 'out'). Drank heavily and noisily; joined in noisy revelry.—"The wild haunting melodies were heard while the mighty men *caroused* at the banquet."—Peter Hugh Reed.

**carp'ing** (kahrp'ing). Faultfinding; censorious; caviling.—"The examples which I shall give are offered in no spirit of *carping* criticism."— Harry S. Truman.

**car'riage** (kar'ij). Deportment; bearing; manner of holding or carrying the head and body.—"Like his walk, his *carriage*, everything about him suggested power."—Thomas Wolfe.

**caus'tic** (kawce'tik). Sarcastic; satirical; sharp and biting; severe; stinging; acrimonious.—"He made bitter, *caustic* speeches."—Bruno Frank.

**cel'i bate** (sel'ĭ bāte). Unmarried; single.—"He had not known many women and had remained *celibate* under the eyes of Buddha."—Pearl S. Buck.

**chafed** (chāfe't). Fretted; become irritated; shown soreness and vexation. —"They had *chafed* under the control of Holland."—Deneys Reitz.

**cha grin'** (shuh grin'). The vexation of wounded pride; disappointment that humiliates.—"These victories on the part of our enemies were expected, and caused no *chagrin*."—Percy C. Magnus.

**char'y** (chair'i). Cautious; wary; watchful; circumspect; careful; shy of doing something; reluctant.— "When they first arrive from the training school they're often a little *chary* about going to church."— Frederic Sondern, Jr.

**chev"a lier'** (shev"uh leer'). A knight; hence, a chivalrous man; a cavalier; a gallant gentleman.—"His quaint and old-world courtesies have made him a modern *chevalier*."—George F. Gahagan.

**chiv'al rous** (shiv'ăl rŭs). Possessing the characteristics of the ideal knights of the age of chivalry; gallant and helpful; courteous and considerate; brave and generous.—"Sensitive, *chivalrous*, proud, the little Marquis moves through the somber fabric of the story."—Alexander Woollcott.

**chol'er ic** (kol'er ik). Hot-tempered; fiery; irascible; easily made angry; wrathful.—"He has a *choleric* temper, and lusty vigor."—Amy Loveman.

**ci vil'i ty** (si vil'ĭ ti). Politeness; courtesy; a cold, formal act or expression. —"Everything was refused, but with a curious *civility*."—André Maurois.

**clean'li ness** (klen'li ness). Cleanness; habitual freedom from dirt and rubbish; tidiness; unsoiled condition.— "Would Prairie Lake be like this— sleepy, slightly prim in its *cleanliness?*" —Jerry Brondfield.

**co"cotte'** (kō"kot'). A woman of low morals; a prostitute; a strumpet.— "He had, says his biographer slyly, the taste of a *cocotte*."—Carlos Baker.

**com'a tose** (kom'uh tōce). Lethargic; abnormally sleepy; in a stupor.—"It should be the duty of the president to awaken to life a *comatose* department." —Charles Seymour.

**com'i ty** (kom'ĭ ti). Friendliness and courtesy; kindly consideration for others; goodwill.—"An interfaith *comity* must be realized in communities of mixed religious populations."—F. Ernest Johnson.

**com pla'cent ly** (kŏm plāy'sĕnt li). In a pleased and satisfied way.—"We cannot pursue *complacently* our customary life."—Cordell Hull.

**com plai'sant** (kŏm plāy'zănt). Courteous; willing to please; agreeable; obliging; affable; polite.—"The occasional interludes of relaxation were under his *complaisant* management."—H. G. Wells.

**com pli'ant** (kŏm plī'ănt). Having a tendency to yield to others; ready to conform to control or authority; wont to acquiesce; submissive.—"If the writer's ideology was *compliant* to the prevailing mood, the absence of these fundamentals was overlooked."—J. Donald Adams.

**com po'sure** (kŏm pō'zhur). Tranquility; calmness; serenity.—"We may look with some sense of *composure* at the progress which has been made."—Winston Churchill.

**con"de scen'sion** (kon"dē sen'shŭn). Courtesy to inferiors; a patronizing manner.—"I appeared at crowded auditions wearing an immaculate suit and an air of amused *condescension*."—Noel Coward.

**con nu'bi al** (kŏ nū'bi ăl). Relating to matrimony; matrimonial; conjugal; having to do with marriage; pertaining to husband and wife.—"When they took their curtain calls together, surely there was a mild, *connubial* glow."—Gretchen Finletter.

**con'se quence** (kon'sē kwence). Importance with reference to what follows; hence, distinction; social rank.—"There was a certain air of acknowledged *consequence* about them, and they talked as if they were accustomed to have their opinions listened to."—Helen C. White.

**con viv"i al'i ty** (kŏn viv"i al'ĭ ti). A gay fellowship; a festive sociability.—"Solitary reading is not so much fun as bookish *conviviality*."—Paul V. McNutt.

**co quet'tish ly** (kŏ ket'tish li). Like a flirt; in a way to attract the attention, especially of men.—"Her *coquettishly* arranged hair was adorned with a blue silk ribbon."—Axel Munthe.

**cor dial'i ty** (kor jal'ĭ ti). Friendliness; kindliness; friendly warmth of manner.—"All contributions are characterized by wholehearted brotherhood and *cordiality*."—Pedro de Alba.

**cor'pu lent** (kor'pū lĕnt). Fat; fleshy; portly; very stout; obese.—"He had the elastic grace too often favored by *corpulent* dignitaries."—Franz Werfel.

**cos'set ed** (koss'et ed). Petted; fondled; pampered.—"His mood was the opposite of self-pity, a feeling that his life had been too *cosseted* and furlined."—John Buchan.

**cour'te san** (kor'tē zan). A court mistress; a prostitute.—"Her husband was not paying court to some established *courtesan* nor setting up a separate temporary apartment."—Pearl S. Buck.

**cox'combs"** (koks'kōmes"). Fops; conceited, vain men; pretentious, silly men.—"These Spartans in their roughness are as affected as our own *coxcombs*."—Caroline Dale Snedeker.

**coy'ly** (koy'li). Shyly; coquettishly; diffidently; demurely; with shrinking modesty.—"She *coyly* took a bath in a jungle waterfall."—Bennett Cerf.

**crav'ing** (krāve'ing). A yearning; a longing; a natural inherent desire; an excessive silent begging.—"There is a *craving* for recognition of one's ability and accomplishments which is a greater force than financial reward alone."—Herman W. Steinkraus.

**crest'fall"en** (krest'fawl"ĕn). Dispirited; dejected; with hanging head; cowed.—"Pretty soon, *crestfallen* and bitter, he was applying for Relief."—Louis Bromfield.

**crotch'et y** (kroch'ĕ ti). Full of perverse fancies; whimsical; eccentric; capricious and short-tempered.—"He was still likely to be *crotchety*, still quick to take offense at a slight."—Thomas Wolfe.

**cu pid'i ty** (kū pid'ĭ ti). Avarice; an inordinate desire for wealth; greed.—"He appealed to his *cupidity*, and sold it to him as a gold brick."—Donald G. Cooley.

**cur mudg'eon** (kur muj'ŭn). A miserly or churlish person.—"Mr. Ickes makes reformer and *curmudgeon* practically synonymous."—Luther Huston.

**curt** (kurt). Rudely brief in speech or manner; abrupt; brusk.—"She was known to be somewhat *curt* and distant with everyone."—Edith Wharton.

**cyn'i cal** (sin'i kăl). Given to sneering at evidences of virtue; sarcastic; skeptical.—"The guests are very *cynical* about their legislature."—Henry W. Toll.

**cyn'i cism** (sin'ĭ siz'm). Contempt for the generosity or virtues of others; a disposition to doubt good motives in human conduct; the expression of this doubt.—"Prostration and *cynicism* followed the plunge into war."—Orville Prescott.

**dal'li ance** (dal'i ănce). Flirting; amorous trifling; fondling; wasting time with wanton caresses.—"As for his *dalliance* with Mary Chaworth, that was of course unhappy."—André Maurois.

**dec'o rous** (dek'ō rŭs). Suitable for the occasion; conventionally proper.—"When the Queen was signaled they resumed the more *decorous* exercise."—P. W. Wilson.

**de co'rum** (dē kō'rŭm). Propriety or decency, as in manner or conduct; formality.—"A high-spirited youth, he was little mindful of college *decorum*."—Amy Loveman.

**def'er ence** (def'ur ĕnce). Great respect; respectful yielding; courteous regard for the opinion of another; consideration.—"She took us in hand with a combination of authority and *deference*."—George V. Denny, Jr.

**de mean'or** (dē meen'ur). Behavior; conduct; manner; way of acting.—"Instantly the animal's whole *demeanor* changed."—Nash Buckingham.

**de mon'stra tive** (dē mon'struh tiv). Inclined to strong expression of feeling or opinion; effusive.—"The mother is naturally very *demonstrative* and expresses her feelings with intense emotion."—William Lyon Phelps.

**de mure'ly** (dē mūre'li). Sedately; decorously; modestly; primly; staidly; gravely.—"She looked *demurely* down at her hands and spoke in a small plaintive voice."—Pearl S. Buck.

**de spon'den cy** (dē spon'dĕn si). Depression; a state of disheartenment; decrease of hope.—"If I were to set them high, I might raise false hopes; if I set them low, I might cause undue *despondency* and alarm."—Winston Churchill.

**de sign'ing** (dē zīne'ing). Scheming; artful; crafty; intriguing.—"Ill-natured historians have called the Empress Josephine a *designing* woman."—Douglas E. Lurton.

**dif'fi dence** (dif'ĭ dĕnce). Modesty; shyness; humility.—"I submit with *diffidence* and confidence that an efficient administration has been provided."—Winston Churchill.

**dil'a to"ry** (dil'uh tō"ri). Given to delay; tardy; slow; causing delay.—"If we continue to be *dilatory* in our actions, our aid may come too late."—James B. Conant.

**dis cern'ment** (di zurn'mĕnt). Keenness of judgment; insight.—"Here is a critic of high moral seriousness and cool, fastidious *discernment*."—Irwin Edman.

**dis cre'tion** (diss kresh'ŭn). Cautious and correct judgment; prudence; care and caution in speech and action.—"*Discretion* is the better part of valor only when you hope to have the chance to fight again."—Archibald MacLeish.

**dis grun'tled** (diss grun't'ld). Disappointed or vexed; discontented; put in a bad temper.—"There were farmers and their wives who were *disgruntled* and unhappy."—Ruth Gruber.

**dis heart'en ing** (diss hahr't'n ing). Discouraging; weakening to the spirit or courage.—"Nothing further was done in the matter. The situation was *disheartening*."—Alexander P. de Seversky.

**di shev'eled** (di shev"'ld). Disarranged; in loose disorder; hence, ruffled.—"His neatly parted hair becomes progressively *disheveled* as he darts from studio to studio."—Elizabeth Starr.

**dis"re pute'** (diss"rē pūte'). Loss of reputation or honor; discredit; lack of respect and character; lowered estimation.—"He said poets and painters had both felt the *disrepute* into which they had been forced in the boom years."—Edward A. Weeks.

**dis sem′bler** (di sem′bler). One who makes a pretense of something; a person who disguises his thoughts or purposes; one who puts on false appearances; a dissimulator.—"Thou art a brave *dissembler*, but art expressly come, nevertheless, to sit at his feet."—Caroline Dale Snedeker.

**dis′so lute ness** (diss′ō lūte něss). Profligacy; immorality; wasteful extravagance.—"The experience of the past tells us that floods of universal *dissoluteness* follow war."—Edward J. Meeman.

**dis traught′** (diss trawt′). Distracted; greatly excited; crazed; in a state of violent excitement.—"The *distraught* lady pleaded for help in an unusual case."—Louis A. Stone.

**doc′ile** (doss′il). Easy to manage; tractable.—"If these are to survive, it will not be because the Constituencies return tame, *docile*, subservient Members."—Winston Churchill.

**drowsed** (drouz′d: 'ou' as in 'out'). Dozed; was half asleep; was sleepily passing the time.—"In the sunny garden she *drowsed* over the classics."—Lloyd C. Douglas.

**drow′sy** (drou′zi: 'ou' as in 'out'). Heavy with sleepiness; sleepy; lethargic; half-asleep.—"The town, so *drowsy* a moment before, was now alive and running for its very life."—Stewart H. Holbrook.

**dudg′eon** (duj′ŭn). Resentment; sulky displeasure; ill humor.—"He lost patience, and in high *dudgeon* summoned the architect."—Bodo Wuth.

**dupes** (dūpes). People misled through accepting the improbable; tricked or deceived people.—"His *dupes* among us have sought to make footholds for him here."—Franklin Delano Roosevelt.

**ec cen′tric** (ek sen′trik). A person who is peculiar, strange, erratic, odd.—"The *eccentric* is different, but he is different because he is off center."—Roland H. Bainton.

**ef fu′sive** (e fū′siv). Demonstrative; gushing; showing warm feeling.—"The demeanor of my visitors, which had been courteous, but cool, now became almost *effusive*."—W. Somerset Maugham.

**eg′o ism** (ē′gō iz'm). The doctrine that the supreme end of human conduct is the perfection or happiness of the self, or ego; love of self.—"His *egoism* is aggressive, and the first person singular is the word that recurs most frequently in his conversation."—W. Somerset Maugham.

**e′go tism** (ē′gō tiz'm). The habit of speaking or thinking continually of oneself; self-conceit; selfishness; the frequent use of the words 'I' and 'my.'—"I regard this doctrine as the supreme expression of human *egotism*."—L. P. Jacks.

**e ma′ci at″ed** (ē māy′shi āte″id). Very thin from loss of weight; starved-looking; having lost much flesh; lean-looking.—"She was *emaciated*, half-dead from her long ordeal of prison privation."—Dorothy Canfield Fisher.

**em bar′rassed** (em bar′ăst). Involved in difficulties; hampered; abashed.—"The League is *embarrassed* by not knowing whether your Government will co-operate or not."—Herbert Morrison.

**em bit′tered** (em bit′erd). Made bitter or resentful; aggravated; exasperated; acrimonious.—"There is little that is easy about life. To become *embittered*, however, is indeed tragic and unfortunate."—George Matthew Adams.

**en dear′ing** (en deer′ing). Making dear or precious to someone; causing a person to become an object of great love and devotion.—"His charm and comic manners must have been *endearing* to her, for she remained with him."—Paul Cranston.

**en grossed′** (en grōce′t′). Absorbed; completely occupied.—"Most of us have been so *engrossed* with the White House that we have quite forgotten the home units on which the White House must depend for counsel."—W. J. Cameron.

**en′mi ties** (en′mi tiz). Hostile conditions; antagonisms.—"They try to reawaken long-slumbering religious *enmities*."—Franklin Delano Roosevelt.

**en vi′ron ment** (en vī′rŭn měnt). Surroundings; external circumstances; all the outside conditions and influences and things that affect people as a whole.—"The government is desirous of doing everything it can to create an *environment* in which private investment is encouraged."—Harry L. Hopkins.

**eq′ua bly** (ek′wuh bli). In an even, quiet tone; steadily; in a tranquil, undisturbed way.—"'True,' he said *equably.* 'At such a distance she cannot hear.'"—Samuel Hopkins Adams.

**e″qua nim′i ty** (ē″kwuh nim′ĭ ti). Composure; evenness of temper; calmness. —"The rabbi took this ignominious proceeding with absentminded *equanimity.*"—Franz Werfel.

**e rot′ic** (ē rot′ik). Amorous; relating to passionate love.—"These quacks promise health and give a little *erotic* stimulation by commercializing psychology."—Morris Fishbein.

**es cap′ism** (ess kāpe′iz'm). The habit of turning the mind to activities, imaginations, or some kind of entertainment in order to escape from realities or routine work.—"It is only through the medium of the screen that these workers can indulge in a little essential *escapism.*"—Hilary St. George Saunders.

**eth′i cal** (eth′i kăl: 'th' as in 'thin'). Pertaining to rules of right and wrong conduct; in agreement with professional standards of conduct.— "Being *ethical* among doctors is practically the same thing as being a Democrat in Texas or a Presbyterian in Scotland."—Irvin S. Cobb.

**et′i quette″** (et′i ket″). The usages of polite society; social customs; rules and forms of propriety of action.— "Friendly people have good manners no matter how ignorant they are of the laws of *etiquette.*"—Sidonie Matsner Gruenberg.

**e va′sive** (ē vāy′siv). Dodging or evading a question or argument; seeking to escape from a truth or statement; elusive; wanting in frankness.— "Everywhere he got the same *evasive* answer."—Franz Werfel.

**ex act′ing** (eg zakt′ing). Making urgent demands; requiring precise results.—

"He is an *exacting* man though he does not appear severe."—Lord Beaverbrook.

**ex″hi bi′tion ism** (ek″si bish′ŭn iz′m). An inclination to make a public display in order to attract attention to oneself; a tendency to a self-satisfied parade of personal attractiveness.— "It was as if, no matter what they did in a gesture of defiant *exhibitionism,* the world would go on accepting them."—Louis Bromfield.

**ex hil″a ra′tion** (eg zil″uh rā′shŭn). Stimulation; enlivenment; animation; cheerfulness; liveliness.—"Refreshment and *exhilaration* of the spirit comes from contact with beauty in music, sculpture, and painting."— Virginia C. Gildersleeve.

**ex po′nents** (eks pō′nĕnts). Those who explain or represent the principles of something.—"They are advocates and *exponents* of craft unionism, and they resent industrial unions."— John L. Lewis.

**ex′tro verts** (eks′trō vurts). Those whose interests are centered in the actions and things of the outside world; people who are not given to introspection or self-examination.— "The neurotic wants to be like the average normals, the *extroverts* whom he envies."—Louis E. Bisch.

**fas tid′i ous** (fass tid′i ŭs). Overnice; very particular about form or details. —"*Fastidious* fellows are appearing in the evening in dinner jackets."— Lucius Beebe.

**feigned** (faind). Pretended; assumed; simulated; unreal.—"She spoke with a *feigned* air of knowingness."—Edith Wharton.

**fem′i nists** (fem′ĭ nists). Those who advocate the equality of women with men.—"The ardent *feminists* on our board were concerned about the status of women after the war."— Lucy R. Milligan.

**fil′i al** (fil′i ăl). Befitting a son or daughter; due from children to parents.—"The group is characterized by strong *filial* piety."—Karl R. Bendetsen.

**flair** (flair). Talent or aptitude; special taste or liking.—"His real strength lies in his *flair,* which can't be put down in black and white."—John Buchan.

**flip′pan cy** (flip′ăn si). Lack of mental gravity; unseemly lightness.—"Is *flippancy* a useful or even legitimate device in discussing public questions?"—Herbert Hoover.

**flip′pant** (flip′ănt). Pert and trifling; smart and disrespectful; shallow and impertinent; treating serious matters with a lack of gravity.—"There were, for instance, the politicians who were *flippant*, arrogant, and threatening in their language."—Dorothy Thompson.

**flound′ers** (floun′derz: 'ou' as in 'out'). Stumbles and struggles uncertainly; acts clumsily and makes mistakes; hence; muddles along. —"The heroine *flounders* awkwardly, half-unwillingly, almost as if by accident, in the role."—Dorothy Canfield Fisher.

**foi′bles** (foy′bl′z). Personal weaknesses; slight faults of character; failings.—"We get their whims, *foibles*, and disputes, as well as their strategy and tactics."—Stephen Vincent Benét.

**for lorn′ly** (fŏr lorn′li). Miserably; as though without help or hope; pitiably; abjectly; as though friendless and forsaken.—"He stood *forlornly*, staring through the rain across the yellow water."—Pearl S. Buck.

**for′mal** (for′măl). Conventional; ceremonious; adhering scrupulously to social form or custom; used only on stiff, precise occasions.—"The use of my *formal* given name indicated that he was not on the best of terms with me."—A. J. Cronin.

**fri vol′i ty** (fri vol′ĭ ti). Frivolousness; silly, trifling behavior; acts that lack seriousness or sense; levity.—"Not even the most severe critic of wartime *frivolity* can raise an eyebrow at this restaurant."—Lucius Beebe.

**fro′ward** (frō′werd). Wayward; perverse; obstinately disobedient; willful; intractable; refractory.—"No one likes a *froward* child."—Malcom Babbitt.

**fust′y** (fuss′ti). Old-fashioned; out of date; like an old fogy; moldy or musty with age.—"She had an unbalancing personality even to an old *fusty* pedagogue like myself."—Samuel Hopkins Adams.

**gal′lant ry** (gal′ăn tri). Bravery; respectful courtesy; chivalrousness; courtliness; polite attention to all women; dashing courage.—"He had that kind of *gallantry*—courageous and aware."—Anne Morrow Lindbergh.

**gape** (gāpe). To open the mouth wide; to stare with mouth open; to stare in this way at something strange.— "They gathered outside the wire enclosure to *gape* at the prisoners."— Roy Chapman Andrews.

**ge″ni al′i ty** (je″ni al′ĭ ti). Kindness of disposition; cheerfulness; warmth.— "The President received me with cordial *geniality*."—Lord Cecil.

**gen teel′** (jen teel′). Refined; polite; well-bred; belonging to high society. —"She began as a rebel against this *genteel* tradition."—Joseph Wood Krutch.

**gour′mand** (gŏor′mănd). A person who is fond of good food; a judge of good fare; an epicure.—"He was too fat, but food tempted and tortured him, as it does any *gourmand*."— Malcom Babbitt.

**gour″mets′** (gŏor″māze′). Epicures; people who appreciate really good food and are connoisseurs in eating and drinking.—"Many *gourmets* will agree that clams and mussels are among the most delectable of the bivalves."—L. H. Fowler.

**gra′cious** (grā′shŭs). Agreeable; full of charm; courteous and kindly; polite; pleasant and humane.—"He signified with a *gracious* inclination of the head that she might follow him." —Elizabeth Goudge.

**grat′i fied** (grat′ĭ fīde). Pleased, as by satisfying a desire or need; delighted; happily satisfied.—"I am most *gratified* by the support of the delegation."—Marvin Jones.

**griz′zled** (griz″ld). Gray; streaked with gray; hence, gray-haired.— " 'The big mistake,' said one *grizzled* ancient, 'was to let women start growing things.' "—Dorothy Canfield Fisher.

**grouch** (grouch: 'ou' as in 'out'). A fit

of ill-temper or surly discontent; a mood of grumbling sullenness; a state of complaining sulkiness.—"I waked with a *grouch*, stiff muscles, and a sour taste in my mouth."— John Myers Myers.

**ha bit'u at ed** (huh bit'ū āte id). Accustomed; made familiar by use or habit; familiarized.—"The inhabitants have become so *habituated* to this order of priority as to be unaware that it exists."—L. P. Jacks.

**har'di hood** (hahr'di hŏŏd). Sturdy courage; audacity; venturesomeness; boldness; daring; firmness of mind.— "We want young men of intellectual *hardihood*."—Thomas W. Lamont.

**hau teur'** (hō tur'). Haughtiness; disdainful pride; arrogant manner; lofty or lordly spirit or behavior.— "The cool *hauteur* of the exclusive inn in its attitude toward applicants was not mere snobbery."—Lloyd C. Douglas.

**heart'en ing** (hahr't'n ing). Giving courage to; encouraging; cheering or giving strength and spirit; inspiriting. —"I often turn to Jefferson and find the *heartening* language of the Americanism for which generations of our forebears fought and died."—Claude Bowers.

**hoy'den** (hoy'd'n). A boisterous, bold girl; a romping, rude girl; a tomboy. —"Could you imagine that such a demure lady had been a *hoyden* in her youth?"—Donald G. Cooley.

**hu mane'** (hū māne'). Showing kindness; benevolent; charitable.—"We will request gifts so that *humane* agencies can continue to help."— Charles P. Sullivan.

**hu man"i tar'i ans** (hū man"ĭ tair'i-ănz). Those who are broadly philanthropic and humane; those devoted to the welfare of mankind.—"Sometimes we find engineers who are *humanitarians*, uplifters, and philosophers."—Arthur E. Morgan.

**hu mil'i at"ed** (hū mil'i āte"id). Humbled; mortified; abashed; chagrined. —"I returned to my useless solitude in the old tower, *humiliated* and despondent."—Axel Munthe.

**hy"per crit'i cal** (hī"pur krit'i kăl). Overcritical; too critical of, or in-

clined to find fault with, small mistakes; unduly exact.—"How can one find the heart to be *hypercritical* about anything?"—John J. Green.

**hy"per sen'si tive** (hī"pur sen'sĭ tiv). Very easily hurt or offended; very keenly impressionable; having excessively sensitive feelings.—"It is impossible to change the habit patterns of childhood—the supercharged and *hypersensitive* character of the nervous system."—Louis E. Bisch.

**i de'al ism** (ī dē'ăl iz'm). The habit of forming standards of excellence and striving after their realization; following ideals; acting from a standpoint of what ought to be.—"There is need in politics for *idealism*."—Lloyd C. Stark.

**i den'ti ty** (ī den'tĭ ti). Who or what a person is; equality with itself; a distinctive character or similarity.— "Your individuality is your spiritual *identity*."—Emmet Fox.

**im ag'i na"tive** (i maj'ĭ nā"tiv). Romantic; showing imagination; given to using the creative faculty of the mind; constructive.—"He is a tremendously effective business head— hard-working, *imaginative*, conscientious."—Marquis W. Childs.

**im'be cile** (im'bē sil). Feeble-minded; childish; mentally impotent; stupid; mentally deficient; foolish.—"She looked up indignantly at the *imbecile* smile on the face in the picture."— Edith Wharton.

**im mod'est** (im mod'est). Bold; lacking in decency; not modest; indelicate; indecorous.—"The *immodest* allusions to nausea and victuals were the permitted liberties of old family servants."—Stephen Vincent Benét.

**im pas'si ble** (im pass'ĭ b'l). Unfeeling; incapable of suffering; impassive; apathetic.—"She was always *impassible*, haughty and distant."—George F. Gahagan.

**im per'ti nent** (im pur'tĭ nĕnt). Rude; out of place; meddlesome; offending propriety; presumptive; inappropriate.—"There was a certain dignity about him that made a lot of questions seem *impertinent*."—Christopher La Farge.

**im prac'ti cal** (im prak'ti kăl). Not

practical; not useful; incapable of applying knowledge or judgment; having theoretical, instead of usable, ideas.—"She lived in a world of dreams, and knew that her husband found her *impractical*."—Rose Feld.

**im pres'sion a ble** (im presh'ŭn uh b'l). Easily influenced; capable of being inculcated or molded.—"You have invested four of the most *impressionable* years of your life in college education."—Robert H. Jackson.

**im"pro pri'e ties** (im"prō prī'ĕ tiz). Improper acts; unsuitable actions or expressions; words or deeds that are not in accord with the standards of good society.—"The book shimmers and sparkles with the most sophisticated pro- and *improprieties*."— Fanny Butcher.

**im'pu dence** (im'pū dĕnce). Insolence; brazenness; bold rudeness; shameless disrespect; pert boldness.—"The hero's *impudence* and perilous conversation struck us as refreshing."— Will Cuppy.

**in"ca pac'i ty** (in"kuh pass'ĭ ti). Incapability; want of competency; disability; lack of power.—"Imagine yourself retired for physical *incapacity* at thirty."—Dale Carnegie.

**in"con sid'er ate** (in"kŏn sid'er it). Thoughtless; showing a lack of thought and consideration for others; disregarding the feelings of others.— "'Forgive me,' he said, self-reproachfully. 'I have been very *inconsiderate*.'" —Lloyd C. Douglas.

**in"con sol'a ble** (in"kŏn sōle'uh b'l). Disconsolate; unable to be comforted; hopelessly sorrowful; dejected; not to be comforted.—"For three years she lay on her bed, *inconsolable*, peevish, embittered by her trouble."—Lloyd C. Douglas.

**in"de co'rum** (in"dē kō'rŭm). Want of decorum or seemliness; impropriety; lack of good taste and etiquette. —"To bring up the subject of religion in that mixed group was gross *indecorum*."—Donald G. Cooley.

**in dig'ni ties** (in dig'nĭ tiz). Affronts; insults; acts that degrade or mortify; offenses against personal dignity or respect; slights.—"I can almost for-get the *indignities* I have suffered."— Rachel Field.

**in dul'gent** (in dul'jĕnt). Lenient; charitable; tolerant; yielding weakly to desires of others.—"They are supposed to have been made undisciplined and selfish by too *indulgent* parents."—Anne O'Hare McCormick.

**in'fan tile** (in'făn tīle). Having the characteristics of infants or infancy; childish.—"The group fear of the size and power of machinery is *infantile*."—W. J. Cameron.

**in"fi del'i ty** (in"fĭ del'ĭ ti). Unfaithfulness; adultery; violations of the marriage vows.—"She is worried about her husband's *infidelity*."— Rosemary Benét.

**in firm'** (in furm'). Feeble, as from age; sickly; weak and faltering.—"In the growing demand of the aged, the classification is not limited to the *infirm* or the helpless."—Paul F. Cadman.

**in gen'u ous** (in jen'ū ŭs). Frank; candid; naïve; sincere; artless.—"In his *ingenuous* and patently honest statement the Marshal admits he cannot form a Government."—Anne O'Hare McCormick.

**in'grate** (in'grāte). An ungrateful person; one who is not thankful.— "Aaron Burr was a traitor and an *ingrate*."—Donald G. Cooley.

**in gra'ti at"ing** (in grā'shi āte"ing). Winning confidence or favor from someone; trying to secure a good reception; trying to please.—"An *ingratiating* salesman called on me." —Harvey T. Harrison.

**in hos'pi ta ble** (in hoss'pi tuh b'l). Not extending a welcome; not affording shelter; lacking the disposition to receive and entertain kindly and generously.—"It is hard to be *inhospitable* even to objectionable people."—Ainslee Mockridge.

**in quis'i tive** (in kwiz'ĭ tiv). Curious; asking questions to gratify curiosity; prying; inquiring; peering into; searching.—"There was hardly anything that their *inquisitive* eyes did not find to be paintable."—Adriaan J. Barnouw.

**in sen'si tive** (in sen'sĭ tiv). Unimpressionable; without deep feeling; not easily affected by outside influences. —"The Colonel, who was *insensitive* to details, continued to be proud of his home."—Edith Wharton.

**in'so lent ly** (in'sō lĕnt li). Disrespectfully; impudently; rudely; insultingly.—"He stared *insolently* into the face of the young interloper."—Lloyd C. Douglas.

**in"sub or"di na'tion** (in"sŭ bor"dĭ nā'-shŭn). Disobedience; rebellion; mutiny; refusal to submit to authority.— "More than half of them were once commissioned officers who, for rank *insubordination* or other irregularities, are now in disfavor with the Government."—Lloyd C. Douglas.

**in teg'ri ty** (in teg'rĭ ti). Uprightness of character; honesty; soundness.— "They are engaged in a life struggle to preserve the liberties and *integrity* of the New World."—Anne O'Hare McCormick.

**in tem'per ate** (in tem'pur it). Not temperate or moderate; excessive; unbridled; immoderate; unrestrained. —"Lord Byron was given to *intemperate* fits of anger."—S. L. Scanlon.

**in tol'er ance** (in tol'ur ănce). Refusal to allow or permit beliefs or actions which are contrary to one's own plan of life; bigotry; want of liberality; unwillingness to put up with something of which one does not approve. —"It will be a task to extirpate this spirit and régime of *intolerance*."— Winston Churchill.

**in'tro verts"** (in'trō verts"). Those whose emotions are self-centered; those who continually engage in self-examination.—"Many are suffering from ingrown minds. It has become the fashion to call them *introverts*."— Joseph Jastrow.

**in tu'i tive** (in tū'ĭ tiv). Instinctive; natural; knowing or perceiving without resorting to the reasoning powers; directly perceptive through sense, without reasoning.—"I had an understanding of people which was penetratingly *intuitive*."—Thomas Sugrue.

**in vei'gle** (in vee'g'l). Persuade by deception or flattery; entice by beguiling; coax.—"Ingenious, resourceful,

and aggressive, they *inveigle* their way into factories all over the country."— Frank J. Taylor.

**in vig'or at"ing** (in vig'ur āte"ing). Strengthening; animating; giving energy and vigor; hence, stimulating; exhilarating.—"On the subject of making pictures he was forthright and *invigorating*."—Hilary St. George Saunders.

**ir'ri tat"ed** (ir'ri tāte"id). Vexed; impatiently annoyed; provoked.— "Britain and ourselves are such close relatives that we sometimes become *irritated* with each other."—Edward J. Meeman.

**jaun'ty** (jawn'ti). Having a self-satisfied, careless air; sprightly; perky and smart; saucy.—"A brownish bird with a gray breast and a *jaunty* chestnut cap bobbed up."—Bennie Bengston.

**jo cose'** (jō kōce'). Merry and facetious; humorous; playful; jocular; sportive; waggish.—"The reporters were in *jocose* mood as their vessel chugged slowly down the harbor."— Emma Bugbee.

**jo'vi al ly** (jō'vi ă li). Expressing gaiety and good-humor; merrily; hilariously.—"The author *jovially* tells a story on himself."—Dorothy Canfield Fisher.

**ju di'cious ly** (joo dish'ŭs li). Wisely; sensibly; making use of good, sound judgment; in a well-advised, discreet way; sagaciously; prudently.—"He has built up his community by lending money liberally and *judiciously*." —J. P. McEvoy.

**lack"a dai'si cal** (lak"uh dāy'zi kăl). Listless; languid; feebly sentimental. —"A *lackadaisical* attitude has resulted in a crisis."—J. Edgar Hoover.

**lan'guid** (lang'gwid). Listless; wanting in strength or force; limp from exhaustion; without animation.— "Even in its death throes the *languid* expression never left the face of the sloth."—V. Wolfgang von Hagen.

**lar'ce nous** (lahr'sĕ nŭs). Thievish; given to defrauding others; full of plans for committing thefts.—"The serious situation failed to melt the *larcenous* heart of the racketeer."— George F. Gahagan.

**lax** (laks). Slack; remiss; not using due care.—"A few individuals grew *lax* in the performance of their specific duties."—J. Lester Perry.

**list′less** (list′less). Spiritless; lacking interest; indifferent; too tired to care or exert oneself; languid.—"He was *listless*, because he saw no future in his humdrum life."—Emil Lengyel.

**mag″na nim′i ty** (mag″nuh nim′ĭ ti). Greatness of soul or heart; generosity in feeling or behavior towards others; nobility of mind; elevation above what is petty.—"To effect this settlement requires moral resolution and great *magnanimity*."—Walter Lippmann.

**mal″ad just′ment** (mal″uh just′mĕnt). Lack of adaptation to circumstances. —"As cases of *maladjustment* occur, they are referred to the commission." —John Gabriel.

**mal″a droit′ly** (mal″uh droyt′li). Awkwardly; clumsily; in a blundering way; with a lack of skill or ingenuity. —"He told him he thought he was conducting the whole affair *maladroitly*."—A. S. M. Hutchinson.

**ma lin′ger** (muh ling′ger). Feign sickness or inability; shirk.—"Civilians will have to stand to their jobs, and any who *malinger* or run away will be shot."—Westbrook Pegler.

**man′ner isms** (man′er iz′mz). Adherence to particular manners or styles; particular ways of speaking or behaving; odd habits; unusual gestures. —"There is nothing in his bearing or *mannerisms* to indicate that he is heir to a great fortune."—Richard W. Abbott.

**mar′i tal** (mar′i tăl). Pertaining to marriage; matrimonial.—"He deserted her after several years of *marital* incompatibility."—Samuel Z. Orgel.

**mar″ti net′** (mahr″ti net′). A very strict disciplinarian; a person who enforces obedience and order very rigorously.—"It is the story of a stormy, brainy *martinet*."—Bell Irvin Wiley.

**ma ter′nal** (muh tur′năl). Motherly; pertaining to a mother; inherited from one's mother.—"She was guided by some sound *maternal* instinct.— Henry James Forman.

**maud′lin** (mawd′lin). Foolishly and effusively affectionate; silly in an emotional way.—"When we try to apply intelligence it is often sidetracked by *maudlin* sentimentality." —George Barton Cutten.

**mel′an chol″y** (mel′ăn kol″ĭ). Morbidly gloomy; sad; dismal.—"It will be our long history that will come to an abrupt and *melancholy* end."— Winston Churchill.

**mel′lowed** (mel′ōde). Matured; softened by experience; softened and developed by age; made more gentle and sweet by time.—"Her stern good sense was at last *mellowed* with wisdom."—Ellen Lewis Buell.

**met′tle some** (met″l sŭm). Full of mettle; spirited; fiery; full of spirit and courage; ardent.—"This *mettlesome* yearling needed a light hand on the rein."—André Maurois.

**mien** (meen). The external appearance; demeanor; bearing; carriage; manner.—"There appeared a column of soldiers marching with swinging stride and confident *mien*."—John D. Rockefeller, Jr.

**minc′ing** (mince′ing). Uttered with affected primness or preciseness, or with exaggerated elegance or refinement; affectedly refined.—"With *mincing* words about national interests, these people foster their own designs."—Frank C. Walker.

**minx** (mingks). A wanton woman; a pert girl or woman; a flirt; a forward girl.—"Mercenary *minx* that she was, she had simply come to ask for money."—Elizabeth Goudge.

**mis′an thrope** (mis′ăn thrōpe). A hater of mankind; a person who distrusts and avoids human beings; one who dislikes human society.—"She was disowned by her kind and became not a *misanthrope* but an individualist."—May Lamberton Becker.

**mis og′y ny** (mi soj′ĭ ni). Hatred of women.—"She sowed the seeds of an enduring *misogyny* when she said, 'If only you had been a dear little girl.' " —H. G. Wells.

**mock′er y** (mok′ur i). Ridicule; derisive action or speech; impudent mimicry; banter; making fun of something.—"Of course, much of the laughter is *mockery*—that is what a satirist is for."—Edward A. Weeks.

**mope** (mōpe). To be silent and out of spirits; to abandon oneself to depression; to be dejected and despondent. —"Time was when the strategy of American business was to *mope* in its tents."—John Chamberlain.

**mor′bid** (mor′bid). Taking an excessive interest in matters of an unwholesome nature; unhealthy; diseased.—"Any candid observer can testify to the corrosive power of this *morbid* appetite for power."—John W. Davis.

**mo′ron** (mō′ron). An adult person whose mental capacity is only that of a child of twelve or younger; a child whose mentality is arrested or undeveloped.—"Everybody is a famous man unless he is a *moron*."— Harry Hansen.

**mo rose′** (mō rōce′). Gloomy and moody; bitter and dissatisfied; sourly austere.—"He was silent and *morose*, a problem to the doctors."—John H. Fulweiler.

**moun′te bank** (moun′tē bangk: 'ou' as in 'out'). A charlatan; a person who practices deception by tricks and humbug; a quack; an impostor, pretending to possess some skill.— "The *mountebank* was paid to go away without performing the miracle."—H. W. Haggard.

**na ïve′** (nah ēve′). Ingenuous; simple; unsophisticated; childlike; artless.— "Our *naïve* self-sufficiency sometimes breaks down."—Harry Emerson Fosdick.

**na ïve″té′** (nah ēve″tāy′). Simplicity; ingenuousness; artlessness; unspoiled sincerity and frankness.—"*Naïveté* and sophistication, satire and something lyrical may all be present at once."—Howard Devree.

**non′cha lance** (non′shuh lănce). Indifference; jaunty unconcern; casual imperturbability; gay carelessness.— "He stepped with easy *nonchalance* into the focused glare of the headlights."—Franz Werfel.

**non″con form′ist** (non″kŏn for′mist). One who does not conform to the doctrine of an established church; one who fails to bring his views into

harmony with established usage.— "As far as the amenities of society were concerned, Samuel Johnson was a *nonconformist*."—Sterling McCormick.

**nos tal′gi a** (noss tal′ji uh). Severe homesickness.—"I have a sort of *nostalgia* for competition."—Leon Henderson.

**nos tal′gic** (noss tal′jik). Very homesick; morbidly anxious to return to a former place or state.—"Man becomes *nostalgic* and looks back to primitive America as to a Garden of Eden."—Bayard Christy.

**no″to ri′e ty** (nō″tō rī′ĕ ti). The state of being widely known and talked about, generally unfavorably; ill-fame; being well-known for something discreditable.—"The desire for *notoriety* has started many boys on the wrong path."—Donald G. Cooley.

**oaf′ish** (ōfe′ish). Loutish; awkward; stupid; doltish; ungainly.—"He had a call from two *oafish*, unprepossessing young men."—H. G. Wells.

**o bei′sance** (ō bāy′sănce). Deference; acts or gestures of deep respect; homage; submissive obedience.— "She did not teach the children to pay him proper *obeisance* as the head of the family."—Rose Feld.

**ob strep′er ous** (ŏb strep′ur ŭs). Unruly; making a great disturbance; noisy; disorderly; difficult to manage. —"He was the most *obstreperous* patient ever admitted to a naval hospital."—Don Wharton.

**ob tru′sive** (ŏb trōō′siv). Forward; intrusive; inclined to push in or obtrude; disposed to thrust himself upon attention.—"He is an insolent, *obtrusive* boor."—Emmet Holloway.

**of fi′cious ness** (ŏ fish′ŭs ness). Intrusion into what is not one's concern; an informal connection with official matters.—"We were soon exposed to all the evils of bureaucracy, *officiousness*, and action based on theoretical thinking."—Edward A. O'Neal.

**o′gre** (ō′gur). A monster or giant who was fabled to eat human beings; hence, a very ugly and cruel man.— "The tramp, framed in the doorway, looked like some frightening *ogre*."— Douglas Brewster.

**o pin'ion at"ed** (ō pin'yŭn āte"id).
Obstinately attached to an opinion;
self-willed; dogmatic; having and
asserting very definite convictions.—
"The book is *opinionated*, but its
opinions are those of the time."—
May Lamberton Becker.

**op"por tu'nist** (op"ŏr tū'nist). One
who takes advantage of opportunities
and circumstances without much
regard for fixed principles or possible consequences.—"My opponent's
latest subterfuge brands him as a
political *opportunist*."—Albert W.
Hawkes.

**or'gy** (or'ji). A wild revelry; a carousal;
excessive indulgence.—"They determined to share in the prevailing
*orgy* of extravagance."—Edmund A.
Walsh.

**pan'der ers** (pan'dur urz). Those who
act as go-betweens in love affairs;
hence, procurers; those who further
the illicit acts of others.—"The
*panderers* climbed to power by trading
the birthright of the mass man."—
Mark M. Jones.

**pa ro'chi al ism** (puh rō'ki ăl iz'm).
Narrowness of view; provincialism;
limited viewpoint.—"To be a patriot
meant a larger loyalty as against the
*parochialism* of a local mind."—
Harry Emerson Fosdick.

**pa thet'ic** (puh thet'ik: 'th' as in
'thin'). Arousing compassion; pitiful; exciting pity or sorrow; of the
emotions.—"The *pathetic* relationship between the Baron and herself
gave the play much of its charm."—
Austin Wright.

**pa'thos** (pāy'thoss: 'th' as in 'thin').
The quality that arouses emotion or
passion; suffering.—"National moni-
tors are often nurtured upon the
*pathos* of a people."—T. V. Smith.

**pec"ca dil'los** (pek"uh dil'ōze). Slight
or trifling sins; small faults; little
offenses.—"Mobs have killed their
fellow men sometimes for mere
*peccadillos*."—Harold L. Ickes.

**pee'vish** (pee'vish). Irritable and fretful; cross and complaining; querulous and moody; ill-tempered and
touchy.—"The peace was wrecked
by his *peevish* factionalism."—William Allen White.

**pen'sive ness** (pen'siv ness). Dreamy
thoughtfulness; serious or sad reflection; a state of melancholy thought
or musing.—"She was lovelier in
this *pensiveness* than he had ever seen
her."—Lloyd C. Douglas.

**pe nu'ri ous ness** (pē nū'ri ŭs ness).
Stinginess; miserliness; meanness in
the use of money; parsimony.—
"There is a strange mixture of
*penuriousness* and lavishness in the
Nizam."—Jay Nelson Tuck.

**per'son a ble** (pur'sŭn uh b'l). Of attractive appearance; comely; well-
favored; pleasant to look at.—"That
*personable*, and to me always profoundly annoying, actor was calming
himself with a cigarette."—Alexander Woollcott.

**per sua'sive** (pur swāy'siv). Having
the power to win over by entreaty or
reasoning; having the tendency to
influence or convince.—"The Prime
Minister dwelt on the point in his
very patient and *persuasive* speech."
—Winston Churchill.

**pert** (purt). Saucy; bold and free in
speech; impudent.—"She is a *pert*
but attractive young lady."—Lewis
Nichols.

**per verse'ness** (pur vurce'ness). Acting
in a wilfully wrong or contrary way;
waywardness; petulant obstinacy;
unreasonable stubbornness.—"The
premature chill of *perverseness* had
nipped the germinating seeds, but
had not quite killed them."—André
Maurois.

**pes'si mists** (pess'ĭ mists). Persons given
to desponding views; those who look
on the worst side of things.—"Most
manufacturers are not *pessimists*, they
are realists."—Walter D. Fuller.

**pet'ti ness** (pet'i ness). Meanness;
undue attention to trifles; nar-
row-mindedness. — "Understanding
should drive out bitterness and *petti-
ness* in the face of a common peril."—
E. C. Bancroft.

**pet'u lant** (pet'ū lănt). Fretful; perverse; peevish; subject to fits of
crossness; querulous.—"It was a
*petulant* little sound, like gnomes at
work."—Virginia S. Eifert.

**phil"an throp'ic** (fil"ăn throp'ik: 'th'
as in 'thin'). Relating to the desire to

promote the happiness and betterment of mankind; benevolent; charitable.—*"Philanthropic* work is my hobby."—Benjamin Lazrus.

**phleg mat'ic** (fleg mat'ik). Apathetic; impassive; indifferent; stolid.— "Sculpture is a more static, a more *phlegmatic* art than painting."— Lorado Taft.

**piqued** (peekt). Provoked; angry at being slighted; wounded in pride; nettled.—"I was still *piqued* because I had heard of the Scouts and the shooting from others."—Christopher La Farge.

**pit'i ful** (pit'i fool). Pathetic; piteous; pitiable; miserable; calling forth pity; heart-rending.—"They tried to persuade each other that his sons were a source of pride to the community so they themselves would not seem quite so *pitiful* as they really were."—Bruno Frank.

**plac'id** (plass'id). Smooth; unruffled; calm; peaceful; undisturbed.—"The nasal chant drifted to me across the *placid* water."—C. Wellington Furlong.

**plau'si ble** (plaw'zĭ b'l). Seeming likely to be true; appearing worthy of trust.—*"Plausible* reasons for quitting are always at hand."—W. J. Cameron.

**poise** (poyze). Balance; hence, equilibrium; dignity of manner or behavior; equanimity; repose of bearing.— "His cool classical *poise* seems to have kindled with a faint reflection of romantic fervor."—George F. Whicher.

**pol'i tic** (pol'ĭ tik). Discreet; wary; prudent; artful; wisely adapted to an end; diplomatic.—" 'Your point is well taken,' he conceded. Then he became slyly *politic.*"—Gene Fowler.

**pos ses'sive** (pŏ zess'iv). Showing the desire to possess; expressing control or ownership; indicative of having or holding as a possession or right.— "Under his half-civilized surface he was as primitive and *possessive* as any of his Pathan ancestors."—Maud Diver.

**pre co'cious** (prē kō'shŭs). Unusually forward and mature; mentally developed much earlier than usual.— "How any girl so young could have been so *precocious* was a mystery explainable only by recourse to such patronizing words as prodigy."— Orville Prescott.

**pre"dis po si'tion** (prē"diss pō zish'ŭn). Susceptibility; tendency; inclination; a state of being predisposed or having a natural bent.—"Most women admit a *predisposition* for a male of compelling personality."—Jess Stearn.

**pre oc'cu pied** (prē ok'ū pīde). Engrossed in thought; mentally absorbed or engaged in something that takes precedence of everything else. —"American industry has been *preoccupied* in creating a continuous flow of new products."—Alfred P. Sloan, Jr.

**pre"pos sess'ing** (prē"pŏ zess'ing). Making a favorable first impression; inspiring a preconceived liking or opinion; attractive; pleasing.—"In profile she had somewhat the look of a bird of prey, but full face she was *prepossessing.*"—W. Somerset Maugham.

**pre sent'a ble** (prē zen'tuh b'l). In suitable condition for company; fit to be seen in society; of decent appearance.—"The boys said that they weren't *presentable* enough to come in."—Douglas E. Lurton.

**pre sump'tion** (prē zump'shŭn). Overconfidence; blind self-assertion; effrontery or unpleasant boldness; arrogance.—"I have before met a youngster who displayed such offensive *presumption.*"—Emmet Holloway.

**prob'i ty** (prōbe'ĭ ti). Strict moral honesty and integrity; uprightness.— "Last but not least ranks *probity* in thought and action."—Madame Chiang Kai-shek.

**promp'ti tude** (promp'tĭ tūde). Speed in acting or making a decision; promptness; readiness of action; the habit or fact of acting without delay. —"They were provided, with a *promptitude* which gave rise to some suspicions, with service at home."— L. P. Jacks.

**prud'er y** (prood'ur i). Extreme propriety in conduct; primness; modesty, especially, when affected or priggish.—"The eyes of your souls have been opened, *prudery* has been erased from your minds."—William Elliott.

**pru'ri ent** (prōōr'i ĕnt). Given to indulging in lascivious longings and lewd thoughts; full of lustful cravings. —"This author with a *prurient* mind seems to have done his research in the sewers of Paris."—Hugh E. Blackstone.

**puck'ish** (puk'ish). Mischievous; resembling Shakespeare's elf who was always full of pranks.—"It was a silly situation and one that tickled the *puckish* sense of humor of my friend."—Roy Chapman Andrews.

**pu'er ile** (pū'ur il). Characteristic of childhood; childish; silly; thoughtless.—"It is futile and *puerile* for Democrats to blame our grief on Republicans."—Edmund A. Walsh.

**punc til'i ous ly** (pungk til'i ŭs li). Scrupulously; very carefully with regard to small details or punctilios; in a way that paid strict attention to points of honor or behavior; obeying all forms of etiquette precisely.—"He *punctiliously* practiced the same sort of justice in dealing with his slaves." —Lloyd C. Douglas.

**pup'pet** (pup'et). A person slavishly subject to the will of another.— "They created a separate State which its *puppet* King has not dared to visit."—Eduard Beneš.

**quail** (kwāle). Lose courage; shrink; cower; tremble; quake, as though in great danger; be afraid.—"There is no tendency among the American people to *quail* before the size and grimness of their job."—Wendell L. Willkie.

**quak'ing** (kwāke'ing). Trembling; shaking; shuddering with fear; quivering with emotion.—"At this time other motion-picture stars were *quaking* because voice had come to the screen."—Gene Fowler.

**quer'u lous** (kwer'ū lŭs). Disposed to complain; quarrelsome; fretful; complaining.—"I heard the first *querulous* voices of those who carped at the order."—William Allen White.

**quiz'zi cal** (kwiz'i kǎl). Mock-serious and questioning; teasing; odd.—"I can imagine the *quizzical* smile on the face of Abraham Lincoln if he should listen to my feeble words, making him out to be a modern prophet."—Stewart W. McClelland.

**ram'shack"le** (ram'shak"l). Tumbledown; likely to fall to pieces from age or neglect; unsteady; rickety; shaky. —"When we at last began it was only in a half-hearted, *ramshackle*, confused manner."—Winston Churchill.

**ras'cal ly** (rass'kǎl i). Like a rascal or worthless fellow; knavish; mean; base; dishonest.—"He is a common type of *rascally* tax-collector, disloyal to everybody."—Lloyd C. Douglas.

**ra'tion al ize** (rash'ŭn ǎl īze). To give a reasoning and understandable explanation of; to make conformable to reason; to attribute creditable motives to.—"In order to *rationalize* the agreement, the labor leaders persuaded the Senator to draw up a resolution."—Edward H. Collins.

**re ac'tion** (rē ak'shŭn). A partial or total response to some kind of stimulation; an action in response to some word or deed.—"I have given you some of the Washington *reaction* to the President's speech."—William L. Shirer.

**re buffs'** (rē buffs'). Repulses; snubs; rejects advice.—"Pity the man who gets mad and *rebuffs* his critic."— Richard S. Reynolds.

**rec"on cil"i a'tion** (rek"ŭn sil"i āy'shŭn). The act of being reconciled or restored to friendship after a disagreement; a settlement of differences; a bringing together or reuniting harmoniously.—"After three weeks of anxiety a *reconciliation* was effected." —W. Somerset Maugham.

**rec'ti tude** (rek'tǐ tūde). Uprightness in principles and judgment, correctness of procedure; honesty.—"The engineer is contented to be a man of great *rectitude* of conduct for his employer."—Arthur E. Morgan.

**re miss'** (rē miss'). Slack or careless in matters requiring attention; neglectful; lax in duty.—"We should be *remiss* if we were to leave anything undone which will tend to assure peace."—Cordell Hull.

**re pose'** (rē pōze'). Quietness and ease; composure; dignified calmness; restful manner; freedom from anxiety and excitement; state of being at rest. —"Americans are notorious for their lack of *repose*."—John J. Green.

re sent'ment (rē zent'měnt). Anger and indignant displeasure on account of a real or fancied injury; a feeling of indignation at an insult or wrong. —"You become sick only if you permit and encourage self-pity, fear, *resentment*, anger, worry and other nocuous emotions."—Winfred Rhoades.

re source'ful (rē sorce'fōōl). Quick-witted; full of ideas that can be resorted to for aid or support; able to think out the best ways to do things; full of expedients.—"Through his *resourceful* little sister he had his chance."—Ellen Lewis Buell.

res'tive ness (ress'tiv ness). Impatience of control; fidgetiness; restlessness; uneasiness.—"I sympathize with the *restiveness* of the financial community in periods of market lassitude."—Ganson Purcell.

rev'er ie (rev'ur i). A dreamy, musing state; dreamy thoughts; daydreaming; a fantastic delusion or train of thought; a state in which one is oblivious to surroundings.—"She would drift into moods of *reverie* and stare into vacancy."—John Buchan.

ro tund' (rō tund'). Rounded; plump; rounded out; hence, slightly fat.—"I met the tall spinster and her somewhat more *rotund* widowed sister."—George V. Denny, Jr.

ruf'fi an (ruf'i ăn). A lawless, cruel, and brutal fellow; a rough, turbulent bully; a desperado.—"The taxi was bearing down upon them with a *ruffian* at the wheel."—Henry J. Powers.

sad'ists (sad'ists). Those who are sexually perverted and derive pleasure from torturing others, especially those they pretend to love.—"There is no reason why murderers and *sadists* should escape merely because they are numerous."—Lord Vansittart.

sa ga'cious (suh gāy'shŭs). Discerning; shrewd; intelligent; able; sage.— "These I thought were wise words from a *sagacious* and alert man."— William Philip Simms.

sar don'ic (sahr don'ik). Derisive; sneering; scornful; bitterly sarcastic. —"Nothing in the show catches the *sardonic* point of view so well as the petulant acting of Billy Kond."— Brooks Atkinson.

sa'ti ate (sāy'shi āte). Gratified; filled to repletion; fully satisfied; surfeited; sated.—"They looked upon that profound, *satiate*, helpless slumber."— Don Marquis.

scorn'ful (skorn'fōōl). Full of scorn or disdain; contemptuous; mocking; disdainful.—"His heart was *scornful* behind his smiling face."—Pearl S. Buck.

sed'en tar"y (sed'ĕn ter"i). Sitting much of the time; accustomed to work in a sitting posture.—"This middle-aged lawyer is a *sedentary* fellow, and he needs the tonic of using his arms and legs."—Bruce Barton.

se'nile (see'nīle). Of great age; very old and weak; infirm; doting.—"The picture of *senile* innocence, she blinked down into his face."—Sigrid Undset.

sen"si bil'i ties (sen"sĭ bil'ĭ tiz). Tendencies to feel hurt or offended; susceptibilities to outside influences; sensitive and acute feelings; capability of being deeply moved.—"She turns the simplest word into a dart aimed at her *sensibilities*."—Rachel Field.

sen"si tiv'i ty (sen"sĭ tiv'ĭ ti). Sensitiveness; power to perceive and feel. —"This is our chance to prove that we possess the necessary courage and *sensitivity* to picturize the facets of the undertaking."—Harry M. Warner.

sen'su ous ness (sen'shŏŏ ŭs ness). Enjoyment of the pleasures of the senses; perception by the senses; sense impressions; appeals to the senses.— "The author's prose is as economical as it is tingling with *sensuousness*."— Iris Barry.

sen"ti men'tal (sen"tĭ men'tăl). Dominated by a mental attitude which is influenced by emotion rather than reason; showing deep, tender feeling; mawkishly tender or emotional.—"I should have foreseen that this mighty fellow would not surrender with a *sentimental*, prosaic statement."—Gene Fowler.

**se ren'i ty** (sē ren'ĭ ti). Unruffled calm; placid composure.—"The unity and *serenity* of France today do honor to the human race."—William C. Bullitt.

**ser vil'i ty** (sur vil'ĭ ti). Cringing submission; obsequiousness; slavish behavior; the fawning attitude of a menial.—"Wherever he went the others treated him with groveling *servility*."—Louis Bromfield.

**shrewd** (shrōōd). Keen-witted; clever; astute; sagacious; discerning.— "They played a *shrewd* hand in the struggle for commercial air power in Latin America."—Cornelius V. Whitney.

**sin'gu lar** (sing'gū lur). Unusual; strange; peculiar to one person; odd. —"The garden was cultivated by a *singular* being named Jim."—Don Marquis.

**si'ren** (sī'rĕn). Bewitching; using deception to entice to danger; fascinating; alluring as the Greek Sirens.— "It might have been easy for us to delude ourselves into accepting the *siren* song of propaganda."—Manuel J. Quezon.

**slan'der** (slan'dur). A false tale or report uttered maliciously and designed to injure the reputation of another; defamation; false and injurious statements.—"I will call upon the law that covers wanton and malicious *slander*."—S. L. Scanlon.

**slat'tern ly** (slat'urn li). Untidy and slovenly; negligent and dirty in dress and ways.—"Every dusty *slatternly* Chinese woman in the town had many babies, and only his Mary had none."—Pearl S. Buck.

**slov'en ly** (sluv'ĕn li). Lazy and untidy; dirty and careless in habits and appearance; unkempt; messy.—"He is married to a *slovenly* and nagging wife."—May Lamberton Becker.

**slug'gard** (slug'urd). A person who is very lazy and sluggish; a drone; one who is habitually idle.—"There is no place in an active society for a *sluggard*."—Douglas Brewster.

**slug'gish** (slug'ish). Lazy; lacking in energy, like a sluggard; inert; not easily roused; torpid; indolent; slothful.—"The Government had thrown all manner of sops to the old Adam in this *sluggish* heart."—Alexander Woollcott.

**smug'ly** (smug'li). Smoothly; complacently; showing self-satisfaction.— "Shall we *smugly* and foolishly ignore the plain facts and wrap ourselves in delusion?"—Tom Connally.

**sniv'el ing** (sniv''l ing). Crying in a snuffling way; pretending to be contrite; being emotional in a maudlin way; whining; making a show of grief.—"If he were really in a tight place it wouldn't help to have her in the back seat *sniveling* for comfort."— Anne Morrow Lindbergh.

**spir'it ed** (spir'i ted). Full of life and animation; full of spirit; lively; animated or fiery.—"The subjects of religion and politics will always start a *spirited* argument."—Malcom Babbitt.

**spon"ta ne'i ty** (spon"tuh nee'ĭ ti). Action without premeditation; natural action arising from a sympathetic impulse; an action resulting from a sudden inner prompting; hence, natural impulsive feeling.—"He can say these phrases with a *spontaneity* and immediacy."—Marc Connelly.

**spruce** (sprōōce). Smart; trim; well-groomed.—"A *spruce*, neat appearance is obligatory in the armed forces."—Morton Freud.

**squeam'ish ness** (skweem'ish ness). Oversensitiveness; fastidiousness; scrupulousness; finicalness.—"Some feel that this compassion, which they may prefer to call *squeamishness*, has gone too far."—Percy Aldridge Grainger.

**stealth** (stelth). Secret action or movement; a clandestine or furtive procedure; a sly or concealed manner of acting.—"I did this clandestinely and by *stealth*, without saying anything about it to my nurse."— Irvin S. Cobb.

**suave** (swahv). Smoothly agreeable; affably persuasive; soothingly pleasing; bland; gracious.—"He was always *suave* and unhurried."—Roy Chapman Andrews.

**sub ser'vi ence** (sŭb sur'vi ĕnce).

**Truckling**; accepting an inferior position; willingness to take a second place.—"The continuing *subservience* of aviation to surface service, alarmed him."—Alexander P. de Seversky.

**sub ver′sive** (sub vur′siv). Destructive; tending to cause ruin; undermining to morals or faith; corrupting.— "Debates and *subversive* talk took place over the pots of beer."—Jules Romains.

**suf′fer ance** (suf′ur ănce). Patient endurance; tolerance of something not liked or wanted; negative consent.— "It was only by *sufferance* on the part of the authorities that the émigrés were allowed to stay in town."— Donald G. Cooley.

**su″per cil′i ous** (sū″pur sil′i ŭs). Exhibiting haughty contempt or indifference; arrogant; disdainful; scornfully superior.—"The typical Englishman, as seen through American spectacles, was a haughty, *supercilious* person."—Lord Cecil.

**su″per fi″ci al′i ty** (sū″pur fish″i al′i-ti). Shallowness: that which is on the surface only and has no depth; partial knowledge; cursoriness.— "Perhaps it was that curious simplicity and *superficiality* which saved her."—Louis Bromfield.

**su pe″ri or′i ty** (sū peer″i or′i ti). Showing a consciousness of being greater or better: a display of characteristics more excellent or preferable; predominance.—"She did not quite like her tone of *superiority* with her mother."—Edith Wharton.

**su pine′** (sū pīne′). Inactive; indifferent; having no interest or care; listless.—"We are seeking to build a world peace upon intelligent effort rather than upon *supine* sentimentality."—Francis B. Sayre.

**swarth′y** (swor′thi: 'th' as in 'the'). Having a dark or sunburned complexion; dark-skinned; dusky.— "Who could doubt those *swarthy* men knew Tenedos and Darien?"—John Masefield.

**tan′trum** (tan′trŭm). A petulant fit of bad temper: a display of ill humor, or temper, or petulance that is sudden and of short duration.—"His hands wouldn't function properly, and he had a roaring *tantrum*."— Oren Arnold.

**te′di ous ly** (tee′di ŭs li). Tiresomely; wearily; irksomely; boringly; monotonously; wearisomely.—"Instead of *tediously* shaving your wax records of re-use, the old record will be erased magnetically while you are dictating the new one."—Stanley S. Jacobs.

**tem′per a ment** (tem′pur uh měnt). Individual peculiarity; character; nature or disposition.—"The dance tunes are spirited and in keeping with the *temperament* of the people."— Eamon de Valera.

**ten′sion** (ten′shŭn). Mental strain; strained relations; a condition of nervous anxiety.—"The practice of pioneer virtues has been stimulated in the heightened *tension* of today."— May Lamberton Becker.

**tes′ti ly** (tess′tĭ li). Fretfully; irritably; in a touchy way; petulantly.— " 'That's woman's talk,' he said *testily*."—Dorothy Canfield Fisher.

**traits** (trāts). Distinguishing features or qualities of mind or character; personal characteristics.—"*Traits* which would have won their way to class honors are now put to hard work."— William Trufant Foster.

**tran′quil** (trang′kwil). Calm; quiet; peaceful; free from disturbances.— "Even in *tranquil* and prosperous times there is a constant shifting of trade channels."—Franklin Delano Roosevelt.

**trans port′ed** (trance port′ed). Carried away with great emotion; carried away by strong feeling: conveyed from one place to another, mentally or physically.—"The entire conception *transported* the listener into another sphere."—Olin Downes.

**treach′er ous** (trech′ur ŭs). Traitorous; hence, unreliable; deceptive; having an appearance that is untrustworthy. —"I could see a *treacherous* looking thunderstorm."—F. H. Christensen.

**un bi′ased** (un bī′ăst). Free from prejudice; impartial; fair; not favoring one side more than the other.—"He can give you practical, factual, *unbiased* advice."—Charles F. Collisson.

**un civ′il** (un siv′ĭl). Ill-mannered; impolite; rude; not civil; discourteous; ill-bred.—"It's a relaxation to be *uncivil* once in a while."—Douglas Brewster.

**un couth'** (un kōōth'). Marked by awkwardness of bearing or appearance; odd; ungainly; outlandish.— "A Chinese boy of *uncouth* appearance was allotted the task of serving the coffee."—Shanmukham Chetty.

**un gain'ly** (un gain'li). Awkward; clumsy; lacking grace or ease of movement.—"No woman who walks the earth need be *ungainly*."—John J. Green.

**un"re strained'** (un"rē straind'). Free from a check or restraint; not curbed; unchecked; not held back.—"He is released from these limitations, made free of the subhuman world of *unrestrained* feeling and uncriticized belief."—Aldous Huxley.

**up'right** (up'rīte). Morally correct; just and honest; strictly honorable; righteous.—"Clerics of *upright* character and men with red noses feel equally at home in that tavern."— Ainslee Mockridge.

**ur ban'i ty** (ur ban'ĭ ti). Courtesy; suavity; smooth politeness; blandness; pleasant refinement.—"He was never out of temper, never embarrassed. He treated him with the extreme of *urbanity*."—Stephen Vincent Benét.

**ux o'ri ous** (uks ō'ri ŭs). Showing excessive devotion to one's wife; foolishly submissive to a wife.—"The *uxorious* schoolmaster was not really absurd but simply tiresome."— Austin Wright.

**vac'il lat"ing** (vass'ĭ lāte"ing). Wavering; fluctuating; unsteady; changeable; irresolute.—"He considered those methods *vacillating* and tinged with insincerity."—H. G. Wells.

**vac"il la'tion** (vass"ĭ lā'shŭn). Fluctuation of mind; irresolution; indecision; wavering opinions.—"Many years of *vacillation* and uncertainty have largely provoked the evils from which we suffer."—Winston Churchill.

**vag'a bond** (vag'uh bond). A person who has no fixed home and wanders from place to place; a wanderer; a tramp.—"François Villon was an engaging *vagabond* and a gracious poet."—Jack Bond.

**ve'nal** (vee'năl). Ready to sell honor or principles; mercenary; open to bribery and corruption.—"These revolutionary movements are based on the assumption that human beings are *venal* and criminal."—Dorothy Thompson.

**vul gar'i ans** (vul gair'i ănz). Vulgar people; people whose tastes and manners are coarse and offensive.— "The ingenious reason was given by some *vulgarians* that he was trying to supplant a member of the team." —Louis Adamic.

**wag'gish** (wag'ish). Mischievous; funny; droll; jocose; sportive.—"In my *waggish* way, I might observe that this would lend credence to a dark suspicion."—Alexander Woollcott.

**whim"si cal'i ty** (hwim"zi kal'ĭ ti). A quaint, fanciful, or odd idea; quaint humor.—"Lincoln met recurring disaster with *whimsicality* to muffle the murmur of a bleeding heart."— T. V. Smith.

**win'some** (win'sŭm). Pleasing: attractive; possessing a winning, captivating character: charming; giving pleasure.—"This animal is a *winsome* creature."—Luis M. Alzamora.

**wist'ful ness** (wist'f'l ness). Longing; thoughtful musing; yearning for something that is not likely to be granted.—"The moods of the flute range from *wistfulness* to jollity, from ecstasy to despair."—Rene Le Roy.

## ONE-MINUTE REFRESHER

We sometimes surmise that we know words better than we do. Here are ten simple selections from this chapter. After each selection three choices are given. Underline, in each case, the one word or phrase of the three that is *nearest* in meaning to the key word.

1. *banality:* (a) The quality of being commonplace. (b) of being ancient. (c) of being unpleasant.
2. *chagrin:* (a) amusement. (b) humiliating vexation. (c) great courage.
3. *cupidity:* (a) love. (b) timidity. (c) greed.
4. *misanthrope:* (a) an African quadruped. (b) an old relic. (c) a hater of mankind.
5. *diffidence:* (a) an argument. (b) shyness. (c) bad temper.
6. *morose:* (a) sullen. (b) swamp-like. (c) poor.
7. *foibles:* (a) a type of game. (b) fantastic stories. (c) slight faults of character.
8. *cosseted:* (a) fondled. (b) fooled. (c) fated.
9. *captious:* (a) apt to be upset. (b) apt to be taken prisoner. (c) apt to find fault.
10. *probity:* (a) a court inquiry. (b) something capable of proof. (c) strict honesty.

*Answers:* 1 — a;  2 — b;  3 — c;  4 — c;  5 — b;  6 — a;  7 — c;  8 — a; 9 — c;  10 — c.

# CHAPTER V

## THESE WORDS ARE CLOSE IN MEANING

THERE IS no way that I can exaggerate or overemphasize the part that synonyms will play in your word-building plan.

The acquisition of synonyms will do more than any other thing to give strength, flexibility and vitality to your speech and to your writing; precision and accuracy to your reasoning.

The American language is your heritage. It is the greatest language of power and culture the world has ever seen, and one of its most priceless possessions is the beautiful distinction of its synonyms.

We speak of synonyms as words of similar meaning, and we say "similar," as you know, because no two words can have exactly the same meaning.

Each group of synonyms is strung like a series of beads on one central idea, but each word in the group presents a slightly different face of this idea, and in direct proportion as you can command the group, you will be able to express your thoughts about that idea with exactitude.

Let us summon the word "stubborn" to the witness stand, and then cross-examine a few of the other members of its group: *Obstinate, obdurate, implacable, decisive, recalcitrant, inexorable, contumacious, pertinacious, headstrong.*

Here is what they tell us about themselves:

A *headstrong* person is one who will not be stopped in what he is doing, while *obstinate* and *stubborn* people refuse to follow the wishes of others. A very agreeable person can be *obstinate* for the moment on a single point at issue, but *stubbornness* is more nearly habitual. A person is *obdurate* when he sticks to his purpose in spite of moving and emotional appeals; he is *recalcitrant* when he "kicks back" and is stubbornly rebellious; while the *contumacious* are proud and insolent in their defiance. A *pertinacious* demand can bring an *obstinate* refusal. When we approve of an *inexorable* judgment we call

57

it *decisive, firm, inflexible, resolute.* When we condemn it we term it *obstinate, stubborn, implacable.*

Here we have a list of words gathered around the single term "stubborn," but each one of these words has a carefully shaded difference in meaning and gives a new angle to the main thought. As a matter of fact, these words are like adjoining but sharply bounded territories that unite to make up the general common-wealth of "stubbornness."

The riches of our language in these synonyms are almost beyond belief, and give continuing evidence of the power and the fertility of our speech. At times, these synonyms add up to prodigal totals. In Roget's *Thesaurus* 82 synonyms are recorded for the word *vice*, 176 for *resent*, 230 for *take.*

The different types of exercises that will help you expand your vocabulary are legion in number, but I can assure you there is no practice that will build it so rapidly as a study of synonyms. It will give you the virtuosity that a concert pianist has in his art.

Try testing yourself with the much-abused word *big* and see what substitutions you can make in the following list:

| | |
|---|---|
| A big business | A big statue |
| A big house | A big job |
| A big intellect | A big room |
| A big war | A big disaster |
| A big cave | A big waste |
| A big occasion | A big desert |

Here are a few suggestions:

| | |
|---|---|
| A tremendous business | A colossal statue |
| A huge house | A prodigious job |
| A massive intellect | A spacious room |
| A gigantic war | A stupendous disaster |
| A mammoth cave | A prodigal waste |
| A momentous occasion | A vast desert |

In each case isn't the picture given by the substitution more sharp, more accurate? The word "big" conveys only the idea of size. The other words indicate different kinds of size.

Practice this game of substitution, occasionally, when you are reading. Here, for example, is the substitution method as applied to a passage from the novel *Trelawney* by Margaret Armstrong. Many of the substituted words are too commonplace to be recorded in this volume, but this paragraph will indicate the method:

"His supper over—it was an excellent (fine, delicious, admirable, tasty, capital, choice, first-class, superior) meal—he disposed himself for a siesta (rest, sleep, nap). The couch was soft (yielding, comfortable, agreeable, pleasant, delightful, satisfactory, commodious), but he was accustomed (used, habituated) to napping in the most uneasy (uncomfortable, disturbed, unquiet, disordered, untranquil) spots."

You can employ this scheme during the day with outdoor advertising billboards, with car-cards in the busses and subways, or while you are reading the advertisements in the daily papers or magazines. The high-priced advertising men have chosen what they believe to be the best word for the occasion. See whether you can better their choice. You can continue this exercise as you read your newspaper. In the body of this chapter is a quotation from George H. Houston, president of a huge locomotive works: "I had the *temerity*," he said in an interview, "to make this estimate some weeks ago." When you run across a statement in the daily press that contains such an interesting word cross-examine yourself. Is *temerity* the best word for the purpose? Exactly what does it mean? Would *audacity* do? How about *hardihood?* What other synonyms are there?

Exercises like these will stretch your vocabulary in an amazing fashion, and it can be done easily and swiftly. Consult your dictionary, if you must, to prove that the word you have substituted makes sense. This is important, since synonyms cannot always be interchanged successfully. The words *give, impart* and *confer* are synonyms, but you don't *impart* a Christmas gift to a friend, nor do you *confer* a punch in the jaw on an enemy.

When Madame Chiang Kai-shek crossed and re-crossed our country on her lecture tour she took our nation by storm. She was immediately ranked as one of the great women of the age. She had glowing ideals and a radiant spirit, but she didn't dress them in shabby garments. She clothed them in a language so superb that it was startling and became front page news. She, a foreigner, knew the power of the language that is our birthright, and when she wanted to delineate an idea, she would pick and choose her synonyms with the skill of an artist selecting colors from his palette.

This synonymic chapter is exceptionally important, and should invite your close study. The first twenty-five groups I have discussed in detail. Directly after these more lengthy treatments, the synonyms are merely listed in family groups, *but* the definitions have been so devised that the reader will be able to detect both the similarities in meaning that run through the words of any given group, and also the differences in meaning between members of the same family.

## Words That Are Close in Meaning

**a ban'don** (uh ban'dŭn). To give up persons and things after association with them.—"The time came when he was forced to *abandon* his associates and strike out for himself."—George F. Gahagan.

Synonyms for *abandon:* The word *abandon* often implies previous responsibility. You *abandon* a friend who has depended upon you, but you can also *abandon* a ship or your bad habits. You *resign* from an office, you don't *abandon* it. A king *abdicates* his throne. We can *forsake* God, but we cannot *abandon* him. *Forsake* means leaving what was once beloved and familiar. *Discontinue* is to give up by bringing to an end; we *discontinue* our subscription to a magazine. We *cede* a point in an argument, or, a nation will *cede* territory to its neighbor. To *abjure* is, literally, to give up by taking an oath; to *discard* is to throw away as useless; to *renounce* is to give up by making a declaration; to *relinquish* is to give up reluctantly something that we like; to *forego* is usually to deny oneself: "I will *forego* the pleasures of the trip."

**al le'vi ate** (ă lee'vi āte). Lessen or lighten physical or mental troubles.—"The program is imperative to *alleviate* shortage."—Paul McNutt.

Synonyms for *alleviate: Lighten* implies making a weight less; in a figurative sense we *lighten* a person's burden of sorrow: we *moderate* our anger or our demands, or the storm *moderates*, that is, lessens in force. When we *alleviate* (Latin *ad + levare*, lift up, lighten) a man's trouble, we literally lift it to or towards ourselves. When we *relieve* a man of his worry, we lift it or carry it away from him. We *alleviate* suffering. We *relieve* the sufferer. We *reduce* a debt or a swelling, *assuage* the pangs of hunger. Our grief *mitigates* (etymologically, "becomes soft") with the years; the fury of a storm or of a fever *abates*, or, in its Latin meaning, "is beaten down." But we don't *moderate* a trouble, or *abate* a pain, or *mitigate* our temper, or *alleviate* a man. When we *allay* pain, we *a*, "away," *lecgan*, "lay," or "put the pain away."

**al lure'** (ă lūre'). Draw or attract by some charm, or by a promise of pleasure or advantage.—"Even at seventy Ninon D'Enclos had the power to *allure* young men."—Ellery Marsh Egan.

Synonyms for *allure:* We may *attract* someone to us by accident; we *allure* them by plan and intent. The simple word *lure*, however, often has an unpleasant implication. A woman may *allure* a man with her charm, but she *lures* him to destruction. To *entice* is to *attract* artfully and skillfully, and to *tempt* is to *attract* to wrongdoing by promises of reward. The words *inveigle, decoy, cajole* and *seduce* all have slightly sinister connotations. *Inveigle* is to attract by blind leads or guile; *decoy* by snare or bait; *cajole* by deception or flattery; while one who *seduces* is usually winning a person over from good to evil. Those who *captivate* have captured the fancy through some irresistible influence; those who *fascinate* hold the object at the mercy of the attraction. We *enchant* by a magic influence; we *charm* with a power that gives great pleasure.

**al″ter ca′tion** (awl″tur kā′shŭn). A sharp and angry debate; a dispute; an argument; wordy contentions; wrangling.—"The air was loud with profane talk and Asiatic *altercation*."—Caroline Dale Snedeker.

Synonyms for *altercation:* Used in its best sense, an *argument* is a presentation of reasons, facts and proofs, either for or against an opinion, a statement or a measure. A congressman makes an *argument* in favor of a bill. A *debate* is an orderly presentation of *arguments* for and against by two or more sides. A *contention* is often an opinion stated without the bitterness that attends an *altercation:* as, "it is my *contention* that God exists." A *dispute* is a sharp, angry *argument;* a *dissension*, a violent *disagreement*. When we *wrangle* or *squabble* or *bicker* we are being undignified, petty and petulant; but a *brawl* is a wordy *quarrel* that often ends in a fight. A group can have an angry *controversy* if they prefer, but usually a *controversy* is merely a strenuous *discussion;* and a *discussion* is a conversation about the pros and cons of a situation.

**ar′ti fice** (ahr′ti fiss). An ingenuous contrivance, trick or expedient. —"The people should not be misled by *artifice* or subterfuge."— Robert E. Wood.

Synonyms for *artifice:* The words *fraud, guile, imposture* and *subterfuge* connote deceptive *devices* that are malicious, mean or evil in intent. *Imposture* is a deceitful act or *contrivance* to gain an end, an imposition. *Fraud* is an underhand or secret robbery or deception. *Guile* is crafty cunning for securing advantage or gain. "He was a man without *guile.*" *Subterfuge* (Latin *subter* "under," *fugere* "to flee") is a move to escape or conceal something. A *trick* can be mischievous and sometimes mean, but *wile* is a trick that beguiles or wheedles. When we employ a *maneuver*, we are engineering a clever movement, as in war. *Ruse* and *finesse* can be innocent or guilty. A *ruse*, which is a crafty means or *device* to divert from a purpose, may be carried out with great *finesse*, that is, it can be subtly misleading. A *device* is simply a clever contrivance to promote some end: as, "the gearless shift on automobiles is a clever *device*"; while an *invention* is a *device* that is the result of study and research.

**as sert'** (ă surt'). To state positively, though without proof, sometimes in a challenging way.—"In the face of possible opposition, I will *assert* that my theories are sound."—James Gordon Dustin.

Synonyms for *assert:* When we *assert* something, we are apt to be making a challenging statement which others may deny. To *aver*, on the other hand, is to make a statement from positive knowledge. Witnesses *attest* to a crime, while conquerors *proclaim* their victories to the whole world. To *pronounce* is to state as an opinion or judgment, and to *claim* is to assert something that should be acknowledged. We *maintain* our point against argument; we *allege* that something happened when we have no proof but we believe that we are capable of furnishing proof; we *propound* a theory as a basis for consideration. To *avow* is to make open acknowledgment, often in the face of opposition; to *avouch* is to guarantee, and to *asseverate* is to state very solemnly and sometimes excitedly.

**av"a ri'cious** (av"uh rish'ŭs). Greedy of gain or wealth: keen to get and to keep: grasping.—"We have battled with the *avaricious* and ruthless for eleven years."—Harold L. Ickes.

Synonyms for *avaricious:* The *covetous* are eager to get something away from its possessor or owner; the *parsimonious* are *stingy* and wish to keep what they have. An *avaricious* person is usually both *covetous* and *parsimonious.* He who is *rapacious* is excessively *covetous* and apt to seize what he desires by force. The *miserly* stint themselves to make their gains by petty savings; the *niggardly* stint others and refuse to spend; the *penurious* are *economical* in a mean way and affect poverty.

**blem'ish es** (blem'ish iz). Disfiguring marks or stains on a surface; imperfections; faults.—"Any leather contains *blemishes* of various degrees."—I. M. Kay.

Synonyms for *blemishes:* A *blemish* is a superficial fault that mars the beauty of an object. A *flaw* or a *taint* is in the structure. We can say that there is a *flaw* or a *taint* in his character, but we speak of a *blot* or a *stain* upon his reputation. A *speck* is a tiny mark that *spots* or *stains;* a *spot* and a *blot* are larger, and a *daub* is a large smear. A man's character and a piece of metal can both be *tarnished* and so lose their luster. In a figurative sense, a *blemish* is the result of wrong actions or deeds, but a *brand* or a *stigma* is inflicted by others.

**can'did ly** (kan'did li). Freely and openly: without bias or partiality: truly and justly.—"They will be remedied most easily by recognizing them calmly and *candidly.*"—Walter Lippmann.

Synonyms for *candidly:* We speak *frankly* when we speak courageously, expressing our feelings without restraint; we act *fairly* when we act with justice and truth; we deal *honestly* when we have no intention to deceive. *Impartially* is an adverb that indicates no favor to one side more than another; *sincerely* means without hypocrisy or pretense; *artlessly* means unaffectedly and without guile. Those who deal *openly* are hiding nothing. *Ingenuously* means freely and innocently; *naïvely*, simply and unconventionally; *unreservedly*, without holding back any part.

**ec cen'tric** (ek sen'trik). Turning aside or varying from the usual custom or method: out of the ordinary.—"He was an outlandish, ill-kempt, *eccentric*, and completely charming human being."—Ainslee Mockridge.

Synonyms for *eccentric: Eccentric* comes from the Greek *ek*, "out of," and *kentron*, "center": that is, an *eccentric* man is "off center," *unusual* in a *strange* way; if such a one is called *abnormal* (Latin *ab*, "away from," and *norma*, "rule"), he is an exception to the rule. The word *odd*—"an *odd* person" or "an *odd* accident"—means someone or something that cannot be paired off with anything and is, therefore, *peculiar* or *unusual. Singular*, in the sense of *unusual*, is alone of its kind. An *erratic* person or object has "wandered away from the beaten track," he is uncertain and unpredictable. *Outlandish* things are "foreign looking"; *bizarre* things, of a strange but fanciful shape; while *grotesque* things are also strange, but badly misshapen and absurdly incongruous. *Quaint* denotes that which is pleasingly *odd* and perhaps old-fashioned, and *queer* signifies something out of the usual course of events. *Unique* has no like or equal, and a *strange* thing is something hitherto unknown.

**e quiv′o cal** (ē kwiv′ō kăl). That may be understood in different ways: of doubtful or questionable meaning.—"On account of the uncertainty about territory this form of aid wore a more *equivocal* face."—Frederick Lewis Allen.

Synonyms for *equivocal:* Things *doubtful* are open to question, as the Latin base *dubito,* "am uncertain," would indicate. Things *dubious* are questionable and under suspicion, as "a *dubious* reputation." Anything *questionable* needs proof before it can be accepted. *Ambiguous* (Latin *ambi,* "around," *ago,* "drive") signifies that which can be interpreted in more than one way. An *ambiguous* statement may be unintentionally obscure; an *equivocal* statement is often purposely deceptive. *Uncertain* is used in the sense of "not sure to happen," "of which knowledge is doubtful"; *enigmatical,* when the answer must be guessed as a riddle; *indefinite,* when the number or size is doubtful because it cannot be accurately determined. Things *obscure* are not clear to the mind or eye; things *perplexing* are confusing, puzzling or filled with uncertainty; things *suspicious* are questionable and not to be trusted.

**fluc′tu ate** (fluk′chŏŏ āte). Move or roll back and forth, or up and down, irregularly or alternately.—"He lived a feverish life, and we watched him *fluctuate* from failure to success and back to failure again."—Ellery Marsh Egan.

Synonyms for *fluctuate: Undulate* and *fluctuate* are from two Latin words *unda* and *fluctus* that both mean "wave," but *undulate* more nearly preserves the original meaning. A rug may *undulate* in the wind. The ocean *undulates.* But our feelings or our fortunes *fluctuate;* they rise and fall, come and go. *Waver* (Anglo-Saxon *wafian,* "wave") means to shrink back from a former decision, or to move to and from. We can *waver* uncertainly in our minds; the line of infantry *wavers* under attack; or a flame will *waver* in the breeze. Those who *vacillate* move or decide first one way and then another in weak uncertainty as to what to do; those who *hesitate* speak or move as though uncertain how to decide or proceed. Pendulums *oscillate* (Latin *oscillare,* "swing"); piano strings *vibrate.* When persons or things *swerve,* they deviate from a line or a rule; when they *veer,* they change suddenly from one course to another. The temperature, or the weather, or a person's feeling or taste *varies.*

**hin′der** (hin′dur). To prevent or delay motion, growth or progress.—"The lack of the proper vitamins will greatly *hinder* the growth of children."—Ainslee Mockridge.

Synonyms for *hinder:* To *retard* is to slow up progress or action by any means whatsoever; to *prevent* is to keep from action or growth; to *obstruct* is to keep from progress by placing some obstacle in the way; and to *oppose* is to try to *prevent* or *delay.* The *obstructed* roads may *retard* the hostile forces, but it may also be that we will not have sufficient troops to *oppose* the enemy and so *prevent* them from reaching their objective. *Hamper* is to delay by load or restraint; *impede,* by obstacle or burden; *thwart,* by a counter move; *baffle,* by causing confusion; while to *frustrate* (from the Latin *frustra,* "in vain") is to bring to complete and final failure. That which is *baffled* may yet succeed: that which is *frustrated* can never succeed.

**his′to ry** (hiss′tō ri). A record or systematic account of past events: a story or narration.—"*History* repeats its mistakes, but each time the bill is higher."—Bertram M. Myers.

Synonyms for *history:* An *account* is a statement of facts, a report or story; a *chronicle,* an account of events in the order of their occurrence; while *annals* are the *records* of events year by year. Public *records* and documents are kept in *archives.* A *biography* is an account of a person's life, while in an *autobiography* (Greek *autos,* "self") the *account* is written by the person himself. A *register* is a *record,* usually official, containing details and entries of items. A *narrative* is a story of happenings in the order in which they have occurred and it may often be nothing more than an anecdote; a *recital* is the telling in detail of some event or events; and a *memoir* is an account of personal experiences written by the person himself. All of these things, *chronicles, memoirs, biographies* and such, are the material of *history.*

**in her′ent** (in heer′ĕnt). Existing as a permanent, inseparable element: belonging as an original part by its very nature.— "Every region of the world possesses its own *inherent* difficulties." —Sumner Welles.

Synonyms for *inherent:* That which is *essential* belongs to the nature or quality of a thing or person and is indispensable to it, as a clutch is an *essential* part of an automobile. Things *intrinsic* are not accidental, but pertain to the nature or essence of a person or thing: we say that the *intrinsic* value of a copper coin is slight, or we speak of the *intrinsic* honesty of a man. An element or quality is *inherent* permanently in a person or a thing and is an integral part of it. We speak of his *inherent* love of truth, or of his *intrinsic* excellence. *Intrinsic* pertains to the essence of a thing; *inherent* to its quality. *Inborn* characteristics are born in a person; those *inbred* are inherited and deeply rooted; those that are *congenital* belong as a property of the thing or person and have existed since birth. What is *ingrained* is fixed deeply in the very fiber. *Native* qualities belong on account of place of birth or race, and *innate* qualities are natural and not acquired.

**ire** (īre). Anger; wrath; strong resentment.—"Racial prejudice always stirs his *ire*."—Henry J. Powers.

Synonyms for *ire: Fury* is a rage so excessive that it borders on madness, but *indignation* is an impersonal and unselfish displeasure, a deep and intense anger directed against something shameful. Those who impose upon subject races stir our *indignation*, but the violent and unjust attacks of an enemy whip us into a blind *fury*. *Resentment* is due to a slight or injury; *exasperation*, to long continued irritation, where *anger* boils over. *Wrath* is usually the result of provocation; *rage* forgets discretion; and *passion*, in the sense of *anger*, implies deep emotion. *Petulance, impatience* and *irritation* are lesser forms of *anger:* they are temporary and from immediate causes. *Petulance* is a peevish annoyance; *impatience* is a state of restless irritability because of delay or opposition; *irritation* is an excited form of impatience, generally caused by something that rubs us the wrong way.

**mis for′tune** (miss for′chŏŏn). Adverse fortune for which the sufferer is not always directly responsible.—"*Misfortune* attended his every move."—Bradwell E. Tanis.

Synonyms for *misfortune:* A *mishap* is an unlucky accident, but *adversity* is a serious and continuous type of misfortune. A *calamity* is a sudden and severe misfortune, but a *disaster* is sudden, severe and unusual. *Affliction* is trouble that causes mental or bodily distress, while a *chastening* is a disciplinary experience. We say that a person who has bragged about his money and lost it has received a *chastening;* we speak of a person who is deaf as having an *affliction. Bereavement* is a loss, usually through death; *tribulation*, a suffering that continues, often the result of oppression; a *visitation* is a severe trial and possibly a punishment; a *mischance* is simply something that has gone wrong, a piece of bad luck.

**mul″ti far′i ous** (mul″ti fair′i ŭs). Of great diversity: of many and various kinds: having great variety.—"As years go on, the laws of any nation become *multifarious* and confusing."—Emory L. Fielding.

Synonyms for *multifarious: Manifold* suggests doing many things, performing several functions at one time, having many and various uses. *Multifarious* emphasizes the diversity or unlikeness, as well as the number, of the elements involved. We speak of *"manifold* copies of a letter" but "the *multifarious* colors of the autumn leaves." *Multiform*, directly from the Latin *multus*, "many" and *forma*, "shape," means having many forms, shapes or appearances. The word *multiple* suggests the idea of more than one of like things, as "the *multiple* strands of a carpet," while *multiplex* (Latin *plico*, "fold") means made up of many parts, but also contains the idea of "complex," as "general laws are necessarily *multiplex.*" With *multitudinous* we suggest vast numbers, as "the *multitudinous* waves of the sea"; but *multifold* implies many times doubled, mutiplied.

**plen'te ous** (plen'tē ŭs). Yielding a rich supply; plentiful; abundant.—"The Creator of this beautiful world made *plenteous* provision for all its inhabitants."—Louis Ludlow.

Synonyms for *plenteous:* When anything, such as a gift of money, is *plenteous*, it is ample for all needs; when it is *lavish*, it is more than enough and given freely; when it is *prodigal*, wastefulness is usually implied. An *affluent* person has an abundance of riches; the *generous* are open-handed. We speak of *luxuriant* hair, streams *teeming* with fish, *copious* tears and *liberal* donations; but, curiously, while all these words mean "abundant," we do not speak of *copious* donations, *liberal* crops, *luxuriant* tears, or heads *teeming* with hair. *Luxuriant* refers to growth; *teeming* to production or bringing forth; *liberal* to giving or expending; *copious* to thought, language or supply.

**pro pen'si ty** (prō pen'sĭ ti). An inclination or tendency towards a condition or action; a mental and sometimes unfavorable disposition towards something.—"There is a certain *propensity* to become preoccupied with the details at the expense of the issues of general policy."—Walter Lippmann.

Synonyms for *propensity: Penchant* (from the French *pencher*, "to incline") means a strong *inclination*, leaning, or attraction towards something as, "a *penchant* for art." *Proclivity* (Latin *pro*, "forward," *clivus*, "sloping") signifies a natural or constitutional *disposition* or *tendency* that is forceful, as "a *proclivity* to steal." When we have a *tendency* we literally "lean on" something or move towards it. Some people have a particular "leaning towards" or *inclination* for the stage; some have an *inclination* to evil. Those with a *predilection* have "chosen before" and therefore have a favorable *prepossession* for something, an *inclination* to like it. If you have a fixed *tendency* or *bent* for something, such as business, your mind and interest have taken this direction and you have a liking for it; whereas a *bias* is a mental *inclination* or prejudice, often without reason, and sometimes unfair. A *predisposition* is a state of being inclined beforehand; a condition favorable or liable to something.

**re prove′** (rē prōōve′). To blame; to censure in order to correct; to criticize adversely to the face of the person censured.—"We should always *reprove* a child, a servant or an employee in private."—Charles Henry Weston.

Synonyms for *reprove:* To *admonish* deals with the future, and warns against anticipated mistakes or the repetition of wrong acts: "Moses *admonished* the Children of Israel." To *chide* is to *reprove* gently. *Chide* and *admonish* are the mildest forms of the *reproving* words. When we *censure*, we do not always express our adverse judgment to the person *censured;* but when we *rebuke*, we *censure* a person directly, sharply and severely. When we *expostulate* with people, we reason with them earnestly about their faults, and appeal to them to change; while when we *remonstrate* with someone, we plead protestingly and give reasons against wrong actions. To *reproach* is to *censure* or *criticize* openly and with a deep feeling of anger or sorrow. We can *reproach* others or ourselves. To *reprimand* is to give formal and official reproof, and to *condemn* is to adjudge and to hold wrong. Those whom we *upbraid* are sharply *rebuked* and are deserving of blame. Those whom we *berate*, we *rebuke* or *censure* in an abusive or angry way.

**rev″o lu′tion** (rev″ō lū′shŭn). A movement or fundamental change that overthrows a system or government and substitutes a new one.—"A *revolution* in South America is usually handled in a gentlemanly and bloodless fashion."—Charles Henry Crozier.

Synonyms for *revolution: Rebellion* (Latin *re,* "again"; *bellum,* "war") is a fight against authority or government; when a *rebellion* is successful, it becomes a *revolution* (Latin *re,* "again," "back"; *volvo,* "roll," "turn"). A *riot* is a temporary outbreak of lawlessness on the part of civilians; in a *strike* the outbreak is exercised against business management; a *mutiny* is a rebellion against military or naval authority. *Sedition* is the plotting, *rebellion* is fighting, against the existing government; and such actions may result in *anarchy*, that condition of disorder where there is no law or government in power. A *revolt* is a sharp, short fight against conditions or allegiance, while an *insurrection* is an armed uprising of brief duration in an effort to seize power.

**sum'mit** (sum'it). The highest point or degree: the extreme or topmost level obtainable.—"We had a series of dizzy and breathtaking adventures before we reached the *summit*."—Henry T. Powers.

Synonyms for *summit:* The word *peak* signifies the highest point in state or condition, while *pinnacle* suggests a height that is dizzy or insecure, or a slender, pointed spire. When an ascending series has reached the highest point of intensity, we call that point the *climax*, from the Greek word *klimax*, "ladder." *Culmination* (Latin *culma*, "top") is the attainment of the highest point or position; *acme* is the highest point, but the word usually implies perfection. We say "that is the *acme* of literary style," "the *culmination* of his career," "the *climax* of a play." *Meridian*, *zenith* and *apogee*, in their most common meanings, refer to the heavens. *Meridian* is the highest position of the sun at midday; *zenith*, the point in the heavens directly overhead; *apogee*, the point in the orbit of a celestial body which is farthest from the earth, the highest possible or farthest point. *Apex* is the pointed or angular end or highest point, while a *summit* is relatively rounded, often the topmost of the series comprising a mountain range.

**tran'sient** (tran'shĕnt). Passing quickly out of sight or existence: of short duration.—"The management looks upon the immediate heavy traffic as a *transient* thing."—J. B. Hill.

Synonyms for *transient:* A *fugitive* prisoner or a *fugitive* pleasure is one that is literally (Latin *fugio*, meaning "run") running away. We wish to hold on to things that are *fugitive*, but they escape us, while things that are *fleeting* pass swiftly by. Pleasure is *transient*, but the life of man is *transitory*, that is, it is brief by its very nature. The word *ephemeral* (Greek *ephēmeros*, for a day) indicates a duration more brief than *transitory*, and often implies a slight contempt, as, "the tawdry book had only an *ephemeral* popularity." Things that are *evanescent* have little substance and vanish, like the *evanescent* rainbow, before our eyes. *Temporary* is a more practical term to indicate a thing that lasts only a short time. We do not speak of an *evanescent* job, but a *temporary* job.

**wis'dom** (wiz'dŭm). Ability to use or exercise knowledge and wise judgment: the power of true discernment through the exercise of the highest moral and intellectual facilities.—"Knowledge is static, *wisdom* is active and moves knowledge, making it effective."—William J. Mayo.

Synonyms for *wisdom:* A person is naturally endowed with *understanding, foresight, prescience, insight, sagacity, discernment* and *judgment;* but he must acquire *erudition, knowledge, enlightenment, reason. Prescience* is a *knowledge* of the future; *foresight,* the capacity to foresee and prepare for the future: *prudence* is the exercise of caution and economy in our daily affairs, although there may be emergencies when it is the better part of *wisdom* to throw *prudence* to the wind. *Knowledge* is the sum of acquired information and the perception of facts, and *wisdom* is *knowledge* with the capacity to make due use of it; *enlightenment* is advancement in *knowledge,* usually along moral and intellectual lines, as "the 19th Century was an age of great *enlightenment";* *erudition* indicates specialized, scholarly or bookish *knowledge,* and *reason* includes those faculties that enable one to distinguish between the true and the false. A person of *insight* sees the inner nature of a thing; a person of *discernment* has the faculty of discriminating accurately. A person of *judgment* makes correct decisions; a person of *sagacity* has keen penetration and judgment; a person of *discretion* is prudent and careful in his decisions.


## More Words That Are Close in Meaning

**haz'ard ous** (haz'urd ŭs). Exposed to danger of risk or loss that is beyond control.—"We must not place too much dependence on the *hazardous* course of importation."—James E. Murray.

**per'il ous** (per'ĭ lŭs). Full of peril; full of immediate or impending danger. —"Every ship captain feeling his way through *perilous* channels owes a debt of gratitude for his safety to Gustaf Dalen."—Erik Wästberg.

**pre ca'ri ous** (prē kāy'ri ŭs). Depending on insecure or uncertain future contingencies; dependent on chance or hazard.—"The price for failure may easily be a *precarious* existence in a world dominated by brute force." —Frank M. Dixon.

**un sta'ble** (un stāy'b'l). Inconstant in result; fluctuating; lacking in stability; not dependable.—"The drug proved to be *unstable,* and uncertain in its reaction. '—Earlene M. Cornell.

**dor'mant** (dor'mănt). In a state of sleep; present but inactive.—"Worries about an attack are now *dormant.*"—Delos C. Emmons.

**la'tent** (lāy'tĕnt). Present but not visible.—"There is another *latent* evil in the bill."—Thomas E. Dewey.

**po ten'tial** (pō ten'shăl). Possible but not actual; able to exist but not yet existing.—"The great *potential* value of the battleships isn't generally understood."—Joseph K. Taussig.

**con"tu ma'cious**    (kon"tū mā'shŭs). Rebellious; refractory; stubbornly perverse; contemptuous of authority; insolently obstinate.—"She was described as that restless, roving, disobedient, *contumacious* female."—Robert Sencourt.

**de ci'sive** (dē sī'siv). Deciding; having a definite result; settling or putting an end to some uncertainty; positive; conclusive.—"Stalingrad was one of the most *decisive* battles of the war."—Bruce Ellsworth.

**im pla'ca ble** (im plāy'kuh b'l). Irreconcilable; unyielding; inexorable; merciless.—"Through you, as one of the *implacable* foes of tyranny, I am happy to transfer these implements of war."—Dwight D. Eisenhower.

**in ex'o ra ble** (in ek'sō ruh b'l). Unyielding; implacable; relentless; not able to be influenced or changed.— "They had in mind, without doubt, the *inexorable* progress of neighborliness which has long been under way in this hemisphere."—Henry A. Wallace.

**ob'du rate** (ob'dū rĭt). Unyielding; stubborn; hardhearted; obstinately pursuing a purpose in spite of appeals.—"He had such respect for the judgment of that *obdurate* Annabella." —André Maurois.

**ob'sti nate** (ob'stĭ nit). Stubborn; headstrong; hard to control; unyielding; opinionated; wilful; refusing to move.—"The simple words made no impression on the *obstinate* brat."—Hendrik Willem Van Loon.

**per"ti na'cious ly** (pur"tĭ nā'shŭs li). Obstinately; stubbornly; inflexibly; persistently; tenaciously.—"For all his mockery of England, he clung *pertinaciously* in little things to the old customs of his country."—André Maurois.

**re cal'ci trant** (rē kal'si trănt). Rebellious; refractory; obstinately defiant; resisting authority stubbornly.— "The teacher was struggling to pull up some *recalcitrant* child."—Dorothy Thompson.

**au dac'i ty** (aw dass'ĭ ti). Impudence; boldness; daring.—"To submit to unjust aggression is to encourage the enemy in his criminal *audacity*."— Charlotte of Luxembourg.

**te mer'i ty** (tē mer'ĭ ti). Venturesome boldness; recklessness; rashness; audacity; presumption.—"I had the *temerity* to make this estimate some weeks ago."—George H. Houston.

**co los'sal** (kō loss'ăl). Enormous; huge; like the gigantic statue at Rhodes.— "The amount of shipping required for the transportation is *colossal*."— Robert E. Wood.

**gi gan'tic** (ji gan'tik). As big as a giant; huge; enormous; colossal; immense; of giantlike proportions.— "We must have time to settle our *gigantic* long-view questions."—Herbert C. Hoover.

**mam'moth** (mam'ŭth: 'th' as in 'thin'). Very large; huge; of unusual size as the mammoth or extinct elephant.— "He will not use the power and influence of this *mammoth* nation to promote or create war."—John L. Lewis.

**mas'sive** (mass'iv). Powerful in scope and effect; weighty and solid.— "Neither reason nor coaxing has had the slightest effect against the *massive* obstinacy of the powers that be."— Winston Churchill.

**pro dig'ious** (prō dij'ŭs). Enormous in size or degree; vast; immense; unheard of.—"A *prodigious* outcry was caused by it."—Somerset Maugham.

**spa'cious** (spā'shŭs). Of vast extent; capacious; large; of indefinite size.— "I do not deny these teachers their *spacious* and important place in the preparation for America's tomorrow."—Irving T. McDonald.

**tre men'dous** (trē men'dŭs). Very great; extraordinary; awe-inspiring; causing astonishment by its magnitude or power.—"They are doing *tremendous* things—stupendous things."—H. G. Wells.

**vast** (va(h)st). Of great extent; enormous; immense; very, very large.— "His beard arrived first and then the rest of his *vast* bulk."—Jan Struther.

**dis crep'an cies** (diss krep'ăn siz). Disagreements; states or points of variance.—"This organization would obviate *discrepancies* and differences, confusion and delay."—Owen J. Roberts.

**dis crim"i na'tion** (diss krim"ĭ nā'shŭn). Discernment of distinctions; penetration of differences.—"New forms of trade *discrimination* have arisen."—Franklin Delano Roosevelt.

**dis par'i ties** (diss par'ĭ tiz). Differences in kind or condition.—"Recognizing the wide *disparities* in the various areas, the board may make additional allowances."—George W. Taylor.

**dis sim″i lar'i ties** (dis sim″ĭ lar'ĭ tiz). Things in which we are unlike.—"We have been stressing our *dissimilarities* and emphasizing our differences."—George B. Cutten.

**dis tinc'tions** (diss tingk'shŭnz). Distinguishing marks or qualities; marks of honor; superiorities.—"They were ignorant of tradition and unimpressed by *distinctions* of rank."—Edith Wharton.

**in″e qual'i ties** (in″ē kwol'ĭ tiz). Conditions of being unequal; examples of lack of uniformity or evenness.—"Even in the best democracy there will always be *inequalities* of opportunity."—Donald G. Cooley.

**ni'ce ties** (nī'sĕ tiz). Refinements; subtleties; delicate distinctions; exact discriminations.—"He spoke very well, almost too perfectly, with grammatical *niceties* that were slightly pedantic."—André Maurois.

**com pact'** (kŏm pakt'). Condensed; closely consolidated.—"Let me give you a *compact* synopsis now and the details later."—Alfred M. Landon.

**con cise'** (kŏn sīce'). Brief; clear and clean-cut, without any superfluous words.—"These drafters prepare the bills in proper form, with *concise* wording to prevent loopholes."—Thomas C. Desmond.

**la con'ic** (luh kon'ik). Using as few words as possible; bluntly brief.—"They are suffering more from these attacks than is apparent in the *laconic* reports."—David Lawrence.

**pith'y** (pith'i). Expressing the gist of the matter in few words.—"The headlines must be short and *pithy*."—R. W. Jepson.

**sen ten'tious** (sen ten'shŭs). Axiomatic; containing many aphorisms or maxims; pompously-formal or moralizing.—"Grieg's manner was impulsive, but never *sententious*."—Percy Aldridge Grainger.

**sum'ma ry** (sum'uh ri). Performed without delay or ceremony; dispensing with unnecessary details.—"A great deal of this *summary* criticism is merely a fad."—André Maurois.

**terse** (turce). Short and to the point, but tasteful and finished.—"The picture is *terse* and brief, with thrilling moments of incident and action."—Elsa Maxwell.

**cap'i tal** (kap'ĭ tăl). Excellent; of the best kind; admirable; first-rate.—"'That's a *capital* plan,' said the boss."—Ainslee Mockridge.

**car'di nal** (kahr'dĭ năl). Of basic or fundamental importance.—"The *cardinal* pattern of their policy will be to retain an iron hand over every industry engaged in the production of armaments of war."—William J. Donovan.

**dom'i nant** (dom'ĭ nănt). Governing or commanding; ruling or controlling.—"Reduction of the elk herd became the *dominant* issue."—Victor H. Cahalane.

**pre dom'i nant** (prē dom'ĭ nănt). Superior in influence, power, or effectiveness; prevailing over others.—"The three *predominant* groups of our national life are agriculture, labor, and industry."—Sidney Hillman.

**prime** (prīme). First in rank, order, or importance; hence, chief; best.—"Jugoslavia is the *prime* illustration."—Dorothy Thompson.

**prin'ci pal** (prin'sĭ păl). Chief; main; first in importance; most important.—"The *principal* source of profit was the bar."—Jules Romains.

**su preme'** (sū preem'). Highest in importance; greatest.—"That will be our first and *supreme* task, and nothing must lure us from it."—Winston Churchill.

**ca dav'er ous** (kuh dav'ur ŭs). Like a corpse; looking like a dead person.—"These birds had bald *cadaverous* heads and long wrinkled necks."—Arthur Koestler.

**ghast'ly** (gast'li). Having a death-like appearance that terrified.—"Vines crawled in every direction across the *ghastly* jumble of whitish stone."—S. Dillon Ripley.

**gris'ly** (griz'li). Horrifying; causing terror or dread; savage-looking.— 'We are permitted to guess the ature of the dread conspiracy and the status of the *grisly* figures."— Will Cuppy.

**grue'some** (groo'sŭm). Causing a kind of horror that makes one shudder; suggesting gloomy or frightful thoughts.—"On the front line death never ended his *gruesome* harvest."— George S. Patton, Jr.

**hid'e ous** (hid'ē ŭs). Very shocking; frightful; horrible; dreadful; revolting.—"Several innocent persons have died *hideous* deaths as a result of drinking poison liquor."—J. Edgar Hoover.

**ac com'pan i ment** (ă kum'puh nimĕnt). That which goes with something else or is associated with it; hence, an instrumental part to support a voice; a subordinate part that is instrumental or vocal.—"The music for voice and piano *accompaniment* is given for each carol."—May Lamberton Becker.

**ad den'dum** (ă den'dŭm). An addition; a thing added; a supplement, a brief added note.—"The presence of beauty in this form is never treated as a mere *addendum* to the values of life." —L. P. Jacks.

**ad'junct** (aj'ŭngkt). Something joined or added that is not a real part of the thing but may be a vauable addition.—"Grade labeling is not a reform but an essential *adjunct* to successful price regulation."—J. K. Galbraith.

**ap pend'age** (uh pen'dij). A subordinate or subsidiary part or attachment.—"She lost what character she had and became merely the *appendage* of a tradition."—Louis Bromfield.

**ap pur'te nances** (ă pur'tē nǎn'siz). Objects belonging or pertinent to a principal thing as accessories.— "There must be a convenient pantry and a pleasant kitchen with all *appurtenances* thereto."—Emily Post.

**aux il'ia ries** (awg zil'yuh riz). Persons or things that help or aid in some capacity.—"The rack and torture chamber have been revived as accepted *auxiliaries* of law and order." —Jonah B. Wise.

**bane'ful** (bāne'fool). Causing great harm; deadly.—"Some say that a *baneful* precedent will be established."—Franklin Delano Roosevelt.

**noi'some** (noy'sŭm). Very offensive, particularly to the sense of smell; bad-smelling.—"Now he would escape the *noisome* odors of the battlefield."—George F. Gahagan.

**nox'ious** (nok'shŭs). Causing injury to health; morally harmful.—"The use of *noxious* gases in war is a hideous commentary on civilization."— Franklin Delano Roosevelt.

**ob nox'ious** (ŏb nok'shŭs). Objectionable; of a character to give offense.— "He has every right to fight what he deems an *obnoxious* law."—Robert Marion La Follette.

**per ni'cious** (per nish'ŭs). Causing harm; working mischief or evil; having the power of destroying or injuring.—"The *pernicious* practice of name-calling is aggravated in the field of international politics."—John W. Bricker.

**be smirched'** (bē smurch'd'). Smeared with stains; smirched to dim the brightness; dishonored.—"It seems strange to me that my own good name should be *besmirched* on such evidence."—George W. Mills.

**con tam'i nat"ed** (kŏn tam'ǐ nāte"id). Made impure by contact or admixture; corrupted spiritually.—"Some people take the attitude that politics is something sordid from which they would be, in some way, *contaminated*." —Lloyd C. Stark.

**de filed'** (dē fīle'd'). Rendered foul or dirty; befouled.—"They have invaded and *defiled* the country."— Winston Churchill.

**sul'lied** (sul'id). Soiled; stained; made impure.—"His life is *sullied* with heinous sins, his soul is dark."—Axel Munthe.

**taint'ed** (taint'ed). Tinged with poison; impregnated with something harmful.—"They have *tainted* our

democracy with autocratic demands."
—Fred I. Kent.

**vi'ti at"ed** (vish'i āte"id). Of which the quality has been impaired or made impure.—"The heavier *vitiated* water slowly sinks to the bottom and the purer water rises."—Frank J. Meyers

**flu'ent** (flū'ĕnt). Ready in speaking or writing; speaking or writing without hesitation.—"We know this man to be a *fluent* liar."—Samuel Grafton.

**gar'ru lous** (găr'ū lŭs). Given to talking too much and about trifles, in a tedious, rambling way.—"The great doctor saw that *garrulous* folk did not waste his time."—William Elliott.

**glib** (glib). Smooth-tongued; using words flippantly or superficially.—"Americans are rightly suspicious of the *glib* politician."—Lawrence Hunt.

**lo qua'cious** (lō kwā'shŭs). Using an incessant flow of words; given to continual talking.—"Thank Heaven, he was free from *loquacious* friends."—John Buchan.

**ver bose'** (vur bōce'). Using many unnecessary words; wordy; containing more words than are needed.—"He can reach heights of *verbose* wrath over the misdeeds of a union functionary in Podunk."—James B. Carey.

**vol'u ble** (vol'ū b'l). Having a flow of words in speaking; using words easily and smoothly.—"His young aide was a small man, brilliant and *voluble*."—Lyman Bryson.

**bom bas'tic** (bom bass'tik). Making use of extravagant or ranting phrases.—"His ability to silence these *bombastic* and verbose men is unequalled."—Edward R. Murrow.

**gran dil'o quent** (gran dil'ō kwĕnt). Pompously eloquent; making use of lofty words and tall talk.—"He had dropped his slightly *grandiloquent* tone."—Pearl S. Buck.

**gran'di ose** (gran'di ōse). Having an imposing style; pompous.—"The official was explaining in rather a *grandiose* fashion that he would be delighted to show us the institution."—Edward R. Murrow.

**mag nil'o quent** (mag nil'ō kwĕnt). Boasting; uttered in a boastful, vainglorious manner.—"Their pretentious phrasing and their constant use of *magniloquent* clichés is familiar."—Ludwig Lewisohn.

**tur'gid** (tur'jid). Swollen; inflated; hence, ostentatious.—"This *turgid*, poisonous backwash actually has been called the wave of the future."—Albert N. Williams.

**in"com pre hen'si ble** (in"kom prē-hen'sĭ b'l). Not capable of being comprehended; not possible to understand.—"American loneliness made for a pleasure in welcoming strangers which is *incomprehensible* to people in the established communities of the Old World."—James Truslow Adams.

**in ex'pli ca ble** (in eks'pli kuh b'l). Not capable of being explained; that cannot be accounted for.—"Her *inexplicable* rise is one of the great phenomena in history."—Jan Christiaan Smuts.

**in scru'ta ble** (in skrōō'tuh b'l). Not able to be understood or fathomed; defying interpretation.—"Many ills were accepted as the workings of an *inscrutable* Providence."—I. Ogden Woodruff.

**mys'tic** (miss'tik). Secret; having a hidden meaning or significance.—"I longed to be there in the *mystic* hours when darkness might lay its balm upon tired eyes."—John Haynes Holmes.

**oc cult'** (ŏ kult'). Mysterious; dealing with secret agencies.—"It seemed as if the beast was a phantom possessed of some *occult* power."—Roy Chapman Andrews.

**rec'on dite** (rek'ŭn dīte). Too deep for ordinary comprehension; profound; beyond ordinary perception.—"The book relates to the dawning period in Greek art and it clarifies a *recondite* subject."—Royal Cortissoz.

**tran"scen den'tal** (tran"sen den'tăl). Surpassing ordinary comprehension; supernatural.—"Do we not continue to witness the *transcendental* beauty of the sunset?"—John D. Rockefeller, Jr.

**an tag′o nisms** (an tag′ō niz′mz). Opposing principles; active conflicts or oppositions.—"There are natural *antagonisms* of interest which divide their peoples."—Winston Churchill.

**an tip′a thy** (an tip′uh thi: 'th' as in 'thin'). A deep and instinctive mental or physical dislike for a person or thing, causing recoil from it.—"The sexes are closer together instead of farther apart, and there is no rivalry or *antipathy*."—Mary Agnes McGeachy.

**a ver′sion** (uh vur′zhŭn). A permanent distaste or intense dislike coupled with a desire to avoid.—"I have always approached biographical novels with a mixture of *aversion* and distrust."—J. Donald Adams.

**dis taste′** (diss tāyste′). Disapproval; dislike; displeasure.—"I can well understand the *distaste* with which many Indians are likely to regard the scheme."—Lord Halifax.

**re pug′nance** (rē pug nănce). A deepseated and opposing distaste.—"This *repugnance* was more than physical, but she hoped for a readjustment."—Willa Cather.

**dis may′** (diss māy′). Consternation; loss of courage caused by fear of something to come; disabling alarm. —"Instead of plaudits, they are receiving dead cats, aged tomatoes, old boots, and other tokens of *dismay*."—Samuel Grafton.

**hu mil″i a′tion** (hū mil″i āy′shŭn). Abasement; reduction to an inferior position in the eyes of others; a lowering of self-respect.—"In the flush on his sister's face he thought he saw the *humiliation* he would always bring on his people."—Morley Callaghan.

**mor″ti fi ca′tion** (mor″tĭ fi kā′shŭn). A state of vexation or depression caused by shame that one has let others see some weakness or ignorance.—"My relief was mixed with *mortification* at having been so afraid."—John Myers Myers.

**i o′ta** (ī ō′tuh). A particle; a very small amount.—"Not an *iota* of State

powers should be yielded."—Herbert R. O'Conor.

**mol′e cules** (mol′ē kūle′z). Minute particles; the smallest portions into which a substance can be divided without chemical change; units of matter.—"Yet there is movement in all things—atoms and *molecules* forever in movement."—George Matthew Adams.

**scin til′la** (sin til′uh). A spark; hence, a speck, something so small that it can scarcely be seen; a very slight trace of something.—"They found that the facts were supported by more than a *scintilla* of evidence."—O. R. McGuire.

**shreds** (shredz). Small torn strips; fragments; torn pieces; scraps.—"Everywhere, again, treaties and agreements were being torn to *shreds*."—Carlos Martins.

**whit** (hwit). A speck; an atom; the smallest degree.—"It will not matter a *whit* whether we are politicians or business men."—Wayne Coy.

**cring′ing** (krinj′ing). Bowing in servility or cowardice; shrinking and crouching in fear or humility.—"The dog came to me, whimpering and *cringing*."—Donald G. Cooley.

**fawn′ing** (fawn′ing). Basely humble; slavishly flattering or toadying.—"The mayor and other notables had rushed to the banquet with *fawning* haste."—Franz Werfel.

**ob se′qui ous** (ŏb see′kwi ŭs). Complying or agreeing in a slavish, fawning way.—"To the end he remained calm and unruffled, civil but not *obsequious*." — Somerset Maugham.

**truck′ling** (truk′ling). Yielding in a servile, fawning way; currying favor obsequiously.—"They are always *truckling* to the rich."—Lloyd C. Douglas.

**es′sence** (ess′ĕnce). The real nature of anything; the chief character.—"Courage and fidelity are the *essence* of his being."—Winston Churchill.

**gist** (jist). The main point; the substance of a matter; the real ground or point of a longer statement.—"They approved the resolution embodying the *gist* of the agreement."—Claude Pepper.

**nu'cle us** (nū'klē ŭs). A kernel; hence, a center of development.—"An Anglo-American working partnership is the *nucleus* of the United Nations."—Clive Baillieu.

**pith** (pith). The central tissue of plants; hence, the most important part, the essential part.—"The *pith* and charm of the autobiography is in the personality of the writer."—Henry Seidel Canby.

**quin tes'sence** (kwin tess'ĕnce). The purest and best part; the highest form or embodiment; the most perfect example; the concentrated essence.—"I accept this as the *quintessence* of all compliments I have ever received."—Wendell Willkie.

**ad'age** (ad'ij). A traditional saying or proverb handed down from the past and widely used.—"For centuries the world accepted the biblical *adage* that the man who soon parted with his money was a fool."—William Bennett Munro.

**aph'o rism** (af'ō riz'm). A brief, pithy statement of a general truth.—"Education has many facets. With this *aphorism* as a cue, we are making a number of experiments."—Fairfield Osborn.

**ap'o thegm** (ap'ō them: 'th' as in 'thin'). A short, pithy saying that is instructive.—"To paraphrase a famous *apothegm*, he holds that what is new will not be important, and what is important will not be new."—Gerald Johnson.

**dic'tum** (dik'tŭm). An authoritative or positive utterance.—"They might well reflect on Nietzsche's *dictum* 'The coldest of all monsters is called the State.' "—Nicholas Murray Butler.

**max'im** (mak'sim). A brief statement of a truth that is drawn from experience and self-evident.—"Our traditional *maxim* is 'The people form the foundation of the country.' "—Generalissimo Chiang Kai-shek.

**pre'cepts** (pree'septs). Prescribed rules of conduct; laws to guide behavior or action.—"When are we to become civilized, according to the *precepts* taught by Christ?"—George Matthew Adams.

**tru'ism** (trōō'iz'm). An obvious truth; a platitude.—"The Chairman, whom I have just quoted, announced a *truism*."—James E. Murray.

**con"tra dic'to ry** (kon"truh dik'tō ri). That are contrary or deny one another; mutually opposed.—"He had already confused them by issuing *contradictory* directions."—Ursula Parrott.

**in con'gru ous** (in kong'grōō ŭs). Not adapted to the occasion; inappropriate; unsuitable.—"The deposit would not have seemed *incongruous*, but just and fitting."—Archibald MacLeish.

**in"con sis'tent** (in"kŏn siss'tent). Not agreeing with itself; unable to stand together.—"Either the Board is misinterpreting the law, or the law itself is *inconsistent* or contradictory." —C. E. Wilson.

**ir rec"on cil'a ble** (ir rek"ŏn sīle'uh-b'l). That cannot be reconciled or brought into harmony.—"In neither of the countries are the issues *irreconcilable*."—Walter Lippmann.

**be nev'o lence** (bē nev'ō lĕnce). Desire for the good and well-being of others; charitableness.—"The life of Christ is a long record of persecution but His love and *benevolence* shine through it all."—Generalissimo Chiang Kai-shek.

**clem'en cy** (klem'ĕn si). A tendency to show mercy or indulgence; lenity towards offenders.—"Why should parole, or some form of *clemency*, be extended in one community and not in another?"—J. Edgar Hoover.

**com pas'sion** (kŏm pash'ŭn). Sympathy with those who suffer; pity for distress and suffering with a willingness to bring relief; condolence.—"This fighting book is rich with universal *compassion* and righteous indignation."—Sterling North.

**le'ni en cy** (lee'ni ĕn si). Forbearance; mercifulness; gentleness.—"The officials continued to undo the Field Marshall's *leniency* toward civilians." —Albert Perry.

**be wil′der ment**    (bē wil′der mĕnt). Confusion caused by many and various matters all claiming immediate attention.—"There was agitation, uncertainty, and *bewilderment* after the crash."—Cassius E. Gates.

**di lem′ma**  (di lem′uh). A perplexing choice between two equally undesirable alternatives.—"The people demand the help of the business world in this present *dilemma*."—C. M. Chester.

**per plex′i ty**  (pur plek′sĭ ti). Puzzled uncertainty; mental confusion; distracted embarrassment.—"They advanced slowly, stopping frequently to parley, their faces full of *perplexity*."—Lloyd C. Douglas.

**plight**  (plīte). A distressed or complicated condition or state.—"We must not take time out to gloat over the *plight* of that country."—Franklin Delano Roosevelt.

**pre dic′a ment**  (prē dik′uh mĕnt). A difficult, embarrassing, or puzzling situation.—"Officials in Washington are anxious to prevent a recurrence of this *predicament*."—George E. Daniels.

**quan′da ry**  (kwon′duh ri). A state of uncertainty or perplexity as to the next move.—"The great educators themselves seem to be in a *quandary*." —Edward A. Filene.

**co′ma**  (kō′muh). A state of prolonged unconsciousness or insensibility caused by disease or injury.—"He had sunk into a deep *coma* from which his emergence was most unlikely."— Lloyd C. Douglas.

**leth′ar gy**  (leth′ur ji). Stupor; a state of apathy and indifference; apathetic and gloomy drowsiness.—"The city had fallen into economic *lethargy*."— Margery Wilson.

**stu″pe fac′tion**  (stū″pē fak′shŭn).  A stunned and overwhelmed state.— "Attempts to explain, detractions, and then *stupefaction* had followed." —H. G. Wells.

**stu′por**  (stū′pur). A condition of the body in which the senses or faculties are deadened or greatly dulled.— "They lived through these terrible years in mental *stupor* or apathy."— H. J. Van Mook.

**tor′por**  (tor′pur). Suspended animation or vitality; apathy.—"He said that their *torpor* and indifference in the face of all this was really criminal."—Robert Marion La Follette.

**re served′**  (rē zurvd′). Self-restrained in speech or manner.—"He was so *reserved* that the conversation lagged and finally ceased altogether."— George F. Gahagan.

**ret′i cent**  (ret′ĭ sĕnt). Apt to keep one's own counsel and not discuss matters with others.—"Either they preferred to meet elsewhere or else they were merely *reticent*."—Jules Romains.

**se cre′tive**  (sē kree′tiv). Inclined to secrecy or lack of frankness, especially about personal affairs.—"The fact that he was expected to be *secretive* about the romance annoyed him."—Gene Fowler.

**tac′i turn**  (tass′ĭ turn). Disinclined to talk.—"The head boy was *taciturn*, fair, and good-looking."—H. G. Wells.

**un″com mu′ni ca″tive**  (un″kō mū′nĭ-ka″tiv). Disinclined to impart information; not disposed to converse. —"When he ventured on several commonplace remarks she was attentive but *uncommunicative*."—Lloyd C. Douglas.

**ap′ti tude**  (ap′tĭ tūde). A potential ability; a natural propensity; a natural or acquired gift or ability.— "*Aptitude* tests must be given."— Carl A. Gray.

**ca″pa bil′i ties**  (kā″puh bil′ĭ tiz). Abilities to learn and understand; qualifications to develop efficiency and power; undeveloped faculties; competent powers.—"Our boys have retained both their *capabilities* and their dignity."—Ernie Pyle.

**com′pe tence**  (kom′pē tĕnce). Qualification to meet all demands; ability to work promptly and well.—"He is a business man of high *competence* himself."—Winston Churchill.

**dex ter′i ty**  (dex ter′ĭ ti). Skill in using the hands; expertness.—"The manual *dexterity* of the girls makes them more effective than men in certain jobs."—Mrs. Henry Morgenthau, Jr.

**ef fi′cien cy** (e fish′ĕn si). The quality of capable production; active power to produce a result.—"How long can men work without losing *efficiency* by fatigue and strain?"—Paul V. Mc-Nutt.

**be fit′ting** (bē fit′ing). Suitable; appropriate; fit for; proper for.—"The clothes are not *befitting* to a vagrant." —Lloyd C. Douglas.
**meet** (meet). Ethically suitable; morally fitting and proper.—"It is *meet* that we should give thanks for our good fortune."—Donald G. Cooley.

**se date′** (se dāte′). Demure; sober; grave; serious; calm and quiet; tranquil and composed.—"He is a *sedate* and colorless fellow who has forgotten how to laugh."—Stanley Walker.
**staid** (staid). Of a very steady and sober character; expressive of a fixed gravity and soberness.—"The block between Fifth and Sixth Avenues was *staid* and aristocratic."—Vilas J. Boyle.

**ab′so lute** (ab′sō lūte). Free from restriction or relation; positive; unequivocal.—"Believing is an *absolute* condition. Either you believe or you don't."—Oren Root, Jr.
**ar′bi trar″y** (ahr′bĭ trer″i). Decisive but unreasonable; dependent on will, whim, or discretion.—"There should be no *arbitrary* exclusion of these films."—Harry M. Warner.
**ar′ro gant** (ar′ō gănt). Boastful; overbearing; offensively demanding.— "This outlook about science is an *arrogant* assumption."—Eric A. Johnston.
**au thor′i ta″tive** (aw thor′ĭ tā″tiv). Possessing the right to command and enforce obedience.—"We have one statement from a highly *authoritative* source: the Pope's statement of December 24th."—Elmer Davis.
**co er′cive** (kō ur′siv). Tending to restrain by force or fear—"The people of a democracy, when the need is clear, can exercise self-discipline without *coercive* legislation."—Paul V. McNutt.

**dic″ta to′ri al** (dik″tuh tō′ri ăl). Resembling dictators or those who exercise supreme and entire control.— "Strikes have been called arbitrarily by *dictatorial* business agents."—Eric A. Johnston.
**dog mat′ic** (dog mat′ik). Pertaining to dogma and what is held as a definite opinion; excessively opinionated.— "My reputation is built up on an impregnable basis of *dogmatic* reiteration."—George Bernard Shaw.
**haugh′ty** (haw′ti). Disdainfully proud; unapproachable; consciously and contemptuously proud of some superiority.—"The university was a stronghold of select and *haughty* student guilds."—Jules Romains.
**im per′a tive** (im per′uh tiv). Obligatory; urgent; very necessary.—"It seemed *imperative* to reassure the American people that their government was telling them the truth."—Elmer Davis.
**im pe′ri ous** (im peer′i ŭs). Commanding; compelling; requiring implicit obedience.—"The history of the past gives us *imperious* warning of what happens when a free people relinquishes liberty."—George F. Barrett.
**mas′ter ful** (mass′tur fŏŏl). Fond of authority; domineering.—"It was sweeping along revolutionaries, *masterful* men, and weaklings."—H. G. Wells.
**o″ver bear′ing** (ō″vur bair′ing). Forcing others to do what one wishes; aggressively arrogant; overwhelming. —"They dislike the erratic, brutal, and *overbearing* discipline of the unions."—Westbrook Pegler.
**per emp′to ry** (pur emp′tō ri). Admitting no refusal; leaving no choice; expressing a command that must be obeyed.—"One day a *peremptory* invitation was sent to him to take over the Finance Ministry."—Emil Lengyel.
**ty ran′ni cal** (ti ran′i kăl). Despotic; resembling the injustice and severe oppression of a tyrant.—"He understands very well the insecurities on which *tyrannical* assurance is based." —Marjorie Farber.

**churl′ish** (chur′lish). Mean; crabbed;

rude in manner; uncivil in speech.—
"To enquire why he had not thought
of it in the first place seemed like
*churlish* quibbling."—Ellen Lewis
Buell.

**glum** (glum). Dismally silent; doggedly
gloomy.—"I sat as *glum* as Queen
Victoria through the whole performance."—Woolcott Gibbs.

**gruff** (gruf). Rough in voice or manner;
hoarse and deep.—"He slackened his
ace with a *gruff* laugh."—Edith
Wharton.

**sple net'ic** (splē net'ik). Suffering from
spleen; hence, peevishly malicious;
spitefully stern and harsh.—"Driven
constantly to write for bread, it was
easy to be gossipy, *splenetic*, to make
anecdote do for substance."—Ludwig Lewisohn.

**sul'len** (sul'ĕn). Gloomy-tempered and
unsociable; obstinately ill-humored;
resentfully silent.—"Those who do
not work for these higher wages are
envious and *sullen*."—Hugh Butler.

**sur'ly** (sur'li). Rude and ill-tempered;
always ready to take offense; habitually resentful of any intrusion.—"A
fat man waddled out of the crowd
and confronted him with *surly* arrogance."—Lloyd C. Douglas.

**las civ'i ous** (lă siv'i ŭs). Lustful; having
wanton desires.—"Pharaoh's child,
though somewhat *lascivious*, was not
devoid of sentiment."—Thomas
Mann.

**lech'er ous** (lech'ur ŭs). Addicted to
the desire for the indulgence of sex;
morally depraved.—"A preliminary

victory is scored by the *lecherous* town-
bachelor."—Iris Barry.

**lewd** (lūde). Unchaste; indecent; licentious.—"The Postal Laws and Regu-
lations prohibit the mailing of *lewd*
books and pictures."—J. Donald
Adams.

**ob scene'** (ŏb seen'). Offensive to delicacy and modesty; impure.—"He
felt uncomfortable, as though he had
taught a child to say innocently an
*obscene* thing."—Pearl S. Buck.

**sa la'cious** (suh lā'shŭs). Having a tendency toward sexual love and intercourse.—"These types of popular
entertainment are yielding to slightly
*salacious* plays."—Ludwig Lewisohn.

**sen'su al** (sen'shoŏ ăl). Given to indulgence in the pleasures of the senses;
fond of bodily pleasures; overindul-
gent to the appetites.—"He was
*sensual*, therefore he longed for the
invisible."—Thomas Mann.

**hulk'ing** (hul'king). Bulky; of clumsy
build; heavy.—"The old bull seals
are great *hulking* fellows, rolling in
fat."—Roy Chapman Andrews.

**pon'der ous** (pon'dur ŭs). Very large
and weighing a great deal; huge;
heavy and difficult to move.—"His
home was no longer an ill-lit house
with *ponderous* furniture."—R. W.
Symonds.

**un wield'y** (un weel'di). Not easy to
wield or manage; clumsy; hard to
handle; cumbersome.—"He tugged
the *unwieldy* tube out of the trough,
and for an interval rowed hard."—
Lloyd C. Douglas.

## One-Minute Refresher

Some of the twelve words listed below have as many as twenty or thirty synonyms apiece. Many of these synonyms are too well known to be included in this book. Nevertheless, it will be a good test of your facility in recalling words if you will try to write down at least five synonyms for each word given. Take plenty of time and don't be surprised if you fail in some cases. This exercise will be extremely difficult for most people.

1. indolent _____ _____ _____ _____ _____
2. stupor _____ _____ _____ _____ _____
3. capacious _____ _____ _____ _____ _____
4. complacent _____ _____ _____ _____ _____
5. restitution _____ _____ _____ _____ _____
6. leniency _____ _____ _____ _____ _____
7. degenerate _____ _____ _____ _____ _____
8. revere _____ _____ _____ _____ _____
9. malevolence _____ _____ _____ _____ _____
10. hazardous _____ _____ _____ _____ _____
11. transient _____ _____ _____ _____ _____
12. disparities _____ _____ _____ _____ _____

*Answers:* (1) slothful, lazy, idle, lethargic, loafing, languorous, inactive. (2) insensibility, inertness, apathy, phlegm, dullness, torpor, numbness, unconsciousness, sluggishness, impassiveness. (3) spacious, wide, huge, immense, expansive, extensive, roomy, great. (4) contented, satisfied, cheerful, relaxed, easy, serene, peaceful, calm. (5) return, restoration, reparation, atonement, indemnity, recompense. (6) clemency, mercy, forgiveness, favor, gentleness, tolerance, moderation, mildness, indulgence, forbearance. (7) deteriorate, retrograde, decline, disintegrate, decay, rot. (8) respect, honor, worship, esteem, venerate, admire, approve. (9) hate, malignity, resentment, venom, virulence, savagery, brutality, spleen, malice, spite. (10) perilous, risky, dangerous, precarious, venturesome. (11) transitory, fleeting, evanescent, passing, ephemeral, impermanent, brief, fugacious, momentary, temporary. (12) dissimilarities, unlikenesses, diversities, divergencies, inequalities, differences, variations, variables.

# CHAPTER VI

## CAN YOU PRONOUNCE THEM?

IT IS really not hard to learn to pronounce correctly and well. A smooth and cultured pronunciation can be developed with absurd ease if you are willing to spend an almost infinitesimal amount of time in forming new habits.

Train yourself to listen more attentively to the better speakers over the air or in the movies or at the theater. Try to catch the little shades of sound as you go along. Repeat them to yourself and endeavor to fix them in your mind.

Put a ring around words that you are uncertain about when you are scanning a newspaper or a magazine. Or, if you are reading the current best seller jot down the words that puzzle you on the inside cover of the book or on a slip of paper. Look them up in the latest dictionary that you can find, and record them with their pronunciations, including their accents, in your pocket note-book if you prefer. Since diacritical marks are hard to interpret, it is sometimes helpful to invent a rhyme for the word in question, as *cache*, "cash." Go over these doubtful pronunciations while you are waiting for a bus, or before you go to sleep at night. They are like shining eels and are apt to slip out of your memory into the sea.

When listening to professional speakers or to the best actors, it would be well to attend not only to their pronunciations, but also to the clarity with which they enunciate every syllable, and to the way they modulate their voices.

These three items, pronunciation, enunciation and modulation, are important mechanical factors that go into the technique of making yourself understood. These are vital parts of our communications system and they must be kept clear and in order if we wish to speak with power and authority.

We can be meticulous in pronunciation, but if we clip and mumble our words, whatever we are trying to say will be weakened.

81

But even when we pronounce and enunciate with great care, if the voice is monotonous the hearer will soon lose interest.

Modulation, or the varying key and tone of the voice, is an invaluable art to learn. The vocal cords are the strings of a violin and the words are the musical notes.

I call to mind, as an example, an acquaintance who can say the single word "hello" over the telephone in such fashion that it radiates the charm of personality I know he has. He makes a stranger feel that here is someone that it would be a pleasure to meet.

Modulation and emphasis also contribute importantly to the meaning of what a person is saying. The one short word "go" can be so sounded as to indicate fear, affection, disgust, entreaty, command, hope, hatred, terror. And in a lighter way, an attractive girl can murmur "Good-night" with those subtle modulations and overtones that make you know she doesn't want you to go at all. She merely wants to be kissed!

Give habitual thought to these things. All it will take will be a few of those moments that others waste. And, besides, you will find the whole practice a pleasant and a profitable pastime.

Listen to your own voice and appraise it. Cup your hand behind your ear and say something. Stand close in a corner of your bedroom and speak. Then you will hear your voice as others hear it. How does it sound to you? Are you using the lower register? Read out loud and it will help you immensely. Most people like to be read to. Ask your listener to criticize you frankly and to catch you when you slur your words.

Many of the words in our language are so illogical in their pronunciations, so absurd and often so without reason, rhyme or law, that we may need to take on a small store of patience if we are planning to smooth out our syllables.

Imagine the patience that would be needed by someone who didn't know our language. Suppose a foreigner were facing for the first time such words as *bough, cough* and *colonel,* what reasonable hope could he have of pronouncing them correctly? By what stretch of the imagination would he guess that *choir, one* and *quay* were pronounced "kwire," "wun" and "kee"? Or that *choose* would rhyme with *lose* instead of *loose,* and that *chose* would rhyme with *grows* instead of *lose?* And who invented these fantastic pronunciations: *tomb, comb; how, tow; come, home; four, tour, sour?* Or arranged the pronunciations in the sentence: "The *maid said* it was a *plaid* dress"?

We can comfort ourselves that the road we have to travel is not as long as that of a foreigner. We start with great advantages. And yet, even among those of us who are native-born, there are still so few who are sure that their pronunciations are at all times sufficiently clear and accurate. When, for instance, a shift of sound will turn a plain word like *bow* from a low obeisance into a tie that men wear, and when a transfer of accent from the first to the last syllable can change the word *record* from a noun to a verb, we will realize what an important factor pronunciation is in the practical matter of being understood.

While this art of pronunciation is a vital one, we still shouldn't take it as seriously as some schoolmarms do, and so run the danger of becoming timid or self-conscious or stuffy about it. The line between "correct" and "incorrect" is a thin one that is always in motion. We can witness words that are changing their pronunciations right before our eyes. It used to be "correct" to say *ration*, with a long "a" as in station. This, at least, was the "preferred" pronunciation. But the tide is coming in for the *ration* that rhymes with "passion," and the next dictionary will probably record the latter as the "preferred" pronunciation. Things like these are determined by common usage.

There is a geography of pronunciation too, and the accident of birth is bound to give a twist to your tongue. If your father and mother were born on the Eastern or Western Seaboards you, in all probability, will call *chocolate* "chock-uh-lit" and you will pronounce the proper name *Harry* to rhyme with "marry." On the other hand, the vast majority of the hundred million people who live between the Alleghanies and the Coast Range say "chawk-uh-lit" and they rhyme *Harry* with "merry."

Which ones are correct? They are all "correct."

Every locale in the United States has its language peculiarities. Beyond this, there is not one of us who pronounces a given word in precisely the same way that others do. We too have our individual dialects.

In spite of these localized pronunciations and these personal habits, the way you pronounce your words and the tone of your voice will inevitably place you in a class and a caste. Mispronunciations make an unfortunate impression. They blur your personality, and they prove that your education is limited. So go to work on your speech; take a deep and genuine pride in it and people will respect you as you yourself respect others whc have developed a skill in this art.

Above all, go forth with confidence. As my friend Walter Houston says: "Whenever and wherever you speak, *intend to be heard!*"

All of the words that are assembled in this chapter appear elsewhere in this volume with their definitions and illustrative sentences. They are presented here for your study as a drill in pronunciation. With some of the words more than one pronunciation is allowable but the generally preferred form is given. In some cases accent presents the only difficulty.

## Can You Pronounce Them?

| | | | |
|---|---|---|---|
| abdominal | (ab dom′ĭ năl) | apache | (uh pash′), |
| abeyance | (uh bāy′ănce) | | a criminal |
| aborigines | (ab″ō rij′ĭ neez) | aphasia | (ă fāy′zhi uh) |
| abracadabra | (ab″ruh kuh-dab′ruh) | aphrodisiac | (af″rō diz′i ak) |
| | | apogee | (ap′ō jē) |
| absolutism | (ab′sō lūte iz′m) | appurtenances | (ă pur′tĭ năn″siz) |
| absorbing | (ăb sor′bing) | arraigned | (ă raind′) |
| acceded | (ak seed′ed) | aspirant | (ass pīre′ănt) |
| acclimatized | (ă klī′muh tīze′d) | Augean | (aw jee′ăn) |
| accoutered | (ă kōō′turd) | auxiliaries | (awg zil′yuh riz) |
| accusatory | (ă kū′zuh tō″ri) | aversion | (uh vur′zhŭn) |
| acoustics | (uh kōōce′tiks) | aviary | (āy′vi er″i) |
| acuity | (uh kū′ĭ ti) | avoirdupois | (av″ur dū poize′) |
| acumen | (ă kū′měn) | azure | (azh′ur) |
| adajio | (uh dah′jō) | | |
| adherents | (ad heer′ĕnts) | baccalaureate | (bak″uh law′rē-āte) |
| adjudication | (ă jōō″di kā′shŭn) | | |
| adjured | (ă jōōrd) | bacchantes | (bă kan′teez) |
| admirable | (ad′mĭ ruh b′l) | balderdash | (bawl′der dash) |
| aegis | (ē′jiss) | balm | (bahm) |
| aeons | (ē′ŏnz) | basal | (bāse′ăl) |
| aeronautical | (āy′ur ō naw″ti-kăl) | bathos | (bāy′thoss) |
| | | bayou | (bī′ōō) |
| Aesculapian | (ess″kū lāy′pi ăn) | behooves | (bē hōōve′z′) |
| aesthete | (ess′theet: 'th' as in 'thin') | beneficent | (bē nef′ĭ s′nt) |
| | | beneficiary | (ben″ē fish′i er′i) |
| afflatus | (ă flāy′tŭs) | benign | (bē nīne′) |
| agoraphobia | (ag″ō ruh fō′bi uh) | benison | (ben′i z′n) |
| alignments | (uh līne′měnts) | bequeathed | (bē kweethe′d: 'th' as in 'the') |
| allegro | (ah lāy′grō) | | |
| almoner | (al′mŭn ur) | berserk | (bur′surk) |
| ambivalence | (am biv′uh lĕnce) | bestial | (bess′chăl) |
| ambulatory | (am′bū luh tō″ri) | bizarre | (bi zahr′) |
| anabasis | (uh nab′uh siss) | blackguard | (blag′ahrd) |
| analogous | (uh nal′ō gŭs) | blazoned | (blāy z′nd) |
| animadversion | (an″ĭ mad vur′-zhŭn) | braggadocio | (brag″uh dō′shi ō) |
| | | Brobdingnagian | (brob″ding nag′i-ăn) |
| antibody | (an′ti bod″i) | | |
| antiphonal | (an tif′ō năl) | brochure | (brō shūre′) |
| Apache | (uh pach′ē), an Indian | bruit | (brōōt) |
| | | brusquely | (brŭsk′li) |

| | | | |
|---|---|---|---|
| bulwark | (bŏŏl'werk) | critique | (kri teek') |
| burgeoned | (bur'jŭnd) | Croesus | (kree'sŭs) |
| burlesquing | (bur lesk'ing) | culinary | (kū'li ner″i) |
| | | curmudgeon | (kur muj'ŭn) |
| cabal | (kuh bal') | cyclical | (sī'kli kăl) |
| caballeros | (kah″bahl yāy'- | cynosure | (sī'nō shŏŏr) |
| | rōze) | czars | (zahrz) |
| cabana | (kuh bah'nuh) | | |
| caches | (kash'iz) | dais | (dāy'iss) |
| cacophony | (kuh kof'ō ni) | debacle | (dē bak″l) |
| cadres | (kad'riz) | debauching | (dē bawch'ing) |
| calumniated | (kuh lum'ni āte″- | debouched | (dē bŏŏsh'd') |
| | id) | decorum | (dē kō'rŭm) |
| caparisoned | (kuh par'ĭ sŭnd) | deign | (dāne) |
| carnage | (kahr'nij) | deleterious | (del″ē teer'i ŭs) |
| carnivorous | (kahr niv'ō rŭs) | deliquesces | (del″ĭ kwess'ez) |
| cashier | (kash eer') | demesne | (dē māne') |
| causality | (kaw zal'ĭ ti) | demoniacal | (dē″mō ni'uh kăl) |
| cautery | (kaw'tur i) | descried | (dē skrīde') |
| cavalcade | (kav″ăl kāde') | desideratum | (dē sid″ur āy'tŭm) |
| cavil | (kav'il) | despicable | (dess'pi kuh b'l) |
| censorious | (sen sō'ri ŭs) | desuetude | (dess'we tūde) |
| centrifugal | (sen trif'ū găl) | devotees | (dev″ō teeze') |
| cerebral | (ser'ē brăl) | diaphanous | (dī af'uh nŭs) |
| cerements | (seer'mĕnts) | dichotomy | (dī kot'ō mi) |
| chalets | (sha lāyz') | dimensions | (dĭ men'shŭnz) |
| chameleon | (kuh mē'lē ŭn) | diminution | (dim″i nū'shŭn) |
| charnel | (chahr'nĕl) | diplomacy | (di plō'muh si) |
| Charon | (kair'ŏn) | disfranchises | (diss fran'chīze ez) |
| chasms | (kaz'mz) | disheveled | (di shev″'ld) |
| chef-d'oeuvre | (shāy dur'vr') | disparate | (diss'puh rāte) |
| chiaroscuro | (ki ah″rō skū'rō) | dissidents | (diss'ĭ dĕnts) |
| chicanery | (shi kāne'er i) | divas | (dē'vuhz) |
| chimera | (kī mee'ruh) | diverting | (dĭ vur'ting) |
| choleric | (kol'ur ik) | divest | (dĭ vest') |
| Cimmerian | (si meer'i ăn) | docile | (doss'il) |
| Circe | (sur'sē) | domicile | (dom'ĭ sil) |
| cleanliness | (klen'li ness) | dotage | (dōte'ij) |
| coherent | (kō heer'ĕnt) | dourly | (dŏŏr'li) |
| comely | (kum'li) | dramaturgy | (dram'uh tur″ji) |
| comminatory | (kŏ min'uh tō″ri) | ductile | (duk'til) |
| comparably | (kom'puh ruh bli) | | |
| composite | (kŏm poz'it) | egregiously | (ē gree'jŭs li) |
| condign | (kŏn dīne') | eleemosynary | (el″ē mos'i ner'i) |
| condolence | (kŏn dō'lĕnce) | elision | (ē lizh'ŭn) |
| conduits | (kon'dits) | empirical | (em pir'i kăl) |
| conjugal | (kon'jŏŏ găl) | empyrean | (em″pi rē'ăn) |
| consuetudes | (kon'swē tūde'z) | endemic | (en dem'ik) |
| consummate (adj.) | (kŏn sum'it) | entirety | (en tīre'ti) |
| contumely | (kon'tū mē″li) | environment | (en vī'rŭn mĕnt) |
| conversant | (kon'vur sănt) | ephemeral | (ĕ fem'ur ăl) |
| corroborated | (kŏ rob'ō rāte″id) | epilogue | (ep'ĭ log) |
| coup | (kŏŏ) | epitome | (ē pit'ō mē) |
| covert | (kuv'urt) | equipoise | (ē'kwĭ poyze) |
| cozened | (kuz″'nd) | equitable | (ek'wi tuh b'l) |
| crabbed | (krab'id) | escapades | (ess″kuh paidz') |

| | | | |
|---|---|---|---|
| esoteric | (ess″ō ter′ik) | heretic | (her′ĕ tik) |
| essay (verb) | (e sāy′) | hermaphrodites | (hur maf′rō dītes) |
| euphoria | (yū fō′ri uh) | holocaust | (hol′ō kawst) |
| euthanasia | (yū″thuh nāy′zhi- | homogeneous | (hō″mō jee′nē ŭs) |
| | uh) | hostage | (hoss′tij) |
| exacerbate | (eg zass′ur bāte) | hyperboles | (hī pur′bō leez) |
| exhaustively | (eg zawce′tiv li) | | |
| exhilaration | (eg zil″uh rā′shŭn) | idealism | (ī dē′ăl iz′m) |
| exorcised | (ek′sor sīze′d) | illustrative | (i luss′truh tiv) |
| extempore | (eks tem′pō rē) | imbroglio | (im brōle′yō) |
| | | imperious | (im peer′i ŭs) |
| façade | (fa sahd′) | impotence | (im′pō těnce) |
| fanfaronade | (fan″fuh rŏn āde′) | impresario | (im″pruh sah′ri ō) |
| fealty | (fee′ăl ti) | impugn | (im pūne′) |
| feigned | (faind) | inaugurated | (in aw′gū rāte″id) |
| feint | (faint) | inchoate (adj.) | (in kō′it) |
| feloniously | (fē lō′ni ŭs li) | incognito | (in kog′ni tō) |
| fêted | (fāte′ed) | incomparable | (in kom′puh- |
| fiasco | (fē ass′kō) | | ruh b'l) |
| fjords | (fyordz) | indecorum | (in″dē kō′rŭm) |
| flaccid | (flak′sid) | indices | (in′dĭ seez) |
| flagitious | (fluh jish′ŭs) | indictment | (in dīte′měnt) |
| forays | (for′āyz) | indisputable | (in di spū′tuh b'l) |
| forte (strong point) | (fort) | indissoluble | (in di sol′ū b'l) |
| fragmentary | (frag′měn ter″i) | inebriety | (in ē brī′ĕ ti) |
| frenetic | (frē net′ik) | inexplicable | (in eks′pli kuh b'l) |
| fulsome | (fool′sŭm) | inextricably | (in eks′tri kuh bli) |
| furibund | (fū′ri bund) | infamous | (in′fuh mŭs) |
| | | infinitesimal | (in″fin ĭ tess′ĭ măl) |
| garish | (gair′ish) | ingenious | (in jeen′yŭs) |
| gaucheness | (gōshe′ness) | inimical | (in im′i kăl) |
| gauge | (gāje) | inimitable | (in im′ĭ tuh b'l) |
| gelid | (jel′id) | initiate | (i nish′i āte) |
| generic | (jē ner′ik) | insouciance | (in sōō′si ănce) |
| genie | (jee′ni) | intaglio | (in ta(h)l′yō) |
| germane | (jur māne′) | integral | (in′tē grăl) |
| ghouls | (gōolz) | internecine | (in″tur nee′sin) |
| glacial | (glāy′shăl) | interrogatory | (in″tě rog′uh tōri) |
| glistened | (gliss″nd) | interstices | (in tur′sti sez) |
| gnarled | (nahrl′d) | intricate | (in′trĭ kit) |
| gourmand | (gōor′mănd) | intrigue | (in treeg′) |
| gourmets | (gōor′māze′) | inundated | (in′un dāte″id) |
| gratis | (grāy′tiss) | inveighed | (in vāde′) |
| gravamen | (gruh vāy′men) | inveigle | (in vee′g'l) |
| gregarious | (grē gair′i ŭs) | irascibility | (i rass″ĭ bil′ĭ ti) |
| grimaces | (gri māy′siz) | irrefutable | (ir re fū′tuh b'l) |
| guise | (gīze) | irrelevant | (ir rel′ē vănt) |
| gyrations | (jī rā′shŭnz) | irreparable | (i rep′uh ruh b'l) |
| | | irrevocably | (i rev′ō kuh bli) |
| habiliments | (huh bil′ĭ měnts) | itinerary | (ī tin′ur er″i) |
| halcyon | (hal′si ŭn) | | |
| harangue | (huh rang′) | jalousied | (zhal″ōō zeed′) |
| harem | (hair′em) | jejune | (jē jōon′) |
| hauteur | (hō tur′) | jeopardy | (jep′ur di) |
| heinous | (hāy′nŭs) | jocund | (jok′ŭnd) |
| herculean | (hur kū′lē ăn) | joust | (just) |

| | |
|---|---|
| jurisprudence | (jŏŏr″iss prōō′-dĕnce) |
| katabasis | (kuh tab′uh siss) |
| kudos | (kū′doss) |
| lagniappe | (lan yap′) |
| laity | (lāy′ĭ ti) |
| lamentable | (lam′ĕn tuh b'l) |
| lascivious | (lă siv′i ŭs) |
| laudable | (lawd′uh b'l) |
| leonine | (lee′ō nīne) |
| lesions | (lee′zhŭnz) |
| Lethe | (lē′thē: 'th' as in 'thin') |
| liaison | (lē āy′zŭn) |
| lieu | (lū) |
| limned) | (limd) |
| literally | (lit′ur ă li) |
| logistic | (lō jiss′tik) |
| Logos | (log′oss) |
| longitude | (lon′jĭ tūde) |
| Lothario | (lō thair′i ō: 'th' as in 'thin') |
| lucubrations | (lū″kū brā′shŭnz) |
| macabre | (muh kah′b'r) |
| machinations | (mak″ĭ nā′shŭnz) |
| maestro | (mī′strō) |
| maligned | (muh līne′d′) |
| mandatory | (man′duh tō″ri) |
| maneuvering | (muh nōō′vur ing) |
| mansuetude | (man′swē tūde) |
| masochism | (maz′ŏk iz′m) |
| mediatory | (mee′di uh tō″ri) |
| mediocre | (mee′di ō″ker) |
| mellifluous | (mĕ lif′lŏŏ ŭs) |
| memorabilia | (mem″ō ruh bil′i-uh) |
| mesa | (māy′suh) |
| miniature | (min′i uh chŏŏr) |
| minions | (min′yŭnz) |
| miscegenation | (miss″e je nā′shŭn) |
| misogamist | (mi sog′uh mist) |
| misogyny | (mi soj′ĭ ni) |
| mnemonic | (nē mon′ik) |
| moguls | (mō gulz′) |
| monogamous | (mō nog′uh mŭs) |
| moribund | (mor′ĭ bŭnd) |
| multifarious | (mul″ti fair′i ŭs) |
| musicale | (mū″zi kahl′) |
| myopics | (mī op′iks) |
| myrmidons | (mur′mi dŏnz) |
| naïvete | (nah ēve′tāy′) |
| narrator | (na rāy′ter) |

| | |
|---|---|
| nefarious | (nē fair′i ŭs) |
| nemesis | (nem′ē siss) |
| nepenthe | (nē pen′thē: 'th' as in 'thin') |
| nepotism | (nep′ō tiz'm) |
| nescience | (nesh′i ĕnce) |
| niceties | (nī′sĕ tiz) |
| nihilists | (nī′ĭ lists) |
| nirvana | (nir vah′nuh) |
| nonchalance | (non′shuh lănce) |
| noxious | (nok′shŭs) |
| numismatics | (nū″miz mat′iks) |
| obesity | (ō bess′ĭ ti) |
| obligato | (ob″li gah′tō) |
| obloquy | (ob′lō kwi) |
| Occident | (ok′sĭ dĕnt) |
| ochlocracy | (ok lok′ruh si) |
| onerous | (on′ur ŭs) |
| onomatopoeia | (on″ō mat″ō pē′-yuh) |
| onus | (ō′nŭs) |
| ophthalmology | (of″thal mol′ō ji: 'th' as in 'thin') |
| optometrist | (op tom′ē trist) |
| orgy | (or′ji) |
| orisons | (or′i zŭnz) |
| orthoepists | (or′thō e pists: 'th' as in 'thin') |
| otiose | (ō′shi ōce) |
| oubliettes | (ōō′blē ets′) |
| overt | (ō′vurt) |
| pachyderm | (pak′i durm) |
| palled | (pawld) |
| palliative | (pal′i uh″tiv) |
| panegyrics | (pan″ē jir′iks) |
| pantomime | (pan′tō mīme) |
| paradigms | (par′uh dimz) |
| pastiche | (pass teesh′) |
| patent (open) | (pāy′tĕnt) |
| patina | (pat′i nuh) |
| pediatricians | (pē″di uh trish′-ănz) |
| pellucid | (pĕ lū′sid) |
| penalized | (pee′năl īze'd) |
| penology | (pē nol′ō ji) |
| perfervid | (pur fur′vid) |
| persiflage | (pur′si flahzh) |
| perverted (adj.) | (pur vur′ted) |
| perverts (noun) | (pur′vurts) |
| phantasmagoria | (fan taz″muh-gō′ri uh) |
| pharmacopoeia | (fahr″muh kō-pee′uh) |
| philippics | (fĭ lip′iks) |

| | | | |
|---|---|---|---|
| photogenic | (fō tō jen'ik) | schisms | (siz'mz) |
| picturesque | (pik"choͦor esk') | schizophrenia | (skiz"ō free'ni uh) |
| piquant | (pee'kănt) | scion | (sī'ŭn) |
| plagiarism | (plāy'ji uh riz'm) | secreted | (sē kreet'id) |
| podiatrist | (pō dī'uh trist) | seismic | (sīze'mik) |
| poignant | (poyn'yănt) | sempiternal | (sem"pi tur'năl) |
| portended | (por tend'ed) | senescence | (sē ness'ĕnce) |
| portents | (por'tents) | senile | (see'nīle) |
| potable | (pō'tuh b'l) | seniority | (seen yŏr'ĭ ti) |
| precedence | (prē seed'ĕnce) | sentient | (sen'shĕnt) |
| precedents | (press'ē dĕnts) | seraglio | (sē ra(h)l'yō) |
| preferable | (pref'ur uh b'l) | sesame | (sess'uh mē) |
| premature | (prē"muh choͦor') | silhouetted | (sil"oͦo et'id) |
| prescient | (prē'shi ĕnt) | sinecure | (sī'nē kūre) |
| project (verb) | (prō jekt') | slough (bog) | (slou) |
| project (noun) | (proj'ekt) | slough (to shed) | (sluf) |
| proletariat | (prō"lē tair'i ăt) | solace | (sol'ĭss) |
| propitiate | (prō pish'i āte) | soubriquet | (soͦo'bri kāy) |
| pseudonym | (sū'dō nim) | splenetic | (splē net'ik) |
| psychiatry | (sī kī'uh tri) | stalwarts | (stawl'werts) |
| psychic | (sī'kik) | stertorous | (stur'ter ŭs) |
| puerile | (pū'er il) | subtler | (sut'ler) |
| purport (noun) | (pur'port) | succinctly | (suk singkt'li) |
| purports (verb) | (pur ports') | supine | (sū pīne') |
| purulent | (pū'roͦo lĕnt) | surfeit | (sur'fit) |
| putsch | (poͦoch) | suzerainty | (sū'zĕ rain ti) |
| | | swarthy | (swor'thi: 'th' as in 'the') |
| quandary | (kwon'duh ri) | | |
| queues | (kūze) | sycophant | (sik'ō fănt) |
| quietus | (kwī ee'tŭs) | | |
| | | tautologies | (taw tol'ō jiz) |
| rapine | (rap'in) | technique | (tek neek') |
| ratiocination | (rash"i oss"i nā'shŭn) | telepathy | (tē lep'uh thi: 'th' as in 'thin') |
| rationale | (rash"ŭn a(h)'lē) | temerarious | (tem"ur air'i ŭs) |
| recluse | (rē kloͦoce') | temperament | (tem'pur uh-mĕnt) |
| reconnaissance | (rē kon'ĭ sănce) | | |
| recrudescence | (rē kroͦo dess'ĕnce) | tenebrous | (ten'ē brŭs) |
| recuperative | (rē kū'pur āy"tiv) | tenuity | (ten ū'ĭ ti) |
| redoubtable | (rē dout'uh b'l) | thesaurus | (thē saw'rŭs: 'th' as in 'thin') |
| refluent | (ref'lū ĕnt) | | |
| regime | (rĭ zheem') | timbre | (tim'ber) |
| reminiscences | (rem"ĭ niss'ĕn siz) | transient | (tran'shĕnt) |
| renaissance | (ren"e sahnce') | trauma | (traw'muh) |
| renascence | (rē nass'ĕnce) | traversing | (trav'urce·ing) |
| replicas | (rep'li kuhz) | trucial | (troͦo'shăl) |
| reputable | (rep'ū tuh b'l) | truncated | (trung'kāte id) |
| rescind | (rē sind') | turgid | (tur'jid) |
| robots | (rō'bŏts) | tyrannical | (ti ran'i kăl) |
| rodomontade | (rod"ō mon tāde') | tyro | (tī'rō) |
| sabotage | (sab"ō tahzh') | ukases | (ū kāce'iz) |
| sacrilegious | (sak"rĭ lē'jŭs) | umbrage | (um'brij) |
| salient | (sāy'li ĕnt) | unconscionable | (un kon'shŭn uh-b'l) |
| satiety | (suh tī'ĕ ti) | | |
| scabrous | (skāy'brŭs) | unctuous | (ungk'choͦo ŭs) |

| | | | |
|---|---|---|---|
| unfrequented | (un″frē kwen′ted) | vignettes | (vin yets′) |
| untoward | (un tōrd′) | villainous | (vil′ĭn ŭs) |
| usurious | (ū zhŏŏr′i ŭs) | viragoes | (vi rā′gōze) |
| | | vitiated | (vish′i āte″id) |
| vagary | (vuh gair′i) | volatile | (vol′uh til) |
| vapid | (vap′id) | | |
| versatile | (vur′suh til) | wanness | (won′ness) |
| vertiginous | (vur tij′ĭ nŭs) | wastrel | (wāce′trĕl) |
| viable | (vī′uh b'l) | writhed | (rīthe′d: 'th' as in |
| viands | (vī′ăndz) | | 'the') |
| vicarious | (vī kair′i ŭs) | | |
| vicissitudes | (vĭ siss′ĭ tūdez) | yeoman | (yō′men) |

## One-Minute Refresher

Here's a pronunciation teaser-test for you. Quite a number of the twenty words in the next paragraph are too simple in meaning to be included in the defined word lists of this book. But all of the italicized words rate high among the most mispronounced words of our language. See how many you can get.

His expression was *dour* and his manner *brusque*. "The accident down by the *quay* was *lamentable*," he said with a *grimace*. The man driving the car was of *athletic* build, but, at the moment, his hold on the wheel must have been *flaccid*, or he might have been suffering from some *inexplicable vagary*. Anyhow he had a *genuine* aversion to driving a car. In addition he was of an *incomparably mischievous* and *garrulous* type. His girl companion, a *vaudeville* actress, was in *dishabille* at the time. The *demise* of the two was *simultaneous*. It was fortunate that he was killed as his *status* before the law would have been serious, as his record showed that he had previously committed a *heinous* crime under an *alias*.

*Answers:* dour (dōōr), brusque (brŭsk), quay (kee), lamentable (lam′ĕn-tuh b'l), grimace (gri māce′), athletic (ath let′ik), flaccid (flak′sid), inexplicable (in eks′pli kuh b'l), vagary (vuh gair′i), genuine (jen′ū in), comparably (kom′-puh ruh bli), mischievous (miss′chĭ vŭs), garrulous (gar′ū lŭs), vaudeville (vōde′vil), dishabille (diss″uh beel′), demise (dē mīze′), simultaneous (sī″mŭl-tay′nē ŭs), status (stāy′tŭs), heinous (hāy′nŭs), alias (āy′li ăss).

# CHAPTER VII

## THESE ARE YOUR WORKADAY WORDS

WHEN WE SAY that an *executive* wishes to *protest* against your letter of *complaint* because he feels that your unjustified *query* will *impair* his credit, we are dealing with words of high utility. These are the dray horses of our language that must pull the heavy carts of the world's commerce.

While such words are familiar to the majority of people, it would be unsafe to stigmatize them as "commonplace." Each one, no matter how humble it may be, is like a tiny piece of matter that is violently alive and active with electrons. Each word, written or spoken, is a major miracle made up of many minor miracles.

Let's pick a word at random out of this chapter and examine it in our laboratory with an appraising and expert eye. "We have been successful," says Thomas E. Dewey, "in tearing their *alibi* to shreds."

We all know the meaning of the word "alibi." It is as commonplace a term to us as it is to the crime-boys and racketeers who use it to their advantage. We are so used to seeing it that we slip and glide all too easily over the strange symbols that make it up, not realizing that the word itself, and every one of its parts, have some rather pretty stories bound up in them.

In the first place this word is composed of four different letters of the alphabet, "a," "l," "i," and "b."

Where, then, may have these written symbols originated?

"A" happens to be the first letter of "alibi." But there are those who say that it doesn't just "happen" to be the first letter of our alphabet and one of the commonest vowel sounds of the ancient languages. Here is the story.

Our alphabet, as we all know, has been handed down to us, and came through the Romans and the Greeks supposedly from the Phoenicians some 3,000 years ago. The Phoenician alphabet was composed of letters that are almost recognizable pictures of familiar objects. The original wavy lines of our now formalized "M," as an instance, are said to have represented the ocean to these daring explorers. Their "O" was the eye that you see with, while "K," with its fingers, is thought to have signified a spread and open hand. In "C" they claim that we have the crooked neck of a camel; in "D" the supposed flap of a tent; "E" a window with the side-bar gone; "H," a fence.

The most important commodity, to these ancients, though, was food, and for this, the Phoenicians chose the ox, "alef" (ah'lef), or, rather, what looks like the head of the ox, and this symbol was their "A," and stood first in their alphabet. At that early time, the "A" was aslant like the horns of the animal. It seems that the Greeks, later on, turned the picture over and added the cross-bar to make our "A."

The "L" of "alibi" was known as "lamed" (lah'med) to the Phoenicians, and they drew it in such a fashion that it looked something like the ox-goad or whiplash with which they drove the cattle. In this case, it was the Romans who formalized the letter and the whiplash in "L" is no longer so easily apparent.

The letter "I," the most commonly repeated vowel sound in the English language, was, in all likelihood, the Phoenician symbol for a finger, while the "B" or "beth" in Phoenician, resembles a crude house. After food, shelter was most important. Curiously we still have "beth" preserved in the town-name Bethlehem, "the house of food."

These are the letters that make up the plain word "alibi" and "alibi" itself has a picture within it. In its Latin translation this word means "another." That is, you were in another place when the murder was committed!

So beware of taking even the plainest word for granted. Each one can be exciting. Each one will unfold like a flower. Even the dullest word will take on color and interest if we search out its history. And in many of the sentences that are listed under "Your Workaday Words" you will discover how a skilled user of language can employ a well-worn word in such a way that it is no longer dull and drab.

The three words, "abstain," "hardihood," and "smirked" can scarcely be said to belong to the aristocracy of language, but note how they are set in phrases by W. L. Mackenzie King, Thomas W. Lamont, and William L. Shirer.

"We, in Canada, were free to make war or to *abstain* from making war."

"We want young men of intellectual *hardihood*."

"The Fascism that *smirked* at the decadent Democracies crumbled like a cracker."

Skill in their settings, therefore, can often show bright new facets of many of the words that may seem somewhat trite to you in the following list.

## THESE ARE YOUR WORKADAY WORDS

**a bat′ing** (uh bāte′ing). Diminishing; reducing; lessening.—"International law is a system of agreements among nations made for the purpose of *abating* the horrors of warfare."—Newton D. Butler.

**ad′ver sar″y** (ad′vur ser″i). Opponent; enemy; foe; a person opposing another; an antagonist.—"She studied her *adversary*. He was big and obviously bad tempered."—Emma Bugbee.

**a kim′bo** (uh kim′bō). Having hands on hip and elbows turned outward.— "He halted with sandaled feet wide apart and arms *akimbo*."—Lloyd C. Douglas.

**al′i bi** (al′ĭ bī). A plea or evidence that a person was somewhere else when a deed was committed.—"Having been in the gaol for over a year they had been able to establish their *alibi*."—Axel Munthe.

**al ter′na tives** (awl tur′nă tivz). Offerings of two things, one of which must be chosen.—"Mankind is tragically confronted once more by the *alternatives* of freedom or serfdom."—Cordell Hull.

**a massed′** (uh mass′t′). Heaped up or accumulated, as a fortune; gathered together or collected, as materials.— "Need more evidence be *amassed* that this is extremely useful?"—James F. Bender.

**a muck′** (uh muck′). Making frenzied attacks on everyone in sight.—"The simple folk hid Jews in their homes because the persecutors had run *amuck*."—George N. Shuster.

**an′tics** (an′tiks). Brisk movements; odd behavior.—"The *antics* of the attacking war ships fascinated me."— Robert S. Beile.

**ar′a ble** (ar′uh b′l). Capable of being cultivated; fit for plowing or tilling. —"The United States tills half of her potentially *arable* land."—Donald A. MacLean.

**a ro′mas** (uh rō′muhz). Agreeable odors; fragrance; pleasant smells.— "Children of all ages thrilled to the *aromas* wafted from the kitchen."— Edwin C. Hill.

**as″cer tain′a ble** (ass″er tain′uh b′l). Able to be learned for a certainty; able to be found out or determined; able to be freed from doubt.—"Her book contains the absolute truth so far as the truth is *ascertainable*."— Stanley Walker.

**as sump′tion** (ă sump′shŭn). A taking for granted; an assuming or supposing; a presumption.—"The only reason to accept him would be the *assumption* that he could establish a strong rule."—Ernie Pyle.

**au then′tic** (aw then′tik: 'th' as in 'thin'). Reliable; according to facts; genuine.—"This I recognized immediately as being *authentic* wisdom." Noel Coward.

**a vail′a ble** (uh vail′uh b′l). Capable of being used advantageously; at one's disposal.—"We have still to learn how to make these things *available* to all."—David Sarnoff.

**a vert′ed** (uh vurt′id). Prevented; warded off; avoided; prevented the effects of, by turning aside.—"The moral lesson would have been priceless and it might have *averted* a quarrel."—Lord Vansittart.

**baf′fle** (baf″l). To thwart; to foil; to defeat by perplexing.—"The problem was enough to *baffle* a more able man than he."—Lew Holt.

**ban′died** (ban′did). Passed along or

back and forth; given and received; exchanged; discussed. — "These phrases have been *bandied* about very freely."—Paul G. Hoffman.

**ban′tam** (ban′tăm). Diminutive; very small; small-sized.—"There was something bright and quick in his *bantam* eye which discouraged too much catechism."—Christopher Morley.

**bar′ren** (bar′ĕn). Sterile; producing only stubby growth; not fertile; bare.—"The mountains were *barren*, covered only with a scanty green."—Pearl S. Buck.

**bar′ri er** (bar′i ur). Obstruction; an obstacle to prevent passage.—"Radio is the one means of communication to which international boundaries present no *barrier*."—David Sarnoff.

**bau′ble** (baw′b'l). Something worthless and showy; a trifle having very little value; a fancy article of no real worth, but glaring and showy.— "The book is the year's most glittering *bauble*."—Fanny Butcher.

**be lit′tling** (bē lit′ling). Detracting from; depreciating; minimizing.— "Let there be no *belittling* of this issue."—Sumner Welles.

**be night′ed** (bē nīte′id). Involved in physical, mental, or moral darkness and gloom; ignorant.—"We want no repetition of the fanaticism of those *benighted* medieval times."—Ralph W. Sockman.

**be reft′** (bē reft′). Deprived of something beloved or valuable; made desolate through loss.—"Had all religious and military themes been taken from artists of the past, it would have left them sadly *bereft*."—Monroe E. Deutsch.

**be set′** (bē set′). Harassed; embarrassed; attacked on all sides; hemmed in; encompassed; set upon.—"Your mother is not well and I am everywhere *beset* by difficulty."—Stephen Vincent Benét.

**bilg′y** (bil′ji). Having the smell of foul water that collects in the bottom of the hulls of ships.—"The ferries are chugging into the *bilgy* backwaters of our harbors."—Donald Culross Peattie.

**blanch** (bla(h)nch). Turn white; become very pale with fright; become pallid; turn suddenly white.—"The children's pinched faces *blanch* at the roar of the new monsters of the air." —Wood Netherland.

**boon** (bōōn). A blessing; a good thing bestowed.—"The information would prove a *boon* to the nation's production effort."—Alvin E. Dodd.

**boun′te ous** (boun′tē ŭs: 'ou' as in 'out'). Plentiful; generous; liberal.— "Without a rather *bounteous* supply of both sense and capital, there cannot be full employment."—T. C. Hannah.

**bro mid′ic** (brō mid′ik). Commonplace; obvious; like a platitude.— "The saying has become threadbare and *bromidic*."—Merle Thorpe.

**brunt** (brunt). The main shock or stress; the hardest part.—"Australia is bearing the *brunt* of the activities in the Pacific."—Herbert V. Evatt.

**bur′nish ing** (bur′nish ing). Polishing; making shiny by rubbing.—"The butler busied himself *burnishing* the brass around the fireplace."—John Patterson.

**butt** (but). Object or person aimed at; a goal; a target at which criticism or ridicule is aimed.—"He laughs with equal exuberance whether friends or enemies are the *butt* of the joke."— Eric A. Johnston.

**cal′cu late** (kal′kū lāte). To reckon; to compute; to add, or determine by other mathematical processes.—"It took time to *calculate* the amount of damage that the hurricane had done."—Tom Pennell.

**car′cass** (kahr′kuhss). The dead body of an animal; a corpse; the dead body of a man, fish or bird.—"We had to drive the jays from the *carcass* while we worked on the butchered animal."—Bennie Bengston.

**char″ac ter is′tics** (kar″ăk tur iss′tiks). Distinguishing features or marks.— "We were rapidly writing the *characteristics* of our age on the pages of a new civilization."—Ernest Bevin.

**cleav′age** (kleev′ij). A split or division; a separation.—"Good times have been obstructed by class *cleavage*."— William F. Russell.

**com mu′ni ty** (kŏ mū′nĭ ti). A sharing;

a participation; a sharing together; a common ownership: a likeness; a common character or fellowship.— "The Balkan States have a *community* of interest that should be joined."— Bruce Ellsworth.

com′pa ra bly (kom′puh ruh bli). Similarly; correspondingly; conformably.— "The giant Clippers would all operate at *comparably* low fares."— Juan T. Trippe.

com′pen sate (kom′pen sāte). Counterbalance as an equivalent; make equal return to; pay suitably; make up for as payment to someone.— "The increase does not *compensate* the workers for real wages."—Philip Murray.

com plex′i ty (kŏm plek′sĭ ti). A complication; something that is difficult; an intricacy.— "The report has opened up many technical questions of the greatest *complexity*."—Raymond B. Fosdick.

com′pli cat″ed (kom′plĭ kāte″id). Made more complex or difficult.— "Military security is *complicated* by the conditions of modern naval warfare."—Elmer Davis.

com ply′ (kŏm plī′). To obey; to consent to; to agree with; to act in accordance.— "We have wired the President that we are willing to *comply* with the suggestions."—Edward R. Burke.

com pose′ (kŏm pōze′). To make up; to form; to constitute.— "The audience seemed to *compose* a whole community, a little town."—Thomas Wolfe.

com pound′ed (kom pound′ed: 'ou' as in 'out'). Composed; formed; made up of a combination of elements.— "The old-time immaculate hero, who was *compounded* of all the virtues, would be laughed off the stage."—George Jean Nathan.

com pres′sion (kŏm presh′ŭn). Condensation; grouping closely together. —"By culture I do not mean the *compression* or concentration of the pedant."—Owen D. Young.

con fid′ed (kŏn fīde′id). Entrusted; committed.— "We have *confided* to our government far-reaching powers over our lives and our welfare."— Thomas E. Dewey.

con″fir ma′tion (kon″fur mā′shŭn). Corroboration; verification; establishment; a making more sure or firm by an act or word; assurance by additional proof; sanction.— "She nodded her head slightly in *confirmation*."—Thomas Wolfe.

con ge′nial (kŏn jeen′yăl). Agreeable; pleasing; having similar tastes and needs; sympathetic; having kindred interests; suitable; agreeing together. —"Spain was the home of his spirit. In Spain he could feel his nature rooted in a *congenial* soil."—George F. Whicher.

con ges′tion (kŏn jess′chŭn). An overcrowded condition.— "The vacation period begins on Tuesday in order to eliminate *congestion* of transportation facilities."—Charles A. Kirk.

con serv′ing (kŏn surv′ing). Keeping from loss; protecting; preserving.— "The disturbing movements appear attributable to the desire to seek a more certain medium of *conserving* wealth."—Leon Fraser.

con sol′i dat″ing (kŏn sol′ĭ dāte″ing). Making firm and solid; organizing and strengthening.— "The enemy has been *consolidating* his position."— John A. Beasley.

con trib′ut ing (kŏn trib′ ūte ing). Sharing in effecting a result; helping to bring about or accomplish.— "A *contributing* factor in the success was the perfect coordination of the attack."—Henry L. Stimson.

con vey′ (kŏn vāy′). Carry from one place to another; transport; transmit; deliver to another place.— "Words are transmission lines that will *convey* the power of ideas."— William A. Temple.

cope (kōpe). Contend or strive on equal terms; fight successfully.— "You are confronted with facts with which you must *cope*."—Frank L. Rowland.

cor ral′ing (kō ral′ing). Penning up; driving into a corner; pressing hard; rounding up.— "Officials are busy throughout the country *corraling* delegates."—Harrison E. Spangler.

cor″re spond′ing (kor″ē spond′ing). Similar and similarly placed.— "Earnings for the first two months of this year were better than in the *corresponding* months a year ago."— R. G. A. van der Woude.

**coun"ter mand'ing** (koun"ter mand'- ing: 'ou' as in 'out'). Recalling by a contrary order; canceling; revoking a previous order or command. —"The President hotly resented the *countermanding* of his orders."— Malcolm Douglas.

**cred'it a ble** (kred'it uh b'l). Deserving credit; meritorious; bringing honor. —"I have no doubt that his tale of praiseworthy activities is a very long one and a very *creditable* one."— Winston Churchill.

**cul'ti vat"ed** (kul'tǐ vāte"id). Devoted time and thought to; improved and developed by study, exercise, and training.—"His voice was better trained and he had *cultivated* a new kind of vehemence."—Edmund Wilson.

**de fine'** (dē fīne'). Make the meaning clear; describe; explain; state the meaning of; hence, make characteristics or outlines clear.—"Trying to *define* those eyes, he had arrived at the conclusion that they were chiefly distinguished by their loneliness."— Lloyd C. Douglas.

**de lib'er at"ed** (dē lib'ur āte"id). Considered carefully; weighed over in the mind; taken counsel; debated; pondered; meditated.—"He had *deliberated* upon this phenomenon until he had arrived at the explanation of his own attitude."—Lloyd C. Douglas.

**de lu'sion** (dē lū'zhŭn). A false impression; a false belief or opinion; a misconception; a mistaken idea.—"She was told to pray for deliverance from *delusion*."—Thomas Sugrue.

**delv'ing** (delv'ing). Digging deeply; penetrating; making laborious research.—"At this moment any *delving* into statistics becomes futile."— H. A. Burgers.

**de notes'** (dē nōtes'). Indicates; signifies; means; is a sign; marks.—"The absence of cotton textile legends *denotes* an early stage in Worth Street evolution."—W. Ray Bell.

**dep"ri va'tion** (dep"rĭ vā'shŭn). Loss; the act or state of taking away by force or of keeping from having something.—"We are only on the fringes of this undertaking as far as personal *deprivation* at home is concerned."— James F. Byrnes.

**de tach'ment** (dē tach'mĕnt). Isolation; separation; aloofness; dissociation from surroundings.—"Were I to drift down again I would not have that sensation of bodily *detachment*." —Roy Chapman Andrews.

**de'vi ous** (dē'vi ŭs). Leading away from a straight course; turning aside; diverging; varying.—"It is expected that *devious* attempts will be made to weaken our effort."—Philip Murray.

**dis"ad van'tag es** (diss"ăd va(h)n'ti- jiz). Unfavorable conditions; inconveniences; discreditable sides; handicaps; lack of benefits.—"The fort had its *disadvantages*, but it was a safer and more attractive place than the city."—Lloyd C. Douglas.

**dis"as so'ci ate** (diss"ă sō'shi āte). Separate from connection or association; disconnect from relation; dissociate. —"I cannot *disassociate* this place from sad memories."—Emory L. Fielding.

**dis"a vow'** (diss"uh vow'). Refuse to acknowledge; disclaim; deny.—"It is the incurable ambition of the novelist to be lifelike, he will not *disavow* it."—H. G. Wells.

**dis close'** (diss klōze'). Make known; reveal; divulge; lay bare.—"We should both *disclose* our affairs fully." —Eric A. Johnston.

**dis'lo cate** (diss'lō kāte). Disarrange; put out of joint.—"If Western civilization is going to engage in war and *dislocate* our whole machinery of living, we are bound to have hard times."—Thomas W. Lamont.

**dis trac'tion** (diss trak'shŭn). Diversion of the mind; interruption.— "The training of pilots can proceed without *distraction* or impediment."— Winston Churchill.

**dis use'** (diss ūce'). Discontinuance of use; lack or cessation of use.—"The old well and its mossy bucket had long since fallen into *disuse*."—Sterling McCormick.

**di vert'ed** (di vurt'ed). Turned aside or deflected.—"The Conference was one of the first activities that was

ever *diverted* from ordinary channels."
—W. A. Patterson.

**drudg′er y** (druj′ur i). Dull, wearisome, or menial work.—"When zest departs, labor becomes *drudgery*."— Owen D. Young.

**du′bi ous ly** (dū′bi ŭs li). Doubtfully; mindfully uncertain as to the result; uncertainly.—"We cannot fight tentatively or *dubiously* against men who are fighting under a frenzy of fanaticism."—Wendell L. Willkie.

**ef fect′ed** (e fekt′ed). Brought about; accomplished; caused; produced; put into action; achieved.—"Not wishing to betray his complete ignorance of the subject, he *effected* a diversion by proposing a change of scene."— Edith Wharton.

**el′i gi ble** (el′i ji b'l). Capable of being chosen or elected; qualified; fit or suitable to be chosen.—"Large numbers will be *eligible* for various types of vocational training."—H. C. Coombes.

**em brac′ing** (em brāce′ing). Inclusive; comprehensive; taking in as parts of a whole.—"We must quicken our words into a specific, *embracing* program."—Cordell Hull.

**en list′** (en list′). Engage for military or naval service; hence, to gain the interest and assistance of; get the support of; obtain the aid of.—"He wants to *enlist* the co-operation of all governments that have territorial interests."—Henry C. Wolfe.

**en meshed′** (en mesht′). Entangled in a network or meshes; ensnared as in a net or trap.—"His voice coils about his hearers until they are *enmeshed* and spellbound."—Gertrude Atherton.

**e quiv′a lent** (ē kwiv′uh lĕnt). The equal in meaning or kind; significant likeness; similar or interchangeable name.—"The common European harriers are the *equivalent* of our marsh hawk."—Hugh Birckhead.

**er rat′ic** (e rat′ik). Not conforming to rules; irregular; eccentric.—"Water is *erratic* in its tendency to evaporate, dissipate, or return, as the humidity of surrounding atmosphere decreases or increases."—E. V. Crane.

**e vap′o rat″ed** (ē vap′ō rāte″id). Passed off in vapor; disappeared like vapor. —"The thrill and the interest simply *evaporated*."—W. J. Cameron.

**e va′sion** (ē vā′zhŭn). An escape by subterfuge or artifice; a contrived avoidance.—"Running away from your problems is a cowardly *evasion*." —Emmet Fox.

**ex cep′tion al** (ek sep′shŭn ăl). Unusual; quite out of the ordinary; uncommon; forming an exception to the general rule; hence, superior to others.—"How rarely one finds these qualities in even an *exceptional* child." —Henry James Forman.

**ex er′tions** (eg zur′shŭnz). Efforts; acts of putting some power into vigorous action; exercises needing strength and vigor.—"He and I rested from our *exertions* while they cleaned and cooked the fish."—Ira Wolfert.

**ex″po si′tion** (eks″pō zish′ŭn). Presentation in detail; display; showing clearly and materially.—"Implications contain more intrigue to the eye and the spirit than *exposition*."— Frederic Taubes.

**ex tinct′** (eks tingkt′). Extinguished; inactive; no longer erupting.— "These blue lakes used to be craters of the *extinct* volcano."—Virginia S. Eifert.

**ex tract′** (eks trakt′). Draw out; choose out; take out; select.—"They *extract* what is theirs and reject what is not." —J. Donald Adams.

**fac to′tum** (fak tō′tŭm). A man of all work; a person who has many and various duties to perform; a person who does all kinds of work.—"Under the guidance of the old *factotum* we set off on the trip."—May Lamberton Becker.

**fa′vor it ism** (fāy′vur it iz′m). A show of partiality or favor; favoring or liking one more than others; manifesting fondness that is unreasonable or unfair.—"One touch or show of *favoritism* and you have failed as a parent."—Hugh E. Blackstone.

**fea′si ble** (fee′zĭ b'l). Practicable; capable of being done successfully.— "The surest way for the Government to advance sound and general recovery is by keeping its cost and taxes as low as *feasible*."—Eugene G. Grace.

**fell** (fell). Cut down as a tree; hence, knock down; beat down.—"He could never *fell* an opponent with a single punch."—Arthur Daley.

**fer til'i ty** (fur til'ĭ ti). A state of producing abundantly; power to produce; fruitfulness; power to yield good crops.—"A large farm offers possibilities for increasing soil *fertility*."—Charles F. Collisson.

**fet'tered** (fet'urd). Chained; shackled; confined; restrained; bound; hampered.—"Because of my lameness, I might feel quite *fettered*."—Lloyd C. Douglas.

**flails** (flāle'z). Separates the grain by beating with an implement consisting of a kind of wooden blade attached loosely to a handle; threshes; beats. —"The sharp gravel of the hail *flails* the harvest and rends the trees asunder."—Thomas Mann.

**flex"i bil'i ty** (flek"sĭ bil'ĭ ti). Readiness to yield to influence; capability of being modified or changed.—"History is filled with unforeseeable situations that call for some *flexibility* of action."—Franklin Delano Roosevelt.

**foil'ing** (foyl'ing). Outwitting; frustrating; defeating; balking; rendering ineffectual.—"The girl reporter is not forever *foiling* villains or falling in love with city editors."—Emma Bugbee.

**form'a tive** (form'uh tiv). Having the power of building or forming; impressionable.—"I spent the *formative* years of my life among your people." —Madame Chiang Kai-shek.

**gleaned** (gleen'd). Gathered item by item carefully; picked patiently; gathered bit by bit.—"Holly, ground-pine, and mountain laurel should be *gleaned* sparingly, if at all, as these are facing extermination."—Earlene M. Cornell.

**grap'ple** (grap"l). A close hold, as in wrestling; a fight at close range.— "We must prepare for the time when they advance into deadly *grapple*."— Winston Churchill.

**gra tu'i tous ly** (gruh tū'ĭ tŭss li). Freely; without provocation; voluntarily; without reason or need.— "They constitute an advantage *gra-*

*tuitously* offered to the enemy."— George Fielding Elliot.

**gra tu'i ty** (gruh tū'ĭ ti). A tip for service; a present in return for some service; a voluntary gift.—"Her earnings went to the house except for what *gratuity* she might be given." —Roy Chapman Andrews.

**hag'gling** (hag'ling). Disputing; chaffering; caviling; wrangling.—"We must not indulge ourselves in the wasteful luxury of *haggling* over the blame."—Everett Chapman.

**ham'per ing** (ham'pur ing). Hindering; cumbering; embarrassing; restraining.—"The hostility is now being used as an excuse for *hampering* labor's devotion to the great effort." —Alex Rose.

**hand'i caps** (han'di kaps). Conditions imposed to equalize the chances of competitors in contests; hence, any disadvantages making success more difficult.—"These nations have overcome tremendous *handicaps*."— Henry L. Stimson.

**hand'i work"** (han'di wurk"). Work done by the hands; work performed personally.—"You set as much store by your *handiwork* as we do."— Queen Elizabeth of England.

**hap'haz"ard** (hap'haz"urd). Accidental; chance; random.—"The formation of our government was no *haphazard* affair."—George W. Maxey.

**heck'le** (hek"l). Ask troublesome questions in order to embarrass a speaker; bother with comments or gibes.— "I can't mix purpose with fun, and people *heckle* me for it."—William Saroyan.

**hes'i tan cy** (hez'ĭ tăn si). Hesitation; uncertainty; the tendency to hold back in an undecided way; irresolution; vacillation.—"Why should you have the slightest *hesitancy* about telling her?"—Emmet Holloway.

**hewn** (hūne). Cut with an edged tool; fashioned or shaped by blows with a sharp instrument; formed by hewing.—"It was scarcely more than a post roughly carven and *hewn*."— Caroline Dale Snedeker.

**hin'drance** (hin'drănce). That which hinders or restrains; something that holds back or obstructs; an impediment or check.—"Our pundits decided that youth was best served by 'expressing itself' and doing what it pleased without let or *hindrance*."—Channing Pollock.

**hordes** (hordz). Motley multitudes of human beings; swarms; wandering crowds.—"Great *hordes* of panic-stricken refugees fled the towns."—John Cudahy.

**hov'er** (huv'ur). Stay near one place in the air; remain suspended at one place; hang in the air about one spot.—"The helicopter can move forward, backward and sideways, and even *hover*."—Eugene E. Wilson.

**hum'drum"** (hum'drum"). Without interest; tedious; monotonous; wearisome.—"The bee-hive theory of society, with its *humdrum* allotment of tasks, has no attraction for him."—John W. Davis.

**i den'ti cal** (ī den'ti kăl). Absolutely the same; exactly alike.—"Most experiments when repeated under *identical* conditions gave the same results."—Irving Langmuir.

**ig nored'** (ig nōre'd). Took no notice of; disregarded; paid no attention to; refused to notice.—"The stretcher bearers *ignored* curses, bullets, bombs, and shell fire alike."—Richard Llewellyn.

**il lu'sion** (i lū'zhŭn). A misleading appearance; a false impression.—"To suppose that we are not involved in what is happening is a profound *illusion*."—Winston Churchill.

**im mod'er ate ly** (im mod'ur āte li). More than is proper; excessively; intemperately; beyond reasonable bounds.—"She likes dances, not *immoderately* but as other young girls do."—Rebecca West.

**im pair'** (im pair'). Diminish the value of; weaken; lessen.—"These dangers *impair* the faith without which freedom cannot prevail."—Cordell Hull.

**im pos'ture** (im poss'chŏor). Fraud; deception; trickery; imposition or trick to gain an end.—"There were many mountebanks and magicians, and every conceivable type of *imposture* flourished."—Lloyd C. Douglas.

**im pres'sive** (im press'iv). Tending to produce an impression and hold the attention; exciting emotion or admiration; having the power to make an imprint.—"When he got into the Fire Department he came to show us his new uniform, and his helmet was very *impressive*."—Stephen Vincent Benét.

**im pru'dent** (im prōō'dĕnt). Lacking discretion; ill-advised; lacking provision for the future.—"An *imprudent* policy might mean the loss of jobs." —John L. Collyer.

**in crust'ed** (in kruss'tid). Covered with a crust or hard coat; overlaid; crusted; thickly covered.—"The hinges were deeply *incrusted* with paint."—John P. Marquand.

**in cur'** (in kur'). Bring upon oneself; encounter.—"Here comes a letter proposing that I shall *incur* the risk of being elected Governor of California."—Upton Sinclair.

**in"dis tin'guish a ble** (in"diss ting'-gwish uh b'l). Not able to be distinguished or told apart from something else; unable to be recognized as different.—"I can remember only one part in which he seemed *indistinguishable* from the character he was impersonating."—Edmund Wilson.

**in dus'tri ous** (in duss'tri ŭs). Diligent; perseveringly busy; habitually occupied; painstaking; hard-working.— "One got the impression that the *industrious* army had overdone its task of reconstruction."—Jules Romains.

**in"e ras'a ble** (in"ē rāce'uh b'l). Incapable of being rubbed out or erased; that cannot be rubbed out or obliterated; impossible to remove.—"The heavy pencil marks proved to be *inerasable*."—Malcom Babbitt.

**in'fer ence** (in'fur ĕnce). Deduction; impression; conclusion.—"I do not wish to leave the *inference* that I believe railroad employees should work for low wages."—R. W. Brown.

**in form'a tive** (in for'muh tiv). Instructive; giving news or knowledge; giving items of information.—"This piece of historical recreation is a swift paced, *informative* story."—Virginia Kirkus.

**in ge'nious** (in jeen'yŭs). Inventive; clever; skilful; cleverly planned; well conceived; characterized by ingenuity.—"He devised an *ingenious* chart which almost automatically keeps the advertising campaign functioning according to plan."—A. H. Dente.

in"of fen'sive (in"ŏ fen'siv). Harmless; not offending or annoying; unobjectionable; giving no offense.—"What are you worrying about? He's *inoffensive* enough."—Jules Romains.

in sep'a ra ble (in sep'uh ruh b'l). Not capable of being separated; that cannot be disjoined or viewed apart.— "The whole history of the composer is *inseparable* from his people."— Olin Downes.

in tact' (in takt'). Complete and unimpaired; untouched; uninjured.— "The House has preserved its function and authority *intact*."—Winston Churchill.

in ter'pret (in tur'pret). Give the meaning of; explain; construe.—"We often *interpret* some provisions of the Bill of Rights so that they override others."—Herbert Hoover.

in tru'sion (in trōō'zhŭn). An entry without permission or welcome; coming unwanted and without invitation; forcing an entrance when not wanted.—"The coming of a stranger was not an unwelcome *intrusion* into a closed circle."—James Truslow Adams.

in vert' (in vurt'). Turn inside out or upside down; reverse or change to an opposite condition or position.— "It was natural that the rejected leader should *invert* himself in another swift transformation."—H. G. Wells.

in var'i a bly (in vair'i uh bli). In a uniform way; unchangeably; unchangingly; in a way that does not change or vary.—"It has not been the principles of George III but the principles of Pitt, Burke, and Fox that have almost *invariably* prevailed in our Empire."—Malcolm MacDonald.

in ves'ti gat"ed (in vess'tĭ gāte"id). Examined thoroughly; made a patient search; inspected carefully.—"In the sandpit I *investigated* the family life of a group of bank swallows."—Bennie Bengston.

ki osks' (kē osks'). Open Turkish pavilions; hence, light ornamental booths or structures used as newsstands or bandstands.—"The quaint newsstand *kiosks* dotted the main streets of Paris."—Bradwell E. Tanis.

lan'guor (lang'gur). Weak, listless feelings; lack of vigor; general lassitude; sluggishness.—"Her face was rarely out of my mind with its sudden brilliance and its sudden *languor*."— John Buchan.

lieu (lū). Place; stead.—"I have no intention of accepting phrase-making in *lieu* of fighting American qualities."—Percy C. Magnus.

liv'er y (liv'ur i). A particular uniform worn by servants; a special or peculiar garb or uniform provided for household servants, especially menservants.—"The coachman in the picture is in full *livery*."—John Hanbury-Williams.

loomed (lōōm'd). Appeared indistinctly above the surface of sea or land; came gradually into sight in the distance.—"Guatemala's volcanoes *loomed* below us."—W. Stephen Thomas.

mag'net (mag'net). Something possessing a very strong power of attraction. —"It seemed as though some powerful *magnet* were drawing at the very heart of this country."—Newton D. Butler.

man'a cled (man'uh k'ld). Fettered; handcuffed; shackled; chained with manacles.—"Some of the poor wretches had heavy chains about their necks and both hands tightly *manacled*."—Roy Chapman Andrews.

mea'ger (mee'gur). Inadequate; deficient in strength; poor; scanty.— "The achievement is too *meager* and insecure."—Francis B. Sayre.

me thod'i cal ly (mē thod'i kăl li: 'th' as in 'thin'). According to a general or established way or order; according to an arranged system or method. —"The armored divisions slowly and *methodically* took up their stations."— Winston Churchill.

midg'et (mij'et). Very small; diminutive.—"As soon as the *midget* bottles appeared, other customers ordered them."—Joseph H. Choate, Jr.

**min'gled** (ming'g'ld). Intermixed; blended; intermingled; mixed; combined.—"The library had a *mingled*, mysterious smell of old leather, stored books and piles of magazines."— Edwin Way Teale.

**mi nute'ly** (mĭ nūte'li). Very particularly or exactly; in every small detail. "Never before has the world known so *minutely* what war means."—Jane Addams.

**mis guid'ed** (miss gīde'id). Misinformed; taken in by wrong advice; led astray or into making mistakes; hence, wrongly judged; mistaken.— "They would not be warned; it was *misguided* of them."—Stephen Vincent Benét.

**mis haps'** (miss haps'). Unfortunate or unlucky accidents; misadventures. —"All the value that anyone can get out of an accident is experience in how to avoid similar *mishaps* in the future."—A. J. R. Curtis.

**mis lead'ing** (miss leed'ing). Leading astray or into error; deluding; giving a wrong impression.—"He believed the report to be confusing and *misleading*."—William M. Jeffers.

**mo lest'** (mō lest'). Disturb in any injurious way; interfere with.—"The enemy was so roughly handled that he dare not *molest* their departure."— Winston Churchill.

**mol'ten** (mōle'tĕn). Melted; reduced to fluid by heat.—"Between the solidly frozen crystalline state and the fluid *molten* state, the flow of these materials varies."—E. V. Crane.

**mor'sels** (mor's'lz). Small quantities; little pieces.—"The *morsels* of wisdom are distilled from a long life spent in the pursuit of wisdom."—Orville Prescott.

**mot'tled** (mot''ld). Marked with spots or streaks of different shades or colors; blotched or variegated in appearance.—"When a fawn is born its coat is *mottled* with white spots." —Hebe Bulley.

**muf'fled** (muf''ld). Covered so as to deaden the sound; wrapped up to prevent from seeing; hence, dulled; repressed; deadened; made less distinct.—"The book is enormously simplified in method despite its contacts with the roughness and the *muffled* tumult of life."—Ludwig Lewisohn.

**neg'a tive ly** (neg'uh tiv li). In a way that abstains from action or refuses to accept what is proposed.—"This far-reaching power of the Senate under our Constitution has been used *negatively*. We propose that the Senate act positively."—Joseph H. Ball.

**no'ta ble** (nō'tuh b'l). Remarkable; worthy of note; conspicuous; striking; noticeable.—"It is a *notable* experience to find a book so profoundly unified, so distinguished."— Stark Young.

**ob scure'** (ŏb skūre'). Darken or hide from view; to make indistinct.—"A good catchword can *obscure* analysis for fifty years."—Oliver Wendell Holmes.

**ob serv'ant** (ŏb zur'vănt). Attentive; mindful; quick to notice; carefully watchful; noticing everything.—"He sat back *observant* and let his companion explain."—H. G. Wells.

**ob'sta cle** (ob'stuh k'l). Hindrance; impediment; difficulty; something that stands in the way.—"Their parents, I'm afraid, are the *obstacle*." —Edith Wharton.

**on'er ous** (on'ur ŭs). Burdensome or oppressive.—"The board will try to obtain relief from provisions that we regard as *onerous*."—Joseph L. Dubow.

**or de'als** (or dee'ălz). Trying and difficult experiences.—"We must pledge that we will steadfastly follow, through all the *ordeals* that face us." —Brehon B. Somervell.

**out wit'** (owt wit'). To defeat by greater cunning; to frustrate by surpassing in cleverness.—"Commerce has a way of purging itself of its own ills, if not too much bound by man's attempt to *outwit* natural laws."— W. L. Clayton.

**o'vert** (ō'vurt). Open; public; outwardly manifest; unconcealed.— "*Overt* criticism was dangerous and suppressed."—H. G. Wells.

**pal'pi tat"ing** (pal'pĭ tāte"ing). Pulsating or beating more rapidly than usual, especially the heart; throbbing; quivering.—"Here's his little wife *palpitating* at the footstep of Another Man—the man with the United States Mail!"—Violet Moore.

**par″a pher na′li a** (par″uh fur nāy′li-uh). Accessories of equipment; apparatus; belongings.—"High tariffs, embargoes, quotas, clearing offices, and other similar manifestations are but the *paraphernalia* of war."—Ivy Lee.

**par tic′i pate** (pahr tiss′ĭ pāte). To have a share in common with others. —"Only the representatives of management and labor are permitted to *participate* in the discussions."—H. A. Enochs.

**pa′tron ized** (pāy′trŭn īze′d). Treated with condescension; treated as an inferior; helped in a condescending way.—"They do not want to be *patronized* or dominated by the policies of any nation."—Thos. J. Watson.

**pen′e trat″ing** (pen′ē trāte″ing). Having the power to penetrate or to enter the mind; hence, discerning; acute; keen and piercing; astute; shrewd; sagacious.—"Her questions were searching and *penetrating*."—Henry James Forman.

**per′me ates** (pur′mē ātes). Spreads right through; pervades; saturates.— "The preliminary victories were achieved by the spirit which *permeates* all the armed forces."—Joseph C. Grew.

**per sis′ten cy** (pur siss′tĕn si). Continuance of effort; perseverance; continuance in spite of opposition.— "The social rule must be live and let live, and those who break this rule with *persistency* must be liquidated." —George Bernard Shaw.

**pit** (pit). Put in competition or rivalry; set in opposition.—"If you were to *pit* the British Commonwealth plus the United States against the rest of the world, it would be a very lop-sided world."—Jan Christiaan Smuts.

**plugged** (plug′d). Stopped, or made tight, as with a peg or wedge.—"As we *plugged* up one hole the boat burst a seam elsewhere."—Paul S. Willis.

**pon′der ing** (pon′dur ing). Weighing in the mind; considering thought-fully; meditating over.—"Anxious farmers are *pondering* their fate."— Alben W. Barkley.

**prac′ti ca ble** (prak′ti kuh b'l). That can be put into practice or used for an intended purpose; usable.—"The government gave tangible proof of its readiness to translate its desire into *practicable* form."—Cordell Hull.

**pre cau′tion** (prē kaw′shŭn). Prudent thought beforehand; provision for emergency; previous care or forethought; caution beforehand; a measure to prevent harm.—"Vaccination of the population was undertaken as a *precaution*."—Raymond B. Fosdick.

**pre cise′** (prē sīce′). Exactly stated; strictly accurate; exact; punctilious; scrupulously particular.—"To be *precise*. Ascension Island is 1448 miles from Natal."—John Gunther.

**pref″er en′tial** (pref″ur en′shăl). Possessing a priority; showing greater favor; showing or giving preference. —"They have frequently given *preferential* treatment to our competitors." —Henry J. Kaiser.

**prej′u dice** (prej′yŏŏ diss). A biased opinion; a preconceived judgment; a decision without reason or justice.— "It will be a time of demagoguery and *prejudice*."—Herbert Hoover.

**pre vail′** (prē vāle′). To be victorious; to prove triumphant; to have real influence and predominate; to become general and wide-spread.— "This despotism must fall if real peace is to *prevail*."—Albert Einstein.

**prod′ded** (prod′ed). Poked or thrust on with a goad; instigated; aroused mentally.—"He has *prodded*, jibed, and driven others on to war."— Gerald P. Nye.

**prof′fered** (prof′urd). Offered for acceptance; tendered; offered.—"The economic satisfactions *proffered* by an advancing civilization and dependent upon peace are futile to oppose the summons to arms."—Charles Evans Hughes.

**pro test′** (prō test′). Enter a formal dissent; remonstrate against; voice an objection to; declare untrue.—"No good American will calmly sit by and not *protest* waste and extravagance." —James S. Kemper.

**pro trude′** (prō trood′). Project; stand out; stick out; are thrust forth.— "From every point of observation guns *protrude*."—John Steinbeck.

**prow′ess** (prou′ess: 'ou' as in 'out'). Strength, skill, and courage in battle; bravery; daring; superior ability.— "This boy's world is a land of competition and combat where he can prove his *prowess*."—Herbert Hoover.

**puls′es** (pulce′iz). Rhythmic beatings of the arteries; hence, tendencies or movements indicative of feelings or opinions.— "Shelley quickened our *pulses*, and Browning interpreted us to ourselves."—George Wharton Pepper.

**quad roon′** (kwod roon′). A person having one-fourth negro and three-fourths white blood; the offspring of a white person and a mulatto or half-negro person.— "The warm coloring of the *quadroon* can create a beauty that is hard to match."—Donald G. Cooley.

**quar′tered** (kwor′turd). Placed in a temporary shelter, lodging, or residence; provided with lodgings; sheltered in a specified place.— "The American soldiers found themselves *quartered*, four cots to a room, in a luxurious hotel."—Frederick Lewis Allen.

**que′ry** (kweer′i). Inquiry; doubt; question.— "We accept the challenge of *query*, permitting divergent views the right of discussion."—Madame Chiang Kai-shek.

**quest′ing** (kwest′ing). Seeking; searching; examining; inquiring.— "We must have enough *questing*, intellectually honest minds to do the work." —Thomas Parran.

**quirk** (kwurk). A sarcastic turn; a twist or quibble; an evasive turn.— "By some peculiar *quirk*, men talk as if the Federal Government is a sovereign body, above and apart from the people."—James William Fulbright.

**ran′dom** (ran′dŭm). Chance; casual; without definite intention; haphazard.— "I am going to end my *random* comments with a completely modern example."—Dorothy Canfield Fisher.

**ranked** (rankt). Held a specified place or grade.— "Kansas *ranked* fourth in the production of petroleum for many years."—Alfred M. Landon.

**re al′i ties** (rē al′ĭ tiz). Actualities; persons or things that really exist; truths; actual conditions.— "I have seen many peoples face to face with the most bitter *realities*."—William C. Bullitt.

**re buke′** (rē būke′). A reproof; a sharp expression of disapproval; a reprimand.— "It only takes a moment to administer a *rebuke* but a long time to forget it."—Harold R. Stark.

**re cep′ta cle** (rē sep′tuh k'l). Anything that serves as a container; any bag, basket, or other container; a place in which to put things.— "The effect of this canned culture is a mind that is a *receptacle* of superficial rubbish."— Pearl Buck.

**rec″og ni′tion** (rek″ŏg nish′ŭn). Acknowledgment; favorable notice; acceptance as having a claim to attention; acknowledgment of appreciation.— "During these travels his friend urged him to undertake serious roles and therewith find *recognition* comparable to his powers."—Gene Fowler.

**re coil′** (rē koyl′). To start back in dismay or loathing; shrink back.— "We instinctively *recoil* from words or pictures that expose brutality."— Lucy Milligan.

**rec′on cile** (rek′ŏn sīle). Adjust the differences or inconsistencies of; harmonize.— "We cannot possibly *reconcile* the principle of democracy with the principle of governmental omniscience."—Lewis H. Brown.

**re count′** (rē kount′: 'ou' as in 'out'). Relate or tell in detail; give an account of; tell the particulars of.— "These passages in poetry *recount* a parallel story of oppression."—Iris Barry.

**re cum′bent** (rē kum′bĕnt). Reclining; leaning; resting; lying against; reposing.— "To our left was the Capitol, *recumbent* on its hill of dark-foliaged trees."—John Dos Passos.

**re dress′** (rē dress′). Satisfaction for wrong done; reparation; a remedy or setting right.— "These men felt that they had been taxed without represen'ta'tion and they sought *redress* of grievances."—Henry A. Wriston.

**re frain'** (rē frain'). Abstain from action; restrain; forbear; hold back.— "I cannot *refrain* from reiterating my gratification."—Franklin Delano Roosevelt.

**ref'uge** (ref'ūje). Shelter; protection; cover; safety from distress or danger. –"Confronted with danger, we take *refuge* in old formulas."—Frederick L. Schuman.

**rel'a tive** (rel'uh tiv). Intelligible only in relation to something else; depending for meaning on a connection with something else; comparative; not absolute.—"Time, like everything else, is *relative*."—Thomas W. Pangborn.

**re li'ance** (rē lī'ănce). Dependence; trust; confidence.—"The *reliance* upon subcontracts and supplies has been a basic principle of the automotive industry."—C. E. Wilson.

**re lin'quish** (rē ling'kwish). Surrender something we like; give up; abandon; withdraw from.—"We will not *relinquish* a ray of splendor of our dreams." —A. A. Berle, Jr.

**re mon'strance** (rē mon'strănce). Expostulation; reproof; protest.—"You will find that my *remonstrance* is mild compared to that of the Director of the Budget."—Herbert Hoover.

**ren'der** (ren'dur). To give; to furnish; to give in return; to contribute; to bestow or provide.—"Mr. Eden's sympathetic understanding of international affairs and his sincerity enable him to *render* great service."— Thos. J. Watson.

**ren'o vat"ed** (ren'ō vāte"id). Made new; renewed; freshened up; restored to a good condition; made over or repaired.—"A former firehouse was given by the city, and *renovated* and equipped by donations."—Mark A. McCloskey.

**re nowned'** (rē nound': 'ou' as in 'out'). Celebrated; famous; widely known; having a great reputation.— "He liked the idea that a place so *renowned* and ancient belonged to him."—Edith Wharton.

**re plen'ish** (rē plen'ish). To fill again; to get fresh supplies; to stock up with new supplies.—"The ships have to go to their own bases to *replenish*."— Ernest J. King.

**rep'u ta ble** (rep'ū tuh b'l). Having a good reputation; honorable; of good character; respectable; creditable.— "We persuaded the court that we were *reputable* citizens."—Arthur Garfield Hays.

**res"er va'tion** (rez"ur vā'shŭn). A tacit limitation or exception about matters; the withholding of something or keeping something back that may change a decision or meaning.— "The ambassador spoke bluntly and made his statements without a single *reservation*."—Douglas E. Lurton.

**res'i due** (rez'ĭ dū). A remainder or surplus after a part has been separated; a remaining part.—"Such stories leave a *residue* of bad feeling and serve to keep our nations apart." —Mrs. Alfred J. Mathebat.

**res"ig na'tion** (rez"ig nā'shŭn). Submission to what cannot be changed; surrender to the inevitable; acquiescence in something that it is useless to resist.—"He goes off to camp with more *resignation* than eagerness."— Brooks Anderson.

**re sort'ing** (rē zort'ing). Having recourse to; using something as a means; seeking help from.—"There is a demand that injustice be corrected by *resorting* to the sword."— Franklin Delano Roosevelt.

**res'pite** (ress'pĭt). An interval of relief from suffering or penalty.—"The reindeer finds *respite* from the torments of flies in man-built smudges." —Frederica de Laguna.

**re spond'ed** (rē spond'ed). Answered the call; acted in response; replied.— "The men *responded* in numbers far exceeding our calculation."—Anthony Eden.

**re stor'a tive** (rē stōre'uh tiv). Tending or able to bring back to a former state; capable of restoring and renewing.— "It is a *restorative*, invigorating thing to give thanks."—W. J. Cameron.

**re straint'** (rē straint'). Self-repression; control over one's actions; check, or repression of action; tendency to hold back.—"Each hesitated to start a battle, but Porky's *restraint* outlasted the skunk's."—Alan Devoe.

**re stric′tions** (rē strik′shŭnz). Limitations; restraints.—"War brings many *restrictions* on our freedom."—Eric A. Johnston.

**re sume′** (rē zūme′). Recommence; take up again; continue from where we left off; begin again after interruption.—"Shall we, when our men come home, step aside, and *resume* economically and industrially almost where we left off?"—Fannie Hurst.

**re tard′ing** (rē tahrd′ing). Causing to move more slowly; hindering; delaying.—"It does not mean a *retarding* of effort, the slowing down of promising work."—Raymond B. Fosdick.

**re trac′ing** (rē trāce′ing). Going back over; going over again in an opposite direction; tracing back to a starting point.—"The older woman left them and began slowly *retracing* her steps toward her house."—Lloyd C. Douglas.

**re″tro ac′tive** (re″trō ak′tiv). Affecting past acts and obligations; applying to what is past.—"They refused to accept the *retroactive* accumulating liability."—Charles O'Neill.

**re vamp′** (rē vamp′). Make something over; use old materials to remake something.—"None of these tools can be effective unless we *revamp* the processes of government."—Franklin Delano Roosevelt.

**re veal′ing** (rē veel′ing). Divulging; disclosing or making known what was kept secret.—"The survey is the most *revealing* exhibition of what we thought was going on in education."—Nicholas Murray Butler.

**re ver′sals** (rē vur′sălz). Changes back to the contrary; decisions in an opposite direction.—"Definite *reversals* by the Court of important decisions in the field of taxation come readily to mind."—Homer Cummings.

**re vive′** (rē vīve′). Come back to life; take on fresh vigor; regain strength and courage; gain new life and spirit. —"If the so-called liberal arts subjects which have been laid on the shelf for a while are worth having they will *revive* quickly when peace returns."—William Mather Lewis.

**ros′ter** (ross′tur). A list of officers and men enrolled for duty.—"There is now being prepared a *roster* of all scientific men."—Harlan True Stetson.

**rub′ble** (rub″l). Broken fragments of stone, masonry, and other materials. —"There were many whole districts where nothing remained but an occasional chimney, with all the rest *rubble*."—Joseph E. Davies.

**scant′i ly** (skan′tĭ li). Insufficiently; sparingly; deficiently; meagerly; scarcely sufficiently.—"She remembered the *scantily* clad savages in the great tapestry."—Edith Wharton.

**scav′en gers** (skav′ĕn jurz). Animals or birds that feed on carrion; vultures and other birds that feed on decaying matter.—"Some birds serve as insect-regulators, and some are *scavengers*." —Walter P. Taylor.

**shirked** (shurkt). Meanly avoided; evaded; left for someone else to do.— "The responsibilities of citizens and leaders cannot be *shirked* without running the risk of disaster."—O. C. Carmichael.

**sig′ni fied** (sig′nĭ fīde). Denoted; implied; showed by a sign; meant.— "His men did not seem to understand what the action *signified*."—Franz Werfel.

**smirked** (smurkt). Smiled self-complacently; smiled in a silly, self-satisfied way; simpered.—"The Fascism that *smirked* at the decadent Democracies crumbled like a cracker."—William L. Shirer.

**spe′cies** (spee′shiz). A kind, sort, or variety.—"To destroy the reservoirs of capital is a *species* of madness equalled only by that of thirsty people destroying reservoirs of water."— George W. Maxey.

**spec′u late** (spek′ū lāte). To form conjectures; to theorize; to consider the different aspects.—"It is too early to *speculate* on the enemy's hope of resistance or escape."—Clement R. Atlee.

**spi′ral** (spī′răl). A winding and advancing curve; a coil; a circling round a center.—"Experience demonstrates that once the inflationary *spiral* is under way, it is almost impossible to check it."—Alfred P. Sloan, Jr.

**stag'nant** (stag'nănt). Foul from standing still a long while; smelly from want of motion; impure or offensive for lack of a current.—"A blast of outer air had freshened the *stagnant* atmosphere of the drawing-rooms."—Edith Wharton.

**stemmed** (stem'd). Resisted; made progress against; checked.—"The air force not only *stemmed* the tide, but carried the armies forward."—Winston Churchill.

**stim'u lus** (stim'ū lŭs). Something that rouses the mind or spirits; an incentive; a stimulation or spur.—"College has meant to you the sharpening of wits in debating and the *stimulus* of inspiring lectures."—George B. Cutten.

**stint** (stint). Restriction of the amount; limitation of a share; limit.—"We have called on our congregations to give without *stint* to our country."—Maurice H. Eisendrath.

**strain** (strain). Constraint; pressure; unnatural tension.—"You have imposed just that much more *strain* on productive facilities."—Chester W. Nimitz.

**striv'ing** (strīve'ing). Making efforts; trying hard; working earnestly; endeavoring; struggling.—"He was aware that they were *striving* to make themselves heard."—L. P. Jacks.

**sub side'** (sŭb sīde'). Cease from agitation; quiet down; settle.—"The atoms gradually *subside* to their normal states."—Karl T. Compton.

**sub stan'tial ly** (sŭb stan'shăl i). Essentially; materially; in the main; considerably.—"His taxes should not be *substantially* less in Florida than in Illinois."—Mark Graves.

**suc'cu lent** (suk'ū lĕnt). Juicy, as a plant; fleshy and thick; rich in tasty fluids.—"The plant lice feasted on the *succulent* sap of the vines."—Wallace L. Ware.

**sup plant'** (suh plant'). To displace; to replace, or put something in the place of.—"The purpose of the clearing union is to *supplant* gold as a governing factor, but not to dispense with it."—Lord Keynes.

**sup'ple** (sup''l). Flexible; easily bent; pliable; limber; pliant; yielding.—

"The shoulder joint of the hummingbird is unusually *supple*."—Charles H. Blake.

**sur mount'ed** (sur mount'ed: 'ou' as in 'out'). Conquered; risen superior to; overcome by force of will.—"We have *surmounted* many serious dangers."—Winston Churchill.

**sym'bol ize** (sim'bŭl īze). Represent figuratively or by symbols; typify; stand for; express by means of symbols or characteristics.—"These orphaned children *symbolize* what Madame Chiang Kai-shek is doing to bring about a world where children can live respectable lives."—Wendell L. Willkie.

**sym'pho ny** (sim'fō ni). Concord or agreeable blending.—"Harmony is essential to a *symphony* of people."—Jonah J. Goldstein.

**tam'per er** (tam'pur ur). One who interferes or makes alterations, especially foolish or perverting ones.—"The idealist is the more insidious *tamperer* with entertainment than the dictator."—Gilbert Seldes.

**taw'dri ness** (taw'dri ness). Gaudiness; showiness without elegance; lack of taste; cheap finery.—"The taste for *tawdriness*, we feel, is temporary and will exhaust itself."—W. J. Cameron.

**ten'dered** (ten'durd). Formally offered; presented for acceptance.—"Grateful acknowledgment is *tendered* to the organizations and members who have been most helpful."—W. Ray Bell.

**tex'ture** (teks'choor). Composition; constitution; general make-up; structure; union of constituent parts.—"In his ultimate *texture* he was a far profounder modernist than his leader."—H. G. Wells.

**thatch'ing** (thach'ing). A roof formed of reeds, straw, palm leaves or the like, arranged so as to shed water.—"The green leaves served for the *thatching* of the house."—Kenneth P. Emory.

**tink'ered** (tingk'urd). Made fruitless attempts to improve or set in order.—"The Government has *tinkered* with our money until the investor is afraid to make commitments."—E. F. Smith.

**tot'ter ing** (tot'ur ing). Shaking and leaning over as if about to fall; unsteady; having lost stability.—"Only as we take ourselves in hand as never before can we bring strength to a *tottering* world."—Thomas W. Lamont.

**trans form'ing** (trance form'ing). Changing completely; metamorphosing; of a kind that changes the whole nature.—"New people can be produced only through the *transforming* power of vital religion."—George L. Carpenter.

**trans fu'sion** (trance fū'shŭn). Transference; transmission; imparting; transferring from one to another.—"Never was the *transfusion* of intellectual courage from the youth of our universities to our society more needed."—Robert H. Jackson.

**tran spired'** (tran spīre'd'). Became known; leaked out; became gradually public.—"The news of the débacle *transpired* and soon became common property."—Malcom Babbitt.

**trib'ute** (trib'ūte). Warm praise; an offering of respect and gratitude.—"I also pay *tribute* to the large army of workers who labored with you."—Eugene Reybold.

**tri'fles** (trī'f'lz). Things of little value or importance.—"They are *trifles* in themselves, but they add up to an enormous difference in the morale of our men."—Mrs. Alfred R. Bachrach.

**trun'dle** (trun'd'l). Roll along, as though on wheels; bowl along, as a hoop; roll along freely.—"They would collect the children, shove them into a car, and *trundle* home."—Homer Croy.

**twinge** (twinje). A sudden sharp pain; a darting local pain; a twitch; a pang.—"She felt a *twinge* of uneasiness."—Anne Morrow Lindbergh.

**typ'i cal** (tip'i kăl). Having the nature or character of a representative object; symbolic; characteristic; representative.—"He is a *typical* Yankee, which means that idealism and shrewd self-seeking are nicely balanced in his temperament."—Henry Seidel Canby.

**un"a ware'** (un"uh wair'). Not aware; unconscious; ignorant; not cognizant; unmindful.—"The subconscious mind (or the unconscious) is that part of your mentality of which you are *unaware*."—Emmet Fox.

**un"con cerned'** (un"kŏn surnd'). Free from anxiety; indifferent; not showing any concern or care; having an easy mind.—"The crowd remained silent, apparently filled with *unconcerned* curiosity."—Franz Werfel.

**un"der mined'** (un"dur mīnd'). Weakened; overthrown in an underhand way; ruined; enfeebled and gradually destroyed.—"They have organized subversive movements and *undermined* in advance the nations they planned to invade."—William L. Green.

**un due'** (un dū'). Excessive; immoderate; inappropriate; improper; unwarranted.—"The *undue* bustle of the Americans disturbed the British visitors."—Douglas Brewster.

**un er'ring ly** (un ur'ing li). Making no mistakes; unfailingly.—"The minds of the justices go *unerringly* to the mark."—Sherman Minton.

**un flinch'ing** (un flinch'ing). Unyielding; not shrinking or drawing back; steadfast; not giving way.—"The discussion is honest, earnest, and *unflinching*."—William Allen White.

**u'ni son** (ū'ni sŭn). Agreement and accord; perfect harmony.—"Two of the horses are pulling in *unison* today; the third is not."—Franklin Delano Roosevelt.

**un ri'valed** (un rī'v'ld). Having no competitor or rival; matchless; peerless; unequaled.—"The shore stations afforded *unrivaled* opportunities for study."—Roy Chapman Andrews.

**un told'** (un tōld'). Too great to be counted or numbered; inexpressible; so great that it cannot be estimated.—"He who 'bridleth not his tongue' can do *untold* injury to his nation's military and political welfare."—William Mather Lewis.

**us'age** (ūce'ij). Habitual use; customary or long-continued employment; way of using; treatment.—"The meanings and the pronunciations of words are determined almost entirely by common *usage*."—Ellery Marsh Egan.

**van'tage** (van'tij). Superiority; a position of advantage or opportunity. —"The discussion gave an opportunity for the pseudopatriots to seize a point of *vantage*."—Charles Evans Hughes.

**veered** (veerd). Gradually changed direction, as the wind; turned; swerved; shifted.—"V-like the spreading ripples *veered*."—John Masefield.

**verge** (vurje). The extreme edge; the brink; the border.—"He has led your country to the horrid *verge* of ruin."—Winston Churchill.

**ver'i fy** (ver'ĭ fĭ). Prove to be true; confirm; check the correctness of; test the accuracy of.—"Count the whole row, then close the eyes and name the numbers. Open the eyes again and *verify* your guess."—Aldous Huxley.

**ver'sions** (vur'zhŭnz). Translations; modified descriptions; accounts or statements.—"The plans are not alternative ideas but different *versions* of the same idea."—Frederick Phillips.

**vic'tim ized** (vik'tim īze'd). Made a victim of; swindled; defrauded; cheated.—"He began to feel *victimized*. Evidently the evening was going to rest heavily on him."—Christopher Morley.

**weird** (weerd). Strange; eerie; uncanny; witchlike.—"The scene was *weird* and unearthly like a picture of the Eternal Pit."—Roy Chapman Andrews.

**whets** (hwets). Sharpens; gives a keen edge by friction.—"As the strife goes on, man *whets* his blade afresh."—William Addleman Ganoe.

**wield** (weeld). To manage with full effect, as a weapon; to handle easily and with full power.—"These men are pitting their strength of muscle and nerve to *wield* machines against machines."—Henry H. Arnold.

**wind'rows"** (wind'rōze"). Rows (as of hay) raked together to dry before being rolled into cocks.—"The grain lay in *windrows* on the still, green countryside of Bourgoyne."—Henry J. Powers.

**win'nowed** (win'ōwe'd). Blown off like chaff from the grain; hence, separated or sorted out; sifted; fanned out.—"The School was a fair example of the chaff of mentally unsettled people that was being *winnowed* out of the social order."—H. G. Wells.

**wrought** (rawt). Effected; worked; fashioned into shape; accomplished by work.—"The things Jefferson *wrought* and fought for have been condemned to extermination by brute force."—Claude Bowers.

## ONE-MINUTE REFRESHER

Each of the six words in this list can be substituted for one of the italicized phrases that appear in each of the following sentences. If often happens that one right word is more effective than several words and will contribute to force and to clarity.

a. confided    d. dubiously
b. incur     e. unflinching
c. impair     f. molest

1. The failure slowed him up but it did not *hurt the chances of* his final success. The failure slowed him up but it did not _____ his final success.

2. He said I should not *expose myself to* the risk of accident. He said I should not _____ the risk of accident.

3. She looked at me *in an uncertain way*. She looked at me _____.

4. The enemy did not *interfere with* their messengers. The enemy did not _____ their messengers.

5. We have *given over* to our government great powers. We have _____ to our government great powers.

6. He faced the danger with courage that *did not weaken or waver*. He faced the danger with _____ courage.

*Answers:* 1 — c; 2 — b; 3 — d; 4 — f; 5 — a; 6 — e.

# CHAPTER VIII

## WHEN YOU GET SERIOUS ABOUT FINANCE
## AND BUSINESS

THE DEFINITIONS of the words that surround business and finance are more accurate than those governing the more careless terminology of our daily life, although they do not approximate the word-accuracy of the scientific fields.

Nevertheless when we say: "An *accredited* representative"; "an *affiliated* company"; "an *accruing* value"; "*amortization* payments," we must know within reason what we are talking about or the wheels of industry would slow up and stop. The definitions and the delimitations of these words must be reasonably clear in our minds. Many a business lawsuit has been won or lost on the turn of a definition. To us as laymen, for instance, it is not a matter of critical importance whether a tomato is defined as a vegetable or a fruit. But in the industry itself this dispute grew into a famous legal case that was carried to the Supreme Court of the United States where it was decided that a tomato was a vegetable. Again, a decision of the Court of Customs and Patent Appeals said that bacteria are animals in spite of the fact that most biologists claim that they are plants! And in each of these cases every available dictionary was called into court and the definitions quoted.

In order better to understand the value and the vital importance of sharp, clear meanings, let us undertake the extraordinarily difficult task of constructing a definition. The process will throw some light on the problem.

How would you, a business man or woman, define the term "commodity"?

Well, a "commodity," you might say, "is a type of manufactured goods that one man sells to another."

This, of course, would be highly incorrect.

Does a commodity have to be sold? Can't it be bought? Also

109

this definition implies that one male adult has to sell it to another male adult.

Try again!

"A *commodity* is a type of manufactured goods that is bought and sold."

Let's examine this definition.

Milk is a *commodity*, but this product could hardly be called "manufactured goods," and must it be bought and sold to be a commodity? Can't it be traded in? And shouldn't it have value?

So once more.

"A *commodity* is an article of value that is for purchase or sale or that may be traded in."

We are now close to a sound definition of the most common meaning of this term, but there is still one flaw. A house or a factory could hardly be called a "commodity." It would appear that a commodity must be something smaller that can be moved.

So, finally:

"A *commodity* is a movable article of value that is for purchase or sale or that may be traded in."

And here we have arrived at one usable and fairly water-tight definition of the word "commodity," but the process will show you how incredibly hard it is to so tie a word to its meaning that it will not pull away from its moorings!

Of course in business and finance, in buying and selling and in barter and trade, words and their meanings have an exceptional importance. We are no longer dealing with them as literary instruments or as pleasant conversational counters. In business, words are the tools of trade. They mean money. This truth can be most vividly observed in the profession of advertising for in advertising words are used to sell goods at a profit.

Now from the earliest beginnings of language it has always been considered important to name things well, on the assumption that words can alter things. This superstition is still with us. You doubt it? Then why are you apt to knock wood just after you have bragged: "I have never had an automobile accident in my life"? You see you are a little afraid that your mere statement about an "accident" may alter your luck. Speak of the devil, as the saying is, and he is sure to appear.

The advertising experts have discovered that words *can* alter things—at least in the minds of potential customers—and they practice their magic on us daily.

The advertiser rarely sells toilet paper, for instance. He sells "bathroom tissue." There are no "second-hand" cars. They are "reconditioned" and "reprocessed." Clothing is never "cheap." It is "under-priced." Steamship lines no longer sell third-class tickets: they are now "tourist" class. The embalmer and undertaker has long ago become a "funeral director" or a "mortician," and an undertaking establishment has changed to a "funeral parlor." A radio program is never *paid* for by anyone. It is "sponsored," or "comes through the courtesy of." We don't sell shirts and drawers to the girls. We sell them "chemises" and "step-ins," and "under-things."

To borrow an example from the semanticist, S. I. Hayakawa, it would be easy to tell which would be the more effective placard in a meat market: "Finest quality filet mignon," or "First class piece of dead cow." And could you imagine how much tuna fish would be bought under its old name of "horse-mackerel"?

A year or two ago a number of philologists were asked by a theatrical manager to invent a "dignified word to describe the formal and rhythmic disrobing of the body in public." His client, as you have probably guessed, was a strip-teaser. The girl said it would help "the verbally underprivileged members of my profession" because, in her own words, "I saw right away what was holding up the progress of strip-teasing. We just had the wrong word!"

The results of naming things well can be measured in dollars.

Let me quote the factual evidence of this from the book *You've Got to Sell Glamor*. "Three times more men purchased a gray hat called *Tyrolea* than when unnamed. Ten times more women buy a shade of hosiery when it is called *Gala* than when it is offered as plain beige. And the doggy shades in hosiery, *Spaniel, Collie,* and so on, sell ten to twenty times more than the unnamed shades."

The mastery of these words of commerce by a business man or a business woman is, obviously, a very practical affair.

**a bey′ance** (uh bāy′ănce). Suspension; temporary inaction.—"We are holding such things in *abeyance* since we have asked Mr. Newton to take over."—Harold L. Ickes.

**ac ces′so ry** (ak sess′ō ri). Supplemental; additional; aiding in a subordinate way.—"*Accessory* equipment was designed and purchased."—Paul Stayboldt.

**ac cred′it ed** (ă kred′it ed). Authorized; furnished with credentials.— "We stand ready to confer immediately with *accredited* representatives of the company."—Edward Heckelbech.

**ac cre′tion** (ă kree′shŭn). An accumulation or external addition.—"We have freed a substantial part of our commerce from an *accretion* of excessive trade barriers."—Eugene P. Thomas.

**ac cru′ing** (ă krōō′ing). Accumulating; coming as a natural result, as by business.—"Of course, advertising has an *accruing* value."—Victor C. Schwab.

**af fil′i at″ed** (ă fil′i āte″id). Associated; connected.—"His organization is no longer *affiliated* with ours."—William L. Green.

**a gen′da** (uh jen′duh). A record of things to be done; a program of business to be discussed at a meeting; papers to be read or items for discussion.—"An *agenda* which includes fact-finding questions is prepared ahead of time."—A. H. Dente.

**a grar′i an** (uh grair′i ăn). Pertaining to lands of fields and their tenure and general distribution.—"The mind of the *agrarian* age was definitely set against research in any branch of science."—Edward A. Filene.

**al lot′ment** (ă lot′mĕnt). A special share set apart for a particular person or purpose, by lot; an apportioned part; a share; a distribution of assigned parts.—"Unto thee wealth shall come, the *allotment* of land, the goodly land."—Caroline Dale Snedeker.

**a mor″ti za′tion** (uh mor″ti zā′shŭn). Gradual reduction of a debt through contributions to a fund invested in such a way that its accumulations will cancel the debt at maturity.— "Real estate companies urge that practically all mortgages provide for periodic *amortization* payments."— Thomas S. Holden.

**an nulled′** (ă nuld′). Canceled; made void; nullified; done away with; reduced to nothing; invalidated.— "The loan is *annulled* if I sell the story."—Louis Adamic.

**ap por′tioned** (ă pōr′shŭnd). Divided or assigned proportionally; allotted. —"A part of these taxes should be *apportioned* among the States."— Mark Graves.

**ap praise′** (ă praize′). Make a valuation of; estimate the worth of; set a price on.—"We are never able to measure, or *appraise*, the full value of influence."—George Matthew Adams.

**ap″pre hend′ed** (ap″rē hend′ed). Feared; conjectured; supposed; anticipated.—"Losses have been greatly less than we *apprehended*."—Winston Churchill.

**ap pren′tice** (ă pren′tiss). A learner or beginner; a person who is bound by agreement while learning a trade or profession.—"From the lowest *apprentice* seaman to the highest ranking officer, the Navy is a volunteer organization."—Adolphus Andrews.

**ap prised′** (ă prīze′d′). Informed; notified.—"Only a very few can be *apprised* of all the facts."—Frank Knox.

**ap pro″pri a′tions** (ă prō″pri āy′-shŭnz). Sums of money set apart for some special use.—"The armed services have the *appropriations* which control the letting of contracts."— Philip Murray.

**ap prox′i mate ly** (ă prok′si mit li). Nearly, but not exactly; from a rough estimate; nearly estimated.— "Enrollments have dropped *approximately* twenty per cent."—William Pearson Tolley.

**ar′ti sans** (ahr′tĭ zanz). Trained workmen; superior mechanics.—"Honest competition always stimulates the best *artisans*."—Emmet Holloway.

**as say'** (ă sāy'). An analysis; a test; appraisal.—"Labor cannot avoid the necessity of a political *assay* of the work."—John L. Lewis.

**as sessed'** (ă sest'). Made an estimate of; put a valuation on; determined the value of.—"He has very acutely *assessed* his own limitations in this respect."—J. Donald Adams.

**as sign'ment** (ă sīne'mĕnt). A special piece of work prescribed for a particular person or group; a fixed task given; the work allotted to a certain group as a duty.—"Reaching that high level of output is going to be the toughest *assignment* this nation ever tackled."—Paul G. Hoffman.

**av"o ca'tions** (av"ō kā'shŭnz). Occupations; usual business pursuits.—"Your men will return to their productive *avocations*."—Dwight D. Eisenhower.

**a vowed'** (uh voud': 'ou' as in 'out'). Acknowledged; openly declared.—"It is the *avowed* objective of each plan to eliminate foreign exchange controls on current account."—Winthrop W. Aldrich.

**bar'tered** (bahr'turd). Carried on trade by exchange of goods instead of using money; exchanged one commodity for another; hence; sold for something that is considered an equivalent.—"Assuming that our liberty is safe, we have unconsciously *bartered* some phase of it for what we conceive to be security."—Winthrop W. Aldrich.

**ba zaars'** (buh zahrz'). Oriental market-places or rows of shops; streets of small shops; any assemblage of shops. —"Mohammed learnt all he knew in trading *bazaars*."—James Thomas.

**ben"e fi'ci ar"y** (ben"ē fish'i er"i). A person who receives a gift or advantage; one who receives a benefit or help.—"Did he ever confer a great gift upon someone and request the *beneficiary* to keep it a secret?"—Lloyd C. Douglas.

**boo'ty** (bōō'ti). The spoils of war; plunder.—"*Booty* was great. The enemy left heavy 40-mm batteries." —Eugene M. Landrum.

**cap'i tal ize** (kap'ĭ tăl īze). Turn into capital or resources; hence, convert into something that can be utilized for the sake of advantage; turn into something that can be used for profit. —"People around the table are fascinated. The trainers *capitalize* this interest to drive home the application to their own work."—Stuart Chase.

**car'a van** (kar'uh van). A large van; hence, a company of travelers or the conveyances in which they travel.— "The Army determines whether the evacuation is accomplished by train, bus, or automobile *caravan*."—Karl R. Bendetsen.

**car'tels** (kahr'telz). Combinations of business or industrial firms in order to control prices; pools to fix rates.— "The right of private enterprises to form huge international *cartels* controlling materials for its own benefit, must be abolished."—Mrs. J. Borden Harriman.

**cat'e go"ries** (kat'ē gō"riz). Classes of things; divisions for classification.— "Federal taxes fall into three principal *categories*—consumer taxes, personal taxes, and taxes on corporations."—Franklin Delano Roosevelt.

**cer'ti fy"ing** (sur'tĭ fī"ing). Giving certain knowledge of; attesting; verifying.—"I am *certifying* this case to the National War Labor Board."—Frances Perkins.

**ces sa'tion** (se sāy'shŭn). A stop; a ceasing; a pause; an end or discontinuance.—"Pet dealers reported no *cessation* in the demand for these cats."—Stephen Vincent Benét.

**chat'tel** (chat"'l). An article of personal property; a movable.—"A worker could be sold with the land as if he were a *chattel* attached to it."—Edward F. McGrady.

**chi can'er y** (shi kāne'ur i). Trickery; deceitful actions; unfair and sharp practice; false and misleading arguments.—"The boy knew enough English to resent the brutal *chicanery* with which they were sold as indentured servants."—Edward A. Weeks.

**cli"en tele'** (klī"ĕn tel'). A body of patrons or clients; a group of customers; a following.—"To build up a southern *clientele*, we planned an advertising program."—Frank Case.

**cof'fers** (kof'urz). Strong chests, boxes, or trunks for money and other valuables; funds or treasury.—"In ancient Rome graft also filled the *coffers* of the racketeers."—Douglas E. Lurton.

**col lat'ed** (kŏ lāte'id). Collected, verified, and arranged in order; placed all sheets, as of a manuscript or book, in exact order to be bound.—"When she got the sheets *collated*, she pressed a foot lever which operated a stapling machine."—Stuart Chase.

**col lat'er al** (kŏ lat'ur ăl). From the same source but subordinate; additional; connected, but secondary to the main thing.—"There was some small *collateral* benefit."—Bradwell E. Tanis.

**com mod'i ties** (kŏ mod'ĭ tiz). Movable articles of value that are for purchase or sale or that can be traded in.—"In the initial period we shall be confronted with shortages of many *commodities*."—Fiorello H. La-Guardia.

**com pos'ite** (kŏm poz'it). Made up of separate parts; combined.—"The advisory committee is a *composite* expert."—Charles Evans Hughes.

**con'claves** (kon'klāves). Secret councils or meetings; private assemblies or societies; cabals; private meetings. —"The custodians of capital have neglected the *conclaves* of the idealists where men and women are seeking security."—Paul F. Cadman.

**con di'tion al** (kŏn dish'ŭn ăl). Subject to, or depending on, something else; made on certain terms; limited by conditions or modifying circumstances.—"The agreement was tentative and *conditional*."—Hugh E. Blackstone.

**con'duits** (kon'dits). Channels or pipes for conveying liquids, gas, cables, or electric wires; underground tubes for the passage of electric wires.—"The fire started in the building through faulty electrical *conduits*."—Emory L. Fielding.

**con fed'er a'tion** (kŏn fed"ur āy'shŭn). A league; an alliance; a combination or union for mutual support or for a special purpose.—"The three things —ideal aims, businesslike methods, sportsmanlike principles—form the strongest *confederation* of spiritual forces ever introduced into human affairs."—L. P. Jacks.

**con ferred'** (kŏn furd'). Held a conference; consulted.—"I have *conferred* with everybody in sight."—Frances Perkins.

**con ser'va tive** (kŏn sur'vuh tiv). Adhering to the existing order; opposed to change; safe and moderate.—"The directors have decided to adopt a *conservative* dividend policy."— George T. Christopher.

**con sign'ment** (kŏn sīne'měnt). Something forwarded or delivered to someone, to be cared for in some way; something given in charge of someone, committed to his care.—"A considerable *consignment* of these goods left for Spain."—Anthony Eden.

**con stric'tion** (kŏn strik'shŭn). The state of being drawn together, contracted, or bound; hence, tightness; compression; a shrinking or restriction.—"There was an absence of returns, a *constriction* of credit."— H. G. Wells.

**con"sul ta'tion** (kon"sŭl tā'shŭn). A meeting for conference; the act of interchanging information or advice. —"In *consultation* with the representatives, we reviewed the findings of the day."—William Maxwell Aitken.

**con'tra band** (kon'truh band). Goods that are prohibited or excluded, as by military law.—"Neutral ships not carrying *contraband* were held immune from attack."—Francis B. Sayre.

**con triv'ance** (kŏn trīve'ănce). A device or appliance; an invention; a mechanism adapted for a special purpose.—"The boy had rigged up a *contrivance* to open the door from his bed."—Bertram M. Myers.

**con vene'** (kŏn veen'). Call together; convoke; summon to assemble.— "The commission will *convene* an immediate hearing."—Ralph T. Seward.

**con vert'i ble** (kŏn vur'tĭ b'l). Interchangeable; capable of being changed. —"The new money must not be freely *convertible* into gold."—Lord Keynes.

**con″vo ca′tion** (kon″vō kā′shŭn). An assembly; convention; organization; a council or meeting.—"I will take an old proverb for the text of this *convocation* address."—W. H. Cowley.

**co-or″di na′tion** (kō or″di nā′shŭn). Harmonious operation or adjustment.—"*Co-ordination* depends on the personalities involved."—Charles G. Ramsey.

**cor rob′o rat″ed** (kŏ rob′ō rāte″id). Confirmed; made more certain; strengthened; given additional proof; established.—"The identification was *corroborated* by the Arab name."—Willy Ley.

**crafts′men** (krafts′mĕn). Skilled mechanics; artisans; those who work at an art or trade with their hands.—"The average salary for teachers is less than the reward offered to carpenters and other skilled *craftsmen*." —Robert Gordon Sproul.

**cre den′tials** (krē den′shălz). Certificates of authority; references; testimonials; letters of recommendation. —"We had *credentials* from the Secretary of the Interior and were treated royally."—Thomas Barbour.

**de fi′cien cies** (dē fish′ĕn siz). Defects; imperfections; inadequacies; shortages.—"Practice drills are held for the purpose of bringing out any *deficiencies* in the system."—Hugh A. Drum.

**de frayed′** (dē frāy′d′). Paid; settled. —"Funds collected will go directly to the purchase of kits, all expenses being *defrayed* by the Association."—Michael Lerner.

**de fla′tion ar″y** (dē flā′shŭn er″i). Relating to the reduction in the amount of medium of exchange, or of purchasing power.—"The margin of resources must be substantial to relieve the *deflationary* pressure which results from anxiety."—Lord Keynes.

**de pre″ci a′tion** (dē prē″shi āy′shŭn). A decrease in value, especially the lowering of the purchasing value of standard coinage.—"No one can benefit from a competitive race in the *depreciation* of currencies."—Henry Morgenthau, Jr.

**de rived′** (dē rīve'd′). Drawn from the source; obtained from the original.— "Practically all the products derived from petroleum are also *derived* from coal."—James D. Francis.

**des′ig nat″ed** (dez′ig nāte″id). Named and appointed; selected for a purpose; specified and identified by name.—"Capital funds are received in trust for the benefit of institutions specifically *designated*."—Frank D. Loomis.

**di′a grams** (dī′uh gramz). Mechanical plans, drawings, outlines.—"The newspapers supply maps and *diagrams*, explications and explanations." —Henry A. Wriston.

**dis burse′ment** (diss burce′mĕnt). Expenditure; paying out.—"It is not difficult to visualize the steadying effect in this *disbursement* of compensation funds."—John G. Winant.

**dis′count** (diss′kount: 'ou' as in 'out'). Give less than full credit to; take at less than full value; allow for exaggeration in; take a certain amount off.—"There are those who *discount* his advertised ability."—S. L. Scanlon.

**dis cred′it ed** (diss kred′it ed). Disbelieved; distrusted; hence, undervalued, disparaged.—"Almost everything that the employer now does for the employees is being *discredited*."— Eugene G. Grace.

**dis man′tling** (diss man′t′ling). Stripping of equipment and fixtures.— "Terminating the Bureau means *dismantling* the plants located in many communities."—Aubrey Williams.

**dis pos′al** (diss pōze′ăl). Power of control or distribution; readiness for use or service.—"History has put at our *disposal* extensive information about the way of living of our great ancestors."—Alexis Carrel.

**doc′u ment** (dok′ū mĕnt). A piece of written or printed matter conveying information or evidence.—"This report is a momentous *document*."— Edward R. Murrow.

**ec′o nom′ic** (ek″ō nom′ik). Pertaining to money matters or wealth, or to means and methods of living wisely; pertaining to the management of public funds, labor, taxes, etc.—

"There can be no political freedom where *economic* freedom is lacking."—Harold L. Ickes.

**e con'o my** (ē kon'ō mi). Management of affairs; organization of resources of various groups; a practical administration of industrial resources.—"The first herculean task was to build up a sound *economy* in the nation."—George F. Gahagan.

**em bar'go** (em bahr'gō). Authoritative stoppage of foreign commerce or of any special trade.—"The program included an *embargo* on that nation."—Cordell Hull.

**em bez'zle ment** (em bez″l měnt). Fraudulent appropriation to one's own use of property belonging to others; theft of money held in trust.—"In such crimes as *embezzlement* and forgery our record stands no comparison with stable nations."—Herbert Hoover.

**e mol'u ments** (ē mol'ū ments). Profits from some office or position; remuneration or advantages connected with an office or service; gains; general advantages.—"Would he surrender his income and his *emoluments* except in an emergency?"—Harold L. Ickes.

**en'ter prise** (en'tur prīze). Boldness and energy in practical affairs.—"Under the stimulus of individual initiative and *enterprise* industry has expanded."—John W. Davis.

**eq'ui ties** (ek'wǐ tiz). Values of properties in excess of mortgages; the values of properties above any charges against it or liens on it.—"The value of *equities* in farms, houses, and other real estate has fallen to a new low."—Frank Gannett.

**ex ac'tions** (eg zak'shǔnz). Compulsory levies; requirements; demands.—"You must show respect for all religious *exactions* in these countries."—Emily Post.

**ex cess'** (ek sess'). That which passes the ordinary or required limit; an overplus.—"The price would have been well in *excess* of the book value."—Charles P. Cooper.

**ex pro'pri at″ed** (eks prō'pri āte″id). Taken from a private owner for public use; taken away from an individual for use by the state.—"The houses of many residents have been *expropriated* and new houses built for them elsewhere."—Frederick Lewis Allen.

**ex tor'tion ate** (eks tor'shǔn āte). Oppressive; exorbitant; grossly excessive.—"Make up your mind that taxes will always be *extortionate*."—Emmet Holloway.

**fab″ri ca'tion** (fab″rǐ kā'shǔn). Manufacture; act of building.—"For the *fabrication* of landplanes and fly boats the cost is about the same."—Theodore P. Hall.

**fac sim'i le** (fak sim'ǐ li). An exact copy or reproduction.—"The automatic telegraph machine transmits the telegram so that a *facsimile* copy of it arrives at the distant end of the wire."—Leila Livingston Morse.

**fac ti'tious** (fak tish'ǔs). Artificial; conventional; manufactured; trumped up.—"No *factitious* means can be found for basing this trade on the belief that the American Hemisphere can become self-sufficient."—Eugene P. Thomas.

**fis'cal** (fiss'kǎl). Financial; pertaining to the treasury or finances of a government.—"These functions are all associated in giving reality to any governmental *fiscal* and monetary policies."—Beardsley Ruml.

**for'age** (for'ij). Food suitable for cattle or horses.—"We solve problems of storage of fruit, *forage*, fiber, and industrial crops."—Sigmund Sameth.

**frat″er ni za'tion** (frat″ur nī zā'shǔn). Friendly association as brothers and comrades; coming together into fellowship as intimates.—"He will share his fate with other workers and there will be an enormous *fraternization*."—Dorothy Thompson.

**gra'tis** (grāy'tiss). Free of charge; gratuitously; for nothing; without recompense.—"The organization had agreed to teach poor boys *gratis*."—McCready Huston.

**gross** (grōce). Entire or total, without deductions, not net; whole, undiminished by expenses, etc.—"Such facts as net earnings, *gross* sales, and working capital are valuable yardsticks."—Chaplin Taylor.

**hand′i crafts** (han′di krafts). Trades or arts requiring skill with the hands; manual skill; expertness in handwork.—"A return to horses and *handicrafts* means a return to the old level of population."—Aldous Huxley.

**hus′band** (huz′bănd). Manage frugally; handle thriftily; save for future need; use economically.—"After this prodigal waste of raw materials we must *husband* our resources."—Jack Bond.

**in cer′ti tude** (in sur′tĭ tūde). Uncertainty; absence of assurance; insecurity.—"The business entered a period of *incertitude*."—Ainslee Mockridge.

**in dem′ni ties** (in dem′ni tiz). Payments in compensation for loss or damage.—"The peace must not be drawn in bitterness or unpayable *indemnities*."—Wendell L. Willkie.

**in fla′tion** (in flā′shŭn). Expansion so as to exceed just value; hence, overissue of currency and its results; a rise in prices that seems impossible to stop.—"*Inflation* probably is the most terrible economic disaster we can suffer."—Alfred P. Sloan, Jr.

**in″ge nu′i ty** (in″jē nū′ĭ ti). Skill in planning or originating; inventiveness; cleverness in contriving or designing.—"The Board was organized to do an entirely new job, and so was compelled to use creative *ingenuity*."—Stuart Chase.

**in i′ti a″tive** (i nish′i āy″tiv). The ability for original conception and independent action; first steps; originating and leading.—"This has called for improvisation and local *initiative*."—Barbara Ward.

**in″no va′tion** (in″ō vā′shŭn). The making of a change in something established; the introduction of something new.—"The procedure is somewhat novel. If it is an *innovation*, it appears to be a happy one."—Lord Keynes.

**in′roads** (in′rōde′z). Encroachments; raids; forays; attacks; incursions or entrances with the object of taking.—"We are making too great *inroads* on our food rations."—Donald G. Cooley.

**in sol′ven cy** (in sol′věn si). Bankruptcy; a condition in which one is unable to pay debts or meet the claims of creditors.—"The three shops wallowed in and out of *insolvency* in the hands of a bicycle repairer, a shoemaker, and a greengrocer."—H. G. Wells.

**in″ter cep′tion** (in″tur sep′shŭn). The seizure of something on the way before it is allowed to proceed to its destination; an arresting or seizing by authority; an interruption in the course of something.—"Bermuda was made a censorship center for the *interception* and examination of mail."—Frederick Lewis Allen.

**in′ter course** (in′tur korce). Exchange of ideas; commerce; communication.—"The economic life of nations needs a large sphere and very active *intercourse*."—Eduard Beneš.

**la gniappe′** (lan yap′). A small present given by tradesmen to customers in some parts of America.—"As a bonus or *lagniappe* she has included in her new book five stories and one poem which never before have appeared in book form."—John O'Hara.

**mam′mon** (mam′ŭn). Riches; wealth thought of as an evil influence; worldliness or wealth personified.—" 'Frankly I would make you friends with the *mammon* of unrighteousness,' he said."—L. P. Jacks.

**mar′gin al** (mahr′jĭ năl). Connected with goods produced and sold at such a small profit that the sale scarcely covers the cost of production; hence, close to the limit; that yield a very small return.—"It stratifies groups so that elements in the population are limited either to menial or *marginal* occupations."—G. E. Sokolsky.

**mer′can tile** (mur′kăn til). Commercial; pertaining to merchants; having to do with trade.—"Industry calls for full cooperation of those engaged in *mercantile* pursuits and in the professions."—E. W. Palmer.

**mer′ce nar″y** (mur′sē ner″i). A person serving or working only or chiefly for pay or reward.—"A man without a principle is a mere *mercenary*."—T. V. Smith.

**merg′er** (mur′jur). A combination of a number of interests or organizations.

—"The *merger* would be a violation of the principles and teachings of the Prayer Book."—William T. Manning.

**min'i a ture** (min'i uh chŏŏr). On a very small scale; reduced in size or extent.—"These special workshops for the handicapped are *miniature* industrial plants in themselves.—E. W. Palmer.

**mint'age** (min'tij). The act of minting, or making and stamping as money; making metal into the current coin of a country; coinage.—"It was no Julian or Augustian coin—it came of a later *mintage*."—Stephen Vincent Benét.

**mis car'riage** (miss kar'ij). Mismanagement; failure to reach a desired end; failure of a plan or of an objective.—"Everyone was on the alert to detect the author of this strange *miscarriage* in the world's affairs."—L. P. Jacks.

**mod"i fi ca'tions** (mod"ĭ fi kā'shŭnz). Variations in one or a few particulars; changes in some parts.—"*Modifications* and additions are incorporated for specialized operations."—Lawrence D. Bell.

**mo nop"o lis'tic** (mō nop"ō liss'tik). Having the exclusive right or privilege for some particular work, or the control, as of a commodity, which allows prices to be raised.—"A just people's peace cannot dwell side by side with *monopolistic* practices."—Harold L. Ickes.

**ne go"ti a'tions** (nē gō"shi āy'shŭnz). Conferences for the purpose of arranging terms; parleys.—"Continued *negotiations* will bring final results."—John L. Lewis.

**nep'o tism** (nep'ō tiz'm). The show of favoritism to nephews or other relatives; undue favor to relatives; grants of privileges or positions to relatives.—"He would do nothing for his brothers, so that there would be no talk of *nepotism*."—H. G. Wells.

**nom'i nal** (nom'ĭ năl). Existing in name only; hence, too small to be considered; inconsiderable; virtually nothing.—"In the light of today we can say that the price we paid for Alaska was a *nominal* sum."—Ellery Marsh Egan.

**nov'ices** (nov'iss iz). Beginners in any business or occupation; inexperienced people.—"How many members of the next legislature will be absolute *novices?*"—Henry W. Toll.

**ob tain'** (ŏb tain'). Are prevalent; are general; are established; prevail.—"Those who remain are paid lower wages than *obtain* elsewhere."—David L. Cohn.

**o'ver tures** (ō'vur chŏŏrz). Tentative proposals intended to lead to further negotiations.—"Never fear that compassionate *overtures* will be wasted."—Bruce Barton.

**pat'ri mo ny** (pat'rĭ mō ni). An inheritance from a father or an ancestor.—"The middle classes squandered the spiritual and moral *patrimony* which had been conserved by the older feudal ages."—George N. Shuster.

**pa'tron age** (pāy'trŭn ij). Support given by a sponsor; regular business given by customers or clients; financial support or custom given by a clientele.—"*Patronage* of genealogists is brisk among the members of the hereditary societies."—Horace Claremont.

**pend'ing** (pend'ing). Remaining undecided; not yet settled; waiting to be completed; awaiting adjustment; hence, overhanging or imminent.—"He gives an intelligent statement about the *pending* issues in our politics."—William Allen White.

**pen'sion ers** (pen'shŭn urz). Persons living on regular payments given to them after retirement for past services; those who receive a pension or stated allowance for injuries or special service.—"These ancient *pensioners* wore a blue uniform with big silver buttons."—Christopher Morley.

**per'qui sites** (pur'kwi zits). Incidental profits from service beyond what is due as salary; also, income or salary.—"In these universities the professors had to teach what the students wished to hear; otherwise the benches were empty and the *perquisites* lacking."—Raymond H. Geist.

**pre'cious** (presh'ŭs). Costly; of great

value; highly prized; esteemed as rare.—"The creative power weighs each coin, hoarding the *precious*, shoving dross away."—Donald Culross Peattie.

**pre fab'ri cat"ed** (prē fab'rĭ kāte"id). Constructed or made of standardized parts which can be assembled or put together after they reach their destination to form a complete structure. —"The whole idea of the *prefabricated* ship is open to question as a serious peace-time project."—Lincoln Colcord.

**pre'mi um** (prē'mi ŭm). A price above the nominal value; a sum above par; hence, 'at a premium' or 'in great demand'; very valuable because quite rare.—"The genuine Siamese cats were at a *premium*."—Stephen Vincent Benét.

**pre rog'a tives** (prē rog'uh tivz). Unquestionable rights; generally admitted privileges.—"The disadvantages are that the unions would try to usurp management's *prerogatives*." —Donald Dallas.

**pri or'i ty** (prī or'ĭ ti). Precedence; right of way in front of others.— "Educational rehabilitation must be given *priority* along with food and medical care."—Alonzo F. Meyers.

**pro ce'dure** (pro see'dūre). A course of action; the methods of conducting a business.—"Now we get to actual hiring which is usually a *procedure* of many steps."—W. W. Finley.

**pro cur'a ble** (prō kūre'uh b'l). Capable of being obtained by any means; that may be procured or obtained by effort.—"He resolved to write to his brother for the best edition *procurable*."—Stephen Vincent Benét.

**pro cure'ment** (prō kūre'měnt). The act of obtaining; acquisition; the task of getting by effort or means.— "Officials in charge of labor *procurement* say that these boys are doing a wonderful job."—Carrol C. Hall.

**proj'ect** (proj'ekt). A scheme or plan; something mapped out in the mind, as an undertaking.—"Low-cost power furnishes energy for the operation of the *project*."—Harold L. Ickes.

**pro pri'e tors** (prō prī'ĕ turz). Persons who are the exclusive owners of

something; owners.—"Among the executive group are included such positions as presidents, general managers, and *proprietors*."—Chaplin Tyler.

**pur suits'** (pur sūtes'). Businesses; vocations; kinds of employment.—"Reconstruction will involve a shift in the work and *pursuits* of millions of people."—Matthew Woll.

**pur vey'ors** (pur vāy'urz). Those who furnish or supply something.—"All these *purveyors* of information may be used to create strife as well as goodwill."—George F. Zook.

**quit'tance** (kwit'ănce). A release from debt; something tendered by way of requital; a discharge from an obligation; a receipt.—"Here is your *quittance* for the money that you owe."—Douglas Brewster.

**re cessed'** (rē sest'). Suspended business for a short time; had a short intermission; ceased work for a time; did not meet in session.—"The column in the paper was halted after Congress *recessed*."—Clare Boothe Luce.

**re ces'sion** (rē sesh'ŭn). The act of going backwards; a withdrawing.— "Perhaps there may be a brief period of economic *recession*."—Wendell L. Willkie.

**re cip'i ent** (rē sip'i ĕnt). One who receives; one who accepts a gift.—"One man's money may be taken and given to another to the great satisfaction of the *recipient*."—John W. Davis.

**re cip'ro cal** (rē sip'rō kăl). Mutual; shared by both sides; having an interchange of privileges and advantages.—"The *reciprocal* trade agreements program places us in a position where we have something positive to offer other nations."—Franklin Delano Roosevelt.

**re claimed'** (rē klaimd'). Brought back (wild land) to a cultivated state; brought (waste land) to a good condition.—"Many thousands of acres of Palestine have been *reclaimed* by the Jews and put to fertile production." —Frederick C. Painton.

**rec'om pensed** (rek'ŏm penst). Paid for; given an equivalent to; compensated; repaid; indemnified.—"These trips often involved expenditures for new clothes and luggage for which she was never *recompensed*."—Emma Bugbee.

**re couped'** (rē kōopt'). Recovered; regained as compensation; made up for.—"The net volume of business could not all be *recouped*."—Louis K. Comstock.

**re mu'ner a"tive** (rē mū'nur āy"tiv). Profitable; affording satisfactory payment; paying.—"There are diversified laws in every state that prevent the alien from engaging in *remunerative* work."—Harold Fields.

**re trench'** (rē trench'). Reduce or curtail expenses; cut down expenditures; hence, economize.—"The economist advised that the company *retrench*." —W. H. Cowley.

**re vert'** (rē vurt'). Turn back; return to some former condition.—"Eliminate advertising, and the world would quickly *revert* economically to the dark ages."—Lenox R. Lohr.

**sal'vage** (sal'vij). To save from destruction; to rescue from being wasted.—"When we understand the importance of saving kitchen fats, millions of people will begin to *salvage* every spoonful."—Esther Lloyd-Jones.

**sar to'ri al** (sahr tō'ri ăl). Pertaining to a tailor; of tailored garments; tailoring.—"These new textiles will have some individual characteristics that will enliven our *sartorial* habits."—Francis Westbrook, Jr.

**sen ior'i ty** (seen yŏr'ĭ ti). Superiority in status or standing secured by length of service for a corporation or business; priority of rights or privileges as a reward for long faithful service.—"Nothing, in my opinion, is more sacred in railroad employment than *seniority*."—William Hard.

**spec'i fy** (spess'ĭ fī). State in detail; mention definitely; state in explicit terms; name as special items.— "These criticisms are too general. Please *specify* your objections."— John J. Green.

**spon'sor ship** (spon'sur ship). The act of making oneself responsible for the statements or doings of another.—

"This *sponsorship* leaves the society free to carry out its musical plans."— Marshall Field III.

**sta bil'i ty** (stuh bil'ĭ ti). Steadfastness; established firmness; durability; constancy; steady strength of character. —"The success of an enterprise depends to a great extent on the *stability* of the employees."—Sterling McCormick.

**sta tis'tics** (stuh tiss'tiks). Facts systematically gathered and classified which relate to a particular class or interest and which can be stated in numbers; numerical facts about people or things.—"*Statistics* show that only fifty million citizens of the United States can trace their ancestry to England, Scotland, and Northern Ireland."—Emory L. Fielding.

**sti'pend** (stī'pend). An allowance or salary; a fixed sum paid at regular intervals; a yearly payment.—"It was the Sonata in F major that secured for Grieg a life-long *stipend* from the government."—Percy Aldridge Grainger.

**stip'u lat"ed** (stip'ū lāte"id). Specified, as the terms of an agreement; definitely arranged.—"This tax would provide for withholding *stipulated* amounts from incomes as they are earned."—Eric A. Johnston.

**sub sid'i ar"ies** (sŭb sid'i er"iz). Auxiliaries; companies controlled by a parent organization.—"The corporation *subsidiaries* have been entirely free of labor disturbances."—Myron C. Taylor.

**sub'si dies** (sub'sĭ diz). Pecuniary aid granted by the government to a person or group producing something for the public benefit.—"Some people have dubbed incentive payments *subsidies*, thinking thereby to condemn them."—James L. Byrnes.

**sub'stance** (sub'stănce). Material possessions; wealth; property.—"A man of poverty among men of *substance*, he also produced some forty paintings whose genius remained unrecognized for several years."—Edwin Seaver.

**su"per sedes'** (sū"pur seedz'). Takes the place of by reason of superior worth or right; replaces.—"Formation of this committee *supersedes* the situation created by the correspondence."—Winston Churchill.

**sus cep'ti ble** (sŭ sep'tǐ bl). Capable of being influenced or acted upon; of such a nature as to be easily affected; capable of undergoing.—"The acres are *susceptible* of irrigation with available water supplies."—Harold L. Ickes.

**tac'tics** (tak'tiks). The science and art of military and naval maneuvers; hence, adroit management for accomplishing an end; clever devices or their application; methods of proceeding.—"Bungling *tactics* have created confusion and injured our standing."—Hugh Butler.

**ten'der** (ten'dur). Money offered as payment; recognized currency.—"Among the primitives of West Africa cowry shells were legal *tender*."—Hebe Bulley.

**trends** (trendz). General directions or courses; prevalent tendencies; inclinations.—"From past experience we can derive concrete facts and *trends* that aid in forecasting futures."—Lewis H. Brown.

**un"der write'** (un"dur rīte'). To guarantee or assume responsibility for.—"I am not willing to *underwrite* the war policy of another nation."—Hugh S. Johnson.

**u'ni form** (ū ni form). That does not vary; consistent; having a standard that does not change.—"The people want a *uniform* currency."—Albert J. Beveridge.

**un sound'** (un sound': 'ou' as in 'out'). Not valid; not of true value; not firmly fixed; lacking strength and solidity.—"Gresham's law still holds. *Unsound* money will always drive out sound money."—Bertram M. Myers.

**u'su rer** (ū'zhŏŏ rur). A moneylender; a person who makes money loans, charging an exorbitant rate of interest.—"The *usurer* was biting his nails and not saying anything at all."—Stephen Vincent Benét.

**u su'ri ous** (ū zhŏŏr'i ŭs). Of extremely high interest for the use of money; of a premium for the use of money beyond the rate established by law.—"He now began to pay at the *usurious* rates demanded."—Gene Fowler.

**vest'ed** (vest'ed). Held for a special time or in a special way and not subject to any contingency.—"No political appetites or *vested* interests must stand in the way."—Winston Churchill.

**vin'tage** (vin'tij). The yield of a vineyard; especially the finest wine from a special district in a very good year.—"The period of fermentation is not the time to test the quality or to appraise *vintage* of the wine."—Harvey T. Harrison.

**waive** (wāve). Give up temporarily, as a right or claim; forego; do without.—"Workers should not be allowed to *waive* vacations and draw additional pay."—Paul V. McNutt.

## ONE-MINUTE REFRESHER

The key words that are printed in italics are terms that are in this chapter. After each phrase or sentence are three words. Underline the word that is nearest in meaning to the key word.

1. He received a handsome *stipend:* prize; reward; payment.
2. The company *defrayed* all the expenses: paid; disallowed; reduced.
3. Advertising has an *accruing* value: lessening; helpful; accumulating.
4. They are engaged in *remunerative* work: heavy; continuing; profitable.
5. Let us *appraise* the probable results: flatter; estimate; criticize.
6. She surrendered her *emoluments:* perfumes; payments; patrimony.
7. When she got the cards *collated:* cleaned; separated; arranged.
8. They took up the *agenda:* contract; program; argument.
9. The committee disapproved of this *disbursement:* ruling; dismissal; expenditure.
10. He was an *accredited* representative: authorized; unacceptable; faithful.

*Answers:* (1) payment; (2) paid; (3) accumulating; (4) profitable; (5) estimate; (6) payments; (7) arranged; (8) program; (9) expenditure; (10) authorized.

# CHAPTER IX

## FOREIGN WORDS ARE YOUR GRACE NOTES

No LANGUAGE can be absolutely complete in and of itself. No matter how broad and inclusive it may be in the wealth and variety of its terms, there will always be small gaps that need a filling. The French language, with all its versatility, has no words for *home, baseball* or *cocktail,* so it has adopted our words as labels for these ideas. We have no exact duplicates in English for *carte blanche* or *faux pas,* so we have borrowed these from the French.

Some of the words in this chapter are no doubt already a part of your verbal equipment. Others may be new to you. Of course there will be many of these words and phrases that you may never care to use conversationally but it will still be a cultural satisfaction to know their meanings when you chance to meet them in your reading or when you hear them.

There are many who wonder at the need for these loan-words and even resent their presence. Such people forget that we not only have these visible foreign visitors among us, but that more than three hundred thousand foreign words, now disguised and invisible, have been assimilated into our language during its long history.

We think understandably, but somewhat loosely, of the American language as being Anglo-Saxon in its nature and origin. Of course its lusty roots do strike deep into the rich Chaucerian soil and into the primitive speech of the Angles and the Saxons who invaded old England. But when we realize that, among the more than one hundred and thirty million citizens of our vast American nation, there are not many more than fifty millions who can trace their family beginnings directly to Great Britain and Northern Ireland, and that about eighty millions are of French, Dutch, Scandinavian, Russian, German, Czechoslovakian, Italian, Polish, Negro, Asiatic and other foreign extractions, we shall see that our speech must be as composite as our blood. And so it is.

The sturdiness of our American language is due in part to a

heritage that stretches back to ancient Rome and Greece, and its present robustness is evidenced by its growing sum of loan words and by its constant and avaricious borrowings from the treasuries of other nations.

To tell the story of these innocent and light-fingered pilferings would be repetitious. Let's identify just a few of them with their countries of origin for our present pleasure.

In each case these scanty lists are no more than samples of thousands of others.

We have long ago taken and made as our own the common words *embargo, tornado, mosquito, alligator, sarsaparilla* and *hurricane* from the Spanish; *carnival, motto, cornice* and *cameo* from the Italian: *law, writing* and *wrong* from the Scandinavian. The Dutch have given us such salty words as *scum, freebooter, yacht, boodle, cruise, buoy* and *furlough;* the Irish contributed *slogan, bog, whisky, smithereens* and *clan;* the Persians, *azure, awning, divan, magic.* We turn to Africa for *canary* and *gorilla;* to Brazil for *jaguar* and *tapioca;* while the South Sea Islands have made us richer with *taboo* and *tattoo.*

Now I am going to call on one ambassador each to represent ten other nations that belt the earth:

| | | | |
|---|---|---|---|
| kiosk...... | Turkey | boomerang.... | Australia |
| mammoth.... | Russia | coffee........ | Arabia |
| molasses..... | Portugal | geyser....... | Iceland |
| bronco...... | Mexico | quartz....... | Germany |
| typhoon..... | China | zebra........ | Abyssinia |

Such words as these have become part and parcel of our speech. They are the loyal emigrés who have taken out their citizenship papers and have changed their pronunciations and often their spellings to fit in with our American way of life. There are others though—*début* and *cliché* are examples—which have remained faithful to their native country, as do many immigrants, and have retained their foreign accent.

Words of this latter type cannot, in all fairness, be considered as "literary" and affected. Even though they have not been assimilated, they still serve a real purpose and are used with telling effect by men and women of culture and intelligence.

When Grover Whalen states that New York City is no "*parvenu* of elegance," he is using a French word for which we have no adequate translation, and when Eduard Beneš says, "That nation must surrender all territories which she has seized. To my mind this is definitely a *sine qua non* of permanent peace," he is employing a

Latin phrase that would take many more words to express in our language.

Such words as these, naturally, should never be used unless there happens to be no English equivalent. And their pronunciations must be practiced until they are meticulously correct. Of course, whoever employs the words and phrases in this chapter must be easy and confident in their use.

## FOREIGN WORDS ARE YOUR GRACE NOTES

*(For key to pronunciation of foreign words see page x)*

**ab″at toirs′** (ab″ă twahrz′). Slaughter-houses; large buildings or sheds where animals to be used for food are killed.—"The great *abattoirs* slay the animals that make up a part of the city's meat supply."—Theodore Dreiser.

**ad ho′mi nem** (ad hom′i nem). To the man or individual; hence, aimed at a person's prejudices rather than at his intellect.—"He stirred up racial hatred with arguments of the *ad hominem* type."—Malcom Babbitt.

**ad in″fi ni′tum** (ad in″fi nī′tŭm). Endlessly; without any limit.—"One could multiply these instances *ad infinitum*."—Gordon Heriot.

**ad in′ter im** (ad in′tĕ rim). In the mean time; during the interval; meanwhile; temporary.—"This was only an *ad interim* arrangement."—Emory L. Fielding.

**ad lib′i tum** (ad lib′ĭ tŭm). At pleasure; as one desires; to any extent.—"The unknown wilderness lay westward before him, where the lost tribes wandered *ad libitum*."—Hervey Allen.

**ad nau′se am** (ad naw′shē am). To the point of disgust or revulsion; so as to sicken or disgust.—"We hear today, *ad nauseam*, the epithet, 'Fascism.'"—Merwin K. Hart.

**à″ la mode′** (ah″ luh mōde′). In the fashion; fashionable; modish.—"Sleeveless dresses were *à la mode* for all occasions."—Donald G. Cooley.

**al fres′co** (al fress′kō). Open-air; in the open air; outdoor.—"His *al fresco* performances have attracted some of the greatest throngs ever to witness

an operatic production."—Ronald F. Eyer.

**al′ter e′go** (al′tur ē′gō). Second self; other self; hence, intimate friend.—"He leaned on him for friendship and entertainment. He had become his *alter ego*."—Lloyd C. Douglas.

**a mour′** (uh mōōr′). A love-affair, often an illicit one; a secret love intrigue.—"With a stupid laugh he hinted at a romantic *amour*."—W. Somerset Maugham.

**an′i mus** (an′ĭ mŭs). An animating or inciting thought or purpose; animosity.—"Methods were accepted, except where they were felt to be an unworthy *animus* riding on a worthy cause."—Owen D. Young.

**an′no Dom″i ni** (an′ō dom″ĭ ni). In the year of our Lord or of the Christian Era.—"*Anno Domini* is generally written in an abbreviated form as A.D."—Ellery Marsh Egan.

**a″pri o′ri** (ā″pri ō′ri). Prior to experience; previous to examination; presumptively.—"Everything cannot be reckoned out *a priori* in each emergency."—Walter Lippmann.

**ap″ro pos′** (ap″rō pō′). Suited to the time and occasion; with regard or referring to; as suggested by.—"One of my friends assured me, *apropos* of the newspaper story, that no such resolution had been passed."—James Duane Squires.

**ar ca′na** (ahr kāy′nuh). Secrets; mysteries.—"The *arcana* of the basements and cellars altered the whole complexion of the day."—H. G. Wells.

**ar′got** (ahr′got). Slang; the popular use of odd expressions; the peculiar words or phrases used by certain classes of people.—"Some of our most respectable words have come from the *argot* of the gangsters."—Sterling McCormick.

**ar tistes'** (ahr teests'). Professional singers or dancers; professional actors, and the like.—"Upon the walls of the theater hung large tinted photographs of the *artistes.*"—Hilary St. George Saunders.

**at'el ier** (at'ĕl yāy). Workshop; studio; workroom of an artist.—"His *atelier* was small, but it had an all-important north window."—Donald G. Cooley.

**au" fait'** (ō" fāy.'). Familiar with the facts; hence, proper; in good taste; in good form.—"She generally dropped out before we went to the restaurant as the place wasn't considered *au fait* for women then."—Roy Chapman Andrews.

**au" re voir'** (ō" re vwahr'). Till we meet again; good-by till our next meeting.—"I said good-by and *au revoir* to twenty years of sturdy democracy and social awareness."—Jan Masaryk.

**bad"i nage'** (bad"ĭ nij'). Raillery; playful ridicule or banter; good-natured chaffing.—"Above these pianissimo passages are heard the clink of glasses, the striking of matches, and *badinage.*"—Clarissa Lorenz.

**bag"a telle'** (bag"uh tel'). Trifle; a thing of little worth or importance.— "Money was the merest *bagatelle* in these elections."—George Barton Cutten.

**bagn'ios** (ban'yōze). Houses of ill fame; brothels.—"Blatant girls accosted him from the windows of the *bagnios* in Rio."—Hugh E. Blackstone.

**bas"-re lief'** (bah"-rē leef'). Sculpture or carving that is less than half the true depth; sculpture in which the figures only stand out slightly from the background.—"Most concepts of mine in relation to wood take the form of *bas-relief.*"—Maurice Glickman.

**bas"ti na'do** (bass"ti nāy'dō). An Oriental punishment, beating the soles of the feet, usually with a stick; a beating with a cudgel or stick.—

"One of his tyrants inflicted the *bastinado* on him, and as Peel was writhing beneath the raining blows, Byron came up."—André Maurois.

**ba'ton** (bă ton'). A short rod or wand used by conductors to beat time.— "Nikisch had instinctive and imperious mastery of the *baton.*"—Serge Koussevitsky.

**beau' i de'al** (bō' ī dē'ăl). The beautiful model; the highest type of excellence; the ideal beauty.—"This actress is the *beau ideal* of present-day Hollywood."—Emmet Holloway.

**beau" monde'** (bō" moNd'). High society; the world of fashion; fashionable society.—"It was a distinguished party and the *beau monde* was well represented."—S. L. Scanlon.

**beaux"-arts'** (bō"-zahr'). The fine arts; painting, drawing, architecture, sculpture.—"He is a wealthy, traveled, cultured gentleman and a lover of the *beaux-arts.*"—Charles Henry Crozier.

**beaux gestes'** (bō zhests'). Magnanimous actions; graceful gestures; ingratiating deeds.—"The *beaux gestes* of Lord Chesterfield are still acclaimed."—George F. Gahagan.

**bel"-es"prit'** (bel" ess"pree'). A person of wit and spirit; a highly cultured and brilliantly humorous person; wit.—"From a silent, retiring youth he grew into a *bel-esprit* and a good sportsman."—Emmet Holloway.

**belles"-let'tres** (bel"-let'r'). Works of literary art; writings that are purely literary; criticism of literature.— "That definition of humanities with its polite learning and *belles-lettres* is redolent of an age far removed from ours—and not only in time."— Monroe E. Deutsch.

**bête" noire'** (bāte" nwahr'). An object of abhorrence; a person or thing intensely disliked; a bugbear.—"All through my life, mathematics has been my *bête noire.*"—Roy Chapman Andrews.

**bi"be lots'** (bē"blōze'). Small artistic objects of art; curious articles of virtu.—"The green-and-white enamel star had long lain among his *bibelots* and looked like a foreign order."—E. F. Benson.

**bil'let-doux'** (bil'āy-dōō'). A love letter; a lover's note.—"She hid the *billet-doux* under a pile of handkerchiefs in her bureau drawer."—Donald G. Cooley.

**bla"sé'** (blah"zāy'). Sated with pleasure; surfeited with excessive indulgence.—"Napoleon's career flashed like a meteor on the dark horizon of a tired and *blasé* world."—Ennis P. Whitley.

**bo'na fi'de** (bō'nuh fī'dē). In good faith; without deceit.—"It is understood that the consignment must be *bona fide.*"—Fiorello H. La Guardia.

**bo nan'za** (bō nan'zuh). Anything that is very profitable and yields a rich return.—"I hope no one will think that this is a *bonanza* crop—that it offers a chance to get rich quick."—Tom L. Wheeler.

**bons" mots'** (boN" mō'). Clever sayings; terse witticisms.—"Such a conventional formula did not apply to this slick coiner of epigrams and *bons mots.*"—Elsa Maxwell.

**bon" ton'** (boN" toN'). Good breeding; the fashionable world or style; the society manners.—"In their habits and manners they tried to ape the *bon ton* of their new neighbors."—Charles Henry Crozier.

**bon" vi"vant'** (boN" vē"vahN'). An epicure; one who loves good food and living; a gourmet.—"The one-time ambassador to Washington was a *bon vivant* and table eclectic."—Donald C. Peattie.

**bou'doir** (bōō'dwahr). A lady's private sitting-room, often connecting with her bedroom.—"He was leaving his wife's *boudoir* when their daughter halted him."—Lloyd C. Douglas.

**bou'le vard** (bōō'luh vahrd). A broad city avenue, specially designed for pleasure-walking or driving.—"I know of at least one photo-electric traffic light, placed where a bridle path crosses a busy *boulevard.*"—C. C. Furnas.

**bour'geois** (bōōr'zhwah). The middle class; tradesman or townsman.—"The *bourgeois* often became a rank opportunist. He believed in power and profit only."—George N. Shuster.

**ca"bal le'ros** (kah"bahl yāy'rōze). Spanish gentlemen; cavaliers.—"The romantic *caballeros* were thought to make ardent love by moonlight and strum the guitar all day long."—John B. Glenn.

**ca ba'na**(kuh bah'nyuh).A small house; a bathhouse.—"Every *cabana* at the Beach Club was rented long before the water was warm enough to tempt even the hardiest."—Lucius Beebe.

**cach'es** (kash'iz). Hiding places, generally holes, used by explorers for storing provisions for future use.—"Their meat *caches* were full of walrus carcasses.—Frederica de Laguna.

**ca"fé'** (ka"fāy'). A restaurant; a coffee-house.—"Many dancers in the *café* were killed in the fire."—Hilary St. George Saunders.

**ca"ma ra'de rie** (kah"muh rah'duh rē). Comradeship; loyalty; good fellowship.—"He is dealing with sea officers, not desk officers; and his style rises in response to their *camaraderie* to give us this picture of the new navy in action."—Fletcher Pratt.

**ca"naille'** (kuh"nal'). The lowest class; the rabble; riffraff; an unruly mob; the vulgar multitude.—"No doubt they'll find out that I served beer to the *canaille.*"—Jules Romains.

**carte" blanche'** (kahrt" blahnsh'). An authorization signed in blank to be filled in by the recipient; hence, full power.—"Secret police visiting warehouses with a *carte blanche* for investigations violate the very essence of democratic principles."—Winthrop A. Aldrich.

**ca'sus bel'li** (kāy'sŭss bel'ī). A cause for war; an event or occurrence that justifies a declaration of war; an act that warrants the start of hostilities.—"Any dispute easily becomes envenomed to the point of being made a *casus belli.*"—Aldous Huxley.

**cause" cé lè'bre** (kawse" sāy lāy'br'.) A celebrated case (in law); a lawsuit or trial that excites much attention.—"When you enter the great reception room you are apt to meet either the hero or the villain of the latest *cause célèbre* on Capitol Hill."—Elsa Maxwell.

**cau″se rie′** (kō″ze rē′). A chat; an informal talk; an informal address; a free or unconventional criticism.— "We listened for a weary hour to his *causerie* on Russia."—Malcom Babbitt.

**ca′ve at emp′tor** (kāy′vē at emp′tor). Let the buyer beware; hence, no responsibility is accepted for the purchaser's dissatisfaction, he buys at his own risk.—"It is a world in which the principle of *caveat emptor* applies recurrently in relationships of love, friendship, or family."—James T. Farrell.

**char″gé′ d′af″faires′** (shahr″zhāy′ dă′-fair′). A substitute for an ambassador; a deputy ambassador; an officer in charge of diplomatic business in the absence of a minister; a diplomatic representative.—"He informed the *chargé d'affaires* of the government's decision."—George Polk.

**cha″ri va′ri** (shah″rē vah′rē). A burlesque serenade consisting of a medley of sounds made with tin horns, pans, or other metal kitchen ware.—"He and the rest of the gang were generally in on *charivari* parties and Hallowe'en depredations."—Don Marquis.

**chef″-d'oeu′vre** (shă″-dur′vr′). A masterpiece; a chief work or very excellent production, surpassing others.— " 'The Man with the Hoe' was the *chef-d'oeuvre* of the poet, Edwin Markham."—R. L. Dawson.

**chic** (sheek). Elegance and good taste; smartness; stylishness.—"Life at the Colony pursues the even tenor of respectability and *chic*."—Lucius Beebe.

**ci″ce ro′ne** (siss″ĕ rō′nē). A guide who conducts tours and gives information; hence, a guide who understands.— "It was strange to see Mr. Landon, the advocate of clarity, sitting mum, while Mr. Hoover, taking the role of barker, or *cicerone*, told the world what he thought Mr. Landon thought."—Samuel Grafton.

**ci″-de vants″** (see″-de vahNz′). Former occupants; those who formerly had the positions.—"Some are new men. Some men who have come back. *Ci-devants*."—H. G. Wells.

**cir′ca** (sur′kuh). About; as nearly as the date is known.—"Although the exhibit was marked '*circa* 1350,' the tools were probably of even earlier date."—Bertram M. Myers.

**claque** (klak). Hired applauders in a theater.—"The packed galleries included a professional *claque*."—L. J. Dickinson.

**cli″chés′** (klee″shāyz′). Fixed forms of expression; trite remarks; hackneyed phrases.—"How often one hears the military *clichés* that we cannot fight today's war with tomorrow's weapons."—Alexander P. de Seversky.

**clique** (kleek). An exclusive or clannish set; a coterie.—"The ruling *clique* was too blind to face the issues."— Arthur Menken.

**co″gno scen′ti** (kō″nyō shen′tē). Connoisseurs; experts or critical judges in some particular field of art or commerce.—"The *cognoscenti* look down their patrician noses at this intransigent school of painting."—Malcom Babbitt.

**co me″di enne′** (kō mee″di en′). An actress who plays in comedy; an actress who plays amusing parts.— "Miss Law is a born *comedienne*."— Austin Wright.

**comme″ il″ faut′** (kō″ meel″ fō′). As it should be; correct; proper.—"A black dinner coat and striped trousers are *comme il faut* at an afternoon wedding."—Hugh E. Blackstone.

**con″fi dant′** (kon″fĭ daNt′). A person to whom secrets are confided or entrusted.—"By imperceptible gradations, he had become the *confidant*, the arbiter of our difficulties."— Samuel Hopkins Adams.

**con′freres″** (kon′frairz″). Colleagues; fellow members of an association.— "Our delegates try to dissuade our Latin American *confreres* from their suspicion."—Dennis Chavez.

**con′gé** (koN′zhāy). Dismissal; leave-taking; a formal farewell.—"This sudden *congé* came as a great surprise to all."—Donald G. Cooley.

**con″nois seur′** (kon″i sur′). A competent critical judge of something, as art, music, wine.—"The wine-drinker tends to be something of a *connoisseur*."—Joseph H. Choate, Jr.

**con quis'ta dors** (kon kwiss'tuh dorz). Leaders of the Spanish conquest of Mexico and Peru; conquerors.— "Cordoba was founded by one of the *conquistadors.*"—G. Jones Odriozola.

**con ser"va toire'** (kŏn sur"vuh twahr'). A school of art or music.—"The *conservatoire* closed at once, so I arranged a concert tour that winter."—Willa Cather.

**con'tre temps"** (kon'truh tahNz"). An embarrassing incident; an awkward occurrence; an unlucky mishap; a temporary stoppage.—"Colorful persons march through these stories of escapades and *contretemps.*"—Amy Loveman.

**cor tège'** (kor tāyzh'). A procession; a train of attendants; a retinue.— "Paid mourners precede the funeral *cortège.*"—William Alfred Eddy.

**co'te rie** (kō'tĕ rĭ). A set of persons who meet habitually; a clique.—"If the President accepts the advice of that little *coterie,* he will wage an undeclared war."—Burton K. Wheeler.

**coup** (kōō). A master stroke; a brilliant stratagem.—"Her biggest *coup* was her marriage to the Count."—Harry Hansen.

**coup" de grâce'** (kōō" de grahce'). Finishing stroke; death blow; final and decisive blow.—"German sympathizers disappeared and the Lusitania gave neutrality the *coup de grâce.*"—Roy Chapman Andrews.

**coup" d'é"tat'** (kōō" dāy"tah'). A sudden or unexpected stroke of policy or statesmanship, often one that overthrows the existing government.— "We all recall the *coup d'état* by which Napoleon III made himself Emperor."—George Wharton Pepper.

**cui sine'** (kwē zeen'). Cooking department; style or quality of the cooking. —"Half the travelers would depart praising, instead of cursing the *cuisine.*"—Joseph H. Choate, Jr.

**cul"-de-sac'** (kul"-duh-sak'). A blind alley; a passage or narrow gorge open only at one end.—"One evening we camped in a rocky *cul-de-sac* of the hills."—Eleanor Lattimore.

**da'ta** (dāy'tuh). Actual or assumed facts; information.—"It requires the assembling of considerable *data* to indicate a significant trend."—Malcolm F. Hawkes.

**deb"o nair'** (deb"ō nair'). Affable; courteous and gay; complaisant.— "The American soldier and sailor have never lacked a gay, *debonair* disregard of danger."—Monroe E. Deutsch.

**de"bris'** (de"bree'). Rubbish; accumulated fragments; ruins.—"The mother was gathering pickings from the *debris.*"—Richard Llewellyn.

**dé"but'** (dāy"bew'). A first appearance on the stage or before the public; a formal entrance upon a career.— "Our *début* in England was in historic Bristol."—John Finley Williamson.

**dé col'le té"** (dāy kol'tāy"). Low-necked; leaving the shoulders and neck bare; cut low in the neck.— "The green silk of her dress was becoming even though its lines were not *décolleté.*"—Rachel Field.

**dé"cor'** (dā"kore'). All that makes up the decorative ensemble of a room or stage.—"Neither the mannered acting of the star nor the Victorian *décor* saves the show from being a comparative dramatic débacle."—Howard Barnes.

**de fac'to** (dē fak'tō). In reality; actually and really existing.—"The Committee will soon be recognized as the *de facto* temporary government."— Johannes Steel.

**de luxe'** (dē lŏŏks'). Of superfine quality; of great elegance or magnificence; specially lavish; involving great expense.—"Through this process of reproduction the complete story was ready for immediate dispatch. Here was espionage *de luxe!*" —Francis Rufus Bellamy.

**dem'i-monde** (dem'i-moNd). The class of society to which women of doubtful reputation and standing belong. —"He was disposed to mystery and a curiosity about society and the *demi-monde.*"—H. G. Wells.

**dé noue'ment** (dāy nōō'mahN). The unraveling of a plot or story; the outcome; hence, catastrophe.—"Then came the *dénouement.* The great work of Hernandez was bound and then buried in the stacks of the library of the Escorial."—Victor W. von Hagen.

**de no'vo** (dē nō'vō). Anew; afresh; from the beginning.—"We have made a grievous mistake. We must go back and start *de novo.*"—Charles Henry Crozier.

**de ri"gueur'** (de rē"gur'). Necessary for good form; required by etiquette; according to the best taste; hence, imperative.—"Wasn't it *de rigueur* for every writer with serious pretensions to have no faith in anything save, possibly, the gospel according to St. Marx?"—J. Donald Adams.

**der"nier" cri'** (dair"nyāy" kree'). The latest cry; hence; the last word or the newest fashion.—"Doll-like hats were the *dernier cri* in the summer of that year."—Douglas Brewster.

**de trop'** (de trō'). Too much or too many; hence, not wanted; in the way.—"The couple patently regarded her as very much *de trop.*"—Maud Diver.

**de'us ex ma'chi na** (dē'ŭs eks mak'inuh). A god from a machine; hence, something that comes just in the nick of time to overcome a difficulty; a providential intervention; something introduced to solve a problem.—"The puppy tracks down saboteurs and is the *deus ex machina* for a happy ending to the book."—Rose Feld.

**dil"et tan'te** (dil"ĭ tan'ti). A dabbler in art matters; a superficial amateur.—"Nero was a *dilettante* in the classics."—Edmund A. Walsh.

**dis"ha bille'** (diss"uh beel'). Negligent attire, as a loose robe or undress garment; a loose dressing gown or negligée.—"She was a whirlwind of emotionalism robed in flowing *dishabille.*"—A. S. M. Hutchinson.

**dis tin'gué** (diss tang'gāy). Distinguished-looking; of distinguished or superior air or bearing; distinguished in manner and carriage.—"The stranger's appearance was undeniably *distingué.*"—Douglas E. Lurton.

**dis trait'** (diss trāy'). Absent-minded; distracted; diverted; inattentive.—"When he saw her she seemed subdued and *distrait.*"—Samuel Hopkins Adams.

**di"ver"tisse"ment'** (dē"ver"teece"mahN'). Amusement; a short performance; a diversion; entertainment; something pleasing and diverting.—"The new comedy is a nice, inoffensive little *divertissement* with some amusing spots in it."—Burton Rascoe.

**dol'ce far nien'te** (dol'chay fahr nyen'tāy). It is sweet or pleasant to do nothing; hence, delightful or pleasant idleness.—"The *dolce far niente* of the Hawaiian holiday contrasted sharply with the rush and turmoil of New York."—Bruce Ellsworth.

**dou"ble en"ten'dre** (dōō"b'l ahN"-tahN'dr'). A word or phrase of double meaning; an ambiguous expression; a phrase having another meaning which is often indecent.—"That is the crackling kind of wit that strains at a *double entendre.*"—Harry Hansen.

**é clat'** (āy klah'). Brilliance; glory; renown; notoriety; celebrity; social distinction.—"Such *éclat* for her if you went in your robes of office!"—E. F. Benson.

**é"lan'** (āy"lahN'). Brilliant or impetuous ardor or dash; eagerness to act.—"The *élan* of the troops is still very high."—Dwight D. Eisenhower.

**é"lite'** (āy"leet'). The choicest part, especially of a society or army.—"They propose class government by *elite* selected by the government."—Herbert Hoover.

**em"bon"point'** (ahN"boN"pwaN'). Stoutness; corpulence; plumpness.—"He was a short, compact figure, and a little inclined to a localised *embonpoint.*"—H. G. Wells.

**é"mi"gré'** (āy"mee"grāy'). An emigrant; a fugitive from the French Revolution; a refugee; one who flees from his native land.—"He couldn't possibly call himself a French *émigré* unless he wore a powdered wig."—Willa Cather.

**en"ceinte'** (ahN"saNt'). Pregnant; with child; soon to bear a child.—"The management of tuberculosis when a woman is *enceinte* is not so difficult as we were led to believe."—George G. Ornstein.

**en"fant" ter"ri'ble** (ahN"fahN" te"-rē'bl'). Terrible child; a child who asks embarrassing questions, always says the wrong thing at the wrong

time, and is a general nuisance.—
"When he broke into business he was
the *enfant terrible* of the trade."—
Sidney Carroll.

**en masse'** (on mass'). In a body; all
together; in a mass.—"The settlement descended on us *en masse*."—
Arthur C. Twomey.

**en'nui** (ahN'nwee). Boredom; a feeling of weariness resulting from lack
of interest; listless discontent; tedium.—"The sloth swims with the
same *ennui* and disdain for quickened
movement that it displays toward
everything in life."—V. Wolfgang
von Hagen.

**en pas"sant'** (ahN pah"sahN'). In
passing; by the way; in the course of
doing things.—"Let's consider these
small problems *en passant*. Our critical discussions will come later."—
Donald G. Cooley.

**en rap"port'** (ahN ra(h)"pore'). In
sympathetic or harmonious relation;
in close communication or connection.—"He ought to be fairly *en
rapport* with the situation since he has
been standing there for some time."
—Theodore Dreiser.

**en sem'ble** (ahN sem'bl'). Of all performers playing together to render
concerted music; of several instruments together.—"*Ensemble* playing
is an excellent means of perfecting
reading-fluency."—Jan Smeterlin.

**en suite'** (ahN sweet'). In a set or
series; connected with one another.—
"The rooms reserved for us were *en
suite*."—Tom Pennell.

**en"tente'** (ahN"tahNt'). An understanding or agreement; a friendly
understanding between parties or
states based on more or less formal
agreements or declarations.—"The
new *entente* is the result of a visit by
the Mexican film star."—Fred Stanley.

**en"tou"rage'** (ahN"too"rahzh'). Associates, companions, or followers collectively.—"Glance at Napoleon after
Waterloo as he stands surrounded by
the little remnant of his *entourage*."
Bruce Barton.

**en"tr'acte'** (ahN"trakt'). The interval
between two acts; an interlude between acts of a play or opera.—

"During the *entr'acte* they strode
about the main lounge."—André
Maurois.

**en'trée** (ahN'trāy). Privilege of entering; admission; freedom to enter;
right of entry.—"She had *entrée* with
Soviet officials."—Ernestine Evans.

**en"tre nous'** (ahN"truh noo'). Between
us; between ourselves; in confidence.
—"In all decency this story should
remain *entre nous*."—George F. Gahagan.

**en"tre pre neur'** (ahN"tre pre nur').
One who originates and manages an
enterprise.—"If the Government becomes the great *entrepreneur* or risk-
taker, the private incentive to assume
risk in the hope of gain gradually
dies."—Emil Schram.

**es'pi o nage** (ess'pi ō nij). The practice
of spying; offensive surveillance.—
"This League was intended to serve
as a reserve force for *espionage* activities."—Martin Dies.

**es"prit' de corps'** (ess"pree' de kor').
Common devotion of members to an
organization.—"*Esprit de corps* has
always been very high in the regiment."—Ben J. Northridge.

**ex ca the'dra** (eks kuh the'druh: 'th'
as in 'thin'). Speaking from a seat
of office or professor's chair; authoritative; exercising official authority.—
"You can be extempore in this
assignment rather than *ex cathedra*."
—Christopher Morley.

**ex"po sé'** (eks"pō zāy'). An embarrassing disclosure of something discreditable; an undesirable exposure.—
"It is actually an *exposé*, in which he
takes interior decoration for a ride."
—Iris Barry.

**ex trav"a gan'za** (eks trav"uh găn'-
zuh). A fantastic literary or dramatic
composition; an elaborate and spec-
tacular drama or show.—"The brilliant *extravaganza* weaves satire deftly
into its tale of the rich South American."—Amy Loveman.

**fait" ac"com"pli'** (fāy"ta" koN"plee').
An accomplished fact; something already done; a thing that is finished
and presumed to be irrevocable.—
"They accepted the situation as a
*fait accompli*, and set to work."—
Thomas C. Boushall.

**faux" pas'** (fō" pah'). A false step; hence, a mistake or error, especially a breach of social etiquette or a slip in conventional behavior; a violation of good breeding.—"This makes you feel foolish; you have made an absurd *faux pas.*"—L. P. Jacks.

**fies'ta** (fyess'tah). A religious festival; a feast-day; a holiday in memory of a saint.—"The Chinese discovered the principle of the rocket centuries ago when their gunpowder was used for *fiesta* instead of fighting."—Edward Laroche Tinker.

**fi na'le** (fē nah'lē). The last act or scene; the end; the concluding chapter.—"She was found out, and the *finale* was obvious."—Michael Mac-Dougall.

**fi nesse'** (fē ness').Refinement.—"Many operations are made on higher-priced shoes to give them *finesse.*"—I. M. Kay.

**flâ"neurs'** (flah"nurz'). Those who lounge or wander aimlessly; idlers; hence, intellectual triflers.—"Just then twenty-five elephants, all unnoticed by these infuriating young *flâneurs,* were standing on their heads."—Alexander Woollcott.

**force" ma"jeure'** (force" mah"zhur'). Irresistible force; superior power; main force.—"He was ousted by *force majeure* and has never resigned."—William Philip Simms.

**for tis'si mo** (for tiss'i mō). Very loud; hence, an extra loud sound; great emphasis.—"So much optimism calls forth the sharpest reaction, so much *fortissimo* makes one long for silence."—Ludwig Lewisohn.

**fra'cas** (frāy'kuss). Uproar; noisy fight; brawl; disorderly quarrel.—"The policeman who strolled through the hollow just about that hour quieted the *fracas.*"—Christopher Morley.

**fu'rore** (fū'rōre). Rage; overmastering anger; angry excitement.—"I know what a *furore* this may create in other shipbuilding nations."—Henry J. Kaiser.

**gam'in** (gam'ĭn). A street Arab; a neglected child of the streets.—"My shoes were shined by the most charming little *gamin.*"—George F. Gahagan.

**gauche'ness** (gōshe'ness). Left-handedness; hence, awkward action; clumsiness; awkwardness.—"He was looking at him, obviously annoyed by his *gaucheness.*"—John P. Marquand.

**gen're** (zhaN'r). Style, sort, or class.—"Few novels in this *genre* are more rewarding."—Mary A. Miles.

**ha bit"u é'** (huh bit"yū āy'). A constant visitor; a frequenter; one whose visits have become a habit.—"The doctor was a *habitué* of the coffee house.—H. W. Haggard.

**ha'rem** (hair'em). The apartments for women in a Mohammedan's house; a seraglio; all the females occupying the harem; the home of wives and concubines.—"He selects a private station on the shore, destined to be the site of his prospective *harem.*"—Roy Chapman Andrews.

**hoi" pol loi'** (hoy" pŏ loy'). The masses; the common people; the rabble.—"In these days it seems as though some of our intellectuals are almost as gullible as the *hoi polloi.*"—H. W. Prentis, Jr.

**hon"o rar'i a** (on"ō rair'i uh). Honorary payments for professional services; rewards for gratuitous services; fees or privileges given as an honor.—"The scant *honoraria* from the publication did not last long."—Louis Adamic.

**hors" de com"bat'** (or" de koN"bah'). Out of the combat or fight; disabled from the battle.—"It proved to be the last round of the fight, and the champion, to use a literary phrase, was *hors de combat.*"—S. L. Scanlon.

**hors" d'oeu'vre** (or" dur'vr'). An appetizer; a relish; a dish served to create or increase appetite; hence, something that adds zest.—"The colonel dismisses the book as a literary *hors d'oeuvre.*"—Fred Allen.

**im"passe'** (im"pahce'). A blind alley or cul-se-dac; hence a way or condition that seems impassable; a serious inescapable predicament; a deadlock.—"If an *impasse* is reached, management and representatives of labor should assume responsibility for determining how a solution shall be reached."—M. W. Clement.

**im ped"i men'ta** (im ped"ĭ men'tuh).

**Things** that encumber or hinder; encumbrances that impede progress or movement; hindrances; things that retard action.—"To go there was to move westward without the baggage or the *impedimenta* of the past."—Hervey Allen.

**im promp'tu** (im promp'tū). Made, done, or uttered on the spur of the moment; offhand; extemporaneous. —"They are trying to create an impression that lawyers can be outwitted by the *impromptu* common sense of the poor but honest heroes of drama."—William L. Ransom.

**in am"o ra'ta** (in am"ō rah'tuh). A sweetheart; a woman with whom one is in love or enamored; a woman beloved; a woman in love.—"Nor should his *inamorata* resent this."—Frank Sullivan.

**in"com mu"ni ca'do** (in"kŏ mū"ni-kah'dō). Cut off from outside communication; in solitary confinement. —"I have affidavits in my possession that people are being held *incommunicado* for days."—Robert Marion La Follette.

**in ex tre'mis** (in eks trē'miss). In the last extremity; dying; at the point of death; at the last gasp.—"There is something about the type of soul that turns to religion *in extremis* which is not pleasing."—Theodore Dreiser.

**in"gé"nues'** (aN"zhā"newze'). Actresses who play artless and ingenuous roles.—"The critic described the speech of our stage *ingénues* as consisting of honeyed tones enunciated through a mouthful of baked potatoes."—Frank H. Vizetelly.

**in re** (in rē). In the matter of; with regard to; concerning; in the case of. —"There was an unusual amount of interest during the testimony *in re* White versus Cameron."—Bruce Ellsworth.

**in sou'ci ance** (in sōō'si ănce). Careless unconcern; indifference.—"I was appalled at the tone of the piano, but I preserved an air of *insouciance*."—Noel Coward.

**in to'to** (in tō'tō). Altogether; entirely; in the whole; without reservation.— "Naturalism, as fathered by Zola, ac-cepted scientific determinism *in toto*." —J. Donald Adams.

**ip'so fac'to** (ip'sō fak'tō). By the fact itself; in the very act; by the very nature of the case.—"Anyone daring to doubt him on this point was *ipso facto* a traitor to the future greatness of the city."—Louis Adamic.

**jeu" d'es"prit'** (zhĕr" dess"pree'). A witty sally; humorous trifle; a fanciful play of wit.—"Many a *jeu d'esprit* fell from the lips of Oscar Wilde."— Morgan Deming.

**joie' de vi'vre** (zhwah' de vee'vr'). Joy in being alive; hence, keen enjoyment of life; zest; agreeable excitement.—"He was a likeable person, simple, full of *joie de vivre* and the worship of beauty."—Roy Chapman Andrews.

**lais"sez"-faire'** (lāy"sāy"-fair'). Non-interfering; inactive; do nothing; unregulated by government.—"Some of the harshness of the *laissez-faire* system was being modified by a socialist movement."—Edward J. Meeman.

**la'res and pe na'tes** (lāy'reez pē nāy'-teez). Household gods; hence, prized possessions; valued personal or household goods.—"Wherever my father's sons and daughters have gone, they have carried these chicken dumplings of ours like *lares and penates* to new homes."—Robert P. Tristram Coffin.

**lav"a liere'** (lav"uh leer'). A piece of jewelry, consisting of an ornamented pendant on a chain; hence, a loose, hanging ornament.—"That button has been hanging for a year like a moose's *lavaliere*."—Gene Fowler.

**Le'bens raum"** (lāy'bĕnz roum": 'ou' as in 'out'). Space for living; hence, additional land or territory deemed necessary for the expansion of emigration or the business of a nation; room to expand and grow.—"She finally sought spiritual *Lebensraum* outside her own country."—Mary Ross.

**leg"er de main'** (lej"er de māne'). Sleight of hand; a trick or deceptive performance that depends upon dexterity.—"The happiness of a great many people cannot be arranged for by merely actuating the financial *legerdemain* of some new notion of the State's accounting."—Mark M. Jones.

**lése″-ma″jes″té′** (leez″-mah″zhess″tāy′). A crime against the sovereign power; an offense against the dignity of a ruler; an insult; treason.—"He was harried by the inquisitive police because he had published a sentence that seemed to savor of *lèse-majesté.*" —W. H. Chamberlin.

**lit″té″ra″teur′** (lē″tāy″rah″tur′). A literary man; one who engages in literature as a profession; a man of letters.—"The author is a gay and brilliant *littérateur* with a style as fresh as the day after tomorrow."— Malcom Babbitt.

**lo cale′** (lō kahl′). Locality, especially with reference to the surrounding features.—"They aligned themselves with the best social families of the *locale* where they proposed to do business."—Gordon Heriot.

**ma laise′** (ma lāze′). Uneasiness; discomfort; indisposition of the body without any actual disease; a general, indefinable unrest and uneasiness.— "It did not take him long to realize the advancing *malaise* of his world." —H. G. Wells.

**ma té″ri el′** (muh te″ri el′). Materials collectively, as for military use; supplies and equipment.—"The nation reinforced its *matériel* and men by sea and air."—Henry L. Stimson.

**mé″lange′** (māy″lahNzh′). A mixture; a miscellaneous combination; an intermingled number.—"There is a bewildering *mélange* of small cat-like animals in both hemispheres."— Edwin H. Colbert.

**mé″nage′** (māy″nahzh′). A household; the persons that compose a household; domestic management; those who live in one house.—"I was anxious to learn how a *ménage* without benefit of clergy worked in the Orient."—Roy Chapman Andrews.

**mé″sal″liance′** (māy″zal″yahNce′). A misalliance; a mismating; a marriage with a person who is a social inferior; an improper or unsuitable marriage.—"Let us suppose that the odds are 3 to 1 against the dreaded *mésalliance.*"—L. P. Jacks.

**mé″tier′** (māy″tyāy′). Trade; profession; one's special line or calling.— "It is a question of *métier*—the doctor daily deals with man and his environment."—Iago Galdston.

**mi″lieu′** (mē″lĭ′uh′). The center or middle; hence, environment or surroundings; the setting.—"The *milieu* for her stories is the deep South."— Joseph Henry Jackson.

**mi nu′ti ae** (mi new′shi ē). Very small and unimportant details; minute, precise particulars.—"The workers lose all sense of proportion in a wave of *minutiae.*"—William Elliott.

**mi rage′** (mi rahzh′). An optical illusion; a reflection that appears like real objects, but inverted.—"Faith must be made tangible in the lives of those over whom a foreign *mirage* has cast a spell."—Lisa Sergio.

**mise″ en scène′** (mē″ zahN sāne′). The setting of a play; the arrangement of the players and scenery on the stage; the scenery and paraphernalia used in presenting a play.—"She has surrounded herself with fine and celebrated players and a meticulous *mise en scène.*"—Howard Barnes.

**mo′dus o″pe ran′di** (mō′dŭs op″ĕ-ran′di). A way of working; a mode of operating; the way a thing works or operates.—"No one can help but marvel at the *modus operandi* of an airplane."—Donald G. Cooley.

**mo′dus vi ven′di** (mō′dŭs vi ven′di), A mode of living; a temporary arrangement pending settlement.—"It is fatuous to talk of a compromise or a *modus vivendi* with such a dictator." —Robert G. Sproul.

**mo rale′** (mō rahl′). A state of mind with reference to courage, hope, and self-reliance; mental condition as regards confidence and zeal.—"*Morale* is built upon confidence."—W. W. Finley.

**mor″a to′ri um** (mor″uh tō′ri ŭm). A period during which a debtor is authorized to suspend payments.— "He urged us to give a five-year *moratorium* on debt payments."— Joseph T. Robinson.

**mo″tif′** (mō″teef′). The leading feature in any work; the theme; the principal idea.—"The gaining of power for personal ends is the key to their entire life *motif*."—Joseph Jastrow.

**mu ez′zin** (mew ez′in). A Mohammedan priest who calls the faithful to prayer from a minaret of one of the mosques.—"The *muezzin* intoned the call to prayer."—C. Wellington Furlong.

**née** (nāy). Born; noting the maiden name (surname at birth) of a married woman.—"By his bedside sat Margaret, *née* Wolfstone."—L. P. Jacks.

**ne plus ul′tra** (nē pluss ul′truh). The furthest point attainable or which anyone can reach; the summit of achievement or success; the highest pitch.—"When the doctor was elected president of the American Medical Association he felt that he had reached the *ne plus ultra* of his career."—Charles Henry Weston.

**no′blesse″ o″blige′** (nō′bless″ ō″-bleezh′). Nobility obliges; hence, nobility of birth or high rank carries with it an obligation to be honorable and generous in behavior; privilege involves responsibility.—"Some vague blend of noble and ignoble motives, of masochism and *noblesse oblige* always held her back."—Jan Struther.

**nom′ de plume″** (nom′ de plo͞om″). The name under which an author writes; a pen name; a pseudonym.—"He was contributing articles under a *nom de plume*."—Victor Keen.

**non com′pos men′tis** (non kom′pŏss men′tiss). Not of sound mind; mentally unbalanced; having lost mental control.—"The woman kidnaper was proved to be *non compos mentis*."—Charles Henry Crozier.

**non seq′ui tur** (non sek′wi tur). An inference that does not follow from the premises; a fallacy resulting from applying a wrong conclusion.—"It is a *non sequitur* to imply that the difference in result was due to diversities in the relations of the Executive to the legislature."—Thomas Reed Powell.

**nou″veau′ riche′** (no͞o″vō′ reesh′). A person who has recently become rich; a parvenu.—"Conspicuous waste is often a sign of the *nouveau riche*."—Bradwell E. Tanis.

**nu″ance′** (new″ahnce′). A slight shade of difference in a color or shade; hence, a subtle difference in meaning.—"A term into which much has been compressed may convey the wrong *nuance*."—George N. Shuster.

**op′ti mum** (op′tĭ mŭm). Most favorable for the production of the best results; best, as regards conditions.—"The *optimum* time for photographing birds at their nests is from three to six days after the eggs have been hatched."—Eliot Porter.

**ou″tré′** (o͞o″trāy′). Eccentric; strikingly odd and extravagant; outside the limits of propriety; wanting in decorum.—"To speak kindly her costume was *outré*."—Bradwell E. Tanis.

**pal″an quin′** (pal″ăn keen′). An enclosed litter or hammock-like conveyance carried by poles on the shoulders of men, and used chiefly in India and China.—"The officer enjoyed the unique experience of being carried through the streets in a *palanquin*."—Ainslee Mockridge.

**par ex′cel lence** (pahr ek′sĕ lahnce). Pre-eminently; beyond comparison; ranking above all others; by virtue of the greatest excellence.—"This is the prescription *par excellence* for the tired heart."—Peter J. Steincrohn.

**par′ve nu** (pahr′vē new). One who has risen suddenly from the ranks; that which has attained a position above that for which it is fitted; an upstart.—"New York City is no *parvenu* of elegance."—Grover Whalen.

**pas sé′** (pa(h) sāy′). Past; out of date; antiquated; past its prime; past its usefulness or interest.—"He does not need to be told that the subject is *passé*."—Joseph Wood Krutch.

**pat′ois** (pat′wah). A dialect peculiar to a district; the use or pronunciation of words that are unlike the literary language of that locality.—"Scholars told me that I spoke French with a provincial *patois*."—John P. Marquand.

**pen″chant′** (pahN″shahN′). A strong inclination; a liking; a leaning towards or in favor of something.—"His elusive memory for names is buttressed by a *penchant* for identify-

ing performers with suitable nick-
names."—Paul D. Green.

**pe'ons** (pee'ŏnz). Common laborers;
unskilled workers; laborers working
to pay off a debt.—"To *peons* these
comforts were grandeurs."—May
Lamberton Becker.

**per cap'i ta** (pur kap'i tuh). By heads;
hence, for each person.—"The higher
their *per capita* wealth, the greater
their purchasing power."—John B.
Glenn.

**per se** (pur see). By or in itself; for its
own sake.—"I appreciate that you
cannot follow this advice *per se.*"—
Frank L. Rowland.

**per so'na non gra'ta** (pur sō'nuh non
grāy'tuh). A person who is not
acceptable; a diplomatic representative who is not satisfactory or welcome in the country to whose government he is accredited.—"Being a
journalist he would be *persona non
grata* in both these countries."—
C. J. Spriggs.

**per"son nel'** (pur"sŏ nel'). The persons employed in some business or
service.—"An investigation is under
way and changes in *personnel* will be
made."—J. Lester Perry.

**pe tite'** (pĕ teet'). Small; diminutive;
little; of small and dainty build.—
"His wife was dark, piquant, *petite*,
attractive.—Theodore Dreiser.

**pièce" de ré"sis"tance'** (pe ess" duh
rā"ziss"tahNce'). The chief dish of a
meal; the most substantial dish at a
meal; a rare or choice morsel; the
chief thing in a collection.—"One
*pièce de résistance* of the whale world
measures only about one twelfth
of an inch in length."—Elon Jessop.

**pi'quant** (pee'kănt). Having a sharp
taste; hence, sharp and stinging, but
stimulating.—"This rebuke from the
old veteran was *piquant.*"—Albert
Perry.

**po grom'** (pō grom'). A massacre, riot,
or pillage instigated by a central
government; especially one directed
against the Jews.—"The Cardinal
mounted his pulpit to protest against
the brutal *pogrom.*"—George N.
Shuster.

**po seurs'** (pō zurz'). Those who pose
or strike attitudes; those who are

given to attitudinizing; affected
people.—"He ignores the sneers of
the *poseurs.*"—Westbrook Pegler.

**pot"pour'ri** (po(t)"pŏor'i). A medley;
a hotchpotch; a mixture; a stew of
meat and vegetables, or of other mixtures.—"Here is a *potpourri* with all
its wide range of ingredients, served
piping hot for the gourmet."—Ruth
Blodgett.

**pour"boire'** (pŏor"bwahr'). Money to
buy a drink; hence, a tip; a gratuity.
—"I slipped the taxi-driver a small
*pourboire.*"—Henry J. Powers.

**pour" par"ler'** (pŏor" pahr"lāy'). A
discussion that is informal; a preliminary conference or consultation
preceding negotiations.—"Before the
formal meeting a small group of the
leaders had a *pour parler.*"—Ellery
Marsh Egan.

**pri'ma fa'ci e** (prī'muh fāy'shi ē). On
the first appearance; at first view; at
first sight or based on a first impression.—"The prisoner was easily convicted on *prima facie* evidence."—
Malcom Babbitt.

**pro'té gés** (prō'tĕ zhāz). Those cared
for in some special way by another;
those under the care and protection
of some friend or patron.—"There
was nothing she had to teach that her
*protégés* could not have discovered for
themselves."—J. Donald Adams.

**pro tem'** (prō tem'). For the time being; for the present; temporarily.—
"We are *pro tem* the trustees of this
inheritance."—Mark M. Jones.

**pu'is sance** (pew'i sănce). Power; force;
might; ability to conquer.—"The
best authority for that period says
that he was on the point of rising into
a far greater state of *puissance.*"—
Herbert Ravenel Sass.

**qua'si** (kwāy'sī). Appearing as if; simulating in appearance; resembling; in
a certain degree.—"The relation
between employer and employee
is a *quasi*-public affair."—Myron C.
Taylor.

**quid pro quo** (kwid prō kwō). Tit for
tat; something for something; something in place of something else.—
"As a *quid pro quo* Russia has undertaken apparently not to interfere

with the European imperialist system."—Ralph Wallace.

**qui vive′** (kee veeve′). The challenge of a French sentinel, "Who goes there?" hence, alert; watchful and on the lookout for something to happen.—"She was frank, bright, vividly alert, always on the *qui vive.*" Bradwell E. Tanis.

**rac″on teur′** (rak″on tŏŏr′). A person who can tell a good story and tell it well; a skilled story-teller; a relator of anecdotes.—"He is a journalist, warrior, and *raconteur.*"—Stanley Walker.

**rai″son′ d′ê′tre** (rāy″zoN′ dāy′tr′). Reason for the existence of something; purpose that justifies, or an excuse for existing; an aim or object that caused existence.—"Like most other things in heaven or on earth, it has a *raison d'être.*"—James F. Bender.

**rap port′** (ra pōre′). A sympathetic relationship; accordance; conformity.—"My aim was to establish a *rapport* of fatality between each of the personalities and their backgrounds." —Salvador Dali.

**rap″proche″ment′**     (ra(h)″prosh″- mahN′). The act of getting together; restoration of cordial relations.—"The world was gratified at the obvious co-operation and *rapprochement* between the two countries."—Nicholas Murray Butler.

**re cher″ché′** (re sher″shāy′). Sought with extra care; hence, much sought after; choice; rare; very elegant and refined.—"We went to the small and *recherché* curio shop, with the talisman."—Samuel Hopkins Adams.

**re con′nais sance** (rē kon′ĭ sănce). An examination or survey of a tract of land to find out the strength and position of an enemy, or the nature and resources of the district.—"Our air *reconnaissance* reports constant and growing reinforcements of enemy strength."—Douglas MacArthur.

**re duc′ti o ad ab sur′dum** (rē duk′- shi ō ad ab sur′dŭm). Proof of the absurdity or falsity of something by producing a consequence that is logically absurd and impossible.— "The notion of a planned economy finally reached its climax, and its *reductio ad absurdum,* in the vogue of technocracy."—Walter Lippmann.

**ren′dez vous** (rahn′dĕ vōō). A meeting or appointment to meet; a meeting-place.—"They lead the people bravely forward to each successive *rendezvous* with destiny."—T. V. Smith.

**ré″su mé′** (rāy″zew māy′). A recapitulation; a summary; a summing up; an abstract or epitome.—"An official of Savo gave a *résumé* of the war."— Ira Wolfert.

**ris″qué′** (reece″kāy′). Bordering on impropriety; verging on indecency and suggestiveness; involving risk of offense.—"The play was *risqué* and wickedly witty."—Douglas E. Lurton.

**rou″é′** (rōō″āy′). A debauched or corrupt person; a dissolute man; a rake; a person who is immoral, intemperate, and dissipated.—"François Villon was a wicked and charming *roué.*"—Tom Pennell.

**sa fa′ris** (suh fah′riz). Hunting expeditions; traveler's caravans; journeys for a special purpose, as exploration. —"The firm specializes in outfitting the *safaris* of big-game hunters."— Homer W. Smith.

**sa′ga** (sah′guh). A legendary or heroic story; a story of heroism.—"His new book is a kind of lyric *saga* of the American folk."—Lewis S. Gannett.

**sa″lon′** (sah″loN′). A reception in a fashionable French home; an assembly of important guests; a social reunion of distinguished people.— "They came so often and stayed so long and talked so hard that he began to feel himself the host of a Parisian *salon.*"—Elizabeth Goudge.

**sang′-froid′** (sahN″-frwah′). Composure in trying circumstances; coolness in danger; freedom from agitation or disturbance; calmness in the face of an ordeal.—"She met the crucial emergency with all of the dignity and the *sang-froid* of a Charlotte Corday facing the guillotine."— Charles Henry Crozier.

**sa vants′** (sa vahNz′). Men of special learning; scholars.—"Poland, with its thinkers and *savants,* has furnished its contribution to the spiritual patrimony of the world."—Pius XII.

**sa"voir'-faire'**   (sa(h)"vwar'-fair'). Quickness to perceive and do the right, proper, and graceful thing; tact; knowledge of what to do and say, and readiness to act.—"The charming Madame du Barry had at all times *savoir-faire*."—Jack Bond.

**sé"ance'** (sāy"ahNs'). A session; a sitting; a meeting for the sake of deliberation or investigation.—"After all the ceremonies and delays, I had expected that we should have a long *séance* together."—Irvin S. Cobb.

**se ragl'io** (sē ra(h)l'yō). A harem; a walled palace for a Sultan; the place where wives and concubines live in some eastern countries.—"It was a sordid *seraglio* in the Arab quarter of Algiers."—Donald G. Cooley.

**se"ri a'tim** (seer"i āy'tim). In series; point by point; taking one thing after another; in connected order.— "George recited her faults to her *seriatim*, almost like a bookkeeper reading off his orderly figures."— John J. Green.

**si es'tas** (si ess'tuhz). Midday or after-dinner naps.—"The Latin Americans are fond of their afternoon *siestas*."—John B. Glenn.

**si'ne qua non'** (sī'nē kwāy non'). An essential; a necessity; an indispensable condition.—"That nation must surrender all territories which she seized. To my mind this is definitely a *sine qua non* of permanent peace." —Eduard Beneš.

**soi'-di"sant'** (swah'-dē"za(h)N'). Self-styled; pretended; would-be.—"This nationalistic spirit manifested itself in the petty persecution exercised by *soi-disant* patriots."—Clare Godfrey.

**soi"gné'** (swah"nyay'). Well-groomed; cared for in a painstaking, assiduous way.—"Its denizens would infinitely rather be *soigné* than serene."— Florence Haxton Bullock.

**sot'to vo'ce** (sōt'tō vō'chā). In an undertone; under the breath; aside. —"He kept up a *sotto voce* endorsement to the sentences that came clear and emphatic from the speaker."— H. G. Wells.

**soup"çon'** (soop"soN'). A slight suggestion; a very small taste; a minute quantity.—"He guides her abstrac-tion from the unworthy, the deceptive *soupçon* of false excitement."— Florence Haxton Bullock.

**spi"ri"tu"el'** (spē"rē"tū"el'). Marked by refinement and grace; characterized by the higher and delicate qualities of mind; ethereal; refined.—"It was a sensitive face, with an expression more *spirituel* than any I have ever seen."—Malcom Babbitt.

**sta'tus quo"** (stāy'tŭs kwō"). The existing state of things; the unchanged position.—"We are told by the smug spostles of the *status quo* that the Supreme Court has nullified some of the acts."—Alben W. Barkley.

**sub ro'sa** (sub rō'zuh). Privately; confidentially; in strict confidence; secretly.—"It's not a new discovery. They're teaching it, *sub rosa*, in the new universities."—H. G. Wells.

**sum'mum bo'num** (sum'ŭm bō'nŭm). The supreme or chief good; the highest good from which other benefits are derived.—"We seek knowledge—for itself alone, apparently— as a kind of *summum bonum*."—John Haynes Holmes.

**sur veil'lance** (sur vāle'ănce). The act of watching or overseeing; close watch over something.—"Supervision and *surveillance* have their limits." —Arthur E. Morgan.

**tem'po** (tem'pō). Relative speed or rate of movement; characteristic manner or style.—"The aim is to increase the *tempo* of education and training."—Randall Jacobs.

**ter'ra fir'ma** (ter'uh fur'muh). Dry land; solid ground; firm earth.— "When I land back on American *terra firma* it is with the mixed feelings of relief and criticism with which a native returns."—Edward A. Weeks.

**ter'ra in cog'ni ta** (ter'uh in kog'ni tuh). An unknown or unexplored country or district.—"The world outside our little college town literally was *terra incognita*."—Roy Chapman Andrews.

**tête-'à-tête'** (tāte'-uh-tāte'). A private conversation between two people; a private interview; a confidential chat.—"Four or five times he was an appreciative guest, and then it

seemed time to arrange a *tête-à-tête.*"
—H. G. Wells.

**tour" de force'** (tōōr" de force'). A feat of strength or skill; an ingenious work.—"The book is a brilliant *tour de force* both of logic and imagination."—John Chamberlain.

**tout" en"sem'ble** (tōō"tahN"sahN'-bl'). The general appearance or effect.—"Her dress, her shoes, her coiffure, the *tout ensemble*, had a gracious and pleasing effect."—Ainslee Mockridge.

**tout" le monde'** (tōō" le moNd'). All the world; everybody; everyone.— "Who then is vain? The answer is simple. '*Tout le monde.*' "—Donald G. Cooley.

**tun'dra** (tun'druh). Rolling, treeless, and often marshy plains of Siberia and other arctic regions.—"Vast camps have been built on land created out of the swamps and *tundra* of the arctic.—Joseph E. Davies.

**ven det'ta** (ven det'uh). A blood-feud or quarrel in which the family of the person killed or injured takes revenge on the slayer or his relatives.— "Kentucky feuds and their shootings are close cousins to the *vendetta* of Italy."—Sterling McCormick.

**ver'bum sap** (vur'bŭm sap). A colloquial shortening of the Latin phrase 'verbum sat sapienti (est),' or, a word to the wise is sufficient.— " '*Verbum sap,*' he said, and abandoned the horse and turned to the door."—H. G. Wells.

**vers' li bre** (vair' lē'br'). Verses in which variable rhythm is substituted for definite meter; free verse; verse that is cadenced but not confined to a regular metrical form.—"*Vers libre* can be just a lazy way of writing poetry unless you are a great artist." —Henry T. Powers.

**vi'ce ver'sa** (vī'sē vur'suh). The order of terms being reversed.—"They seek to turn capital against labor, and *vice versa.*"—Franklin Delano Roosevelt.

**vir"tu o'so** (vur"tū ō'sō). A master of art-technique, as a skilled musician; a person possessing great technical skill.—"Perhaps you think it is only in our period that the so-called '*virtuoso* conductor' takes liberties with tempi."—Serge Koussevitsky.

**vis"-à-vis'** (vee"-zuh-vee'). A person who is face to face with another, or opposite to another.—"My *vis-à-vis* at one of the tables was served with a quarter-bottle."—Joseph H. Choate, Jr.

**vi'va vo'ce** (vī'vuh vō'sē). By word of mouth; by spoken words; orally.— "He could not answer any of the first four questions actually addressed to him *viva voce.*"—Christopher Morley.

**vox" po'pu li** (voks" pop'yū li). The voice of the people; public sentiment.—"What a world this would be if it were run by those who sign their letters to the editor '*vox populi!*' "— Donald G. Cooley.

**wan'der lust"** (va(h)n'dur lōōst"). Longing to wander and travel; irrepressible urge to move from place to place.—"*Wanderlust* was strong, and he persuaded his father to give him money with which to make his way to America."—Ronald F. Eyer.

**welt'schmerz"** (velt'shmerts"). World pain and sorrow; weariness of life; discontent with things in general; pessimism.—"The book is a timely tract, not oversoftened by its sub-theme of *weltschmerz.*"—Margaret Parton.

**zeit'geist"** (tsīte'gīst"). The spirit of the time; the drift or tendency of the intellectual and moral characteristics of an era or epoch.—"The *zeitgeist* is just as likely to be a spirit of evil as a spirit of good."—Aldous Huxley.

## ONE-MINUTE REFRESHER

Fill each space in the ten sentences with the one foreign word that best fits the meaning. As you do this pronounce the word out loud for practice.

|   |   |
|---|---|
| a. virtuoso | f. a priori |
| b. raconteur | g. connoisseur |
| c. motif | h. saga |
| d. status quo | i. chic |
| e. bon mot | j. belles-lettres |

1. The many adventures of the crew on their long voyage read like a _____ of the sea.

2. Her dress was in the mode and her whole appearance was _____.

3. He is a man of the world, rich with life and anecdote and vastly entertaining as a _____.

4. Burning ambition for power was the life _____ of Napoleon.

5. Heifitz is a violin _____ with a most exquisite touch.

6. He passed by the more popular reading of the day and devoted himself to the polite learning that can be derived from _____.

7. The ambassador was an accomplished _____ of modern art.

8. Change is the watch word of radicals, but the conservatives are usually content with the _____.

9. We are told that miracles are impossible. This is an _____ assumption.

10. The conversation of Oscar Wilde sparkled with many a witty _____.

*Answers:* 1 — h;  2 — i;  3 — b;  4 — c;  5 — a;  6 — j;  7 — g;  8 — d; 9 — f; 10 — e.

# CHAPTER X

## THESE WORDS HAVE OPPOSITE MEANINGS

THERE ARE thousands of words in our language that have no companion words of opposite meanings. But if a person is determined to use words significantly and effectively he should be able to command opposites whenever they exist.

You may be able to think of "vigilant" when you want to, but if you can't recall such an antonym as "unwary" when you need to you will be handicapped by that much. "He was 'unwary,' " is much more effective than "he was 'not vigilant.' " If you know "prudence" it is equally important to be able to remember "indiscretion." The west side of the city has "affluence"; the east side, "pauperism." One duty is "obligatory"; another is "optional." This statesman has reached the "zenith" of his career; that statesman has fallen to the "nadir."

This versatility is one of the attributes of those who use words well and it will be a vital supplement to your own knowledge of the subject. Make yourself deft in this and in every branch of language, for, after all, the measure of a man is his skill in the use of words of culture, of power, and of high utility.

Of course the most accurately opposed words are the positive words that are turned into negatives by such prefixes as "in," "un," "dis," "il," "ir," "a" and "mis," as: judicious, *in*judicious; essential, *un*- or *non*essential; integration, *dis*integration; logical, *il*logical; reverent, *ir*reverent; typical, *a*typical; apprehension, *mis*apprehension.

We can draw upon the body of this chapter for one example of the negative "ir," where Fred C. Moffat comments on "rational" investment, and the philosopher, Bertrand Russell, complains of "*ir*rational propaganda."

A more interesting and effective opposition of words occurs in the following quotations, and note how well these political speakers choose and place their words:

141

"A peace," says Frank Knox, "temporarily enjoyed by a people without courage and honor is but a *prelude* to certain disaster."

While Burton K. Wheeler says: "I fear the *aftermath* of war."

Again we find contrasted words of opposite meanings in these sentences:

"The answer lies in part in the incessant, *vehement* emphasis on the need for everyone to learn more and more thoroughly his immediate task."—Maurice Hindus.

and—

"The people are unpredictable, sometimes *apathetic* almost to the point of numbness."—John Gunther.

Of course almost all of these terms have more than one word to express their opposite meanings. "Rational" is opposed, not only by "irrational," but also by "insane," "unreasonable," "preposterous," "ridiculous," "absurd," "senseless." Over against "prelude" would be "postlude," and contrasting with "vehement" would be "calm," "lifeless," "impassive," "stoical," "stolid."

While these words that we have used as examples seem to possess directly opposite meanings, they are opposite only at certain points. Just as no two words in our language are exactly alike in meaning, so, and in similar fashion, no two words can be *exactly* opposite in meaning.

We can illustrate this point by picking a few sharply contrasting words out of the dictionary: black, white; sacred, profane; concord, discord; ingress, egress; celebate, libertine; literal, figurative; ordinal, cardinal.

These pairs *seem* like direct opposites, and yet it only takes a moment's consideration to realize that the opposite of a "black-out" is not a "white-out"; and that while you can speak of the "concord" of nations it would sound strange to talk of the "discord" of nations; and that a man's language may sometimes be "profane," but it is never called "sacred"; and while you may be accused of having a "literal" mind you could hardly ever be said to possess a "figurative" mind!

Words, you see, are not a mathematical science. They are an art. They are like our fellow-men, and we must learn to understand word nature just as we do human nature.

After all how could two words ever have precisely opposite meanings? Or precisely the same meanings? The true meanings of words are only approximated in the dictionaries. Meanings are highly personal things, hidden away in our minds and ringed about with special associations. As a matter of actual fact there is no single word in our language that means exactly the same thing to two or more people.

If I say the word "milk," it calls up pleasant associations. I am speaking of something that I like. But when the word "milk" was mentioned to the late John Barrymore, he exclaimed, "Milk? Milk? I tried it once and it turned to chamois in my stomach."

This word meant one thing to him. Another thing to me.

Again. Joe likes to catch fish. You like to eat fish. I sell fish. So when someone mentions "fish" to us, I think of the price of the commodity, you recall the *filet de sole bonne femme* you had at the Marguery, and Joe dreams of the salmon he snagged last year on the Gaspé Peninsula. It is the same four-letter word in each case but it has conveyed three different meanings to three people.

This is quite natural and understandable, as the meanings of words are influenced by our experiences and interwoven with our memories. No two persons have ever learned the same word under precisely the same circumstances, with the same background, or apprehended the new term in the same time period.

These considerations all add to the enthralling subject of words and they show you that your vocabulary is a highly personal possession.

Read this chapter with thoughtful care and determine for yourself from time to time where the opposite pairs recorded here meet and where they miss.

## These Words Have Opposite Meanings

**a ban'doned** (uh ban'dŭnd).   Given over to vice; dissolute; very wicked; profligate; immoral.—" 'It's the dream of my life to be taken for an *abandoned* hussy,' she answered."—W. Somerset Maugham.

**re deemed'** (rē deem'd').   Regained possession of by paying a price; rescued from sin and its consequences; delivered from evil by renouncing it. —"If we are to save civilization, it must first be *redeemed*."—Karl Morgan Black.

**ab bre'vi at"ed**   (ă bree'vi āte"id). Shortened; made quite short; hence, very short.—"The native women wore nothing but *abbreviated* skirts of dark cloth."—Eric Sevareid.

**e lon'gat ed** (ē long'gāte id).   Lengthened; stretched out; extended; made longer.—"We walked through neighborhoods of brick houses with *elongated* windows."—John Dos Passos.

**a bet'ted** (uh bet'ed).   Encouraged; helped; aided; supported; assisted; upheld; incited; fomented.—"His spreading reputation was financed and *abetted* by propaganda."—H. G. Wells.

**dis suad'ed** (di swāde'id).   Advised against; diverted by argument or appeal.—"A man who has a low I.Q. should be *dissuaded* from trying to study medicine."—Carl A. Gray.

**ab"nor'mal** (ab"nor'măl).   Unusual;

not according to the normal rate; hence often, above the average.— "The railroads' *abnormal* earnings should be placed in reserves."— R. B. White.

**sub nor′mal** (sub nor′măl). Below the normal or usual standard; lower than the regular or natural level.— "One of the characteristics of appendicitis is a *subnormal* temperature." —Hugh E. Blackstone.

**ab ste′mi ous** (ab stē′mi ŭs). Marked by self-restraint in giving up pleasures, food and drink; abstaining voluntarily from indulgence of appetites; avoiding excess; eating and drinking very sparingly.—"The habits of Mahatma Gandhi could always be called *abstemious* to the last degree."—Ellery Marsh Egan.

**glut′ton ous** (glut″n ŭs). Greedy; voracious; inclined to feast or eat too much; apt to gormandize.—"The fish developed as a keen, *gluttonous* hunter."—Brooke Dolan.

**ab′sti nence** (ab′stĭ nĕnce). Self-denial; giving up food or pleasures; doing without something; fasting.— "He had excused the afflicted children from their duty of *abstinence* during Lent."—Stephen Vincent Benét.

**in″e bri′e ty** (in″ē brī′ĕ ti). Drunkenness; inebriation; intoxication.— "There are limits even to the elastic hospitality of *inebriety*."—John Myers Myers.

**a bun′dance** (uh bun′dănce). A plentiful supply; a great number or quantity.—"Unbalanced *abundance* can bring the most terrible kind of scarcity."—James A. Farley.

**dearth** (durth). Scarcity; lack; scarceness; inadequate supply.—"Hitherto there has been a *dearth* of expedients in the business of a probation officer."—Sanford Bates.

**ac cord′ance** (ă kor′dănce). Agreement; harmony; conformity; compliance.—"We need a President who has a clear program for America to solve the basic problems in *accordance*

with the principles of our system."— Joseph H. Ball.

**dis′cord** (diss′kord). Disagreement; dissension; want of harmony; strife; contention.—"Confusion and bitterness and *discord* have been the result of this vacillation."—Wendell L. Willkie.

**af′fa ble** (af′uh b′l). Friendly; courteously pleasant; complaisant; benign. —"*Affable* phrases encouraged the applicants."—André Maurois.

**con ten′tious** (kŏn ten′shŭs). Quarrelsome; disputatious; fond of argument or strife; persistently starting disputes.—"When a man reaches 70 he is conventionally supposed to become less *contentious* and more philosophical."—Harold L. Ickes.

**af fin′i ty** (ă fin′ĭ ti). Chemical attraction; close relation; natural inclination.—"The materials employed must have some degree of *affinity* for each other."—E. L. Hemingway.

**re pul′sion** (rē pul′shŭn). Repugnance; refusal to mix with or accept; great dislike; extreme aversion; a repelling or driving apart.—"I have heard it said that the relationship of business to the fine arts is not affinity, but *repulsion*."—L. P. Jacks.

**af″fir ma′tion** (af″ur mā′shŭn). A solemn declaration or statement; assertion; confirmation; testimony.—"We need a ringing *affirmation* in the fundamental soundness of our own institutions to produce prosperity for all." —Thurman W. Arnold.

**ne ga′tion** (nē gā′shŭn). Absence of something definite; nullity; the opposite of affirmation or of some positive thing.—"It is fear that we have to overcome, fear and denial and *negation*."—Louis Bromfield.

**af′flu ence** (af′lū ĕnce). A profuse or abundant supply; wealth.—"The available market was big enough to assure *affluence* for the privileged few."—Edward A. O'Neal.

**pau′per ism** (paw′pur iz′m). Poverty; abject need; lack of necessities.—"He will put the unemployed to work; he will abolish *pauperism*."—John L. Lewis.

**af'ter math"** (af'ter math"). Consequences, often very serious ones.—"I fear the *aftermath* of war."—Burton K. Wheeler.

**pre'lude** (prel'yōod). That which foreshadows a coming event; an introductory movement.—"A peace temporarily enjoyed by a people without courage and honor is but a *prelude* to certain disaster."—Frank Knox.

**ag gran'dize ment** (ă gran'diz mĕnt). The act of becoming greater and more important.—"I might have been tempted to charge the United States of North America with some form of imperialistic desire for selfish *aggrandizement*."—Franklin Delano Roosevelt.

**deg"ra da'tion** (deg"ruh dā'shŭn). Reduction in rank or dignity; decline of reputation; disgrace; shame.—"That way lies certain defeat and *degradation*."—William L. Batt.

**ag'gra vate** (ag'ruh vāte). To make worse; to increase.—"Subsidies do not prevent the real causes of inflation, they *aggravate* them."—Paul S. Willis.

**as suage'** (ă swāje'). Lessen; mitigate; give relief to; soothe; pacify; calm; make quieter or milder.—"You and I *assuage* each other's egotisms."—H. G. Wells.

**a lac'ri ty** (uh lak'rĭ ti). Cheerful willingness and promptitude; briskness; eager and lively action.—"He took his place with *alacrity*, his face beaming with interest."—Pearl S. Buck.

**in ert'ness** (in urt'ness). Inactivity; sluggishness; inherent disinclination to be active; torpidity; lack of energy.—"He preferred to dream, to swim, and, above all else, to let himself sink benumbed into a seeming *inertness*."—André Maurois.

**al layed'** (ă lāde'). Abated; calmed; lessened; moderated; checked.—"The public zest for magic is *allayed*."—Raymond Moley.

**in ten'si fied** (in ten'sĭ fīde). Increased in force and energy; made more violent; heightened in intensity.—"From then on, the campaign of terror was *intensified*."—Oswald Garrison Villard.

**al lur'ing** (ă lūre'ing). Attracting; enticing; captivating; tempting.—"India is more *alluring* and perhaps the easier prey."—Girja Shankar Bajpai.

**re pul'sive** (rē pul'siv). Repelling; causing aversion; arousing dislike; exciting disgust or horror; very offensive.—"Her mother and sister would find no end of tedious if not actually *repulsive* things for her to do."—Helen C. White.

**am"bi gu'i ty** (am"bi gū'ĭ ti). A word or expression that is capable of being interpreted in more than one way.—"Conscience can back up the worst kind of conduct as well as the best. The reason for this *ambiguity* is plain."—Harry Emerson Fosdick.

**pre ci'sion** (prē sizh'ŭn). Accuracy of definition; definiteness.—"No one was able to answer the question with much *precision*."—Winston Churchill.

**am'i ca ble** (am'i kuh b'l). Friendly; promoting good will; cordial; peaceable.—"From now on the will and the mechanics for immediate and *amicable* adjustments are at hand."—Charles E. Wilson.

**hos'tile** (hoss'til). Antagonistic; of an enemy; unfriendly; showing enmity or hatred.—"These *hostile* groups are each fighting against the other."—Wendell L. Willkie.

**am'ple** (am'p'l). Fully sufficient to meet all requirements; abundant; extensive.—"Copies should be illustrated with *ample* sketches or photos."—A. J. R. Curtis.

**in"suf fi'cient** (in"sŭ fish'ĕnt). Inadequate; scanty; lacking in amount or detail; deficient in needful facts.—"Precious nights of toil were spent in mastering the hard facts so necessary and so *insufficient* for the making of a doctor."—Axel Munthe.

**an"te ce'dents** (an"tē seed'ĕnts). Ancestry; previous conduct or history of forefathers.—"The government keeps no record of the religious affiliations or racial *antecedents* of its employees."—W. M. Kiplinger.

**prog′e ny** (proj′ĕ ni). Offspring; children; descendants.—"We make him a citizen, and use our records to assist his *progeny*."—Marshall E. Dimock.

**an te′ri or** (an teer′i ur). Prior; earlier.—"Irish melodies reach back to a period *anterior* to the dawn of musical history."—Eamon de Valera.

**pos te′ri or** (pos teer′i ur). Later in time; coming after in an order or series; subsequent in point of time.—"Constantine was *posterior* to Nero."—Douglas Brewster.

**ap″a thet′ic** (ap″uh thet′ik: 'th' as in 'thin'). Without emotion or feeling; impassive.—"The people are unpredictable, sometimes *apathetic* almost to the point of numbness."—John Gunther.

**ve′he ment** (vee′ĭ mĕnt). Forceful; deeply felt; very urgent and passionate.—"The answer lies in part in the incessant, *vehement* emphasis on the need for everyone to learn more and more thoroughly his immediate task."—Maurice Hindus.

**ap″pro ba′tion** (ap″rō bā′shŭn). Approval; commendation; praise; acceptance as satisfactory; sanction.—"Whoever had started this wild pandemonium, it was apparent that it lacked the hero's *approbation*."—Lloyd C. Douglas.

**der″o ga′tion** (der″ō gā′shŭn). The act of detracting or disparaging; the lessening of good repute.—"The *derogation* of General Mitchell was limited to the top flight of the military services."—Alexander P. de Seversky.

**ar′dent** (ahr′dĕnt). Intense; fervent; glowing.—"He animated an *ardent* philanthropy with the keenest and brightest intellectual powers."—Winston Churchill.

**im pas′sive** (im pass′iv). Apathetic; showing no feeling; devoid of any signs of emotion; expressing indifference.—"The faces of the men were stupid and *impassive*."—Pearl S. Buck.

**as per′sions** (ass pur′shŭnz). Injurious imputations; slanderous reports; malicious charges; defamations.—"They are trying to stir up trouble by casting *aspersions* on our womenfolk."—Westbrook Pegler.

**plau′dits** (plaw′dits). Expressions of applause; acclamations; shouts of approval; bestowal of praise.—"Too often early *plaudits* later become criticism."—Hattie Caraway.

**as sur′ance** (ă shŏŏr′ănce). Undoubting conviction; full confidence.—"Because there was no *assurance* that these sacrifices counted in the effort, there was distrust and friction."—Leon Henderson.

**mis giv′ing** (miss giv′ing). A feeling of doubt, premonition, or apprehension; anxiety; suspicion.—"Reports of new secret weapons once filled us with dread and *misgiving*."—James H. McGraw.

**as tute′** (ass tūte′). Keen in discernment; shrewd; sagacious.—"I think there is a general feeling that bankers are *astute*."—Charles L. Kaufman.

**gul′li ble** (gul′ĭ b'l). Easily imposed upon; easily cheated or taken in; credulous; simple; capable of being gulled or tricked.—"The midgets sometimes display miniature furnishings for effect on *gullible* spectators."—Robert W. Marks.

**ben″e fac′tion** (ben″ē fak′shŭn). An act conferring a benefit; a boon, or benefit.—"A condition which promotes a profitable business is a public *benefaction*."—Eugene G. Grace.

**det′ri ment** (det′rĭ mĕnt). Anything that impairs, injures, or causes damage or loss.—"Large numbers of refugees could be absorbed without *detriment*, indeed with advantage."—Lord Samuels.

**blithe′ly** (blīthe′li: 'th' as in 'the'). Cheerfully; gladly; gaily; happily.—

"Too many people go *blithely* ahead without any previous training."—Sam A. Lewisohn.

**dis con'so late ly** (diss kon'sō lāte li). Dejectedly; cheerlessly; forlornly; gloomily; inconsolably; desolately; sadly.—"I sat down *disconsolately* at a small table by myself."—Roy Chapman Andrews.

**bois'ter ous** (boyce'tur ŭs). Noisy and tempestuous; vociferous and rough. —"He was six feet of solid brown and *boisterous*, two-fisted masculinity."—Leland Stowe.

**sub dued'** (sŭb dūde'). Reduced in power; toned down; made less intense; repressed; subjugated; controlled.—"He went slowly back to the box, dimly aware of the *subdued* stir going on behind the stage."—Elizabeth Goudge.

**bra'zen** (brāy'z'n). Impudent; shameless; harsh sounding; impudently bold.—"Her enemies are always waiting, sometimes insidious, sometimes *brazen*."—Paul Shipman Andrews.

**un"as sum'ing** (un"uh sūme'ing). Modest; diffident; not putting on airs; unpretentious; shy.—"These portraits have an *unassuming* charm of their own."—Helen Comstock.

**breed'ing** (breed'ing). Good manners; polite behavior; evidences of careful education and training; distinctive characteristics of good birth.—"Some of the young men had considerable pretensions to elegance and *breeding*."—Helen C. White.

**vul gar'i ty** (vul gar'ĭ ti). Coarseness of behavior; lack of good breeding; lack of refinement in conduct or speech; grossness; unrefined manners.—"*Vulgarity* accompanied our feverish industrial expansion."—Walter R. Agard.

**bux'om** (buk'sŭm). Plump and comely; cheerful and full of health; vigorous and jolly.—"There was one *buxom*, masculine woman with her male companion."—Louis Bromfield.

**gaunt** (gawnt). Starved-looking from want of food; emaciated; thin and pinched-looking; wan and bony.—"One was an old, goat-toothed Briton, lean and *gaunt*."—John Masefield.

**ca pri'cious** (kuh prish'ŭs). Fickle; changeable; characterized by unreasonable changes of mood; fitful.—"Adventure and excitement there is, but only within the bounds permitted by gods more *capricious* than those of the Greeks."—Mary Ross.

**in al'ter a ble** (in awl'tur uh b'l). Unchangeable; incapable of being altered or modified.—"I take up my pen now to assure you of the *inalterable* regard and friendship of myself and my son."—André Maurois.

**cal'low** (kal'ō). Not yet feathered, as a bird; hence, not fully grown; inexperienced; youthful.—"A spirit which thinks itself too fine for the rough uses of the world is too young and *callow* to do a man's work in the world."—Thomas Wolfe.

**so phis'ti cat"ed** (sō fiss'tĭ kāte"id). Worldly-wise; having no natural simplicity; artificial and subtle.—"It was still a staple which could be profitably sold in *sophisticated* Manhattan."—John Ferris.

**cen trip'e tal** (sen trip'ē tăl). Moving toward the center; developing from without toward the center or inward; tending toward.—"The *centripetal* forces of integration are mutual good will, faith in the principles of the American Republic, and our economic system."—H. W. Prentis, Jr.

**cen trif'u gal** (sen trif'ū găl). Tending away from a center; radiating out; moving outward away from a center. —"The *centrifugal* forces of social disintegration that would tear us apart are always stronger than the centripetal forces that bind us together in national unity."—H. W. Prentis, Jr.

**chas'ti ty** (chass'tĭ ti). Purity; virginity; continence; virtue.—"They spurn and violate *chastity* and respect for the personality of others."—Denna Frank Fleming.

**in con'ti nence** (in kon'tĭ nĕnce). Lack of restraint; unchastity; inability to control passions or appetites.—"It is just healthy *incontinence*. Chastity now is out of fashion."—H. G. Wells.

**co her'ent** (kō heer'ĕnt). Connected; consistent; made up of related parts; logically joined or connected.—"He found that a weary body had made his brain incapable of *coherent* thought."—John Buchan.

**in"co her'ent** (in"kō heer'ĕnt). Inconsistent; confused; unable to coordinate; disconnected in thought and action.—"He was dumb, *incoherent*, unable to give reasons."—John Masefield.

**com'pe tent** (kom'pē tĕnt). Adequate; capable; able; possessing natural qualifications; having ability and authority.—"He has become a *competent* administrator and a clever advocate."—Louis H. Hacker.

**in ca'pa ble** (in kāy'puh b'l). Incompetent; not capable; possessing very little ability; unfit; inefficient; unqualified; hence, unable.—"The town proved to be *incapable* of producing anybody willing to go with them."—Nevil Shute.

**com"pre hen'sion** (kom"prē hen'shŭn). Understanding; a mental grasp of facts and meanings.—"*Comprehension* must be the soil in which shall grow all the fruits of friendship."—Franklin Delano Roosevelt.

**mis"ap pre hen'sions** (miss"ap rē hen'shŭnz). Misunderstandings; wrong conceptions; mistaken ideas; failures to grasp or understand.—"Her perpetual *misapprehensions* were a standing joke with everybody."—Edith Wharton.

**com pat'i ble** (kŏm pat'ĭ b'l). Capable of existing together; harmonious.—"This policy is most *compatible* with democratic institutions."—Henry L. Stimson.

**in"com pat'i ble** (in"kŏm pat'ĭ b'l). Discordant; opposed; incapable of existing together harmoniously; inconsistent.—"As long as the individ-

ual complies with the party rules he can be an excellent member of the party and behave like a criminal. The two are not *incompatible*."—Dorothy Thompson.

**com mend'a to"ry** (kŏ men'duh tō"ri). Expressing praise; expressive of approbation; putting a favorable opinion into words.—"The speech, on the whole, was flattering and *commendatory*."—Sterling McCormick.

**dis par'ag ing** (diss par'ij ing). Speaking of slightingly; undervaluing.—"I am making some criticisms of a *disparaging* character upon some aspects of our defense."—Winston Churchill.

**con'cave** (kon'kāve). Hollow and rounded, as the interior of a curve or circle; incurved; vaulted.—"The walls, although mostly *concave*, curving in all directions, are well-nigh ideal for murals."—Louis Adamic.

**con'vex** (kon'veks). Curved as the outside of a circular figure; curved out, like the outside of a sphere.—"In the *convex* driving-mirror she could see, dwindling rapidly, the patch of road where they had stood."—Jan Struther.

**con form'i ty** (kŏn for'mĭ ti). Agreement; harmony; compliance with accepted standards of conduct; action according to required forms or rules.—"The colleges were then intended to discipline the minds of a select group of students into *conformity* with the conventions of their day."—Lewis Gannett.

**var'i ance** (vair'ĭ ănce). Disagreement; difference; lack of harmony.—"I do not think anything I say will be at *variance* with what you have heard from my lips in former times."—Maxim Litvinoff.

**con strict'ed** (kŏn strikt'ed). Drawn together or compressed; cramped; bound; contracted.—"It is a conflict between liberal ways of life and narrowly *constricted* ones."—Francis B. Sayre.

**ex pan'sive** (eks pan'siv). Effusive; unrestrained; capable of enlarging;

broad in sympathies.—"He is likely to be *expansive* about himself and his country."—James Truslow Adams.

**con'stant** (kon'stănt). Always remaining the same under the same conditions; invariable.—"The analysis of the material from any given source is fairly *constant*."—J. H. Chesters.

**var'i a ble** (vair'i uh b'l). Apt to change or vary; uncertain; changeable; inconstant; subject to change.—"The caloric value will be *variable* depending essentially on the volume of the food stuffs utilized."—George G. Ornstein.

**con'gre gat"ed** (kong'grē gāte"id). Collected together; assembled; gathered. —"Civilians are *congregated* in these resorts and cities."—Henry H. Arnold.

**dis persed'** (diss purst'). Scattered; separated; distributed; spread out in different places.—"If your listeners are widely *dispersed* encourage them to come closer together."—Daniel P. Eginton.

**con clu'sive** (kŏn klōō'siv). Decisive; final; putting an end to doubt or question; convincing.—"We could not have more *conclusive* evidence that there is a solid understanding." —Walter Lippmann.

**in"con clu'sive** (in"kŏn klōō'siv). Indecisive; not leading to a conclusion or result; not decisive.—"The first claim is *inconclusive*."—William T. Collins.

**con'fi dent** (kon'fĭ dĕnt). Self-reliant; certain; firmly trustful; full of assurance; assured.—"Success soon gave him a *confident* manner."—Bertram M. Myers.

**tim'or ous** (tim'ur ŭs). Timid; fearful of danger; easily frightened.—"Some children tend to react to feelings of insecurity with *timorous*, self-conscious behavior."—Samuel Z. Orgel.

**cra'ven** (krāy'vĕn). Cowardly; full of fear.—"Idle and futile is the voice of the weak nation, or the *craven* nation, when it clamors for peace."—Frank Knox.

**un daunt'ed** (un dawn'ted). Fearless; intrepid; courageous; unafraid; undismayed; refusing to be discouraged.—"*Undaunted*, they continued to write amateur shows for churches and clubs."—David Ewen.

**cres cen'do** (krĕ shen'dō). Gradual increase of power.—"The air power roars in an ever heightening *crescendo*."—James H. Doolittle.

**di min"u en'do** (di min"ū en'dō). Gradually lessening in volume of sound; gradually diminishing in force.—"It is quite difficult for pianists to make a quick *diminuendo* on a trill."—Orville A. Lindquist.

**cre du'li ty** (krē dū'lĭ ti). A proneness to accept what is improbable; a disposition to believe on slight evidence.—"The pendulum of human emotion has swung first towards exaggerated *credulity* and then towards equally exaggerated incredulity."—James B. Conant.

**in"cre du'li ty** (in"krē dū'lĭ ti). Unbelief; doubt; indisposition to believe; skepticism.—"She gave a sniff of *incredulity* as she listened to the story."—Edith Wharton.

**curbed** (kurb'd). Controlled; held in subjection.—"Petty sins if not *curbed* can become great."—Walter K. Kellenberg.

**un bri'dled** (un brī'd'ld). Unrestrained; uncurbed; violent; uncontrolled.—"The new capitalism is shedding the last traces of its memory of *unbridled* individualism."—Eric A. Johnston.

**cul'pa ble** (kul'puh b'l). Deserving of blame or censure; faulty.—"Those who set the policies are the *culpable* officials."—James E. Murray.

**mer"i to'ri ous** (mer"i tō'ri ŭs). Deserving of reward; praiseworthy; entitled to gratitude or honor; worthy of merit.—"If believing is a merit in itself, it is certainly more *meritorious* to believe something that is hard to believe."—Don Marquis.

**cur tail'ment** (kur tail'mĕnt). A cutting short; a retrenchment; a reduction.—"This bill represents a *curtailment* of an important social protection."—Thomas E. Dewey.

**en hance′ment** (en hance′mĕnt). Increase; advance.—"The struggle has found expression in the *enhancement* of the people's welfare."—Adolf A. Berle, Jr.

**de cried′** (dē krīde′). Said disparaging things about; discredited; belittled; condemned.—"Our enemies have *decried* and sought to destroy our religious faiths."—Herbert C. Hoover.

**eu′lo gized** (ū′lō jīze'd). Extolled; praised very highly; lauded; commended.—"The professor was being *eulogized*."—Betty Smith.

**de fam′a to″ry** (dē fam′uh tō″ri). Slanderous; scandalous.—"The bill will provide punishment for any *defamatory* and false statements."—Walter A. Lynch.

**laud′a to″ry** (lawd′uh tō″ri). Expressing high praise.—"Notwithstanding these *laudatory* remarks I intend to assume a democratic attitude."—Harvey T. Harrison.

**dis″al lowed′** (diss″ă loud′: 'ou' as in 'out'). Disapproved; rejected; prohibited; refused acceptance; not allowed or sanctioned.—"These backgrounds would entail prohibitive costs or costs *disallowed* by restrictions."—William Dozier.

**sanc′tioned** (sangk′shŭnd). Approved authoritatively; ratified; permitted; authorized.—"No further price increases are to be *sanctioned*."—Franklin Delano Roosevelt.

**dis creet′** (diss kreet′). Judicious; careful; having good judgment in action and speech; speaking only at opportune moments; avoiding mistakes and keeping one's own counsel.—"Rubens had to conduct some *discreet* conversations with the politicians."—Frederic Taubes.

**in″ju di′cious** (in″jōō dish′ŭs). Unwise; indiscreet; imprudent; ill-advised; lacking in judgment.—"He wondered whether his master thought this remark was *injudicious*."—Lloyd C. Douglas.

**dis″en gag′ing** (diss″en gāje′ing). Releasing something that is held; detaching; loosening; freeing from entanglement; extricating.—"The copilot starts by *disengaging* his safety belt."—Francis Vivian Drake.

**en tan′gling** (en tang′gling). Catching in a trap or snare; hence, preplexing; complicated; involving; leading to difficulties.—"These commitments are not more *entangling* than those which we have already taken."—Winston Churchill.

**dis fig′ured** (diss fig′yŏŏrd). Spoilt the beauty of; marred; defaced; injured or impaired the appearance of."—In the great room below the gallery damp stains *disfigured* the walls."—Elizabeth Goudge.

**em bel′lished** (em bel′isht). Ornamented; decorated; made beautiful by additional ornamental features.—"Many are the statues of military heroes which great art has *embellished*."—Monroe E. Deutsch.

**dis″in clined′** (diss″in klīne'd′). Not inclined or disposed; averse; unwilling.—"I don't actually dislike golf, but I am *disinclined* to play it."—Bradwell E. Tanis.

**prone** (prōne). Mentally inclined or disposed; liable.—"We are *prone* to think of the electric locomotive as a comparatively recent creation."—C. M. A. Stine.

**dis in″te gra′tion** (diss in″tē grā′shŭn). Gradual wasting and decay; breaking up; destruction of unity.—"This philosophy led us to business chaos and in the direction of social and political *disintegration*."—Hugo L. Black.

**fu′sion** (fū′zhŭn). Blending; coalition; fusing together; union; alliance.—"What particularly lifts these painters to an honorable level is their *fusion* of sincerity and truth."—Royal Cortissoz.

**dis pir′it ed** (diss pir′it ed). Disheartened; depressed; discouraged.—"Her narrative does not give any real insight into what life is like for the

depraved and *dispirited* multitudes."
—Florence Haxton Bullock.

**vi va′cious** (vī vā′shŭs). Lively; animated; full of life and spirits; merry; light-hearted;sparkling.—"The dominating rhythm is *vivacious* and burbling."—William J. Calvert, Jr.

**dog′ged ly** (dog′ed li). Sullenly persistent; tenaciously; stubbornly determined.—"The people coolly and *doggedly* solve their problems."—Gordon W. Allport.

**ir res′o lute ly** (i rez′ō lūte li). In an undetermined, undecided way; hesitatingly; doubtfully; waveringly; vacillatingly.—"At first he held this rude cross *irresolutely* in his hands."—Franz Werfel.

**dy nam′ic** (dī nam′ik). Producing activity; efficient; making use of force. —"The so-called *dynamic* nations intend to expand by fair means or foul."—Dorothy Thompson.

**stat′ic** (stat′ik). At rest; not moving forward; quiescent.—"Life seems to remain *static* for thousands of years and then to shoot forward with amazing speed."—Robert A. Millikan.

**ef fec′tu al ly** (e fek′chŏŏ ă li). Adequately; in a way that produces an intended result; efficaciously; in a way that answers the purpose.—"If I was a treat for him to look at he concealed his feelings very *effectually.*"—Irvin S. Cobb.

**in″ef fec′tu al ly** (in″e fek′chŏŏ ă li). Uselessly; vainly; unavailingly; without producing any effect.—"Her mother *ineffectually* called after her."—Edith Wharton.

**em′i grate** (em′ĭ grāte). To leave a home or country in order to settle permanently in another.—"People of the professional type are most inclined to *emigrate.*"—Dorothy Thompson.

**im″mi grat′ed** (im″ĭ grāte′id). Came into a country of which not a citizen in order to settle there; moved into a country in order to establish permanent residence there.—"They had *immigrated* to America many years before."—Bruce Ellsworth.

**e″nig mat′i cal** (ē″nig mat′i kăl). Puzzling; inexplicable; perplexing; baffling; mysterious; that cannot be understood.—"He remained in a pose of *enigmatical* attention."—H. G. Wells.

**lu′cid** (lū′sid). Intellectually clear; easy to understand; clearly expressed; bright and normal.—"The style of the biography is *lucid* and good."—James Truslow Adams.

**en no′bling** (en nō′bling). Raising to a higher level; making noble; exalting. —"Can anything we are called upon to do compare with the heroic sacrifice that is *ennobling* the common people?"—Thomas W. Lamont.

**mor′ti fy ing** (mor′tĭ fī ing). Humiliating; vexatious; humbling; deadening.—"These episodes are *mortifying* to national pride."—James Rowland Angell.

**er′u dite** (er′ŏŏ dīte). Very learned; scholarly.—"These are thoughts only, not *erudite* opinions and conclusions formed after deep and prolonged study."—Madame Chiang Kai-shek.

**un tu′tored** (un tū′turd). Untaught; ignorant; uninstructed; unschooled. —"One needs to distinguish the cultivated person from the ignorant and *untutored.*"—Daniel P. Eginton.

**es″o ter′ic** (ess″ō ter′ik). Adapted exclusively for the initiated and enlightened few; understood by only a select few; secret.—"I must have recourse to the *esoteric* knowledge of the breeders."—Peter Schmuck.

**ex″o ter′ic** (ek″sō ter′ik). Intelligible to the uninitiated; belonging to outsiders; suitable for the public; hence, easily understood.—"The Gnostic sects believed in the existence of esoteric and *exoteric* teachings, the latter reserved for the many, the former for the few."—Aldous Huxley.

**ex trin′sic** (eks trin′sik). Outward; outside; external; coming from without; not inherent.—"*Extrinsic* stimuli are found in food substances, proper temperature, moisture, etc."—Edwin G. Conklin.

**in trin'sic** (in trin'sik). Belonging to the nature or essence of a thing; real; essential; true.—"He should try to understand society as an *intrinsic* unity."—Pius XII.

**ex'o dus** (eks'ō dŭs). A departure; a going forth from one's country.—"There must be an *exodus* of these refugee children."—Hyman Judah Schachtel.

**in'flux** (in'fluks). A continuous flowing in.—"The *influx* of new materials into the building field may become an important factor."—Arthur A. Hood.

**ex pres'sive** (eks press'iv). Significant; carrying much feeling or expression; conveying special emphasis or expression.—"The philosopher Emerson defended slang as being forceful and *expressive*."—Malcom Babbitt.

**in"ar tic'u late** (in"ahr tik'ū lāte). Dumb; unable to express oneself clearly.—"If the realtors become *inarticulate* now the habit of government rule over private property will become fixed."—Cyrus Crane Willmore.

**fe lic'i tous** (fē liss'ĭ tŭs). Happily expressed; appropriate; apt; happy in effect.—"He caught the changeful moods of the music in the most *felicitous* and subtle manner."—Olin Downes.

**lu gu'bri ous** (lū gū'bri ŭs). Doleful; exaggeratedly solemn; mournful.—"The story is tangled and *lugubrious*, with much to be said on either side."—John Gunther.

**fick'le** (fik"l). Liable to change; changeable; unstable; vacillating; variable.—"There were long spells of *fickle* weather between winter and summer."—Ralph Parker.

**im mu'ta ble** (i mū'tuh b'l). Unchangeable; invariable; permanent; incapable of change.—"The laws of economics are as *immutable* as those of mathematics."—Louis Bromfield.

**fic ti'tious** (fik tish'ŭs). False; counterfeit; that do not really exist.—"Se-curity holders should not be permitted to be misled by entries showing *fictitious* assets."—Milo R. Maltbie.

**ver'i ta ble** (ver'ĭ tuh b'l). True; genuine; actual; real.—"He has to his credit a *veritable* giant—a mural landscape 150 feet in length."—Homer Croy.

**fig'ur a tive"ly** (fig'yŏŏr uh tiv"li). In a typically mental rather than a literal sense, hence symbolically.—"Groups of the human family have broken camp; they are on the march, both literally and *figuratively*."—J. Hillis Miller.

**lit'er al ly** (lit' ur ă li). According to the letter, hence, exactly as to fact or detail; according to the exact import or meaning.—"We must do *literally* everything in our power to increase the supplies."—Edward R. Stettinius, Jr.

**fin'i cal** (fin'i kăl). Very precise and fussy; overnice or fastidious in dress or habits; affecting an unduly dainty manner; too refined.—"The author portrayed him as a feminine type of man with *finical* habits."—Malcom Babbitt.

**un kempt'** (un kempt'). Untidy; disheveled; of neglected appearance.—"The patients were *unkempt* and unshaven."—George W. Mills.

**flus'tered** (fluss'turd). Confused and flurried; excited and befuddled; in a bustling, agitated state.—"The tiny cabin was crowded and hot, the visitors bewildered, the chairman of the committee *flustered*."—Emma Bugbee.

**im"per turb'a ble** (im"pur tur'buh b'l). Calm; unexcitable; incapable of being disturbed; not easily agitated.—"The *imperturbable* officer lined up the lot and calmly collected their knives."—Eric Sevareid.

**fra'grance** (frāy'grănce). A pleasant scent; a sweet-smelling odor; agreeable, pleasing redolence.—"As he wandered down the glen he recalled their walk along the same path in its summer *fragrance*."—Edith Wharton.

**stench** (stench). A very offensive odor; a stink; a very bad smell; a foul odor. —"The air was filled with the bitter *stench* of burning metal."—Richard Llewellyn.

**fu ne′re al** (fū neer′ē ăl). Very solemn and sad; suitable for a funeral; gloomy; dismal; mournful; doleful. —"He says that even her *funereal* titles were sardonic exclamations on the part of an individual at the idea of her own demise."—J. Donald Adams.

**ju′bi lant** (jōō′bĭ lănt). Exultant; joyful; exultingly glad; elated with happiness.—"Another 10,000 tons of paper per annum would make all these publishers *jubilant*."—Frank Swinnerton.

**grave** (grāve). Important; momentous; of serious import; formidable.— "Have you considered the *grave* responsibilities you incur?"—Bruce Ellsworth.

**triv′i al** (triv′i ăl). Of little importance; insignificant; petty.—"Underneath this seemingly *trivial* incident in world affairs were the rivalries that made Europe a battleground."— John Cudahy.

**il leg′i ble** (il lej′ĭ b'l). Very difficult to read; not legible; not easy to read; not very plain or decipherable; unreadable.—"He often repeated a sentence which gave her a second or two to polish off her notes, almost *illegible* from the speed of her writing."—Emma Bugbee.

**leg′i ble** (lej′ĭ b'l). Easy to read; readable; written in a clear, well-formed script.—"His name, burned into a cypress plank, was not plainly *legible*."—Lloyd C. Douglas.

**il lit′er a cy** (il lit′ur uh si). The state of being untaught; the inability to read and write.—"Wandering scholars frustrated the design to reduce the people to *illiteracy*."—Eamon de Valera.

**lit′er a cy** (lit′ur uh si). Ability to read and write; a knowledge of letters; hence, educational condition.—"We cannot hope to raise the *literacy* of other nations and fail to roll back ignorance in our own communities." —Henry A. Wallace.

**log′i cal** (loj′i kăl). Pertaining to the science of correct thinking; of the art of reasoning or the use of argument; hence, reasonable; in accordance with correct reasoning; clearly inferred from circumstances.—"Each episode was a *logical* outgrowth of what went before."—Roy Chapman Andrews.

**il log′i cal** (il loj′i kăl). Contrary to the rules of correct reasoning; not reasonable; not according to reason, sound sense, or the science of proof; not logical.—"The German women believed, with that strange *illogical* hope that seems natural to women, that they would have a home and a husband."—Pearl Buck.

**mo′bile** (mō′bil). Freely movable; able to change position very easily.—"The actress has the most expressive and *mobile* features I have ever seen."— Donald G. Cooley.

**im mo′bile** (im mō′bil). Unmovable; fixed; motionless; not able to move. —"The grasshopper has five *immobile* eyes that are so placed that it can see in all directions at once."— H. Radclyffe Roberts.

**par″ti al′i ty** (pahr″shi al′ĭ ti). Special liking; favoring one more than others; prejudice in favor of someone; predilection.—"I only hoped that they would show no *partiality*, but be as fair to me as they were to him."— Irvin S. Cobb.

**im par″ti al′i ty** (im pahr″shi al′ĭ ti). The quality or character of being unbiased and just; fairness; showing no favoritism.—"They will preserve the *impartiality* of our courts."— Winston Churchill.

**ob′vi ous ly** (ob′vi ŭs li). Clearly; plainly; easily seen; perceptibly.— "He made his points too *obviously*, underlined his effects with too heavy a hand."—Dorothy Canfield.

**im″per cep′ti bly** (im″pur sep′tĭ bli).

Without being seen or recognized.—
"The solution will come almost *imperceptibly.*"—Francis B. Sayre.

**pi′ous** (pī′ŭs). Devout; religious; godly; devoted to God and religious acts; showing a reverential spirit.—"Naturally they show their most *pious* face to the West."—Dorothy Thompson.

**im′pi ous** (im′pi ŭs). Having no reverence for sacred or private things; lacking respect; irreverent or undutiful.—"One of those *impious* girls might cry out if they saw the curls on the dressing-table."—EdithWharton.

**om nip′o tence** (om nip′ō tĕnce). Unlimited and universal power: unlimited power within a certain sphere, or of a certain kind.—"People in distress over-estimate the *omnipotence* of legislation."—George W. Maxey.

**im′po tence** (im′pō tĕnce). Weakness; feebleness; lack of physical or moral power; helplessness.—"Successive surrenders would end by impressing the idea of *impotence* and submission upon the people's mind."—André Maurois.

**po′tent** (pō′tĕnt). Powerful; convincing; efficacious; able to influence; having authority; mighty.—"These first-hand reports have proved a *potent* influence."—Charles Thomson.

**im′po tent** (im′pō tĕnt). Lacking in power; weak; feeble.—"The result of this one-sided arrangement was a chronically *impotent* French cabinet." —John Chamberlain.

**qual″i fi ca′tion** (kwol″ĭ fi kā′shŭn). That which fits a person for something.—"Signing a check has remained the principal *qualification* of a United States Secretary of the Treasury."—Will Rogers.

**in com′pe tence** (in kom′pē tĕnce). General lack of ability or capacity; unfitness.—"The demand for power to compel is a confession of *incompetence* to lead."—Eugene E. Wilson.

**ques′tion a ble** (kwess′chŭn uh b′l). Doubtful; uncertain; open to question or doubt; dubious; liable to be called in question.—"We have no sure knowledge, but at the least his actions appear *questionable.*"—Ellery Marsh Egan.

**in″con test′a ble** (in″kon tess′tuh b′l). Indisputable; unquestionable; undeniable; hence, certain.—"We must accept the *incontestable* fact that war cannot be localized."—Maxim Litvinoff.

**staunch** (stawnch). Constant; faithful; true; loyal; unwavering.—"He was a *staunch* believer in the conservation of wildlife."—John H. Baker.

**in con′stant** (in kon′stănt). Changeable; fickle; variable; not constant; unstable.—"Some thought the fetters kept the *inconstant* goddess from running away, others admitted that they were for punishment."—Caroline Dale Snedeker.

**man′i fest** (man′ĭ fest). Evident; apparent; obvious.—"Benefits are already becoming *manifest* and will continue to grow."—Cordell Hull.

**in″con spic′u ous** (in″kŏn spik′ū ŭs). Not attracting attention; not obvious; not easily discerned; keeping out of public notice.—"He must be as *inconspicuous* as possible and keep his work confidential."—Thomas C. Desmond.

**pru′dence** (prōō′dĕnce). Wise forethought or caution in practical affairs; sagacity and good judgment; discretion; economical use of resources.—"This lack of *prudence* amounted to a crime."—Winston Churchill.

**in″dis cre′tion** (in″diss kresh′ŭn). Indiscreetness; imprudence; lack of foresight or judgment.—"We believe him in his *indiscretion* and know he won't fail."—H. G. Wells.

**pro pi′tious** (prō pish′ŭs). Attended by favorable circumstances; kindly disposed; auspicious; favorable.—"He wanted to ask him something, tell him something, but did not feel the moment *propitious.*"—John Buchan.

**in op″por tune′** (in op″ŏr tūne′). Unfitting; unseasonable; untimely; inappropriate; inconvenient; unsuitable.—"The present moment is a singularly *inopportune* time to cherish tender scruples."—J. Donald Adams.

**sig nif′i cant** (sig nif′ĭ kănt). Important; containing some special meaning; standing as a sign for something; expressing something of value, or momentous.—"The Supreme Court decision prevented the Government from trying another *significant* case."—Thurman Arnold.
**in″sig nif′i cant** (in″sig nif′ĭ kănt). Unimportant; trifling; trivial; slight.— "The first model was so well designed that only *insignificant* changes in it have ever been made."—Erik Wästberg.

**tan′gi ble** (tan′jĭ b'l). Able to be touched and felt; real; evident; actual, not illusive.—"There are, fortunately, *tangible* advantages on our side."—Warren J. Clear.
**in tan′gi ble** (in tan′jĭ b'l). That cannot be touched; not easily grasped by the mind.—"The kinship of the Americas, *intangible* in itself, is based on the tangible fact of a common land."—Henry A. Wallace.

**val′id** (val′id). Founded on sufficient legal force; lawfully binding; effective; supported by authority.—"This decree is not *valid* in North Africa." —Henri H. Giraud.
**in val′id** (in val′id). Not valid or effective; indefensible; without any force or authority; groundless.—"The question is *invalid* because the studios do not change every book."—William Dozier.

**ra′tion al** (rash′ŭn ăl). Having the ability to think and reason clearly, hence, judicious; based on reason; intelligent.—"Attention to the intrinsic values rather than to marked prices is an essential to *rational* investment."—Fred C. Moffatt.
**ir ra′tion al** (ir rash′ŭn ăl). Unreasonable; not possessing or not using reasoning powers; hence, absurd; foolish.—"We cannot start too soon to combat *irrational* propaganda."— Bertrand Russell.

**per′ti nent** (pur′tĭ nĕnt). Relevant; properly bearing on the matter; applicable and to the point.—"The *pertinent* facts and considerations relating thereto are these."—Sumner Welles.
**ir rel′e vant** (ir rel′ē vănt). Unrelated; not applicable to the matter; not to the point; inappropriate; not adapted to the purpose.—"We soon lose the feeling that the groupings are incongruous and *irrelevant*."—William Allen White.

**joc′und** (jok′ŭnd). Merry; cheerful; pleasant and jocular; having a blithe and gay manner or disposition; mirthful.—"A fat, friendly, *jocund* priest met us."—Charles Henry Crozier.
**plain′tive** (plāne′tiv). Mournful; sorrowful; expressing sadness; melancholy.—"As for the Stanzas to Augusta, he found these intolerably *plaintive*, and parodied them mercilessly."—André Maurois.

**jus″ti fi′a ble** (juss″tĭ fī′uh b'l). Shown to be right and just; capable of being shown to be fair and fit; worthy to be approved.—"Seniority rules that keep older men and women in jobs are, in the main, *justifiable*."—E. W. Palmer.
**un war′rant ed** (un wawr′ănt ed). Unjustifiable; not defensible; unauthorized; not guaranteed; not assured.— "The general declared that in *unwarranted* criticism of any Ally we are simply playing into the hands of the enemy."—Frederick C. Painton.

**strin′gent** (strin′jĕnt). Rigid; severe; strict; constrained; bound closely to requirements.—"Since our space limitations are *stringent*, we have been forced to confine our efforts to school children."—Kenneth S. Rice.
**le′ni ent** (lee′ni ĕnt). Merciful; clement; indulgent; forbearing; kind.— "You have been so *lenient* in permitting me to exercise my fancy on the studio."—John Barrymore.

**max'i mal** (mak′sĭ măl). Highest; greatest possible.—"Our debt had reached its *maximal* point."—Malcom Babbitt.

**min'i mal** (min′ĭ muhl). Least; in the least possible degree; as little as possible.—"To physicians, this indicates that it will do its best work on *minimal* or moderately advanced patients, before the system is completely infected."—Ralph Wallace.

**men da'cious** (men dā′shŭs). Addicted to lying; deceitful; false; lying.— "This revolution has been characterized as the meanest and most *mendacious* revolution the world has ever known."—Arthur Garfield Hays.

**ve ra'cious** (vē rā′shŭs). True; accurate; conforming to the truth; honest; truthful.—"This exquisitely wise and humorous book is as close to a *veracious* and universal biography of scholarly youth as this generation is likely to enjoy."—Christopher Morley.

**mer'ci ful** (mur′si fŏol). Full of mercy or willingness to spare and forgive; exercising more kindness than justice requires; compassionate; humane; forbearing.—"It was possible that a *merciful* judge would spare them."— W. Somerset Maugham.

**ruth'less** (rōoth′less). Pitiless; cruel; showing no mercy; merciless.—"This drama of *ruthless* gang violence occurred just a few weeks ago."—J. Edgar Hoover.

**mod″ern is'tic** (mod″urn iss′tik). Expressive of modern types; characteristic of up-to-date designs and materials.—"On the film one could see the small plateau and the dark *modernistic* mass of the hotel."— Thomas Kernan.

**out mod'ed** (owt mōde′id). Out of fashion; no longer approved; not in vogue any longer.—"This approach demands the scrapping of *outmoded* prejudices."—Fraser Bond.

**na'dir** (nāy′dur). The point of the celestial sphere directly beneath where one is standing; hence, the lowest possible point or depth.—"At the *nadir* of my despair a solitary singer appeared."—William J. Calvert, Jr.

**ze'nith** (zē′nith). The point in the celestial sphere that is exactly overhead; hence, the peak or highest point of anything.—"Rachmaninoff left this world at 'the *zenith* of his power." —Alexander Brailowsky.

**ob lig'a to″ry** (ob lig′uh tō″ri). Morally binding; legally required; imposing an obligation or duty.—"We would not make any automatic and *obligatory* commitments in regard to them."—Winston Churchill.

**op'tion al** (op′shŭn ăl). Depending on choice; not compulsory; left to a person's choice; alternative.—"The officers who opposed fixed requirements now favor *optional* distribution."—Frank D. Loomis.

**o pac'i ty** (ō pass′ĭ ti). Non-transparency; the quality or state of not allowing light to pass through; opaqueness.—"The piece of glass had the *opacity* of onyx."—Donald G. Cooley.

**trans par'en cy** (trance pair′ĕn si). Something that allows light to pass through it; something transparent or diaphanous; something without opacity.—"He passed the spot where she stood as if she were mere *transparency*."—Margaret Lee Runbeck.

**o paque'** (ō pāke′). Letting no light through; hence, obscure; dark; unintelligent; unintelligible.—"The meaning of the act is being smeared over with the usual *opaque* coating of official pronouncements."—Freda Kirchwey.

**pel lu'cid** (pĕ lū′sid). Transparent; easy to understand; clear.—"Starting with the simplest and most *pellucid* of styles, he hid himself more and more in a billowing cloud of words."—Ludwig Lewisohn.

**os″ten ta'tious ly** (oss″ten tā′shŭs li) Pretentiously; in a way that attracted notice or made a public display; pompously.—"He learnt the inadvisability of quitting the game *ostentatiously* and vindictively."—H. G. Wells.

**un″ob tru′sive ly** (un″ŏb trōō′siv li). Without seeking to attract attention; without putting themselves forward; unassumingly; without ostentation. —"*Unobtrusively* they rode the lines as passengers, their noses pressed against the windows."—Frank J. Taylor.

**par″si mo′ni ous** (pahr″sĭ mō′ni ŭs). Stingy; niggardly; penurious; sparing in spending money.—"She had gained several small favors from her *parsimonious* employer."—Edith Wharton.

**wast′rel** (wāce′trĕl). Spendthrift; wasteful; profligate.—"Will you be the *wastrel* heirs of a glorious patrimony?" —Irving T. McDonald.

**pa tri′cian** (puh trish′ăn). Belonging to the aristocracy or nobles.—"I am thinking of the beautiful *patrician* mansions in Italian towns."—William Ralph Inge.

**ple be′ian** (plē bee′yăn). Pertaining to the common people; hence, of a lower class; inferior; common; vulgar.—"It was considered *plebeian* to speak Russian except to servants."— Roy Chapman Andrews.

**pro lif′ic** (prō lif′ik). Abundantly productive; freely reproductive.—"The well is not as *prolific* as it used to be.— Charles L. Kaufman.

**ster′ile** (ster′ĭl). Barren; unproductive; unfruitful; incapable of producing results.—"His leadership would be a *sterile* thing were it not based on the enormous stability given China by her peasantry."—Bruce Ellsworth.

**ra′di ant** (rāy′di ănt). Brightly shining; beaming with joy; sending out or disseminating rays of happiness and love.—"He hoped to meet the crippled girl with the *radiant* face and the golden voice."—Lloyd C. Douglas.

**som′ber** (som′bur). Dark and gloomy; partly deprived of light; murky; dusky.—"Threading the *somber* gorge, we reached the outpost."—Eleanor Lattimore.

**un war′y** (un wair′i). Incautious; taking no precautions against danger; unguarded; not on the lookout.— "We no longer stalk the forest to pounce upon *unwary* prey."—George Barton Cutten.

**vig′i lant** (vij′ĭ lănt). Watchful; careful; active; alert.—"Understandable ceiling prices and *vigilant* enforcement should hold the line."—Prentiss M. Brown.

## ONE-MINUTE REFRESHER

There are a number of opposite meanings for each of the eight words listed below. See if you can recall and write down at least five. In a few cases you may find this exercise exceptionally difficult. But don't begrudge too much the time that you spend. You are working towards a great accomplishment.

1. propitious
2. constant
3. approbation
4. vehement

5. consonant
6. prudence
7. affluence
8. veracious

*Answers:* 1. adverse, antagonistic, forbidding, harsh, hostile, ill-disposed, repellent, inauspicious, unfavorable, unfriendly. 2. changeable, infrequent, variable, impermanent, irregular, unfaithful, unreliable, unsteady, fickle, inconstant. 3. derogation, disapproval, odium, displeasure, disaffection, dislike, dissent, distaste, blame, censure, obloquy, disparagement, depreciation, condemnation, disapprobation. 4. apathetic, calm, composed, immobile, indifferent, quiet, lethargic, sluggish, unemotional. 5. antagonistic, contrary, contradictory, irreconcilable, incongruous, inharmonious, incompatible, inconsistent, discordant, inconsonant. 6. indiscretion, carelessness, recklessness, negligence, improvidence, foolhardiness, incautiousness, imprudence. 7. pauperism, poverty, destitution, need, penury, privation, want, beggary, indigence, mendicancy. 8. mendacious, false, deceptive, untruthful, lying, fraudulent, deceitful, dishonest, disingenuous.

# CHAPTER XI

## YOUR NOUNS OF POWER

NOUNS OF POWER can be used by the expert with terrific force. I remember a startling instance of this. A few years ago I was a guest at a coffee plantation that bordered one of the jungles on the Pacific slope of Guatemala.

The padron and I often passed the long tropical evenings in discussions of international politics.

On one occasion he asked: "Do you know why your President is so popular with us down here?"

I answered with an exploratory "No."

"Well," he replied, "all of your Presidents before him have spoken of 'America' meaning only the United States. *He*, for the first time in our history, said 'the Americas,' and that magic word suddenly included all of us and sent an electric thrill down through the Latin Republics from the Mexican border to the tip of Cape Horn."

We sometimes claim that one small word holds enough TNT to blow up the world. Here is an example of just one small letter, the letter "s," which turned a singular noun into a plural and generated such astounding power that it could help gain millions of friends for us to the South. And yet the actual physical force of a word as it comes out of a person's mouth has been computed as one-thousandth of one millionth of one horse power!

On another occasion early in the days of World War II, a sign was posted at the dock of a New Jersey ferry slip that read, "Smoking is Forbidden." The passengers who were smoking all hurried by the placard with no more than an indifferent glance. One late afternoon as we walked off the boat we saw that a new sign had been put up. This one read: "Smoking is SABOTAGE." That single noun, "sabotage," instantaneously snuffed out every cigarette in sight.

These are sharp examples that prove the truth of Mark Twain's old phrase. "The difference," said he, "between the right word and the almost right is the difference between lightning and the lightning bug."

Examples of this artistry in the use of nouns can be found again and again in the writings and the speeches of the influential men and women of our time.

It is no accident, for instance, when John Haynes Holmes says: "The social order cracks up in one vast *cataclysm* of ruin and death." Nor is it just a matter of chance when Orville Prescott writes: "Scornful *diatribes* almost drowned out the loud cheers."

These men, and the many others whom you will find quoted in this chapter, had these nouns to draw upon when the occasion arose.

Those who use words well and can choose the right word instead of the almost right word were not born with this ability. They possibly even had no natural aptitude. They knew that a limited vocabulary presented a cruel and unnecessary handicap and they studied consciously to overcome that handicap.

The nouns printed in the next few pages are the living, lusty products of the genius of our language. You will find that some of them are as sensitive as an apothecary's scales. Others are as blunt as cudgels, or as sharp as knives, or as salty as the sea.

If you too will study to possess the nouns that are listed here and if you will become so adept in their use that you can command them to your purpose, you will have learned one more secret of the power of words.

## YOUR NOUNS OF POWER

**a bom″i na′tion** (uh bom″ĭ nā′shŭn). Something to be loathed; that which is hateful and repugnant.—"It is hateful, it is distasteful, it is an *abomination*, and we ought to get rid of it."—Clarence Darrow.

**ac″qui si′tion** (ak″wi zish′ŭn). The act of obtaining; possession.—"The *acquisition* of huge territories is not a synomym for winning a war."—Dorothy Thompson.

**ac′ri mo ny** (ak′rĭ mō ni). Sharpness or bitterness of speech or temper.—"Some people maintain that the absence of hope would prevent the *acrimony* of a losing fight."—Madame Chiang Kai-shek.

**ad″u la′tion** (ad″ū lā′shŭn). Servile flattery; extravagant praise.—"Such universal *adulation* must seem desirable."—John W. Davis.

**ad ver′si ty** (ad vur′sĭ ti). Hardship; continual misfortune; distress; disaster; calamity.—"People resting in prosperity sink; nations fighting to chip footholds in the ice-cliff of *adversity* rise."—Allan Nevins.

**af flic′tion** (ă flik′shŭn). Distress of mind or body; great suffering or grief.—"He has been stricken down by an *affliction*."—Winston Churchill.

**ag″i ta′tion** (aj″ĭ tā′shŭn). Violent emotion; disturbance of mind or body; excitement; perturbation.—

"He noted how curious it was that any kind of *agitation* always fired his courage anew."—André Maurois.

**ag'o ny** (ag'ō ni). Anguish; extreme mental or bodily suffering; torture; an intense struggle of mind or body. —"The world is emerging from the *agony* of its Gethsemane."—Jack Bond.

**an"i mos'i ty** (an"ĭ moss'ĭ ti). Enmity; hostility; ill will.—"Despite the outward signs of peace between the two groups, some sub-surface *animosity* persists."—M. S. Rukeyser.

**a"plomb'** (uh"plom'). Self-assurance; confidence; poise and self-possession. —"He presided throughout the evening with the *aplomb* of a corporation lawyer."—John H. Fulweiler.

**ap"per cep'tion** (ap"ur sep'shŭn). Keen mental perception; intellectual power used to create awareness through all the senses; the connecting of new with former knowledge.— "The faculty of *apperception* was highly developed in the painter, Angelica Kauffmann."—Douglas Brewster.

**ar ray'** (ă rāy'). An imposing display of persons or things; an impressive series; a regular arrangement.— "There was an *array* of fine friends at the wedding."—W. Somerset Maugham.

**ar'son** (ahr's'n). The spiteful or malicious burning of a dwelling or other structure.—"The loss of property by destruction by *arson* reaches an incredible sum."—Edmund A. Walsh.

**as cend'an cy** (ă sen'dăn si). Supreme influence; domination; sway; most influential control; paramount power over.—"He came quickly to rejoice in the *ascendancy* of this swift, urgent man."—Caroline Dale Snedeker.

**as per'i ty** (ass per'ĭ ti). Harshness or sharpness of temper; severity; irritability; acrimony.—"There was a touch of *asperity* in his voice."— Emma Bugbee.

**as sev"er a'tions** (ă sev"ur āy'shŭnz). Emphatic assertions; affirmations; solemn statements; earnest and positive declarations.—"The premeditation of his preparations for war gave the lie to all his *asseverations* of peace-

ful intentions."—Louis P. Lochner.

**as"si du'i ty** (ass"i dū'ĭ ti). Close and continuous application and effort.— "I know with what constancy and *assiduity* the propaganda factories manufacture stories."—Carlton J. H. Hayes.

**a troc'i ties** (uh tross'ĭ tiz). Shocking cruelties; outrageously cruel deeds.— "I heard of the horrible *atrocities* perpetrated in the rape of Nanking."— Joseph C. Grew.

**au"then tic'i ty** (aw"then tiss'ĭ ti: 'th' as in 'thin'). Genuineness; reliability; undisputed origin; validity.—"These attempts at *authenticity* are often frustrated by self-styled experts."—Hilary St. George Saunders.

**ba'bel** (bā'b'l). A confusion of many voices and languages; tumult.—"In this *babel* of strange voices not one voice was raised in genuine sympathy for the middle class."— Howard G. Fuller.

**bal'der dash** (bawl'dur dash). An empty and pretentious flow of words; nonsense.—"All such talk seems ridiculous *balderdash* when applied to America."—James Rowland Angell.

**bed'lam** (bed'lăm). A wide scene of uproar and confusion; an incoherent tumult; formerly the name of an old priory in London which was turned into a lunatic asylum.—"Today the *bedlam* of the world beats in everyone's ears."—Hugh McK. Landon.

**be he'moth** (bē hē'moth). An enormous creature described in the Bible; probably the hippopotamus.—"In the deceptive shadows of the forest the cougar looked like a *behemoth*."— Donald G. Cooley.

**big'ot ry** (big'ŭt ri). Obstinate and intolerant attachment to a cause or creed.—"It is *bigotry* of all sorts that I have fought and hated all my life." —Thomas E. Dewey.

**bil'lings gate"** (bil'ingz gāte"). A London fish market which was notorious for bad language; hence, coarse and abusive talk; violent invective; vulgar, vituperative language.—"She poured out a flood of *billingsgate* that would better fit the tongue of an angry fishwife."—Malcom Babbitt.

**bo'vine** (bō'vīne). An ox; a cow; a bovine animal; a steer.—"They rope the *bovine* and get it down with a minimum of trouble."—Ernest Douglas.

**brag'gart** (brag'urt). A vain boaster; one who brags; a person who is fond of making vainglorious statements.— "We are confident that you now know him for a *braggart*, a gasbag, and an impostor."—H. I. Phillips.

**brut'ish ness** (broōt'ish ness). Behaving like a brute or savage; coarseness; grossness; barbarity; brutal cruelty. —"What we are doing has been attempted before but it has made little or no impression on the *brutishness* and stupidity of mankind."—L. P. Jacks.

**cal'um ny** (kal'ŭm ni). A false, malicious accusation or report; a slander. —"It was a lie as black, a *calumny* as foul and atrocious, as ever issued from a human throat."—Eugene V. Debs.

**car'nage** (kahr'nij). Extensive and bloody slaughter.—"The King knew that no military purpose could justify further *carnage*."—John Cudahy.

**ca rous'al** (kuh rouz'ăl: 'ou' as in 'out'). A drinking party; a drunken revel; a boisterous feast or revel.— "This was not an ordinary brawl; this was a general, united *carousal*." —Thomas Mann.

**cas"ti ga'tion** (kass"tǐ gā'shŭn). Severe rebuke or criticism.—"He singles them out for *castigation*."—L. J. Dickinson.

**cat'a clysm** (kat'uh kliz'm). A sudden upheaval or overwhelming change.— "The social order cracks up in one vast *cataclysm* of ruin and death."— John Haynes Holmes.

**ce ler'i ty** (sē ler'ǐ ti). Speed; swiftness; rapidity; quick motion.—"I never knew an elevator to progress to the ninth floor with such *celerity*."— Irvin S. Cobb.

**cen'sure** (sen'shur). Condemnation; strong disapproval; adverse criticism. —"They keep up a constant paean of praise of all things American, and un-American has become a comprehensive term of *censure*."—Bertrand Russell.

**cha'os** (kāy'oss). Complete disorder; the confused state of the unformed universe; hence, a state of utter confusion and disorder.—"She has vanished into the cruel limbo of a world in *chaos*."—George N. Shuster.

**char'la tans** (shahr'luh tănz). Pretenders to knowledge; quacks; impostors. —"Many *charlatans* try to attribute to government Omniscience and Omnipotence."—Lionel Robbins.

**cli'max** (klī'maks). A culmination; the highest point in a series; a turning point; highest point of intensity.— "The battle has reached a *climax*."— Dwight D. Eisenhower.

**com pul'sion** (kŏm pul'shŭn). Coercion; the act or state of being obliged or forced to do something.—"This is not an issue between voluntarism and *compulsion*."—Robert P. Patterson.

**com punc'tion** (kŏm pungk'shŭn). Self-reproach for wrong doing; slight regret.—"We've got to teach these men to kill without *compunction*."— Charles L. Soctt.

**con cus'sion** (kŏn kush'ŭn). Violent shock; severe shaking; great jar.— "Skyscrapers in Japan are ingeniously built to withstand the *concussion* of earthquakes."—Joseph Clark Grew.

**con"dem na'tion** (kon"dem nā'shŭn). Censure; the act of pronouncing guilty; strong disapproval.—"Cardinal Hinsley was uncompromising in his *condemnation* of wicked deeds and evil schemes."—Richard Downey.

**con"fis ca'tion** (kon"fiss kā'shŭn). The act of seizure as a forfeit.—"Argentina's officials are against *confiscation* of these ships."—Herbert Clark.

**con"fla gra'tion** (kon"fluh grā'shŭn). A great and extensive fire.—"When on the western prairies a *conflagration* starts, men fight fire with fire."— Harry Emerson Fosdick.

**con"ster na'tion** (kon"stur nā'shŭn). Sudden overwhelming fear or alarm; confused terror; terrifying amazement.—"We shall see a flow of munitions that will strike relentlessly at our enemies, to their *consternation* and utter dismay."—John J. Jouett.

**con vic'tion** (kŏn vik'shŭn). A firm belief; a state of being convinced.—"I have an inner *conviction* that we Americans have learned our lesson." —Thomas W. Lamont.

**de bauch'er y** (dē bawch'ur i). Sensuality; indulgence in impurity; moral corruption; licentiousness; intemperance; carousal.—"Why do you yourself bray before them in their dance of *debauchery?*"—Thomas Mann.

**de ca'dence** (di kāy'děnce). Process of deterioration; decline; decay.—"The myth of European *decadence* is shattered."—Joseph C. Grew.

**dep"re da'tions** (dep"rē dā'shŭnz). Robberies; acts of plundering and ravaging.—"Very serious *depredations* were committed on the east coast of America."—Winston Churchill.

**der"e lic'tions** (der"ě lik'shŭnz). Failures in duty; wilful omissions; neglect of duty; shortcomings.— "Certain *derelictions* short of crime are so special to the society that 'toils not' as to indicate cause and effect."—Channing Pollock.

**de serts'** (dē zurts'). Deserved punishments; merited returns; penalties for wrong doing or rewards for good behavior.—"He was getting his just *deserts* under the law of divine retribution."—Dorothy Thompson.

**des"o la'tion** (dess"ō lā'shŭn). A state or condition of dreariness, affliction, and devastation.—"War causes desecration and *desolation*."—Francis J. Spellman.

**de spoil'er** (dē spoyl'ur). Plunderer; robber; one who seizes the belongings of others.—"They would welcome the opportunity to put a bayonet into the *despoiler* of their ancestral homeland."—George E. Sokolsky.

**des"ti tu'tion** (dess"tǐ tū'shŭn). Extreme poverty; a condition of lack and want, being utterly devoid of all resources and the means of living.— "The slow process of losses may end in an impoverished death bed before actual *destitution* supervenes."—H. G. Wells.

**de ter"mi na'tions** (dē tur"mǐ nā'shŭnz). Resolutions; resolves; firm decisions; fixed purposes.—"We have new *determinations* that our future

shall surpass even our past."—Fannie Hurst.

**de ter'rent** (dē ter'ěnt). Prevention or restraint from action, as by fear of consequences.—"Perhaps the greatest present *deterrent* to world cooperation is a tendency to admit its desirability, but to say it is impossible to work out."—Harold E. Stassen.

**de tract'ors** (dē trak'turz). Defamers; slanderers.—"For all my imitators, for all my *detractors*, I have one unique response, a good drawing."—Salvador Dali.

**di'a tribes** (dī'uh trībe'z). Abusive dissertations; invectives; bitter discussions.—"Its critical reception was mixed, scornful *diatribes* almost drowning out a number of loud cheers."—Orville Prescott.

**dic'tate** (dik'tāte). An authoritative prompting; a rule or maxim.—"It is our heart's *dictate* to safeguard the deposit which we have been commissioned to keep."—Pius XII.

**dis patch'** (diss patch'). Speed; prompt performance and completion of work. —"We must act with greater *dispatch* and great efficiency."—James F. Byrnes.

**dis"pu ta'tions** (diss"pū tā'shŭnz). Discussions; debates; controversies; argumentations.—"I avoid those religious *disputations* like the plague."— Hendrik Willem Van Loon.

**dis"so lu'tion** (diss"ō lū'shŭn). The act of dissolving or melting away; a breaking up into parts or separating; a falling to pieces; a coming to an end.—"Our old American society is really in *dissolution*."—John Buchan.

**dolt** (dōlt). A very dull stupid person; a blockhead; a dunce.—"The *dolt* set off, shambling down the road."— Lloyd C. Douglas.

**dull'ard** (dul'urd). A very dull or stupid person; a person of slow understanding; a dolt.—"Some of the faculty will be intensely interested in the difficulties of the *dullard*."— Charles Seymour.

**dy nam'ics** (dī nam'iks). The movements of physical and other forces; the forces producing or governing activity.—"The *dynamics* of his personality had been directed into channels different from mine."—Roy Chapman Andrews.

**ec'sta sy** (ek'stuh si). Mental exaltation; extravagant and overpowering emotion; rapture; overmastering joy. —"There seems to be some climatic influence at work that produces a soaring *ecstasy* of yearning wistfulness."—Percy Aldridge Grainger.

**ef'fi ca cy** (ef'ĭ kuh si). Effectiveness; power to produce the intended result; potency or force.—"We will make the burglar doubt the *efficacy* of burglary, then the world will become safe for good people."—Rebecca West.

**ef flu'vi a** (e flōō'vi uh). Ill-smelling exhalations, as from decaying matter or sewers; invisible emanations that are noxious.—"There was an old conception that the *effluvia* given off from lungs and from human skin was poisonous."—Howard W. Haggard.

**ef fron'ter y** (e frun'tur i). Audacity; boldness; presumptuousness; undue liberty.—"The government has the *effrontery* to spend money lavishly for the making over of other nations."— Hugh Butler.

**ef ful'gence** (e ful'jĕnce). Radiance; splendor; beaming brightness; diffusion of light.—"The shop windows glowed with brightness. Nothing I have ever seen could compare with this *effulgence*."—Hilary St. George Saunders.

**e la'tion** (ē lā'shŭn). Jubilant state of mind; high spirits; happy pride; exultation; excitement following success.—"She spoke with the *elation* of one who is a connoisseur of foul weather."—Christopher Morley.

**e lim"i na'tion** (ē lim"ĭ nā'shŭn). Removal or casting out; exclusion; a getting rid of.—"A great deal of thought has been given to the *elimination* of interference in television broadcasting."—Robert Eichberg.

**e man"ci pa'tion** (ē man"si pā'shŭn). Liberation from bondage or dependence; making free.—"We believe that the ultimate *emancipation* of the people depends upon their right to work out their own destiny."— Ernest Bevin.

**e nor'mi ty** (ē nor'mĭ ti). Great wickedness; atrocity; depravity; outrageousness; enormous or monstrous sin.—"Not until the crime had been committed did I realize the *enormity* of it."—Lloyd C. Douglas.

**en thrall'ment** (en thrawl'mĕnt: 'th' as in 'thin'). Enslavement; slavery; bondage; servitude.—"To contemplate this state of existence is to envisage a new era of economic *enthrallment*."—Raymond H. Geist.

**en thu'si asts** (en thū'zi asts: 'th' as in 'thin'). People who have very keen interests in something; those who are filled with enthusiasm and zeal for some course or cause; ardent adherents; zealots.—"He moved his home so that his daughters, who were keen tennis *enthusiasts*, could live nearer to the champion."—Keith Monroe.

**e"qui lib'ri um** (ē"kwĭ lib'ri ŭm). A state of balance produced by the counteraction of two or more forces. —"A social order within a nation must strive not so much for unattainable equality as manageable *equilibrium*."—Owen D. Young.

**ex"al ta'tion** (eg"zol tā'shŭn). A mental state of great joy; ecstatic emotion; rapture; elation.—"They left him in a daze of *exaltation*."—Franz Werfel.

**ex as"per a'tion** (eg zass"pur āy'shŭn). Extreme anger; great irritation; intense and continued aggravation; bitter vexation.—"I might have saved my *exasperation*, for the incident was typical of many to follow."— W. Stephen Thomas.

**ex'i gen cies** (eks'ĭ jĕn siz). Pressing needs or demands; critical conditions.—"We have agreed not to remain longer than military *exigencies* require."—Francis J. Spellman.

**ex'ple tive** (eks'plē tiv). An oath; an exclamation, often profane; an expression, often a swear word, used as emphasis.—"He turned to fling back a snorting *expletive* over his shoulder." —Stephen Vincent Benét.

**ex ter"mi na'tion** (eks tur"mĭ nā'- shŭn). Total destruction; complete eradication; utter annihilation.—"It is a sober report on systematic *exter-*

*mination* by starvation."—Edmund Wilson.

**ex tinc′tion** (eks tingk′shŭn). A putting an end to something; a destroying. —"We have reached the stage where restriction and curtailment means *extinction*."—Walter D. Fuller.

**ex trem′i ty** (eks trem′ĭ ti). Greatest need or peril; greatest danger; extreme distress; the utmost or farthest point of endurance.—"It was in the days when England was in her most dire *extremity*."—Bradwell E. Tanis.

**ex u′ber ance** (eg zū′bur ănce). Superabundance of action or the like; overflowing energy.—"We know that hey fought with the same fearless *xuberance*, the same combative exaltation."—Frank Knox.

**fan′fare** (fan′fair). A noisy parade; a showy display.—"The men who sail the vessels go about their appointed tasks with the minimum of *fanfare*." —Frank J. Taylor.

**fas″ci na′tion** (fass″ĭ nā′shŭn). Enchantment; charming allurement; strong attraction.—"I can never forget the *fascination* I felt when hearing the performance of Rachmaninoff for the first time."—Artur Schnabel.

**fa tal′i ty** (fa tal′ĭ ti). A disaster causing death; a calamity resulting in death; a fatal or destructive misfortune ending in death.—"It is fantastic that a ship could explode in mid-ocean without a single *fatality*." —Ellery Marsh Egan.

**fe lic′i ty** (fē liss′ĭ ti). Great happiness; blissfulness; a state of comfort and contentment.—"A man without a heart and soul cannot enjoy spiritual *felicity*."—Henry W. Taft.

**fer′ment** (fur′ment). Excitement or agitation; tumult; stirring up.— "There has not been such a *ferment* of ideas for a generation."—Barbara Ward.

**fe roc′i ty** (fē ross′ĭ ti). Fierceness; savageness; fierce cruelty; brutal wildness.—"He recorded all with a kind of lurid imagination and with nothing less than *ferocity*."—Royal Cortissoz.

**fer′vor** (fur′vur). Ardor; zeal; enthusiasm; intensity of feeling.—"Moved by democratic *fervor*, Bolivia declared

the existence of a state of war."— Enrique Penaranda.

**fi as′co** (fē ass′kō). A complete or humiliating failure.—"In our ears ring the taunts of mockery and the reproach of *fiasco*."—Winston Churchill.

**fi nal′i ty** (fī nal′ĭ ti). A final, conclusive, or decisive act or determination. —"Peaceful solutions of *finality* must be sought in the appropriate tribunal."—William L. Green.

**for′ti tude** (for′tĭ tūde). Strength of mind to meet pain, peril, or adversity; resolute courage; firm endurance.—"We must learn again the patience and *fortitude* that armed our ancestors."—William O. Douglas.

**fren′zy** (fren′zi). Madness; delirium; fury; mental excitement.—"He knew that his army, in a *frenzy* of desperation and despair, might revolt."— John Cudahy.

**frus tra′tion** (fruss trā′shŭn). Failure; defeat; prevention from accomplishment.—"There sometimes come moments of fatigue, and occasionally, even a sense of *frustration*."—Jan Christiaan Smuts.

**gam′ut** (gam′ŭt). The whole range of anything; a complete series.—"Between these extremes is the whole *gamut* of variations." — Robert Gordon Sproul.

**gas″con ade′** (gass″kŏn āde′). Boasting; bragging talk; braggadocio; bluster. —"A simple question on my part brought forth a torrent of *gasconade*." —Donald G. Cooley.

**gib′ber ish** (jib′ur ish). Meaningless chatter; incoherent gabble; foolish and unintelligible talk.—"We are threatened with the second Fall of Man, the fall from reason to *gibberish*."—William Alfred Eddy.

**gibes** (jībe′z). Taunting words; sneering remarks; scoffs; sarcastic expressions.—"After a few attempts to talk to her and some *gibes*, they let her alone."—Sigrid Undset.

**griev′an ces** (greev′ăn siz). Causes of grief or sorrow; wrongs; injustices.— "Then will be the time to deal with the *grievances* of the discontented nations."—Winston Churchill.

**gus′to** (guss′tō). Enjoyment and appreciation that is full of zest; keen enjoyment and relish; hearty appreciation. —"The things he is personally interested in go forward with brilliance and *gusto*."—Walter Lippmann.

**ha rangue'** (huh rang'). A vehement speech; a ranting oration.—"His hour-long *harangue* was without a single constructive suggestion."—Joseph T. Robinson.

**har'ri dan** (har'ĭ dăn). A hag; a vixenish old woman; a vixen; a haggard old woman.—"That old *harridan* of an aunt of yours has been talking melodrama."—Helen C. White.

**hav'oc** (hav'ŭk). General destruction; devastation; ruin.—"He may carry *havoc* into the Balkan States."—Winston Churchill.

**hel'lions** (hel'yŭnz). People given to deviltry and bad deeds.—"Our men are determined that his *hellions* will never again crash their lines."—Roane Waring.

**hire'ling** (hīre'ling). A mercenary; one who works for money only and has no interest in the result of his work.—"The case must not be tried secretly before some *hireling* of a despot, but publicly before a jury."—Monroe E. Deutsch.

**hoax** (hōke'z). A trick or deception; a practical joke.—"This is another *hoax*, as unreal as a reported invasion from Mars."—Franklin Bliss Snyder.

**hov'els** (hov'ĕlz). Huts; small, mean dwellings; wretched houses.—"He visited the sick and sat for hours in airless caves and *hovels*."—Helen C. White.

**hy poc'ri sy** (hi pok'rĭ si). Extreme insincerity; the feigning to be what one is not.—"Jane Austen never says anything directly against *hypocrisy* or pretentiousness."—Dorothy Canfield Fisher.

**ig"no ra'mus** (ig"nō rā'mŭs). An ignorant pretender to knowledge; an ignorant person.—"Somebody has got to start something, and it may have to be some intrepid *ignoramus*."—Edward A. Filene.

**im men'sity** (i men'sĭ ti). Vastness; boundless extent; immeasurable space; hugeness; limitless expanse.—

"The houses and fields were small and solitary upon the *immensity* of these ever broadening arms of land."—Pearl S. Buck.

**im'pact** (im'pakt). A collision or forceful contact.—"The *impact* of a strike is felt throughout the nation.—Sidney Hillman.

**im'pe tus** (im'pē tŭs). Driving energy; momentum; vigor; force.—"Battle awaited you, and into it you threw the strength and courage of your young manhood with such an *impetus* as to turn the whole tide of war."—Francis J. Spellman.

**im"por tu'ni ty** (im"por tū'nĭ ti). Repeated demands; insistent and troublesome asking; annoying pertinacity. —"Never before has the power of *importunity* been so perfectly demonstrated."—Paul F. Cadman.

**im"pre ca'tions** (im"prē kā'shŭnz). Curses; invocations of evil on someone; maledictions; execrations; words calling forth calamities.—"As he stumbled on through the darkness, the raging *imprecations* followed him as far as the old gate."—Lloyd C. Douglas.

**in fer'no** (in fur'nō). The infernal regions; hell; hence, a place of torture, a hellish place.—"Following the roar of explosions, great clouds of smoke and later leaping flames rose over the *inferno*."—Francis B. Sayre.

**in junc'tion** (in jungk'shŭn). An urgent admonition; authoritative instruction; an order.—"It seemed odd that several different persons should be given the same touching *injunction*."—Somerset Maugham.

**in"si pid'i ty** (in"si pid'ĭ ti). Dullness; monotony; lack of interest; flatness; vapidity; tastelessness.—"She realized the *insipidity* of inspecting plants in the company of a suspicious head gardener."—Edith Wharton.

**in sis'tence** (in siss'tĕnce). Urgent pressure; emphatic demands; persistent repetition of a statement.—"We approve labor's *insistence* on the development of a great system of free public education."—Matthew Woll.

**in'tri ca cies** (in'trĭ kuh siz). Complexities; complications; perplexing and involved states; difficult details.—

"Her father, a tea and oil merchant, had never learned the *intricacies* of customs and accounting."—Pearl S. Buck.

**in vec'tive** (in vek'tiv). A violent accusation; railing abuse; bitter condemnation.—"Victor Hugo excoriated Napoleon III with magnificent *invective*."—Orville Prescott.

**in vin"ci bil'i ty** (in vin"si bil'ĭ ti). State of being unconquerable; condition of strength that cannot be weakened or overcome by anyone.—"She is counting on each of us to delay our effort long enough for her to consolidate her potential *invincibility*."—Joseph C. Grew.

**i ras"ci bil'i ty** (i rass"ĭ bil'ĭ ti). Extreme irritation; hot anger; choler; hot-tempered annoyance.—"He was full of the pent-up *irascibility* of the past weeks."—Robert G. Chaffee.

**jeop'ard y** (jep'ur di). Danger; peril; exposure to death or injury.—"His life is too valuable to be put in *jeopardy*."—Lloyd C. Douglas.

**ju"bi la'tion** (jōō"bĭ lā'shŭn). Rejoicing; exultation; noisy and joyous festivity.—"His birthday was cause for *jubilation* and celebration."—Mark Eisner.

**jug'ger naut** (jug'ur nawt). The idol of Vishnu drawn on a heavy cart under whose wheels devotees would throw themselves; hence, any custom or creed that demands ruthless sacrifice.—"The *juggernaut* was too strong. It had prepared itself for seven long years."—Yates Stirling, Jr.

**jus"ti fi ca'tion** (juss"tĭ fi kā'shŭn). Justifying; good excuse or reason; ground that shows something to be right and just; defense or vindication.—"There is no reasonable *justification* for the new taxes."—Bertram M. Myers.

**knav'er y** (nāve'ur i). Deceitfulness in dealings; fraud; trickery; dishonesty; roguery.—"The chapters of our history are crammed with accounts of conspiracy, patriotism, bravery, and *knavery*."—John Kieran.

**lag'gard** (lag'urd). Loiterer; one who moves slowly and falls behind.—"The American Bar Association is proving itself to be no *laggard* in considering the situation."—George R. Farnum.

**lar'ce ny** (lahr'sĕ ni). Small thefts; taking and carrying away things unlawfully.—"Small boys were contemplating the *larceny* of a mince pie or a cake."—Edwin C. Hill.

**lev'i ty** (lev'ĭ ti). Lack of seriousness; trifling thoughtlessness; frivolous gaiety; lack of mental gravity.—"Let me also warn you against the *levity* and nonsense which he likes."—André Maurois.

**li"a bil'i ty** (lī"uh bil'ĭ ti). Something to one's disadvantage; something that detracts from strength instead of adding to it.—"An unfit man at the front is a *liability*, not an asset."—George Barton Cutten.

**lib'er tine** (lib'ur teen). One who does not restrain his desires or appetites; a dissolute or immoral person.—"We call the alien a *libertine*, the instigator of everything that means license."—Harold Fields.

**lust** (lust). Strong desire; eagerness; excessive appetite; inordinate or vigorous inclination.—"He likened the *lust* for material success to the serpent in the fable that ate up all the other serpents."—Ludwig Lewisohn.

**lust'i ness** (luss'ti ness). Vigor; healthfulness; robustness; strength and liveliness.—"San Francisco is tinged with the color of the Orient and the *lustiness* of the pioneers."—Harrison Smith.

**mag'nate** (mag'nāte). A person of rank and power; a great man; an important person; a notable and prominent person in a large industry.—"He tells the story of a mighty French automobile *magnate*."—Bennett Cerf.

**mag'ni tude** (mag'nĭ tūde). Great size; vastness; immensity.—"It should be possible to finance the program without increasing the *magnitude* of current treasury deficits."—Harold G. Moulton.

**mal"e dic'tions** (mal"ē dik'shŭnz). Invocations of evil; curses.—"The political party heaped *maledictions* upon the existing order."—William Allen White.

**mal′e fac″tors** (mal′ē fak″turz). Criminals; evildoers; felons.—"This levy on the people is collected by an army of *malefactors* who make their living through crime."—Edmund A. Walsh.

**ma lev′o lence** (muh lev′ō lĕnce). The character of having an evil disposition towards others; maliciousness; evil intentions; spitefulness.—"We witnessed the cruel *malevolence* of a barbarian."—Eugene V. Debs.

**ma lig′ni ty** (muh lig′nĭ ti). Very great malice; great harmfulness; malevolence; maliciousness; virulent ill-will.—"If he had not been so occupied with his own personality, he might have remarked the extreme *malignity* of the face before him."—H. G. Wells.

**ma′ni ac** (māy′ni ak). A madman; a lunatic; an insane person; a crazed and raving madman; a person affected with mania.—"There goes the *maniac* who started all this racket!"—William L. Shirer.

**mas′sa cre** (mass′uh kur). Slaughter; indiscriminate killing of numbers of people.—"Slavery became a substitute for *massacre*."—Harry Emerson Fosdick.

**maun′der ing** (mawn′dur ing). Grumbling; murmuring incoherently; muttering.—"Mawkish *maundering* will not equip us for our battle through life."—Madame Chiang Kai-shek.

**max′i mum** (mak′si mŭm). The greatest quantity or number; the greatest possible number.—"He has the gift of compressing the *maximum* of words into the minimum of thought."—Ramsey MacDonald.

**maze** (māze). Embarrassment; perplexity; confusion; bewilderment.—"Tangled and lost in the *maze* of his own emotions, he knew not which way to turn."—Emory L. Fielding.

**mê″lée′** (māy″lāy′). An affray; a general hand-to-hand fight; a skirmish; a confused, mixed-up fight among a number of persons.—"Any attempt to carry out these reconstructions would result in a general *mêlée*."—L. P. Jacks.

**men′ace** (men′iss). A threat; an impending evil.—"If the poison is allowed to remain, a serious *menace* to life may result."—John D. Rockefeller, Jr.

**men dac′i ty** (men dass′ĭ ti). Lying; falsity; untruth; deceit; untruthfulness.—"It is a ringing call to resist the loathsome creed that any man by *mendacity* and crimes may ride on the backs of his fellow men over the sacred things of life."—Claude Bowers.

**mi nus′cule** (mi nuss′kūle). A very small ancient writing or letter; hence, miniature; very small scale.—"In these sketches he gives you his world —primitive, lovely, sordid, in *minuscule*."—Florence Haxton Bullock.

**min′ions** (min′yŭnz). Servile favorites; hence, slavish creatures.—"It is a battle to the death against the multiple *minions* of crime."—J. Edgar Hoover.

**mis′cre ants** (miss′krē ănts). Evil-doers; villains; depraved people; unscrupulous and base people.—"His fate may serve other *miscreants* with the reminder that the wages of sin is death."—Winston Churchill.

**mi′ser li ness** (mī′zur li ness). Stinginess; a state of accumulating money and goods and living miserably; a reluctance to part with any possession.—"Our *miserliness* does not lie in the value we place upon our money or our lives."—Frederick L. Schuman.

**moil** (moyl). Drudgery; toil; confusion; trouble; turmoil.—"Had the East been beaten in this bloody *moil?*"—Thomas Wolfe.

**mo′ment** (mō′mĕnt). Importance; consequence; far-reaching weight or influence.—"Labor unions are facing problems of great *moment*."—Jack Bond.

**mo men′tum** (mō men′tŭm). Impetus of a moving body; energy gained by motion.—"The supreme cause is now gathering *momentum* as it rolls forward to its goal."—Winston Churchill.

**mon stros′i ties** (mon stross′ĭ tiz). Things unnaturally distorted, malformed, or enormous; abnormal forms or growths.—"The *monstrosities* began where the personal knowledge of the artist ended."—Willy Ley.

**mu nif'i cence** (mū nif'ĭ sĕnce). Lavish generosity; great liberality; extreme bountifulness.—"I have heard your *munificence* to the nurse described as a false emphasis."—L. P. Jacks.

**nem'e sis** (nem'ē siss). The goddess of chastisement and vengeance; hence, retribution; downfall, brought about by just punishment.—"Your inertia may spell your own *nemesis*."—Charles L. Kaufman.

**non en'ti ty** (non en'tĭ ti). A person of no importance; a nobody; a person of very little importance or account.—"She won't be thrown away on this poor *nonentity*, at all events."—Edith Wharton.

**ob lit"er a'tion** (ŏb lit"ur āy'shŭn). Destruction so as to leave no trace; abolishment.—"Anything short of total *obliteration* of the enemy as a nation will be a compromise."—Westbrook Pegler.

**ob liv'i on** (ŏb liv'i ŭn). Forgetfulness; the state of being forgotten; the act of erasure from memory.—"Their names are now shriveled by the fires of *oblivion*."—P. W. Wilson.

**ob scen'i ty** (ŏb sen'ĭ ti). Indecency in word and act; offensive and immodest language or actions; lewdness.—"These men reduced themselves to a common denominator of boorishness, *obscenity*, and truculence."—Edmund Wilson.

**ob tuse'ness** (ŏb tūce'ness). Dullness; lack of perception; insensitivity; stupidity.—"She marvelled once more at the *obtuseness* of the most brilliant men."—Edith Wharton.

**o'di um** (ō'di ŭm). Something hated; offensiveness; great disgust; reprobation or condemnation incurred by a person or an action; opprobrium.—"Impeachment brought the office to its lowest point, and Grant added the *odium* of corruption."—Avery Craven.

**of'fal** (off'ăl). Garbage; worthless rubbish; refuse of any kind.—"The pigeons clucked as they picked for *offal* in the cobblestones."—Helen C. White.

**on'slaught"** (on'slawt"). A violent hostile attack; a furious assault.—"Behind this armored and mechanized *onslaught* came a number of infantry divisions."—Winston Churchill.

**op pro'bri um** (ŏ prō'bri ŭm). Disgrace or scornful reproach caused by shameful conduct; infamy; ignominy; disdainful or abusive reproach.—"America does not share this general *opprobrium*."—Orville Prescott.

**os'tra cism** (oss'truh siz'm). Exclusion from all intercourse; banishment from all privileges and favors; prohibition from participation.—"Independent spirits are subjected to official browbeating and *ostracism*."—H. W. Prentis, Jr.

**out'rage** (owt'rāje). An act of shocking violence or cruelty.—"The same kind of *outrage* against every form of signed compact was repeated on a far larger scale."—Winston Churchill.

**o va'tion** (ō vā'shŭn). An enthusiastic reception; a burst of welcoming applause; a spontaneous outburst of welcome.—"They greeted him that morning with the murmured *ovation* and the trampling of feet."—Jules Romains.

**pal'lor** (pal'ur). Paleness; lack of color; pallid or wan appearance.—"They had wanted to paint the building red, but the landlord opposed the idea, and so it had the dingy *pallor* of its neighbours."—H. G. Wells.

**pan"de mo'ni um** (pan"dē mō'ni ŭm). A place remarkable for disorder and uproar.—"A national workshop must be either a gigantic workhouse under rigid discipline or a huge *pandemonium* of uncontrolled idleness."—George W. Maxey.

**pang** (pang). A keen, piercing pain; a sudden, sharp pain; a twinge; a throe of mental anguish.—"Conscience gave him no *pang*—he merely wondered how the captain would work it out."—Franz Werfel.

**par'a gon** (par'uh gon). A model of excellence; a type of something perfect.—"It is man's superior brain that makes him the *paragon* of animals."—Edwin Grant Conklin.

**per di'tion** (pur dish'ŭn). Eternal death; torment; hell; utter destruction; damnation; hence, ruin; loss.—

"It is man's *perdition* to wish to be safe in a static world, when he should be ready to die for a truth in a world of flux."—Allan Nevins.

**per'fi dies** (pur'fĭ diz). Acts of faithlessness; treacherous actions; deeds that violate faith or allegiance.— "Byron himself had experienced how far mean *perfidies* can go towards spoiling a life that should have been one of beauty."—André Maurois.

**per'pe tra"tors** (pur'pē trā"turz). Persons guilty of committing crimes; those who perform or do something, especially something bad or wicked. —"The *perpetrators* of these crimes shall answer for them."—Franklin Delano Roosevelt.

**per"ti nac'i ty** (pur"tĭ nass'ĭ ti). Tenacity of purpose; steady adherence to a pursuit or opinion; persistency.—"If we possess the *pertinacity* to bring it into being, what was yesterday regarded as impossible becomes today the reality."—Madame Chiang Kai-shek.

**per'verts** (pur'vurts). Corrupted people; renegades; apostates; those who forsake religion or principles; people who lead immoral lives.—"He died in the hands of those unutterable *perverts*."—Sigrid Undset.

**phe nom'e non** (fē nom'ē non). A fact or event that can be observed and can be scientifically explained; an extraordinary event or thing.—"The spring migration of birds is a much less marked *phenomenon* on the Pacific coast than in the eastern States."— John H. Baker.

**pil'lage** (pil'ij). Open robbery; the act of plundering.—"He launched his armies upon new fields of slaughter, *pillage*, and devastation."—Winston Churchill.

**pit'tance** (pit'ănce). A very small portion; a small allowance; a meager allowance or dole.—"None of them should receive compensation—anyhow not more than a *pittance*."— Lord Vansittart.

**pol lu'tion** (pŏ lū'shŭn). Defilement; impurity; uncleanness; contamination.—"He decided that the *pollution* of the water might have come from the hands of the drillers."—Elinor Graham.

**pol troons'** (pol trōōnz'). Mean or spiritless cowards; dastards; craven men; lazy idlers.—"It was to the Empire's advantage to have such *poltroons* in high office throughout all the provinces."—Lloyd C. Douglas.

**por ten'tous ness** (por ten'tŭs ness). Gravity; solemnity; ominousness; significance.—"But the author needs this slow-motion *portentousness* to carry off her absurd story."—Edmund Wilson.

**po'ten tate** (pō'tĕn tāte). A person having great power; a person in authority; a ruler.—"The local *potentate* was a fat, amiable gentleman."— Franz Werfel.

**pre pon'der ance** (prē pon'dur ănce). Excess of influence or power; superiority; an overbalance.—"The proposal would give Britain a slight *preponderance* of voting power."— Redvers Opie.

**pro cras"ti na'tion** (prō krass"tĭ nā'-shŭn). The act or habit of putting off till a future time; delay; dilatoriness. —"That kind of *procrastination* is not mere perversity."—Leon Fraser.

**prod'i gies** (prod'ĭ jiz). Persons having remarkable powers or talents; extraordinary people; abnormally clever people.—"She concluded we must be *prodigies*."—Gretchen Finletter.

**pro fes'sions** (prō fesh'ŭnz). Open declarations; avowals; affirmations of faith in something; acknowledgments. —"*Professions* of democracy in America have never meant much more than they have anywhere else."— Don Marquis.

**pro fun'di ty** (prō fun'dĭ ti). Depth; profoundness; great depth.—"He is an intelligent performer, pretending to no excessive emotional *profundity*." —Stephen Somervell.

**pro fu'sion** (prō fū'zhŭn). Abundance; bountiful supply; generous quantity. —"In most parts of Latin America flowers grow in riotous *profusion*."— Henry A. Wallace.

**pro nounce'ment** (prō nounce'mĕnt: 'ou' as in 'out'). A declaration or formal announcement; a solemn or formal statement.—"It was a solemn *pronouncement* listened to with breathless interest."—Douglas E. Lurton.

**pug nac′i ty** (pug nass′ĭ ti). Disposition to fight; combativeness; love of fighting.—"I am not forgetting the gratification that war gives to the instinct of *pugnacity*."—George Bernard Shaw.

**pur′port** (pur′port). Meaning; gist; implication; significance; general tenor.—"Even though the talk reduced the first classroom period by several minutes its *purport* was devastating."—Christopher Morley.

**qui e′tus** (kwī ee′tŭs). A final quittance or settlement; hence, a silencing of life; death; also, a decisive blow.— "The good American word *quietus* probably owes its life and currency to Shakespeare's 'Hamlet.' "—Christian Gauss.

**ram page′** (ram pāje′). Boisterous agitation; a dashing about with anger or violence; a wild and reckless outbreak.—"Everything he was doing meant he would pretty soon go on a *rampage*."—Cordell Hull.

**ra pac′i ty** (ruh pass′ĭ ti). The act of seizing what is coveted; greed; grasping actions; extortion.—"Great patriots struggled in vain against the *rapacity* of some of the people."— Gordon Heriot.

**rec′re ant** (rek′rē ănt). A coward; a faithless person; a deserter; a traitor to a cause.—"He became convinced that he would be a *recreant* and a sinner if he deserted his post."—Don Marquis.

**re crim″i na′tion** (rē krim″i nā′shŭn). Abuse; abusive argument; accusation.—"Let us remember that *recrimination* and hatred will lead us nowhere."—Madame Chiang Kaishek.

**re nun″ci a′tion** (rē nun″si āy′shŭn). Giving up; abandoning pursuits or habits; self-denial; sacrifice.—"The way to a joyful and happy state is through *renunciation* and self-limitation everywhere."—Albert Einstein.

**re″per cus′sions** (rē″pur kush′ŭnz). Rebounds; reverberations; reciprocal effects; results in return for something.—"Such a system would have great *repercussions* in the world economic system."—Henry A. Wallace.

**re proof′** (rē prōōf′). Censure for faults; expression of blame or disapproval; a reprimand or rebuke.—"The generals had to face the stern *reproof* of Napoleon."—Jack Bond.

**re ver″ber a′tions** (rē vur″bur āy′shŭnz). Echoes of sound; prolonged and recurring sounds.—"My windows rattled with *reverberations* from the explosions."—Arthur Menken.

**re vil′ings** (rē vīle′ings). Defamations; abusive speeches; railings against something or someone; using vilifying language.—"Recriminations and *revilings* get nowhere."—M. W. Clement.

**re vul′sion** (rē vul′shŭn). A violent recoil; a sudden reaction; a quick change of feeling; a sudden withdrawal.—"The major pushed away the pack of passports with a gesture of *revulsion*."—Franz Werfel.

**ri gid′i ties** (ri jid′ĭ tiz). Resistances to change; inflexibilities; strict customs; firm and unchangeable rules.—"Both industry and labor were protected by economic *rigidities*."—Edward A. O'Neal.

**ro′bots** (rō′bŏts). Automatons; figures that work mechanically and heartlessly.—"If we harness the human mind we shall have *robots* instead of workers."—Dorothy Thompson.

**roist′er er** (royce′tur ur). A noisy reveler; a blustering, boisterous merrymaker.—"In this rural community one *roisterer* can make enough disturbance to sound like a whole battalion."—Frederick Lewis Allen.

**ruck** (ruk). The common herd; the crowd of ordinary people who are out of the running; the multitude of commonplace people.—"The young and the ambitious battle to get out of the *ruck* of mankind."—Douglas E. Lurton.

**sab′o tage″** (sab′ō tahzh″). The act of doing poor work that will cause damage; injuring or wrecking parts of machinery in order to cause accidents or to interfere with work or production.—"They planned a program of *sabotage*."—Westbrook Pegler.

**sat″u ra′tion** (sat″ū rā′shŭn). Such a state of repletion that nothing more can possibly be added.—"There is a point of *saturation* for wages and hours, and if you go beyond that point you will destroy the employment and, therefore, destroy yourself."—Daniel Tobin.

**scoun′drels** (skoun′drĕlz: 'ou' as in 'out'). Unprincipled rascals; worthless, dishonorable, and mean people; villains.—"On the screen he consorted with *scoundrels* and criminals." —Lucius Beebe.

**scru′ti ny** (skrōō′tĭ ni). Close investigation; careful observation and examination; critical inspection.—"That is a strong statement but it will stand strict *scrutiny*."—Ralph Starr Butler.

**scur ril′i ties** (skŭ ril′ĭ tiz). Indecent remarks; coarse jokes; obscene buffoonery; vulgar, offensive acts.— "They jingled in their pockets the loose coin of their stale *scurrilities*."— Thomas Wolfe.

**sev′er ance** (sev′ur ănce). Sundering; cutting apart; separation; breaking off.—"They have accomplished one of their main objectives—the *severance* of communications."—Hanson W. Baldwin.

**se ver′i ty** (sē ver′ĭ ti). Extreme strictness; harshness; sternness; sharpness; rigor in operation; unsparing austerity.—"The *severity* of his punishment matched his crime."—John J. Green.

**shrews** (shrōōz). Scolding women; termagants; women who have a nagging, quarreling disposition.—"When they really go sour they make the most unconquerable *shrews* in the world."—Christopher Morley.

**sig nif′i cance** (sig nif′ĭ kănce). Meaning; importance; consequence; signification.—"This personal friendship between the Chief Executives of our two nations seems to me not only of practical benefit but also of profound *significance*."—Franklin Delano Roosevelt.

**sol″i dar′i ty** (sol″ĭ dar′ĭ ti). Coherence and oneness in nature and interests; union of responsibilities.—"They are deaf to appeals to reason, to friendship, to human *solidarity*, and they

beat the drums of hatred and conquest."—William C. Bullitt.

**spleen** (spleen). Bad temper; spitefulness; anger; malice.—"The ancients used to think that earthquakes were caused by a wrathful god venting his *spleen* on a people that needed chastening."—Roland T. Bird.

**splen′dors** (splen′durz). Magnificent shows; glories; bright and radiant sights.—"There are few *splendors* to equal a sunrise or sunset over the harbor of Naples."—Sterling McCormick.

**squal′or** (skwol′ur). The dirt and wretchedness of thriftless poverty; misery and neglected dirt.—"The millions of our people who have come out of the *squalor* of unemployment will never go back."—Henry A. Wallace.

**stal′warts** (stawl′wurts). Big and strong men who do not waver; sturdy partizans; stout and brave supporters.— "Some of the Republican *stalwarts* have had to swallow hard in order to stomach this new fare."—James A. Farley.

**stam′i na** (stam′i nuh). The supporting vitality; vigor; strength; ability to endure; endurance.—"These unconquered men and women are a living testament to the *stamina* of the human spirit."—Joseph C. Grew.

**stead′fast ness** (sted′fast ness). Constant faith and devotion to duty; tenacity of purpose; unwavering stanchness and steadiness.—"We thank the courageous Chinese for their unfailing *steadfastness*."—Robert C. Clothier.

**ste ril′i ty** (stĕ ril′ĭ ti). The condition of having no reproductive power and being free from living organisms; freedom from germs; hence, purity. —"The sealed package preserves *sterility* right up to the moment of application."—C. A. Breskin.

**stig′ma** (stig′muh). A mark of disgrace; a stain on character; a mark, sign, or brand.—"Some men seem to feel there is a *stigma* attached to them when they remain on the farm."—Eric A. Johnston.

**strin′gen cy** (strin′jĕn si). Strictness; severity; rigor; lack of supplies;

scarcity.—"This period of *stringency* is perhaps passing."—Winston Churchill.

**sub lim′i ty** (sŭb lim′ĭ ti). A state of exaltation; grandeur; nobility of attainment; majesty; awe-inspiring excellence or beauty.—"Solemnity, *sublimity*, languor, and conscious power naturally tend toward a slow movement in the rate of speech."—Daniel P. Eginton.

**sub′ter fuge** (sub′tur fūje). That to which one resorts for escape; a false excuse; artifice; an emergency means of evading censure.—"There can be no unity if the people are forced into it by *subterfuge*."—Hamilton Fish, Jr.

**su″per flu′i ties** (sū″pur flōō′ĭ tiz). Things not needed; articles that are superfluous; supplies that are unncessary.—"Wigs were ordered off, other *superfluities* discarded."—Albert Perry.

**su per′la tives** (sū pur′luh tivz). Words expressing supreme excellence; expressions of the highest degree of comparison; phrases or words lauding something above all others.—"Customers do not want *superlatives* in the description of products."—Arlie L. Hopkins.

**sup″pli ca′tion** (sup″li kā′shŭn). Entreaty; humble request; earnest beseeching; solicitation; begging; pleading.—" 'Water, water,' said the voice from above, in desolate *supplication*."—Stephen Vincent Benét.

**su prem′a cy** (sū prem′uh si). The state of being highest in power or authority; a position of superiority to all others; a rank so high that it cannot be exceeded.—"It is as if the increase of women reporters menaced one of the last stands in male *supremacy*."—Helen Rogers Reid.

**sure′ty** (shŏŏr′ti). Certainty; sure knowledge; security; sureness.—"The sketch of the figure was mangificent in its energy and its *surety*."—Helen C. White.

**ta boos′** (tuh bōōze′). Prejudices; things that one ostracizes; forbidden or prohibited things.—"We are confronted with a practical situation and yet many people seem to be satisfied to sit toying with their *taboos*."—Nicholas Murray Butler.

**tar′tar** (tahr′tur). A very irascible person; a person who has a violent temper; hence, a person who is too strong for his attacker.—"A certain toastmaster, noted for his jibes, caught a *tartar* when he introduced a well-known after-dinner speaker."—Daniel P. Eginton.

**taunt** (tawnt). A bitterly insulting reproach; a sarcastic remark; a sneer; scornful language.—"His scientific creed was illustrated in his reply to this *taunt*."—Harlow Shapley.

**te nac′i ty** (tē nass′ĭ ti). A firm and fast hold of rights or principles; an unyielding and strong hold; persistency.—"The British may have blundered but their *tenacity* is everywhere apparent."—Harry Hansen.

**throes** (thrōze). Violent pangs or pains; anguishing struggles; agonies.—"We have witnessed the spectacle of some nations already in the *throes* of economic poverty."—Cordell Hull.

**ti′rades** (tī′rāde′z). Prolonged declamatory speeches, generally censuring or complaining.—"It is little use uttering *tirades* against anti-Semitism."—Cardinal Hinsley.

**trav′ail** (trav′āle). Anguish or distress encountered in achievement; suffering.—"Out of the agony and *travail* of economic America the Committee for Industrial Organization was born."—John L. Lewis.

**trep″i da′tion** (trep″ĭ dā′shŭn). A state of trembling fear; perturbation; involuntary agitation.—"I do not address you for the first time with any less *trepidation* because the subject is one with which I have recently become familiar."—Lord Keynes.

**trib″u la′tion** (trib″ū lā′shŭn). A condition of affliction and distress; a long and severe trial or sorrow.—"In the time of our *tribulation* you have surely shown that compassion which is the mark of the good neighbor."—Queen Elizabeth of England.

**tur′bu lence** (tur′bū lĕnce). Disturbance; commotion; disorder; tumult.—"She captures the wildness of the times and the *turbulence* of men's emo-

tions and ambitions."—Lewis Gannett.

**tur'moil** (tur'moyl). Tumult; confused disturbance; sounds of trouble.
—"Out of the present *turmoil* will
come order and peace."—Francis J.
Spellman.

**tur'pi tude** (tur'pi tūde). Baseness;
depravity; inherent wickedness; vile-
ness.—"Recent examples of scandal
and *turpitude* served to strengthen
previous impressions."—William F.
Russell.

**ty phoon'** (tī fōon'). A violent storm or
hurricane, especially a destructive
spiral wind-storm in the China seas;
a tornado or cyclone.—"We rolled
across the China Sea to Manila in
the wake of a *typhoon*."—Roy Chapman Andrews.

**tyr'an ny** (tir'uh ni). Despotism; masterful and severe use of power; cruel
or unjust acts of authority.—"To you
*tyranny* is as hateful as it is to us."—
Queen Elizabeth of England.

**up heav'al** (up heev'ăl). The overthrow of an established order; social
uprising and agitation.—"Germany
has caused a world *upheaval* twice in
a quarter of a century."—Ernest
Bevin.

**ur'gen cy** (ur'jĕn si). Need for prompt
attention; demand for immediate
action.—"I have used all the arguments of *urgency* and I have endeav-
ored to explain many of the processes
in detail."—Winston Churchill.

**u"sur pa'tion** (ū"sur pā'shŭn). The act
of seizing and holding without right
or legal authority; unlawful seizure
of power or position.—"To have the
States stripped of their power through
Federal *usurpation* would be the
greatest calamity in American history."—Herbert R. O'Conor.

**ut'ter most** (ut'ur mōst). The utmost;
that which was of the highest quality
or degree; the most possible; the
most in their power.—"The snarling
critics did their *uttermost* to destroy
the play."—Tom Pennell.

**va cu'i ty** (vă kū'ĭ ti). Emptiness; vacancy of mind or attention; lack of
intelligence; lack of ideas; mental
inactivity; inanity; stupidity.—"In
answer to my presumably intelligent

question I received a look of complete *vacuity*."—Donald G. Cooley.

**vam'pires** (vam'pīres). Fabulous beings said to suck the blood of the
living while they slept; hence, those
who live upon others by draining
them of their mental and physical
possessions.—"The letter V also
stands for the *vampires* who suck
the blood of others."—Monroe E.
Deutsch.

**van'dal ism** (van'dăl iz'm). Actions
like those of the Vandals who pillaged Gaul and Rome; hence, ruthless and wilful destruction or deface-
ment of works of art, or things of
beauty.—"*Vandalism* of this type on
Hallowe'en is a disgraceful tradition."—Francis Maloney.

**ve loc'i ty** (vē loss'ĭ ti). Celerity; speed,
rapid motion.—"The metal entering
through the opening must have a
high *velocity*."—E. W. Harding.

**ven'om** (ven'ŭm). Spitefulness; malice;
malignity; virulence.—"Presently.
with a certain *venom*, I asked, 'Are
all your countrymen like these in the
hotel?' "—Louis Bromfield.

**ve rac'i ty** (vē rass'ĭ ti). Truthfulness;
honesty; accuracy.—"The Founda-
tion did not enquire into the *veracity*
of the information it received."—
Sister Kenny.

**vi cis'si tudes** (vĭ siss' ĭ tūde'z). Complete changes in fortune; alterna-
tions; great variations in circumstances.—"The lords of human destiny attempted to walk the turbulent
waves of human *vicissitudes*."—Edmund A. Walsh.

**vin dic'tive ness** (vin dik'tiv ness). A
spirit of revenge; a desire to retaliate.
—"There should be no *vindictiveness*
in victory."—Elmer Davis.

**vi ra'goes** (vi rā'gōze). Quarrelsome
women; termagants; turbulent, bad-
tempered women; vixens.—"The
heaven and the hell, the tennis-
playing sylphs and the gin-drinking
*viragoes*—the smoke of the city sus-
tains them both."—L. P. Jacks.

**vi ril'i ty** (vi ril'ĭ ti). The vigor and
strength (of manhood); forcefulness.
—"The *virility* of American industry
is something to give us great heart."
—Donald M. Nelson.

vit″ri ol′ics (vit″ri ol′iks). Caustic speeches; biting criticisms.—"Ours is not a field for flamboyance and *vitriolics*."—Paul V. McNutt.

vi tu″per a′tions (vī tū″pur āy′shŭnz). Abusive faultfindings; railings; wordy cries of abuse; severe scoldings; revilings.—"There had been loud *vituperations* from the rowers as they steered their boat between the towered moles of masonry."—Gertrude Atherton.

vo lup′tu ous ness (vō lup′tū ŭs ness). Sensuous gratification; luxurious pleasure.—"There is a *voluptuousness*

and a rhythmic fascination to this music."—Peter Hugh Reed.

zeal (zeel). Earnest effort; fervor; enthusiastic devotion; eager interest.— "None of this kept him from performing his official and patriotic duties with the greatest *zeal*."— Bruno Frank.

zeal′ots (zel′ŭts). Those who are over-enthusiastic; those who support something very ardently; fanatics.— "We are not embarking in a mad scramble for naval supremacy as claimed by anti-preparedness *zealots*."—Clark H. Woodward.

## One-Minute Refresher

Can you make new words? Then change the nouns that you have just had in this chapter into their adjective equivalents. The noun "strength," for instance, would change to its adjective form "strong." This is a simple task and easily accomplished, but if you do it swiftly, say in thirty seconds, it will serve as a limbering up exercise for your vocabulary.

CHANGE THE NOUN INTO THE ADJECTIVE

1. tyranny
2. bigotry
3. cataclysm
4. pugnacity
5. desolation

6. virility
7. felicity
8. adversity
9. braggart
10. audacity

*Answers:* 1. tyrannical 2. bigoted 3. cataclysmic 4. pugnacious 5. desolate 6. virile 7. felicitous 8. adverse 9. braggart 10. audacious.

# CHAPTER XII

## WHEN YOU ARGUE ABOUT POLITICS AND WORLD AFFAIRS

In times of national stress the so-called political words become of more than ordinary importance.

If we intend to qualify as intelligent citizens of our own nation or of the world at large we must inform ourselves as to the meanings of these words. Our leaders are continually speaking to us and we should be certain as to what they are trying to tell us.

Says James M. Cox: "A senatorial *cabal* was formed, a sufficient number of senators pledging their opposition."

What is a "cabal"?

Says Eduard Beneš: "We in Europe assumed that your great President Wilson had *plenipotentiary* powers."

What are "plenipotentiary" powers?

Says Madame Chiang Kai-shek: "Never for a moment should we confuse democracy with *ochlocracy*."

What is "ochlocracy"?

Says David Sarnoff: "We have to look to the *autocracies* of Europe to see what such government control of broadcasting may mean."

What is the difference between an "ochlocracy" and an "autocracy"?

Says H. H. Kirk: "These states make use of a *bicameral* legislature."

What kind of legislature is that?

If we are planning to examine these questions of policy and to decide about them and to vote on them, we *must* know the terminology that is being used by the men and women who are carrying on these public discussions.

There is a further danger and a grave one in this political terminology that we must be on our guard against. There is a group of words that demagogues use to fool us with, danger-words that have led charlatans to power. Besides this these words have probably caused more personal bitterness, broken friendships, mayhem, murder, barroom fights and wars than any other words in the entire English language.

The special words that I am speaking of occur in all departments of our life, but our political vocabulary is particularly filled with them.

A recognition of the danger that these words present—I call them Ghost Words—is so vitally important that I want to subject them to a careful analysis. A complete understanding of how to treat them will lead to clearer thinking on every subject and will prevent many a violent and futile argument.

Let us bring a few of the more lethal ones into our laboratory for examination.

Here they are: regimentation, bureaucracy, plutocracy, ideology, authoritarian, autocracy, jingoism, totalitarianism.

Then there are such simple and innocent appearing ones as: freedom, justice, truth, liberty, equality, labor, capitalist, monopoly, peace, progressive, reactionary, inflation.

What angry verbal battles have swirled and surged around these words!

And why not?

Even the briefest examination will make the trouble clear.

We will choose a single specimen, "communism," and, for comparison, we will set it against the noun, "table," that comes from an entirely different class and category.

The word "table," of course, is a concrete term that calls up a definite picture. It refers to a familiar object that we can see and touch. We have long since agreed that a table is a piece of furniture with one or more legs and a flat top to hold things on. There is no dispute about this. There can be none. If someone goes further and claims that a certain table is more than six feet long, a measuring tape settles the matter. No argument is possible.

The word, "communism," however, is of another breed. This word refers to no object that we can put a finger on. It is an abstraction that calls up an idea, not a picture. The literal word "table" appeals to our understanding. The figurative word "communism" appeals to our emotions. "Communism" is something that you can't see or photograph; you can't even define it satisfactorily, because the true definition is not in any dictionary. It is in you and you and you. The meaning of "communism" is personal and individual and is based, in part, upon your private opinions and is colored by your pet prejudices. I have given to it and to its kith and kin the general name of Ghost Words because they are all words of unreality, astral spirits without flesh or blood or physical body. These are the biggest sinners among the Fictions.

It may be interesting to show one of these words at work.

An eager young man, for instance, will say: "I'm afraid of communism in America."

All right. What is he *really* afraid of? The communism of Karl Marx, as laid down in *Das Kapital?* Communism as interpreted by Lenin? By Trotsky? Communism as practiced by the former Cominterns? Or by the Communist Party in America? The communistic theories of Stalin's earliest days? His theories today? Tomorrow? Does the young man really *know* what he is afraid of? Or is he just making a loud noise?

These Ghost Words have a legitimate value and use. We couldn't talk about communism unless there were such a word. But we should be careful not to use this type of word as though it represented a definite object like a table, for there is "no thing" there. At least no one thing. The word "communism" is merely a convenient shorthand symbol that stands for the varying ideas and theories of millions of Russians and other peoples, and the myriad practices that go to make up a highly complicated and constantly changing manner of living. We can't talk "all" about any such vast subject as this.

It is, therefore, stupid and absurd to get passionate about anything as fuzzy and foggy as abstract words. They are too vague in outline to be the subject of heated debate, and like our early maps, they hold, within their boundaries, vast unexplored regions where we may too easily get lost.

There is only one possible technique to follow in discussing the misty topics that are represented by these abstract words, and if you aren't afraid of inviting the dislike that attaches to a cross-examining attorney, you can use it.

Some years ago the term "New Deal" was invented. By their dictionary definitions "New" and "Deal," taken together, can't possibly signify anything that makes sense, unless they should be spoken by a bridge or poker player who wants a new deal at cards. Nevertheless, the mere mention of these words proved a bombshell in many a gathering.

Let us see how we can treat words like these so that they will not explode.

We will pretend that someone has just said, "I hate the New Deal."

Now a passionate argument will start unless we leave the clouds and go down the ghostly verbal ladder to where we can have one foot on the ground. So we will ask:

"What, particularly, don't you like about the New Deal?"

"I don't like the President."

(At least we have arrived at an object that can be seen and photographed. But the answer is still too general, for a President must certainly have done something during his term, or in his private life, that would meet the approval of a fair-minded man. So—)

"What particular act of the President do you object to?"

"I object to his policies in Puerto Rico."

(Here we are getting closer to the events of the real world which we can both see.)

"What specific policy don't you like?"

"His sugar policy."

At last we are standing on solid ground. We have translated the mystic and meaningless words, "New Deal," into some one thing that they represent. We have found a topic that we can discuss with profit if we happen to know anything about the general subject of sugar policy, the history of the sugar industry in Puerto Rico, the exports, imports, the government decisions, the results of the decisions, and the more successful "sugar policies," if any, that have been followed by other nations in similar situations.

As a rule, when we walk down the semantic ladder this way, from the abstract and general, where the talking is loose and emotional, to the concrete and objective, where our conversation must deal with facts, you and I and the others will often discover that we cannot name or quote a single authority, or marshall any convincing statistics for the occasion, or bring the weight of one lone paragraph from a recognized book to our aid. We may find, to our embarrassment, that we actually don't know so much as one important item about the subject, and, in the argot of the street, we might as well shut up.

Watch out for these Ghost Words. Keep a careful eye on those of our national leaders who use too many of them. You will hear a politician mouthing empty phrases that are studded with such high-sounding words as "liberty," "security," "equality." Again and always, ask yourself these questions: Liberty to do *what?* Security from *what,* and how and when is he going to get it for us? Equality with whom and in what respects?

Terms of this type can be turned to very queer ends, and often have been. Hitler knew the power of abstract words over his people, and he drugged the populace with them while he seized his dictatorship. "For at the sound of certain words," said the philosopher, Schopenhauer, many years ago, "the German's head begins to swim, and, falling straightway into a kind of delirium, he launches into high-flown phrases that have no meaning whatsoever."

So beware of these Ghost Words. Learn to listen to them with appraising ears and to use them cautiously. Keep in mind that they are no more than abbreviations for a way of life. Don't argue about a word like "Freedom." No such over-all quality ever existed. Always ask "Freedom from what?" and then, when you have your answer, argue about *that*, if you happen to be informed on the subject.

Arguments based on Ghost Words can go on all night. By morning you will know that you have been terribly excited, but you won't be quite sure as to what you have been excited about.

After all, most of us *think* we are thinking when we are merely *feeling*. We think with our emotions and decide with our prejudices. We usually act first and then we try to figure out reasons why we behaved that way. We rarely change our fundamental beliefs. Rather than do this we will spend our whole lives gathering facts to substantiate the opinions we were born with.

Do you doubt any of these statements? Then cross-examine yourself. What is your religion? Is it *your* religion or did you inherit it from your parents? Are you opposed to sending your child to a "Progressive School"? Why? Can you produce half a dozen *authoritative* facts to bolster your opinion? And, incidentally, while we are on the subject, will you tell me what *is* a "Progressive School"? Can you write the definition of one in twenty words? In fifty? You will probably find it absolutely impossible as, once again, "progressive" is a Ghost Word signifying nothing. Why are you voting for Jack Windlestraw for President? Have you read his speeches with thoughtful care? Can you explain your position factually and without emotion? *Are* you explaining the stand you have taken, or are you just making unpleasant sounds?

Anything you believe because you were born into a certain family and locale is a prejudice, a pre-judgment, and is open to question. We usually see things in terms of our training and our interests and when we think we are "thinking" we are usually just re-arranging our prejudices.

The archeologist works to his conclusions with pick and shovel and by patient research. The astronomer speculates and figures for years before announcing the position of a new star. The doctor hesitates to venture an opinion without a minute examination and then, often, is not sure. A lawyer reads volumes of precedents before giving his advice. The scientist sits down before a fact with the humility and the open mind of a little child. But ask any of us laymen how to run a government or a war and we will instantly present you with a basketful of opinions.

We *must* learn to distinguish between an *opinion* and a *fact*. There are so few among us who do. Fewer even than you think. We are prone to say: "I *know* that that is the wrong way to do it," and we sincerely believe that we have stated a fact. Listen to the disputes around you. You will hear a multitude of Ghost Words without sensible meanings, a plethora of opinions, but so pitifully few facts. In any argument, if we eliminate glib personal opinions and stick to such facts as would have a chance of being accepted as evidence in a law court, I'm afraid we would have little to say!

Of course, we shouldn't take this too seriously. After all, conversation is often just an instrument of good will and of friendship, like a dog wagging his tail, and opinions can be entertaining if we recognize that they *are* opinions.

The purpose of this chapter then, beyond adding to your word supply, is to encourage a more careful consideration of the meanings of words and a much more studied attention to the science of straight thinking. Words of culture have so much more power when the thinking behind them is straight. And, concomitantly, a democracy has so much more security when its citizens have acquired an intelligent appreciation of the values of the words that are used by its statesmen and political mentors. Many of these words are offered to you in the pages to come.

**ab′di cate** (ab′di kāte). Give up voluntarily; renounce power or office.— "Ideas and principles, as well as kings, can *abdicate*."—Nicholas Murray Butler.

**ab″o li′tion** (ab″ō lish′ŭn). The act of putting an end to; extinction.—"The League does not possess the means for the complete *abolition* of war."—Maxim Litvinoff.

**ab′ro gat″ed** (ab′rō gāte″id). Annulled by authority or by later enactment.— "Japan had *abrogated* the Washington treaty and was building more ships."—Eugene Worley.

**ab′so lut ism** (ab′sō lūte iz′m). Despotism; the doctrine of unlimited control vested in an autocrat; the practice of absolute government; absoluteness.—"The idea that *absolutism* might be the necessary way to a world republic had been floating in men's minds."—H. G. Wells.

**ad her′ents** (ad heer′ĕnts). People devoted to a cause or leader; followers; partisans; supporters.—"Some scientists and some *adherents* of religion may lack high ideals, but this is no just condemnation of either science or religion."—Edwin Grant Conklin.

**aides** (aidz). Naval or military officers who assist a superior officer in his duties.—"His conferences with our President, with our Secretary of State, and with their *aides*, are another advance in the exchange of men, methods, ideas and ideals."— Thos. J. Watson.

**a lign′ments** (uh līne′mĕnts). The positions in line on the side of a special cause.—"Final *alignments* of both political sides have been made.— Jan Christiaan Smuts.

**al le′giance** (ă lee′jănce). Loyalty to 'a government or cause; faithfulness; devotion; fidelity.—"These unselfish ideals command the *allegiance* of all classes."—Winston Churchill.

**am″bus cade′** (am″bŭss kāde′). Ambush; lying in wait in a concealed spot to surprise or attack an enemy. —"The early American Indian was expert at the art of *ambuscade*."— Ellery Marsh Egan.

**a me′lio rat″ed** (uh meel′yō rāte″id). Made more endurable; mitigated; improved.—"There will be no peace until the unjust terms are *ameliorated*."—William E. Borah.

**a mend′ment** (uh mend′mĕnt). A change in a bill by adding or omitting something therein.—"Under the *amendment* a few prices are raised and others are lowered."—Lew Hahn.

**am′nes ty** (am′ness ti). A pardon for offenses; an overlooking of misdeeds. —"It finally became necessary to grant something like a general *amnesty* in the matter."—Don Marquis.

**am phib′i ous** (am fib′i ŭs). Suited to both land and water.—"An enormous *amphibious* expedition was embarked in hundreds of ships."— Franklin Delano Roosevelt.

**a nab′a sis** (uh nab′uh siss). A military advance into a country; a going up with a military force into another country.—"After the battle of Stalingrad came the magnificent *anabasis* of the Russians that thrilled the world."—Douglas Brewster.

**an′ar chy** (an′uhr ki). Disorder and utter disregard of government.— "There was a general state of *anarchy* out of which grew the catastrophy of war."—Sumner Welles.

**An′glo philes** (ang′glō fīles). Those who greatly love and admire England and everything English.—"There are a limited number of extreme *Anglophiles* who put the interests of Great Britain above those of the United States."—Robert E. Wood.

**An″glo pho′bi a** (ang″glō fō fō′bi uh). An aversion to England or the English; hatred or dread of everything English.—"This man was leaving a trail of *Anglophobia* wherever he went and was stirring up trouble for the British in Syria."—Kingsbury Smith.

**an nex′** (ă neks′). To join or add a smaller to a larger thing; to subjoin or unite as a subordinate part; to attach in ownership.—"Great nations are always tempted to *annex* their weaker neighbors."—Henry J. Powers.

**ar′bi ters** (ahr′bi turz). Arbitrators;

chosen umpires; persons having full power to settle disputes; judges.—"The Statute of Westminster recognizes the Dominions as self-governing nations and as *arbiters* of their own fate."—Viscount Cranborne.

**ar'bi trate** (ahr'bĭ trāte). To settle a controversy by empowering persons chosen by both parties to hear the dispute and decide the matter.—"The committee will vote to *arbitrate* the matter with the companies and the commission."—Michael J. Casha.

**ar'go sies** (ahr'gō siz). Fleets of ships; large merchant vessels sailing together; numbers of richly laden ships under one command.—"During the season when the great *argosies* were becalmed, he went off into the heat of the Sahara."—Jay Allen.

**ar ma'da** (ahr mah'duh). A fleet of war-vessels.—"We have put into the air the greatest *armada* the world has ever seen."—Frank Knox.

**ar'se nals** (ahr'sē nălz). Public establishments for manufacturing or storing arms and munitions of war.—"Each hour will add guns and shells to our *arsenals*."—Frank Knox.

**as pir'ant** (ass pīre'ănt). A seeker for honors or position; one who eagerly desires to attain something great; a candidate for office.—"To become a politician, and eventually, maybe, a statesman, the *aspirant* must start by ringing door bells."—Fred W. Parker.

**as sem'ble** (ă sem'b'l). Collect in one place; gather together; come together; convene; congregate.—"The delegates to the party convention had begun to *assemble*."—Tom Pennell.

**a sy'lum** (uh sī'lŭm). A place of refuge or shelter.—"I denounced the Administration for imposing new restrictions on our already limited offer of *asylum* to the victims."—Norman Thomas.

**au thor"i tar'i an** (aw thor"ĭ tair'i ăn; 'th' as in 'thin'). Upholding authority against individual liberty; advocating and encouraging obedience to authority even when in opposition to liberty of the individual.—"This was more apparent in what were called the *authoritarian* communities than in those which claimed to be democratic."—H. G. Wells.

**au toc'ra cies** (aw tok'ruh siz). Absolute or despotic governments.—"We have to look to the *autocracies* of Europe to see what such government control of broadcasting may mean."—David Sarnoff.

**au ton'o my** (aw ton'o mi). The power, right, or condition of self-government.—"The act grants them a large measure of *autonomy*."—Edmund D. Lucas.

**av"oir du pois'** (av"ur dū poize').—A system of weights of the United States and Great Britain; a system of weights in which the pound is sixteen ounces.—"The Cullinan diamond weighed a pound and a third *avoirdupois*."—Samuel G. Gordon.

**bas'tion** (bass'chŭn). A projecting part of a fortification having two faces and two flanks.—"The great *bastion* of Singapore was lost."—Frank Knox.

**bel'li cose** (bel'i kōse). Pugnacious; warlike; fond of fighting.—"They have of late grown *bellicose*."—Bainbridge Colby.

**bel lig'er ent** (bĕ lij'ur ĕnt). Warlike; engaged in warfare.—"Those airmen brought every square mile of the *belligerent* nations into the zone of combat by their bombing."—Henry H. Arnold.

**bi cam'er al** (bī kam'ur ăl). Consisting of two chambers or branches.—"These states make use of a *bicameral* legislature."—H. H. Kirk.

**bi lat'er al** (bī lat'ur ăl). Having two sides; two-sided; affecting two sides or parties in an agreement.—"It has broadened into a United Nations organization which will render *bilateral* arrangements within the circle unnecessary."—Anne O'Hare McCormick.

**bi par'ti san** (bī pahr'tĭ zăn). Made up of members of two parties; representing both sides; composed of delegates from each side.—"A *bipartisan* committee was immediately formed."—Ellery Marsh Egan.

**biv'ou ac** (biv'ŏŏ ak). A temporary encampment without shelter.—"It was midnight before they struck the outlet and they had another wretched *bivouac* in the rain."—John Buchan.

**bloc** (blok). A group, as of politicians, formed to foster special interests.— "The farm *bloc* attacks me for keeping prices too low."—Prentiss M. Brown.

**bond'age** (bon'dij). Slavery; serfdom; servitude; compulsory subjection or captivity.—"Then the children of Israel were delivered out of their *bondage*."—Bradwell E. Tanis.

**boun'ties** (boun'tiz: 'ou' as in 'out'). Grants or allowances from the government.—"*Bounties* for not raising this or that were paid out of the public treasury."—De Witt Emery.

**breach** (breech). A break or rupture; a violation; a breaking up.—"It may be said that this was not a *breach* of our understanding."—Anthony Eden.

**bu reauc'ra cy** (bū rok'ruh si). Government by rigid and arbitrary control as contrasted with what is generally known as private initiative. —"I do not hesitate to say that if America takes the road marked 'stabilization,' *bureaucracy* will be the first step."—Alfred P. Sloan.

**ca bal'** (kuh bal'). A group of persons secretly united to plan and carry out intrigues or conspiracies.—"A senatorial *cabal* was formed, a sufficient number of senators pledging their opposition."—James M. Cox.

**ca'dres** (kad'riz). Frameworks; skeleton organizations; the officers, sergeants, etc. of regiments kept in reserve for possible expansion.—"He was trying, by extensive and secret activities, to keep the *cadres* of the old army in good order in preparation for a future one."—Jules Romains.

**Ca'liph** (kāy'lif). The ruler of a Moslem state; a Mohammedan civil or religious head of state; originally, a successor to Mohammed.—"This incredible man claims to be the descendant of the first *Caliph* of Mohammed."—Jay Nelson Tuck.

**cam"a ril'la** (kam"uh ril'uh). A cabal or clique; a group of unofficial advisers who have secret powers; a junto.—"The *camarilla* planned the revolution behind closed doors."— Emory L. Fielding.

**ca pit"u la'tion** (kuh pit"ū lā'shŭn). A conditional surrender.—"They imposed on France first a *capitulation* and then a regime of dictatorship."— Charles de Gaulle.

**car'a vels** (kar'uh velz). Small sailing vessels; light fast sailing ships.— "*Caravels* freighted with wonder have come even from far Cathay."— Alexander Woollcott.

**caste** (kast). A social class or division.—"No official *caste* has developed except the guild of professional politicians."—H. W. Dodds.

**chau'vin ism** (shō'vin iz'm). Exaggerated patriotism; warlike patriotism; vainglorious or extravagant show of patriotism; supporting a fighting attitude in foreign affairs; jingoism. —"That savage *chauvinsim* many have fallen into."—Edmund Wilson.

**chau"vin is'tic** (shō"vin iss'tik). Pertaining to one who is extravagantly patriotic; vaingloriously patriotic.— "The Church knows what Caesars a *chauvinistic* worship of the State will breed."—Edward A. Walsh.

**ci ta'tion** (sī tā'shŭn). A specific mention conferring honor.—"With profound pride I accept for them this rare and distinct *citation*."—Samuel P. Ginder.

**ci vil'ian** (si vil'yăn). For the use of those who are neither soldiers nor sailors; of all persons not in the army or navy.—"This has built up a tremendous need for essential *civilian* products."—Charles R. Hook.

**co"a li'tion** (kō"uh lish'ŭn). An alliance of persons, parties, or states.— "The times call for what might be termed a *coalition* government."— C. M. Chester.

**code** (kōde). A systematized body of law; a set of rules; a group of principles.—"They have not even the *code* which first-rate soldiers observe toward a brave enemy."—A. A. Berle, Jr.

**co'horts** (kō'horts). Armed bodies of soldiers, originally the tenth part of a Roman legion; companies or groups.—"The *cohorts* of his brothers had passed Tweedsmouth."—Brooke Dolan.

**col lab'o rat"ing** (kŏ lab'ō rāte"ing).

Working in combination with others or cooperating with them.—"By *collaborating* with the rest of the world to put resources fully to work, we shall raise our own standard of living."—Henry A. Wallace.

**col′leagues** (kol′eegz). Fellow members of an official body; associates.—"I will meet again at the British Embassy and confer with our *colleagues*." —Lord Beaverbrook.

**com min′gle** (kŏ ming′g'l). To mingle or blend together; to mix together.— "Small frictions often arise when different races are forced to *commingle*."—Ainslee Mockridge.

**com′mon er** (kom′ŭn ur). One of the common people; one of the untitled; formerly, a member of the English House of Commons.—"William Jennings Bryan liked to be called 'The Great *Commoner*.'"—S. L. Scanlon.

**Com′mon wealth″** (kom′ŭn welth″). A body of people united on a basis ol voluntary agreement; a politicaf union of states or countries having common interests and viewed as equals in authority.—"If the principle of 'might is right' were established throughout the world, the freedom of England and the whole British *Commonwealth* of Nations would be in danger."—King George VI of England.

**com′mu nal** (kom′ū năl). Pertaining to a community or political division.— "The Mohammedans pursue an independent *communal* policy."—Edmund C. Lucas.

**com′mune** (kom′ūne). A small division for local government; a self-governing community; also the people of such a place or region.—"Twenty years of usurpation by Rome have destroyed the autonomy of the *commune*."—Anne O'Hare McCormick.

**com mu′ni ty** (kŏ mū′nĭ ti). The people of a village, town, or state; a particular region and the common interests connected with it.—"Women today have far more complicated *community* obligations than they used to have."—Mary Agnes McGeachy.

**com′pact** (kom′pakt). An agreement; a covenant; a contract.—"They made a secret *compact* with each other and determined on a course of action."— Douglas E. Lurton.

**com pa′tri ots** (kŏm pāy′tri ŭts). Fellow countrymen.—"American people share the sense of loss of the Polish people at the tragic death of General Sikorski and his distinguished *compatriots*."—Cordell Hull.

**com peers′** (kom peerz′). Equals in rank or birth; peers; companions; associates.—"It is not among mean people, but among his *compeers* of the great, that he wishes to be first."— Thomas Wolfe.

**com pos′ing** (kŏm pōze′ing). Reconciling; arranging; settling; quieting; calming.—"The states of the world have groped forward to find something better than the old way of *composing* their differences."—Franklin Delano Roosevelt.

**con cert′ed** (kŏn sur′ted). Planned, arranged, or contrived together; combined.—"The delegation cooperated in the effort to achieve *concerted* action."—Marvin Jones.

**con cil′i ate** (kŏn sil′ĭ āte). To win the friendship of; to win over; to gain favor of.—"This alliance may find it profitable to be polite to the Yankee, and even to *conciliate* him."—H. L. Mencken.

**con″do min′i um** (kon″dō min′i ŭm). Joint dominion or control; government or ownership by two or more powers; a country or region governed by more than one power.—"The Sudan is a well-known example of a vast *condominium*."—Douglas Brewster.

**con′quests** (kong′kwests). Conquered lands or territories; persons or things overcome by force, and appropriated. —"This conception was elaborated to consolidate their *conquests* and to prepare for new ones."—L. P. Jacks.

**con sen′sus** (kŏn sen′sŭs). A collective opinion; a general agreement.—"It was the *consensus* that he was a grand actor."—Bertram M. Myers.

**con′sort** (kon′sort). A wife or husband; especially the wife or husband of a king or queen.—"Prince Albert, the *consort* of Queen Victoria, never shared her throne."—Bradwell E. Tanis.

**con spir'a cy** (kŏn spir'uh si). An agreement between two or more persons to do an evil act.—"There is a *conspiracy* on the part of financial interests and politicians to prevent a settlement."—John L. Lewis.

**con stit'u en cy** (kŏn stit'ū ĕn si). A body of voters; the district that elects or appoints a representative member to Congress.—"They appealed to the emotions and thoughts of their *constituency*."—Edward L. Bernays.

**con"sti tu'tion al** (kon"stǐ tū'shŭn ăl). In accordance with established law; consistent with the fundamental principles of the country; lawful; authorized by the principles by which a country is governed.—"A cablegram requested that it consider granting the vote to women by *constitutional* amendment."—L. S. Rowe.

**con"tro ver'sial** (kon"trō vur'shăl). Contentious; pertaining to disputes or argument.—"The amount of time devoted to the discussion of *controversial* public issues might be regulated."—Neville Miller.

**con voked'** (kŏn vōke't'). Called together; assembled by a summons; summoned to meet together.—"The leaders *convoked* an old-fashioned, New England town meeting."—Hugh E. Blackstone.

**cor'don** (kor'dŏn). An extended line, as of men, ships, forts, etc.—"What is desired is to form a protective *cordon* about possessions that are in danger."—Rex G. Tugwell.

**cos"mo pol'i tan** (koz"mō pol'ĭ tăn). Common to all the world; not local or limited.—"The patriotism of a great *cosmopolitan* nation must be large enough to obliterate racial distinction."—Jane Addams.

**cour'i er** (kōōr'i ur). A person who accompanies travelers to arrange the details of their journey; a messenger; an attendant who takes charge of accommodations and arrangements for travelers.—"Vernon, the perfect *courier*, enquired at the bureau for letters."—Maud Diver.

**czars** (zahrz). Emperors or absolute monarchs; rich despotic rulers; autocratic governors.—"Our chances to become *czars* of industry grow more remote."—Thomas Parran.

**de bac'le** (dē bak"l). A route or collapse; a stampede; a sudden downfall.—"They had their backs to the sea which led to a complete *debacle*."—Henry L. Stimson.

**de fec'tions** (dē fek'shŭnz). Desertions; abandonment of allegiance or duty.—"There was great unrest among the men and even *defections* from their ranks."—Dorothy Thompson.

**del'e gat"ed** (del'ē gāte"id). Committed or entrusted; assigned; gave over (authority to him to act).—"The President *delegated* full plenipotentiary powers to his emissary."—Malcom Douglas.

**de lib"er a'tions** (dē lib"ur āy'shŭnz). Slow and cautious decisions and actions.—"You carry with you in your *deliberations* the hopes of millions of human beings."—Franklin Delano Roosevelt.

**dem"a gog'ic** (dem"uh goj'ik). Pertaining to unprincipled leaders who seek to gain influence by pandering to the prejudices of the people.—"When *demagogic* politicians set out systematically to ruin corporations, who gets hurt?"—M. S. Rukeyser.

**dem"on stra'tion** (dem"ŭn strā'shŭn). A public expression or exhibition of welcome, approval, or condemnation; an outward show or manifestation.—"There was an enthusiastic *demonstration* in front of the palace at Potsdam."—Sterling McCormick.

**de'pots** (dee'pōze). Warehouses or storehouses; military stations for collecting personnel and materials; also, railroad stations.—"Storage *depots* of large capacity are being constructed by the Army."—Joseph B. Eastman.

**dep"u ta'tion** (dep"ū tā'shŭn). A person or persons acting for others; a delegation.—"The Prime Minister received a *deputation* from the League of Nations Union."—R. W. Jepson.

**des'pot ism** (dess'pŏt iz'm). Absolute power; autocracy; tyranny.—"It is the age-old struggle of innate *despotism* against innate liberty."—William J. Cameron.

**dig'ni tar"ies** (dig'nǐ ter"iz). Men holding high official positions; men of high rank in Church or State.—"He kept pulling up his stockings in front of some British *dignitaries*."—Albert Perry.

**di plo'ma cy** (di plō'muh si). Tact; skill in managing affairs between nations; the art of securing advantages in negotiations without stirring up hostility.—"Two distant regions of the world have come within the range of our *diplomacy*."—Walter Lippmann.

**dip"lo mat'ic** (dip"lō mat'ik). Pertaining to tact and skill in conducting negotiations.—"The real task of *diplomatic* defense is to make military defense unnecessary."—A. A. Berle, Jr.

**di rec'tive** (dǐ rek'tiv). Something that points the way; an order that points out the direction to be followed or course to be pursued.—"The policy is based on a *directive* from the chiefs of staff."—Kingsbury Smith.

**dis"af fec'tion** (diss"ă fek'shŭn). Disloyalty; discontent; estrangement; unfriendliness.—"There was serious *disaffection* among the groups and the leader had requested that loyal members should hear plain words."—Franz Werfel.

**dis fran'chis es** (diss fran'chīze ez). Takes away from a citizen the rights or privilege of voting or holding office.—"Any American election which *disfranchises* ten million voters is not electing a truly representative, a truly democratic government."—Harley M. Kilgore.

**dis sent'ing** (di sent'ing). Disagreeing in opinion; withholding approval.—"Congress passed that resolution without a *dissenting* vote."—Nicholas Murray Butler.

**di vi'sive** (dǐ vī'siv). Expressing division; indicating distinctions; causing discord; creating dissension.—"A *divisive* movement started in the Republican Party."—Douglas E. Lurton.

**do min'ion** (dō min'yŭn). Supreme authority; sovereignty; power of control; rule; predominance.—"When you understand human nature, you will have *dominion* over it."—Emmet Fox.

**dos'si ers** (doss'i urz). Bundles of papers which contain records; sets of documents.—"There are fundamental differences of principles involved which all the *dossiers* of diplomacy cannot obscure."—Robert I. Gannon.

**dy'nas ties** (dī'năss tiz). A succession of sovereigns in one line of family descent governing the same country.—"We must try to avoid the pitfalls in which former *dynasties* and systems have fallen."—Madame Chiang Kaishek.

**ech'e lon** (esh'ĕ lon). A naval or military arrangement in which the men are drawn up in parallel lines to the right and left of those in front, like a ladder or series of steps.—"We were able to get in touch with the rear *echelon* in the jungle two miles behind us."—Edward Lincoln Smith II.

**em'is sar"y** (em'ǐ ser"i). A person sent on a mission; a secret agent.—"Not till the night of May 27th did he send an *emissary* to the army."—John Cudahy.

**en dorse'ment** (en dorce'mĕnt). An act of ratification or approval; sanction; support.—"His three-time election is taken as a good *endorsement* of his ability as an executive."—Alfred M. Landon.

**en'ter pri ses** (en'tur prīze iz). Projected tasks or work; undertakings.—"Federally-owned *enterprises* are under way."—Franklin Delano Roosevelt.

**en'voy** (en'voy). A diplomatic agent sent on a special mission by his government.—"We shall await further developments before sending an *envoy* to the island."—Cordell Hull.

**eq'ui ta ble** (ek'wi tuh b'l). Characterized by fairness and just dealing; impartial.—"This government requires only that foreign countries shall accord our nationals fair and *equitable* treatment."—Franklin Delano Roosevelt.

**ex pa"tri a'tion** (eks pā"tri āy'shŭn). Exile; banishment; permanent withdrawal from one's native land.—"There had set in the movement of protest by *expatriation*, not unknown in an older America."—Ludwig Lewisohn.

**ex″ploi ta′tion** (eks″ploy tā′shŭn).Self-
ish employment for one's own use or
advantage; selfish use.—"There can
be no world cooperation unless measures are taken to prevent the *exploitation* of the under privileged peoples."
Mrs. J. Borden Harriman.

**fac′tions** (fak′shŭnz). Parties of persons
combined for a common purpose;
often, small cliques within a party.—
"The employee is in between various
*factions* seeking in one way or another
to gain control."—Eugene S.Grace.

**fac′tious** (fak′shŭs). Seditious; causing
strife or stirring up disputes; partisan;
given to opposition.—"There is a *fac-
tious* element in every labor union."
—John J. Green.

**fe′al ty** (fee′ăl ti). Fidelity; devoted
loyalty; faithfulness.—"The psychology back of federal legislation is that
the citizen's loyalty and *fealty* to the
nation stands over against his loyalty
to his particular state."—Owen J.
Roberts.

**fed″er a′tions** (fed″ur āy′shŭnz). National unions or sovereign states
formed by uniting local governments
under a sovereign power, while leaving each part free to manage its own
affairs whenever these do not interfere with the good of the whole.—
"Tribes grew into *federations*, and
*federations* into nations."—W. J.
Cameron.

**Feu′dal ism** (fū′dăl iz′m). A medieval
system of homage and service of
tenants.—"They insist that liberty,
like *Feudalism*, must now be abandoned."—Herbert Hoover.

**fi′at** (fī′at). A positive and authoritative command that something be
done.—"There was fear that governmental *fiat* would replace the decisions of business men."—Winthrop
W. Aldrich.

**fil′i bus″ter** (fil′ĭ buss″tur). The act of
delaying or obstructing legislation by
continual speaking to consume time,
or by other methods.—"They were
asked whether a *filibuster* is a procedure of referring a bill back to a
committee."—H. H. Kirk.

**flour′ish ing** (flur′ish ing). Thriving;
prosperous; increasing in wealth;
growing in extent and power.—"I

do not mean that *flourishing* international commerce is in itself a guarantee of peaceful international relations."—Cordell Hull.

**for′ays** (for′āyz). Raids; marauding expeditions.—"Skirmishes and *forays*
have taken place on the ground and
in the air."—Winston Churchill.

**for′mu lat″ed** (for′mū lāte″id). Stated
in exact, concise, and systematic
form; expressed in clear terms, as a
formula.—"The President *formulated*
his seven-point program."—Owen
D. Young.

**ge″o pol′i tics** (jē″ō pol′i tiks). The science which treats of the dependence
of both the home and foreign politics
of a nation upon the physical surroundings.—"They went about as
living symbols of the might of German *geopolitics*."—Bruno Frank.

**ger″ry man′der ing** (jer″i man′dur-
ing). Altering a boundary unfairly;
making unnatural or arbitrary restrictions in a country; dividing election districts unfairly.—"*Gerrymander-
ing* has not taken place in Northern
Ireland but in Eire."—D. L. Savory.

**gib′bet** (jib′et). A kind of gallows on
which executed criminals were often
left hanging as an example to others.
—"In the French Revolution many
a grisly body hung from a *gibbet*."—
S. L. Scanlon.

**gu″ber na to′ri al** (gū″bur nuh tō′ri-
ăl). Pertaining to a governor.—"I
glared at the Farmers' Alliance appearing in *gubernatorial* offices."—
William Allen White.

**he gem′o ny** (hē jem′ō ni). Leadership,
or supreme command.—"The United
States would have to agree not to
form a *hegemony* in South America."
—Dorothy Thompson.

**hel′ots** (hel′ŏts). Slaves; serfs; bond-
men.—"They are wholly unaware of
the mad arrogance of desiring those
immigrant stocks to remain inarticulate *helots*."—Ludwig Lewisohn.

**hench′men** (hench′mĕn). Servile assistants; faithful followers; political
followers, seeking personal profit.—
"Office holders and *henchmen* secretly
corralled delegates."—Harrison E.
Spangler.

**hos′tage** (hoss′tij). A person held as a

pledge, as in war, for the performance of some agreement.—"For every one taken as a *hostage* or executed, others will rise at once to take over."—Alexander Loudon.

i″de ol′o gies (ī″dē ol′ō jiz). Fanciful speculations; dreamy theorizing; visionary ideas.—"We must not involve ourselves in a quarrel about *ideologies*."—Winston Churchill.

im′mi grant (im′ĭ grănt). Entering a country to settle there, and to reside permanently.—"The *immigrant* peoples have chosen to become citizens."—Henry A. Wallace.

im peach′ (im peech′). To charge with a crime or misdemeanor in office; to accuse of treason; to bring an accusation against, before a competent tribunal.—"There have been many threats to *impeach* a President, but the denunciation has never been carried out."—Ainslee Mockridge.

im pe′ri al (im peer′i ăl). Belonging to an emperor or empire; of an emperor.—"He was released from prison by these conquering, *imperial* soldiers."—Henry James Forman.

im pe′ri al ism (im peer′i ăl iz′m). A system of supreme authority and power; seeking to extend dominion over other countries.—"The nations are laying the foundations for new war by their obvious intention to perpetuate their own *imperialism*."—Norman Thomas.

im′ple ment (im′plē mĕnt). Carry into effect; fulfill; carry out; accomplish. —"You have the opportunity to *implement* these same ideals."—Madame Chiang Kai-shek.

im″por ta′tion (im″por tā′shŭn). Something that is imported or brought in from abroad; a commodity introduced from a foreign country.—"This new *importation* gave the trade a fresh impetus."—Henry J. Powers.

im″po si′tion (im″pō zish′ŭn). The act of levying or exacting by force or influence; the placing of a burden.—"We shall have fought in vain if governmental control prolongs the subordination of individual enterprise by the *imposition* of harmful limitations."—Eugene P. Thomas.

im″pre scrip′ti ble(im″prē skrip′tĭ b'l). Inalienable; that cannot legally be taken away.—"Let us stand foursquare on our *imprescriptible* rights."—Bertram M. Myers.

in au′gu rat″ed (in aw′gū rāte″id). Invested with an office; hence, commenced; begun; set in motion; entered upon.—"This split-second program thus *inaugurated* was to occupy my every movement."—Hilary St. George Saunders.

in″di vid′u al ism (in″dĭ vid′ŭ ăl iz′m) Personal independence of action and character; the doctrine that freedom of individuals is as important as group freedom.—"Wars are won by this much-defamed, rugged *individualism*."—Herbert Hoover.

in″flu en′tial (in″flōō en′shăl). Exerting an influence; powerful; effective; able to affect or sway.—"Public opinion shall again be *influential*."—Eduard Beneš.

in fu′sions (in fū zhŭnz). Admixtures; mixtures that have been poured in.—"We are a young country with *infusions* of blood from many nations."—Cordell Hull.

in sig′ni a (in sig′ni uh). Medals, badges, and other distinguishing marks of high office or honor.—"The Declaration of Independence and the Constitution of the United States are our high *insignia* of state."—W. J. Cameron.

in′sti tut″ed (in′stĭ tūte″id). Set up; originated and organized; began and established; set on foot.—"The Truman Committee *instituted* an enquiry."—Emmet Holloway.

in″sti tu′tions (in″stĭ tū′shŭnz). Established orders, laws, and usages.—"Without the *institutions* of representative government the charters of the people's rights cannot be saved."—Archibald MacLeish.

in sur′gent (in sur′jĕnt). One who takes part in forcible resistance to the constituted authorities.—"How they do love an *insurgent*—when he is in the other party!"—William E. Borah.

in″ter de pen′dence (in″tur dē pen′-dĕnce). Mutual reliance; reciprocal dependence; reliance on and trust in each other.—"We recognize a mutual *interdependence* of our joint resources."—Franklin Delano Roosevelt.

**in″ter ne′cine** (in″tur nee′sin). Involving mutual slaughter; sanguinary; deadly to both sides.—"The modern Jap soldier is a product of centuries of *internecine* warfare."—Warren J. Clear.

**in trigue′** (in treeg′). Working for an end by underhand means; a plot or deceitful scheme.—"Some were seduced by *intrigue*."—Winston Churchill.

**ir″ri ga′tion** (ir″ĭ gā′shŭn). Artificial watering of land by means of canals, ditches, etc.; bringing water to farm lands and crops by cutting ditches to carry the supply.—"*Irrigation* works, roads, and temples were admirable."—Luis M. Alzamora.

**jin′go** (jing′gō). Pertaining to a person who advocates a warlike policy in foreign affairs; chauvinistic.—"The motto on the new stamp is a bit *jingo*, you'll admit."—Christopher Morley.

**ju″ris dic′tion** (jŏŏr″iss dik′shŭn). Sphere of authority; territory over which a power or right extends.—"He is concerned only with his own interests in his own *jurisdiction*."—Westbrook Pegler.

**league** (leeg). Agreement; alliance; union for mutual assistance; hence, 'in league with' or 'allied with.'—"He is in *league* with the future."—Clare Boothe Luce.

**le ga′tion** (lē gā′shŭn). An embassy; a minister of state and his assistants; a diplomatic mission; the official residence of a legate or diplomatic minister.—"Passports were handed to him for himself and the *legation* personnel."—George Polk.

**long′shore″man** (long′shōre″măn). A man who helps to load ships at a port; a stevedore; a man who works at wharves.—"She was looking pensively into the middle distance at the figure of the personable *longshoreman*."—Alexander Woollcott.

**mach″i na′tions** (mak″ĭ nā′shŭnz). Hostile plans or plots; artful schemes. —"I do not believe that the revolutions which have shaken the world

were merely the *machinations* of evil men."—Dorothy Thompson.

**mag″a zine′** (mag″uh zeen′). A strong building or place of storage for gunpowder and other military supplies. —"From the powder *magazine* the flight continues."—Joseph C. Grew.

**mal′con tents″** (mal′kŏn tents″). Discontented, rebellious people; people dissatisfied with the existing state of affairs; political or social agitators.— "They were the same rude, wild *malcontents* that followed any warlord." —Pearl S. Buck.

**man′date** (man′dāte). An authoritative requirement; a command; a legal order from high authorities.— "I am not outside my country with any *mandate* or with any means to help suffering people."—Francis J. Spellman.

**ma neu′ver ing** (muh nōō′vur ing). Making adroit moves; employing military tactics to gain some advantage.—"The electron tube transmits and receives vocal messages in the *maneuvering* tanks and officers' cars." —James H. McGraw, Jr.

**mar′tial** (mahr′shăl). Pertaining o, or connected with, military operations. —"They have *martial* qualities, but they do not like the drill."—Winston Churchill.

**me′di at″ing** (mee′di āte″ing). Interposing between parties in order to reconcile them; acting as an intermediary; acting as a go-between or connecting link to effect an agreement.—"We may yet find the means of *mediating* between the combatants." —Winston Churchill.

**mil′i tant** (mil′ĭ tănt). Of a warlike tendency; combative; engaged in strife; ready to fight.—"Now I know why the man is so *militant*."— Christopher Morley.

**mon′e tar″y** (mŏn′ē ter″ĭ). Financial; of coinage or other currency; consisting of money; pecuniary.—"Towards the end of the year, thanks to Byron's *monetary* aid, the Greek fleet was fitted out."—André Maurois.

**muf′ti** (muf′ti). Ordinary or civilian dress worn by someone who is generally in uniform; plain clothes worn by those entitled to wear a uniform.

—"I found a higher percentage of our youth in uniform attending religious services than they did when they were in *mufti*."—Barnett R. Brickner.

**mus'ter** (muss'tur). To summon and gather together, as troops; to bring together.—"Equip him with the best to *muster* him into military service." —Carl A. Gray.

**ni'hil ists** (nī'ĭ lists). Those who advocate the social doctrine that denies all authority.—"The *nihilists* believed in progress by catastrophe."— Robert Maynard Hutchins.

**nul″li fi ca'tion** (nul″ĭ fi kā'shŭn). Abolishment of the value of something; the claim of a State to make null and void a federal law of which it disapproved.—"A strict constructionist and enemy of privilege, he checked *nullification* and destroyed the bank."—Avery Craven.

**ob jec'tive** (ob jek'tiv). An object aimed at; a goal or point to be reached.—"The right to a job at fair wages and the support of the government to that end is another major *objective*."—Thomas E. Dewey.

**ob″li ga'tions** (ob″lĭ gā'shŭnz). Requirements imposed; legal bonds; necessary duties.—"These treaties will formally define the mutual *obligations* of the parties."—Lord Halifax.

**och loc'ra cy** (ok lok'ruh si). Rule of the multitude; government by the populace; mob rule.—"Never for a moment should we confuse democracy with *ochlocracy*."—Madame Chiang Kai-shek.

**of fen'sive ly** (ŏ fen'siv li). By serving as a means of attack from which to launch aggressive acts to enforce other conditions; aggressively.—"The island is equally important to us, *offensively* and defensively."—Alexander A. Vandergrift.

**ol'i gar″chies** (ol'i gahr″kiz). Forms of government in which supreme power is restricted to a few.—"In *oligarchies*, militarism has leaped forward, while in those nations which have retained democracy, militarism has waned." —Franklin Delano Roosevelt.

**op press'** (ŏ press'). Impose hardships upon unjustly; tyrannize over; place burdens on; treat cruelly.—"The vast armaments which disfigure our civilization *oppress* all peoples."—Ivy Lee.

**ou″bli ettes'** (ōō″blē ets'). Deep dungeons into which prisoners were lowered through a trap door at the top; secret dungeons without doors or any means of outlook.—"The political police had its prisons and its *oubliettes*."—H. G. Wells.

**par'i ty** (par'ĭ ti). Equality; equivalent position; like state or value.—"That *parity* in the air has always been considered the minimum of our safety." —Winston Churchill.

**par'ley** (pahr'li). Hold a conference; discuss terms; confer.—"We will never *parley;* we will never negotiate with that man."—Winston Churchill.

**par'ti zan ship** (pahr'tĭ zăn ship). Adherence to a separate party or faction.—"These perilous days demand cooperation between us without trace of *partizanship*."—Franklin Delano Roosevelt.

**pa ter'nal ism** (puh tur'năl iz'm). Fatherly care or control, as exercised by a government over the affairs of a people.—"Experience had taught them that political freedom and individual liberty were more essential than any kind of *paternalism*."— Henry W. Taft.

**pa″tri ar'chal** (pāy″tri ahr'kăl). Having a man as head of the family and ruler of the tribe; pertaining to such a government.—"Most societies of today are *patriarchal* in character."— O. R. McGuire.

**pe'on age** (pee'ŏn ij). A system of labor that was like slavery.—"The President took the first effective steps to abolish child *peonage*."—Hugh S. Johnson.

**pleb'i scite** (pleb'i sīte). An expression of the will of the people, by their votes on a matter of public interest; the decree of the people.—"It is utterly foolish to talk about a *plebiscite* on war."—Frank Knox.

**plen″i po ten'ti ar'y** (plen″i pō ten'shi er″i). Invested with full authority by a government.—"We in Europe assumed that your great President Wilson had full *plenipotentiary* powers."—Eduard Beneš.

**plu toc'ra cy** (plo͞o tok'ruh si). The wealthy classes; those who control government by their wealth.—"We cannot have a band of drones in our midst, whether they come from the ancient aristocracy or the modern *plutocracy*."—Winston Churchill.

**prec'e dents** (press'ē dĕnts). Established modes of procedure; examples justifying actions which follow.— "The President, with his thorough knowledge of American naval history, did not choose *precedents* at random."—Elmer Davis.

**pre fer'ment** (prē fur'mĕnt). Promotion or appointment to a higher rank or office; the act of advancement to a better position.—"If you elect me, you will have elected a man who has made no promises of *preferment* to any group."—Charles Edison.

**pre'mi er** (prē'mi ur). The prime or principal minister of state; the prime minister of England or of one of her dominions; the responsible head of a cabinet in a government.—"Has there ever been a greater *premier* of England?"—Emmet Holloway.

**prin"ci pal'i ties** (prin"sĭ pal'ĭ tiz.) Territories of a reigning prince; hence, powerful influences; supreme states.—"The stout old Puritan has fought his last battle against *principalities* and powers."—L. P. Jacks.

**probed** (prōbe'd). Searched through; scrutinized thoroughly; carefully and deeply investigated; examined beneath the surface.—"Activities having to do with this matter are liberally *probed* by the Committee."—Stanley High.

**proc"la ma'tion** (prok"luh mā'shŭn). A public authoritative announcement; an official declaration or publication.—"The King's *proclamation* was in the name of Canada."—W. L. Mackenzie King.

**pro'to col** (prō'tō kol). The original copy of a transaction or diplomatic document; also the etiquette department of the Ministry of Foreign Affairs.—"But to know how to seat properly, as per *protocol*, a half a dozen Ambassadors, their wives, plus

members of the Cabinet, Senate, Congress, Army and Navy is to be an endowed genius."—Elsa Maxwell.

**pro vin'cial isms** (prō vin'shăl iz'mz). Peculiarities of a province; narrow opinions, sayings or manners peculiar to a district.—"Patriotism broke down local *provincialisms*."—Harry Emerson Fosdick.

**pro vi'sion al** (prō vizh'ŭn ăl). Conditional; temporary; for the time being; adopted tentatively to provide for a temporary necessity, but subject to change.—"In these zones they have asked to be recognized as a *provisional* government."—William L. Shirer.

**purg'ing** (purj'ing). Purifying or cleansing from whatever is impure or superfluous; clearing and cleaning.— "It is great to have a part in *purging* an old system of abuses."—Hugo L. Black.

**putsch** (poͦoch). A small rebellion; an unsuccessful outbreak or uprising of the people.—"The beer hall *putsch* of Hitler led to the destruction."— Anne O'Hare McCormick.

**quar'ter** (kwor'tur). Clemency; mercy to a captured enemy; forbearance.— "No *quarter* will be allowed that small minority of aliens who seek to undermine our institutions."—Marshall E. Dimock.

**ral'ly ing** (ral'i ing). Collecting and restoring order; assembling for a common purpose; arousing to action; uniting for a fresh effort.—"The nations failed to establish a *rallying* point."—John Curtin.

**rap'ine** (rap'in). The taking of property by force; spoliation; robbery; plundering.—"Unless one were hardened to these tales of bloodshed and *rapine* one simply could not believe them."—George N. Shuster.

**rat"i fi ca'tion** (rat"ĭ fi kā'shŭn). The act of giving official or authoritative sanction; confirmation; approval.— "The treaty must come back to the Senate for *ratification*, amendment, or rejection."—Joseph H. Ball.

**re ac'tion ar"y** (rē ak'shŭn er"ĭ). Favoring an opposite movement or counter policy; marked by action in an opposite direction.—"The grandeur of the *reactionary* monarchy and its collapse are both covered in the novel."—Orville Prescott.

**rec"i proc'i ty** (ress"ĭ pross'ĭ ti). Mutual cooperation; exchange of privileges; mutually interchangeable obligations.—"Our prosperity and peaceful existence will be determined in large measure by whether we can live on terms of decent friendship and *reciprocity* with this new Russian colossus."—Leland Stowe.

**re ci'sion** (rē sizh'ŭn). Canceling; repealing; annulment; rescinding.— "The sudden *recision* of the agreement was a shock to all parties."—Hugh E. Blackstone.

**rec"la ma'tion** (rek"luh mā'shŭn). A reclaiming or restoration to a former state; a process of recovering or bringing back to a good and useful condition.—"After forty years of the most drastic *reclamation* struggle in America, they have disarmed the river."—Tom Hughes.

**re gime'** (rāy zheem'). A system of government; a social system; a mode of administration.—"Under that *regime* women are forced from their homes into factories."—Pearl S. Buck.

**reg'i men** (rej'ĭ men). A systematized course of living; control; a system of governing; a prescribed rule.—"A realization is spreading that a new theory of living and an untried *regimen* are being forced upon us."— Annie Nathan Meyer.

**reg"i men ta'tion** (rej"ĭ men tā'shŭn). Formation into groups, as into a regiment; the process of organization according to a system.—"The American in the making would have had scant use for blueprints, bureaucrats or *regimentation*."—James Truslow Adams.

**re'gion al** (rē'jŭn ăl). Of a region or division; sectional; belonging to an entire region.—"Their calculations do not extend beyond the functions of the *regional* bosses."—Westbrook Pegler.

**rep"a ra'tion** (rep"uh rā'shŭn). Amends; atonement; restoration after injury; compensation for wrong. —"Here, then, we see the beginnings of a process of *reparation*, and of the

chastisement of wrongdoing."—Winston Churchill.

**re pa'tri at"ed** (rē pāy'tri āte"ed). Restored to their own country; brought back to land of birth.—"They allowed the enemy diplomats and agents plenty of time and freedom before they were *repatriated*."— Walter Lippmann.

**re pri'sals** (rē prī'zălz). Forcible seizures from an enemy by way of retailiation or indemnity; injuries in payment for injuries.—"We British will never seek to take vengeance by wholesale mass *reprisals*."—Lord Simon.

**re sourc'es** (rē sorce'iz). Available property, products, and supplies; wealth and powers of achievement.— "Today we are in the contest with all the strength and the vast *resources* of our great nation."—John D. Rockefeller, Jr.

**re voke'** (rē vōke'). Recall; rescind; repeal; withdraw or take back; annul by taking back.—"The Board can issue, *revoke*, recall, cancel, or void any of these books."—Marie Smith.

**sacked** (sakt). Plundered; looted; carried off the contents; robbed by force.—"The rabble broke into the city and *sacked* and raped and pillaged."—Henry James Forman.

**schisms** (siz'mz). Divisions into groups or sects; separations into hostile companies on account of divergent opinions.—"*Schisms* and hatred stalk in the land."—Alfred M. Landon.

**se ces'sions** (sē sesh'ŭnz). Withdrawals from a group; acts of seceding or retiring from a party or organization.— "The public became gradually accustomed to professorial *secessions*."— L. P. Jacks.

**se di'tion** (sē dish'ŭn). Language or conduct directed against the government; hence, plotting against authority.—"Very few traitors and spies were convicted under the *Sedition* Act."—Rodney L. Mott.

**serf'dom** (surf'dŭm). Bondage; slavery, compulsory servitude.—"This is a struggle between liberty and *serfdom*." —Percy C. Magnus.

**ser'vi tude** (sur'vĭ tūde). Slavery; bondage; serfdom; forced labor.— "It was a real and actual state of *servitude.*"—Winston Churchill.

**sig'na to"ries** (sig'nuh tō"riz). Those who sign and are bound with other signers by the terms of a document or agreement.—"The three great powers were *signatories* to the treaty." —Charles Henry Crozier.

**sov'er eign ty** (sov'ur ĭn ti). Supreme authority; dominion; control.— "Every nation has *sovereignty* of its skies."—Clare Boothe Luce.

**spoils** (spoylz). The gains of a successful party in an encounter; perquisites or profits from some undertaking.— "The *spoils* of victory will be the responsibilities of a new world and a new kind of peace."—Percy C. Magnus.

**spo"li a'tion** (spō"li āy'shŭn). Plunder; pillage; destruction; act of despoiling; authorized robbery in war.— "The *spoliation* of the ancient Norman towns was one of the tragedies of history."—George F. Gahagan.

**strat'a gems** (strat'uh jemz). Maneuvers to outwit an enemy; changes of position to deceive a foe; devices for gaining advantage.—"He used a variety of *stratagems* to evade the enemy concentrations."—Charles J. Rolo.

**strat'e gy** (strat'ē jee). The science of military position and the employment of means for gaining advantage; the use of stratagems and maneuvers.—"The *strategy* under which we are operating is one of mutual help."—Claude R. Wickard.

**sub'ju gat"ing** (sub'jŏŏ gāte"ing).Conquering; subduing; making subservient; enslaving.—"They may not in the end be found capable of *subjugating* and exploiting the four hundred millions of Chinese."—Winston Churchill.

**tac ti'cian** (tak tish'ŭn). One who employs tactics or the art of maneuvering to gain an end; one who uses clever devices to accomplish something; a skilful manager.—"He is a *tactician* unable to grasp strategic implications."—Max Werner.

**tit'u lar** (tit'chŏŏ lur). In name or title

only, not an active officer; nominal only, not in reality.—"He is still the *titular* head of the Republican party." —A. L. Miller.

**to tal"i tar'i an ism** (tō tal"ĭ tair'i ăniz'm). Government of a country by one party or faction.—"*Totalitarianism* is insidiously boring from within the temple of our liberties."—Harold L. Ickes.

**trai'tor ous** (trāy'tur ŭs). Guilty of treason; like a traitor; faithless; perfidious; treacherous. — "There were *traitorous* moderates, he thundered."—Helen C. White.

**trea'son** (tree'z'n). Violation of allegiance to country or ruler; disloyalty to one's country; assistance to enemies of one's country.—"The charge is *treason* and attempted murder."— Stephen Vincent Benét.

**tri um'vi rate** (trī um'vi rāte). A group or coalition of three men who unitedly exercise authority or control; government by three; a group of three.— "The *triumvirate* of God, Gold, and Glory motivated our forefathers to lay down their lives to reserve all power to the people."—T. C. Hannah.

**tru'cial** (trōō'shăl). Of the nature of a truce or respite; that call for cessation of fighting during negotiations; bound by conditions of a truce.— "Most of the misunderstandings would be speedily forgotten were we disposed to make *trucial* advances."— William S. Walsh.

**tyr'an nize** (tir'ă nīze). Rule as tyrants; govern with unjust severity; commit acts of oppression; use power cruelly.—"They had seized the government and pretended to *tyrannize* over honest people."— Helen C. White.

**u kas'es** (ū kāse'iz). Official decrees; government proclamations.—"Hundred of persons were awaiting trials for violating these *ukases.*"—George W. Maxey.

**ul"ti ma'tum** (ul"tĭ māy'tŭm). The final terms offered; a last proposal or demand.—"Without a declaration of war, without even an *ultimatum,* the bombs rained down." — Winston Churchill.

**un'der lings** (un'dur lingz). Subordinates; people of lower position or rank; inferiors; under-officials.—"The governors and their *underlings* counted upon the missionary efforts to win the friendship of the Indians."—G. Jones Odriozola.

**u″ni cam'er al** (ū″ni kam'ur ăl). Consisting of only one chamber or legislative body.—"The one-house or *unicameral* legislature has never been given a trial by any state under present conditions."—Hubert R. Gallagher.

**u″ni ver sal'i ty** (ū″nĭ vur sal'ĭ ti). Unrestricted adaptability; unlimited versatility; wholesale comprehensiveness; the state of being all-embracing. —"*Universality* is not the solution for our security problem."—Jan Christiaan Smuts.

**u to'pi an** (ū tō'pi ăn). Ideal; having an imaginary perfection; like Utopia, an ideal commonwealth or existence. —"There will be no commitments to *utopian* schemes incapable of practical fulfillment."—Joseph P. Kennedy.

**van'guard″** (van'gahrd″). The advance-guard of an army; the front troops; the van; soldiers marching in front to clear the way; hence, those in the forefront of any company.— "He is the leader of the *vanguard* of the air forces against the archenemy."—C. Wellington Furlong.

**vas'sal** (vass'ăl). Tributary; politically dependent; subject.—"This amendment to all intents and purposes made Cuba a *vassal* state of this country."—Gordon Heriot.

**vul'ner a ble** (vul'nur uh b'l). Capable of being wounded; open to attack or injury; assailable.—"We are in some ways more *vulnerable* to air attack than any other country— once we can be reached."—Winston Churchill.

**yeo'men** (yō'mĕn). Men who owned free land; farmers cultivating their own farms; higher class retainers. —"John Wyclif was responsible for organizing peasants, workers, artisans, and *yeomen* into groups."— H. W. Prentis, Jr.

## ONE-MINUTE REFRESHER

Here are ten words that have to do with national or international affairs. Following this list are ten synonymous phrases. Fill in the proper word after each descriptive phrase:

a. emissary
b. demagogic
c. dossiers
d. abrogated
e. Anglophile

f. cabal
g. oligarchy
h. autonomy
i. ochlocracy
j. bicameral

1. The type of government that is run by mob rule is called a (an) _____.

2. They are a group of persons secretly united to plan and carry out conspiracies. They are a (an) _____.

3. They are unprincipled leaders who seek to gain influence by pandering to the prejudices of the people. They are _____ politicians.

4. He loves England and everything English. He is a (an) _____.

5. He is an accredited agent sent on a mission. He is a (an) _____.

6. They are bundles of papers that contain records. They are _____.

7. That nation has a legislature consisting of two chambers or branches. It has a _____ legislature.

8. Japan annulled by authority the Washington treaty. Japan _____ the treaty.

9. They have a government in which the supreme power is restricted to a few. Their government is called a (an) _____.

10. They gave to that small nation the right and power of self-government. They gave that nation a large measure of _____.

*Answers:* 1 — i; 2 — f; 3 — b; 4 — e; 5 - a; 6 — c; 7 — j; 8 — d; 9 — g; 10 — h.

# CHAPTER XIII

## THESE ARE YOUR WORD FAMILIES

WE SOMETIMES are inclined to think of words as unrelated and individual creations. As static entities. Words don't just happen. They live and grow according to fixed laws; they are born and they die; they marry and have vast progenies.

One of the most fascinating, engaging and colorful topics in the study of words is the search for the stories that lie behind them, and that so often tie them intimately one to another.

I have gathered together in this chapter a few of the many families and have segregated them with the parent root at the head of each section.

The families are not complete. The cousins and uncles and aunts are much too prolific to be included in this volume. The Latin root *spect* from *spectare* (to see), for instance, has actually given us 256 different English words at the last counting; such serviceable ones as *spec*ify, *spect*rum, *spect*ator, in*spect*, *spect*acle, retro*spect*, all with the idea of "see" or "sight" buried in them.

These sample families are merely indicative of the wealth that research can uncover, and I will ask you to look at other words in this book and see whether you can detect some root that may lead to the brothers and sisters that these words may have.

There is an English brood, and a fascinating one, that was spawned by the Latin word *plicare*. The translation of the word is "to fold." The problem that you find so "com*plicat*ed" has been folded in with something else and is hard to untangle. A sup*plic*ant folds his knees before you. When you ex*plic*ate a thing you unfold it. You lay it open, and you therefore "explain" it, but if you are faced with du*plic*ity, watch out. *Duo* means "two." Something may easily be concealed within the second fold! Sim*plic*ity of course is only one fold and conceals nothing. While if you have any com*plic*ity with a murder it means that you are *com* (with) *plic* (folded) or you are folded or tangled up with it.

This search for the stories in words, and the family ties between words, is more than an engaging hobby. By this search we can better understand the meanings of words, and we are certain to arrive at finer discriminations. When we know that the translation of the Latin word *torquere* is "to twist," such words as "*tor*ment" and "*tort*uous" take on a new significance. We then realize that a smart "re*tort*" is one that twists and turns a remark back against the one who has just said it. And we see clearly that "ex*tort*ed" money has been twisted and wrung from the victim by pain and by force.

Words, like people, must be known to be understood. The more you can see *all around* a word, the better you know its pronunciation, its varying meanings, its history and its family connections, the more that word will become your private and personal possession.

There may be an appreciable effort that will be necessary to this accomplishment, but we all know that it is by little disciplines that we arrive at a major success.

The first eleven discussions of the word families on the next few pages are done at some length in order to make their family connections perfectly clear, and to enrich them I have included many simple words that do not appear elsewhere in this volume. Directly after these the families are merely listed in groups, but the definitions in these lists are so arranged that it will be easy for the reader to locate the common root that ties each family together.

## These Are Your Word Families

CAPUT is a Latin noun that means "head." Its root appears in the following words in the forms *cap, capit, cipit, cip.*

It is quite easy to trace *caput* and its meaning "head" through our English words. The City of Washington is the *capit*al, or "head," of the United States; a *capit*al letter stands at the "head" of each printed sentence; a *cap*tain stands at the "head" of his troops; and in architecture the piece that stands at the "head" or top of a column or pilaster is called the *capit*al. In ancient days punishment by death usually meant the headsman's axe; now *capit*al punishment is more often in the electric chair. When a person loses his head in an accident, he is said to have been de*cap*itated, and sometimes the accident is caused by his being too pre*cip*itate, in such a hurry that he has gone into something literally "head first." A pre*cip*ice also looks as though it had plunged down "head first." We have taken over the Latin phrase *per capita* without change. When we say "so much *per capita*," we mean "by heads," or one for each individual.

DUCERE is a Latin verb that means "to lead" or "to draw." Its root appears in the following words in the forms *duc*, *duk* or *duct*.

This makes it clear to us that when a girl is se*duc*ed, she is led (*ducere*) aside (*se*) from the straight path, and when a boy is in*duct*ed into the army, he is "led into" it. When a metal is soft, like gold, and can be led or drawn out into a wire it is *duct*ile. No clever de*duct*ion is required to find the meaning of "lead" in the royal title *duke*, or even in Il *Duce*, the one-time self-appointed "leader" of the Italian people. Again, when I con*duct* you through this study of words, I am attempting to "lead" you with me and it will con*duce*, or "lead" you, to good results. If you, in turn, in*duce* a friend to come into your home, you are "leading" him in, and if you ask him for some comments on your house this may e*duce* or "lead out" a complimentary remark. Ab*duct*ors "lead" or carry people away (Latin *ab*, away) by force; and when we make de*duct*ions about the kidnaping, we are following a line of reasoning that "leads from" (Latin *de*, from) a group of theories or facts to a conclusion. When you are intro*duc*ed to a person, it means that you have been "led within" (Latin *intro*, within) the circle of that person's acquaintance. And when a child has been e*duc*ated, his inner qualities and abilities have been "led out."

FACERE is a Latin verb that means "to make" or "to do." Its root appears in the following words in the forms *fact*, *fic* and *fy*.

A *fact*ory is a place where goods are manu*fact*ured, and if they are well-made the producers will certi*fy*, or "make certain" (Latin *certus*. certain) that the shipment will give satis*fact*ion. When we know that certi*fy* means "make certain" and that digni*fy* means "make worthy" (Latin *dignus*, worthy) it will be easy for us to guess at the meanings of simpli*fy*, glori*fy*, falsi*fy*, uni*fy*, justi*fy* and beauti*fy*. Those who paci*fy* others are really "peace-makers" (Latin *pax*, peace), and those who dei*fy* others are truly "god-makers" (Latin *deus*, god). An edi*fic*e is a building (Latin *aedes*, house) and a forti*fic*ation is a structure that has been "made strong" (Latin *fortis*, strong). The Latin terms that combine to form our English words magni*fic*ent, arti*fic*ial and bene*fic*ial originally meant "made large," "made arty," "made well." If a frightening event should terri*fy* you and petri*fy* you, it "makes terror for you" and "makes you into stone" (Latin *petra*, rock).

GENERE is a Latin verb that means "to give birth to" or "to produce." Its root appears in our English words as *gen*.

There is an army of these *gen* words open to discovery. The first chapter of the Bible, for instance, is the book of *Gen*esis and this shows that the story it tells goes back to the "birth" of the world. If we should be inteiested in the early beginnings of our own family, we are touching on the subject of *gen*ealogy or the knowledge of family origins (Greek *logy*, study or science). Again, if a person should be suffering from a con*gen*ital disease it is a disease he was "born with." If we happen to be a *gen*tleman or *gen*erous or *gen*teel, we were just "born" that way, and it may be thanks to the fortune of eu*gen*ics, or being "well-born." The Greek prefix *eu* means "well." Of course, if you should de*gen*erate, you will have fallen from (Latin *de*, from) your position at "birth," and if you are unre*gen*erate, you have fallen so low that you don't want to reform or "be born again." If you are that type your pro*gen*y, or your children who follow you, may suffer. There are inventors in the world who are in*gen*ious and have the "inborn" power to accomplish things, and if they are clever enough they may become *gen*iuses.

GRAPHEIN is a Greek verb that means "to write." Its root appears in our English words in the forms *graph* and *gram*.

When we tele*graph* or send a tele*gram*, we are "writing far away" (Greek *tele*, far). When we "write" on paper we often use pencils made of *graph*ite. With the *graph*ophone we are "writing with sound" (Greek *phone*, sound), and with the helio*graph*—the instrument that is used for sending messages by means of the sun's rays thrown from a mirror—we are "writing with light." An author will auto*graph* his latest book for you; that is, he will "write" his name on the fly-leaf himself (Greek *autos*, self). And a good conversationalist will give you a *graph*ic description of his trip, one that will be just as vivid as though it were "written" down. The word *ge* in Greek means earth, and geo*graph*y would then be a "writing" about, or description of, the earth. Should you be interested, a *graph*ologist will give an estimate of your character and your type of personality by studying a sample of your hand "writing." When a famous person dies, a laudatory epi*graph* will often be "written" or carved upon his tomb.

LIGARE is a Latin verb that means "to bind." It appears in the words below in the forms *lig*, *ligat*, *ly*, *li*, *leag*, *loy*.

This root does not appear in many English words, but where it *does* appear it is particularly vivid. If we are *li*able for a certain debt, that debt is "binding" upon us until it is paid, and a *li*en on our property is legal and "binding." In our lives we are faced with certain ob*lig*ations that we are ob*lig*ed to fulfill because we are "bound" thereto by reason of duty, law, loyalty, gratitude or simple good faith. A *ligat*ure is a surgical thread that the surgeon uses to tie or "bind" off blood-vessels during an operation, and *ligat*ure is also a tough tissue that ties or "binds" bones together. We discover things "bound" together in a metal al*loy* or a *leag*ue, and even the word al*ly* comes from the Latin *ad* (to) and *ligare* (to bind), and so nations that are al*lies* are "bound" together.

MANUS is a Latin noun that means "hand." It appears in the following words in the forms *manu*, *mani*, and *man*, and in its French form *main*.

Today *manu*factured articles are largely made by machinery, but the word *manu*facture carries within itself the record of those days when everything had to be "made by hand" (Latin *factura*, a making). When you have a *mani*cure, you are merely having "hand-care." When slaves are e*man*cipated or freed, they are taken from the "hands" that held them and their *man*acles or "hand-cuffs" are stricken off. The meaning of *manu*al labor is easy to see, but a *manu*al is a small "handbook." When you *mani*pulate your car through traffic, you are using the English form of a Latin word that means "filling your hands." When you *mani*pulate any piece of machinery, it is *mani*fest that you have your "hands full," and a thing that is *mani*fest is so clear and so near that you can reach for it and pick it up with your "hands." This same meaning of "hand" runs through *man*ners, originally the use of your "hands," and *man*date, written orders that were presented by "hand." If you *main*tain your position in an argument, or if you *main*tain a home, you literally (Latin *tenere*, hold; *manu*, by hand) keep hold of it with your hands.

MERGERE is a Latin verb that means "to dip." Its root appears in our English words as *merg* and *mers*.

We often hear of business *merg*ers, and this simply means that great corporations have *merg*ed and have so been "dipped" or sunk into a larger unit or *merg*er, and have in this way lost their individual identities. There are a number of modified Latin prefixes that attach themselves to *mergere* such as *sub*, under; *e*, out; *im*, in. When an object is sub*merg*ed it is "dipped" below the surface and is swamped, inundated, overwhelmed. When it comes up and into view again it is said to e*merg*e, and some things that come up suddenly often present e*merg*encies that call for immediate action on our part. Im*mers*ed is a more gentle form of *mergere* and doesn't necessarily indicate that the object or person has to be "dipped" entirely under. People who are baptized are im*mers*ed and an individual can be im*mers*ed in study.

PHONE is a Greek noun that means "sound." It appears in the following words in the forms *phone* and *phon*.

Our common word tele*phone* literally means "far away sound"; the mega*phone* that is used by the announcer in sporting events signifies "powerful sound" (Greek *mega*, large or powerful); and the micro*phone* of the radio is a "small sound" (Greek *micro*, small) but it carries with it the further meaning of a small sound that can be made more powerful. With gramo*phone* we have the Greek form *gram*, write, combined with "sound," so the gramo*phone* "writes sound." If the music that comes over the air is pleasing, we call it eu*phon*ious (Greek *eu*, well or good). If, on the other hand, the sound should be discordant and ugly, this is known as caco*phon*y or "bad sound" (Greek *kakos*, bad). In some forms of music, particularly in church services, we speak of anti*phon*al music, as when an anthem is sung alternately by the choir and the congregation. Here the sounds are opposed (Greek *anti*, against) to each other. The word *phon*etics covers the science of "speech sounds," the "sounds" of our language.

SCRIBERE is a Latin verb that means "to write." Its root appears in our English words as *scrib* or *script*.

The simplest combinations of this root are found in the English word *scrib*ble, to "write" hastily or carelessly, and in the *script* of the theater or the motion picture, or the ancient *scrib*e who patiently "wrote" or tran*scrib*ed his manu*script*s. The word *script*, of course, is an abbreviated form of manu*script*, and a manu*script* is something that was originally "written by hand" (Latin *manu*, by hand). Now we have typewritten manu*script*s. From all this we can easily guess that the *script*ures are holy "writings." We can sub*scrib*e to an idea and thus endorse it or "underwrite" it, or we may sub*scrib*e for a magazine, which naturally implies that we are "writing" our name under it, giving a "written" promise to pay for it. Those who are circum*scrib*ed are hemmed in and narrowly limited, for a circle has been "written" all around them (Latin *circum*, around). The army con*script* has had his name "written" down together with (Latin *con*, with) others and is so enlisted by compulsion.

VIDERE is a Latin verb that means "to see." Its root appears in our English words in a multitude of forms that are fascinating but often difficult to trace and detect. Some Latin and Greek roots come into our language almost unchanged. The root *"vid,"* however, has been twisted into such spellings as *vis, vie vey, vy, wis, wiz* and *wit,* but each one of them still holds the meaning of "see" within it.

Those who are *wise* can "see" clearly and therefore have *wis*dom. The *wiz*ard and the *wit*ch are shrewd and have sharp *wit*s and their *vis*ion is sometimes supernatural. Pro*vid*ence (Latin *pro,* forward) is the power to "see ahead," and e*vid*ence (Latin *e* or *ex,* out) is something a lawyer draws out of a *wit*ness so that it can be "seen." A *vie*w is a scene that we sur*vey* or "look over," and when we super*vis*e a job we "look over" that also. We "oversee" it. When we re*vis*e our opinion of a person, we are really "seeing" and judging him again, and should we en*vy* a person we are literally "seeing against him," or looking at him askance. And, of course, the in*vis*ible can't be "seen" at all.

## Additional Word Families

### AMARE

A Latin verb that means "to love." Its root appears in the following words in the forms *am, amat:*

**am'o rous** (am'ō rŭs). Passionately in "love"; very affectionate; doting.— "An *am*orous bull whale may be very amusing to us but to his lady friend he is doubtless as exciting as a matinée idol is to a débutante."— Roy Chapman Andrews.

**en am'ored** (en am'urd). In "love" with; fascinated or charmed by; delighted with.—"At the same time he is still en*am*ored of the farm tradition."—James Truslow Adams.

**am'a to"ry** (am'uh tō"ri). "Loving" passionately and sexually; "loving" erotically.—"Her *am*atory adventures had been numerous."—Don Marquis.

**par'a mour** (par'uh mŏŏr). A "lover"; generally one who "loves" illicitly; one who illegally takes the place of husband or wife.—"You imperil our whole tribe with your black par*amour*."—Thomas Mann.

### CEDERE

A Latin verb that means "to yield," to "withdraw," or "to move." Its root appears in the following words in the forms *ced, cess:*

**cede** (seed). "Yield" or give up something; surrender title to rights or property.—"China, with all other liberty-loving nations, will gladly *ced*e such of its sovereign powers as may be required."—T. V. Soong.

**re cede'** (rē seed'). "Withdraw" or "move" back; hence, become more distant.—"The boundaries of the great unknown re*ced*e with every advance of knowledge."—Arthur Meighen.

**se cede'** (sē seed'). "Withdraw" from a religious body or political organization; formally resign from a union or association.—"From time to time Texas threatens, jokingly, to se*ced*e from the Union."—Donald G. Cooley.

**con ced'ed** (kŏn seed'ed). Admitted to be true; "yielded" or acknowledged; granted.—"The program is generally con*ced*ed in the industry to have done the best job in carrying messages."—A. S. Burrows.

**ac ced'ed** (ak seed'ed). "Yielded" to; given consent to; assented to; agreed to.—"There is justice as well as wisdom in the American position acceded to at Moscow."—Arthur Krock.

**ces'sion** (sesh'ŭn). A "yielding" or giving up to another; a handing over; a surrendering, especially of a piece of land or the rights to property.—"This forced cession of territory can lead to a future war."—George F. Gahagan.

**con ces'sion** (kŏn sesh'ŭn). The act of "yielding"; a giving in to something; an acknowledgment.—"The duck knew his own bedtime, but that was his only concession to country life."—Paul Cranston.

**con ces'sions** (kŏn sesh'ŭnz). Grants of land or the rights connected with it; lands or rights "yielded" or given up to them.—"Hungary and Poland will receive concessions of territory." —H. V. Kaltenborn.

**ac'cess** (ak'sess). Entrance; a passage or path provided by something "yielding" or "withdrawing"; a way to go in.—"We provided safe and free access for the workers to their jobs."—Westbrook Pegler.

**ac ces'si ble** (ak sess'ĭ b'l). Attainable; easy to reach because an entrance has been provided or "yielded" so that one can go in; affording passage or entrance.—"The seat of administration might well be some point like Panama, readily accessible by sea and air to all continents."—Harold E. Stassen.

**in"ter ced'ed** (in"tur seed'ed). Mediated; interposed; pleaded that someone "yield"; asked a favor from one person for another.—"He successfully interceded with the manager to save the girl's job."—Dan Parker.

## CLAUDERE

A Latin verb that means "to shut" or "to close." Its root appears in the following words in the forms claus, clud, clus, clois:

**claus"tro pho'bi a** (klawce"trō fō'bi uh). A morbid dread of being "shut" in or unable to escape; a fear or horror of "closed" places.—

"An urge to spread the gospel to the four corners of the earth produced in him a kind of national claustrophobia."—Robert Humphreys.

**ex clud'ed** (eks klōōd'id). "Shut" out or kept out; debarred; prevented from entering.—"Because of their system, I am excluded."—André Maurois.

**pre clud'ed** (prē klōōd'id). "Shut" out by some kind of barrier placed ahead; hence, impeded; rendered ineffectual by a preceding action.— "No plane was damaged to an extent that precluded its proceeding to its destination."—James H. Doolittle.

**con cludes'** (kŏn klōōdz'). Brings something to a "close" by "shutting" off anything further; forms a decisive judgment; "closes" an argument by inferring.—"He concludes that smoking after meals brings on a certain pleasure and favors digestive activities."—Robert H. Feldt.

**in clu'sion** (in klōō'zhŭn). Enclosure as part of a whole; something included or to be "inclosed" within.— "I'll mark that down for inclusion in my program."—Sterling McCormick.

**se clu'sion** (sē klōō'zhŭn). Isolation or aloofness; a keeping in retirement, "shut" off, or apart from others.— "They were newly hatched from the egg of Oriental seclusion."—Roy Chapman Andrews.

**re cluse'** (rē klōōce'). One who "shuts" himself off from his fellow men to live a secret or "shut" in life because he likes solitude or for religious reasons; a hermit; an anchorite; a cloistered nun.—"He says that the scholar of today is a selfish recluse who pursues learning solely for private pleasure or fame."— Maurice Baum.

**clois'tered** (kloyce'turd). "Shut" off from the outside world, or, as in the following quotation, confined to one place or purpose. The cloisters of a monastery or convent are covered walks where monks or nuns can get air and exercise "shut" off from outsiders.—"I am interested in art that is not *clois*tered and set apart."—Nelson A. Rockefeller.

## CURRERE

A Latin verb that means "to run." It appears in the following words in the forms *curr, curs, cours, cor:*

**con curred'** (kŏn kurd'). "Ran" together, hence, agreed in opinion; assented to; acquiesced.—"The statement was alleged to have been con*curr*ed in by the secretary."—William M. Jeffers.

**con cur'rent** (kŏn kur'ĕnt). Occurring, existing, or "running" together at the same time.—"The invasion of the Malay Peninsula was almost exactly con*curr*ent with the attack on Pearl Harbor."—Thomas C. Hart.

**oc cur'rence** (ŏ kur'ĕnce). An event or happening; a taking place; a "running" toward, or coming to pass; an incident.—"If a revolution was threatened you could bet on its oc*curr*ence; if an agitation was in progress you could bet on its success."—L. P. Jacks.

**cur'ren cy** (kur'ĕn si). General acceptance, prevalence, or recption as a result of moving or "running" freely; general esteem or standing.—"Such a language can acquire life and *curr*ency only if there is a recognition of the role it can play."—Christian Gauss.

**cur'so ry** (kur'sō ri). Rapid and superficial; "run" through in a rather hasty way.—"You can ask your doctor to make a *curs*ory examination of your eyes as a part of his routine physical examination."—Harry S. Gradle.

**pre cur'sors** (prē kur'surz). Those who "run" ahead of others as harbingers or heralds. These forerunners are often not people but signs which give some intimation of coming events.—"These symptoms of hate and intolerance are sure pre*curs*ors of cleavages."—James E. Freeman.

**cur'sive** (kur'siv). "Running" or flowing, as applied to a style of writing in which the strokes are joined or "run" together and the angles of the letters

rounded.—"The *curs*ive writing used in the copybooks many years ago certainly produced legible handwriting."—Bruce Ellsworth.

**ex cur'sive** (eks kur'siv). "Running" out or away; rambling; wandering; making excursions or digressions from the point.—"The speech was so ex*curs*ive that it lost all direction and meaning."—Malcom Babbitt.

**dis cur'sive** (diss kur'siv). Passing or "running" from one subject to another; ranging over a wide field.—"The book is a collection of the somewhat random and dis*curs*ive thoughts of a very great musician."—Gerald W. Johnson.

**con'course** (kon'korce). A "running" together or in company with; hence, an assemblage; a gathering or crowd; a throng.—"These bearded trees resembled an interminable con*cours*e of old men attending a public funeral."—Hilary St. George Saunders.

**dis cours'es** (diss korce'iz). Long discussions or lectures; treatises "running" to and fro over different phases of a subject.—"There are books that in the guise of fiction are persuasive dis*cours*es on philosophy."—Irwin Edman.

**re course'** (rē korce'). A "running" back to, or a resort to, for help or security; an appeal for protection.—"If unity is to be achieved, it cannot be through re*cours*e to the past, but through concentration upon the goal ahead."—Henry P. Van Dusen.

**suc'cor** (suk'ur). A "running" to place something under as a support; hence, a "running" to the aid of or to help; assistance or relief in time of need or danger.—"It shall not be said that he denied suc*cor* to the friendless."—Stephen Vincent Benét.

## FRANGERE

A Latin verb that means "to break." Its root appears in the following words in the forms *frag, fract, frail, fring:*

**frag'men tar"y** (frag'mĕn ter"i). Composed of detached or "broken" pieces or fragments; made up of incomplete or unfinished parts.—"She was intent upon transcribing *frag*mentary notes."—Mark Sullivan.

**frag′ile** (fraj′ĭl). Easily "broken" or destroyed; frail; delicate.—"One's physical resources had ebbed to low tide, and one's *frag*ility had made common cause with such other *frag*ile things as hummingbirds and heliotrope."—Lloyd C. Douglas.

**frac′tious** (frak′shŭs). Likely to "break" out in a fit of irritation; peevish; fretful; perverse; restive. —"They haven't the slightest notion why they waste their time with *frac*tious calves."—Ernest Douglas.

**re frac′to ry** (rē frak′tō ri). Apt to "break" away from control; unruly; ungovernable; resistant.—"The world is re*fract*ory to moral teaching such as we have to offer."—L. P Jacks.

**in frac′tion** (in frak′shŭn). An act of "breaking" or violating; disregard; violation.—"Never again must the civilized world tolerate unilateral in*fract*ion of treaties."—Anthony Eden.

**frail′ties** (frail′tiz). Qualities or states of being easily "broken" or weak; hence, moral infirmities; liabilities to err; weaknesses.—"Despite its faults and *frail*ties, capitalism glows with the colors of perfection when compared with the other two systems."— Eric A. Johnston.

**in fringed′** (in fring′d′). Violated; disregarded; "broken" in upon; intruded on; trespassed upon.—"Civil liberties are often in*fring*ed."—S. Bernard Wortis.

## GRADI

A Latin verb that means "to step" or "to go." Its root appears in the following words in the forms *grad, gress:*

**grad′u at″ed** (grad′ū āte″id). Marked out in "steps" or degrees; divided into grades or spaces according to scale; marked with degrees of measurement.—"The measuring glass

was *grad*uated down to fractions of ounces."—Emory L. Fielding.

**gra′di ent** (grāy′di ĕnt). The rise and fall; the "going" up and down as though by degrees or "steps"; the rate of increase or decrease; the grade.—"The high potential *grad*ient of the lightning passes up the steel skeleton of the building and slides off the mooring mast into the sky."— Homer Croy.

**ret′ro grade** (ret′rō grāde). That "goes" from better to worse; that "steps" backward or deteriorates; degenerating; decadent.—"I believe there is a sort of retro*grade* evolution going on in my mind."— Axel Munthe.

**in′gress** (in′gress). An entrance; a place to "go" in; power or freedom of entering.—"In all theaters every in*gress* and e*gress* must be kept clear of obstructions."—Jack Bond.

**ag gres′sive** (ă gress′iv). Disposed to vigorous activity to gain an end; pushing; encroaching or forcing an entrance or way to "go" in.—"For centuries God has been seeking to discipline the nations out of ag*gress*ive self-aggrandisement."—Henry Sloane Coffin.

**re gres′sion** (rē gresh′ŭn). A return or a "stepping" back to a lower or less favorable state; a "going" backwards; degeneration.—"It was a sad re*gress*ion from his tough, cheerful army of two years ago."—Albert Perry.

**di gres′sion** (di gresh′ŭn). A turning aside, or "stepping" astray, from the main subject; a deviation; a divergence.—"They claim that freedom is just a di*gress*ion from progress toward Truth."—Bernard A. Brown.

## GREX

A Latin noun that means "flock" or "herd." Its root appears in the following words in the form *greg:*

**gre gar′i ous** (grē gair′i ŭs). Fond of companionship; tending to "flock" together or associate in companies; habitually living together in a community or crowd.—"The river of student life carries all the power that comes from the *greg*arious impulses of human beings."—James Bryant Conant.

**seg′re gat″ed** (seg′rē gāte″id). Placed apart from others; separated from the "herd"; cut off from others; isolated.—"I am not for thrusting off western civilization and becoming se*greg*ated in our independence."—Rabindranath Tagore.

**ag′gre gate** (ag′rē gāte). Gathered into a whole; assembled or gathered together, as a "flock"; collective.—"There is no change in the ag*greg*ate earnings for the two years."—Edward Foss Wilson.

**e gre′gious ly** (ē gree′jŭs li). Excessively; extraordinarily; flagrantly; in a way that surpasses or towers above the "herd" or ordinary men; conspicuously.—"Such a position is e*greg*iously conceited."—Robert M. Hutchins.

## JACERE

A Latin verb that means "to throw" or "to cast." Its root appears in the following words in the forms *jac*, *ject*:

**e jac″u la′tion** (ē jak″ū lā′shŭn). An abrupt or impulsive sound or word uttered or "thrown" out, expressing surprise or any sudden emotion.—"There was a half-audible e*jac*ulation, for this maneuver stirred a memory of brave men."—Lloyd C. Douglas.

**in ject′** (in jekt). "Throw" in as a suggestion; "throw" or force in, as a serum.—"Let me in*ject* the most fundamental of all truths: A recovery after a depression is as inevitable as that day follows night."—Alfred P. Sloan.

**in″ter jec′tion** (in″tur jek′shŭn). An exclamation; a word or phrase "thrown" in between, breaking into a discussion or talk.—"Mr. Baldwin made a chance inter*ject*ion to the effect that he felt a bitter humiliation."—R. W. Jepson.

**pro ject′** (pro jekt′). "Cast" forward; extend forward and beyond.—"It is a place from which we can pro*ject*

ourselves north, east, or west."—Alexander A. Vandergrift.

**con jec′ture** (kŏn jek′chŏŏr). To imagine, surmise, or suppose; to judge from incomplete evidence or from "throwing" together partial facts.—"I ask you to give your imagination free rein and to try to con*ject*ure the situation."—George Barton Cutten.

**de jec′tion** (dē jek′shŭn). Discouragement; depression; a "downcast" state; low, sad spirits.—"Part of the world is ill with de*ject*ion, and mental as well as physical suffering." —Aleš Hrdlička.

**ab′ject** (ab′jekt). "Cast" down in spirits, sunk in a debased condition; hence, servile; slavish; ignoble.—"Europe was terrorized into various forms of ab*ject* submission."—Winston Churchill.

**e ject′ed** (ē jekt′ed). "Thrown" out forcibly; expelled; driven out by force.—"They can be brought to earth only by physical defeat, by being e*ject*ed from the areas they have conquered."—Joseph C. Grew.

## LOQUI

A Latin verb that means "to speak" or "to talk." Its root appears in the following words in the forms *loqu*, *locut*:

**col′lo quy** (kol′ō kwi). A "talking" together; a conversation; a more or less formal discourse; a short "talk." —"He stepped forward saluting, and there was a brief, inaudible col*loqu*y." —Lloyd C. Douglas.

**col lo′qui al** (kŏ lō′kwi ăl). Pertaining to "talking" with others in ordinary, everyday language, as distinguished from using literary or formal language.—"My course of study was through col*loqu*ial contact with real people."—Elbert D. Thomas.

**so lil′o quies** (sō lil′ō kwiz). "Speeches" made alone or to oneself; hence, monologues; "speeches" made as though to oneself.—"The soli*loqu*ies are quite beautiful speeches and poetic in their imagery."—Marc Connelly.

**ob′lo quy** (ob′lō kwi). A "speech" made against or in opposition; a defamation; a vilification; a calumny; a public reproach.—"Despite the ob*loquy* from which his reputation has suffered from official orthodoxies, phrases of his still survive."— Ludwig Lewisohn.

**el′o quence** (el′ō kwĕnce). Fluent, impassioned "speech"; forceful, persuasive language or "speeches."— "Expose school children to *elo*quence, and bring them to look upon it with suspicion."—Bertrand Russell.

**el′o quent ly** (el′ō kwĕnt li). With forceful and fluent language; very expressively; with convincing and impassioned "speech."—"He was perspiring, and swearing *elo*quently while removing a false beard."— Gene Fowler.

**lo cu′tion** (lō kū′shŭn). A style or mode of "speaking" or discourse; a form of expression; phraseology.— "He liked the smooth *locut*ion of the radio announcer."—Bertram M. Myers.

**al″lo cu′tions** (al″ō kū′shŭnz). Formal "speeches," often to groups; addresses by someone in authority; exhortations.—"These objectives accord perfectly with the best traditions of Christian civilization as expressed in recent al*locut*ions of the Supreme Pontiff."—Carlton J. H. Hayes.

**cir″cum lo cu′tion** (sur″kŭm lō kū′- shŭn). The use of more words or longer words than necessary; an indirect way of "speaking"; roundabout expression; an evasive way of saying something.—"Circum*locut*ion means wandering all around an idea, as if it were hot and you were afraid to touch it."—Charles R. Riker.

**in″ter loc′u tor** (in″tur lok′ū ter). The "speaker" between others; a questioner or interpreter; also the man in the middle of the row in a minstrel show who questions the end men.— "He was amazed at the biblical erudition of his inter*locut*or."—André Maurois.

## MITTERE

A Latin verb that means "to send" or "to let go." It appears in the following words in the forms *mit, mitt, miss, mis:*

**re mit′** (rē mit′). "Send" away or down for consideration, decision, or opinion; submit; refer.—"Let's re*mit* this dispute to the referee for his decision."—Ainslee Mockridge.

**com mit′ments** (kŏ mit′mĕnts). Pledges made and "sent" with, or entrusted to do, something; promises to act.— "We shun political com*mit*ments which might entangle us in foreign wars."—Franklin Delano Roosevelt.

**mis′sile** (miss′ĭl). Any object intended to be thrown, "let go," "sent" out, or shot at a distant object or target.— "A destroyer discharges its huge *miss*ile—the torpedo—at close range, and escapes."—Alexander P. de Seversky.

**re mit′tent** (rē mit′ĕnt). "Letting go," abating, or lessening from time to time; "letting go" or diminishing at regular intervals.—"Malaria is a vicious disease and visits upon the victim a re*mitt*ent fever."—Douglas Brewster.

**e mit′ted** (ē mit′id). "Sent" out or forth; gave out; voiced; uttered.— "She e*mitt*ed a murmur of sympathy, for these new people were also alien to her."—Edith Wharton.

**trans mit′ti ble** (trance mit′ĭ b′l). Transferable; that can be "sent" across, handed down, or passed along to others.—"Great fortunes, unfairly made, trans*mitt*ible indefinitely to descendants were sure to excite envy."—Owen D. Young.

**in″ter mit′tent ly** (in″tur mit′ĕnt li). Periodically; "sent" between or "let go" at intervals.—"They gave us depth charges inter*mitt*ently for several hours."—Roy M. Davenport.

**mis′sive** (miss′iv). A note, letter, or other message or communication "sent" from one person to another.— "One strange, sparse *miss*ive had come from his brother."—Stephen Vincent Benét.

**sub mis'sive ly** (sŭb miss'iv li). In a way that "lets go" or "sends" under, or yields control to another; hence, humbly; resignedly; compliantly.— "She stood before me sub*miss*ively as though the ceremony called for respect."—Henry H. Curran.

**ad mis'si ble** (ăd miss'ĭ b'l). Allowable; that may be conceded; such as may be permitted, or "sent" to or through without penalty.—"Many actions that are ad*miss*ible are not in good taste."—Douglas E. Lurton.

**per mis'sive** (pur miss'iv). Allowed; permitted; not forbidden; against which nothing has been "sent" through.—"The private ownership of property is a per*miss*ive, not an inherent, right."—W. L. Clayton.

**re mis'sion** (rē mish'ŭn). A "sending" away or "letting go"; hence, discharge from penalty; delivery from punishment; pardon; forgiveness.— "Re*miss*ion of sins is a tenet of Christianity."—S. L. Scanlon.

**man"u mis'sion** (man"ū mish'ŭn). Emancipation; literally, the "sending" forth of the hand to give formal release from slavery and bondage.— "This is your certificate of manu*miss*ion. You are a free man."— Lloyd C. Douglas.

**sur mise'** (sur mīze'). "Send" or put over or above; hence, form an opinion on very slight evidence; infer or suspect.—"We may sur*mise* what will befall should the conference end in a stalemate."—Eugene P. Thomas.

**prem'ise** (prem'iss). A proposition "sent" before or laid down as a ground or base from which to form a conclusion; a statement previously made setting forth the facts necessary to explain an action.—"The first pre*mise* to these aims is that we recognize the right of Frenchmen to solve the internal problems of France."—Samuel Grafton.

**com'pro mise** (kom'prō mīze). A settlement by mutual concession; an agreement in which each side yields, or "lets go" some points to the opposite side.—"Free men must have opportunity to settle their differences by compro*mise*."— Frances M. Perkins.

**un com'pro mis"ing** (un kom'prō-mīze"ing). Not "letting go" or yielding anything or in any way; strict; inflexible; firm.—"He is direct and uncompro*mising*."— Howard Devree.

**de mise'** (dē mīze'). Death; decease, especially when referring to someone well-known or of great importance. —"I quote this theoretical de*mise* of the human race simply to point out that there are many things in the world more enduring then we are." —C. C. Furnas.

## NASCI

A Latin verb that means "to be born." It appears in the following words in the forms *nasc, nat, gnat:*

**nas'cent** (nass'ĕnt). "Being born" or coming into existence; just starting to develop; beginning to be or to exist.—"This would injure and confuse the *nasc*ent common unification of mankind."—H. G. Wells.

**na'tal** (nāy'tăl). Of "birth" or pertaining to "birth"; dating from "birth." The word is nearly always used in connection with time, but it can refer to place, meaning native. —"The Fourth of July is the *nat*al day of American freedom."—Henry J. Powers.

**con'nate** (kon'āte). "Born" with a person, in a person; "inborn" or congenital.—"The love of rhythm and music is con*nat*e in some peoples."—Ellery Marsh Egan.

**in'nate** (in'nāte). "Inborn"; hence, natural.—"We must cast our lot with those peoples who prize liberty as an in*nat*e right."—Wendell L. Willkie.

**Na tiv'i ty** (nā tiv'ĭ ti). "Birth"; when capitalized, the "birth" of Jesus.— "The Old Testament animals color the legends surrounding the *Nati*v-ity."—Hal Borland.

**cog'nate** (kog'nāte). "Born" in company with others; hence, allied;

related in origin; coming from the same source or root; kindred.— "She was considering cognate matters with appropriate gravity."— Samuel Hopkins Adams.

**im preg′nat ed** (im preg′nāte id). Saturated with another substance; permeated with particles of another substance; literally the word means put into a condition to give "birth." —"The rice grains were found to be impregnated with cultures of bubonic plague."—Harlowe R. Hoyt.

## PLICARE

A Latin verb that means "to fold." It appears in the following words in the forms *pli, plicat, plicit:*

**pli′ant** (pli′ănt). Easily "folded" or bent; flexible, supple, lithe.—"Her waist was slender and *pli*ant."—S. I. Hsiung.

**pli″a bil′i ty** (plī″uh bil′ĭ ti). A tendency to be easily "folded," bent or shaped; a flexibility of character or disposition; a tendency to be easily influenced.—"Elders have a way of over-estimating the *pli*ability of the young."—Robert M. Hutchins.

**im plies′** (im plīze′). Hints at something that is "folded" in; hence, intimates; infers; expresses indirectly.—"Political liberty im*plies* liberty to express one's political opinions orally and in writing."— Albert Einstein.

**ex′pli cate** (eks′pli kāte). To "fold" out, or "unfold"; hence, to explain or interpret; to clear the meaning from obscurity.—"The theologian attempted to ex*plicate* that chapter of the Good Book."—Bradwell E. Tanis.

**im″pli ca′tion** (im″plĭ kā′shŭn). The "folding" in of something inferred; a deduction; something hinted at but not put into exact words.— "His book ends with the im*plicat*ion that there will be further volumes." —Orville Prescott.

**com plic′i ty** (kŏm pliss′ĭ ti). The act or state of being an accomplice, or "folded" in with others; hence, participation, especially in responsi-

bility for wrongdoing.—"Conscious of our own shortcomings, we are not without a sense of com*plicit*y in this war."—Jane Addams.

**du plic′i ty** (dū pliss′ĭ ti). Double-dealing or pretending one thing while being "folded" in with another; hence, tricky or fraudulent deception; deceitful pretension.— "The needed proof of her du*plicit*y was not long in coming."—Michael MacDougall.

**im plic′it** (im pliss′it). "Folded" in, enfolded, or entwined with something; hence, unreserved; complete; unquestioning.—"They had im*plicit* confidence in him."—W. Averell Harriman.

## RUMPERE

A Latin verb that means "to break." Its root appears in the following words in the form *rupt:*

**rup′ture** (rup′chŏŏr). A "breaking" off or breach of peace and accord between people or nations; a disruption.—"Through the *rupt*ure of ties with my homeland I became a sensitive listener to the faint voices that penetrate the walls of occupation."—H. J. Van Mook.

**dis rupt′ed** (diss rupt′ed). "Broken" asunder; torn entirely apart.— "We must rehabilitate those countries whose industrial and economic life has been dis*rupt*ed or shattered." —Charles J. Hardy.

**cor rupt′ed** (kŏ rupt′ed). "Broken" very badly; hence, perverted; depraved; contaminated; changed from good to bad.—"An insane and diabolic militarism has cor*rupt*ed two nations." — Anne O'Hare McCormick.

**e rupt′ed** (ē rupt′ed). "Broke" out or through; caused to burst forth or "break" through and to throw out lava and ashes.—"The intensity of the furious blast which e*rupt*ed Mt. Pelé has seldom been equalled on this planet."—M. S. Dank.

**ir rup′tions** (i rup′shŭnz). Acts of "breaking" in or bursting in; sudden inroads or invasions; violent attacks or incursions.—"The novelist is in conscious subjection to sporadic ir*rupt*ions of his subconscious."— John Galsworthy.

**ab rupt'ly** (ăb rupt'li). Suddenly or unexpectedly because some way or direction "broke" off or ended; all of a sudden.—"Here ab*rupt*ly they came upon a railroad."—Anne Morrow Lindbergh.

### SALIRE

A Latin verb that means "to leap" ro "to jump." It appears in the following words in the forms *sall, sal, sult, sail, sil, (x)ult:*

**sal'lies** (sal'iz). Acts of "leaping" forth; excursions; trips; hence, witty remarks; flights of fancy; remarks that "jump" out suddenly.— "These quaint *sall*ies into current history were seldom dull."—Robert I. Gannon.

**sa'li ent** (sāy'li ĕnt). Outstanding; striking; prominent; conspicuous because they "leap" out or stand out and are noticed.—"What are the true and *sal*ient facts of the finances of the year?"—Winston Churchill.

**re sult'ant** (rē zul'tănt). Happening or following as a consequence of something; ensuing, arising, or "leaping" back as an outcome or result.—"Because of the re*sult*ant relationships, he had gained access to our leading factories."—Francis Rufus Bellamy.

**as sailed'** (ă sail'd'). "Leapt" at suddenly; attacked violently with forceful arguments; overwhelmed with questions or censure.—"I have been frequently as*sail*ed by the publicity director."—Frank R. Kent.

**re sil'i ence** (rē zil'i ĕnce). The power of "leaping" or springing back, or recovering quickly some former position or strength; hence, elasticity of movement; buoyancy; cheerfulness. —"It is necessary that our army be animated by the re*sil*ience of spirit which surged through all earlier American armies."—Henry L. Stimson.

**ex ult'ant ly** (eg zul'tănt li). In a mood of such great rejoicing that one wanted to "jump" for joy; triumphantly; expressing joy at success or advantage gained.—"The first accounts of the affair came e*xult*antly over the radio."—John W. Vandercook.

### SEQUI

A Latin verb that means "to follow." It appears in the following words in the forms *sequ, secut, (x)ecut, su:*

**se'quel** (see'kwĕl). That which "follows"; a continuing part or resumption of a former narrative including most of the same people.—"It is that rare achievement, a *sequ*el to a great success that in no way falls short of its distinguished predecessor."—Orville Prescott.

**se'quence** (see'kwĕnce). A thing which "follows"; or the process of things "following" one after another; a connected series.—"By studying *sequ*ence, we come upon the principles which shape our circumstances." —Raymond Gram Swing.

**con'se quen ces** (kon'sē kwĕn siz). Things that "follow" with other things on which they depend; hence, results; effects.—"Now we are beginning to experience the full con*sequ*ences."—Hugh A. Drum.

**sub'se quent** (sub'sē kwĕnt). "Following" in either time, place, or order; later; succeeding.—"The United States was aflame with the attack on Pearl Harbor and the sub*sequ*ent declarations of war."—Winston Churchill.

**se quen'tial** (sē kwen'shăl). "Following" in succession or as an effect; belonging to a series; serial.—"It was a job of bombing specific targets in a logical, *sequ*ential order."— James H. Doolittle.

**per'se cut"ed** (pur'sē kūte"id). "Followed" through, hence "followed" or pursued in order to afflict or injure, especially on account of religious beliefs; hunted down; tormented.— "They have been suppressed and per*secut*ed for many years."—Dorothy Thompson.

**con sec'u tive** (kŏn sek'ū tiv). "Following" without interruption or in natural order; successive.—"Six consecutive photographs of this sea anemone show the whole process of catching and injesting a small fish." —E. W. Gudger.

**ex ec'u tant** (eg zek'ū tănt). A person who "follows" out, or carries out something to the end; hence, one who performs a task well; a skilled technician.—"The production itself has wasted the talents of its finest executant."—Howard Barnes.

**en sue'** (en sū'). "Follow" into; hence, "follow" as a result or consequence; or "follow" (happen) at a later date. —"I don't even know that labor peace negotiations will ensue."— John L. Lewis.

## SPECERE

A Latin verb that means "to look." Its root appears in the following words in the forms *spect*, *spic:*

**pros'pect** (pross'pekt). Expectation for the future; "outlook"; future probability based on present indications.—"The prospect was black, and the ominous shadows were gathering."—Frank Knox.

**as'pects** (ass'pekts). Ways of "looking" at things; phases.—"Manufacturers have set up a number of committees which are to deal with important aspects of the traffic problem."—Edith Nourse Rogers.

**sus pect'** (sŭss pekt'). Subject to suspicion; "looked" upon with doubt and mistrust; doubtful; meriting distrust.—"A prayer to some seems suspect, as are all attempts to give meaning to the human spirit."— Louis Paul.

**cir'cum spect** (sur'kŭm spekt). Cautious; careful; "looking" carefully at all circumstances; watchful; wary; prudent; taking everything into consideration all round.—"This newcomer seemed to warn him to be circumspect."—Edith Wharton.

**per spec'tive** (pur spek'tiv). The view of things, or facts, in right relations to each other; the distant view; the relation in which parts of a subject are "looked" at mentally.—"It is the pioneering spirit and understanding perspective of the people of the United States which already is making itself felt among other nations of the world."—Franklin Delano Roosevelt.

**in"tro spec'tion** (in"trō spek'shŭn). The practice of self-examination; the act of "looking" within and examining one's own thoughts and feelings. —"He took his seat, lit a cigar and fell into a deep introspection."—L. P. Jacks.

**ret'ro spec'tive** (ret'rō spek'tiv). Reviewing or contemplating the past; "looking" back on things of the past. —"He was wistful enough is his retrospective cry."—Ludwig Lewisohn.

**per"spi cac'i ty** (pur"spi kass'ĭ ti). Acuteness of wisdom and understanding; keen discernment; the "looking" at things or events with clear vision and shrewd discernment; clear perception.—"The surgeon spoke with the fluency due to long practice and with the admirable perspicacity which distinguished him."—W. Somerset Maugham.

## STRUERE

A Latin verb that means "to pile up" or "to build." Its root appears in the following words in the forms *stru*, *struct:*

**con strued'** (kŏn strōōd'). Translated from a foreign language giving the exact meaning and construction; hence, interpreted according to what it has been "built" up to mean; given a meaning according to the construction put on it; taken to mean.—"I don't want what I have said to be construed as a gibe at Democrats."—Harvey T. Harrison.

**in"stru men tal'i ty** (in"strōō men tal'ĭ ti). The agency, or implement by means of which something is "built" in or accomplished.—"Industry is the most important instrumentality in the creation of wealth."—Alfred P. Sloan.

**struc'ture** (struk'chŏŏr). Something "built" up or made of parts arranged together; an interrelation or union of parts.—"We need a breathing space for building later a still broader *struc*ture of peace."—Winston Churchill.

**ob struct'** (ŏb strukt'). "Pile" something in the way to form a barrier or obstacle; block the passage of; hinder or impede action of.—"There are certain religious fanatics who always ob*struct* progress."—Ainslee Mockridge.

**ob struc'tion ists** (ŏb struk'shŭn ists). Those who "pile" up all kinds of obstacles to hinder or hamper legislation.—"He intended to break the gray-haired ob*struct*ionists at the earliest opportunity."—Lloyd C. Douglas.

**con struc'tive** (kŏn struk'tiv). Helpful toward devising, putting together and setting in order; hence, "building" up.—"If each thinking person would make it a point to write one con*struct*ive letter a month to some important official in Washington we'd have representative government."—Frank H. Sparks.

## TENDERE

A Latin verb that means "to stretch." Its root appears in the following words in the forms *tend, tens, tent:*

**dis tends'** (diss tendz'). "Stretches" out or through; expands; dilates.—"The heat dis*tend*s the bomb-case to one and a half times its normal size."—George J. B. Fisher.

**in ten'sive** (in ten'siv). "Stretched" within to a high degree; hence, thorough and deep; earnest and intent; directed emphatically to a single subject.—"An in*tens*ive search uncovered three words ideal for his purpose."—Frank C. Laubach.

**in ten'si ty** (in ten'sĭ ti). A high degree or amount of energy, force, or the like; something "stretched" or strained to an extreme degree.—"The room's utter stillness crackles with in*tens*ity."—May Lamberton Becker.

**ex ten'sive** (eks ten'siv). "Stretched" out so as to be wide and far-reaching; extended in scope or space.—"The damage that was done was ex*tens*ive."—Bertram M. Myers.

**pre ten'sions** (prē ten'shŭnz). Qualities or claims that are "stretched" forward, asking approval; hence, affectations; showy displays.—"Mr. Churchill is always himself everywhere, no pretences or pre*tens*ions."—Bernard M. Baruch.

**in tent'** (in tent'). Something that is "stretched" within; hence, an aim, purpose, meaning, or design.—"If we are to be successful in carrying out the in*tent* of this law, it will be because we are tolerant."—John G. Winant.

**pre ten'tious** (prē ten'shŭs). Making claims to importance or seeking admiration; "stretching" forward all the time in an ostentatious way.—"Science and research are only more pre*tent*ious words for the fun of recording everyday observations."—George A. Petrides.

## TENERE

A Latin verb that means "to hold." It appears in the following words in the forms *ten, tent, tain, tin:*

**ten'or** (ten'ur). The settled course or line of conduct to which something "holds"; hence, the prevailing direction; the general tendency or drift.—"The even *ten*or of their existence was slowed but not stopped."—Dwayne Orton.

**re ten'tive** (rē ten'tiv). Not forgetful; having the power to "hold" afterwards, or remember for future use, what we see, hear and learn—"A re*tent*ive memory is a product of interest, training, and concentration."—Jack Bond.

**de tained'** (dē taind'). "Held" down; kept from proceeding; kept back, delayed, or stopped.—"She tells of the leader of the Moslem revolt who de*tain*ed them to treat his wounds."—Anita Moffett.

**per tain'** (pur tain'). To "hold" through or all over; hence, to belong; to relate to; have reference to; concern.—"There is a tendency to emotionalize the questions of tenure and security so far as they per*tain* to teachers."—Mark M. Jones.

**sus tained'** (sŭss taind'). Supported by something "held" underneath; hence, kept going; continued; maintained.—"Our food production must be strengthened for a huge and long sus*tain*ed effort."—Herbert Hoover.

**con'ti nent** (kon'tĭ nĕnt). "Holding" appetites and sexual desires in check; self-restrained; temperate; chaste. —"I have had to be con*tin*ent while you've had the fun."—H. G. Wells.

### TORQUERE

A Latin verb that means "to twist" or "to turn." Its root appears in the following words in the forms *tort, torô:*

**ex tort'** (eks tort'). To "twist" out or wrest by threats or violence; to exact or wring from someone by intimidation.—"They will make desperate efforts to ex*tort* some compromise peace."—Eduard Beneš.

**re tort'ed** (rē tort'ed). Replied sharply and severely; answered in a quick, caustic way; replied by an accusation, turning the tables on the accuser.—"'You're not dumb,' her mother-in-law re*tort*ed angrily."—Sigrid Undset.

**dis tor'tion** (diss tor'shŭn). A "twisting" away from or out of shape. If mentally, it is a false interpretation; if morally, a perversion; if physically, a misshapen condition.—"There can be no greater misinterpretation and no greater dis*tort*ion of the truth."—John L. Lewis.

**con tor'tion** (kŏn tor'shŭn). A "twisting" together or upon itself; or an unnatural wryness of face or limbs caused by this "twisting."—"He was asked how he prevented the efforts of con*tort*ion from intruding upon the difficult speeches."—Gene Fowler.

**tor'tu ous** (tor'chŏŏ ŭs). "Twisting" or "turning" in several directions; winding about in irregular "turns" or bends.—"Man completed his *tort*uous journey through the lower

forms and emerged on two feet."—George Barton Cutten.

**tor men'tors** (tor men'turz). Those who cause distress and suffering by vexing or annoying others. Originally *tormentors* "twisted" the limbs of their victims on thumbscrews or racks.—"He wanted to find the old woman's *tor*mentors before his train came in."—Willa Cather.

### VENIRE

A Latin verb that means "to come." Its root appears in the following words in the forms *ven, vent:*

**in ter vene'** (in tur veen'). To "come" between; hence, to happen or "come" to pass in a way to cause interruption or stoppage.—"We hope a peaceful settlement will inter*vene* and halt this crisis."—Haile Selassie.

**su"per venes'** (sū"pur veenz'). "Comes" over and above, or in addition; follows closely upon or happens after something.—"Elsewhere in the world where dictatorship has arisen terrorism super*venes*."—James Rowland Angell.

**cov'e nant** (kuv'ĕ nănt). A "coming" together in opinion; an agreement entered into between two or more persons; a compact.—"With the nameless soldier we enter into an earnest co*ven*ant that we will fight until justice is re-established."—Brehon B. Somervell.

**ven'ture** (ven'chŏŏr). An undertaking attended with risk or danger; a business speculation; something that "comes" or to which we "come."—"Schools of music, drama, and ballet will be joining in this new *ven*ture."—Fiorello H. LaGuardia.

**mis"ad ven'ture** (miss"ăd ven'chŏŏr). A bad or unlucky undertaking; a misfortune; a mishap or accident that "comes."—"He should be ashamed to be despondent at the first misad*ven*ture."—Thomas Mann.

**pre ven'tive** (prē ven'tiv). A precautionary measure; something that "comes" before or ahead serving to check, hinder, or stop.—"Good preparation is a good pre*vent*ive for stage fright."—Daniel P. Eginton.

**ad′vent** (ad′vent). The "coming" to or towards; the arrival.—"The ad*vent* of national advertising into the economy of the United States marked one of the greatest social forces in the history of the world."— Lenox R. Lohr.

**cir″cum vent′ing** (sur″kŭm vent′ing). Gaining an advantage by surrounding or "coming" round something with stratagem; outwitting; getting the better of.—"The rich, as usual, have their own way of circum*vent*ing the law."—Lloyd C. Douglas.

**con″tra ven′tion** (kon″truh ven′shŭn). An act that "comes" contrary or in apposition; a violation; a transgression.—"It is an illegal practice in which he has indulged in plain contra*vent*ion of the law."—Bennett Clark.

**con ven′tion al ly** (kŏn ven′shŭn ă li). In a way that "came" together with, or was sanctioned by, custom; formally; in a way that conformed to style.—"We were con*vent*ionally attired and soft spoken."—Arthur Garfield Hays.

**e ven′tu at″ed** (ē ven′chŏŏ āte″id). Resulted; "come" as a consequence or issue.—"Unfortunately there has *event*uated a disruptive movement in the form of agitation for a separate air force."—Thomas C. Hart.

**e ven′tu al″ly** (ē ven′chŏŏ ă″li). Ultimately; finally; in "coming" to the last stages; in the end.—"I hope *event*ually to play a pretty good game."—John D. Rockefeller, Jr.

**e ven″tu al′i ty** (ē ven″chŏŏ al′ĭ ti). A probable "outcome" or result; an event in consequence of something else; a possible happening.—"Every *event*uality is kept in mind, even the possibility of a landing attack by submarine."—John Gunther.

### VOLVERE

A Latin verb that means "to roll" or "to turn round." Its root appears in the following words in the forms *volv, volut, volu:*

**e volve′** (ē volve′). To "roll" out, to "unroll" or unfold; hence, to work out or develop.—"The British Empire is the first in history to e*volve* the idea of self-governing Dominions."— Anthony Eden.

**de volve′** (dē volve′). "Roll" down upon so as to impose a burden of responsibility; be transmitted; be handed down.—"There will de*volve* on the government the major task of helping those countries."—Charles J. Hardy.

**ev″o lu′tion** (ev″ō lū′shŭn). A "rolling" out; a development or growth. —"I travel in the service of Argentine progress and e*volut*ion."—José Arcé.

**con′vo lut″ed** (kon′vō lūte″id). Having many windings, tortuous foldings, and ridges, as though one part had "rolled" on or with another.— "Having a larger or more deeply con*volut*ed brain, a man may indeed be wiser than an oyster."— John Ise.

**cir″cum vo lu′tions** (sur″kŭm vō lū′shŭnz). "Rollings" or turnings around a center; hence, indirect or circuitous ways of thinking, or speaking.—"It is difficult to follow the circum*volut*ions of your reasoning." —Donald G. Cooley.

**vo lu′mi nous** (vō lū′mi nŭs). "Rolled" out until it is big or long; of great bulk; copious; written at great length.—"Certain working theories have been evolved from the *volu*minous data obtained by investigators." —H. L. Kennedy.

### AUTOS

A Greek word that means "self." Its combining form appears in the following words as *auto:*

**au″to bi og′ra phy** (aw″tō bī og′ruh fi). The story of a person's life written by "himself."—"Irvin S. Cobb's *auto*biography was reviewed on a recent broadcast."—John T. Frederick.

**au′to crats** (aw′tō krats). Those who rule by claiming absolute power;

rulers who have unlimited power; despots who rule by "themselves" refusing to allow anyone to share their authority.—"Many *auto*crats of the past have disappeared."—Malvina Lindsay.

**au toc'ra cies** (aw tok'ruh siz). Absolute or despotic governments; governments in which one man keeps all power to "himself."—"We have to look to the *auto*cracies of Europe to see what such government control of broadcasting may mean."—David Sarnoff.

**au tom'a tons** (aw tom'uh tŏnz). "Self-moving" machines; hence, people whose actions are mechanical, involuntary, and without intelligence. —"They have the ability to think for themselves as alert Americans, not military *auto*matons."—Lucien Hubbard.

**au ton'o my** (aw ton'o mi). The power, right, or condition of "self-government"; a state or condition where people govern "themselves." —"The act grants them a large measure of *auto*nomy."—Edmund D. Lucas.

### CHRONOS

A Greek word that means "time." Its combining form appears in the following words in the forms *chrono*, *chron:*

**chro nom'e ter** (krō nom'ē tur). A "time-measuring" instrument; a timekeeper of great accuracy; a clock.—"The ship's *chrono*meter had run down and her radio battery was exhausted."—Robert Dean Frisbie.

**chron"o log'i cal ly** (kron"ō loj'i kǎ li). Referring to the events in the order of "time" in which each occurred.— "*Chrono*logically there are many omissions, but the examples offer a faithful sketch of the eventful years." —W. Ray Bell.

**chron'i clers** (kron'i klurz). Those who register events in the order of the "time" in which they occur; historians; recorders.—"These *chron*iclers were tribal historians."— Hal Borland.

**chron'i cal ly** (kron'i kǎ li). Continuously; all the "time"; habitually; at all "times"; constantly.—"He wore new boots, adding visible discomfort to a countenance already *chron*ically sad."—T. V. Smith.

**syn'chro nized** (sin'krō nīze'd). Regulated and arranged so as to correspond or agree in "time"; made to coincide as to date or "time."—"The handbook should be well written and *synchron*ized with the training routine."—F. R. Atcheson.

**a nach'ro nism** (uh nak'rō niz'm). The misplacing of an event or happening, representing it as occurring out of its proper "time" or date; the presentation of an event in a different "time" from that in which it really took place.—"If this lady reads a current novel she is quick to search for some *anachron*ism which is certain to interest her."—Charles Hanson Towne.

### EIDOS

A Greek word that means "a shape," or "a form," or "a thing seen." It appears in the following words in the forms *idol*, *idyl*, *eido:*

**i dol'a try** (ī dol'uh tri). The worship of idols or images; extreme love or devotion given to a person or thing, to a "shape" or "thing seen" or to a concept.—"They are exponents of a false religion—a religion which is the *idol*atry of individual liberty."— Mortimer J. Adler.

**i dol'a trize** (ī dol'uh trīze). Make an idol or "shape" of something and worship it; regard with great admiration or love.—"It was fortunate for Dr. Johnson that he had a Boswell to *idol*atrize him."—Bertram M. Myers.

**i'dol ized** (ī'dol īze'd). Adored; loved excessively; reverenced as a sacred "shape" or idol.—"When she was under the care of her *idol*ized doctors she felt she was surrounded by sympathy."—Willa Cather.

**i dyl'lic** (ī dil'ik). Simple and picturesque; so pleasing and simple that an idyl or pastoral poem could be written about it; of the natural simplicity that pertains to or belongs to "things seen" in rustic life.—"It was an *idyl*lic marriage. They were sufficient unto themselves."—Paul Cranston.

**ka lei″do scop′ic** (kuh lī″dō skop′ik). Giving a variety of changing "forms," or patterns, or "shapes"; picturesquely diversified.—"The controlled press is not so tirelessly kal*eido*scopic and is better behaved."—Raymond Gram Swing.

## GAMOS

A Greek word that means "marriage." It appears in the following words in the combining form *gam:*

**po lyg′a mous** (pō lig′uh mŭs). "Married" to more than one wife or husband at the same time; having more than one mate at the same time.— "The gray squirrels are usually poly*gam*ous and they are fierce fighters when necessary."—Vernon Bailey.

**big′a my** (big′uh mi). The crime of having two wives or husbands at the same time; "marrying" again while a legal wife or husband is still alive.— "Neglecting to use the Enoch Arden law for a divorce, he had committed big*amy*."—Louis A. Stone.

**mi sog′a mist** (mi sog′uh mist). A person who has a hatred of "marriage." —"The old bachelor liked women but at heart he was a miso*gam*ist." —Donald G. Cooley.

**mo nog′a mous** (mō nog′uh mŭs). Having only one wife; "marrying" only once.—"The Colorados or Red Men are mono*gam*ous."—Christine von Hagen.

## MONOS

A Greek word meaning "one" or "single." Its combining form appears in the following words in the form *mono:*

**mon′o tones** (mon′ō tōnes). Paintings in different shades of a "single" color; monochromes.—"The plates in color are negligible and it is un-

fortunate that they were not replaced by *mono*tones."—Royal Cortissoz.

**mon′o logue** (mon′ō log). A speech uttered by "one" person; a drama for a "single" person; an entertainment by "one" person; a soliloquy. —"He mutters to himself in a low *mono*logue."—Alan Devoe.

**mo not′o nous** (mō not′ō nŭs). Of a wearying sameness; keeping to "one" tone or pitch without change. —"I was nearly crazy with his dreary, *mono*tonous reiteration."— Helen Hayes.

**mon″o ma′ni ac** (mon″ō māy′ni ak). A person mentally deranged on "one" subject; a person who is crazy in "one" respect only.—"I doubt if anyone but a blockhead or *mono*maniac can really be satisfied with his convictions of ten years ago."— H. G. Wells.

**mon′o lith** (mon′ō lith: 'th' as in 'thin'). A "single" large block of stone fashioned as a monument; a stone structure or sculpture formed of a "single" piece of stone.—"It was a *mono*lith with a mosaic surface of slim, fluted bricks."—Alexander Woollcott.

## ONYMA

A Greek word that means "name." It appears in the following words in the form *onym:*

**hom′o nyms** (hom′ō nimz). Words having the same sound or "name" as another word, but a different meaning, a different origin, and often a different spelling.—"Some words are pronounced in the same way but have different meanings. These are called hom*onym*s."—Daniel P. Eginton.

**an′to nym** (an′tō nim). A word of opposite meaning; a word of contrary meaning to another word; a word whose "name" or nature is the opposite of another word.—"The meaning of a word often becomes clearer if we study its ant*onym*."— Ainslee Mockridge.

**a non′y mous** (uh non′ĭ mŭs). Having no acknowledged "name"; of un-

unknown authorship; bearing no "name" or signature.—"The report referred to him as an an*onym*ous British physician."—A. A. Brill.

**pseu′do nym** (sū′dō nim). A "pen-name"; a fictitious "name" used by an author instead of his real "name"; a nom de plume.—"He used the first names of his brother and kid sister as a pseud*onym*."—Bennett Cerf.

**syn on′y mous** (si non′ĭ mŭs). Similar in meaning; equivalent in significance; expressive of or "naming" the same idea.—"The Fuehrer principle has been syn*onym*ous for domination and exploitation."—Generalissimo Chiang Kai-shek.

### SOPHOS

A Greek word that means "wise." Its root appears in the following words in the form *soph:*

**soph′ists** (sof′ists). Teachers of early Greek philosophy; hence, philosophers or lovers of "wisdom"; now, usually, clever but misleading arguers; deceptive reasoners.—"I doubt not the *soph*ists could prove self-deception to rate high among the cardinal virtues."—Lloyd C. Douglas.

**soph′ist ries** (sof′iss triz). Subtly deceptive disputations or reasonings that sound "wise"; tricky and misleading arguments.—"Evasions and *soph*istries do not answer the question."—Alfred M. Landon.

**so phis′ti cate** (sō fiss′tĭ kāte). A person who is "worldly-wise"; one who is experienced in the ways and "wisdom" of the world.—"Never apologize, and never explain, the *soph*isticate warns."—Margery Wilson.

**phi los′o phy** (fĭ loss′ō fi). The love of "wisdom" as leading to the search for it; hence, a system of "wise" and practical guiding rules; knowledge of general principles.—"A nation is a people bound together by a philo*soph*y of life."—Ralph W. Sockman.

**the os′o phist** (thē oss′ō fist: 'th' as in 'thin'). One who believes in the ancient or modern philosophies professing to derive a knowledge of God and the world by direct revelation or intuition, or innate "wisdom."—"There were unusually interesting people around. One winter there was a faith healer and the next there was a theo*soph*ist and the next a Turk."—John P. Marquand.

### TECHNE

A Greek word that means "an art." Its root appears in the following words in the forms *techn, techno:*

**tech′ni cal** (tek′ni kăl). Pertaining to a mechanical "art" or science; pertaining to special facts; pertaining to a method or procedure in some business or condition.—"The House will not wish me to go into *techn*ical details on these points."—Winston Churchill.

**tech nique′** (tek neek′). A manner of performance, as in "art" or science; a special method of procedure.—"There is a *techn*ique for imparting knowledge to others."—F. W. Stein.

**py″ro tech′nics** (pi″rō tek′niks). The "art" of making or displaying fireworks; figuratively, sensational, or very witty, or emotional oratory that suggests fireworks.—"His impassioned speech was filled with all the pyro*techn*ics of a Fourth of July celebration."—Bertram M. Myers.

**tech nol′o gy** (tek nol′ō ji). The science of industrial "art"; theoretical knowledge of industries; or, sometimes, special words used in "art," science, or the like.—"The American way of life cannot withstand more of the exhausting wars which expanding *techn*ology will make possible."—Harold W. Dodds.

## ONE-MINUTE REFRESHER

(A)  The Latin word *videre* (to see) appears in its root forms *vid* and *vis* in hundreds of English words, always carrying the implied meaning of sight and vision. Can you name six English words containing one or the other of these two roots?

1_____  2_____  3_____

4_____  5_____  6_____

(B)  The Latin verb *scribere* (to write) occurs in scores of the words of our language as *scrib* and *script*. Our word *scrib*ble would be an example. Can you recall and write down six of the words that have appeared in this chapter and that contain one of these roots.

1_____  2_____  3_____

4_____  5_____  6_____

(C)  The Latin verb *loqui* means "to speak" and as *loq* and *locut* is hidden in a large group of English words. Can you remember six words from this family that you have just had in this chapter.

1_____  2_____  3_____

4_____  5_____  6_____

*Answers:* (A) pro*vis*o, *vis*it, *vis*itation, en*vis*ioned, *vis*ualize, *vis*ionary, e*vid*ence, *vis*tas, impro*vis*ation, pro*vid*ential.  (B) circum*scrib*e, con*script*, sub*scrib*e, manu*script*, *script*ures, *script*.  (C) inter*locut*or, al*locut*ions, e*loq*uence, ob*loq*uy, soli*loq*uies, circum*locut*ions, col*loq*uial, *locut*ion.

# CHAPTER XIV

## WORDS FOR EVERYDAY LIVING

No words are as "common" as they seem, not even those that are familiar to all people who can read or write. We often use these simple words with a certain surety, but if we were asked to delineate their boundaries we might occasionally find ourselves somewhat puzzled, for as someone once said: "What incorrect, imperfect, inaccurate, primitive, fuzzy and wooly ideas we have about the meanings of words."

In our reading, for instance, we may encounter the phrase, "the *pristine* beauty of the snow," but do we know that "pristine" means "untouched or uncorrupted from the very beginning"? That is, "pristine" snow, must be a first fall of snow. Again, in our conversation, we may refer, casually, to "the *flotsam* and *jetsam* of humanity," but it might be news to be told that "flotsam," in its non-figurative sense, is wreckage found floating on the sea, and "jetsam" is goods cast overboard to lighten a vessel in distress. At times you have heard someone remark that a friend of his is "*hale* and hearty," or that the actions of a certain man are "outside the *pale*," or that a girl's eyes are *limpid*, but how many of us know that "hale" means "whole," and, therefore, sound and healthy, and that when a person is outside the "pale" he is literally outside the "paling" or the protective fence and is by this reason outside the bounds of propriety; and do we know that "limpid" eyes are eyes that are crystal clear?

On another occasion we may read about buildings that are "gigantic," "huge," "immense," but are we so certain of our meanings that we can determine which one of these adjectives would be used to designate the largest building of a group? Or we hear that a series of "calamities," "misfortunes," and "disasters" have befallen a community, but do we know which of these nouns would indicate the greatest distress? These fine discriminations may not be of critical importance, and yet, when we use words as ammuni-

220

tion it is better to hit the bull's-eye, if we can, rather than *almost* hit it.

These simpler words with which we are now dealing are often rich in other meanings and they have a beauty all their own. There is a homely honesty in such abrupt words as "bleak," "bluff," and "brawl." A blunt force is inherent in the terms "lank," "paunch," "welt," "wince," "wench." There is a charm to those humble but longer words, "askance," "elusive," "tranquility."

All of these can truly be called our words for everyday living. Take note of how the experts use them:

"For many years," says Deneys Reitz, "men of our own race have looked *askance* at us because of the views we held."

"The sable staff," says Stephen Vincent Benét, "dominated the brasses like an *elusive* whip, and drew the last exquisite breath of melody from the woodwinds."

"She sat immobile and dignified," writes Pearl S. Buck. "She was a figure of serenity and *tranquility*."

These words are not so common when they are used in uncommon ways. And they can become more interesting if we put them on a dissecting table to examine the parts of which they are made, for even the most elementary words have a definite and orderly structure.

The adjective "puny" is an innocent enough looking subject for experimentation and unless we were to place it under a powerful microscope we would never realize that it was a crystallization of two other words. We frequently hear it said that "he is a *puny* looking individual," and this, as we well understand, means that he is slight or inferior in size, power or importance. Yet under a magnifying glass "puny" breaks up into two French words, *puis*, meaning "then" or "after" and *ne*, meaning "born." If these French words "*puis ne*" are said fast enough and with the French pronunciation (pwee nay), they can easily be corrupted to sound like the English word "puny," which is exactly what happened. If someone, then, were to be so offensive as to tell you that you were "puny," he would mean that you looked as weak and small and helpless as you did on the day that you were born!

The analysis of a more complicated word will add to the value of the discussion. We will choose the familiar adverb "indescribably" for our laboratory examination. If we separate this word into its component parts, it breaks up in this fashion—in-de-scrib-ab-ly. So here we have *in* (meaning "not"), *de* (about), *scrib* (from the

Latin verb *scribere*, "to write"), *ab* (an abbreviation for "able"), *ly* (from the Old English word "lik," which means "like").

Now when we put all the loose parts back together and use the word in such a sentence as "the scene was indescribably beautiful," we mean that this scene is "like" something that we are "not" "able" "to write" "about." That is, this particular scene is so unusual and so remarkable that it passes all powers of description. From this examination and dissection we discover that the five syllable word "indescribable" is, in reality, a telescoped sentence.

Naturally, it would be impracticable for the reader to analyze every word that came into his ken. That would be the occupation of a lifetime. But an occasional excursion like this is helpful, and it will stimulate our imagination and encourage us to dwell with a more careful and curious eye upon these miraculous creations that we call words.

I do urge that you look upon the words in this section with fresh eyes, as though you had never seen them before, and that you consider them with wonder and great curiosity.

## Words for Everyday Living

**a based'** (uh bāce'd'). Made humble; brought down; shamed; mortified; lowered in estimation.—"Mentally he *abased* himself He had been a traitor to his own better nature."—Don Marquis.

**ab lu'tion** (ab lū'shŭn). A thorough washing; a bath; a cleansing.— "There was even a glimpse of the Saturday night *ablution*, seen through back windows."—Christopher Morley.

**a bridge'** (uh brij'). To shorten in any way; to restrain.—"We will oppose any attempts to *abridge*, restrict, or interfere with the functions and rights of free enterprise."—William L. Green.

**ab sorb'ing** (ăb sor'bing). Deeply engrossing; extremely interesting; preoccupying; taking the whole attention.—"English composition can prove to be a most *absorbing* study." —William A. Temple.

**ac cli'ma tized** (ă klī'muh tīze'd). Accustomed to a different climate; habituated to a foreign or new condition of the weather.—"Two game birds—the pheasant and the partridge—have become *acclimatized*."—R. M. Lockley.

**ac com'mo date** (ă kom'ō dāte). To provide for; to lodge.—"It was impossible to *accommodate* more refugees in East Africa."—Lord Cranborne.

**ac com'plished** (ă kom'plisht). Brought to pass; brought to completion.— "The dictators who *accomplished* the revolution did so through their control of radio and the press."—David Sarnoff.

**ac cu"mu la'tion** (ă kū"mū lā'shŭn). A collected mass or pile; an amassing; increase.—"The *accumulation* of habits and tendencies determines character."—Edmund A. Walsh.

**ac knowl'edged** (ăk nol'ejd). Admitted as true; recognized as a fact; assented; confessed; owned to be true.—"He publicly *acknowledged* that a single technical invention had checked his operations."—Vannevar Bush.

**ac quaint'ed** (ă kwain'ted). Familiar with; possessed of a personal knowledge of; intimate enough to recognize.—"Look over your tone language and get *acquainted* with this thing that shouts our secrets to all the world."—Hughes Mearns.

**a cute'** (uh kūte'). Affecting keenly; poignant; crucial.—"We are faced with food shortages, some of them *acute.*"—H. C. Coombes.

**ad'mi ra ble** (ad'mĭ ruh b'l). Estimable; excellent; worthy of admiration; praiseworthy; wonderful.—"There is a mixture of dubious and *admirable* traits in his work."—Royal Cortissoz.

**ad mix'tures** (ad miks'chŏŏrz). Ingredients added to a principal substance to form a mixture; things mingled in as added ingredients.—"All these *admixtures* of other tongues have served to enrich our speech."—William A. Temple.

**ad"van ta'geous** (ad"van tā'jŭs). Profitable; beneficial.—"Restoration to normal conditions would be *advantageous* to all concerned."—Harold L. Ickes.

**af fix'es** (ă fik'siz). Fastens; attaches; fixes; appends or fastens on firmly.— "I do not complain of a system that finds faults and sometimes *affixes* blame."—Lord Beaverbrook.

**a kin'** (uh kin'). Belonging to the same family; related by blood; hence, similar; resembling; of the same kind or nature.—"He puts forward a plea for an art that is *akin* to a weapon, if not a weapon in itself."—John Gould Fletcher.

**al leged'** (ă lej'd'). Asserted to be true; but without giving any proof; said to be; asserted.—"It was charged that the *alleged* conspirators removed the serial numbers."—Francis Biddle.

**al lu'sions** (ă lū'zhŭnz). Indirect references; facts mentioned in passing.— "The Director has made generous *allusions* to the world significance of trade agreements."—Frances Perkins.

**a miss'** (uh miss'). Faulty; out of order; improper; wrong.—"Apart from this flaw there was nothing much *amiss* with the scheme."—Jan Christiaan Smuts.

**a nal'o gous** (uh nal'ō gŭs). Resembling in certain respects.—"We are witnessing an event in human history *analogous* to the sweep of Mohammed and his followers."—John Bryant Conant.

**an'i mat"ed** (an'ĭ māte"id). Moved to action; incited; stimulated; inspired. —"He was *animated* by a passionate desire to enter the ministry."—Morgan Deming.

**ap'pli ca ble** (ap'li kuh b'l). Suitable; capable of being applied or used; appropriate; fitting.—"Work simplification as a technique is *applicable* to other government agencies."— Stuart Chase.

**ap pre'ci a ble** (ă pree'shi uh b'l). Perceptible; recognizable.—"Workable inventories of gasoline stocks no longer exist in *appreciable* quantities in those districts."—Harold L. Ickes.

**ap pre"ci a'tion** (ă prē"shi āy'shŭn). A high valuation; a favorable estimate; a perception of value; true understanding.—"Never before have we Americans been more fervently united not only in love of our country but also in *appreciation* of it."—Francis J. Spellman.

**aq'ui line** (ak'wi lin). Prominent and curved like an eagle's beak; hooked. —"He had an *aquiline* nose, finely cut, and a sensitive, scornful mouth." —Willa Cather.

**art'ful** (ahrt'fŏŏl). Wily; crafty; cunning; deceitful; tricky.—"Was the man before him an *artful* villain?" —L. P. Jacks.

**a skance'** (uh skance'). Disdainfully; sideways, hence distrustfully.— "For many years men of our own race have looked *askance* at us because of the views we held."— Deneys Reitz.

**a skew'** (uh skū'). Turned to one side; in an oblique position; tilted to one side; slanted; crooked.—"Modern styles dictate that a woman's hat must be worn slightly *askew.*"— Bruce Ellsworth.

**as sent'** (ă sent'). Consent; sanction; agreement; acceptance of a proposal. —"She suggested that they consult the farm and a rather dubious *assent* was received."—May Lamberton Becker.

**as sim′i late** (ă sim′ĭ lāte). To take up and incorporate; to absorb.—"Civilization has developed more rapidly than we have been able to *assimilate* it."—J. Hillis Miller.

**as sumed′** (ă sūme′d′). Taken upon oneself; undertaken.—"We have *assumed* the responsibility."—Myron C. Taylor.

**a sun′der** (uh sun′dur). Into different pieces; apart; in different directions. —"The tropical lightning flash ripped the heavens *asunder*."—Tom Pennell.

**at tire′** (ă tīre′). Clothes; dress; array; garments; apparel.—"The young wench loved to deck herself in bizarre and gaudy *attire*."—Jack Bond.

**av′a rice** (av′uh riss). Covetousness; greediness; rapacity; greed of gain; cupidity; desire to acquire.—"A mishap to a family of birds through thoughtlessness or *avarice* is a serious discredit."—Eliot Porter.

**a′vi ar″y** (āy′vi er″i). A large cage for birds; a place or house for keeping numbers of birds.—"The flashing colors and bright sounds of this tropical *aviary* held the children spellbound."—Tom Pennell.

**a wry′** (uh rī′). Askew; crooked; twisted to one side; distorted.—"The photographs caught them with their toes turned in and their open mouths *awry*."—Thomas Wolfe.

**az′ure** (azh′ur). Blue; sky-blue; the clear blue of a cloudless sky; the blue vault of heaven.—"The larks circled up into the abyss of sky, where stars still shone through the dewy *azure*." —Caroline Dale Snedeker.

**bait′ing** (bait′ing). Tormenting; persecuting; harassing; worrying.— "These fellows have been past masters in *baiting* every 'unbeliever' all over the place."—Louis Adamic.

**be hooves′** (bē hōōve′z′). Is needful, right, or essential for.—"It *behooves* us to search our hearts and brace our sinews."—Winston Churchill.

**ber′serk** (bur′surk). Resembling a furious, frenzied fighter.—"Our chauffeur suddenly went *berserk*."— Leland Stowe.

**be stow′al** (bē stō′ăl). The act of conferring a gift; the gift itself; a presentation or a present.—"The *bestowal* of the award, this year, is upon the man who has helped build all three sectors of the system."—Charles E. Wilson.

**bleak** (bleek). Exposed to wind and weather; hence, desolate; cheerless; dreary; depressing.—"This book, at the best, is a rather *bleak* document." —Edmund Wilson.

**blench** (blench). Shrink; quail; flinch; recoil; draw back.—"His wife was a woman of wisdom and dignity before whom even the comic poets would *blench*."—Gertrude Atherton.

**bluff** (bluff). Blunt; abrupt but kindly; outspoken and unconventional; frank and unceremonious.—"She questioned her shrewdly, with a *bluff* friendliness that inspired confidence." —Emma Bugbee.

**blunt** (blunt). Plain-spoken; abrupt and outspoken: unceremonious and frank; curt; brusk; unfeeling or tactless.—"It was necessary to say it that way; being *blunt* was kinder."— John Louis Bonn.

**bol′ster ing** (bōle′stur ing). Supporting; propping up; hence, aiding.— "Uncle Sam thought the rubber plants and seeds would be useful to Brazil in *bolstering* up the long dormant rubber industry."—John Adams.

**bra′vo** (brah′vō). Well done! Excellent! Fine! a cry of excited approval. —"One did not hale a rising sun with applause or cry *bravo* to some blazing meteor."—Rachel Field.

**brawl** (brawl). A loud confused noise; a squabble; a noisy quarrel.— "Something had happened to disturb her, and the result was a superb infantile *brawl*."—Rebecca West.

**bug′a boo″** (bug′uh bōō″). A bogy; a bugbear; an imaginary object causing fright; a false belief or object of terror used to influence by fear.—"I believe there is no more substantial *bugaboo* than the harm resident in children's reading."—J. Donald Adams.

**bun′combe** (bung′kŭm). Nonsense; bombastic speechmaking for political effect; something written or spoken to gain adherents to a cause, or just for applause.—"Younger playwrights sometimes fall for this scholarly *buncombe*."—George Jean Nathan.

**ca'nine** (kāy'nīne). Pertaining to dogs; concerning dogs.—"This group of *canine* myths casts the dog in the role of man's protector."—J. Rodger Darling.

**ca'per** (kāy'pur). Gay, frisky movement; mirthful leap; playful antic.—"I consider it a compendium culled from a life that has been fraught with *caper* and prank."—Fred Allen.

**car'mine** (kahr'min). A rich crimson color; a deep red.—"Her lips were *carmine* and her eyes as hard as those of a harlot."—Donald G. Cooley.

**car'ni val** (kahr'nĭ văl). Gay festivity; riotous merrymaking; noisy feasting. —"The curé had protested the somewhat *carnival* aspect of the proceedings at this shrine."—Helen C. White.

**car'ri on** (kar'i ŭn). A carcass; dead and decaying flesh; putrefying remains of animals or birds.—"During the summer these bears forage around for skunk cabbage roots, mice, marmots, and *carrion*."—Donald Marcy.

**cas cad'ing** (kass kāde'ing). Falling like a series of small waterfalls; pouring over like a steep, broken waterfall.— "It was high above the *cascading* waters of the river."—Bruno Frank.

**case'ment** (kāce'měnt). A window that opens on side hinges like a door.— "The thatched cottage had a wicker bird cage in the *casement* window."— Helen C. White.

**cas'u al** (kazh'ū ăl). Unconcerned; careless; happening by chance; haphazard.—"He can laugh at himself in a *casual*, easy way."—Robert Van Gelder.

**ca'ter** (kāy'tur). To provide for the gratification of something; to supply something desired or needed.—"He chose to *cater* to the demand for miracles born of misery."—James P. Warburg.

**cav'al cade'** (kav"ăl kāde'). A company of riders; a parade.—"I went to the opening of a motion picture *cavalcade* of the most exciting scenes in the history of the past decade."— Arthur Menken.

**cha me'le on** (kuh mē'lē ŭn). A lizard that has the power of changing its color to suit its surroundings.—"I sometimes feel like that unfortunate *chameleon* which got on a Scotch plaid and tried to be all colors at once."— Leon Henderson.

**chide** (chīde). Scold; rebuke; reproach; blame; reprove; admonish.—"They *chide* the girl so much for her little faults that she is becoming bitter."— Hugh E. Blackstone.

**clang'ing** (klang'ing). Making a loud, ringing sound like pieces of metal being struck together; sending forth a harsh, resounding sound.—"In his voice there was the sound of heavy gates *clanging*, closing."—Pearl S. Buck.

**clas'si fy** (klass'ĭ fī). Divide into classes; arrange in groups of the same kind; segregate into divisions having the same or similar characteristics.— "She asked why she should *classify* and file the third copies when two copies were already in the works."— Stuart Chase.

**cleansed** (klenz'd). Made clean; made pure; freed from defilement; thoroughly purged from all impurities. —"Having come so close to death, when it had passed they emerged *cleansed* and purified."—Louis Bromfield.

**cog'i tat"ing** (koj'ĭ tāte"ing). Thinking over; meditating; considering carefully; pondering; reflecting.—"I have been *cogitating* for a bit of poetry to describe the way the book affects me."—Thomas Barbour.

**co"in cide'** (kō"in sīde'). Agree exactly; concur; correspond; agree together.—"The doctor's self-interest and his patient's self-interest *coincide*."—Peter Irving.

**come'ly** (kum'li). Good-looking; pleasing to the sight; suitable; fitting; becoming.—"It is good to see his wit sparkling like a diamond, or the *comely* frocks of the young girls and the joy dancing in their eyes."— L. P. Jacks.

**com mo'tion** (kŏ mō'shŭn). Confusion; noisy disturbance; agitation; tumult; disorder; excitement.—"A fainting woman caused a sudden *commotion*." —Sterling McCormick.

com mun'ion (kŏ mūne'yŭn). Participation; good fellowship; sympathetic communication or intercourse.— "They seemed to share in the *communion* of his happiness and youth." —Thomas Wolfe.

com'ple ment"ed (kom'plē mĕnt"ed). Completed; supplied a deficiency; supplied a lack; filled a requirement. —"They *completed* and responded to each other. Each needed the other in order to keep life from being too commonplace."—Don Marquis.

com"pre hen'sive (kom"prē hen'siv). Inclusive; extensive; of wide scope; broad; including a great deal.— "This Treasury of Science is a first-class production, *comprehensive*, and done with remarkable skill."—Waldemar Kaempffert.

con ceiv'a bly (kŏn seev'uh bli). Imaginably; within the comprehension; hence, easily within the range of possibility.—"Koestler may quite *conceivably* become the great writer of our generation."—Clifton Fadiman.

con ceive' (kŏn seeve'). To form an idea of; imagine; think.—"How superficial then to *conceive* of propaganda as though it were a mere umbrella to keep one dry against a very heavy downpour."—Ivy Lee.

con cerned' (kŏn surnd'). Interested; having to do with the matter; affected or related in some way; having a special interest in the outcome.— "Those theaters would find tremendous backing from parents, teachers, and *concerned* parents."—Dorothy Thompson.

con'crete (kon'kreet). Embodied in actual existence; real and tangible, not abstract or general.—"The men knew they would be answerable for carrying the plan into *concrete* and effective practice."—Winston Churchill.

con'di ments (kon'dĭ mĕnts). Things that add flavor or give relish to food; spices; relishes; sauces; things that season.—"The oldtimer might put you on a diet of molasses seasoned to taste with blue mass and quinine and other attractive *condiments*."—Irvin S. Cobb.

con do'lence (kŏn dō'lĕnce). Expression of sympathy for someone in sorrow.—"May I proffer my humble *condolence?*"—Samuel Hopkins Adams.

con"fi den'tial (kon"fĭ den'shăl). Spoken secretly; intimate; imparting private matters; trusting with secrets. —"The voices changed to low and *confidential* tones."—George F. Gahagan.

con sid"er a'tion (kŏn sid"ur āy'shŭn). Careful thought in order to reach a decision; reflection; deliberation; meditation.—"This important subject needs more *consideration*."— Dorothy Thompson.

con"so la'tion (kŏn"sō lā'shŭn). Comfort; a thing or event that brings relief or solace; a comforting thought or fact.—"He seemed to find a solemn *consolation* in being of service to soldiers."—Willa Cather.

con stit'u ents (kŏn stit'ū ĕnts). Necessary parts or elements.—"Years ago no one knew much about the vitally important *constituents* of our daily food."—Samuel Weiss.

con'sti tute (kon'sti tūte). Make (anything) what it is; make up or give form to.—"Development of an atmosphere of understanding will *constitute* a vast accomplishment."— Cordell Hull.

con ta'gious ly (kŏn tāy'jŭs li). In a way that spreads from one to another; transmittingly; in a way that passes something on to others by contact or communication.—"The President was *contagiously* optimistic."—P. W. Wilson.

con verse' (kŏn vurse'). Have a conversation; talk; interchange thoughts; speak together.—"He was proud at being allowed to hold his father's cane and see him *converse* with the great ones of the city."—Stephen Vincent Benét.

cor'po ral (kor'pō răl). Relating to the body; hence, bodily; personal; of the body.—"A small plot of ground, a few black beans and a chicken or two are enough for the *corporal* needs of the Guatemalan Indian."—Bruce Ellsworth.

coun'ter feit (koun'ter fit: 'ou' as in 'out'). Made to resemble a genuine thing with intent to deceive or defraud; imitated; false, not genuine.— "These orchids will still be here when dictators or their *counterfeit* conquests have vanished."—Bennie Bengston.

**cov'ert** (kuv'ert). Secret; concealed; hidden; insidious.—"We condemn the open and *covert* resistance of administrative officials."—Alfred E. Smith.

**cow'ered** (kou'urd: 'ou' as in 'out'). Crouched tremblingly; shrank back quailing; stooped as if afraid.—"I *cowered* from the open window, nestling under the comforter."—Donald Culross Peattie.

**crack'led** (krak''ld). Made light, sharp, sudden sounds; made a noise like slight but repeated cracks.—"Peter was only fourteen when the musketry *crackled* at Bunker Hill."—Spencer Armstrong.

**cran'ny** (kran'i). A chink or crevice; a narrow opening or fissure; a small cleft or crack.—"It is not safe to reach into a nesting *cranny* of the puffins in the hope of hauling out an egg."—Ben East.

**crouch'ing** (krouch'ing: 'ou' as in 'out'). Stooping low, as a person in fear; cowering with the limbs close to the body.—"Today we are *crouching* behind machines and exchanging shots."—Charles E. Wilson.

**crude** (krōōd). Immature; incomplete; imperfect.—"The telegram is a far cry from the *crude* method of dots and dashes grandfather invented."—Leila Livingston Morse.

**crum'pled** (krum'p'ld). Rumpled; pressed into wrinkles.—"The flag lies *crumpled*."—Douglas MacArthur.

**cu'li nar''y** (kū'li ner''i). Pertaining to cooking; relating to cookery or the kitchen.—"The *culinary* art in turtles has reached a high degree of perfection."—Harold M. Babcock.

**dap'per** (dap'ur). Spruce; trim and smart; natty; small and active.—"This *dapper*, gay, volatile poetaster almost made Boston the Hub of the universe."—Henry Steele Commager.

**daw'dles** (daw'd'lz). Wastes time idly; acts lazily; lingers; loiters.—"The porcupine *dawdles* in the same tree for a whole day if the taste of the bark pleases him."—Alan Devoe.

**de camped'** (dē kampt'). Broke camp; departed suddenly; left secretly; ran away.—"The gypsies *decamped* the next day."—Charles Henry Crozier.

**de cant'ed** (dē kant'ed). Poured off gently from a bottle into a decanter; poured without disturbing the sediment from a plain bottle into a bottle with a glass stopper.—"With affectionate care the monk *decanted* the precious wine."—S. L. Scanlon.

**de cap'i tate** (dē kap'ĭ tāte). Behead, cut off the head.—"The impact will force them to their knees if it does not *decapitate* them."—William Alfred Eddy.

**deign** (dāne). Condescend; stoop patronizingly; think fit; think something worthy of notice.—"He did not *deign* to glance at any of those present."—Franz Werfel.

**del'i ca cies** (del'ĭ kuh sĭz). Dainties; luxuries; choice varieties of food.—"The hippo trampled down the gardens searching for lettuce and other tender *delicacies*."—Homer W. Smith.

**del'i cate** (del'ĭ kit). Easily injured; fragile; sensitive; ticklish; needing very careful handling.—"The social organization does not take much to overturn it. It is extremely *delicate*."—Richard Pattee.

**dem''o li'tion** (dem''ō lish'ŭn). Destruction; overthrow; the act of reducing to a shapeless mass; obliteration.—"Entire populations will be menaced by instruments of *demolition*."—Alexander P. de Seversky.

**de sir''a bil'i ty** (dē zīre''uh bil'ĭ ti). Worthiness of desire; worth-whileness; condition to be wished for.—"There is no connection between the ability to get a job and the *desirability* of going to college."—Robert Maynard Hutchins.

**de tach'es** (dē tach'iz). Disconnects from something else; separates.—"The new bill *detaches* the function of civilian supply from the Production Board."—David R. Craig.

**dig'ni fy** (dig'nĭ fī). Invest with dignity or distinction; give dignity to; impart a more stately quality to.—"Sometimes it is the wiser way not to *dignify* an accusation by an answer."—Bertram M. Myers.

**dis cards'** (diss kahrd'z'). Rejects; dismisses; casts aside, as useless.—"Industry's guidepost to prosperity *discards* the idea that opportunity is dead."—C. M. Chester.

**dis'mal** (diz'măl). Gloomy; cheerless; dreary; miserable; producing depression.—"The hangings and curtains were thick with dust; it was rather a *dismal* place to have a party."—Willa Cather.

**di ver'gent** (dī vur'jĕnt). Going farther apart; deviating; varying.— "However *divergent* our Party interests, however diverse our callings and stations, we have this in common."—Winston Churchill.

**di verse'** (dī vurce'). Differing essentially; capable of various forms.— "The opportunity to exercise our *diverse* talents I like to call the fifth freedom."—Dorothy Kenyon.

**di ver'sion** (dĭ vur'shŭn). Pastime; amusement; entertainment; a diverting or distraction from an occupation to relax or find entertainment; recreation.—"Their chief *diversion*—aside from lounging in the baths—was gambling."—Lloyd C. Douglas.

**di vert'ing** (dĭ vur'ting). Amusing; entertaining; interesting and funny. —"The main thesis of his *diverting* essay is that old furniture has become overvalued."—Iris Barry.

**di vest'** (dĭ vest'). To strip off clothes; hence, free oneself from, get rid of.— "America can enjoy a tremendous future as a maritime operating nation if it can *divest* itself of the shackles of the subsidy system."—Henry J. Kaiser.

**do na'tion** (dō nā'shŭn). A gift; a present; bestowal of gifts.—"Life is a struggle, not a *donation* party."— George W. Maxey.

**do'tage** (dōte'ij). Senility; feebleness of mind, due to age; foolish or childish condition of mind and body caused by old age.—"The old Senator was not in his *dotage*."—Paul G. Hoffman

**dow'a ger** (dou'ur jur: 'ou' as in 'out'). A widow who owns property or has a title from her late husband; an elderly, dignified lady.—"A rich *dowager* was introduced to the first violinist."—Bennett Cerf.

**dry** (drī). Sharp; shrewd; slyly satirical; matter-of-fact and unconscious. —"His wit is as *dry* and sparkling as ever."—Katharine Hanly Bretnall.

**dusk** (dusk). The darker time just before dawn; evening time just before night.—"They joined the staff as literary and dramatic critics, and *dusk* blazed into dawn."—Ludwig Lewisohn.

**eke** (eek). Add to little by little; contrive to make sufficient; try to make do in a scanty way; piece out.—"He raised ducks and chickens for the market to *eke* out his income."— Samuel Hopkins Adams.

**el'e gant** (el'ē gănt). Marked by refinement and grace; correctly rich and in good taste.—"The young man's appearance was positively *elegant*."— Emmet Holloway.

**el"e men'tal** (el"ē men'tăl). Primary, rudimentary; elementary.—"He has not trained his followers to comprehend the *elemental* difficulties of the organization."—S. Stanwood Menken.

**el'e vate** (el'ē vāte). Raise; exalt; ennoble; lift up to a higher place or rank.—"His friend was a passionate idealist who wanted to *elevate* the stage."—Emory L. Fielding.

**e lude'** (ē lūde'). Escape from; evade pursuit; dodge; avoid by dexterity.— "I leaped out of the trench to *elude* him."—Edward Lincoln Smith II.

**e lu'sive** (ē lū'siv). Evasive; tending to slip away; hence, hard to grasp or understand; baffling.—"The sable staff dominated the brasses like an *elusive* whip, and drew the last exquisite breath of melody from the woodwinds."—Stephen Vincent Benét.

**em'bers** (em'burz). Pieces of wood or coal which are still burning after the remainder of the fire has gone out; unextinguished ashes; smoldering, glowing fragments of a fire.—"The peasants were fighting out in the fields away from the flying *embers*."— Helen C. White.

**en gi neered'** (en jĭ neer'd'). Managed; planned and carried out; guided; put through by contrivance; maneuvered.—"Fooling no one, they *en-*

*gineered* his escape."—Roy Chapman Andrews.

**en tire'ty** (en tīre'ti). Completeness; the whole; entireness.—"The article was sent by wireless so it was available in its *entirety.*"—Edwin L. James.

**en treat'ed** (en treet'ed). Pleaded; begged and prayed; petitioned urgently; supplicated.—"At his trial, the Procurator *entreated* the prosecutors to release him."—Lloyd C. Douglas.

**er'go** (ur'gō). Therefore; hence, consequently; for that reason.—"If a heritage cannot be gained in 30 years, *ergo* a man cannot lose one in that time."—William Elliott.

**es″ca pades'** (ess″kuh paidz'). Mischievous pranks or adventures.— 'They read stories that glow with *escapades.*"—William Trufant Foster.

**es tab'lished** (ess tab'lisht). Settled securely; placed on a permanent footing; fixed firmly; instituted; secured beyond dispute.—"Before she had been there a month she had *established* eminent domain over all of us."—Samuel Hopkins Adams.

**es tranged'** (ess trainj'd'). Alienated; made indifferent; made unfriendly. —"Napoleon *estranged* free-spirited men and antagonized the Church." —Ennis P. Whitley.

**ex plic'it ly** (eks pliss'it li). Very plainly; having no reservations or disguised meanings.—"The statute *explicitly* defines the right of workers."—Frances Perkins.

**fa ce'tious ly** (fuh see'shŭs li). Humorously; jestingly; jokingly.—"This labor document was *facetiously* known as the 'Constitution.' "—Westbrook Pegler.

**fa cil'i tate** (fuh sil'ĭ tāte). Make easy; render less difficult; help forward; promote; ease the work of.—"His theory was that this would *facilitate* his task of persuading the statesmen."—William C. Bullitt.

**fa cil'i ties** (fuh sil'ĭ tiz). Aids and conveniences; things that contribute and make attainment easier.—"*Facilities* for advanced education must be evened out and multiplied."— Winston Churchill.

**fa tigue'** (fuh teeg'). Weariness; tiredness; exhaustion from labor or exertion.—"The faces beneath the helmets are frozen with *fatigue.*"—Edward R. Murrow.

**fault'y** (fawl'ti). Imperfect; having a fault or faults; defective; deficient in some way.—"*Faulty* pronunciation is a serious handicap."—Daniel P. Eginton.

**feat** (feet). An act of courage, strength, or skill; a notable act; an achievement.—"The writer has performed an extraordinary *feat* in this book."— Stanley Walker.

**feint** (faint). A trick or pretense in some action; a misleading move; a sham attack.—"The escorts will leave you here. Here you will make your *feint.*"—Edward A. Weeks.

**fe lic'i tate** (fē liss'ĭ tāte). Congratulate; wish happiness and joy to.— "Who would not *felicitate* you on this good fortune?"—Ellery Marsh Egan.

**fêt'ed** (fāte'ed). Honored by entertainment or feasting; honored with festivities; entertained lavishly.—"When his ship arrived, he and his comrades were *fêted* everywhere and received warm hospitality."—Olin Downes.

**filth'y** (fil'thi: 'th' as in 'thin'). Revoltingly dirty; foul; obscene.—"He was in a gleeful mood, telling disgustingly *filthy* stories."—Louis Bromfield.

**fleet** (fleet). Swift; moving quickly; nimble; rapid; fast.—"They tried to follow, but he escaped, the girl *fleet* beside him."—Sinclair Lewis.

**flinched** (flincht). Drew back, as if in pain or afraid; shrank back; winced; wavered.—"For once Pasteur *flinched* before this terrible responsibility."— Paul de Kruif.

**flot'sam** (flot'săm). Goods cast or swept from a vessel into the sea and found floating.—"The waves stretched away round the scene of the wreck: a bit of *flotsam* washed ashore."—Bernard A. Brown.

**fon'dling** (fon'dling). Caressing; petting; showing fondness; handling lovingly.—"The dog took no notice of them, only submitting with an air of polite resignation to their *fondling.*"—Mazo de la Roche.

**fore'bears** (fōre'bairz). Ancestors; fore-fathers.—"For nearly 200 years they and their *forebears* had been a law unto themselves."—Deneys Reitz.

**frol'icked** (frol'ikt). Made merry; had fun; played mirthfully; sported.—"The penguins *frolicked* in the frosty aisles."—Austin Wright.

**fur'bished** (fur'bisht). Polished to make bright; made shiny by rubbing; restored to a fresh appearance; burnished.—"He looked after the captain's horse and *furbished* the weapons."—Hervey Allen.

**fu'tile** (fū'til). Useless; of no avail; expended in vain.—"Life is experience. However, it should not be *futile*."—George Matthew Adams.

**ga'la** (gāy'luh). Festival; gay celebration; festivity or show.—"It was fun to buy a new car and take in the club *gala* without having to worry about how you'd pay your house account."—Stephen Vincent Benét.

**gal'lant** (gal'ănt). Possessing an intrepid spirit; brave.—"We propose to stand by the side of the *gallant* and indomitable French."—John D. Rockefeller, Jr.

**gar'lands** (gahr'lăndz). Wreaths; rings of flowers or leaves twisted together; chaplets; circles of flowers for the head or used as decorations.—"She hung the *garlands* on the fairies' beech in her native country."—Henry James Forman.

**gin'ger ly** (jin'jur li). Very carefully; extremely cautiously; in a very scrupulous or fastidious manner.—"They let themselves *gingerly* down into the water."—John Hersey.

**gleamed** (gleemd). Sent out rays of light; shone out suddenly; flashed; glimmered.—"An occasional light *gleamed* yellow against the blue white of the moonlit snow."—Louis Bromfield.

**glim'mer** (glim'ur). A gleam or small unsteady light; hence, a glimpse; a momentary perception; a slight apprehension.—"I only get the faintest *glimmer* of meaning from his poetry." —Tom Pennell.

**glint** (glint). A gleam; a flash; a glitter. —"I noticed a *glint* of light reflected on the water."—Lowell Bennett.

**glis'tened** (gliss"nd). Sparkled; flashed; glittered; shone; gleamed.—"Her strong white teeth *glistened* like a row of pearls in her merry laughter."—Axel Munthe.

**glit'ter ing** (glit'ur ing). Sparkling; gleaming; glistening.—"The full moon was lighting up the *glittering* waterfalls."—Louis Bromfield.

**glossed** (glost). Made excuses; palliated; smoothed; explained away; made the wrong appear fair or right. —"He has not *glossed* over these unsavory occurrences."—Victor Keen.

**grat"i fi ca'tion** (grat"ĭ fi kā'shŭn). Something that satisfies; indulgence in something; the satisfaction of some craving or desire.—"A man who spends many hours at his desk can have few wants and fewer opportunities for their *gratification*."—Channing Pollock.

**grat'ing** (grāte'ing). Making a rasping noise; producing a harsh, unpleasant sound; rasping; irritating.—"A shrill, *grating* voice like hers will tear your nerves to shreds and tatters."—Henry J. Powers.

**gri mac'es** (gri māy'siz). Distortions of the features; wry faces.—"Noel Coward has a very human side which lies behind the *grimaces* of his Chinese mandarin mask."—Elsa Maxwell.

**grim'y** (grīme'ĭ). Dirty; covered with grime or dirt; soiled; begrimed.—"He dug deep in his own pocket to save the *grimy* house of hope."—Paul de Kruif.

**grope** (grōpe). Feel the way; search by feeling rather than seeing; search in an uncertain way.—"Most of us *grope* our way toward an ideal through the channels of service."—George R. Farnum.

**gross'ness** (grōce'ness). Heavy fatness; lack of refinement; coarseness.—"The *grossness* of the body was redeemed only by the shrewdness of the small blue eyes."—Louis Bromfield.

**grub'by** (grub'ĭ). Dirty; grimy; unclean; slovenly.—"He studied her, wondering what she was doing in so *grubby* an environment."—Samuel Hopkins Adams.

**hack'le** (hak"l). The hairs on the neck

or back of an animal, or the neck feathers of a bird.—"He felt the dog's *hackle* rise under his hands."—Mazo de la Roche.

**hack'neyed** (hak'nid). Commonplace; worn out by frequent use; trite.— "The subject had become too *hackneyed* to be borne."—Jan Struther.

**han'ker** (hang'kur). Have a continual desire; hunger; crave; wish incessantly.—"Let him take it if he wills, I don't *hanker* after it."—Stephen Vincent Benét.

**har mo'ni ous** (hahr mō'ni ŭs). Peaceable; concordant; free from discord or strife; in pleasing agreement; symmetrical; congruous.—"The conception is a masterpiece—daring in motive, farseeing in aim, *harmonious* in design."—L. P. Jacks.

**heed** (heed). Attention; notice; careful consideration; regard.—"Perhaps it is as well that youth doesn't give too much *heed* to the advice of age."— John J. Green.

**her'i tage** (her'ĭ tij). That which is received from one's ancestors; that which is acquired or enjoyed.—"We need not be told that our *heritage* is worth fighting for."—Robert F. Keegan.

**hued** (hūde). Colored; tinted; having particular shades and varieties of colors.—"She paints a richly *hued* picture of student life."—Rose Feld.

**hu mid'i ty** (hū mid'ĭ ti). Dampness; moisture; atmospheric moisture.— "The house was fully equipped with an air conditioning and *humidity* control."—Robert S. Bird.

**il lu'mine** (i lū'min). Light up; illuminate; throw a clear light on; make bright.—"The memory of this undertaking will *illumine* the long future." —Walter Lippmann.

**im pass'a ble** (im pass'uh b'l). Incapable of being passed over or traversed; so that they cannot be used as a means of transit.—"The monsoon season had made the roads *impassable*."—Jack Bond.

**im'puls es** (im'pulce iz). Sudden mental motives or feelings impelling quick action; sudden inclinations to act.— "They are always getting themselves into hot water because their *impulses*

are very vivid."—Elena Miramova.

**in an'i mate** (in an'ĭ māte). Lifeless; without animation or life.—"One may not quibble about the status of *inanimate* things."—Arthur A. Ballantine.

**in"at ten'tive** (in"ă ten'tiv). Heedless; absent-minded; careless; unobservant; neglecting to pay attention.— "The class was drowsy and *inattentive*."—Henry J. Powers.

**in cen'tive** (in sen'tiv). Encouraging; supplying a motive for action; inciting to action; stimulative.—"*Incentive* payments will enable us to increase production without increasing prices."—James F. Byrnes.

**in cin'er a"tor** (in sin'ur āy"tur). A furnace or apparatus for burning rubbish or refuse; a crematory.—"I was thrown off the veranda, picked up, carried off as if to an *incinerator*." —Alexander Woollcott.

**in con"se quen'tial** (in kon"sē kwen'-shăl). Of little consequence or importance.—"Our naval experts will tell you the German Fleet is *inconsequential*."—Burton K. Wheeler.

**in'dex** (in'deks). The forefinger; the finger next to the thumb, so called because used as a pointer, or indicator.—"He would point his *index* to the floor to locate the underground dwellings of the damned."—Axel Munthe.

**in"dis tinct'** (in"diss tingkt'). Blurred; obscured; indefinite; undistinguishable; wanting in clearness.—"The markings on the ancient Egyptian coin were too *indistinct* to read."— Ainslee Mockridge.

**in fec'tious** (in fek'shŭs). Likely to spread; catching; communicable to others; having the quality of being transmitted or passed on to others.— "He was just as fine a sportsman as before, and his spirits were, if anything, more *infectious*."—John Buchan.

**in flict'** (in flikt'). To cause or impose, as if by a blow or suffering.—"We certainly will *inflict* very great damage on the enemy."—Kenneth A. N. Anderson.

**in ju'ri ous** (in jŏŏr'i ŭs). Detrimental in some way; inflicting or liable to inflict injury or harm.—"A recurrence of these conditions would be *injurious* to our country."—J. Edgar Hoover.

**in quir′y** (in kwīre′i). A search or request for information; investigation; an asking for or act of questioning.— "I made *inquiry* as to his new address."—Bradwell E. Tanis.

**in sert′ed** (in surt′ed). Placed or put between other things; introduced; set in or thrust in.—"Someone had *inserted* a small flower between the leaves of the book."—Ellery Marsh Egan.

**in′sight″** (in′sīte″). Intellectual discernment; perception of the inner nature of a thing.—"By exchanging their findings, each dealer has a clearer *insight* into his own problems."—G. A. Sabin.

**in sin″u a′tion** (in sin″ū āy′shŭn). Indirect suggestion; implication; intimation.—"His letter contained a very unpleasant *insinuation*."—Westbrook Pegler.

**in sure′** (in shŏor′). Give assurance of; make sure or certain; secure.—"That will at least *insure* success."—Henry J. Powers.

**in′ti mat″ed** (in′tĭ māte″id). Hinted; suggested indirectly; indicated.— "His tones *intimated* that the interview was at an end."—L. P. Jacks.

**in′tri cate** (in′trĭ kit). Difficult to follow and understand; very perplexing and complicated.—"In the performance of precise and *intricate* operations, women do better work."— Earl Reinhart.

**jests** (jests). Jokes; raillery; acts of mockery; jeering remarks; banter and ridicule.—"The program was gay with little campus *jests* and statistics about the class beauty and the class siren."—Emma Bugbee.

**jet′sam** (jet′săm). Goods thrown overboard to lighten a vessel when in danger of sinking.—"The river, choked with logs and *jetsam*, had none of the beauty of running water."—John Buchan.

**jock′ey ing** (jok′i ing). Maneuvering for advantage; making skilful movements to try to outwit another.— "They scream and curse like mad while *jockeying* for position."—Roy Chapman Andrews.

**lair** (lair). The den of a wild animal; the bed or couch of a wild beast.— "The dragon went off to his *lair* among the hills."—Joan Vatsek.

**lam″en ta′tions** (lam″ĕn tā′shŭnz). Utterances of grief; wailing cries; mournful expressions; bewailing.— "He filled the air with Hispanic *lamentations* every time the nurse entered the room."—T. E. Murphy.

**lank** (langk). Lean; gaunt; slender, straight and thin.—"The *lank*, ambitious young man had found a patron worthy of worship."—Stephen Vincent Benét.

**le′gions** (lee′jŭnz). Large bodies of soldiers; hence, armies; great numbers; multitudes.—"There are whole *legions* of these obnoxious little people." —Robert Allen Ward.

**lei′sure** (lee′zhur). Freedom from necessary occupation; spare time.— "More *leisure* ought to mean more culture."—David Sarnoff.

**lim′pid** (lim′pid). Transparent; clear; lucid.—"Even *limpid* marine water absorbs light."—Hobart E. Stocking.

**lin′ger ing** (ling′gur ing). Protracted; remaining, because reluctant to depart; loitering; hesitating.—"You can remove any *lingering* doubts in your mind about the fighting qualities of the American lad."—Frank Knox.

**loll′ing** (loll′ing). Reclining in a lazy way; leaning in an easy, indolent way against some prop; resting lazily against something.—"The sport, for onlookers, was not a ladylike affair of *lolling* in a grouse-butt with a well-powdered nose."—Jan Struther.

**lout** (lout: 'ou' as in 'out'). An awkward, ungainly fellow; a stupid, clownish fellow; a bumpkin; a clown.—"The *lout* with the donkeys had dragged his caravan out of the weeds."—Lloyd C. Douglas.

**lu′di crous ly** (lū′di krŭs li). Ridiculously; absurdly; laughably.—"The national debt and our surplus of bank funds are at *ludicrously* swollen figures."—W. Randolph Burgess.

**mal′ice** (mal′iss). Ill will; spite; a desire to injure; evil intent.—"They are queer stuff, mean, with a lot of *malice* in them."—H. G. Wells.

**man'gled** (mang'g'ld). Mutilated by ill-treatment; disfigured by cuts or blows; maimed or crushed.—"The gallows had never lacked their shocking burdens of *mangled* human forms."—Hendrik Willem Van Loon.

**mar'i ner** (mar'ĭ ner). A sailor; one who navigates a ship; a seaman.— "His great-uncle was a master *mariner* of Newcastle."—Frank O. Spinney.

**ma'tron ly** (māy'trŭn li). Like a wife or widow; resembling an older married woman; like a woman of age and dignity; like one who supervises women and children in a hospital or other public institution.—"She planted her camp stool at the end of the corridor where she could command her field of duty. She bulged *matronly* in all dimensions."—Christopher Morley.

**mav'er icks** (mav'ur iks). Unbranded animals or motherless calves; hence, unclaimed individuals; those not belonging to any set or caste.—"These people all seemed like outcasts among sheep, *mavericks* who wandered along."—Louis Bromfield.

**me'di a to"ry** (mee'di uh tō"ri). Of the nature of mediation or effecting an agreement; reconciliatory; designed to bring about better relations.—"It is a *mediatory* book, notably urbane, sensible and well-balanced."— George F. Wincher.

**med"i ta'tion** (med"ĭ tā'shŭn). Quiet, continued thought; close thought; turning something over in the mind; contemplation.—"His days were spent in solemn *meditation*."—Ellery Marsh Egan.

**me men'to** (mē men'tō). A hint or reminder to awaken memory; a souvenir; a reminder of an event.— "The scar is a *memento* of his days in lower Greenwich Village."—Will Cuppy.

**me mo'ri al ized** (mē mō'ri ăl īze'd) Commemorated; kept in remembrance; given a memorial to; preserved in memory.—"The death of the beloved officer was *memorialized* in a recent dispatch."—Alfred Mynders.

**met'tle** (met"l). The quality or material of which a thing is composed; hence, "on one's mettle" is "aroused to show great courage and fortitude, the best in one."—"Each economic form will be on its *mettle* to do the best possible job for the service of society."—Edward J. Meeman.

**mim'icked** (mim'ĭkt). Ridiculed by imitating; made fun of by copying; simulated with mocking gestures.— " 'No; really,' she *mimicked* him lightly, as she shook her head."— Edith Wharton.

**mis"in ter'pret ed** (miss"in tur'pret ed). Wrongly understood or interpreted; misunderstood; wrongly explained. —"They are afraid to speak to other people for fear the friendly advance may be *misinterpreted*."—Priscilla Wayne.

**mis mat'ed** (miss māte'ed). Unsuitably married or mated; married to the wrong person; incompatible.— "Many a war-bride finds herself *mismated*."—Hugh E. Blackstone.

**mis no'mer** (miss nō'mur). A name wrongly applied; an inapplicable designation; an incorrect name.— "The term 'factory-built' will always be a *misnomer*—'factory-fabricated and site-assembled' will probably be nearer the truth."—Arthur A. Hood.

**mis use'** (miss ūce'). Wrong use; misapplication; abuse; improper use; use for a wrong purpose.—"It would be a sorry *misuse* of the heroic charity that it should be used to foster hate." —Helen C. White.

**mode** (mōde). Manner; method; way in which something is done; custom. —"This strange mixture is nowhere better illustrated than in his *mode* of travel."—Jay Nelson Tuck.

**mop'pet** (mop'et). A rag doll; hence, a pet name for a small child; a baby.—"He was riding with a group of youngsters, the smallest of whom was a *moppet* of 5 years old."— James F. Bender.

**murk'y** (mur'ki). Darkened or obscured; hazy; dark.—"He was swept down to defeat by greed hiding behind a *murky* smoke screen."—Joseph T. Robinson.

**mus'ty** (muss'ti). Moldy; spoiled by age and neglect; smelling of damp and rottenness.—"The long disused apparatus was *musty*."—Marquis Childs.

**mut′tered** (mut′urd). Uttered indistinctly in a low voice; murmured; spoke in low, sullen tones.—" 'I have never seen him,' her father *muttered*, looking away from them."—Pearl S. Buck.

**mu′tu al** (mū′chŏŏ ăl). Shared and experienced by both sides; reciprocal. —"Our countries have a *mutual* devotion to the ideals of liberty, democracy, and peace."—William C. Bullitt.

**na″ta to′ri um** (nā″tuh tō′ri ŭm). A swimming-school; a swimming pool; a place for natation or swimming; an indoor pool.—"There is a *natatorium* where state swimming meets are held."—Nathan Cohen.

**nau′ti cal** (naw′ti kăl). Pertaining to sailors; of the sea; having to do with navigation or the art of sailing; suitable for wearing at sea.—"He had thought the hat borrowed from a sailor, the loose shirt and the wide breeches aptly *nautical*."—Stephen Vincent Benét.

**nim′ble** (nim′b'l). Agile; moving with quick, sure-footed steps; light and active; sprightly; brisk.—"The chorus girls show a wide variety of *nimble* foot-work."—Howard Barnes.

**non′de script** (non′dē skript). Belonging to no particular class or kind; odd; not easily described.—"Do they want to weaken our economic system into a *nondescript*, unworkable combination of impossibilities?"—F. C. Crawford.

**nook** (nŏŏk). A corner; a hidden spot; a recess; an angle; a sheltered or retired place.—"Each morning I was up early to explore every *nook* and cranny of the island."—Roy Chapman Andrews.

**note′wor″thy** (nōte′wur″thi: 'th' as in 'the'). Remarkable; worthy of notice; worthy of attention.—"It is at least *noteworthy* that he is not only ready to discuss some of the issues but has got out a book of his speeches."—James B. Reston.

**nour′ish ment** (nur′ish měnt). Nutriment; food; that which promotes growth.—"*Nourishment* is good for her, no matter when she takes it."—Henrietta Ripperger.

**nov′el** (nov′ĕl). Of a new kind or nature; hitherto unknown; strange; unusual.—"At the very least it was a *novel* hair-do."—Emory L. Fielding.

**nu tri′tious** (nū trish′ŭs). Nourishing; promoting nutrition.—"There will be enough food for our civilians to have *nutritious* diets."—Claude R. Wickard.

**o be′di ent** (ō bē′di ĕnt). Willingly submissive to control; yielding to authority; obeying commands; compliant. —"There was one bullock that was not so *obedient* as the others."—Mazo de la Roche.

**odd′i ty** (od′ĭ ti). Peculiarity; singularity; that which is strange or unusual; queerness; something odd or peculiar.—"His most striking *oddity* is his mania for salt."—Alan Devoe.

**o′ver cast″** (ō′vur kast″). Clouded over; covered with clouds; dark; gloomy; overshadowed.—"The night was *overcast;* so for some minutes the stretch of road which they must cross would be dark."—Helen C. White.

**pac′i fy** (pass′ĭ fī). To appease or quiet; to allay resentment or confusion; to assuage anger; to calm.— "The sudden appearance of the Prime Minister on the balcony seemed to *pacify* the crowd."—Tom Pennell.

**pa lav′er** (puh lav′ur). Empty talk; public discussion; debate; chatter.— "We have had too much *palaver* about old deals and new."—Alfred M. Landon.

**pal′let** (pal′et). A small mean bed usually of straw; a poor thin mattress.—"After the children got sleepy, she would bed them down on a *pallet*."—Homer Croy.

**pam′pered** (pam′purd). Indulged; coddled.—"Women who are in the service do not want to be *pampered*." —Mildred H. McAfee.

**par tic′i pants** (pahr tiss′ĭ pănts). Sharers; people who share or participate in something; those who take part in something.—"They were aware that above all they were *participants* in a wild venture."—Konrad Heiden.

**pa′trons** (pāy′trŭnz). Those who give

financial support to some enterprise or business; regular customers or clients; those who patronize or support a venture.—"Now that it was almost too late her *patrons* remembered what a smart little ship she was."—Christopher Morley.

**paunch** (pawnch). Belly; stomach; abdomen; protuberant stomach.— "I would not today have my little *paunch* if I burdened myself as you do."—Thomas Mann.

**pe des'tri an** (pē dess'tri ăn). Journeying on foot; walking; moving from place to place on foot.—"The powers should keep pace with progress and extend from the *pedestrian* carrier to the rider."—Oscar L. Young.

**per cep'ti ble** (pur sep'tǐ b'l). Discernible; that may be seen; that can be perceived; evident.—"The program was funny and its effect was immediately *perceptible*."—A. S. Burrows.

**per"fo rat"ed** (pur'fō rāte"id). Pierced with small holes.—"Our technicians developed a system of laying out thousands of feet of *perforated* metal to make landing fields."—Melvin H. Baker.

**per"se vere'** (pur"sē veer'). Persist steadily in doing something difficult; continue striving in spite of opposition; hold to a course of action.— "Not now, not even soon—but if we *persevere* a technique for world peace may be devised."—Bruce Ellsworth.

**pierced** (peerst). Run through or penetrated with a sharp instrument; stabbed; bored through, as with a pointed weapon.—"The hands and feet were *pierced* with large nails."—Theodore Dreiser.

**pit'i a ble** (pit'i uh b'l). Pathetic; calling forth commiseration or contempt; despicable.—"Their efforts to destroy the nation have been *pitiable*." —Eduard Beneš.

**poach'ing** (pōch'ing). Trespassing; intruding unlawfully; encroaching. —"He liked the reply so well that I don't think he ever did much about the *poaching* again."—Sigrid Undset.

**pomp** (pomp). Ostentation; magnificent display; splendor; brilliant show.—"They were hidden away, far from the *pomp* and gold braid and rococo splendors of the city."—Louis Bromfield.

**prates** (prātes). Talks foolishly or vainly about; babbles.—"The administration *prates* about our loss of foreign markets."—George N. Peek.

**preened** (preend). Smoothed and dressed feathers with a beak; tidied up.—"The swallow chattered to itself and *preened* a bit."—Virginia S. Eifert.

**pref'er a ble** (pref'ur uh b'l). More desirable; liked better; preferred.— "Even the election of a Republican president would be *preferable* to the destruction of our democracy."— Harry H. Woodring.

**pre par'a to"ry** (prē par'uh tō"ri). As a preparation; serving to prepare; as an introduction or a making ready.— "He took a refresher course *preparatory* to taking up his new job."— Henry J. Powers.

**pris'tine** (priss'teen). Primitive; primary; hence, original; first; as it was in the earliest stage.—"Having recovered his *pristine* zest for the undertaking, he joked and sang continually."—John Myers Myers.

**pri va'tions** (prī vā'shŭnz). Want of common comforts; absence of necessities; lack of the necessaries and desirable things of life.—"Shortages and *privations* have been accepted by our people in a spirit of which they have a right to be proud."—Anthony Eden.

**priv'i lege** (priv'ĭ lij). A peculiar benefit or advantage; a right or immunity. —"*Privilege*, that sits in high places, has always said that *privilege* is essential to the happiness of the race."— Hugo L. Black.

**prom"e nad'ed** (prom"ē nāde'id). Walked formally and sedately.— "The Prince *promenaded* through Peacock Alley, blissfully unaware of our efforts for his comfort."—Oscar Tschirky.

**pro mis'cu ous** (prō miss'kū ŭs). Composed of parts that are mingled confusedly; hence, miscellaneous; without discrimination.—"They issue a flood of *promiscuous* debentures for public consumption."—Harvey T. Harrison.

**pros'trate** (pross'trāte). Lying prone; hence, brought low; laid low.—"Labor was helpless and its organization *prostrate*."—Hugh S. Johnson.

**pro ver'bi al** (prō vur'bi ăl). Commonly referred to or spoken of; that has become a proverb.—"American hospitality is *proverbial* throughout the world."—Lord Cecil.

**prowl'ing** (proul'ing: 'ou' as in 'out'). Roaming about stealthily; rambling or wandering, as if in search of prey; hunting secretly for something to steal.—"Darkness would give cover for *prowling* men."—Richard Llewellyn.

**pu'ny** (pū'ni). Small; insignificant; weak; of little importance; smaller than usual.—"The cargo ship construction program then under way was a *puny* affair."—Burnham Finney.

**pursed** (purst). Puckered up; drew together; contracted into wrinkles; pressed together into folds like the mouth of a purse.—"He *pursed* his swollen lips and shook his head."—Lloyd C. Douglas.

**qua'ver ing** (kwāy'vur ing). Shaking; trembling; uttering in a quivering, shaking tone; singing or saying in a trembling voice.—"The wail of a porcupine sounds very much like the *quavering* outburst of a baby lying on a safety pin."—Alan Devoe.

**queues** (kūze). Files of people waiting in line in the order of their arrival; waiting lines.—"Long *queues* of people await buses and many stores are closed."—Paul H. Appleby.

**quiv'ered** (kwiv'urd). Trembled; made a slight tremulous motion; quaked; shivered; shook slightly.—"The white clustered city of Tunis still *quivered* in the heat."—Richard Llewellyn.

**rab'ble** (rab"l). A noisy crowd; a mob of disorderly people.—"Outside in the street the *rabble* gathered to cheer."—Bruce Barton.

**rak'ish ly** (rāke'ish li). Jauntily and carelessly; tiltingly; far from the straight or conventional line or position; sportily.—"He was sitting up in bed, his nightcap *rakishly* askew." —Lloyd C. Douglas.

**ram'bles** (ram'b'lz). Roams; walks aimlessly; wanders about; hence, talks or writes about different things without any order or plan; discourses disconnectedly.—"The biography begins in the 80's, and *rambles* down through the decades."—Allan Nevins.

**ran'cid** (ran'sid). Rank; sour; having the taste or smell of oil that has spoiled; stale.—"The tea was flavored with salt and *rancid* butter."— Eleanor Lattimore.

**rash** (rash). Reckless; imprudent; disregarding consequences; acting without caution; being too hasty or taking undue risk.—"It would be *rash* to assume that this protest is the forerunner of a serious break."—Freda Kirchwey.

**re"as sur'ing** (rē"uh shŏŏr'ing). Restoring confidence; giving new courage; assuring anew.—"Though it is not the most important thing to gain weight in tuberculosis, it has a *reassuring* effect on the patient."— George G. Ornstein.

**re clin'ing** (rē klīne'ing). Resting in a recumbent position; lying down; leaning back or supporting oneself comfortably.—"One of the most charming portraits of history is that of Madame Recamier *reclining* on her chaise longue."—Bradwell E. Tanis.

**rec"on noi'ter ing** (rek"ō noy'tur ing). Making a preliminary examination; making a general survey; making a reconnaissance to observe details.— "I'll go out and do a little *reconnoitering*."—Louis Bromfield.

**re flect'** (rē flekt'). Give back as an image or likeness; give back a picture of.—"What his letters *reflect* is a man who, having found a way he had lost, is now happy."—Christopher La Farge.

**re late'** (rē lāte'). Narrate; recite; describe; recount; tell about.—"The adventures he had to *relate* were like an Arabian Nights' tale."—Jack Bond.

**re lease'** (rē leece'). Relief; freedom; a setting free from restraint.—"He might have regarded these events as *release* from the services of the man." —A. S. M. Hutchinson.

**re lent'ing** (rē lent'ing). Becoming less

severe; softening; becoming more merciful and gentle; yielding.—"She paused, *relenting* a little, as he appealed to her better side."—Gene Fowler.

**rel'ish** (rel'ish). Keen appreciation; gratification; liking; appetite.—"The grandfather is dirty and irresponsible, and eats the bread of idleness with *relish*."—Dorothy Canfield.

**re luc'tant ly** (rē luk'tănt li). Unwillingly; resistingly; slowly and after a struggle.—"Nature yields her secrets slowly and *reluctantly*."—David Sarnoff.

**re marked'** (rē mahrkt'). Observed; stated; commented; said.—"He recently *remarked* that he would be the first to wear a mustache."—Charles B. Driscoll.

**rem"i nis'cen ces** (rem"ĭ niss'ĕn siz). The calling to mind and relating of events and incidents; accounts of things remembered; recollections.—"Talk started slowly but rose to a gay confusion of tongues and the interchange of family *reminiscences*."—Edwin C. Hill.

**re pairs'** (rē pairz'). Goes; betakes himself; resorts to; has recourse to.—"Every summer the elderly writer *repairs* to his log cabin by the lake."—Emmet Holloway.

**re press'** (rē press'). Keep forcibly under restraint; suppress; curb; keep down.—"I could not *repress* in my heart a sense of relief and comfort."—Winston Churchill.

**re proach'es** (rē prōch'iz). Rebukes; reproofs; expressions of censure or blame; chidings.—"Be silent in the face of *reproaches*. There are golden compensations for all injustice."—George Matthew Adams.

**re pug'nant** (rē pug'nănt). Offensive to taste or feeling; distasteful; disagreeable; averse.—"Their way may be different from our way or even *repugnant* to our ideas."—Cordell Hull.

**re sem'blance** (rē zem'blănce). External similarity; likeness; similar appearance; similarity in common.—"There was little *resemblance* between the initial plans and the finished product."—George F. Gahagan.

**re serves'** (rē zurvz'). Keeps for a special purpose; sets aside for future use; holds back or in reserve; postpones the use of till later.—"The author *reserves* his bons mots for his books."—S. L. Scanlon.

**re sides'** (rē zīdes'). Dwells; lives; has a home or residence; abides.—"That is where the Bishop *resides*."—Tom Pennell.

**res'o nant ly** (rez'ō nănt li). Resoundingly; in a way that re-echoed; in a way that tended to increase the sound.—"The Colonel laughed *resonantly*."—Edith Wharton.

**res"ti tu'tion** (ress"tĭ tū'shun). The act of restoring something that has been taken away; rendering an equivalent for loss or injury; making good the loss and damage.—"We must exact *restitution* in kind from the enemy."—Lord Maugham.

**re tailed'** (rē tail'd'). Related in detail; recounted; told over again.—"Like a parrot, he could have *retailed* the speech to his friends."—Jules Romains.

**re tal"i a'tion** (rē tal"i āy'shun). Reprisal; requital; a return of like for like.—"This policy is the opposite of *retaliation*. It is a policy of friendly approach to all countries to join us in establishing equality of trade treatment throughout the world."—Franklin Delano Roosevelt.

**re treat'** (rē treet'). Withdrawal; retirement; act of drawing back.—"It could not be divined whether this *retreat* into silence was of a piece with Sabbath observance."—Lloyd C. Douglas.

**ret"ri bu'tion** (ret"rĭ bū'shun). Punishment for wrong deeds; requital for evil; deserved punishment.—"Brute force involves useless sacrifices and *retribution*."—Eduard Beneš.

**rev'eled** (rev'ĕld). Took great pleasure; delighted keenly; took great satisfaction.—"He did not spurn this investigation; he *reveled* in it."—Catherine Drinker Bowen.

**re vers'ing** (rē vurce'ing). Turning the other way; causing to move in the opposite direction.—"They seemed to glory in hurling themselves against an approaching door and *reversing* its direction by brute force."—Jan Struther.

**ro bust′** (rō bust′). Characterized by strength; rugged; powerful.—"That *robust* and truculent poetry is characteristic of the Irish."—J. Hillis Miller.

**romped** (rompt). Ran about and played boisterously; ran and tumbled about in play; fought and chased each other; played roughly.— "These animals lived and *romped* together in the most friendly fashion, never harming each other."—George Matthew Adams.

**ruse** (rōōze). A trick; a stratagem; an artifice; an action intended to deceive or divert from an intention.— "They seemed hurt and sorry when so few fell for their simple *ruse*."— Sigrid Undset.

**rus′tic** (russ′tik). Suitable for the country; simple; artistically rough and unpolished; made of rough-hewn wood.—"His breakfast tray was on a *rustic* table beside him in the garden." —H. G. Wells.

**sac′ri fice** (sak′rĭ fīce). Give up, relinquish, or yield for the sake of another person or thing.—"Each should *sacrifice* for the benefit of all."—Franklin Delano Roosevelt.

**sage** (sāje). A person of recognized wisdom and discretion; a profoundly wise person; a philosopher; a wise counselor.—"The book is the work of a *sage*, rich in good advice."— Thomas Mann.

**sags** (sagz). Loses firmness; sinks under pressure; hence, is depressed; droops; subsides; sinks to a lower level.—"At times the verse *sags* or goes hollow." —Elizabeth Drew.

**sa lu′bri ous** (suh lū′brĭ ŭs). Health-giving; beneficial; healthful; contributing to well-being.—"The hills were aglow with the fruits of *salubrious* vintage."—Wallace L. Ware.

**sal″u ta′tion** (sal″ū tā′shŭn). A greeting; words or gestures expressing greeting or welcome.—"For a long time they confined themselves to a courteous *salutation* in passing."— Franz Werfel.

**sa′vor y** (sāy′vur i). Having a pleasing taste; of a distinctive taste or flavor; appetizing; piquant.—"She cooked up *savory* dishes of onions and broken crusts."—Christopher Morley.

**scav′eng ing** (skav′en jing). Collecting rubbish or refuse from the streets; gathering odds and ends of food that have been thrown out as garbage.— "Ragged skeletons are roving the streets and byways *scavenging* for food."—Ninon Tallon.

**sci′on** (sī′ŭn). A descendant; a young member, especially of a royal family. —"A few days before he had been an almost obscure *scion* of Royalty, the younger brother."—William Mather Lewis.

**scraw′ny** (skraw′ni). Lean and bony; skinny; thin.—"The *scrawny* hog competes with the fat, while good acres stand idle."—L. F. Livingston.

**scut′tled** (skut′ld). Scurried; made to move hurriedly; hurried briskly.— "Children are *scuttled* into underground holes like so many rats."— Wood Netherland.

**sheen** (sheen). Glistening brightness; luster; shine.—"Glimmering in the distance they beheld the silver *sheen* of inviting waters."—William Henry Boddy.

**sheer** (sheer). Pure; exceedingly fine; undiluted.—"Lincoln's writings, by *sheer* beauty and truth, have attained to immortality."—W. J. Cameron.

**shim′mer ing** (shim′ur ing). Gleaming; shining; glimmering in a quivering way.—"He pointed to the *shimmering* towers of another civilization whose builder and maker is God."— William Henry Boddy.

**slash** (slash). A long cut; a gash; a cut or wound made by a sweeping stroke of a knife or sword.—"He came out of the barroom fight with an ugly *slash* across his face."—Jack Bond.

**slith′er ing** (slith′ur ing: 'th' as in 'the'). Sliding; gliding; slipping.— "Early this evening we heard a number of bombs go *slithering* across." —Edward R. Murrow.

**sloth′ful** (slōth′fŏŏl: 'th' as in 'thin'). Lazy; indolent; sluggish; idle.—"We repudiate all ideas of abject or *slothful* defeatism."—Winston Churchill.

**slur′ring** (slur′ing). Disparaging; besmirching; depreciating; defaming;

**traducing.**—"Lincoln was referred to as ignorant by *slurring* contemporaries."—George D. Aiken.

**smoth′ers** (smuth′urz: 'th' as in 'the'). Stifles; suffocates; hence, suppresses or deadens; overpowers.—"A roar of approval and handclapping nearly *smothers* the music."—John Ferris.

**snare** (snair). A trap; a contrivance to entangle; a device for catching and holding; something that entices into difficulties.—"The promised rewards of ambition are a *snare* and a delusion."—Donald G. Cooley.

**snarled** (snahrl′d). Tangled; complicated; mixed up; mentally entangled. —"The instruction sheets are so *snarled* that several keymen think the Government ought to warn us to ignore them."—Sylvia F. Porter.

**sod′den** (sod′'n). Soaked through; saturated with moisture; soggy.—"He found an old woman shivering under damp and *sodden* straw in a fireless cave."—Helen C. White.

**so lic″i ta′tions** (sō liss″ĭ tā′shŭnz). Entreaties or pleas; petitions; acts of requesting or soliciting; appeals.— "For more than three years he had been bombarded with *solicitations* by the agent."—Curtis Zahn.

**sor′did** (sor′did). Mercenary; degraded; base; meanly covetous.— "When the list was published there was no charge of *sordid* procedures." —Martin Dies.

**soughed** (suft). Made a sound like hollow moaning; made a murmuring or sighing sound, as of wind through trees.—"The wind *soughed* in the vaulted courts."—André Maurois.

**spas mod′ic** (spaz mod′ik). Intermittent; fitful; short and violent; occurring at irregular intervals.—"Against these tendencies he waged a *spasmodic* and unavailing war."—Edith Wharton.

**spume** (spūme). Froth; foam; scum; any foaming liquid.—"The southeaster burst over our decks in wild flurries of *spume* and green water."— Alan Burgess.

**spurn′ing** (spurn′ing). Rejecting with disdain; contemptuously refusing to accept.—"He seized the opportunity offered by the occasion while *spurning* its obligations."—L. J. Dickinson.

**star′tling** (stahr′tling). Arousing sudden alarm or fear; causing sudden anxiety or surprise; frightening.— "The commentator had no *startling* news-scoops to offer."—Dorothy Canfield.

**sta′tion ar″y** (stāy′shŭn er″ĭ). Remaining in one place; standing still; having a fixed station or place; getting neither better nor worse.—"I'm still the village stationer—and worse than *stationary*."—Christopher Morley.

**stodg′y** (stoj′ĭ). Dull; short and thickset; hence, heavy; stolid; lacking in interest; hard to arouse.—"It seemed almost incredible that this silent, solemn, *stodgy* province could ever have been haled out of its age-long lethargy."—Lloyd C. Douglas.

**stout** (stout: 'ou' as in 'out'). Strong; hardy; sturdy; forceful.—"He walked beside the donkey with a *stout* thornbush in hand."—Lloyd C. Douglas.

**straits** (straits). Positions of distress and perplexity; difficulties.—"Government and general business are in desperate *straits* for thoroughly trained stenographers."—Elliott M. Smith.

**strewn** (strōōn). Spread by scattering; scattered; disseminated; broadcast; spread abroad.—"A perversity of our mother tongue is the frequency with which silent letters are *strewn* through common words."—Daniel P. Eginton.

**stud′ied** (stud′id). Gazed attentively and thoughtfully at; contemplated; examined carefully; made a study or investigation of.—"She *studied* us silently and looked a bit frightened." —William F. French.

**stunned** (stund). Dazed by a blow or other violence; overwhelmed by shock; bewildered; stupefied; knocked senseless.—"She turned away to harry the butler, leaving him *stunned*."— Stephen Vincent Benét.

**stur′dy** (stur′di). Strong and healthy; robust; hardy; lusty.—"The *sturdy* pioneer was proud of his own strength."—Henry A. Wallace.

**sub ser′vi ent** (sŭb sur′vĭ ĕnt). Useful as a means to promote some purpose; fitted to serve in a subordinate manner.—"Art was *subservient* but not subversive; its mission was to please."—H. G. Wells.

**sub′tler** (sut′lur). More refined; more astute; more acute mentally; more delicate or mysterious.—"Specific education is necessary in recognizing the *subtler* forms of humor."—Winifred H. Nash.

**sug ges′tive** (sŭg jess′tiv). Tending to suggest; fitted to stimulate thought; bringing to mind an idea or feeling.—"Associate the idea with some object that is delightful or in some way *suggestive* of pleasantness."—Aldous Huxley.

**sul′try** (sul′tri). Hot, close, and oppressive; moist and still; sweltering.—"He succeeds in creating a hushed and *sultry* atmosphere."—Ludwig Lewisohn.

**sup′ple ment″ed** (sup′lē ment″ed). Given additions to; provided with extra parts; completed; supplied with what is lacking.—"Unconditional surrender should be *supplemented* with a statement of what our government stands for."—Ralph W. Sockman.

**sur′feit** (sur′fit). Overabundant supply; excess; superfluity; oppressive fulness.—"There was a *surfeit* of bad history decaying in his imagination; he could not see the plain realities."—H. G. Wells.

**sus′pense′** (sŭss pence′). Anxious uncertainty or expectation; temporary cessation; suspension.—"Nature was in a state of *suspense*, awaiting the arrival of spring."—Ainslee Mockridge.

**sus′te nance** (sŭss′tē nănce). Support; hence, food; nourishment; that which gives strength; nutriment; that which supports life.—"Art is like bread or wine or oil, *sustenance* without which the spirit cannot live."—Ludwig Lewisohn.

**syl′van** (sil′văn). Of woods or forests; rural; of groves or trees; rustic.—"The pictures seemed full of mystery, as though withdrawn into a native world of *sylvan* loves and revels."—Edith Wharton.

**tal′ons** (tal′ŭnz). Claws of animals and birds, especially of birds of prey.—"The eagle's enormous *talons* were

open in anticipation of the seizure of the sloth."—V. Wolfgang von Hagen.

**tamped** (tampt). Packed full, as a hole above a blasting charge; rammed down.—"He *tamped* his pipe and lighted it."—Thomas Wolfe.

**tar′di ly** (tahr′di li). Slowly; with delay; dilatorily; reluctantly; at a late date.—"The Middle East has become involved only indirectly and *tardily*."—Nicholas Roosevelt.

**tar′ry** (tar′i). Linger; remain; abide; stay; sojourn.—"We have engaged not to *tarry* longer than military exigencies require."—Carlton J. H. Hayes.

**tart** (tahrt). Sharp or sour to the taste; hence, severe; sharp; cutting; caustic.—"His exclusive position drew *tart* remarks from his compatriots."—Freda Kirchwey.

**taut′ness** (tawt′ness). Tenseness; tightness; distention.—"Make sure that all chains are maintained at proper *tautness*."—George E. Miller.

**taw′ny** (taw′ni). Tan-colored; red-yellow or brownish-yellow.—"The text and beautiful lithographs reproduce the *tawny* hues of the plains country."—Ellen Lewis Buell.

**tend** (tend). Have a tendency; move or incline toward; have a bent or aptitude.—"I don't believe the young people of today are worse than of old. Rather they *tend* to grow better and better."—Emory L. Fielding.

**tep′id** (tep′id). Lukewarm; moderately warm.—"It was *tepid* winter, wretched and miserable—it got on people's nerves more than biting, frosty weather."—Bruno Frank.

**the″o ret′i cal** (thē″ō ret′i kăl: 'th' as in 'thin'). Speculative, as distinguished from practical; based on theory and not on experience.—"There is nothing *theoretical* about the problems of small business. They are real and urgent."—Jesse H. Jones.

**tinged** (tinjd). Imparted a slight color to; colored faintly; hence, modified; changed a little.—"The idea of living in that magic castle had secretly *tinged* her vision of the castle's owner."—Edith Wharton.

**tor′pid** (tor′pid). Sluggish; apathetic; numb; having lost sensibility.—"Her thoughts moved among these problems like *torpid* fish turning about between the weary walls of a too-small aquarium."—Edith Wharton.

**train** (train). A continuous line; succession of connected ideas or things; a sequence; a regular order.—"Later he interrupted his *train* of speech to say that he had just been handed a correction."—Charles B. Driscoll.

**tran quil′i ty** (tran kwil′ĭ ti). Calmness; restfulness; quietness; peacefulness; composure.—"She sat immobile and dignified in her long robe. She was the figure of serenity and *tranquility*."—Pearl S. Buck.

**trekked** (trekt). Traveled, as in ox-wagons; migrated; journeyed into the unknown regions.—"My grandfather *trekked* west from Stockbridge."—Robert A. Millikan.

**trem′u lous** (trem′ū lŭs). Characterized by mental quivering; trembling.—"There was *tremulous* excitement while grandpa skillfully carved the turkey."—Edwin C. Hill.

**tres′passed** (tress′past). Ventured on somebody's property without any right; intruded; encroached.—"In attempting to speak freely, I have *trespassed* on areas properly reserved for theologians."—James B. Conant.

**tri′fling** (trī′fling). Insignificant; small; having little value; unimportant.—"The land was unencumbered except for a *trifling* mortgage."—Willa Cather.

**trudge** (trudje). Walk laboriously; plod along; tramp wearily.—"Beside the ox-carts *trudge* fathers and mothers and children."—Alfred M. Landon.

**trussed** (trust). Bound closely or tightly; made into a tight bundle; fastened or tied.—"This was the pit of oppression and he would lie in it like *trussed* hay."—Stephen Vincent Benét.

**ty′ro** (tī′rō). A beginner; a novice; one who is only in the first or preliminary stages of an occupation.—"It took cold fear, striking at the heart of the nation to teach it that it was a mere *tyro* in the practice of mass production."—Chester H. Lang.

**u″na nim′i ty** (ū″nuh nim′ĭ ti). A state of being of one mind; complete agreement; entire accord; harmony; full agreement in opinion or purpose.—"There was practically literal *unanimity* on the issue."—Mark Sullivan.

**un bos′omed** (un bŏŏz′ŭmd). Disclosed confidentially, as secrets; revealed; confessed secret thoughts or feelings of.—"I have *unbosomed* my soul; now tell us what your religion is."—W. Somerset Maugham.

**un can′ny** (un kan′i). Mysterious; weird; strange.—"The public has an *uncanny* accuracy in estimating the weight that should be attached to the various arguments."—George Gallup.

**un″der go′** (un″dur gō′). Endure; submit to; pass through; be subjected to; suffer.—"If you would like to *undergo* an hour of boredom, ask him about his operation."—Bertram M. Myers.

**un do′ing** (un dōō′ing). Cause of ruin; cause of destruction; loss of prospects or reputation.—"An overweening greed for power was his *undoing*."—Douglas E. Lurton.

**un seem′ly** (un seem′li). Improper; unbecoming; unsuitable; indecent.—"They fought with each other in a most *unseemly* way."—Dorothy Thompson.

**up braids′** (up braidz′). Utters reproaches; reproves; accuses; blames; finds fault with.—"At one moment she is affectionate while at the next she *upbraids* him unmercifully."—Samuel Z. Orgel.

**up hold′** (up hōld′). Support; maintain; defend; give aid to; regard with approval.—"It is absurd to try to *uphold* these foul practices."—Sterling McCormick.

**ur′ban** (ur′băn). Pertaining to a city.—"There are fewer Communists here than in most other large *urban* institutions."—Harry N. Wright.

**ut′ter ing** (ut′ur ing). Speaking; voicing; pronouncing; enunciating.—"We sat at the table, nobody *uttering* a word."—Malcom Babbitt.

**va′grant** (vāy′grănt). Wandering idly; roving; having no aim or course.—"The ruthless ruler burst upon the horizon like a *vagrant* comet."—Hiram W. Johnson.

**var′i e gat″ed** (vair′i uh gāte″id). Having different external appearances; of different varieties; diversified; varying.—"The changes in the old town are almost as interesting as the *variegated* personal stories."—Dorothy Canfield Fisher.

**veg'e tate** (vej'ē tāte). Live in a monotonous, passive way.—"If we can find nothing better to do with freedom than to *vegetate*, why preserve it at all?"—Dorothy Thompson.

**ver'sa tile** (vur'suh til). Subject to change; many-sided; able to do different kinds of things well.—"Of all scientific brain children of recent years none is more *versatile* than the electric eye."—C. C. Furnas.

**waif** (wāfe). A homeless child; a person or animal without home or friends; a stray person.—"The bootblack was a gay and tattered-looking little *waif* with a foreign accent."—Donald G. Cooley.

**wail'ing** (wail'ing). Making mournful sounds; lamenting; crying aloud; weeping because of grief or pain.— "To his knees fled the *wailing* orphan."—Samuel Hopkins Adams.

**wal'low ing** (wol'ō ing). Floundering; rolling about in mud or mire; weltering; surging; gushing forth.—"Then the howling, trampling multitude, the *wallowing* waves of humanity, broke into the Pass between the cliff and sea."—Caroline Dale Snedeker.

**welts** (welts). Wales or raised red streaks made on the skin by lashes from a whip; inflamed marks on the skin or flesh caused by a blow with a stick.—"His coat had been pulled back off his bare shoulders, showing livid *welts*."—Lloyd C. Douglas.

**wench** (wench). A peasant girl; a servant girl; a serving maid; a girl of lowly origin.—"She was a *wench* from the land of Kush."—Thomas Mann.

**whim** (hwim). A caprice; a sudden fancy; a notion; humor; a fantastic inclination; a sudden idea.—"I was going to wander where the *whim* of the moment carried me."—Roy Chapman Andrews

**wiles** (wīle'z). Beguiling tricks; means of cunning deception.—"Enmity has many *wiles*."—Bainbridge Colby.

**wince** (wince). Flinch; shrink back, as though from a blow; draw back, as though in pain.—"He did not build that business. Cast dishonor on its name and he would not *wince*."— W. J. Cameron.

**wisps** (wisps). Small bunches; small bundles, as of straw or hair; twisted pieces or fragments.—"This hairy moss hangs from every branch in mourning *wisps*."—Hilary St. George Saunders.

**wry'ly** (rī'li). In a way that expressed disgust; ironically; as though making a grimace; in a perverse way.—"He smiled *wryly* and shook his head."— Christopher La Farge.

**yield'ed** (yeeld'ed). Gave way; surrendered; gave up; submitted; gave in; resigned.—"Sometimes the troubles *yielded* to the belief, and sometimes the belief *yielded* to the troubles."—L. P. Jacks.

**zest** (zest). Agreeable excitement and keen enjoyment.—"The American radio audience listened with *zest* because they were interested."—James G. Harbord.

## ONE-MINUTE REFRESHER

Here are eight well known words followed by eight sentences. Can you fill in the blank space in each sentence with the particular word that best fits the meaning?

a. berserk

b. repugnant

c. hackneyed

d. retribution

e. ruse

f. ablution

g. resonantly

h. proverbial

1. His style of writing was commonplace, trite and threadbare. His style was _____.

2. My hands were fouled by working on the car so I washed them carefully. I gave them an _____.

3. She was so infuriated that she went into an insane rage. She went _____.

4. When he spoke his voice reverberated throughout the room. He spoke _____.

5. He demanded condign punishment. He demanded _____.

6. The philanthropist's generosity was known throughout the countryside. His generosity was _____.

7. The enemy commandos were captured by a clever trick. They were captured by a _____.

8. The statesman said that the act would be completely distasteful to him. It was _____.

*Answers:* 1 — c;  2 — f;  3 — a;  4 — g;  5 — d;  6 — h;  7 — e;  8 — b.

# CHAPTER XV

## WHEN YOU TALK OF SCIENCE AND THE PROFESSIONS

WHEN WE turn to the terminology of the professions we are entering a field where words, in large part, tend to have more accurate meanings than they do when they are being used in the wide channels of our casual conversations.

In our present day, as an instance, the legal question has arisen as to whether medicine is a "profession" or a "trade." If it should be defined as a "trade," as the Government contends, the American Medical Association would be liable to punitive action under the Anti-Trust Laws. If it should be designated as a "profession" the Association would remain sacrosanct.

What would be your opinion in this case? What is a profession? A trade? What are the differences between the two? The doctor *calls* himself a professional man. Is he one? Is soldiering a profession? If so, why? Is a hack writer on a country newspaper a professional man? How about a politician?

These matters of fine distinctions in word meanings have won and lost lawsuits. They are vital in medicine and in the other professions and sciences.

Please note the clarity of most of these technical words, as they appear in this chapter with their working clothes on. It was easy to understand Wendell L. Willkie when he said, "We are learning that it is not racial classifications nor *ethnological* considerations which bind men together." We know that *ethnology* is the science of the natural races and families of men.

And when Raymond B. Fosdick reports that "In Liberia and other parts of Africa yellow fever is *endemic*," we are clear that the fever is not *pandemic* in Africa, but is localized in certain areas.

And with H. L. Mencken's statement: "I have consulted all sorts of men, including experts in *acoustics*," we are made aware that he has been advising with experts in the science of sound.

It is refreshing to turn from such vague Ghost Words as "discipline," "control," "progressivism," and "the reactionary forces" of the day to the comparative exactitude of such words as "archeology," "oculist," and "physics" with their sharply bounded meanings. It would save us many an angry argument if the terms we bandy about so loosely had half the clarity of those of the professions, of the sciences, and of technological subjects, for most of our heated differences of opinion grow, not out of stupidity or stubbornness but out of a misunderstanding of meanings and an unscientific attitude towards language itself.

The very discipline in vocabulary to which the scientist and others of his ilk have been exposed, has trained them in a clearer type of thinking than that of the average untrained man. It will be an aid to you, also, if you will subject yourself to a similar discipline and if you will particularly strive for accuracy in the definitions and meanings of the following group of words.

## WHEN YOU TALK OF SCIENCE AND THE PROFESSIONS

**ab dom'i nal** (ab dom'ĭ năl). Pertaining to the abdomen; situated in the belly.—"Dr. Ephraim McDowell performed the first *abdominal* operation of its kind in the history of surgery."—J. Howard Pew.

**ab"er ra'tions** (ab"uh rā'shŭnz). Deviations from the customary or natural course; mental wanderings.— "The delusion fosters itself within itself as most ingrowing *aberrations* do."—W. J. Cameron.

**ab ra'sive** (ab rāy'siv). Tending to rub or wear away; likely to grate or scrape.—"The splinters are completely freed to become loose *abrasive* particles."—E. L. Hemingway.

**ac"a dem'ic** (ak"uh dem'ik). Formal and theoretical; unpractical; abstract; unlikely to produce practical results.—"So many other things were of direct personal importance that the war seemed almost *academic*."— Roy Chapman Andrews.

**ab sconds'** (ab skondz'). Departs suddenly and secretly; decamps; goes away and hides from the law.—"One of the Club members becomes unpopular when he *absconds* with $8000

of his bank's money."—James T. Farrell.

**ac com'pli ces** (ă kom'pliss iz). Associates in crime.—"The suffering in Libya is only a foretaste of what we have got to give him and his *accomplices*."—Winston Churchill.

**ac com'plished** (ă kom'plisht). Skilled; proficient; expert; having accomplishments; thoroughly equipped.— "He regretted that they had lost so *accomplished* a master."—Helen C. White.

**a cous'tics** (uh kōōce'tiks). The science of sound; the sound-producing qualities of an auditorium.—"I have consulted all sorts of men, including experts in *acoustics*."—H. L. Mencken.

**ac quit'tal** (ă kwit'ăl). Being set free from a charge of guilt; declaration of discharge from an accusation; pronouncement of innocence; exoneration; exculpation.—"I don't think he has the ghost of a chance of *acquittal*." —Mazo de la Roche.

**ac"tu al'i ty** (ak"chōō al'ĭ ti). Reality; realism.—"Do not let your day dreams take the form of an escape from *actuality*."—Emmet Fox.

**ad dict'ed** (ă dikt'id). Inclined to the pursuit or taking of something.— "The lessons learned from the treatment of persons *addicted* to alcohol may be applied to dietary treatments."—John M. McKinney.

**ad'epts** (ad'epts). Experts; people specially skilled in some art; proficient people; those well-versed in some subject.—"I have always been happy when *adepts* and masters of music liked my work for its affinity with this art."—Thomas Mann.

**ad'i pose** (ad'i pōce). Fatty; of animal fat.—"Is there a living woman so thin that she doesn't worry about excess of *adipose* tissue somewhere?" —Henry J. Powers.

**ad judged'** (ă jujd'). Declared by law; pronounced judicially.—"Although he subsequently earned hundreds of thousands, he still was to be *adjudged* a bankrupt after his death."—Gene Fowler.

**ad ju"di ca'tion** (ă jōō"di kā'shŭn). The act of giving a judicial decision; a decision by a judge.—"These sources of danger are already on the way to peaceful *adjudication*."— Franklin Delano Roosevelt.

**ad min'is ter** (ad min'iss tur). To have the direction of; to manage the enforcement of.—"Under the provisions of law I have the authority to *administer* this act."—John C. Vivian.

**ad"o les'cent** (ad"o less'ĕnt). Approaching manhood or maturity.— "With the *adolescent* years, horizons expand."—George J. Mohr.

**a dul'ter at"ed** (uh dul'tur āte"id). Made impure by addition of other or baser ingredients.—"The doctor takes notice of *adulterated* foods and the like, as the tailor sees missing buttons."—Iago Galdston.

**a"er o dy nam'ic** (āy"ur ō dī nam'ik). Relating to the motion of gases, especially the atmosphere, under the action of force, and to the mechanical effects produced by this motion.— "These designers saved the day for modern design by springing the *aerodynamic* theory upon the public."— Dale Nichols.

**a"er o nau'ti cal** (āy"ur ō naw'ti kăl). Pertaining to navigating the air.—

"We aim to have the best *aeronautical* equipment in the future as in the past."—Eugene E. Wilson.

**ag"o ra pho'bi a** (ag"ō ruh fō'bi uh). Dread of being in wide open spaces; a nervous or morbid dread of public places.—"The root cause of *agoraphobia* is always found in the forgotten childhood past of the patient."— Louis E. Bisch.

**al'che mists** (al'ki mists). Those who transmute or convert base metals into gold.—"Humans who practised the art taken from 'Chema,' the first handbook of chemistry, were called *alchemists*."—Karl T. Compton.

**a'li as es** (āy'li uh siz). Assumed names. —"The lists of names, *aliases*, and descriptions of fugitives are sent to these agencies."—Clyde A. Tolson.

**al'ien ist** (āle'yĕn ist). A specialist in mental diseases; a psychiatrist; a person who is skilled in the study and treatment of insanity.—"He observed that the prominent eyes of the great *alienist* had become moist."— L. P. Jacks.

**al ler'gic** (ă lur'jik). Excessively sensitive; inclined to react in an unfavorable way.—"He said he was afflicted with a neurosis which made him *allergic* to taking orders."—Charles B. Driscoll.

**al"lo path'ic** (al"ō path'ik: 'th' as in 'thin'). Pertaining to a system of medicine which seeks to cure disease by inducing an action of a different kind from that produced by the disease.—"The doctor gives him bitter, *allopathic* medicine."—John P. Marquand.

**am'bu la to"ry** (am'bū luh tō"ri). Pertaining to a walker or walking; able to walk about.—"Hospitals provide facilities for the treatment of bedpatients and *ambulatory* cases."— C. Rufus Rorem.

**am ne'si a** (am nee'zhi uh). Loss of memory; impairment of memory; forgetfulness of identity; a temporary gap in memory.—"The middle class seems to be suffering from *amnesia*, and when it will resume consciousness none yet can say."—Mark M. Jones.

**a moe'ba** (uh mee'buh). A very small

and simple water animal consisting of a single cell or mass of protoplasm which feeds on minute organisms.— "Even an *amoeba* has individuality in that it differs from its fellows."— Lloyd E. Foster.

**a mor'phous** (uh mor'fŭs). Formless; uncrystallized; structureless.—"Some materials may be hot-worked in the *amorphous* state of increasing atomic distances."—E. V. Crane.

**a nat'o my** (uh nat'ō mi). The science of the structure of organisms; the structural make-up of animals or plants; a skeleton.—"On the wall were colored charts showing various portions of the human *anatomy*."— Irvin S. Cobb.

**an″es the′si a** (an″ess thē′zhi uh: 'th' as in 'thin'). Loss of sensation produced by a drug.—"We do not have to send to Europe for our X-ray apparatus, nor do Europeans have to come here for the benefit of *anesthesia*."—Herbert Pell.

**an″i mal′cules** (an″i mal′kūle'z). Tiny animals; minute or microscopic animals or rotifers, so small as to be nearly invisible.—"The microscope revealed that the solution was filled with animalcules."—Bertram M. Myers.

**an′o dyne** (an′ō dīne). An agent or medicine that relieves pain; a drug that soothes; something that assuages or has power to allay suffering.— "His philosophy, far from proving an *anodyne* or a defence, only served to light up the depth of his desolation." —L. P. Jacks.

**an″thro pol′o gists** (an″thrō pol′ō jists: 'th' as in 'thin'). Students of, or specialists in, the science of the physical facts concerning man and his development and history.—"Just why that was so, we must leave to the archaeologists and *anthropologists* to tell."—Henry A. Wallace.

**an′ti bod′y** (an′ti bod″i). A substance that opposes the action of another substance; a substance antagonistic to injurious substances in the body.— "Blood collected by the Red Cross contains an *antibody* effective against measles."—Donald G. Cooley.

**an″ti tox′in** (an″ti tok′sin). A sub-

stance, formed in living tissues, which neutralizes the bacterial poison that produced it."—"If it is a disease, do I see any possibility that it will create its own *antitoxin?*"—Pearl Buck.

**a′pex** (āy′peks). The highest point; the tip or sharp pointed top where lines converge; the vertex of an angle; the concentration point.—"Like the *apex* of an arch, character must be hewn from living rock."—Edmund A. Walsh.

**a pha′si a** (ă fāy′zhi uh). Loss of speech, partial or total impairment of the power of speech due to some disorder in the brain.—"After his stroke the elderly man suffered a mild attack of *aphasia*."—Donald G. Cooley.

**aph″ro dis′i ac** (af″rō diz′i ak). A drug, food or other agent that increases sexual desire.—"The Chinese paid exorbitant prices for the ginseng root because it was supposed to be an *aphrodisiac*."—Roy Chapman Andrews.

**a′pi a rists** (āy′pi uh rists). People who keep bees; bee-keepers; those who have apiaries or sets of bee-hives, or colonies of bees.—"Special schools have been opened for chairmen of collective farms, dairymen, *apiarists*, and others."—Maurice Hindus.

**ap″o plec′tic** (ap″ō plek′tik). Affected with pressure upon the brain, causing sudden loss or diminution of sensation or power to move.—"If he had been told he was behaving like a bad little boy, he would have blown up in an *apoplectic* fit."—Joseph Jastrow.

**ar″che o log′i cal** (ahr″kē ō loj′i kăl). Pertaining to, or engaged in, the study of history from ancient relics.— "Below me lay the excavations made by the *Archeological* Department."— Edmund C. Lucas.

**ar raigned′** (ă raind′). Called into court to answer a charge.—"Instead of being *arraigned* in public, the child is quietly interviewed in private."— John Gabriel.

**a sep′tic** (uh sep′tik). Free from disease germs; having no harmful substance or bacteria; sterilized; purified.— "The last touch had been given to the vitamins of the *aseptic* luncheon." —Alexander Woollcott.

**as phyx′i at″ed** (ass fik′si āte″id). Suffocated; unable to breathe on account of lack of oxygen.—"They were *asphyxiated* in lethal chambers." Edmund Wilson.

**as trol′o gers** (ăss trol′ō jurz). Those who study the reputed influence of the stars on human affairs; those who foretell future events by investigating the aspects of the stars; star-diviners. —"The signs of the zodiac are little used by astronomers and are of interest chiefly to *astrologers*."—Isabel M. Lewis.

**as tron′o mers** (ăss tron′ō murz). Skilled observers of the stars; those who study the size and motions of the celestial bodies.—"Physicists and *astronomers* alike have long been interested in the identification of chemical elements in the sun."—Charlotte E. Moore.

**at′ro phy** (at′rō fi). Wasting or withering away.—"The last leak is the *atrophy* of intelligence produced by stupid, arbitrary censorship."—Wendell L. Willkie.

**au′di to″ry** (aw′dĭ tō″ri). Pertaining to the sense of hearing.—"I suppose I have an *auditory* memory."—George Koltanowski.

**au′ral** (aw′răl). Received by ear; admitted through the hearing faculty. —"*Aural* broadcasting should be retained as a separate and distinct service."—Robert Robins.

**au ric′u lar** (aw rik′ū lur). Pertaining to the ear or hearing; audible; perceived by the ear; of hearing.—"The only appeal was to his *auricular* sense."—S. L. Scanlon.

**au″thor i za′tion** (aw″thur i zā′shŭn; 'th' as in 'thin'). Permission; sanction; authorizing or giving legal power to; legal right; warrant.— "The President does not need *authorization* by statute."—Mark Sullivan.

**bac″ca lau′re ate** (bak″uh law′rē āte). A university degree of bachelor; hence, pertaining to a graduating class at commencement.—"At the *baccalaureate* service she was preoccupied with her responsibilities as a reporter."—Emma Bugbee.

**bac te″ri ol′o gy** (bak teer″i ol ō′ji). The science that deals with bacteria, the tiny living organisms which are sometimes beneficent but sometimes cause disease.—"Since the day of Pasteur the science of *bacteriology* has made giant strides."—James Gordon Dustin.

**ba′sic** (bāy′sik). Fundamental; essential; forming a basis or foundation.— "The plan represents a *basic* study." —Joseph L. Weiner.

**ben″e fi′cial** (ben″ē fish′ăl). Helpful; advantageous; favorable; productive of good.—"High and dry climates are *beneficial* to sinus sufferers."— Jack Bond.

**bi′o log′i cal** (bī″ō loj′i kăl). Relating to the science of life or living organisms.—"The synthetic product has a *biological* activity equal to that of the natural biotin."—J. L. Stokes.

**can′ons** (kan′ŭnz). Laws; critical standards; rules of law; criterions.—"His own life, by all *canons* of art and taste, should have finished when the last sand fell upon the mound they had just left behind."—Stephen Vincent Benét.

**car niv′o rous** (kahr niv′ō rŭs). Feeding on animals; flesh-eating.—"In North America the *carnivorous* animals are much fewer than in the Old World."—Sterling McCormick.

**cat′a lep″sy** (kat′uh lep″si). A sudden seizure or attack causing muscular rigidity; a condition in which the limbs are unable to move.—"He slipped as he was nearing the top, and a kind of *catalepsy* seized the whole sumptuous assembly."—Alexander Woollcott.

**cau sal′i ty** (kaw zal′ĭ ti). The relation of cause and effect.—"The law of *causality* holds true in the psychic sphere as well as in the outer world." —Samuel Z. Orgel.

**cau′ter y** (kaw′tur i). The application of a drug that burns and stings; a burning with a very hot implement to prevent the spread of some poison. —"These methods run the gamut from dietary measures to actual *cautery*."—Don Chalmers Lyons.

**cer′e bral** (ser′ē brăl). Pertaining to the brain; of the brain.—"He suffered a *cerebral* hemorrhage, from which he never fully recovered."—John H. Baker.

**chem′ur gy** (kem′ur ji). The branch of applied chemistry which is concerned with the industrial uses of organic raw materials and farm products.—"The philosophy of *chemurgy* seeks that every American may produce, earn, and consume more."—Wheeler McMillen.

**chi rop′o dist** (kī rop′ō dist). One who specializes in the treatment of minor ailments of the feet.—"I do not know why such outbursts do not intervene in behalf of the *chiropodist*."—Alexander Woollcott.

**chi′ro prac″tor** (kī′rō prak″tur). A person who adjusts joints or the spine as a means of treating disease; one who practises this drugless method of manipulation.—"He had gone over the man like a *chiropractor*."—Leon Ware.

**cir″cum stan′tial** (sur″kum stān′shăl). Consisting of circumstances that give reasonable ground for believing the guilt or innocence of an accused person.—"They published a wealth of *circumstantial* evidence describing the tour."—James Duane Squires.

**clin′ics** (klin′iks). Dispensaries or institions for the treatment of outpatients.—"Boards of Education have psychiatric *clinics* to investigate the causes of maladjustment and recommend treatment."—S. Bernard Wortis.

**co ag′u lat″ing** (kō ag′ū lāte″ing). Congealing; curdling; changing into a clot; changing from a liquid into a dense mass.—"The latex is run into a *coagulating* vat with a little brine and acid, and rubber particles appear."—Harland Manchester.

**co″a lesce′** (kō″uh less′). Combine into one body or community.—"We shall soon enter a period when the stars in the university firmament will slowly tend to *coalesce*."—James Bryant Conant.

**cod″i fi ca′tion** (kod″ĭ fi kā′shŭn). Systemization; reduction to a system of principles and rules.—"As soon as possible the *codification* of international law should be undertaken."—Charles Evans Hughes.

**com bus′tion** (kŏm buss′chŭn). Burning; rapid oxidation.—"Furnaces designed exclusively for oil may have relatively small *combustion* space."—W. C. Schroeder.

**com mut′ed** (kŏ mūte′id). Changed to a less severe penalty or payment.—"The death sentence was *commuted* for some of the prisoners."—Franklin Delano Roosevelt.

**con sist′en cy** (kŏn siss′tĕn si). Degree of firmness; degree of density or solidity; viscosity.—"This yam has the *consistency* of our sweet potato."—Ira Wolfert.

**con tu′sion** (kŏn tū′zhŭn). A bruise affecting the tissue under the skin but not breaking the skin.—"There is a mild *contusion* with a scarcely detectable swelling."—Ainslee Mockridge.

**con″va les′cence** (kon″vuh less′ĕnce). Gradual recovery from illness; period of regaining health and strength.—"I wish to express my heartfelt appreciation of your concern for me during my *convalescence*."—Madame Chiang Kai-shek.

**con′verse** (kon′vurce). Something that exists in reversed relation; hence, the opposite; the contrary.—"Here we have the *converse* of the paradox formulated before."—Aldous Leonard Huxley.

**cor po′re al** (kor pō′rē ăl). Physical; bodily; material; of bodily substance.—"In his own mother the imprisoned spirit was almost more present to people than her *corporeal* self."—Willa Cather.

**cor ro′sive** (kŏ rō′siv). Having the power to gradually eat away, rust, or disintegrate.—"Due to the *corrosive* effects of water, more careful inspections must be made."—Theodore P. Hall.

**cos′mos** (koz′mŏss). The world or universe as an ordered whole; hence, a complete, harmonious system.—"What is good for us is primarily determined by the kind of beings we are as individuals and units of the *cosmos*."—Robert I. Gannon.

**coun′ter part″** (koun′ter pahrt″: 'ou' as in 'out'). Something closely resembling something else; a part that corresponds to another.—"Every chemical in this body of ours has its *counterpart* in the earth upon which we tread."—George Matthew Adams.

**cre a'tive** (krē āy'tiv). Able to bring something into being; that produces from nothing; that causes to exist; productive; inventive.—"The *creative* power of the universe is thought."—Emmet Fox.

**cre'tin ous** (kree'tin ŭs). Having a deformed body and feeble mentality.—"The *cretinous* idiot can be transformed into a child with normal intelligence."—Edward L. Bortz.

**crim"i nol'o gist** (krim"ĭ nol'ō jist). An expert in the study and investigation of crime; a person who makes a scientific study of criminals.—"As a *criminologist*, he held no brief for staring a suspect down."—Bruno Frank.

**cul'prit** (kul'prit). A person guilty of a crime; an offender; one who is accused of a fault or crime; a guilty person.—"The boy was the only possible *culprit*."—Hendrik Willem Van Loon.

**cul'ture** (kul'chŏor). The training, refinement, and civilization of mind, morals, and taste; the result of such education.—"*Culture* is the adze shaping man to fit snugly into the social structure of his day."—William Mather Lewis.

**cur ric'u lum** (kŭ rik'ū lŭm). A prescribed course of study, as in a college; all the courses offered by an educational institution.—"Dick was schooled in the world's hardest *curriculum*—necessity."—Charles B. Driscoll.

**de bil'i tates** (dē bil'ĭ tātes). Weakens; makes feeble or languid.—"A day dream of something you believe is too good to be true *debilitates* the whole mentality."—Emmet Fox.

**de"com po si'tion** (dē"kom pō zish'ŭn). Decay; putrefaction; the process of rotting.—"The processes of *decomposition* have depleted the supply of oxygen."—Henry D. Russell.

**de coys'** (dē koyz'). Lures; enticements; allurements; baits.—"The plant has laid *decoys* about it, so that the insect must freight itself with pollen while supping nectar."—Francis W. Pennell.

**de duc'tive** (dē duk'tiv). Inferential; inferring or deriving as a conclusion; reasoning by deduction.—"At least they come to class resolved to try to use their *deductive* faculties."—Christopher Morley.

**de flect'ed** (dē flekt'ed). Turned aside; deviated; turned from a set course.—"The electrons were *deflected* by magnetic fields."—Karl T. Compton.

**del"e te'ri ous** (del"ē teer'i ŭs). Causing moral or physical injury.—"This particular article is not *deleterious*, but it is inferior in food value."—Fiorello H. LaGuardia.

**del"i quesc'es** (del"ĭ kwess'ez). Melts away; becomes liquid by absorbing moisture from the air; passes away gradually.—"If exposed to the air the element sodium *deliquesces*."—Donald G. Cooley.

**de men'ti a** (dē men'shi uh). Insanity; feebleness of mind; craziness.—"While we fight here, humanity behind us crumbles down to a diseased *dementia*."—H. G. Wells.

**de mon'stra ble** (dē mon'struh b'l). Capable of being demonstrated or established as true; that can be proved; able to be shown or logically proved.—"It is *demonstrable* that the direct rays of the sun are an acute poison to certain types of skin."—Sterling McCormick.

**dep"o si'tion** (dep"ō zish'ŭn). The written testimony of a witness in court; a statement made under oath; a testifying or declaration given under oath.—"I shall not ask you for a *deposition*. It will be best if your name is not brought in at all."—Stephen Vincent Benét.

**de ranged'** (dē rānje'd'). Unbalanced in mind; insane; suffering from mental confusion and disorder.—"Civilized man in the course of time has in many cases become more or less *deranged*."—Aleš Hrdlička.

**der"ma tol'o gists** (dur"muh tol'ō jists). Those who are skilled in the science which treats of the diseases and structure of the skin; skin doctors.—"There is no one formula for a painless, safe, beautiful tan—there are many, say the *dermatologists*."—Martha Parker.

**des′ic cat″ing** (dess′ĭ kāte″ing). Drying up; becoming thoroughly dried and parched.—"Can you see the scene? It was a *desiccating* swampland."—Homer W. Smith.

**de ten′tion** (dē ten′shŭn). State of being forcibly detained or held in custody.—"Following my *detention*, my captors made demands."—Chiang Kai-shek.

**di″ag no′sis** (dī″ăg nō′siss). The determination of the distinctive nature of a disease.—"You can save yourself suffering by an early *diagnosis*."—Harry S. Gradle.

**di′a ther″my** (dī′uh thur″mi: 'th' as in 'thin'). A healing treatment consisting of the application of heat to the tissues under the skin by means of high-frequency electrical currents.—"Most patients seem to find *diathermy* very soothing as well as healing."—Emory L. Fielding.

**di dac′tic** (dī dak′tik). Intended to teach; teacher-like; meant to instruct; instructive.—"At all times the writing is devoid of *didactic* dust."—Bruce Barton.

**di″e tet′ic** (dī″ĕ tet′ik). Related to a regulated course of eating and drinking.—"The international food office would collect world-wide information regarding *dietetic* requirements." —Richard K. Law.

**dif″fer en′tials** (dif″ur en′shălz). Distinctive differences; traits that create a difference.—"Human nature is characterized by enormous *differentials* in endowment."—Ruth Alexander.

**dip′so ma′ni ac** (dip″sō māy′ni ak). A person who has a morbid and often uncontrollable craving for alcoholic drink.—"The book starts as a straight novel about a *dipsomaniac* and ends as a mystery yarn."—Rose Feld.

**dis″a bil′i ty** (diss″uh bil′ĭ ti). Mental or physical incapability of proper or effective action; lack of power to act. —"To learn the rate of complete *disability* in chronic disease is one of the purposes of the survey."—Hugh S. Cummings.

**dis′ci pline** (diss′ĭ plin). To train to obedience or subjection; to train in self-control.—"Students must learn to *discipline* their minds and to be accurate on essential facts."—Virginia C. Gildersleeve.

**dis″til la′tion** (diss″tĭ lā′shŭn). Separation of the evaporating parts of a substance by vaporizing and then cooling the vapor.—"In the stills the oil is extracted by *distillation* with steam."—Tom L. Wheeler.

**doc″u men′ta ry** (dok″ū men′tuh ri). Based on documents or records; derived from written proofs or official papers.—"Her *documentary* melodrama of juvenile delinquency moves fatefully to its end."—Robert Garland.

**e′dict** (ē′dikt). A rule of action proclaimed by authority; a proclamation of command or prohibition.—"The industrial problem will never be solved by *edict*, threat, or Government spending."—Alfred P. Sloan, Jr.

**ed″i fi ca′tion** (ed″ĭ fi kā′shŭn). Instruction or enlightenment; moral uplift; improvement.—"The public is entitled to a supply of good motion pictures for its entertainment and *edification*."—Alexander Markey.

**ef″fer vesce′** (ef″ur vess′). Bubble up; give off bubbles; hiss or foam, as water charged with carbon dioxide.— "Melt a little piece of glacier ice suddenly in a glass and it will *effervesce* like soda water, for it contains more air than ordinary ice."—Albert Carr.

**e lec′tives** (ē lek′tivz). Subjects or courses which students may select to study; optional studies or subjects in a fixed college curriculum.—"College students are given too much freedom in choosing their *electives*."—Ainslee Mockridge.

**e lec′tron** (ē lek′tron). A particle of negative electricity; a component part of the atom and of matter.— "The *electron* tube is the most startling, the most important invention of our time."—Waldemar Kaempfert.

**e lec″tron′ics** (ē lek″tron′iks). The branch of physics which treats of electrically charged particles, and their behavior.—"*Electronics* is the science based on the separation of electron and atom."—Joseph Slepian.

**em'bry o** (em'bri ō). Undeveloped; incipient; rudimentary; embryonic; beginning.—"Just a bit longer and the *embryo* stage will be over."—Elizabeth Goudge.

**em"bry ol'o gy** (em"bri ol'ō ji). The science that deals with the development of the embryo, or germ stages of animals or plants, into organisms.—"*Embryology* is that department of biology that deals with the beginnings of life."—George E. Sinclair.

**e met'ic** (ē met'ik). A medicine or other agent that causes one to vomit.—"Opium was like an *emetic* to me."—Roy Chapman Andrews.

**e mol'li ent** (ē mol'i ĕnt). An external applicant used to soften or sooth the skin.—"The *emollient* was soothing to the wind-burned face."—Donald G. Cooley.

**en act'ing** (en akt'ing). Making into a law; decreeing, as by legislative action; establishing as law.—"Without this *enacting* clause, the bill would be unconstitutional."—Thomas C. Desmond.

**en dem'ic** (en dem'ik). Peculiar to or prevailing in or among some specified country or people; peculiar to a locality, as a disease.—"In Liberia and other parts of Africa yellow fever is *endemic*."—Raymond B. Fosdick.

**en'er vat"ing** (en'ur vāte"ing). Likely to undermine strength and vigor; weakening; enfeebling; debilitating.—"Heat is *enervating*, but so is cold."—Eric A. Johnston.

**en fee'ble** (en fee'b'l). To impair; to make weak or feeble; to make infirm or deficient.—"The resistance to them of a younger generation with its change in taste serves still further to inhibit and *enfeeble* them."—Ludwig Lewisohn.

**en light'en ment** (en līte"n mĕnt). Great moral and intellectual advancement; illumination of the mind; freedom from superstition.—"By culture we mean the development that comes through education and *enlightenment*."—Daniel L. Marsh.

**en"to mol'o gists** (en"tō mol'ō jists). Those who study that branch of zoology that treats of insects.—"*Entomologists* are keenly interested in these tropical plants because they offer a possible solution in the spraying of vegetables."—Laurence Duggan.

**ep"i dem'ic** (ep"ĭ dem'ik). A disease that is wide-spread in a certain district.—"In 1887, the City of New York was threatened with a cholera *epidemic*."—I. Ogden Woodruff.

**e'qui poise** (ē'kwĭ poyze). Equilibrium; even balance; counterbalance of weight or force.—"He was profoundly interested in this principle of *equipoise*."—A. S. M. Hutchinson.

**e"ruc ta'tion** (ē"ruk tā'shŭn). A belching; an emitting of wind from the stomach through the mouth; an ejection.—"Such drinks are apt to produce what is known in polite scientific terms as an *eructation*."—Donald G. Cooley.

**eth'nic** (eth'nik: 'th' as in 'thin'). Ethnological; pertaining to races or groups of races; of the origin and distinctive characteristics of races.—"It does not look as if the *ethnic* composition of Transylvania will count very much when the settlements are made."—Anne O'Hare McCormick.

**eth"no log'i cal** (eth"nō loj'i kǎl: 'th' as in 'thin'). Pertaining to races and families of men.—"We are learning that it is not racial classifications nor *ethnological* considerations which bind men together."—Wendell L. Willkie.

**eu gen'ics** (ū jen'iks). The science of improving the human race by applying the laws of characteristics and inherent tendencies to the selection of marriage mates.—"The Bureau lists many organizations covering *eugenics*, dietetics, and every other kind of public health subject."—Edward L. Bernays.

**eu"tha na'si a** (ū"thuh nāy'zhi uh: 'th as in 'thin'). Painless, peaceful death; a way of producing or inducing death as a relief from pain.—"There are those who defend the practice of *euthanasia* in the case of congenital idiots."—Donald G. Cooley.

**e val"u a'tion** (ē val"ū āy'shŭn). Accurate appraisal; ascertained value; correct estimate of value.—"The *evaluation* of the campaign places a long list of gains on the credit side of our ledger."—Dwight D. Eisenhower.

**ex'cre ment** (eks'krē mĕnt). Refuse matter discharged from animals and birds; feces.—"The parent birds make a habit of removing their fledglings' *excrement* and carrying it away."—Alan Devoe.

**ex cretes'** (eks kreets'). Throws off by normal discharge.—"The normal skin *excretes* water and some waste matter, and secretes a number of different fluids."—R. H. Rulison.

**ex on'er at"ed** (eg zon'ur āte"id). Freed from blame; exculpated; vindicated from accusation.—"Tobacco tar has been *exonerated* as a cause of cancer by numerous experiments."—Robert H. Feldt.

**ex plor'a to"ry** (eks plor'uh tō"ri). Connected with exploring or examining; for the sake of discovery; relating to searching or scrutinizing; used in order to examine.—"The District Attorney was not sure of his ground. All his questions were *exploratory*."—John J. Green.

**ex"tra cur ric'u lar** (eks"truh kŭ rik'ū-ler). Pertaining to what is not included in courses of study but forms part of the life of students in college. —"It was his *extracurricular* activities that ruined him."—S. L. Scanlon.

**fac'tor** (fak'tur). One of the several elements needed to produce a result; a necessary part; an element in a case or situation.—"Later it came into general use as a humanizing *factor* of civilization."—Irvin S. Cobb.

**fac'ul ty** (fak'ŭl ti). The body of instructors in a university or college; the teaching staff.—"A hospital without a medical staff is like a school without a *faculty*."—C. Rufus Rorem.

**fangs** (fangz). Long curved hollow teeth of serpents through which poison is ejected.—"This new wilderness around us is infested with chameleon-like serpents with deadly poison in their *fangs*."—George V. Denny.

**fe'brile** (fee'bril). Feverish; caused by fever; of fever; indicating fever.—"In tuberculosis such acute *febrile* periods are long in duration and a partial starvation would injure the patient considerably."—George G. Ornstein.

**fe lo'ni ous ly** (fē lō'ni ŭs li). Mali-

ciously; with criminal intentions.— "The defendants were charged with knowingly and *feloniously* making castings in a defective manner."— Francis Biddle.

**fis'sion** (fish'ŭn). The act of splitting apart; a breaking into parts; the division of a cell or organism as a means of reproduction.—"The slander grew and multiplied—sometimes by *fission* like a polyp, sometimes by endless extension like a tapeworm." —L. P. Jacks.

**for'fei ture** (for'fĭ chŏor). Loss through some fault, omission, or offense; a penalty or fine.—"For many years we had a law in our State which authorized the seizure and *forfeiture* of intoxicating liquors kept for sale."— Oscar L. Young.

**fos'sil** (foss'il). An animal or plant that has been preserved by being buried a long time in the earth; the hardened remains of prehistoric organisms.— "A *fossil* is, primarily, the preserved remains of an organism."—Percy E. Raymond.

**fu'gi tive** (fū'ji tiv). One who flees, as from pursuit or restraint.—"Georgia charges that this man is a *fugitive* from justice."—Arthur Garfield Hays.

**gal'ax y** (gal'ăk si). An irregular luminous band of innumerable stars encircling the heavens.—"The great *galaxy* we see as the Milky Way has lost its major position in the universe."—Watson Davis.

**gen"e al'o gist** (jen"ē al'ō jist). One who makes a study of records of descent from ancestors; a person who studies direct lines of descent and pedigrees.—"If you are interested in his family tree and coat of arms, the *genealogist* attends to the former, and over the latter two experts disagree." —May Lamberton Becker.

**gen"er al i za'tion** (jen"ur ăl i zā'shŭn). A general inference or conclusion; a general idea or rule.—"Their minds jump from a single case to the *generalization* that studies do not count."— William Trufant Foster.

**gen'er ate** (jen'ur āte). Produce; bring into existence; produce by a process; cause or originate.—"The machines *generate* artificial fevers which improve the circulation."—Waldemar Kaempfert.

**ge ner'ic** (jē ner'ik). General, not specific; characteristic of a class or group; pertaining to a genus or kind of related things.—"The first chapter of Genesis deals with *generic* thought." —Emmet Fox.

**ge"o log'ic** (jē"ō loj'ik). Pertaining to the science of the structure of the earth.—"Major changes in climate through *geologic* ages have long been recognized."—Watson Davis.

**ge'nus** (jee'nŭs). A group of related species; a class group of animals or plants embracing one or more species.—"The *genus* Aster contains about 250 species."—John M. Fogg, Jr.

**glob'ules** (glob'ūle'z). Very small globes or spherical particles looking like small bubbles or tiny balloons.— "A secret method of curing produces tiny *globules*."—Dorothy Whittington.

**grav"i ta'tion** (grav"ĭ tā'shŭn). The force with which all bodies attract each other; the law of tending to move toward some point or center.— "Like *gravitation* in the physical realm, the law of the Lord in the moral realm bends for no one."— Harry Emerson Fosdick.

**gyn"e col'o gy** (jĭ"nē kol'ō ji). The branch of medicine that treats of the functions and diseases of women.— "The discussion of Egyptian *gynecology* is based largely on study of well-known medical papyri dating back to 2000 B.C."—Lewis C. Scheffey.

**hag'gard** (hag'urd). Worn in appearance; emaciated; famishing; wasted by pain and hunger.—"Greece is a gaunt and *haggard* sample of what they are so eager to hand to all the world."—Franklin Delano Roosevelt.

**hal lu"ci na'tions** (huh lū"si nā'shŭnz). Apparent perception of things or sounds which are not really present; illusions; experiences without external objects to correspond.—"The extract of lettuce has some of the virtues of opium without the *hallucinations* that may accompany the latter."—Earlene M. Cornell.

**hem'or rhage** (hem'ō rij). Discharge of blood from a ruptured blood-vessel; severe bleeding.—"Despite the *hemorrhage* he remained conscious."— Edward Lincoln Smith II.

**her'ald ry** (her'ăld ri). The science of armorial bearings and coats of arms; the symbolism of emblazoned arms. —"In the religious realm of *heraldry*, the scallop is the emblem of the Apostle St. James the Great."— Hebe Bulley.

**he red'i ty** (hē red'ĭ ti). Transmission of physical or mental qualities from parent to offspring; qualities derived from forebears.—"*Heredity* and environment combine to shape man's destiny."—James S. McLester.

**her maph'ro dites** (hur maf'rō dītes). Individuals having both male and female organs of reproduction; beings which have the combining characteristics of both sexes.—"At one time in our evolution we were all *hermaphrodites*."—Donald G. Cooley.

**ho'me o paths** (hō'mē ō paths: 'th' as in 'thin'). Those who practice the system of medicine that prescribes minute doses of medicines that would produce in a healthy person the very disease they are treating in the patient.—"She might have added *homeopaths* and vegetarians to the list."— Annie Nathan Meyer.

**hom'i cide** (hom'ĭ sīde). The killing of any human being by another.—"He knew that he would be guilty of *homicide* if he asked of his exhausted soldiers further hopeless resistance." —John Cudahy.

**ho"mo ge'ne ous** (hō"mō jee'nē ŭs). Of the same composition, kind, or nature throughout.—"A *homogeneous* America can become evolved only by making all residents work toward our common welfare."—Harold Fields.

**hon'or ar"y** (on'ur er"i). Conferred as an honor, without the usual requirements and examinations.—"An *honorary* degree from a University is a pleasant gift to receive."—George F. Gahagan.

**hor'o scope** (hŏr'ō skōpe). A chart of the aspect of the heavens giving the relative position of the planets at the instant of a person's birth; also how these are regarded as influencing his life.—"According to the *horoscope* of Alexander II the alexandrite stone is symbolic of misfortune."—Eunice Robinson.

**hor´ti cul″ture** (hor´ti kul″chŏŏr). The cultivation of a garden or orchard.— "The man was interested in *horticulture* and had many books on the subject."—Daniel M. Eisenberg.

**hu man´i ties** (hū man´ĭ tiz). Latin and Greek classics; the branches of polite scholarship; works and authors having aesthetic value; belles-lettres.— "The publication of this new history is an encouraging sign to all students of the *humanities*."—Samuel C. Chew.

**hu mid´i fy ing** (hū mid´ĭ fī ing). Making damp or moist, as the atmosphere.—"New methods of heating, *humidifying*, and drying promise to be necessities in the home."—James H. McGraw.

**hy´brid** (hī´brid). Produced by cross-fertilization; derived from two different varieties or species.—"*Hybrid* rubber plants will soon be flying over jungles en route to Brazil."— John Adams.

**hy″po chon´dri a** (hī″pō kon´dri uh). Morbid depression, especially about one's health; imagination that one is ill or has a disease.—"We have had over ten years of emphasis upon the pathology of democracy with some evidence of consequent *hypochondria*." —Henry W. Wriston.

**hy poth´e sis** (hī poth´ē siss; 'th' as in 'thin'). Something assumed likely to be true; an unsupported theory; a surmise; a provisional supposition.— " 'Was he sincere or just trying to compensate for the weakness of his convictions?' She had a feeling that the second *hypothesis* was the true one."—André Maurois.

**hy″po thet´i cal** (hī″pō thet´i kăl: 'th' as in 'thin'). Tentatively assumed or imaginary; supposed.—"This is no *hypothetical* point which I am raising; it is a very realistic one."—Karl T. Compton.

**hys te´ri a** (hiss teer´i uh). Abnormal excitement, often characterized by paroxysms of alternate laughing and crying; unnatural lack of self-control;

excessive emotionalism.—"These political opportunists and dictators ruled by brutality and *hysteria*."— Louis Bromfield.

**hys ter´i cal** (hiss ter´i kăl). Fitfully emotional; wildly or unnaturally excited.—"He has encouraged them to make sensational *hysterical*, and provoking speeches."—Hamilton Fish, Jr.

**il″le git´i mate** (il″ē jit´ĭ mit). Contrary to law; hence, born out of wedlock; born of unmarried parents.— "We had the eldest son declared *illegitimate*."—André Maurois.

**im´ma nent** (im´uh nĕnt). Indwelling; inherent.—"Death is *immanent* in life."—Alexis Carrel.

**im´mu niz″ing** (im´ū nīze″ing). Protecting against disease; giving immunity to; rendering not susceptible; giving power to resist infection.— "Long-time control was achieved by *immunizing* thousands with the vaccine."—Brehon Somervell.

**im pound´ed** (im pound´ed: 'ou' as in 'out'). Shut up in an enclosure by public authority; hence, seized and held by law.—"The depression arrived and funds were *impounded*."— Victor H. Cahalane.

**in´born″** (in´born″). Born in one; innate; natural; instinctive.—"How fortunate it is that public speaking is not an *inborn* trait but an art to be learned!"—Daniel P. Eginton.

**in dict´ment** (in dīte´mĕnt). A formal written charge or accusation.—"This book is an *indictment* of a shameless era."—Clifton Fadiman.

**in″dis po si´tion** (in″diss pō zish´ŭn). An illness that is only slight and neither deep-seated nor of long duration; a slight disorder in some part of the body.—"The Premier was suffering from nothing serious. Just a mild *indisposition*."—Jack Bond.

**in doc″tri na´tion** (in dok″tri nā´shŭn). Instruction on principles and doctrines.—"I am happy to complete *indoctrination* and shove off for active duty."—Harold E. Stassen.

**in fir´mi ty** (in fur´mĭ ti). Weakness; frailty; feebleness; an infirm or diseased condition; mental, moral, or physical disability.—"A physical *in-*

*firmity* can be turned into an actual asset."—Robert Gordon Anderson.

**in san'i tar"y** (in san'ĭ ter"i). Unhealthy; not sanitary; not favorable to good health; not hygienic; lacking means to preserve health.—"The dusty dentist's office in Naples was the most *insanitary* I had ever seen." —George F. Gahagan.

**in stinc'tive** (in stingk'tiv). Prompted by instinct or natural tendency; caused by a natural feeling or urge; derived from an innate impulse.— "To most people this would be *instinctive* knowledge."—Henry James Forman.

**in teg'u ment** (in teg'ū měnt). A natural covering or envelop, as the skin or coat of an animal; skin, rind, or other covering.—"This doctor friend of mine specializes in improving the touchability of the human *integument.*—Daniel P. Eginton.

**in"ter dict'ed** (in"tur dikt'ed). Prohibited; debarred; forbidden; banned. —"All drinking in the navy was *interdicted.*"—Hugh E. Blackstone.

**in tes'tate** (in tess'tāte). Without having made a valid will; not having legally planned for their possessions in a will.—"An appalling number of persons die *intestate.*"—Emmet Holloway.

**ir'ri tant** (ir'ĭ tănt). That which produces irritation or excites; a stimulant; a substance or agency that causes inflammation or irritates.— "Alcohol is a mild *irritant* to the stomach."—Bradwell E. Tanis.

**ju di'cial** (jōō dish'ăl). Pertaining to the administration of justice; having to do with judges and law courts.— "There was harmony between the executive, *judicial,* and legislative branches then."—Paul Austin Wolfe.

**ju"ris dic'tion al** (jōōr"iss dik'shŭn ăl). Pertaining to the lawful right to exercise authority, or to the territory within which such authority may be legally exercised.—"*Jurisdictional* disputes ought to be deferred."—Henry J. Kaiser.

**ju"ris pru'dence** (jōōr"iss prōō'děnce). The science or philosophy of law and its administration; a system of laws. —"Why should criminal *jurispru-*

*dence* be governed by different procedures in different localities?"—J. Edgar Hoover.

**ju've nile** (jōō'vĕ nil). Youthful; young; not yet grown-up; not of age.— "They requested the Mayor to investigate the recent increase in *juvenile* offenders."—Channing Pollock.

**klep"to ma'ni acs** (klep"tō māy'ni aks). People who have a persistent and uncontrollable impulse to steal although they do not need what they take.— "The company also included a couple of *kleptomaniacs* who used to carry away any object they could lay their hands on."—Axel Munthe.

**le'sions** (lee'zhŭnz). Changes in function or structure of an organ or tissue caused by disease; injuries.—"Many lung *lesions* give scanty symptoms at first."—Charles H. Goodrich.

**lin'e age** (lin'ē ij). Descent in a direct line from a common ancestor; pedigree; race; family.—"A father and a mother and a child of the house and *lineage* of David were in the family town of Bethelem."—Paul Austin Wolfe.

**lore** (lōre). Learning; knowledge; whatever may be taught or learned; a body of facts, tales, or traditions of a nation or on a subject.—"His book is full of curious and often fascinating *lore,* revealing a man striving to know and to experience more."—Gerald W. Johnson.

**maim'ing** (māme'ing). Depriving a person of some part of the body; disabling; mutilating; crippling.— "This reduction in suffering and in *maiming* of employees warrants all the time and expense involved."—Lammot du Pont.

**mal'a dies** (mal'uh diz). Diseases, especially when chronic or deep-seated; illnesses; disordered conditions of mind or body.—"These *maladies* were not local."—Alben W. Barkley.

**mam'mals** (mam'ălz). Animals which have a backbone or spinal column and whose females suckle their young.—"Mammalia may be divided into whales on the one hand, and all other *mammals* on the other."—A. Brazier Howell.

**ma'ni a** (māy'ni uh). Madness; a kind

of mental unsoundness characterized by great emotion; hence, an ungovernable or unreasonable desire; a craze.—"The phrase, 'Do it right' had become almost a *mania* with her."—Pearl S. Buck.

**mas′och ism** (maz′ŏk iz′m). Sexual perversion in which pleasure is derived from being cruelly treated.—"The lovers themselves seem to make a degree of *masochism* necessary to the protagonist in a truly great passion." —Joseph Wood Krutch.

**ma te′ri a med′i ca** (muh tē′ri uh med′i kuh). The branch of medical science that relates to the nature, uses and effects of substances used as curative agents.—"He was taking the examination in *materia medica* in July."—W. Somerset Maugham.

**ma′trix** (māy′triks). The formative cells from which a structure grows; the mass of rock in which a fossil or gem is embedded.—"The fossil was almost completely hidden by the sandy *matrix* in which it was formed." —Edwin H. Colbert.

**ma tu′ri ty** (muh tū′rĭ ti). Full development; a fully grown state; the condition of fully developed power of mind and body; grown-up mentality.—"The accounts deal with men and women whose work is interesting to *maturity* rather than to youth."— Anne T. Eaton.

**meg″a lo ma′ni a** (meg″uh lō māy′ni uh). Insanity in which the patient thinks he is very great and wonderful; a mental condition in which the patient has an exaggerated idea of himself or his importance.—"The criminal folly of Serbian chauvinism and Pan-Serbian *megalomania* are beyond argument."—Orville Prescott.

**mel″an cho′li a** (mel″ăn kō′li uh). A mental derangement characterized by depression and illusions; a state of continued sadness and gloom about everything.—"Her natural tendency toward *melancholia* had been seriously affected by the unpleasant gossip."— Hendrik Willem Van Loon.

**men tal′i ty** (men tal′ĭ ti). Mental activity; habit of mind; power of mind; mental capacity.—"There is no room for that kind of *mentality* in our city."—Fiorello H. LaGuardia.

**met′al lur″gy** (met′uh lur″ji). The science of economically extracting metals from ores, and smelting, refining and alloying them.—"The turbine electrical steam locomotive is a product of pioneering in electrical art and in *metallurgy*."—J. W. Barker.

**me″te or o log′i cal** (mē″tē ŏr ō loj′i-kăl). Relating to the character of the weather and atmospheric changes in particular places.—"I based the conclusion that Germany was the natural air power in Europe upon factors including geographical and *meteorological* conditions."—Charles A. Lindbergh.

**mi″cro-or′gan isms** (mī″krō or′găn-iz′mz). Microbes; bacteria; tiny or microscopic organisms.—"Our scientists were asked to conduct research to determine the most effective treatment for preserving fabrics against attacks by *micro-organisms*."—Henry C. Knight.

**min″er al′o gy** (min″ur al′ō ji). The science of minerals, or substances that are neither animal nor plant.— "This is a problem for a student of *mineralogy*."—Ellery Marsh Egan.

**mis″ap pro′pri at″ed** (miss″ă prō′pri-āte″id). Applied or put to wrong use; appropriated dishonestly; took and used dishonestly; misapplied.—"Shall we say that he *misappropriated* the funds?"—Henry J. Powers.

**mis″be got′ten** (miss″bē got″n). Illegitimate; bastard; born of unmarried parents; hence, generated in an irregular way.—"The *misbegotten* mule, with his out-sized ears has been a standard American joke for more than a century."—Ruth Moore.

**mis″ce ge na′tion** (miss″ĭ jĭ nā′shŭn). Interbreeding of colored and white races; sexual union or mixture of races.—"It is the best novel on the theme of *miscegenation* that I have ever read."—J. Donald Adams.

**mis fea′sance** (miss fē′zănce). The performance in an unlawful or negligent way of something that is really lawful; the wrong use of lawful authority.—"The governor was guilty of gross *misfeasance.*"—Bertram M. Myers.

**mor tal'i ty** (mor tal'ĭ ti). Proportion of deaths in a specified number; death rate.—"The greatest *mortality* was among the young lieutenants who led their men over the top."— George Barton Cutten.

**mu lat'to** (mū lat'ō). The offspring of one white and one Negro parent.— "A *mulatto* woman of exquisite beauty was already on the stage." —Emory L. Fielding.

**mu ta'tion** (mū tā'shŭn). The process of change or alteration in form; variation; a change of characteristics resulting in the creation of a new species.—"Some say that life surmounted the obstacle by the accident of *mutation* and the ultimate survival of the fittest."—Homer W. Smith.

**nar cis'sism** (nahr siss'iz'm). Pleasure derived from admiration of oneself; sexual feeling about one's own body. —"The bright boy of a small town has been caught in some Freudian trap of *narcissism.*"—Edmund Wilson.

**nau'se at"ed** (naw'shē āte"id). Sickened; affected with a desire to vomit; disgusted.—"It was their only nourishment, and they sickened of it; it made them *nauseated.*"—Thomas Mann.

**ne'groid** (nee'groyd). Characteristic of the Negro race; like a Negro; of Negro type.—"Their features are *negroid,* their lips thick, their heads shaped differently."—Albert A. Brandt.

**neu"ras the'ni a** (nū"răss thē'ni uh: 'th' as in 'thin'). Nervous prostration; a derangement of the nervous system attributed to emotional disturbances; nervous debility.—"When the war had ended the *neurasthenia* did not go away"—Louis Bromfield.

**neu rol'o gist** (nū rol'ō jist). A person who is skilled in the treatment of nervous diseases.—"The wife of the famous *neurologist* wrote me that she had found the most beautiful spot." —Charles B. Driscoll.

**neu ro'sis** (nū rō'siss). A functional disorder of the nerves.—"Petty annoyances can cause more *neurosis*

than bombings from planes."— Foster Kennedy.

**neu rot'ic** (nū rot'ik). Suffering from a functional nervous disorder; morbidly unhealthy.—"There should be separate forms for wives and mothers of service men so that they can solve their intricate tax problems without going *neurotic* in the process."— Sylvia F. Porter.

**no'men cla"ture** (nō'mĕn klā"choŏr). A system of names, as used in any art or science, especially classification names of groups or divisions.—"The *nomenclature* of science grows apace during war-time."—S. L. Scanlon.

**nos'trums** (noss'trŭmz). Quack recipes; favorite remedies for special ailments.—"The Bureau of Investigations has a card index listing many quacks, *nostrums,* and fraudulent medicines."—Morris Fishbein.

**no vi'ti ate** (nō vish'i āte). Apprenticeship; period of preparation; state of probation; time of being a novice.— "It was her first important assignment while she was working out her *novitiate.*"—Rose Feld.

**nu"mis mat'ics** (nū"miz mat'iks). The science of coins and medals.—"The hobby of *numismatics* has many distinguished followers."—Charles Henry Crozier.

**nu'tri ment** (nū'trĭ mĕnt). Nourishment; food; that which nourishes and promotes development.—"They tell us that there is very little *nutriment* in white bread."—Jack Bond.

**nur'tured** (nur'choŏrd). Nourished and trained; cared for and educated. —"Your sons will be *nurtured* by the army."—Warren J. Clear.

**o bes'i ty** (ō beece'ĭ ti). Corpulence; excessive fatness.—"We have only time to suggest a few sections such as infections, *obesity,* and diabetes."— Charles H. Goodrich.

**ob ses'sion** (ŏb sesh'ŭn). Persistent preoccupation with a dominating and powerful idea; the influence of an inescapable, haunting idea.—"There is an *obsession* with bloodshed, an insistence that man can be vile."— Iris Barry.

**oc"to roon'** (ok"tō rōōn'). A person whose blood is one-eighth Negro; the child of a white person and one who has a quarter Negro blood.—"She is some sort of West Indian *octoroon*, I believe."—Edith Wharton.

**oc'u lar** (ok'ū lur). Pertaining to the eye; visual; for or by the eyes.—"If the astigmatic person will cultivate habits of *ocular* mobility, he can do much to diminish or even eliminate, his disability."—Aldous Huxley.

**oc'u list** (ok'ū list). A doctor who is skilled in treating diseases and defects of the eye.—"I keep having to squint my eyes to read. I'll have to go back to the *oculist*."—John P. Marquand.

**ol fac'to ry** (ol fak'tō ri). Pertaining to the sense of smell; of smell; having to do with the sense of smell.—"The ability to detect air-borne odors would be useless to a whale, and toothed whales have lost the *olfactory* sense entirely."—A. Brazier Howell.

**om nis'cience** (om nish'ĕnce). Infinite knowledge; knowledge of everything; complete and perfect knowledge.— "Government planning and control might be the solution of all problems if government were beneficent *omniscience* and omnipotence."—Channing Pollock.

**oph"thal mol'o gy** (of"thal mol'ō ji: 'th' as in 'thin'). The science of the eye and its diseases.—"Select a man who holds the certificate of the American Board of *Ophthalmology*."—Harry S. Gradle.

**op'ti cal** (op'ti kăl). Made to assist sight; of the relation of sight and light to each other; ocular.—"The most powerful of present *optical* microscopes might enlarge the appearance of a human hair to the thickness of your wrist."—Wheeler McMillen.

**op ti'cian** (op tish'ăn). One who makes, or deals in, glasses and other instruments to assist vision.—"Many oculists prefer that their patients have their prescriptions filled by an *optician* whom they recommend."— Henry T. Powers.

**op tom'e trist** (op tom'ē trist). One who measures the range of vision of the eye, and its peculiarities.—"You should have your glasses fitted by an *optometrist* or an optician."—Harry S. Gradle.

**or'bit** (or'bit). The path in space along which a heavenly body moves about its center of attraction.—"The comet came within the *orbit* of Mars." —Fred. L. Whipple.

**or'gan isms** (or'găn iz'mz). Organized bodies or material structures made up of parts related to one another in such a way that their relation to the whole governs their relation to each other; animals or plants that resemble these.—"The invading *organisms* are carried to all areas of the body." —George G. Ornstein.

**or'i fic es** (or'ĭ fiss ez). Small openings or cavities; apertures; openings into physical organs.—"One man must keep his eye on the scopes by which the various *orifices* of the body can be explored."—John P. Peters.

**or"ni tho log'i cal ly** (or"ni thō loj'i-kăl i: 'th' as in 'thin'). With regard to the birds of the district; from a scientific acquaintance with the birds found there.—"The islands were less known *ornithologically* than any other part of the world."—Ernst Mayr.

**or"tho don'tic** (or"thō don'tik: 'th' as in 'thin'). Pertaining to the treatment for correcting irregularity or faulty positions of the teeth.—"The timing of *orthodontic* treatment is a difficult problem even for specialists in this field."—G. R. Moore.

**or"tho pe'dics** (or"thō pee'diks: 'th' as in 'thin'). The correcting or preventing of deformities, especially in children.—"Medicine has made extraordinary strides in the therapy of *orthopedics*."—Nathan B. Van Etten.

**os'cil la"tor** (oss'ĭ lā"tur). A device for producing fluctuations in the flow of charges of electricity; a radio-frequency machine which changes mechanical energy into electrical energy.—"No longer does radio equipment have to be taken out of the plane. Now the *oscillator* is taken into the plane and the testing job is done in three minutes."—Lawrence Galton.

**os"te op'a thy** (oss"tē op'uh thi: 'th' as in 'thin'). A system of healing which treats disease by manipulation of misplaced bones.—"He pays considerable attention to this columnist's amiable addiction to *osteopathy*."—Stanley Walker.

**o'zone** (ō'zōne). A gaseous, blue form of oxygen formed by the passage of electricity through the air, and used for purifying air and sterilizing drinking water; hence, pure air.—"I am stretching my muscles and collecting *ozone*."—Roy L. Abbott.

**pa"le on tol'o gist** (pāy"lē on tol'ō jist). A person who studies geological periods and fossils.—"He analyses his friends with the same detached interest that a *paleontologist* might take in a batch of unidentified fossils."—George F. Whicher.

**pal'sied** (pawl'zid). Affected with complete or partial loss of power to move; paralyzed; having the sensation impaired.—"He mopped his perspiring brow, his thin hand trembling as if *palsied*."—Lloyd C. Douglas.

**pan"a ce'as** (pan"uh see'uhz). Pretended remedies for all diseases; remedies to cure all ills.—"There are no *panaceas* under present conditions."—Clarence J. Haverty.

**pan dem'ic** (pan dem'ik). Prevalent over a whole country; widespread over the world; widely epidemic.—"The struggle is on to prevent influenza from becoming *pandemic*."—Tom Pennell.

**par"a noi'ac** (par"uh noy'ăk). Affected with mental unsoundness attended with delusions of persecution or other hallucinations.—"Such *paranoiac* nationalism, if allowed its head, will reduce civilization to a mere shambles."—James Rowland Angell.

**par'a site** (par'uh sīte). An organism that lives in or on another organism.—"The *parasite* infections that may menace us can be avoided."—H. Randolph Halsey.

**par'ox ysm** (par'ŏk siz'm). Sudden or violent emotion; a fit or convulsion.—"We have been able to suffer pain without *paroxysm* only by dosing ourselves with a dangerous opiate."—Hugh S. Johnson.

**path"o log'i cal** (path"ō loj'i kăl: 'th' as in 'thin'). Pertaining to the branch of medical science that treats of diseased conditions, their causes, and nature; hence, morbid, as a result of disease.—"These boys may develop a *pathological* sense of oppression by their parents."—S. Bernard Wortis.

**pec"u la'tion** (pek"ū lā'shŭn). Theft of funds entrusted to one's care; misappropriation of public money; stealing public property; embezzling; pilfering.—"The undiscovered *peculation* of the clerk, the secret tears and the great patience are left behind."—Donald Culross Peattie.

**ped'a gogues** (ped'uh gogz). Schoolmasters; teachers.—"It is up to you as *pedagogues* to determine how this development of mental equipments can best be accomplished."—Frank L. Rowland.

**ped'ant ry** (ped'ănt ri). Ostentatious display of learning; conceited adherence to forms in the application or presentation of knowledge.—"The more sensitive of them regretted that she was rather spoiled by preciosity and *pedantry*."—André Maurois.

**pe"di a tri'cians** (pee"di uh trish'ănz). Physicians specializing in the hygienic care and diseases of children.—"Biologists and *pediatricians* have made great progress in promoting development in the stages after birth."—Edwin G. Conklin.

**ped'i gree** (ped'ĭ gree). Table of descent; lineage; line of ancestors.—"The *pedigree* of his family or the place of his birth does not constitute an American."—Harold L. Ickes.

**pe'nal ized** (pee'năl īze'd). Punished; fined; made to pay a forfeit or suffer a penalty for disobeying rules.—"I gathered that any time he ventured below he was out of bounds and liable to be *penalized*."—Irvin S. Cobb.

**pe nol'o gy** (pē nol'ō ji). The science that treats of the punishment and prevention of crime and of prison management.—"The faults of all our social institutions become the problems of *penology*."—Lewis E. Lawes.

**per"mu ta'tions** (pur"mū tā'shŭnz). The total number of changes in the position of a set of things; the variations in the order of a group of things.—"The perpetual foolish variation of the *permutations* and combinations of 250 cards taken five at a time had no charms for him."—H. G. Wells.

**pes'ti lence** (pess'tĭ lĕnce). Any widespread and fatal infectious malady.—"At the end of any war only death, famine and *pestilence* walk serenely."—William C. Bullitt.

**pet'ti fog"gers** (pet'i fog"urz). Inferior lawyers who resort to mean or tricky ways of doing business; rascally or petty practitioners.—"They fought to the last ditch, but the *pettifoggers* were too many for them."—L. P. Jacks.

**phar"ma ceu'ti cal** (fahr"muh sū'tĭ-kăl). Pertaining to the art or business of compounding drugs and dispensing medicines; hence, from a drugstore.—"Free *pharmaceutical* requirements and free medical attention are features of New Zealand's Social Security arrangements."—Walter Nash.

**phar"ma col'o gy** (fahr"muh kol'ō ji). The science of drugs; the science of the nature, preparation, and effects of medicine.—"It is likely enough that *pharmacology* will be called in as an ally of applied psychology."—Aldous Huxley.

**phar"ma co poe'ia** (fahr"muh kō pee'-uh). A book containing methods of preparing medicines; a stock or collection of drugs.—"From architecture to *pharmacopoeia*, from philology to astronomy, we are indebted to those meditative peoples."—P. J. Searles.

**phi lat'e list** (fi lat'ē list). A stamp collector; one who studies and collects stamps and franked envelopes.—"Button enthusiasts are just as avid for rare specimens as any *philatelist*."—Thelma Shull.

**pho'bi as** (fō'bi uhz). Morbid fears or dreads.—"Persistent or periodic severe nervous symptoms such as depression or *phobias* should be mentioned in the history."—George E. Daniels.

**phys'ics** (fiz'iks). The science that treats of the phenomena associated with matter in general, especially its relation to energy.—"The airplane was born from the science of *physics*."—Herbert Hoover.

**phys"i o log'i cal** (fiz"i ō loj'i kăl). Of the functions of living organisms; pertaining to the workings of organs.—"The ailments of the *physiological* change of life are real and often disabling."—S. Bernard Wortis.

**phy sique'** (fi zeek'). The physical appearance of a person; bodily structure and strength.—"The men of the United States forces who have come to New Zealand have impressed us all by their *physique* and soldierly bearing."—Peter Fraser.

**plain'tiff** (plāne'tif). The complaining party in an action at law; the person who brings a suit against someone.—"This *plaintiff* has less rights than an alien."—John H. Bright.

**plas'ma** (plaz'muh). The fluid part of blood; the colorless part of blood in which the corpuscles float; protoplasm or the life basis in animals.—"The world is hungering for spiritual *plasma* to give it the happy life it craves."—George Matthew Adams.

**po di'a trist** (pō dī'uh trist). One skilled in the science of caring for the feet and the treatment of diseases of the foot.—"What relief a *podiatrist* can give to one's feet!"—Donald G. Cooley.

**pol"i ti'cian** (pol"i tish'ŭn). A person who is versed in the principles of civic administration; one who is interested in intrigues in government science, or uses a political office for private gain.—"He may be a keen *politician*, but one cannot call him a statesman."—Jack Bond.

**po'tion** (pō'shŭn). A drink, often a dose of medicine; a draft or dose of liquid, especially of medicine, poison, or magic.—"He administered the *potion* to the dog, and the remedy seemed to quiet him."—Gene Fowler.

**pred"e ces'sors** (pred"ē sess'urz). Those who have gone before others in point of time; forefathers; ancestors.—"Our high mission obliges us to defend the spiritual heritage of our wise *predecessors*."—Pius XII.

**pre scrip'tion** (prē skrip'shŭn). A remedy for a special condition.—"The *prescription* for our indifference is a rebirth of spirit."—Howard W. Jackson.

**pro fes'sion** (prō fesh'ŭn). An occupation to which one devotes oneself, especially one that calls for special mental or other attainments.—"The *profession* of surgery calls for very sensitive and skilful hands."—Donald G. Cooley.

**pro fi'cien cy** (prō fish'ĕn si). Skill; expertness; advanced state of skill or knowledge.—"The team play over here has reached a high degree of *proficiency*."—Dwight D. Eisenhower.

**pro gen'i tors** (prō jen'ĭ turz). Forefathers; parents; ancestors.—"Henry III is the sum of his *progenitors*."—Robert Humphreys.

**prog no'sis** (prog nō'siss). A prediction or forecast in regard to the course and end of a disease; a prognostication or conclusion in regard to future symptoms.—"This is one case history which requires no *prognosis* except to say that the patient will be as good as new."—Lucy Agnes Hancock.

**prop'a gate** (prop'uh gāte). To cause to multiply; to spread abroad; to produce by generation.—"Nature selects the best to *propagate* the race."—George Barton Cutten.

**pro"phy lac'tic** (prō"fĭ lak'tik). Operating to ward off disease; preventive.—"I refer to the issuance of *prophylactic* equipment."—Henry L. Stimson.

**pro tract'ed** (prō trakt'ed). Unusually extended or prolonged; lengthened.—"There was a failure of further conquests on account of a *protracted* resistance."—William L. Shirer.

**psy chi'a try** (sī kī'uh tri). A branch of medicine that relates to mental diseases and nervous disorders.—"*Psychiatry* has a place in every step of a Navy man's career."—Francis J. Braceland.

**psy"cho a nal'y sis** (sī"kō uh nal'ĭ siss). The diagnosis of mental and nervous disorders by careful analysis of unusual mental reactions, basing the examination on the theory that these reactions are often due to repressed desires which persist unconsciously even though they have been con-sciously rejected.—"Religion, philosophy, metaphysics, and *psychoanalysis* are deeply interwoven into the narrative."—Rose Feld.

**psy"cho log'i cal** (sī"kō loj'i kăl). Of the mind; of the operations, functions and powers of the mind.—"*Psychological* scrutiny showed that the man's mind was like an unfurnished room, devoid of ideas, occupation or interests."—Bruce Barton.

**psy"cho path'ic** (sī"kō path'ik: 'th' as in 'thin'). Relating to excessive sensitiveness, emotional outbursts or instability, or to suspiciousness, doubts and fears; hence, mentally deranged. —"Winston Churchill's reply infuriated the *psychopathic* ruler."—William Elliott.

**psy cho'sis** (sī kō'siss). A mental state or condition; a mental disease.—"In a fog of emotions and appeals we are fast driving into the *psychosis* of war." —Herbert Hoover.

**pu'ber ty** (pū'bur ti). The period in life at which a person becomes capable of bearing offspring; the age when sexual maturity is reached.—"It is no coincidence that dental decay reaches its peak in *puberty*."—Evelyn Wells.

**pun'dits** (pun'ditz). Learned Hindus; hence, learned teachers or men of great learning.—"These *pundits* say that its own precedents do not trouble the Court because it delights in avoiding them."—Hugh S. Johnson.

**pu'ru lent** (pū'rŏŏ lĕnt). Secreting or discharging pus; attended with suppuration or accumulation of sticky yellow matter or pus.—"The pestilence was of a *purulent* type."—Charles Henry Crozier.

**py"ro ma'ni ac** (pī"rō māy'ni ak). A person who has an incendiary mania or a persistent desire to set fire to buildings or things.—"The *pyromaniac* confessed to setting off seven fires for the thrill of it."—Bradwell E. Tanis.

**qui es'cent** (kwī ess'ĕnt). In a state of repose or inaction; still; motionless; quiet.—"After the specimen becomes *quiescent*, no further increase in length is noted."—H. L. Kennedy.

**ra"di a'tion** (rāy"di āy'shŭn). Energy

emitting rays of light or heat; the process of giving out light and heat. —"Luminosity of comets is affected by solar *radiation*."—Fred L. Whipple.

**re cu′per a″tive** (rē kū′pur āy″tiv). Restorative; assisting to recovery; helpful to recovery.—"This kind of planning stimulated the *recuperative* processes necessary to full recovery." —Lewis H. Brown.

**re flec′tion** (rē flek′shŭn). Meditation upon past knowledge or experience; contemplation; quiet intensive consideration of some idea or subject.— "The Church would be profited by a protracted period of silence and *reflection*."—James E. Freeman.

**re′flex es** (rē′fleks iz). Involuntary acts or movements resulting in response to the stimulation of a sense organ.— "Is man merely a combination of *reflexes* worthy of nothing more than to be the servant of the state?"— H. W. Prentis, Jr.

**re mand′** (rē mand′). An order to recommit an accused person to custody after a preliminary examination; a sending back to prison to await a later trial.—"Someone pointed out his name in police-court proceedings, but there had been a *remand*."— W. Somerset Maugham.

**re prieve′** (rē preeve′). The suspension of a sentence; a temporary respite from suffering or death; a postponement or delay of punishment.—"He was going to grant the General a brief *reprieve*."—Albert Perry.

**re tain′ers** (rē tain′urz). Retaining-fees; fees paid or agreements made when engaging the services of a lawyer.—"*Retainers* are cancelled when patriotic duty is involved."— Cassius E. Gates.

**re tort′** (rē tort′). A vessel for heating or distilling substances.—"No test tube or *retort* can teach a man how or with whom to fall in love."—Lord Halifax.

**ru″di men′ta ry** (rōō″dĭ men′tuh ri). Lowest kind of; elementary; primitive.—"The goods were produced under conditions which do not meet *rudimentary* standards of decency."— Franklin Delano Roosevelt.

**ru′di ments** (rōō′dĭ mĕnts). The elementary or first principles or stages; the first steps; the parts learned first; the elements of knowledge.—"The referee wished he knew the *rudiments*."—Daniel P. Eginton.

**sal′low** (sal′ō). Of an unhealthy yellowish color; having a pale, sickly skin; having a dull, muddy complexion.—"The train guard was a thin, *sallow* man with a limp."—Louis Bromfield.

**schiz″o phre′ni a** (skiz″ō free′ni uh). A form of mental derangement which interferes with the unity of the personality and often results in inaction. —"One of the important newer developments in science fields is the shock treatment for *schizophrenia*."— Watson Davis.

**se cret′ed** (sē kreet′id). Hidden from view; concealed; put in a secret place; produced or prepared, as saliva.—"Enough pearly substance is *secreted* around the bead to form the so-called cultured pearl."—Edward Wigglesworth.

**sed′a tive** (sed′uh tiv). Possessing a soothing tendency; calming; allaying irritation; tending to assuage pain.— "The scents were oddly *sedative*, for they moved the blood rather to quiescence than to action."—John Buchan.

**se nil′i ty** (sē nil′ĭ ti). Mental and physical infirmity resulting from old age; a state of weakness and dotage.— "*Senility* has been known to turn men from the ways of crime."—Lucius Beebe.

**sen′so ry** (sen′sō ri). Conveying or producing impulses through the senses; pertaining to sensation.—"The anaesthetic cut off all incoming *sensory* messages."—Edgar Douglas Adrian.

**sen′tient** (sen′shĕnt). Experiencing sensation or feeling; capable of feeling. —"The drama stimulates the thought processes of every *sentient* member of the audience."—Gladys Swarthout.

**shy′ster** (shī′stur). A lawyer who practises in an unprofessional or tricky way; a pettifogging lawyer.—"Even in the professions, it is economic discriminations that produce *shyster* lawyers.—G. E. Sokolsky.

**so″ci ol′o gist** (sō″shĭ ol′ō jist). One who is interested in the origin and development of human society and the details of poverty, marriage, and other problems of community life.— "The *sociologist* was given a hearing and permitted to show the effects of social inheritance on the lives of men."—George B. Cutten.

**so mat′ic** (sō mat′ik). Pertaining to the body; physical; corporeal.—"Many of the spiritual troubles of Thomas Carlyle were *somatic* in their origin." —Donald G. Cooley.

**spasm** (spaz′m). Any sudden or convulsive action or effort; an involuntary or abnormal contraction.—"Disturbing emotions may cause *spasm* in small arteries."—Walter C. Alvarez.

**spe′cial ism** (spesh′ăl is′m). The confining of oneself to a special or particular line of study or work, to the exclusion of other branches; a special or particular field of activity.— "*Specialism* is not the same as specialization. *Specialism* asserts that education for breadth is unimportant."— W. H. Cowley.

**spe cif′ic** (spē sif′ik). A special remedy; something specially fitted to prevent or cure something; anything adapted to bring about a definite result.—"In Dr. Johnson's Letters he recommends his orange-peel *specific* to an accomplished female friend."—Christopher Morley.

**stat′u to″ry** (stat′ū tō″ri). Created or fixed by a specific law.—"This office has no *statutory* authority."—Joseph L. Weiner.

**ster′tor ous** (stur′ter ŭs). Making sounds like snoring, especially as in apoplexy; hoarse and accompanied by a snoring sound made by apoplectics.—"It is not snoring, it is *stertorous* breathing."—Axel Munthe.

**strick′en** (strik′ĕn). Affected by trouble or disease; wounded or struck down by calamity or illness.—"The most casual glance at him would show you that he was a *stricken* man."—Emmet Holloway.

**sub con′scious ly** (sub kon′shŭs li). In a way that lacks intellectual clearness; in a way of which one is only dimly conscious; in a faintly aware condition of something that it is impossible to recall to full consciousness. —"*Subconsciously* one expects to find everything exactly as when one left." —Roy Chapman Andrews.

**su″per fi′cial** (sū″pur fish′ăl). Shallow; marked by partial knowledge; understanding only the obvious.—"From *superficial* books and lack of constant travel between the countries, many misconceptions have arisen."—John B. Glenn.

**sus cep″ti bil′i ty** (suh sep″tĭ bil′ĭ ti). Sensibility; a state of being easily influenced or impressed; capability of receiving a reaction mentally or physically.—"People vary widely in their *susceptibility* to tobacco poisoning."— Victor C. Heiser.

**symp″to mat′ic** (simp″tō mat′ik). Significant; indicative; characteristic; indicating a symptom (of disease); like a sign or token of a particular state or condition.—"When the history of our age is written, I suspect the night clubs will be thought as curious as they are *symptomatic*."— Channing Pollock.

**syn thet′ic** (sin thet′ik: 'th' as in 'thin'). Formed by, or pertaining to, an artificial combination of parts; artificial; imitation.—"We shall have *synthetic* rubber and also substitutes for tin." —Paul V. McNutt.

**te lep′a thy** (tē lep′uh thi: 'th' as in 'thin'). Thought transference; communication of one mind with another without using the channels of sense.—"Perhaps the lesson in geography represented a bit of mental *telepathy*."—Edwin L. James.

**ten′ta cles** (ten′tuh k'lz). Appendages used by invertebrates as feelers or as organs of motion; feelers.—"The hammerhead took the octopus by surprise and nipped off two of his *tentacles*."—Vincent Palmer.

**ther″a peu′tic** (ther″uh pū′tik: 'th' as in 'thin'). Curative; having to do with healing treatment.—" 'Bleeding' as a *therapeutic* agent was supposed to have been discarded a century ago".—George W. Maxey.

**tox″i col′o gists** (tok″si kol′ō jists). Those who study the nature of poisons and their effects and antidotes.

—"*Toxicologists* divide mushrooms into groups by the symptoms they cause."—Donald C. Peattie.

**tra jec'to ry** (truh jek'tō ri). Characteristic of a trajectory, or course, or curve which a body describes when in motion.—"Dad had a club, good enough in its way, but of low *trajectory* potential."—Charles B. Driscoll.

**trance** (trance). A state of insensibility to ordinary surroundings; hypnotic condition.—"The report said that the medium in a *trance* received information from a so-called communicator."—Alexis Carrel.

**trans gres'sion** (trance gresh'ŭn). Sin; crime; offense; misdeed; breaking a law; wrong-doing.—"To punish them for a *transgression*, the nature of which they could not possibly understand, would not be intelligent."—Emmet Fox.

**trau'ma** (traw'muh). A wound; an injury caused to the body by accident or violence.—"These hazards include exposure to toxic gases, and *trauma* in tanks."—James Stevens Simmons.

**tri bu'nal** (trī bū'năl). A court of justice; a judicial body; that which judges and gives a decision.—"The *tribunal* of public opinion is the jury."—Henri Honore Giraud.

**tu'te lage** (tū'tē lij). Guardianship; tutorship; instruction.—"The boy continued his studies under the *tutelage* of a sophomore."—William Trufant Foster.

**un let'tered** (un let'urd). Uneducated; illiterate; ignorant; untaught.— "Putting emphasis on the wrong syllables is a custom very common among the *unlettered*."—Daniel P. Eginton.

**val"e tu"di nar'i ans** (val"ē tū"di nair'-i ănz). Weak, sickly people; those who are always thinking about their health or seeking to recover health; people who are over careful and solicitous about health.—"They were chilled under-sexed *valetudinarians*, deprived of a helpful social and intellectual atmosphere."—Ludwig Lewisohn.

**ven'om ous** (ven'ŭm ŭs). Poisonous; harmful.—"Where there are *venomous* snakes, you must train yourself to examine your surroundings."—Carl F. Kauffeld.

**ver'dict** (vur'dikt). The decision of a jury in a trial; hence, any important decision.—"Many people are still fighting that election and refuse to accept the *verdict*."—Prentiss M. Brown.

**ver'te brates** (vur'tē brātes). Animals having a backbone or spinal column. —"To the *vertebrates* must be attributed the largest contributions to modern civilization."—Walter P. Taylor.

**vi'rus** (vī'rŭs). A morbid poison that is the medium for communicating infectious disease.—"Dr. Francis has found a second kind of *virus* that causes influenza."—Watson Davis.

**vo ca'tions** (vō kā'shŭnz). Regular occupations; callings; professions.— "You may go about your normal *vocations* without fear."—Harold R. L. G. Alexander.

**zo ol'o gy** (zō ol'ō ji). The science that treats of the animal kingdom and animal life.—"The structure of a university should not be a miscellaneous collection of departments from astronomy to *zoology* with all treated as equally important."—Mortimer J. Adler.

## ONE-MINUTE REFRESHER

This may be a bit like a high school or college examination. And yet the education of people who are alert and alive is never a thing of the past. And never finished. See what you can do with these questions.

1. Which two of the following four specialists must qualify as graduate physicians before they take up their professions: the *oculist, optometrist, ophthalmologist, optician?*

2. *Entomologists* are those who are experts in the science that treats of the division of man into races. True or false?

3. *Ethnological* pertains to that branch of zoology that treats of insects. True or false?

4. *Toxicologists* prepare, mount and stuff the skins of animals. Right or wrong?

5. What are the specialties of (a) the *anthropologist,* (b) the *archeologist,* (c) the *philatelist?*

6. What branch of chemistry is *chemurgy?*

7. Among the mentally diseased we have the *paranoiac,* the *megalomaniac* and the *dipsomaniac.* The following symptoms describe the disorders. (a) He has delusions of grandeur. He is a ＿＿＿＿＿＿. (b) He has delusions of persecution. He is a ＿＿＿＿＿＿. (c) He has an uncontrollable craving for alcoholic drink. He is a ＿＿＿＿＿＿.

8. Franklin Delano Roosevelt once said: "These sources of danger are already on the way to peaceful *adjudication.*" What did he mean?

*Answers:* 1. The *oculist* and the *ophthalmologist* must both be graduate physicians. 2. False. *Entomologists* deal with insects. 3. False. *Ethnological* pertains to races of man. 4. Wrong. *Toxicologists* study the nature of poisons and their effects and antidotes. 5. The *anthropologist* studies the science of man, an *archeologist* the science of the remains of past races; a *philatelist* collects stamps and makes a study of them. 6. *Chemurgy* is the branch of applied chemistry which is concerned with the industrial uses of organic raw materials and farm products. 7. He is a (a) megalomaniac, (b) paranoiac, (c) dipsomaniac. 8. The sources of danger will be examined and sensible judgment passed on them.

# CHAPTER XVI

## CAN YOU SPELL THESE WORDS?

IF WE are going to be considered cultured, or even literate, we *must* learn to spell. It is a routine that is expected of us. It would take no imagination to know what would happen to a badly spelled letter of application for a job. And you, yourself, realize how you would rate a person who wrote you a poorly spelled social letter.

Like it or not, speech is class distinction. A man may be ever so well-groomed, good looking, have all the appearance of culture, but let him spell "receive," *recieve* or "their," *there*, and you will immediately place him across the railroad tracks right by the gashouse district.

Unfortunately, then, we are supposed to spell correctly. We can't change the language to suit our convenience. And also we find that we are confronted with one subject that has to be self-taught.

Of course, we also have to face the hard fact that our spelling problems are cruel. When we consider that the sounds of the seven long vowels in our language are respelled for pronunciation in sixty-six different ways, and that there is hardly a letter in our alphabet that doesn't represent from two to eight different sounds; when we consider that the nouns *brother*, *die*, *cloth*, *index* and *penny* all have two plurals apiece, each plural with a different meaning and a different spelling; when we realize that there are twenty ways of writing the sound "sh" (so*c*ial, *ch*ivalry, *s*ugar, etc.), it is easy to know why our English spelling is considered to be almost as heartbreaking as our pronunciation.

I am going to give you only three rules in spelling. They are fairly simple ones, and if you will memorize them they will take care of considerably more than half your mistakes.

RULE 1. Words ending in *e* usually drop the *e* before a suffix beginning with a vowel. Here are a few examples: love, lovable; argue, arguing; guide, guidance. The *e* is also dropped in argument,

267

acknowledgment, abridgment, duly, truly, awful, wholly and in a
few other less common words.

The e, however, is retained in words ending in *ce* and *ge* when
the suffix begins with *a* or *o*, as in noticeable, courageous, and also
in a few other words like dyeing (coloring) and tingeing, in order to
distinguish them from dying (expiring) and tinging (sounding).

RULE 2. Words ending in *y* preceded by a consonant usually
change the *y* to *i* before a suffix, as in try, tries; busy, busily; study,
studied; but *not* in such words as carrying, studying, inasmuch as
the suffix begins with *i* and there would be two *i's* in succession.

Adjectives of one syllable ending in *y* sometimes retain the *y* before -*ly* and -*ness*, as in spryly, dryness.

RULE 3. Words of one syllable, and words accented on the
last syllable, ending in a single consonant preceded by a single
vowel, *double* the final consonant before a suffix beginning with a
vowel, as in stop, stopped; let, letting; confer', confer'ring; expel',
expel'ling.

The consonant is doubled only on an *accented* syllable. If the
accent is changed by adding the suffix, the consonant is not
doubled. This can be illustrated by confer', con'ference; refer',
ref'erence.

There are many other out-running laws that determine our
spelling for us, yet, on the whole, there is so little logic to the subject and there are such a multitude of exceptions, that I sometimes
wonder whether the majority of these laws are worth learning.

What rules, for instance, could possibly make these fantastic
plurals of English nouns seem reasonable to us? staff, staves; ox,
oxen; appendix, appendices; alkali, alkalis; class, classes; dynamo,
dynamos; motto, mottoes; shelf, shelves; man, men; tooth, teeth;
mouse, mice; talisman, talismans; boatman, boatmen; salmon,
salmon.

I realize that I am violating the practices and the canons of
grammar-school teaching when I say it, but it is still my belief
that it takes longer for most people to learn the laws that govern
these plurals than it would take to memorize the plurals themselves
together with the exceptions that always accompany them.

There's only one sure way to master the important and none too
interesting subject of spelling, and that's by patient, painstaking,
persistent practice. Write down the words that bother you in your
vocabulary note-book. Go over them from time to time. Develop
your visual memory, so that when a word has been put into writing
it will "look" wrong to you if it is misspelled. Check the words in

this chapter that particularly trouble you. Rehearse them as you would a five-finger piano exercise.

Many of our strange spellings are the results of printers' errors. Others, such as we find in the word "thought," represent letters that are now silent, but that used to be sounded. Some curious spellings come from words that we have adopted from foreign languages, and that retain a part of their original spellings, such as hemorrhage and lachrymose. Other oddities have been inherited from our own native words.

In the seventeenth century our common word *raccoon* was spelled "rahaugcum," "aracune," and "raro-cun." *Massachusetts* was "Mais-Tschusaeg," *Eternal* was "Aetaernall," and *February*, "Ffebrewarie." While *Mississippi* appeared as "Meche-sebe." At this same time the title *general* was almost unrecognizable as "jinerll." We have shed some of the excess letters, but not all.

There was little pretense of uniformity in spelling before the eighteenth century, and the dictionary of Samuel Johnson was the first guide. Even the learned Doctor contributed many weird spellings to posterity by his arbitrary decisions and his incorrect etymologies. After him came our own Noah Webster. The stupendous influence of his spelling book can be guessed when we know that by 1889 its sales in our country had reached the fabulous total of 62,000,000 copies.

It is true that our language has its difficulties, and yet, with all of the complications, English still possesses many gracious simplicities. We have, for the most part, only two cases to bother with. Our consonants are fairly static, and we can boast of the least complicated systems of pronouns in the world. Best of all we have practically no grammatical gender.

This problem of spelling though, is not too impossible. After all, 90 per cent of the words in English that you see or use won't cause you the slightest bother. Actually three-quarters of all your spelling trouble comes from less than 800 words.

You probably will never gain complete perfection in spelling. There will be little puzzlers that will stick like Scotch burrs in your mind. But since it is still true that a badly misspelled word is one of the world's worst advertisements, you will find it well worth while to use this chapter as a drill book and so reduce your errors to an unimportant minimum.

As with the chapter on pronunciation, these words appear elsewhere in this volume with their definitions, pronunciations, and illustrative sentences.

# CAN YOU SPELL THESE WORDS?

abbreviated
aberrations
abeyance
aborigines
abrogated
abstinence
accelerate
accessible
accessory
acclivity
accolade
accommodate
accruing
accumulation
acknowledged
acquiescence
acquittal
advantageous
agoraphobia
alleged
allegiance
alliteration
allotment
ambidextrousness
ameliorated
amenable
anachronism
analogous
analytically
ancillary
annihilated
annulled
anodyne
anomalies
anonymous
antediluvian
aphasia
aphrodisiac
apocryphal
appalling
apparition
appellation
apportioned
aquiline
archipelago
arresting
asphyxiated
assessed
asseverations
assiduity
assimilate
assonance
auspicious
auxiliaries

avaricious
averred
avoirdupois
baccalaureate
bacchanalian
bagnios
balked
balustraded
banality
battalions
beetling
beleaguered
bellicose
belligerent
besetting
bibliophile
bivouac
bizarre
blackguard
bourgeois
braggadocio
Brobdingnagian
brochure
bruit
buccaneers
buncombe
buoyancy
bureaucracy
burgeoned
burlesquing
buttressed
cacophony
caitiff
calligraphy
camouflage
canard
canons (rules)
caparisoned
caresses
caricature
carillon
carrion
catalytic
catastrophic
catechizing
categories
cautery
censure
chameleon
chauvinistic
chiaroscuro
chicanery
chimera
chiropractor

choleric
choregraphy
chorography
chrysalis
cicerone
claustrophobia
cleansed
coalesce
coercive
cogitating
cognizance
cognoscenti
coincide
collaborating
collateral
colossal
commitments
commodious
compatible
conceivably
conciliate
concrete
concupiscence
concurrent
condign
conferred
conniving
connoisseur
consistency
contemporaneous
contretemps
controversial
convalescence
coquettishly
corollary
corporeal
corroborated
counterfeit
credibility
crepuscule
crescendo
cryptic
curmudgeon
cynosure
debacle
debauching
debilitates
debris
deciphered
deficiencies
deign
deleterious
deliquesces
demesne

demurred
desiccating
desirability
despicable
despondency
deterrent
dichotomy
differentials
differentiation
dilatory
dilettante
discrepancies
discretion
doggerel
drudgery
dudgeon
eccentric
ecclesiastics
echelon
ecstatic
effervesce
efficacious
effluvia
eleemosynary
eligible
ellipsis
embarrassed
emissary
empyrean
enamored
enceinte
ensconced
ephemeral
erratic
escutcheon
eulogized
euphonious
evanescent
exacerbate
excrescence
exonerated
extempore
facetiously
facilities
facsimile
factitious
fallibility
fascination
feasible
feat
feigned
feint
felicitous
fêted

filibuster
fission
fjords
flaccid
flagitious
flippant
florid
forfeiture
fracas
fractious
galaxy
garrulous
genealogist
gnarled
gregarious
grotesque
guise
gynecology
gyrations
habiliments
halcyon
hallucinations
harangue
harass
hauteur
hegira
heinous
hemorrhage
hermaphrodites
hieroglyphics
hirsute
homogeneous
homonyms
humiliation
hybrid
hyperboles
hypochondria
hypocrisy
hysterical
idiosyncrasies
idyllic
illegitimate
illiteracy
imbroglio
immanence
  (indwelling)
immigrant
imminence
  (impending evil)
immobile
immunity
impeccable
impugn
incandescent
incendiary
inchoate

incipient
incorrigible
indelibly
indictment
indissoluble
ineffably
ineffaceable
ingratiating
inimical
initiative
innocuous
inoculate
inseparable
insistence
insouciance
intaglio
intelligentsia
interdependence
interrogatory
inveighed
inveigle
irascibility
iridescent
irreconcilable
irreducible
irresistibly
irretrievably
itinerary
jaundice
jejune
jeopardy
kaleidoscopic
kleptomaniacs
kudos
labyrinth
lachrymose
lackadaisical
lagniappe
legerdemain
leisure
liaison
Lilliputian
limned
literally
littoral
  (of a shore)
machiavellian
maelstrom
maestro
maligned
marauding
massacre
matriarchal
mayhem
melancholy
mephitic

mercenary
meted
mettle (courage)
millennium
minatory
miniature
misconstrued
miscreants
misinterpreted
misogyny
mnemonic
monetary
  (of money)
monitory
  (warning)
morass
myrmidons
naïveté
narrative
nauseated
nautical
necessitate
neophyte
nescience
niggardly
nonchalance
notoriety
novitiate
noxious
obeisance
obesity
obscene
obsolescence
Occident
occurrence
ochlocracy
oculist
officiousness
omniscience
onomatopoeia
ophthalmology
orthoëpists
pachyderm
pageantry
palatial
panegyrics
paradigms
paroxysm
paucity
peccadillos
pellucid
peonage
perceptible
periphery
perspicacious
pertinaciously

pharisaical
pharmaceutical
phenomenal
phlegmatic
picayune
piqued
plebiscite
polygamous
precedence
precocious
predecessors
preened
prejudice
principle
  (a rule of action)
privilege
procurable
prophylactic
propitiate
proselytizing
pseudonym
psychiatry
psychoanalysis
purveyors
pyre
pyrotechnics
qualm
querulous
queues
quiescent
quintessence
quizzical
raillery
razed
  (destroyed)
reclamation
reconnoitering
reiteration
rejuvenescent
reminiscences
renaissance
renascence
repercussions
reprehensible
rescind
resemblance
resuscitated
retaliate
reticence
rhapsodists
rhythmic
Rubicon
rubicund
sacrilegious
salacious
sanguinary

scavenging
schisms
schizophrenia
scintilla
scion
sentient
seraglio
shibboleth
silhouetted
slough
  (shed, cast off)
solicitations
soliloquies
spiritual
  (incorporeal)
spirituel
  (refined)
squeamishness

squelched
stationary
  (fixed)
statistics
stereotyped
straits
stymied
subsidiaries
subtler
succinctly
supercilious
superficiality
supersedes
supplemented
surfeit
susceptibility
suzerainty
svelte

sycophant
symmetry
synonymous
synthetic
tatterdemalion
tautness
temerarious
termagant
terrain
tessellated
thesaurus
tintinnabulations
titillating
tranquillity
transitory
trauma
trekked
trespassed

tyrannize
unintelligible
unctuous
unparalleled
upbraids
uxorious
vacillating
variegated
verisimilitude
versatile
vicarious
vicissitudes
virility
vitiated
waive
writhed
yeomen

## One-Minute Refresher

While this test is not based essentially on the words in this book, it still presents a sturdy challenge to the competent speller. Here is a list of twenty-four words, half of them incorrectly spelled. Twelve of these words should end in "able," twelve in "ible." Check the ones that you believe should be spelled with "ible."

1. imperceptable
2. convertable
3. unpredictable
4. dependable
5. contemptable
6. laudable
7. irrepressable
8. definable

9. flexable
10. divisable
11. reputable
12. digestable
13. detestable
14. suggestable
15. inconceivable
16. delectable

17. reproducable
18. inconsolable
19. pervertable
20. inscrutable
21. compatable
22. deplorable
23. attachable
24. transmittable

*Answers:* Don't be discouraged if you find you haven't done too well with this. Many a good speller has failed miserably. The following words should end in "ible": 1–2–5–7–9–10–12–14–17–19–21–24.

# CHAPTER XVII

## YOUR ADJECTIVES AND ADVERBS OF POWER

THE RICHES of our speech in adjectives and in adverbs can hardly be computed and our American language gives us a luxurious and extravagant selection to choose from. Those who are wise use this wealth to their own great advantage.

In this section adjectives and adverbs of power are shown at work. These words of color and modification should be handled with frugality and skill, and rightly handled they can add great force and authority to a statement.

Here are a few examples of these words in action. Their mere recital gives some indication of their value. Listen:

"The most *blatant* denial"; "the *dastardly* act"; "the *machiavellian* manipulators"; "the *putrid* pestilence"; "the *excruciating* agony."

These words, and such as these, are yours and mine to use, and an expert knowledge of them can give us many ways of expressing our thoughts, thus releasing our natural abilities as they have released the abilities of those who are out in front and leading the procession.

No wonder a language such as ours is being adopted as a universal speech. For being adopted it is. Already three-quarters of the mail of the entire earth is written in English. One-half of the newspapers are now printed in it, and on three-quarters of the radio programs English is the only language spoken. In the far-off year of 1789 a Frenchman had the prescience to predict that English would be the universal language of the future and he prophesied even then that it would be the English of those colonies that were to become the United States of America.

No wonder, too, that the American language has always been admired and envied by the great of other lands.

One time, when Alphonse Daudet was talking to Turgenev, the Russian novelist, about our speech, he suddenly exclaimed:

"What a luxury it must be to have a big, untrodden, barbarian language to wade into!"

The American language, though, is no longer barbarian. It has long since become the civilized and living expression of the body and the spirit of the American people. But even though it has taken its place among the sophisticated languages of the world, the power of our mighty rivers still flows through its veins; it still echoes to the war-whoop of the Indian; it is still redolent with the tang and the argot of the wild west and the gold rush days of '49; it is warm with the love and with the songs of the Negroes; it still throbs with the strife and the passion of the Revolutionary and Civil Wars.

This language, with all its beauty, flexibility, and vitality is yours for the learning. If you are a hard taskmaster on yourself, the work will sometimes be severe. But you will find it endlessly interesting. You will soon get so that you cannot comfortably pass a strange word by. And the general gain to your character, power and precision will be quite incalculable.

The selected words that complete this chapter will add color and culture and great force to your writing and to your speaking, and will help turn a possible language poverty into language wealth.

## Your Adjectives and Adverbs of Power

**a bu′sive** (uh bū′siv). Wrongly used; improper; hurtful; disparaging; offensive; reviling; reproachful.— "There was an *abusive* reference to the British of 1775 as wicked tyrants." —Malcolm MacDonald.

**a bys′mal ly** (uh biz′măl li). Deeply, in a moral and intellectual sense; unfathomably.—"Before 1914 the American people were *abysmally* ignorant concerning international relations."—Nelson P. Mead.

**a cid′u lous** (ă sid′ū lŭs). Rather sour; slightly acid; hence, sour-tempered; bitter.—"The old man turned his head to note the effects of his *acidulous* drollery."—Lloyd C. Douglas.

**ac′rid** (ak′rid). Pungent; stinging to taste and smell; bitter; acid and biting.—"Dark shapes loomed out of the steam and *acrid* fumes."—Elizabeth Fowler.

**ad′a mant** (ad′uh mant). Impenetrably hard; unimpressionable; unyielding. —"We found her still angry and still *adamant*."—Noel Coward.

**ad″a man′tine** (ad″uh man′tin). Of impenetrable hardness; unbreakable; immovable; unyielding; as hard as steel or diamond.—"He stood before the gates riveted with golden hinges to the *adamantine* rock."—Axel Munthe.

**a droit′** (uh droyt′). Skilful in emergencies; quick-witted; clever.—"As the *adroit* orator continued, you could hear the cheers of the party."—William E. Borah.

**ag glom′er ate** (ă glom′ur āte). Gathered into a mass; collected into a heap; densely clustered together.— "An unsightly, *agglomerate* mass of waste, rubble and rubbish blocked the entrance."—Donald G. Cooley.

**a ghast'** (uh gast'). Terrified; frightened; struck with horror; filled with amazed terror.—"The chaplain looked at him, *aghast*."—Franz Werfel.

**an'guish ing** (ang'gwish ing). Agonizing; torturing.—"Last comes the *anguishing* question: When will this end?"—Alexander Loudon.

**ap pal'ling** (ă pawl'ing). Shocking; filled with dismay or horror.—"It is a human achievement unparalleled in history, to have brought the world to such an *appalling* state of confusion."—James A. Farley.

**ar'du ous** (ahr'dū ŭs). Difficult; involving great labor or hardship.—"It was the end of a most *arduous* campaign."—Thomas C. Hart.

**ar'rant** (ar'ănt). Out-and-out; unmitigated; notoriously bad; thoroughgoing; outright.—"Some words are *arrant* tempters to the omission of consonants."—Daniel P. Eginton.

**ar rest'ing** (ă rest'ing). Impressive; arousing attention; striking; attracting notice.—"The statement is both interesting and *arresting*."—Sister Elizabeth Kenny.

**ash'en** (ash'ĕn). Of the color of ashes; pale as ashes; greyish-white.—"The eyes were staring and the face was *ashen*."—Henry J. Powers.

**as'i nine** (ass'ĭ nīne). Stupid; silly.—"It is absolutely *asinine* and ridiculous."—C. S. Snider.

**as"tro nom'i cal** (ass"trō nom'i kăl). Enormously large like the calculations in astronomy; difficult to count because so very big.—"His mail attained *astronomical* dimensions."—H. G. Wells.

**au gust'** (aw gust'). Majestic; grand; imposing.—"Man is his own fate. In this vast realm of the spirit which is man's home, there is no escaping this *august* responsibility of destiny."—John Haynes Holmes.

**aus pi'cious** (awce pish'ŭs). Fortunate; favorable; of good omen; auguring well; propitious.—"All over the earth on that *auspicious* day flags were flying."—H. G. Wells.

**aus tere'** (awce teer'). Severely simple; unadorned.—"The *austere* beauty of Scotland was a welcome relief."—John Buchan.

**au then'ti cat"ed** (aw then'ti kāte"id: 'th' as in 'thin'). Shown to be true; proved to be genuine; attested by authority and confirmed as true.—"*Authenticated* reports of the same kind come from Europe."—Anne O'Hare McCormick.

**av'id** (av'id). Greedy; eagerly desirous.—"We are not *avid* for more territory."—Frank Knox.

**bale'ful** (bāle'fōol). Hurtful; bad; evil; intending harm or evil; pernicious.—"Those deep haunting fears have had a *baleful* influence."—Lewis H. Brown.

**bar bar'ic** (bahr bar'ik). Uncivilized; brutal; savage.—"The prisoners were at times subjected to the most cruel and *barbaric* tortures."—Joseph C. Grew.

**bawd'y** (bawd'i). Lewd; obscene; unchaste; indecent.—" 'I suppose the genuine sea songs are always *bawdy*,' she said."—Christopher Morley.

**be diz'ened** (bē diz"nd). Adorned with cheap splendor; dressed out with gaudy finery; ornamented with tawdry or vulgar trappings.—"He had passed through just such a *bedizened* adventure as he always hoped might be his own."—Stephen Vincent Benét.

**be lea'guered** (bē lee'gurd). Encompassed by force.—"Beneath the darkness of *beleaguered* life they were planning for other people."—L. W. Brockington.

**be nef'i cent** (bē nef'ĭ s'nt). Bringing about or doing good; characterized by kindness.—"As you have already seen, our occupation will be mild and *beneficent*."—Dwight D. Eisenhower.

**be set'ting** (bē set'ing). Attacking on all sides; constantly assailing.—"A civilization that will not fight to destroy *besetting* parasites, does not deserve to live."—James M. Cox.

**bes'tial** (bess'chăl). Like an animal; brutish; savage.—"One can understand this *bestial* savagery only by a glance into history."—Warren J. Clear.

**blast'ed** (blast'ed). Blighted; withered; shriveled; destroyed; ruined;

shattered.—"The *blasted* hopes and immortal aspirations of mankind have not greatly shocked or depressed him."—Orville Prescott.

**bla'tant** (blāy'tănt). Noisy; vociferous; clamorous; obtrusive.—"War is the most *blatant* denial of every Christian doctrine."—Harry Emerson Fosdick.

**blus'ter ing** (bluss'tur ing). Swaggering; uttering vain threats; talking angrily and boisterously.—"We have seen treaties violated by certain *blustering* militant nations."—Brice P. Disque.

**bound'en** (boun'děn: 'ou' as in 'out'). Binding; obligatory; necessary; imposed or required.—"It is your *bounden* duty to demonstrate, because you have to prove the harmony of being in your own life."—Emmet Fox.

**bump'tious ly** (bump'shŭs li). Self-assertively; self-conceitedly; in an aggressively and offensively conceited way.—"*Bumptiously* he presented his claim to all who would listen."—A. S. Burrows.

**cai'tiff** (kāy'tif). Mean and despicable; base and cowardly; wicked.—"It was the *caitiff* act of a *caitiff* man."—Charles Henry Crozier.

**ca jol'ing** (kuh jōle'ing). Alluring; imposing on, as by flattery.—"Radio is persuasive, *cajoling*, and commanding."—Neville Miller.

**ca lam'i tous** (kuh lam'ĭ tŭs). Disastrous; deplorable.—"It would be nothing short of *calamitous* to insist on cutting the number of market inspectors."—Fiorello H. LaGuardia.

**cal'lous** (kal'ŭs). Insensible; hard and unfeeling.—"Public opinion remained *callous* to the pressing need for more ships."—J. W. Greenslade.

**can tan'ker ous** (kan tang'kur ŭs). Perverse; ill-natured; liable to cause trouble.—"Being a *cantankerous* creature, this boat timed her arrival with the Christmas mail late, so as to torture us."—Dillon Ripley.

**cat"a stroph'ic** (kat"uh strof'ik). Pertaining to a sudden misfortune or fatal event; wide-spread and ending in calamity or disastrous changes.—"The *catastrophic* defeats on the eastern front did much to bring Germany to her knees."—Eduard Beneš.

**cav"a lier'** (kav"uh leer'). Offhand; haughty; disdainful; supercilious; free and easy.—"Barrymore carried this *cavalier* treatment of the conventions to what must have been unprecedented lengths."—Edmund Wilson.

**cav'ern ous** (kav'ur nŭs). Like a cavern or large cave; hollow; like a huge cavity or hole.—"I could look down into the *cavernous* nostrils as they swelled out."—Roy Chapman Andrews.

**cen so'ri ous** (sen sō'ri ŭs). Expressing censure or disapproval; faultfinding; given to adverse criticism; judging severely.—"Every word in this letter is open to misconstruction—and would be instantly misconstrued by a *censorious* world."—L. P. Jacks.

**cer"e mo'ni ous** (ser"ē mō'ni ŭs). Formal; performed with impressive acts and ceremonies; punctilious; observing formalities.—"They pull weeds with the same *ceremonious* air that is used in christening a battleship."—John Chamberlain.

**cha ot'ic** (kāy ot'ik). In great disorder; in a state of turmoil and disarray.—"It shows conclusively how *chaotic* the confusion is."—John C. Vivian.

**clan des'tine** (klan dess'tin). Kept secret; surreptitious; underhand.—"The tipster sheet is mysterious, *clandestine*, and boastful."—Peter Schmuck.

**cleft** (kleft). Split; divided; cut open; having a crack or fissure.—"Only her eyes discovered life in them, like the life in eyes of a spirit caught in a *cleft* stone."—Stephen Vincent Benét.

**con gealed'** (kŏn jeeld'). Thick or hardened from cold; stiffened with cold; frozen; curdled or thickened from other causes.—"In that northern climate food became *congealed* very quickly."—Bertram M. Myers.

**co'gent** (kō'jěnt). Compelling belief, assent, or action; powerful; convincing.—"The reasons which were urged were numerous and *cogent*."—Charles L. Kaufman.

**col lu'sive** (kŏ lū'siv). Fraudulent; deceitful.—"*Collusive* agreements between labor organizations and lawless employers by which the public is victimized, should be drastically penalized."—James A. Emery.

**com'ba tive** (kom'buh tiv). Full of fight; contentious; quarrelsome.— "The basis of the new act in Great Britain is a system of industrial relations as cooperative and rational as ours are *combative* and emotional."— Mrs. Eugene Meyer.

**com min'a to"ry** (kŏ min'uh tō"ri). Threatening; denunciatory; accusing; uttering threats of punishment or vengeance.—"Not for some time has so *comminatory* a sermon been hurled at us."—Iris Barry.

**con gen'i tal ly** (kŏn jen'i tăl i). Inherently; innately; constitutionally; naturally, as though from birth.—"They *congenitally* despise the Republican party."—Frank R. Kent.

**con sum'mate** (kŏn sum'it). Perfect; correct; faultless.—"Supplies must flow constantly, and with *consummate* timing."—James F. Byrnes.

**con tempt'i ble** (kŏn temp'tĭ b'l). Despicable; base; deserving scorn.— "There have been *contemptible* efforts toward creating racial intolerance." —Wayne Coy.

**con temp'tu ous** (kŏn temp'chŏŏ ŭs). Disdainful; scornful; haughty; showing contempt, disregard, or insolence. —"There was something intoxicating in this sudden transition from *contemptuous* negligence to interest."— H. G. Wells.

**craft'i ly** (kraf'tĭ li). Cunningly; cleverly and deceptively; guilefully; artfully.—"They say every human being who writes an autobiography exposes himself, no matter how *craftily* he tries to make out a good case."—Irvin S. Cobb.

**crag'ged** (krag'ed). Having many rough, steep, or broken rocks jutting out; having broken cliffs and rugged rocks.—"He heard the broadcast of Siegfried surrounded by the *cragged* majesty of those snow-capped mountains of Vancouver."—Milton J. Cross.

**crass** (krass). Dense; dull; obtuse; lacking refinement; coarse.—"Both parties typified the spirit of a *crass* and godless age."—Edmund A. Walsh.

**cru'cial** (krōō'shăl). Decisive; relating to a difficult choice; critical.—"For all of us it is the *crucial* point at the moment."—Anne O'Hare McCormick.

**cum'ber some** (kum'bur sŭm). Unwieldy; moving with difficulty; burdensome.—"The groups would be so large that they would constitute *cumbersome* administrative machinery."—Emory S. Land.

**das'tard ly** (dass'turd li). Cowardly in a mean and skulking way.—"Criminals responsible for the *dastardly* act of sinking the ship will be brought to justice."—John Curtin.

**daunt'less** (dawnt'less). Fearless; intrepid; undiscouraged; brave.— "Wherever I went I found the same virile spirit of *dauntless* determination."—Anthony Eden.

**de crep'it** (dē krep'it). Worn out; broken down from long usage; weakened with age; very much the worse for long use.—"The *decrepit* vehicle rated a place in the Athenian Museum of Antiquities."—Lloyd C. Douglas.

**de fi'ant** (dē fī'ănt). Disobedient; refusing to recognize or obey authority; showing bold opposition.—"The youth was impudently *defiant* of the proprieties."—Lloyd C. Douglas.

**deft** (deft). Very skilful; dexterous; clever in the use of the hands; handy. —"The berries were picked by the *deft* fingers of the Indian women."— W. Stephen Thomas.

**de lec'ta ble** (dē lek'tuh b'l). Giving pleasure; charming; delightful.— "The text of the book is enlivened by seventy-eight *delectable* line drawings."—Alpheus Smith.

**de lin'quent** (dē ling'kwĕnt). Neglectful of or failing in duty; offending by disobeying the laws.—"We must take the so-called *delinquent* family as it is, and handle the problem."—Elizabeth Wood.

**de"mo ni'a cal** (dē"mō nī'uh kăl). Devilish; fiendish; like demons.—"Waves of savages, *demoniacal* in their ferocity, hit our lines day after day."—Warren J. Clear.

**de mon'ic** (dē mon'ik). Fiendish; like a demon; infernal; devilish.—"There is something monstrous and *demonic* in these evil forces."—Anne O'Hare McCormick.

**de nun'ci a to"ry** (dē nun'si uh tō"ri). Threatening; accusing; censuring.— "The Congressmen were showered with *denunciatory* editorials."—William Green.

**de plor'a ble** (dē plōre'uh b'l). Lamentable; wretched; pitiable; grievous. —"Sanitary conditions in many of the boom towns were *deplorable*."— Charles P. Taft.

**der'e lict** (der'ĕ likt). Remiss; neglectful of obligation.—"I would be *derelict* in my duty if I did not protest."— Charles E. Bradshaw.

**de ri'sive ly** (dē rī'siv li). Mockingly; in a ridiculing way; with scornful laughter.—"He chuckled *derisively* at the question."—Lloyd C. Douglas.

**de rog'a to"ry** (dē rog'uh tō"ri). Expressive of disdain; disparaging; detracting from good repute; belittling. —"The literature was *derogatory* to the Dutch character."—Henrik Willem Van Loon.

**des'pi ca ble** (dess'pi kuh b'l). Contemptible; mean; base; deserving to be despised.—"He would be playing a humiliating role and that would be too *despicable*."—André Maurois.

**de void'** (dē voyd'). Not possessing; lacking.—"Vermeer's paintings are small and *devoid* of pretense; simple intimate interiors, for the most part." —Edwin Seaver.

**dex'ter ous ly** (dek'stur ŭs li). Skilfully; cleverly; adroitly; expertly; deftly. "She spied a faded rose or two on the bushes and twisted them off swiftly and *dexterously*."—Pearl S. Buck.

**di"a bol'i cal** (dī"uh bol'i kăl). Like the devil; fiendish; infernal.—"The American Government will hold those officers personally and officially responsible for these *diabolical* crimes." —Franklin Delano Roosevelt.

**di"a met'ri cal ly** (dī"uh met'ri kăl i). Directly adverse; irreconcilably.— "His action nullifying a federal statute was in a *diametrically* opposite direction."—Hugh S. Johnson.

**di aph'a nous** (dī af'uh nŭs). Transparent; of a texture so fine that it shows the light through; delicate and translucent.—"The colorful butterfly lit for an instant on a flower fluttering his *diaphanous* wings in the sun."— Emory L. Fielding.

**di lap'i dat"ed** (di lap'ĭ dāte"id). Impaired by neglect or misuse; in disrepair.—"Transportation men in Sweden say they are astonished at the *dilapidated* condition of cars."— Allan A. Michie.

**din'gy** (din'ji). Grimy; shabby; dirty-looking; smoky and dull.—"In that *dingy* criminal court, he set us a shining example of common sense." —Sanford Bates.

**dire** (dīre). Extremely calamitous; dreadful; terrible.—"Their armies are in *dire* peril."—Lord Beaverbrook.

**dis pas'sion ate** (diss pash'ŭn it). Unprejudiced; free from passion; impartial; unbiased.—"A *dispassionate* analysis of the facts explodes the theory."—Burton K. Wheeler.

**dis tinc'tive** (diss tingk'tiv). Characteristic; distinguishing; of a special quality.—"The work of this cartographer is *distinctive* yet direct, concise yet comprehensive."—Norman Cousins.

**dol'or ous** (dol'ur ŭs). Sorrowful; mournful; doleful; pathetic.—"You know I am not one of your *dolorous* gentlemen: so now let us laugh again."—André Maurois.

**dough'ty** (dou'ti: 'ou' as in 'out'). Brave; valiant; formidable; strong and able.—"This *doughty* public servant assured the nation that the Navy was ready."—Wendell L. Willkie.

**dour'ly** (dōōr'li). Sullenly; sourly; sternly; severely.—" 'You must mean idols,' he corrected, *dourly*."—Lloyd C. Douglas.

**dras'tic** (drass'tik). Extreme; effective; harshly acting.—"I have made some *drastic* reductions in order to keep expenses as low as possible."— Fiorello H. LaGuardia.

**e bul'li ent** (ē bul'i ĕnt). Boiling up; hence, showing great excitement, manifesting enthusiasm.—"We are a nation of *ebullient* localities."—Eric A. Johnston.

**ec stat'ic** (ek stat'ik). Very joyful;

thrilled; in a state of rapture; enraptured; emotionally exalted.—"They returned *ecstatic* from a summer in the Lake Country."—Margaret Mead.

**ef fec′tive ly** (e fek′tiv li). Efficiently; efficaciously; adequately; in a way that produced the desired result.— "It quietly, steadily, *effectively* put out the smouldering brands of revolution."—Herbert Hoover.

**ef″fi ca′cious** (ef″ĭ kā′shŭs). Capable of producing an intended effect; effective.—"I desire to see the moment when refusal of military service will be the means for an *efficacious* struggle for the progress of humanity."—Albert Einstein.

**e″go tis′tic** (ē″gō tiss′tik). Always referring to oneself; thinking about oneself first; conceited; boastful.— "The art of the bird songsters has three qualities that *egotistic* man prefers to arrogate to himself."— William J. Calvert, Jr.

**e lec′tri fy ing** (ē lek′trĭ fĭ ing). Startling, as though charged with electricity; hence, exciting; deeply stirring; thrilling.—"The book is *electrifying* and as dramatic a story as any in the annals of war."—Lewis Gannett.

**el″e phan′tine** (el″ē fan′tīne). Like an elephant; hence, very large and ungainly; big and clumsy; ponderous; huge and heavy; enormous.—"Compared to the *elephantine* imbecility of the older author, what this young man has written is not bad."—Thomas Wolfe.

**em′i nent ly** (em′ĭ nĕnt li). Perfectly and absolutely; highly; notably.— "They all wear plain clothes and appear to be *eminently* respectable gentlemen."—Edward R. Murrow.

**em phat′i cal ly** (em fat′ĭ kăl ly). Forcibly; positively; with great insistence. —"We wish to stress the urgency as *emphatically* as possible."—Alonzo F. Meyers.

**en rap′tured** (en rap′chŏŏrd). Filled with great delight; charmed; overcome by ecstasy.—"The lovely landscape, stretching before our *enraptured* gaze, had suddenly been shut off by a fog."—John Haynes Holmes.

**en tranced′** (en transt′). Delighted; put in a state of ecstasy; transported with great joy; carried away with wonder.—"He sat staring at the *entranced* girl through uncontrollable tears."—Lloyd C. Douglas.

**ep′ic** (ep′ik). Heroic; noble; grand.— "The world will not forget the *epic* resistance of the Greeks."—Anthony Eden.

**es sen′tial ly** (e sen′shăl li). As an indispensable element; necessarily; on account of its nature.—"The Congress of the United States stands, *essentially*, for the sovereign power of the people."—Enrique Penaranda.

**e the′re al** (ē theer′ē ăl: 'th' as in 'thin'). Like the ether or upper regions; hence, heavenly, spirit-like, exquisite.—"The song of the veery is a soft, tremulous, utterly *ethereal* sound."—Louis J. Halle, Jr.

**ex cru′ci at″ing** (eks krōō′shi āte″ing). Extremely painful; torturing; racking.—"She suffered *excruciating* agony all the way to his office."—J. Howard Pew.

**ex′e cra ble** (eks′ē kruh b'l). Abominable; utterly detestable; very bad.— "The food and wine were at first *execrable*."—John Buchan.

**ex em′pla ry** (eg zem′pluh ri). Worthy to serve as a pattern or type; fit to be imitated; setting an example; hence, commendable.—"In international affairs the Turkish record proved *exemplary*."—Edgar J. Fisher.

**ex haus′tive ly** (eg zawce′tiv li). Thoroughly; fully; minutely; completely covering all points and items.—"He tells, not too *exhaustively*, the story of an exceptionally happy life."— Stephen Somervell.

**ex′i gent** (ek′sĭ jĕnt). Requiring immediate aid; demanding a great deal; exacting; in urgent need.—"But he was still her son, this haughty and *exigent* young stranger who stood aloof from her and passed judgment." —André Maurois.

**ex or′bi tant** (ek zor′bĭ tănt). Excessive; extravagant; going beyond proper limits.—"We gave aid at a price which was *exorbitant*."—Gordon Heriot.

**ex press′ly** (eks press′li). Unmistakably; in plain terms; explicitly; for the direct purpose; particularly.--"Limitation upon the powers of the Federal Government are *expressly* provided for in the Constitution."—David M. Wood.

**ex′pur gat″ed**    (eks′pur gāte″id). Cleared of everything objectionable; divested or stripped of the offensive parts.—"He gave his parents a somewhat *expurgated* report, stressing the improvements and avoiding the other things."—Franz Werfel.

**ex′qui site**    (eks′kwi zit). Delicately beautiful; having unusually refined perception; of very high quality; discriminating.—"Irish music is rich in tunes that imply *exquisite* sensitiveness."—Eamon de Valera.

**fab′u lous ly** (fab′ū lŭs li). Passing the limits of belief; incredibly; astonishingly; unbelievably.—"It is the story of opening *fabulously* rich, virgin country with twentieth-century tools and airplanes."—Ruth Gruber.

**fal la′cious** (fă lā′shŭs). Misleading; deceptive; delusive; illogical.—"I have never listened to more fanatic and *fallacious* reasoning."—Bertram M. Myers.

**fa nat′i cal** (fuh nat′i kăl). Extremely enthusiastic; governed by excessive zeal; unreasonably zealous, especially about religious matters; motivated by inordinate or intemperate enthusiasm.—"The beliefs of their $100,000 a year corporation executive are more than sincere, they are *fanatical*."—Marquis W. Childs.

**far′ci cal** (fahr′si kăl). Absurd; of the nature of a farce.—"The conference is a *farcical* procedure in every respect."—John L. Lewis.

**fat′u ous** (fat′ū ŭs). Stubbornly blind or foolish; illusory; stupidly silly.—"The Church has had to issue a warning against letting oneself be illuded by *fatuous* theories."—Pius XII.

**fec′u lent** (fek′ū lĕnt). Foul; clogged with filth; dirty, smelly, and offensive; filthy.—"Their work took them into the *feculent* slums at the east end of the city."—Donald G. Cooley.

**fe ro′cious** (fē rō′shŭs). Of a fierce and savage nature.—"Their *ferocious* menaces against prisoners of war are

directly related to the change in their military position."—Walter Lippmann.

**fer′vent** (fur′vĕnt). Ardent in feeling; fervid; heartfelt; extremely earnest. —"We have more to fight for than the most *fervent* partisans imagined." —Anne O'Hare McCormick.

**fer′vid** (fur′vid). Ardent; zealous; spirited; vehement; enthusiastic; full of fervor and eagerness.—"With an eloquence too *fervid* to concern itself with the niceties of metaphor he called upon the city to attack the open sore."—L. P. Jacks.

**fes′ter ing** (fess′tur ing). Rankling; causing a sore spot; producing corruption.—"If there are no *festering* centers of grievances, the engineer will have gone far toward meeting the issues."—Arthur E. Morgan.

**fet′id** (fet′id). Giving out an offensive odor; stinking; smelling like something rotten.—"These monstrous plans have hatched from the *fetid* brain of the Dictator."—Wallace L. Ware.

**flac′cid** (flak′sid). Flabby; lacking firmness or elasticity.—"His limbs were as *flaccid* as india-rubber."— John Buchan.

**fla′grant** (flā′grănt). Openly scandalous; notorious; glaring.—"Where there are *flagrant* violations, there will be prosecutions."—Loren Lewis.

**flar′ing** (flair′ing). Burning with an unsteady glare; flaming up suddenly; hence, shining out in glaring or showy colors; displaying ostentation; gaudy; over-conspicuous.—"Then he plunged back into the decorative, now of a coarser and more *flaring* kind."—Ludwig Lewisohn.

**flat′u lent** (flat′ū lĕnt). Inflated; pretentious; windy; puffed up; vainly ostentatious; pompous.—"The speaker substituted words for ideas in his long-drawn-out and *flatulent* address."—Ellery Marsh Egan.

**for′mi da ble** (fōre′mĭ duh b'l). Difficult to accomplish.—"This *formidable* task can be successfully handled only through international cooperation." —Henry Morgenthau, Jr.

**forth′right″** (forth′rīte″). Outspoken; unswerving; straightforward; direct;

decisive.—"The candidate in opposition will have to be *forthright* and positive."—George E. Sokolsky.

**fran′tic** (fran′tik). Frenzied; excessively excited; excitedly anxious.— "A *frantic* race between rising wages and rising prices will only ruin and degrade the worker."—James F. Byrnes.

**frig′id ly** (frij′id li). Stiffly; formally; very coldly; in a forbidding way.— "He looked at her reflectively for a moment and then replied *frigidly.*"— Alice Dixon Bond.

**fu′ri ous** (fū′ri ŭs). Very angry; raging; full of fury; frantic; violent.—"They watched the tournament with side glances at the champions and with *furious* quarrels among themselves." —Axel Munthe.

**gar′ish** (gair′ish). Showy; unpleasantly gaudy; extravagantly gay; glaring.— "The chances of an audition candidate will be less favorable if she presents herself in *garish* clothes and shows bad taste."—Fritz Busch.

**gel′id** (jel′id). Frozen; ice-cold; icy; chilled.—"We were very cold, freezing, *gelid.*"—Donald G. Cooley.

**gla′cial** (glāy′shăl). Icily cold; as frozen and hard as ice.—"One might as well have hoped to fall in love with a beautiful statue of ice, but he tried to discover some approach to that *glacial* summit."— Louis Bromfield.

**gnarled** (nahrl′d). Knotty; twisted; distorted; covered with knots or gnarls; rugged.—"Beside the blossoming trees many dead ones stood. It was a lovely sight, great bouquets of bloom in *gnarled* old hands."— Elinor Graham.

**gor′y** (gōre′i). Covered or stained with blood; bloody.—"We cannot forget is long and *gory* list of broken pledges."—James F. Byrnes.

**griev′ous** (greeve′ŭs). Causing grief or suffering; hence, heinous; very serious; grave.—"We all knew she had made a *grievous* mistake."—Bertram M. Myers.

**gru′el ing** (grōō′ĕl ing). Severe; exhausting.—"On the road ahead lies hard, *grueling* work."—Franklin Delano Roosevelt.

**har′row ing** (har′ō ing). Tormenting to the feelings; wounding; worrying; lacerating.—"They kept up their morale in the most *harrowing* captivity."—H. J. Van Mook.

**hec′tic** (hek′tik). Wild; reckless; extremely hurried; feverish; very exciting.—"Our recreations are *hectic*—at forty or fifty miles an hour."— Lorado Taft.

**hei′nous** (hāy′nŭs). Extremely wicked; atrocious; sinful.—"How *heinous* it would be to train and send overseas great armies of men which we could not supply."—Albert L. Cox.

**hor ren′dous** (ho ren′dŭs). Frightful; fearful; full of horror.—"There is one shocking, *horrendous* error."—Stanley Walker.

**hor rif′ic** (ho rif′ik). Frightful; horrifying; exciting fear or dread; abominable; shocking.—"The nine words ranged from tremulo soprano to a rather *horrific* bass."—Ursula Parrott.

**hyp not′ic** (hip not′ik). Tending to produce a state in which one very readily responds to suggestions or commands given by the person who has brought about the condition; hence, influencing and subjecting to forced acceptance.—"He was dishonest and charlatan, but he knew how to sway the crowd with his *hypnotic* words."—Emery S. Fielding.

**id″i ot′i cal ly** (id″i ot′i kăl li). Foolishly; senselessly; stupidly.—"He doted *idiotically* on his youngest son." —Franz Werfel.

**ig″no min′i ous ly** (ig″nō min′i ŭs li). Humiliatingly; in a way that causes dishonor; degradingly.—"It is the better part of wisdom not to accept failure *ignominiously*, but to risk it gloriously."—Madame Chiang Kai-shek.

**il lic′it** (i liss′it). Not permitted; unlawful.—"The *illicit* traffic in narcotics has cost the American people five times the cost of the Panama Canal."—Edmund A. Walsh.

**il lim′it a ble** (i lim′it uh b′l). Boundless; without limit; limitless.—"We are pouring out the world's savings, and these savings are not *illimitable.*" —Nicholas Murray Butler.

**il lu′so ry** (i lū′sō ri). Misleading; deceiving by false show.—"Time has shown how *illusory* are alliances so far as the maintenance of peace is concerned."—Charles Evans Hughes.

**il lus′tri ous** (i luss′tri ŭs). Famous; renowned; noble; glorious; distinguished; celebrated; honored.—"The *illustrious* dead are here as well as those equally famous and still very much alive."—Iris Barry.

**im pas′sioned** (im pash′ŭnd). Full of emotion and warm feeling; fervent; ardent; stirring.—"This great story of the human drama is set down in an *impassioned* and beautiful manner."—John D. Paulus.

**im pel′ling** (im pel′ing). Driving or urging forward; encouraging or exciting to action; pushing or forcing forward.—"There are a number of *impelling* reasons why the campaign should be supported."—John D. Rockefeller, Jr.

**im pen′e tra ble** (im pen′ē truh b′l). That cannot be pierced; impassable; solid; that cannot be penetrated or passed through.—"The travelers had been marshaled into *impenetrable* queues which writhed slowly about me."—Hilary St. George Saunders.

**im per′ish a ble** (im per′ish uh b′l). Indestructible; not perishable; not subject to decay; everlasting; that cannot come to an end.—"Romance fans us with the wind of its *imperishable* wing."—Samuel Hopkins Adams.

**im pet′u ous** (im pet′ū ŭs). Impulsive; passionate; excitable; hasty; rash; moved by an impetus or driving force.—"He is an *impetuous*, ill-balanced man of the people, a prey to his passions."—Henry Seidel Canby.

**im pos′ing** (im pōze′ing). Impressive because of appearance or power; exerting an influence on account of size or dignity.—"He stepped forward, looking formal and *imposing*, to take the best seat."—Louis Bromfield.

**im preg′na ble** (im preg′nuh b′l). Proof against attack; unassailable; able to resist all assaults.—"Fixed fortifications are no longer *impregnable*."—Franklin Delano Roosevelt.

**in a′lien a ble** (in āle′yĕn uh b′l). That cannot be rightfully taken away.—"The public, through its *inalienable* right to shut off the receiver or turn the dial to another program, will continue to make the rules."—David Sarnoff.

**in cal′cu la ble** (in kal′kū luh b′l). So great that the exact amount cannot be determined; very great.—"The fulfillment of this lofty task would be of *incalculable* advantage to humanity."—Maxim Litvinoff.

**in″can des′cent** (in″kăn dess′ĕnt). White with intense heat; hence, glowing; luminous; brilliant; shining brightly.—"When he is dividing scenes with the embittered grandson, the play reaches its *incandescent* heights."—Howard Barnes.

**in cen′di ar″y** (in sen′di er″i). Pertaining to something that is set on fire or inflamed maliciously; purposely set ablaze.—"The loss due to *incendiary* fires amounted to millions of dollars."—Edmund A. Walsh.

**in ces′sant** (in sess′ănt). Unceasing; continual; never stopping; continuing without interruption.—"From a microphone in the basement he bellowed an *incessant* chant."—Arthur Krock.

**in ci′sive** (in sī′siv). Acute; trenchant; clear-cut; penetrating.—"General Mitchell had an *incisive* mind, with the rare combination of a poetic imagination and an engineering precision."—Alexander P. de Seversky.

**in com′pa ra ble** (in kom′puh ruh b′l). Without equal; not to be compared; peerless; matchless; so great that it is beyond comparison.—"The book is distinguished by reason of its on-the-spot record of the *incomparable* valor of the fliers."—Charles Lee.

**in″con ceiv′a ble** (in″kŏn seeve′uh b′l). Incomprehensible; unthinkable; not possible to conceive or imagine; impossible to contemplate.—"To permit the daughter of his beloved friend to live alone was *inconceivable*." —Gertrude Atherton.

**in″con tro vert′i bly** (in″kon trō vur′tĭ bli). Indisputably; in a manner impossible to disprove.—"We believe the showing of these works of art will demonstrate *incontrovertibly* the community of our material interests."—John Hay Whitney.

**in cor'ri gi ble** (in kŏr'i jĭ b'l). That cannot be corrected; unmanageable; too bad to expect reformation.—"I will not say *incorrigible*, but impenitent."—Winston Churchill.

**in cred'i ble** (in kred'ĭ b'l). Unbelievable; beyond belief; difficult to credit; not capable of belief; too extraordinary to be possible.—"The mountain boys stood looking in wonder at the *incredible* sea."—John Steinbeck.

**in cred'u lous** (in kred'ū lŭs). Unwilling to believe; skeptical; doubtful.—"She was still *incredulous* and spoke uncertainly."—Henry H. Curran.

**in″de fat'i ga ble** (in″dē fat'ĭ guh b'l). Never-tiring; unflagging.—"Most of the credit should go to the U. S. Ambassador whose *indefatigable* patience wore out everybody else."—John Gunther.

**in″de fea'si ble** (in″dē fee'zĭ b'l). That cannot be annulled; not to be made void; incapable of being defeated or undone; that cannot be forfeited or done away with.—"He spoke of the *indefeasible* loyalty of the members to one another and of their union in the sportsmanlike spirit."—L. P. Jacks.

**in del'i bly** (in del'ĭ bli). Ineffaceably; in a way that cannot be removed.—"Retailers are now in possession of hosiery on which the price has been *indelibly* marked by manufacturers."—Lew Hahn.

**in″de ter'mi nate** (in″dē tur'mi nit). Indefinite; vague; not fixed; undecided; irresolute.—"For a time he remained politically *indeterminate*."—H. G. Wells.

**in'di gent** (in'dĭ jĕnt). Very poor; destitute of property or funds; needy; poverty-stricken.—"Nations blessed with abundance are God's providers to the less fortunate and *indigent*."—Donald A. MacLean.

**in″dis pen'sa ble** (in″diss pen'suh b'l). Necessary or requisite for a purpose.—"Those intimate meetings of the high officers of both countries are *indispensable*."—Winston Churchill.

**in dis'pu ta ble** (in diss'pū tuh b'l). Incontestable; not open to dispute or

argument; unquestionable.—"Our victory is *indisputable*. It has already taken place."—Jules Romains.

**in dis'so lu ble** (in diss'ō lū b'l). That cannot be liquefied or melted; hence, perpetually binding.—"France and Britain were in *indissoluble* alliance."—W. Somerset Maugham.

**in dom'i ta ble** (in dom'i tuh b'l). Unconquerable; not to be subdued; unyielding; stubbornly determined.—"The whole community had always feared her *indomitable* will."—Sigrid Undset.

**in ef'fa bly** (in ef'uh bli). In a way that is too lofty or sacred to be expressed by mere words.—"There was something about the grave of the Unknown Soldier in Washington that was *ineffably* beautiful."—John Haynes Holmes.

**in″ef face'a ble** (in″e fāce'uh b'l). Incapable of being erased; that cannot be wiped out or obliterated; incapable of being blotted out.—"There is an *ineffaceable* picture of him in my mind."—Peter W. Rainier.

**in″e rad'i ca ble** (in″ē rad'ĭ kuh b'l). That cannot be completely rooted out or destroyed; that cannot be entirely got rid of; that cannot be utterly removed.—"Between Jew and Moslem, as between Christian and Moslem, there is no *ineradicable* difference."—P. J. Searles.

**in es'ti ma ble** (in ess'tĭ muh b'l). Above price; very valuable.—"We enjoy the *inestimable* privilege of free speech."—Burton Rascoe.

**in″ex haust'i ble** (in″eg zawce'tĭ b'l). Incapable of being used up or completely drained off.—"Brazil has almost *inexhaustible* supplies that we need."—Herman B. Baruch.

**in″ex press'i bly** (in″eks press'ĭ bli). Beyond power of expression; unutterably; in a way that cannot be expressed in words.—"He shook his head as if the recollection were *inexpressibly* precious."—Lloyd C. Douglas.

**in ex'tri ca bly** (in eks'tri kuh bli). In a way that cannot possibly be separated or set free; in a manner from which it is impossible to escape.—"We are Allies, and through us the fate of the East is *inextricably* bound to that of the West."—T. V. Soong.

**in'fa mous** (in'fuh mŭs). Very wicked; notoriously bad; scandalous; detestable; atrocious; shameful.—"*Infamous* advantage was taken of them and many were sold as slaves."—George H. Shuster.

**in fat'u at"ed** (in fat'ū āte"id). Actuated by an extreme love or passion for something; inspired by extravagant devotion which deprives of sound judgment.—"He may pretend that his *infatuated* wanderings are ornithological studies."—Alan Devoe.

**in fer'nal** (in fur'năl). Fiendish; hellish; diabolical; demoniacal; devilish.—"Squatting on the sand he held the *infernal* thing between his knees and detached pieces of deadly mechanism."—Peter W. Rainier.

**in"fin i tes'i mal** (in"fin ĭ tess'ĭ măl). Very minute; so small as to be incalculable for all practical purposes.—"Sacrifices in the cause of peace are *infinitesimal* compared with the holocaust of war."—Franklin Delano Roosevelt.

**in flam'ma ble** (in flam'uh b'l). Combustible; easily made angry; irascible; excitable.—"The son wondered what other mischief his *inflammable* parent had been up to during his own long absence."—Edith Wharton.

**in glo'ri ous** (in glō'ri ŭs). Without glory or distinction; not famous; obscure; characterized by failure; humble.—"We avoid leadership and responsibility by sitting mute and *inglorious* in a corner."—Daniel P. Eginton.

**in im'i ta ble** (in im'ĭ tuh b'l). That cannot be imitated; matchless.—"The Senator has stated it in his own *inimitable* way."—William E. Borah.

**in iq'ui tous** (in ik'wĭ tŭs). Wicked; unjust.—"Pressure groups are *iniquitous* because they undermine national unity."—Emil Schram.

**in nu'mer a ble** (i nū'mur uh b'l). Too many to count; very numerous; very, very many; numberless; too numerous to be counted.—"*Innumerable* problems concerning the production, use, and sale of tobacco have been part of the history of almost

every country for many years."—Lawrence C. Wroth.

**in sen'sate ly** (in sen'sāte li). Marked by a lack of sense or reason; foolishly.—"We *insensately* allowed them to build up this terrible machine."—Winston Churchill.

**in sid'i ous** (in sid'i ŭs). Doing harm or working ill by slow and stealthy means; treacherous; sly; intended to ensnare.—"The inability of a democracy to act quickly is an *insidious* argument."—Wendell L. Willkie.

**in"stan ta'ne ous** (in"stăn tāy'nē ŭs). Acting instantly; without a second's delay.—"The United States has *instantaneous* radio contact with every civilized country in the world."—David Sarnoff.

**in suf'fer a ble** (in suf'ur uh b'l). Intolerable; unbearable; not to be endured.—"He is a stupid fellow, all egoist and ambitions. Lately he has been *insufferable*."—Louis Bromfield.

**in su'per a ble** (in sū'pur uh b'l). Not to be overcome or surmounted.—"The Atlantic Ocean may no longer be an *insuperable* barrier to military invasion of this hemisphere."—William L. Green.

**in"sur mount'a ble** (in"sur mount'tuh-b'l: 'ou' as in 'out'). Insuperable; such as cannot be overcome or conquered; incapable of being overcome.—"Courage is needed to push on when difficulties seem *insurmountable*."—Edmund Ezra Day.

**in ter'mi na ble** (in tur'mĭ nuh b'l). Having no limit or end; endless.—"The list is so *interminable* that it becomes overwhelming."—Harold Fields.

**in tol'er a ble** (in tol'ur uh b'l). That cannot be endured; insufferable; unbearable.—"Many of the *intolerable* burdens of economic depression have been lightened."—Franklin Delano Roosevelt.

**in trep'id** (in trep'id). Unshaken in the presence of danger; fearless; very brave; undaunted.—"The West was won by the efforts of *intrepid* and courageous men from all the Atlantic States."—Herbert Hoover.

**in'un dat"ed** (in'un dāte"id). Covered by a flood; deluged; flooded.—"The country is *inundated*, the dykes are down."—William Haskell.

**in vet'er ate** (in vet'ur it). Deep-rooted; firmly established by long continuance; deep-seated; confirmed by habit; ingrained; ineradicable.—"There is an *inveterate* concealment of grandeur behind a plain exterior."—Margaret Mead.

**in vi'o la ble** (in vī'ō luh b'l). That cannot be violated or broken; incapable of being disregarded or destroyed.—"Their God rules the universe under a system of *inviolable* law and punishes mutineers with death."—L. P. Jacks.

**i rate'** (ī rāte'). Wrathful; enraged; bitterly angry.—"The motion picture gives Mr. Nobody the wings with which to escape the *irate* mother-in-law."—Alexander Markey.

**ir ref'u ta ble** (ir ref'ū tuh b'l). Not able to be disproved; that cannot be refuted or proved false; that cannot be repelled by argument.—"Each test case was backed by *irrefutable* evidence of blood guilt."—Allan A. Michie.

**ir''re me'di a ble** (ir''rē mee'di uh b'l). Incurable; that cannot be remedied; irreparable.—"Britain's plight then seemed *irremediable*."—Dorothy Thompson.

**ir rep'a ra ble** (i rep'uh ruh b'l). For which amends cannot be made; for which there is no compensation; that cannot be remedied or made good.—'The greatest and most *irreparable* loss is of course on the battle field."—James F. Byrnes.

**ir''re pres'si ble** (ir''rē press'ĭ b'l). That cannot be restrained or repressed; that cannot be checked or held back; that cannot be prevented.—"An *irrepressible*, constant odor of garbage was wafting in from outside."—Edith Stern.

**ir''re proach'a ble** (ir''rē prōch'uh b'l). Blameless; not subject to rebuke or censure.—"My country has derived strength and confidence from the far-sighted, *irreproachable* attitude of Brazil."—Franklin Delano Roosevelt.

**ir''re sist'i bly** (ir''rē ziss'tĭ bli). In a way that cannot be counteracted or defeated; hence, so convincingly that they could not be resisted; in a way that defied opposition or resistance.—"The circumstances were so peculiar, so human, and so *irresistibly* comic."—May Lamberton Becker.

**ir''re triev'a bly** (ir''re treev'uh bli). In a way that cannot be repaired or made good; irreparably; incurably; in a way that cannot be recalled or changed.—"They are *irretrievably* and inexpiably implicated in the crimes of the regime."—Walter Lippmann.

**ir rev'o ca bly** (i rev'ō kuh bli). Unalterably; in a way that cannot be changed.—"To be reared in one culture in one society makes one *irrevocably* partake of that culture."—Margaret Mead.

**i'so lat''ed** (ī'sō lāte''id). Placed in a detached situation; cut off from intercourse with others.—"Troops are stationed in *isolated* spots, quite out of reach of ordinary communications."—Madame Chiang Kai-shek.

**la bo'ri ous ly** (luh bō'ri ŭs li). In a way that involves physical or mental exertion; by means of hard work; by putting forth great effort.—"Before most boys have learned *laboriously* to read and write, he had acquired a craftmanship."—Adrian Bury.

**lam'en ta ble** (lam'ĕn tuh b'l). Fitted to be lamented or mourned; deplorable; regrettable.—"Something has got to be done about international communications which are in a rather *lamentable* state."—William L. Shirer.

**lav'ish** (lav'ish). Unstinted; very generous; giving more than enough.—"He was always *lavish* with his wise and stimulating counsel."—H. L. Mencken.

**leer'ing** (leer'ing). Having a sly, malicious, lustful look.—"The main point is how to help one another against the *leering* evil eye of the secret police."—Alexander Loudon.

**le'o nine** (lee'ō nīne). Having the characteristics of a lion; fierce; powerful; majestic.—"He looked rather like a public monument of a *leonine* character."—H. G. Wells.

**le'thal** (lee'thăl: 'th' as in 'thin'). Causing death; deadly; fatal.—"They equip these vigilantes with tin hats, gas masks, and *lethal* weapons."—John L. Lewis.

**li'bel ous** (lī'bel ŭs). Defamatory; slanderous; containing harmful statements.—"They pursued the Senators with malicious falsehood and recklessly *libelous* attacks."—Robert Marion La Follette.

**liv'id** (liv'id). Of a bluish leaden color; ashy-pale; black and blue, as though bruised.—"I saw a *livid* face at the window staring at me with white hollow eyes."—Axel Munthe.

**loathed** (lōthe'd: 'th' as in 'the'). Detested; felt great disgust for; abhorred; disliked.—"She poured him a cup of tepid tea and even drank a cup herself, although there was nothing she *loathed* so much."—Louis Bromfield.

**loath'some** (loathe'sŭm: 'th' as in 'the'). Exciting disgust; calling forth aversion; odious; offensive; repulsive; sickening.—"Those two *loathsome* dominations may well dread their approaching doom."—Winston Churchill.

**low'er ing** (lou'ur ing: 'ou' as in 'out'). Frowning; scowling; sullen; threatening.—"His white face frequently became resentful and *lowering*."—H. G. Wells.

**lu'cra tive** (lū'kruh tiv). Highly profitable; productive of wealth.—"There is a *lucrative* way of handling waste." —Robert S. Aries.

**lu'rid ly** (lū'rid li). In a ghastly, sensational way; dismally; tragically and terribly.—"The adventure story is *luridly* effective."—Orville Prescott.

**lus'cious** (lush'ŭs). Delicious; pleasing to the senses or mind; cloying; sweet and tasty.—"She traces the development of such *luscious* subjects as the fig, the grape, the date."—Ellen Lewis Buell.

**lush** (lush). Fresh and luxuriant; covered with abundant growth and verdure.—"I see a vast valley *lush* with blossoms and blue grass."—Wallace L. Ware.

**lux u'ri ant** (luks ū'ri ănt). Exhibiting excessive growth; exuberant in growth; characterized by abundant growth.—"The wide fields bore a thick, *luxuriant* crop of alfalfa."—Hilary St. George Saunders.

**mach"i a vel'li an** (mak"i uh vel'i ăn). Crafty; treacherous; politically unscrupulous as was Machiavelli, the Florentine statesman.—"My head was filled with the stories of the *machiavellian* manipulators who sat on the thrones of Washington officialdom."—Eric A. Johnston.

**mag nan'i mous ly** (mag nan'ĭ mŭs li). Unselfishly; generously and nobly; in a high-souled way; in a way that showed greatness of soul and a sentiment far above petty motives.— "The Sultan *magnanimously* sent him back to the Christian camp."—Joseph Wood Krutch.

**mag nif'i cent** (mag nif'ĭ sĕnt). Extremely fine and good; grand in appearance, quality, character, and action.—"The Army and Air Force together constitute one *magnificent* fighting machine."—Bernard L. Montgomery.

**ma jes'tic** (muh jess'tik). Stately; kingly; having great dignity; grand and noble.—"He has something of the deep, *majestic* eloquence of the prophets of old."—Stanley Walker.

**ma lev'o lent** (muh lev'ō lĕnt). Malicious; spiteful; wishing evil to come to others; ill-disposed toward others. —"When indignation takes possession of his mind his disposition becomes *malevolent*."—André Maurois.

**ma li'cious** (muh lish'ŭs). Harboring malice or ill will; spiteful.—"The *malicious*, interfering action of the board is designed to prolong the controversy."—John L. Lewis.

**man'da to"ry** (man'duh tō"ri). Obligatory; expressed as a positive command.—"It should be made *mandatory* for new authors of tax instruction sheets to use short words and short sentences."—Sylvia F. Porter.

**mas'ter ly** (mass'tur li). Very skilful; showing the superior skill of a master; worthy of a master; expert. —"With a *masterly* verbal tweak she readjusted the guests who had got out of step."—Jan Struther.

**mawk'ish** (mawk'ish). Lacking strength or vigor; sickening or insipid; sickly. —"To live in these times is to live no *mawkish* sentimental tale."—Dorothy Thompson.

**mel"o dra mat'ic** (mel"ō druh mat'ik). Romantically sensational; containing very exciting incidents.—"I saw them throw kisses to the Statue of Liberty, and this was no *melodramatic* gesture."—Frank Kingdon.

**mem'o ra ble** (mem'ō ruh b'l). Worthy to be remembered; notable; noteworthy.—"The novel lacks any real distinction to make it *memorable*."—Orville Prescott.

**me'ni al** (mee'ni ăl). Servile; serving in some lowly position; low; very humble and mean.—"The man with a high I.Q. must be discouraged from seeking a *menial* job."—Carl A. Gray.

**me"te or'ic** (mē"tē or'ik). Transitorily brilliant; brilliant and flashing for a short time only, as a meteor; having brief periods of great brilliancy.—"With admiring envy he followed the *meteoric* rise of a Bonaparte."—André Maurois.

**me tic'u lous ly** (mē tik'ū lŭs li). Excessively carefully; very particularly; finically; scrupulously; paying great attention to all small details.—"These animated maps of world conquest are as *meticulously* truthful as historians can make them."—Walter Adams.

**min'is ter ing** (min'iss tur ing). Giving service; doing needful things; aiding; helpful.—"One always needs money when one has but recently escaped from the *ministering* clutches of the modern hospital."—Irvin S. Cobb.

**mi rac'u lous** (mĭ rak'ū lŭs). Marvelous; supernatural; wonderful; like a miracle, beyond and surpassing what we deem natural; wonder-working.—"It was to them merely a part of the whole *miraculous* day, though of course not be be understood either."—Pearl S. Buck.

**mo men'tous** (mō men'tŭs). Of great importance; weighty; of great consequence.—"Once again we come to one of those periods in history when *momentous* decisions have to be made."—Mrs. J. Borden Harriman.

**mon'strous** (mon'strŭs). Intolerably hateful; incredibly hideous; having the abnormality and viciousness of a monster.—"The end of this *monstrous* system is now clearly in sight."—Anthony Eden.

**mon"u men'tal** (mon"ū men'tăl). Impressive; lasting as a monument; notable and very large.—"This plain fact is a *monumental* milestone on our onward march."—Winston Churchill.

**mor'dant** (mor'dănt). Biting; hence, sharp; sarcastic; caustic; cutting.—"He has been for years one of the most *mordant* critics of the Russian règime."—Nathaniel Peffer.

**mot'ley** (mot'li). Of different colors; made up of miscellaneous units; clothed in varicolored garments.—"He was walled in with a crowd of alien *motley* people."—Pearl S. Buck.

**mul"ti tu'di nous** (mul"tĭ tū'dĭ nŭs). Consisting of a vast number; very numerous.—"Among the letters were many that suggested *multitudinous* additions to the text."—H. L. Mencken.

**myr'i ad** (mir'i ăd). Composed of a very large indefinite number; innumerable.—"The *myriad* millions of human beings of the Far East are as close to us as Los Angeles is to New York by the fastest trains."—Wendell L. Willkie.

**ne far'i ous** (nē fair'i ŭs). Extremely wicked; atrocious; heinous; villainous.—"There is no place in the city government for any one who would engage in such *nefarious* activities."—Fiorello H. LaGuardia.

**nig'gard ly** (nig'urd li). Stingy; scanty; miserly; meanly small.—"They only got a *niggardly* handout of some square miles of territory."—Baruch Braunstein.

**no to'ri ous ly** (nō tō'ri ŭs li). Manifestly; unquestionably; obviously; in a widely known way.—"He is *notoriously* well armed who has a righteous cause."—Rex G. Tugwell.

**o'di ous** (ō'di ŭs). Exciting great repugnance or disgust; very disagreeable.—"Comparisons may be *odious*."—T. V. Smith.

**o"dor if'er ous** (ō"dur if'ur ŭs). Diffusing or giving out an odor; possessing a strong emanation; having a pene-

trating smell.—"No true Western
thought of these *odoriferous* animals as
noble or useful."—Sherman Baker.

**om'i nous ly** (om'ĭ nŭs li). Menacingly,
like an evil omen; threateningly.—
"The threat hangs *ominously* over the
British Empire."—Claude Pepper.

**ooz'ing** (ōōz'ing). Sending out moisture
in drops like sweat; exuding or discharging moisture slowly.—"There
was no sunshine in the damp and
*oozing* streets on that grey day."—
Helen C. White.

**o'ro tund** (ō'rō tund). Full, clear, and
resonant in voice or utterance; rich
and strong in sound; ringing like
music.—"In *orotund* tones, he announced their marriage."—Lloyd C.
Douglas.

**o"ver whelm'ing** (ō"vur hwelm'ing).
Irresistible; overpowering by sheer
weight of numbers or by force.—
"Victory always depends upon *overwhelming* supplies of all forms of war
materials."—Ernest Bevin.

**pa la'tial** (puh lāy'shăl). Like a palace;
magnificent; fit to be a palace; splendid.—"After his death the *palatial*
residence was converted into apartments."—Roy Chapman Andrews.

**pal'pi tant** (pal'pĭ tănt). Throbbing;
palpitating; pulsating; trembling
with pleasure or fear.—"She felt
again the *palpitant* emotions of a
débutante at her first dance."—
Bradwell E. Tanis.

**pan"o ram'ic** (pan"ō ram'ik). Complete in every direction; like an un-
obstructed continuous scene; like a
series of scenes.—"A *panoramic* view
of the city shows even worse destruction."—Roland T. Bird.

**par'a mount** (par'uh mount: 'ou' as
in 'out'). Superior to all others;
supreme; of chief importance.—
"Among nations, as in our domestic
relations, the principle of interdependence is *paramount*."—Franklin Delano Roosevelt.

**per fer'vid** (pur fur'vid). Very zealous;
ardent; burning; intense; glowing.—
"The pupils of this artist have a *per-
fervid* enthusiasm for their master."—
Emmet Holloway.

**per fid'i ous** (pur fid'i ŭs). Treacherous; involving a breach of faith; de-

liberately false to a trust.—"After the
*perfidious* pact the whole world was
set aghast."—Richard C. Patterson,
Jr.

**per vert'ed** (pur vur'ted). Turned from
its right purpose; diverted; turned
another way; misdirected.—"The
bantering was a cloak for her friend's
affection, a kind of *perverted* abuse
which all understood and in which
all were adept."—Emma Bugbee.

**phe nom'e nal** (fē nom'ē năl). Extraordinary or marvelous; prodigious.—
"Our might must grow even more
than the *phenomenal* growth of the
past months."—James H. Doolittle.

**pit'e ous** (pit'ē ŭs). Arousing compassion; exciting sympathy or pity; pitiful; calling forth sorrow.—"He felt
tender toward the old man, thinking
on his *piteous* unwillingness."—Caroline Dale Snedeker.

**poign'ant** (poyn'yănt). Severely painful; touching; deeply moving; affecting.—"Even more *poignant* is the
destruction that we viewed a little
later in Stepney."—Eleanor Roosevelt.

**pom'pous ly** (pomp'ŭs li). Ostentatiously; in a proud and self-important
way; in a consequential way, as
though very important.—" 'We all
work for the country,' he replied, a
little *pompously*."—Pearl S. Buck.

**pre cip'i tant** (prē sip'ĭ tănt). Rash in
thought and action; hasty; sudden
and abrupt in movement; impulsive;
rushing head-long into action.—
"Don't be so *precipitant* or you will
surely court failure."—Hugh E.
Blackstone.

**pre cip'i tate** (prē sip'ĭ tāte). Extremely
sudden; very abrupt; hasty; rash;
impetuous; without due care or
thought.—"Too *precipitate* an abandonment of controls would spell
disaster."—Clair Wilcox.

**pre cip'i tous** (prē sip'ĭ tŭs). Very
steep; similar to a precipice.—"He
borrowed a rifle and set out with a
unit pushing its way up a *precipitous*
slope."—Elizabeth Bemis.

**pred'a to"ry** (pred'uh tō"ri). Undertaken for plundering; pillaging; robbing and destroying.—"In order to
continue in power that hierarchy

must lead their nation on new *preda-
tory* adventures."—William C. Bullitt.

**pre em'i nent ly** (prē em'ǐ něnt li).
Outstandingly; above all others;
conspicuously.—"This is *preeminently*
a war of science and technology."—
William Pearson Tolley.

**prej"u di'cial** (prej"ŏŏ dish'ăl). Causing prejudice or a biased opinion;
detrimental; hurtful; tending to injure; damaging.—"His first offences
were *prejudicial* to his chances at the
trial."—George F. Gahagan.

**pre pos'ter ous** (prē poss'tur ŭs). Contrary to reason or common sense;
utterly absurd; nonsensical; very
foolish and senseless.—"One hardly
knows how to characterize such
*preposterous* imaginings."—Nicholas
Murray Butler.

**pre sump'tive** (prē zump'tiv). Giving
reasonable or well-founded grounds
for an opinion or belief; creating an
assurance; affording grounds for taking something for granted without
actual proof.—"The evidence was of
a *presumptive* type and not yet based
on ascertained facts."—S. L. Scanlon.

**pre sump'tu ous** (prē zump'chŏŏ ŭs).
Unduly confident; venturesome;
overbold; daring and forward; audacious.—"His grandfather had been
incautious or *presumptuous* enough to
build this metropolitan house amid a
world of wretched huts."—Franz
Werfel.

**prod'i gal** (prod'ǐ găl). Given to wasteful expenditure; addicted to extravagance and waste; yielding in abundance; spending too much; lavish.—
"Country noons are *prodigal* of time
and economical of shadow."—Donald Culross Peattie.

**prod'i gal ly** (prod'ǐ găl i). Extravagantly; lavishly; abundantly; without stint; with great generosity.—
"Able men and women have given
*prodigally* of their time and strength."
—John D. Rockefeller, Jr.

**prof'li gate** (prof'lǐ git). Recklessly extravagant; extremely wasteful; prodigal.—"Our country is wasteful,
*profligate*, yes, but still a great country."—William J. Mayo.

**pro found'ly** (prō found'li: 'ou' as in

'out'). Deeply; reaching far below
the surface; very gravely and deeply.
—"This is a deep-seated factor that
*profoundly* affects the prospects of our
American society."—Edmund E.
Day.

**pro nounced'** (prō nounce'd': 'ou' as
in 'out'). Of marked character;
strongly marked; definitely noticeable; decided.—"That Oscar's fame
has become so *pronounced* is due, in
part, to the fact that he stands as a
bridge between the romantic 90's
and the war-swept 40's."—Frank
Crowninshield.

**pro voc'a tive** (prō vok'uh tiv). Serving to stimulate or excite; arousing;
calling forth feeling or activity.—"It
is filled with fascinating historical
parallels and *provocative* ideas."—
Orville Prescott.

**pu'is sant** (pū'i sănt). Powerful; mighty;
forcible; having great influence or
potency.—"Alcohol is not a stimulant; it is a *puissant* paralyzer, with a
preference for nerves."—George Barton Cutten.

**pun'gent** (pun'jěnt). Affecting the
sense of smell, taste, or touch; biting
or acid; sharp; poignant.—"Forests
breathe anew, and the smell of the
rich earth is *pungent* with fragrance."
—George Matthew Adams.

**pu'tre fied** (pū'trē fīde). Decayed; de-
composed; become rotten or putrid.
—"The wells were polluted by the
thousands of *putrefied* bodies strewn
all over the town."—Axel Munthe.

**pu'trid** (pū'trid). Tainted; having the
fetid odor of decay and corruption;
foul.—"The public saw the *putrid*
pestilence of financial debauchery."
—Alben W. Barkley.

**quench'less** (kwench'less). That cannot be suppressed or subdued; that
cannot be stopped or put an end to;
irrepressible.—"It is a result of his
wide knowledge and *quenchless* curiosity."—Olin Downes.

**rab'id** (rab'id). Furious; raging; violent; fanatical.—"We use our sweat
and blood to shatter the *rabid* attempt of our enemies."—Generalissimo Chiang Kai-shek.

**raff'ish** (raf'ish). Vulgarly pretentious;
low; flashy; disorderly.—"The fuzzy,

*raffish* style of the book has its special appropriateness to the subject."—Edmund Wilson.

**ram'pant** (ram'pănt). Unrestrained; wide-spread; unchecked.—"In many parts of the world disease is *rampant.*" —Raymond B. Fosdick.

**ran'cor ous** (rang'kur ŭs). Full of ill will; showing malignity; expressing spite or enmity; spiteful; malicious. —"The impression produced was one of *rancorous* severity."—William C. Bullitt.

**ra pa'cious** (ruh pā'shŭs). Excessively greedy and covetous; grasping; extortionate; exacting more money than was due.—"The boatman on the river was *rapacious,* and harsh in his demands."—Pearl S. Buck.

**rapt** (rapt). Entirely engrossed; intent; enraptured; deeply absorbed.—"He listened to my plan with *rapt* attention."—Roy Chapman Andrews.

**rap'tur ous** (rap'chŏŏr ŭs). Expressing great joy; ecstatic; enraptured; transported with delight; exceedingly happy.—"His seamed face lighted with a *rapturous* smile."—Lloyd C. Douglas.

**rasp'ing** (rasp'ing). Scraping; grating; making harsh sounds; irritating to the ear.—"The *rasping,* raucous, unmusical sounds were criticized."—Stephen Somervell.

**rau'cous** (raw'kŭs). Harsh-sounding; filled with strident or hoarse noises.— "The last two weeks have been *raucous* ones in Washington. Everybody has been snapping at everybody else."—Raymond Clapper.

**rav'en ing** (rav'ĕn ing). Greedy and hungry; rapacious; voracious; seeking eagerly for prey.—"I have been in the far waste-lands and I have heard the howls of the *ravening* wolves."—Donald G. Cooley.

**rav'en ous** (rav'ĕn ŭs). Eager for food; extremely hungry; voracious; rapacious; greedy.—"He was tingling from his cold bath, and *ravenous* as a hawk for breakfast."—John Buchan.

**re bel'lious** (rē bel'yŭs). Refractory; acting like a rebel; insubordinate; mutinous; in a state of revolt; resistant to authority or circumstances.— "However *rebellious* she felt, she had

made her choice and must live with it."—Rose Feld.

**re doubt'a ble** (rē dout'uh b'l: 'ou' as in 'out'). Formidable; inspiring fear; valiant; worthy of respect.—"John Henry Newman was a *redoubtable* champion of Christian principles against contemporary evils."—Lord Halifax.

**ref'lu ent** (ref'lū ĕnt). Ebbing; flowing back; receding, as the tide.—"There have been many frontiers ever advancing and influencing the 'old settlements' in *refluent* waves."— James Truslow Adams.

**re ful'gent** (rē ful'jĕnt). Resplendent; splendid; brilliant; brightly shining. —"The happy girls eclipsed even the *refulgent* Colonel."—Edith Wharton.

**re lent'less ly** (rē lent'less li). Harshly; without mercy; mercilessly; sternly; pitilessly.—"Unfit human material of all ages is *relentlessly* eliminated."— Bruno Frank.

**re morse'less ly** (rē morce'less li). Pitilessly; cruelly; mercilessly; without compassion.—"The criminals are being hunted down *remorselessly.*"— Douglas E. Lurton.

**ren'e gade** (ren'ē gāde). Traitorous; disloyal; deserting; apostate.—"He is a *renegade* former member."—John L. Lewis.

**re pel'lent** (rē pel'ĕnt). Repulsive or arousing repugnance; distasteful; unattractive; disagreeable.—"Taxation, no matter how *repellent,* is a necessary evil if civilization is to continue."— John J. Merrill.

**rep"re hen'si ble** (rep"rē hen'si b'l). Deserving blame or censure; culpable; blameworthy.—"The attack is obviously *reprehensible* and disgraceful."—J. Roland Sala.

**res'o lute** (rez'ō lūte). Determined; unshaken; bold; firm; inflexible; having a fixed purpose.—"He is an instinctive leader—eloquent and *resolute.*"— Lisle Bell.

**re sound'ing** (rē zound'ing: 'ou' as in 'out'). Echoing; sounding loudly; reverberating; much mentioned.— "She showed that she was not to be impressed by the *resounding* reputations of the great."—Thomas Wolfe

**re splen'dent** (rē splen'dĕnt). Splendid; bright; brilliantly shining.—"It is doing that gives compassion its peculiarly *resplendent* quality. Compassion is active."—Bruce Barton.

**re tal′i a to″ry** (rē tal′i uh tō″ri). Of the nature of a return for some sort of injury received; involving paying back evil with evil; tending to give like for like.—"These remarks are rather *retaliatory* than just."—S. L. Scanlon.

**rib′ald** (rib′ăld). Coarse and indecent; using blasphemous and scurrilous language; jesting irreverently.—"Everything was proceeding as nicely as one could expect from such *ribald* men."—Attilio Gatti.

**rig′or ous ly** (rig′ur ŭs li). Strictly; inflexibly; without any allowance or change.—"The plan was put forward by the Air Ministry, and adhered to *rigorously* and vehemently."—Winston Churchill.

**rue′ful ly** (rōō′fŏŏl li). In a way to cause regret or pity; mournfully; sorrowfully; dolefully.—"After the ship went down one of the officers *ruefully* reminded him of his warning."—Harry Hansen.

**sal′u tar″y** (sal′ū ter″i). Wholesome; beneficial; healthful; useful.—"I cannot refrain from reiterating my gratification that in this, the American republics have given a *salutary* example to the world."—Franklin Delano Roosevelt.

**san′gui nar″y** (sang′gwi ner″i). Bloody; bloodthirsty; attended with much bloodshed.—"It was becoming a very *sanguinary* engagement. Both of his fists were red with blood."—Lloyd C. Douglas.

**sa tan′ic** (sā tan′ik). Like Satan; devilish; wicked; infernal.—"The very grandeur of the crash gave him exactly what he needed—a great role to play, *satanic* though it might be."—André Maurois.

**sca′brous** (skāy′brŭs). Having a rough or knotty surface; hence, not easy to handle decently; impure; lustful; risqué.—"The sailors started their *scabrous* tales of night life ashore."—John Dos Passos.

**scath′ing** (skāthe′ing: 'th' as in 'the'). Damaging; withering; searing.—

"His government has never drawn a more *scathing* criticism than is implied by these peace terms."—Elmer Davis.

**scin′til lat″ing** (sin′tĭ̵ lāte″ing). Sparkling; twinkling; flashing; glittering; sending out sparks or gleams of light.—"The stars shone down in *scintillating* glory."—Gayle Pickwell.

**scud′ding** (skud′ing). Moving swiftly, as before a gale; driving rapidly before the wind.—"A *scudding* rain lashed the windows of the houses."—André Maurois.

**scur′ri lous** (skur′ĭ lŭs). Grossly offensive in an indecent way; vulgar.—"I have investigated the *scurrilous* sheet."—Thomas E. Dewey.

**se pul′chral** (sē pul′krăl). Funereal; suggestive of a tomb or sepulcher; dark and gloomy; dismal.—"All the rooms were chill, melancholy, *sepulchral*."—L. P. Jacks.

**ser′ried** (ser′id). Pressed closely together, as in ranks; in closely packed formation.—"He cried to the *serried* rows on rows of uniformed fanatic youth, 'Strike, and the world will be yours!' "—Dorothy Thompson.

**sin′ew y** (sin′ū i). Supplied with sinews, nerves, or tendons; having strong, tough cords that join muscles to bones; strong; vigorous; brawny.—"I felt two *sinewy* hands on my shoulders and turned to face him."—Samuel Hopkins Adams.

**sin′u ous** (sin′ū ŭs). Winding; turning in and out; hence, devious; rambling.—"Some of us may doubt the artistic validity of these *sinuous* and sometimes untidy rhythms."—George N. Shuster.

**skulk′ing** (skulk′ing). Lurking; moving furtively from place to place; lying hidden.—"He has decreed the death of our citizens wherever his *skulking* assassins of the sea may send them to a watery grave."—Tom Connally.

**so no′rous** (sō nō′rŭs). Resonant; giving out a loud sound; full-sounding; high-sounding; hence, imposing.—"She mused like a statue walled within a *sonorous* cathedral."—André Maurois.

**spar′tan** (spahr′tăn). Heroically brave and enduring like the Spartans;

severely disciplined; undaunted.—
"The military machine has trained
itself in *spartan* simplicity and the
toughness demanded by war."—
Joseph C. Grew.

**spite'ful** (spīte'fŏŏl). Showing spite or
animosity; malicious; full of ill-will;
eager to annoy, thwart, or offend.—
"The women in her plays are as
quarrelsome and *spiteful* as a brood of
unpleasant cats."—Ainslee Mockridge.

**spu'ri ous** (spū'ri ŭs). Not genuine;
false; counterfeit; artificial.—"Let us
not confuse *spurious* liberalism with
the spirit of freedom."—W. J.
Cameron.

**squal'id** (skwol'id). Having a dirty,
neglected appearance; very wretched
and degraded; poor and filthy.—"He
sees Bobby in his *squalid* boyhood
longing for security and comfort."—
Irwin Edman.

**squelched** (skwelcht). Silenced by
humiliating; crushed or discomforted
by some retort; subdued.—"*Squelched*
children seem to offer a sufficient
field of operation for feminine domi-
nance."—Joseph Jastrow.

**state'ly** (stāte'li). Dignified; imposing;
of lofty appearance; majestic.—"He
knew it was full of beautiful things
and that they were grand and
*stately*."—Stephen Vincent Benét.

**stat"u esque'** (stat"ū esk'). Resembling
a statue; like a statue in form; like
carved figures or images.—"The
company about the bed stood *stat-
uesque*, waiting."—Lloyd C. Douglas.

**sten to'ri an** (sten tō'ri ăn). Extremely
loud and powerful; strong-voiced;
loud-sounding.—"He gave a *stento-
rian* growl that produced a profound
silence."—Lloyd C. Douglas.

**stol'id ly** (stol'id li). In a dull, heavy
way; phlegmatically; lacking feeling
and perception; stupidly and impas-
sively.—"The life of the people
moved *stolidly* along a separate path."
—Raymond H. Geist.

**stren'u ous** (stren'ū ŭs). Needful of
strong effort or exertion; very tiring
and exacting.—"The process of root-
ing out the false gods may be long
and *strenuous*."—Anthony Eden.

**stri'dent** (strī'děnt). Giving a loud and
harsh sound; shrill and grating.—
"The world is menaced by brute
force and *strident* ambition."—James
F. Byrnes.

**sub lime'ly** (sŭb līme'li). Nobly;
grandly; majestically; supremely.—
"It is of supreme importance that we
understand how completely, how
*sublimely*, the British are giving of
themselves to this cause."—Paul H.
Appleby.

**sump'tu ous** (sump'chŏŏ ŭs). Costly;
rich; lavish; magnificent.—"This
diet is *sumptuous* compared with the
field ration."—Warren J. Clear.

**su perb'** (sū purb'). Having grand, impressive beauty; surpassing others;
supremely good.—"We feel deeply
the passing of the *superb* musician,
Rachmaninoff."—Pierre Monteux.

**su per'flu ous** (sū pur'flŏŏ ŭs). More
than is needed; beyond what is desirable; needless.—"For those who
heard the concerto it would be *superfluous* to discuss it movement by
movement."—Olin Downes.

**sup'pli ant** (sup'li ănt). Humbly in-
treating; beseeching; earnestly begging.—"I do not appeal in *suppliant*
terms."—Winston Churchill.

**surg'ing** (sur'jing). Swelling as though
agitated; rising like a great wave or
billow; rising high and swelling violently.—"The Archbishop is typical
of a *surging* resurrection within the
human spirit."—P. W. Wilson.

**tan'ta liz'ing** (tan'tuh līze'ing). Fascinating with hopes that cannot be
realized; desirable but out of reach;
tormenting.—"Being so beautiful
and daring, the women are danger-
ously *tantalizing*."—John B. Glenn.

**teem'ing** (teem'ing). Full to overflowing; prolific; swarming; crowded.—
"India has millions of mutually
hostile races and religions in her
*teeming* country."—Ralph E. Flan-
ders.

**tem"er ar'i ous** (tem"ur air'i ŭs). Unreasonably adventurous; very rash;
reckless.—"I don't call that bravery.
I call it being insanely *temerarious*."—
Donald G. Cooley.

**tem pes'tu ous** (tem pess'chŏŏ ŭs). Violent; turbulent; stormy; tumultuous.—"Everyone knows by what

*tempestuous* methods these mountain boys made themselves historic."— May Lamberton Becker.

**te na'cious** (tē nā'shŭs). Tending to hold strongly and firmly; unyielding; apt to retain persistently; retentive. —"The origins of these extravagances were the harder to guess at because of his spiteful memory, *tenacious* of grievances for a very long time."—André Maurois.

**ter'ma gant** (tur'muh gănt). Scolding; quarreling; vixenish; shrewish.— "Even the most *termagant* of aunts was still privately abashed by the enduring calmness of Grandma."— Christopher Morley.

**tit'il lat"ing** (tit'ĭ lāte"ing). Tickling; exciting agreeably; causing pleasant sensations; gratifying to the senses.— "In these new acquaintances he found a *titillating* blend of high living and high thinking."—André Maurois.

**tor ren'tial** (tŏ ren'shăl). Of or resulting from the action of violent streams of water; hence, rainfall that exceeds four inches; like a torrent or flood.— "*Torrential* rains fall throughout the area during the early autumn."— Knight Biggerstaff.

**trag'i cal ly** (traj'i kăl i). Calamitously; distressingly; very sadly; in a way that brought catastrophe.—"Then, *tragically*, at the height of his career, he was mentally stricken."—Gene Fowler.

**tran scend'ent** (tran sen'dĕnt). Surpassing; superior to others; superexcellent; beyond the grasp of the material universe.—"Man while still in the body cannot look upon pure spirit, for the white circle of *transcendent* beauty would strike him blind."—Elizabeth Goudge.

**tri um'phant** (trī um'fănt). Exultant; victorious; jubilant because of a success or triumph; crowned with success.—"It made her feel brilliant and *triumphant*."—Louis Bromfield.

**trump'er y** (trump'ur i). Showy but useless; valueless; worthless; shallow; deceptive.—"The governor might make enough out of it to link me up with any kind of *trumpery* plot."— Stephen Vincent Benét.

**tu mul'tu ous** (tū mul'chŏŏ ŭs). Noisy; boisterous; disorderly and in a tumult; riotous; disturbed; stormy; rough and agitated.—"It is a wild phantasmagoria, a story of *tumultuous* pace."—Edmund Wilson.

**tur'bid** (tur'bid). Having the sediment stirred up; muddy; cloudy; disturbed.—"On the East River the *turbid* waters were catching the mellow light of the summer evening."— John Buchan.

**tur'bu lent** (tur'bū lĕnt). Tempestuous; unruly; greatly disturbed; agitated.—"All were once young and pensive like himself, *turbulent* and tender."—André Maurois.

**un"al loyed'** (un"uh loyd'). Pure; unmixed with anything inferior; having no admixture of anything to debase it.—"The Harrow boys were good judges of character, and after a year recognized that this companion of theirs was of metal *unalloyed*."— André Maurois.

**un bound'ed** (un boun'ded: 'ou' as in 'out'). Without limit; boundless; very great; infinite.—"De Maupassant had an *unbounded* admiration for the old master, Flaubert."—Sterling McCormick.

**un"de ni'a bly** (un"dē nī'uh bli). Indisputably; incontestably; unquestionably.—"The lady was, like her conveyance, large and rather shabby though *undeniably* impressive."— Edith Wharton.

**un gov'ern a ble** (un guv'ur nuh b'l). Impossible to govern or control; unrestrained; hard to rule or hold in check; unbridled; unruly; uncontrollable.—"I have never known anyone whose appetites and temper were both so *ungovernable*."—John J. Green.

**un"im peach'a ble** (un"im peech'uh-b'l). Faultless; blameless; not to be called in question; irreproachable.— "Many believe that judges can discover an *unimpeachable* guide by reading over well-established precedents." —William J. Donovan.

**u nique'** (ū neek'). Rare; uncommon; without equal; matchless.—"In the building of character women have demonstrated a *unique* capacity."— Henry A. Wallace.

**un mit'i gat"ed** (un mit'ĭ gāte"id). Un-qualified; not mitigated or made less severe in any way; not softened; unassuaged; unabated.—"This corruption was especially hopeless and *unmitigated* among the poorer classes."—Ludwig Lewisohn.

**un par'al leled** (un par'uh leld). Un-equaled; unmatched; having no equal; matchless.—"A conspiracy of *unparalleled* circumstances makes it possible for a symposium of women to gather here for these discussions."—Fannie Hurst.

**un plumbed'** (un plumd'). Of which the depth has never been explored; unfathomed; of unknown depths.—"There never was a dearth of theory, that *unplumbed* well of wisdom."—Thomas Wolfe.

**un prec'e dent"ed** (un press'ē dent"-ed). Extraordinary; novel; never experienced before; having no former example.—"An *unprecedented* opportunity exists for the American nations to cooperate to make the spirit of peace a practical and living fact."—Franklin Delano Roosevelt.

**un"pre dict'a ble** (un"prē dik'tuh b'l). Not able to be foretold; hence, likely to do the most improbable things; apt to act in a way that no one could possibly predict or know beforehand.—"We learned from that that our hosts were extremely *unpredictable* and dangerous people."—Eric Sevareid.

**un"pre med'i tat"ed** (un"prē med'ĭ-tāte"id). Not planned beforehand; not designed; not previously thought out or considered.—"Our *unpremeditated* swimming trips had no serious consequences."—Per Höst.

**un scathed'** (un skāthe'd': 'th' as in 'the'). Unharmed; uninjured; without hurt or damage.—"He has come through *unscathed* and triumphant."—J. P. McEvoy.

**un speak'a ble** (un speak'uh b'l). That cannot be expressed in words; inexpressibly objectionable or bad.—"It was an *unspeakable* play, a brash and silly satire."—Tom Pennell.

**un war'rant a ble** (un wawr'ăn tuh-b'l). Unjustifiable; indefensible; that cannot be guaranteed or justified.—"She invented the most *unwarranta-*

*ble* stories about his youth."—H. G. Wells.

**un wont'ed** (un wun'ted). Unusual; not according to custom; extraordinary; not in common use.—"They may make some *unwonted* decree concerning thee."—Caroline Dale Snedeker.

**up roar'i ous** (up rōre'i ŭs). Making an uproar or tumult; making loud, confused noises; accompanied by disturbance and noise; very noisy.—"The heavy father now is a piece of early Americana currently inciting *uproarious* laughter in the theater."—Malvina Lindsay.

**vain"glo'ri ous** (vain"glō'ri ŭs). Boastful; extremely vain or proud; puffed up by vanity; vaunted; ostentatious.—"They will withdraw before it is too late from a *vainglorious* enterprise."—Winston Churchill.

**val'iant** (val'yănt). Strong and intrepid; powerful and courageous; brave; full of valor.—"We nourish the warmest feelings of friendship toward the *valiant* Russian people."—Winston Churchill.

**val'or ous** (val'ur ŭs). Brave; filled with valor and courage; having the strength to meet danger courageously; personally fearless; valiant.—"I have thought of the *valorous* invalids whose bloodless conquests entitle them to a memorial."—Robert Gordon Anderson.

**van'quished** (van'kwisht). Defeated; conquered.—"Under the mandate system only the colonies of the *vanquished* nations were surrendered."—William G. Carleton.

**vaunt'ed** (vawnt'ed). Boasted; bragged about.—"What has happened to our *vaunted* idealism?"—Harold L. Ickes.

**vex a'tious ly** (veks āy'shŭs li). Annoyingly; vexingly; irritatingly; provokingly.—"At night, when she was rolling those *vexatiously* tight bandages round his ailing little heels, she made him repeat Psalms."—André Maurois.

**vi'brant** (vī'brănt). Pulsing with energy; vigorous; resounding.—"The *vibrant* forces of modern science are but waiting the chance to break forth into widening streams of well-being."—Wendell L. Willkie.

**vi′cious** (vish′ŭs). Injurious; in which the effort to overcome one difficulty produces greater difficulties in the original situation; malignant. —"Higher prices result, hence reduced consumption with unemployment still further increased—a *vicious* circle."—Alfred P. Sloan.

**vig′or ous** (vig′ur ŭs). Full of active strength and energy; forcible; full of physical vigor; energetic.—"Foods that require *vigorous* chewing satisfy the stomach faster."—Donald G. Cooley.

**vile** (vīle). Odious; repulsive; evil; disgusting; loathsome; very objectionable.—"They have determined to fight this *vile*, un-American disease to the very end."—Dorothy Thompson.

**vil′lain ous** (vil′ĭn ŭs). Marked by extreme depravity; depraved; having the nature of a scoundrel; detestable. —"This *villainous* force is out not only to destroy Jews but to destroy Christianity."—Alfred Grant Watson.

**vir′u lent** (vir′ū lĕnt). Extremely poisonous; intensely noxious; very deadly; venomous.—"The introduction of *virulent* germs is almost certain to insure a rapid spread of disease." —Harlowe R. Hoyt.

**vir′u lent ly** (vir′ū lĕnt li).Maliciously; venomously, bitterly.—"One group is *virulently* attacking the government's policy."—Dorothy Thompson.

**vi′tal** (vī′tăl). Essential to or supporting life; necessary to existence.— "There are many who put their own interests first and *vital* matters second."—Mrs. J. Borden Harriman.

**vit″ri ol′ic** (vit″ri ol′ik). Like sulphuric acid which burns and scars; hence, caustic; biting; sharp and severely

critical.—"For the rest of the term he ignored him, and then wrote a report that was *vitriolic*."—W. Somerset Maugham.

**vi tu′per a″tive** (vī tū′pur a″tiv). Abusive; faultfinding; railing; reviling; severely censuring; using abusive words.—"He blistered the ears of the man with a choice flow of *vituperative* English."—John Kieran.

**viv′id ly** (viv′id li). Vigorously; clearly; with emphasis; graphically; in a way that gives a strong, clearly defined picture.—"To express oneself *vividly* the Anglo-Saxon words are best."— William A. Temple.

**vix′en ish** (vik′s′n ish). Ill-tempered; quarrelsome; having the characteristics of a vixen or termagant.—"There was the *vixenish* Julia with her obnoxious offspring."—Lloyd C. Douglas.

**vo cif′er ous** (vō sif′ur ŭs). Making a loud outcry; clamorous; noisy; shouting.—"The galleries were in an uproar and *vociferous* in favor of his nomination."—Arthur Krock.

**vo ra′cious** (vō rā′shŭs). Greedy; rapacious; ready to swallow up.—"Our tax bill is not sufficient to meet the *voracious* demands of an extravagant administration."—George W. Maxey.

**wan′ton ly** (won′tŭn li). Without check or restraint; recklessly; waywardly; heartlessly.—"Has the rubber program *wantonly* or unnecessarily stood athwart other essential programs?" —Guy M. Gillette.

**wiz′ened** (wiz″nd). Shrivelled; dried up; shrunken; withered with age.— "The muttering was started by a *wizened* little fellow who had a withered arm."—S. Dillon Ripley.

**za′ny** (zāy′ni). An awkward simpleton or clown; hence, stupid; clownish; like a buffoon or fool.—"Their *zany* doings have become legendary."— Arthur Daley.

## ONE-MINUTE REFRESHER

Adjectives and adverbs have many gradations of power and there are fine distinctions between them. Give careful consideration to the questions that are asked about these eight words and see whether you can write the correct answer to each one.

abusive                   virulently
execrable                 wantonly
calamitous                hectic
ominously                 excruciating

1. When we say that his language is "abusive," how bad it is?
2. Would "execrable" language be worse than "abusive" language?
3. When we speak of a happening as being "calamitous," just what do we mean?
4. Can a bell ring "ominously," and if so, what would be implied?
5. If a man should "virulently" condemn you, just what would he be doing?
6. Once again, suppose he "wantonly" attacked you in his speech; what would that mean?
7. If you had a "hectic" flush how would you look?
8. What is "excruciating" pain?

*Answers:* 1. Such language is harsh, hurtful, reproachfully scurrilous. 2. In a certain sense it would be worse, but the blame would be on the speaker. *Execrable* language is "accursed, damnable, outrageous, abominable. The Latin phrase that it comes from, *ex sacer*, means "not sacred." 3. As you know, this would mean that the happening was characterized by, or of the nature of, or resulting from calamity. 4. Yes, a bell can ring "ominously." The term "omen" comes from a Greek word meaning bird, and birds at that time were watched for prophetic signs. Since so much of our news is bad news, a bell that rings "ominously" is the harbinger of bad news. 5. The word "virulently" comes from a Latin word meaning poison. We recognize it in our language as "virus" which means a germ or the morbid poison of a germ. A man who attacks you "virulently" therefore attacks you in a poisonous and venomous way. 6. This would mean that the man attacked you in a heartless fashion, without reason or consideration, or used lewd words. 7. Your skin would be red and feverish. 8. "Excruciate" has to do with the cross and crucifixion, and so is closely allied to torment and torture. "Excruciating pain" would therefore be "agonizing pain."

# CHAPTER XVIII

## WORDS FOR THE INTELLIGENTSIA

THERE ARE those who feel that long, difficult and abstruse words can perform no useful service for the average person. They consider them as the special vocabulary of the pundits and literati. And still such people might be surprised to know how often they meet such words in their casual reading, and pass them by unnoticed.

The following list of words selected from the contents of the present chapter gives concrete evidence of this. These twelve words appeared in the daily newspapers. They were not hand-picked from the book review, theatrical or high-brow editorial sections, or from the Sunday supplements. I discovered them in the ordinary weekday news columns that are written for mass consumption.

In spite of their commonplace sources these words are extraordinarily hard and the meanings of most of them are unknown to 98 per cent of the reading public. It may comfort you to be told that, if you can identify each one and define it or use it in a sentence, you will prove that you have the vocabulary level of an extraordinary genius, and you can rank yourself as one!

Here are the words:

| | | | |
|---|---|---|---|
| rodomontade | eclectic | exiguous | Procrustean |
| supererogation | susurrus | euphoria | predilections |
| atavistic | casuist | endemic | artifacts |

If you are not familiar with them, look up their pronunciations and definitions that are given in the next few pages, and follow and note the sentences that illuminate them. You will find that many surprisingly difficult words appear and reappear in our press and that they are frequently used by outstanding and successful men and women. If we are to be discerning readers and intelligent citizens, it will help us to understand what our contemporaries are trying to tell us, if we know such words as these.

I do not mean to indicate that the secret of power is to be found in long words. Plain forthright words are usually best for writing. Simple, unaffected and honest ones for speech. Short words, as a rule, have the greater force. Our shining language is so filled with terse, sharp, pungent words: *spade, crass, candid, tax, stop, old, work, fat, foe.* Words such as these have the fire-power of a machine gun. It is generally more effective to say *lie, walk, winding, poor,* than to say *prevaricate, perambulate, anfractuous* or *impecunious.*

But while the short word may often be the better choice, it is important to bear in mind that its long counterpart does not ever mean exactly the same thing.

To "lie," for instance, is to say what one knows to be false. "Prevaricate" is a softer and less offensive term that means to straddle, quibble or evade.

The verb "walk" is clear and understandable to all. "Perambulate" means to *walk around* or *ramble.* You "perambulate" in a garden, but you don't "perambulate" downtown; you walk.

A road may be either "winding" or "anfractuous," but "anfractuous" comes from the same root as "fracture" and means "broken." For this reason an "anfractuous" road is more twisted and tortuous than a winding one.

Again, although "poor" and "impecunious" can mean the same thing, they do not always parallel each other. A person can be poor in arithmetic as well as in worldly goods. When you are "impecunious," however, you have no money. That is all that this word signifies.

It is senseless, of course, to parade big words for their own sake. Such a display always places us in the category with the *nouveau riche* who flashes his money around for effect. Nor should we ever substitute words for ideas. But in all probability there is no such thing as an idea without words to give it form, and some ideas are so large and so intricate that they need important words to interpret them properly.

Abraham Lincoln knew the strength of short words, and he used them with immortal effect in his Gettysburg speech. Winston Churchill learned the efficacy of the small word too. But when we read the speeches of these two men, we are stopped every now and then by an unusual noun or an adjective of grace and distinction, or a verb that has an impact upon us that is physical as well as mental.

All those leaders who command men know the power of important words. Here are a few in action.

"Labor," says John L. Lewis, "is just a *conglomerate* of human beings with ordinary human cravings."

"Our great national dream of a better life for every family," says W. J. Cameron, "is not a political *phantasmagoria*."

"Dictators are *arrogating* to themselves the attributes of the God Almighty," exclaimed John D. Rockefeller, Jr.

And, lastly, Winston Churchill: "I do not think," said he, "that we could have chosen any man more capable of keeping his very large and *heterogeneous* force together."

The right word is a powerful agent, and to know that you have the versatility that will make it possible for you to call upon the right word and fit it to the occasion will give you a courage and confidence of performance that cannot be had so easily in any other way.

We turn now to an assemblage of words that belong to the aristocracy of our language.

## WORDS FOR THE INTELLIGENTSIA

**ab″ne ga′tions** (ab″nē gā′shŭnz). Self-denials; renunciations; denials; abjurations.—"Behind those ill-guarded doors what triumphs, what *abnegations*, what partings pass and are forgotten!"—Samuel Hopkins Adams.

**ab′stract** (ab′strakt). Theory, rather than practice; something apart from the concrete; an idea apart from its application to a particular thing.—"If you fear bureaucracy in the . *abstract*, do not forget that the big companies have problems in bureaucracy also."—Stuart Chase.

**ac ces′sion** (ak sesh′ŭn). Attainment of something added; increase by the addition of something; addition to things already possessed.—"He reports the *accession* of thousands of printed books and pamphlets during the year."—Lawrence C. Wroth.

**ac cliv′i ty** (ă kliv′ĭ ti). Upward slope; an ascending inclination or side of a hill.—"We stood awestruck and abashed at the foot of that fearsome *acclivity*."—Donald G. Cooley.

**ac cords′** (ă kordz′). Harmonies; agreements; conformities; mutual consents.—"She sensed all the shades of personal feeling, the *accords* and an-

tipathies in the household."—Willa Cather.

**ac cou′tered** (ă kōō′turd). Equipped; arrayed; furnished with dress or trappings for war; outfitted with all the requirements for service.—"The main bodies were commanded by junior officers but were not more splendidly *accoutered*." — Lloyd C. Douglas.

**a cu′i ty** (uh kū′ĭ ti). Perception; acuteness; sharpness; penetration; keenness.—"They criticize the policy of those years with surprising *acuity*."—Per Jacobsson.

**a cu′men** (ă kū′mĕn). Quickness of discernment; keenness of intellect.—"Great as was his legal *acumen*, he had not the knowledge or experience to enable him to conduct the technical cross-examination."—Winston Churchill.

**ad um′brate** (ad um′brāte). Foreshadow; indicate vaguely; typify; represent in a sketchy way.—"At least in mathematics you have a chance to see students learning to reason; not just feel, or suspect, or *adumbrate*."—Christopher Morley.

**ad″ven ti′tious** (ad″ven tish′ŭs). For-

eign; not belonging to a person; occurring unexpectedly; casual.—"She
has tougher going with a sketchy and
somewhat *adventitious* role."—Lewis
Nichols.

**af fect'ed** (uh fekt'ed). Were fond of
wearing; liked to have and use; had
a liking or fondness for.—"On his
head was a turban of silk, such as
many gentlemen who had served in
the Indies *affected*."—Stephen Vincent Benét.

**a man″u en'sis** (uh man″ū en'siss). A
secretary; a person who writes from
dictation; one who copies manuscripts.—"Catherine Byron had to
shrug her shoulders and become her
son's *amanuensis*."—André Maurois.

**am″a ran'thine** (am″uh ran'thin). Like
the amaranth or imaginary never-
fading flower; hence, unfading; un-
dying.—"No words can really describe the *amaranthine* beauty of the
Land of the Midnight Sun."—Emmet Holloway.

**am'bi ent** (am'bi ĕnt). Moving around;
surrounding; encompassing.—"The
soft, *ambient* light of the moon spread
across the gay scene."—Donald G.
Cooley.

**am biv'a lence** (am biv'uh lĕnce). A
state of attraction toward someone or
something accompanied by a feeling
of strong dislike; an experience of
love and hatred for a person (or
thing) simultaneously.—"This fierce
*ambivalence*, this terrible alternation
between attraction and repulsion, pol-
lutes the soul."—Ludwig Lewisohn.

**a nath'e ma** (uh nath'ē muh: 'th' as in
'thin'). A ban or curse; hence, something hated and viewed with loathing.—"Fifteen years ago collective
bargaining was the business man's
*anathema*."—Eric A. Johnston.

**an'cil lar″y** (an'sĭ ler″ĭ). Subordinate;
auxiliary; secondary.—"The principal object is to provide a universal
currency. Everything else is *ancillary*
to that."—Lord Keynes.

**a nent'** (uh nent'). In regard to; concerning; about.—"He got into a
quarrel with his local dominie *anent* a
certain passage in the Bible."—Hendrik Willem Van Loon.

**an frac'tu ous** (an frak'chŏŏ ŭs). Tor-

tuous; twisting like a spiral; sinuous;
winding in and out.—"The road
wound its *anfractuous* way through the
rocky and precipitous mountains."—
Ellery Marsh Egan.

**an″i mad ver'sion** (an″ĭ mad vur'-
shŭn). Adverse or carping criticism;
censure; unfavorable remarks; comments expressing blame.—"Had
compulsory servic been decreed at
once, there would have been no
cause for *animadversion*."—A. S. M.
Hutchinson.

**an tith'e sis** (an tith'ē siss: 'th' as in
'thin'). The direct opposite; a contrary.—"Security is a state of mind,
the *antithesis* of fear."—John G.
Winant.

**a poc'ry phal** (uh pok'ri făl). Of doubtful authenticity; spurious; fabulous.
—"This story may well be *apocryphal*,
but I cherish it none the less."—
James B. Conant.

**ap'o gee** (ap'ō jē). The point farthest
from the earth in the orbit of a celestial body; hence, the highest point;
the culmination.—"Great Britain at
that time had reached her *apogee*."—
Robert I. Gannon.

**ap'po site** (ap'ō zit). Appropriate; suitable; pertinent; relevant; fit; adapted
to the purpose.—"He treasured up
the words, but on the whole he did
not at first find them very *apposite*."—
Helen C. White.

**ar'che typ″al** (ahr'kē tīpe″ăl). Of the
original standard pattern or type; of
the original form or prototype; like
the chief or original model.—"Heaven
in the Lord's Prayer is the realm of
Pure Unconditional Being, of *arche-
typal* ideals."—Emmet Fox.

**ar'ro gat″ing** (ar'ō gāte″ing). Taking
or claiming unreasonably; ascribing
proudly and presumptuously; usurp-
ing.—"They are *arrogating* to themselves the attributes of God Almighty."—John D. Rockefeller, Jr.

**ar'ti facts** (ahr'ti facts). Things made
by human art; articles artificially
produced; human workmanship; implements made by primitive people.
—"Where are we to draw the line if
we call the older ones fossils, and reject the later *artifacts*."—Percy E.
Raymond.

as″sig na′tion (ass″ig nā′shŭn). Assignment; appointment; engagement to meet.—"He went off alone in the motor for his *assignation* with the boy from the bicycle shop."—E. F. Benson.

as′so nance (ass′ō nănce). Correspondence or resemblance of sound.— "The flutter of wings and the rustle of disturbed leaves blended in a soothing *assonance*."—Donald G. Cooley.

as trin′gent (ăss trin′jĕnt). Contracting; binding; hence, stern; austere; severe.—"One may be sour and also stupid, but to be *astringent* takes intelligence."—Gerald Johnson.

at″ra bil′ious (at″ruh bil′yŭs). Affected by black bile; hence, melancholy; hypochondriac; acrimonious; full of spite or malice.—"Such an *atrabilious* mood was bound to affect his colleagues."—Bertram M. Myers.

at″a vis′tic (at″uh viss′tik). Pertaining to intermittent heredity; reverting to an ancestral trait or type.—"Something snapped, or some *atavistic* impulse emerged from the deeps, something strong enough to break the tie of a happy marriage."—John Buchan.

at tri′tion (ă trish′ŭn). Grinding down or wearing away.—"They can be conquered only by a progressive *attrition* of their naval power."—Joseph C. Grew.

au′gu ry (aw′gū ri). A portent or omen; a prediction; a sign.—"The advance of the armies into Tunisia is an *augury* full of hope for the future of the world."—Winston Churchill.

a vun′cu lar (uh vung′kū lur). Like an uncle; of an uncle; pertaining to an uncle.—"Uncles, he had discovered, were always filled with *avuncular* ardor at the beginning of their visit."— Elizabeth Goudge.

bar′bate (bahr′bāte). Bearded; having a beard.—"We passed Arabs in dusty sandals, their dark, *barbate* faces inscrutable."—Donald G. Cooley.

bee′tling (bee′tling). Overhanging; lowering; scowling; projecting.— "His *beetling* gorilla eyebrow ridge was a mark of the older males only." —Raymond W. Murray.

be hest′ (bē hest′). Command; authoritative mandate; an injunction.— "One totalitarian method of trading is by the *behest* of fear."—Raymond H. Geist.

ben′i son (ben′i z'n). Benediction; blessing.—"A more inspired play than this would have proved a genuine *benison* to a laggard season."— Howard Barnes.

bi′fur cates (bī′fur kātes). Forks; divides into two branches.—"The road *bifurcates* after it crosses the railroad tracks."—Bruce Ellsworth.

brag″ga do′ci o (brag″uh dō′shi ō). Pretentious boasting; empty brags.— "They have made *braggadocio*, blackmail, and treachery the basis of their international relations."—Robert G. Sproul.

bruit (broōt). To report; to rumor; to spread or publish a report; to noise abroad.—"He had the means to *bruit* this scandal abroad."—Thomas Mann.

cam′er a (kam′ur uh). A judge's chamber; hence, private, secret.—"A small and secret committee worked on the problem in *camera*."—Sterling McCormick.

ca par′i soned (kuh par′ĭ sŭnd). Richly clothed; decorated; covered with gay trappings, as a horse.—"The smolts are covered by shining mail and *caparisoned* for the sea adventure."— Brooke Dolan.

cas′u ist (kazh′ū ist). A person who decides doubtful questions of right and wrong in conduct by injunctions set forth in sacred books or according to an authority on social conventions, rather than on grounds of moral reason.—"The moral problems torturing the scrupulous conscience of this stricken *casuist* were in no way ended by the departure of her husband."— André Maurois.

cat″e gor′i cal ly (kat″ē gŏr′i kăl i). Absolutely; positively; without qualifications; unconditionally; explicitly.—"Let me state *categorically* that the main purpose of our administration is to train them to stand securely on their own feet."—Malcolm MacDonald.

cer′e brate (ser′ē brāte). Think; show

mental activity; manifest brain action.—"Those citizens *cerebrate* with their prejudices and their emotions instead of with their brains."—Harold L. Ickes.

**char'nel** (chahr'něl). Used for dead bodies or bones; sepulchral; burial; mortuary.—"There is a pervasive melancholy, a preoccupation with the tomb and the *charnel* house."—Ludwig Lewisohn.

**chi mer'i cal** (kǐ mer'i kǎl). Visionary; impracticable; fanciful.—"The labor question is at times a shifting ground open to *chimerical* hopes."—Pius XII.

**cinc'tures** (singk'chŏorz). Belts; girdles; hence, deep coverings about the loins.—"The Indian women wore *cinctures* of colored feathers."—Bertram M. Myers.

**cir cu'i tous** (sur kū'ǐ tǔs). Indirect; roundabout.—"History has many *circuitous* and curious passages."—Archibald MacLeish.

**cir"cum am'bi ent** (sur"kǔm am'bi-ěnt). Surrounding; extending all round; encompassing.—"His life is lived in the shadow of a *circumambient* fear."—Ludwig Lewisohn.

**cli mac'ter ics** (klǐ mak'tur iks). Very critical years or periods; times of crisis.—"We have reached one of the *climacterics* of the war."—Winston Churchill.

**cli mac'tic** (klǐ mak'tik). Pertaining to a climax or critical period; marking a crisis; hence, culminating; reaching the highest or most severe point.—"The honors go to her for her *climactic* experience with a devil in human form."—Will Cuppy.

**cog no'men** (kog nō'men). Surname; family name; name or appellation.—"In China a boy could assume another name merely by signing the new *cognomen* on documents or letters."—Elinor Rice.

**col la'tion** (kǒ lā'shǔn). A light meal; a simple repast; a lunch or supper.—"He received us with an elaborate *collation* and sweet champagne."—Roy Chapman Andrews.

**con cat"e na'tion** (kon kat"ē nā'shǔn). A connected series of things or events depending on each other; a number of events linked together; a chain of circumstances or events.—"What a queer *concatenation* of circumstances to doom an Italian patriot to bring up a little Miss Jonathan!"—Edith Wharton.

**con cin'ni ty** (kŏn sin'ǐ ti). Harmony; fitness; mutual adjustment of parts; elegance.—"There is a beauty of its own in *concinnity* of structure."—Charles Henry Crozier.

**con cu'pis cence** (kon kū'pi sěnce). Undue sexual desire; lust.—"Only the *concupiscence* of the flesh can match the unholy lust for gold."—Edmund A. Walsh.

**con fect'** (kŏn fekt'). Prepare; construct; put together; make.—"They *confect* treatises contending that the audience goes to the theatre to be inspired and uplifted."—George Jean Nathan.

**con fig"u ra'tion** (kŏn fig"ū rā'shǔn). Contour; relative position of parts in a pattern or figure; structural arrangement.—"Many more soundings are needed before we can get a detailed picture of the *configuration* of the floor of the Pacific Ocean."—E. S. C. Smith.

**con'flu ence** (kon'flŏo ěnce). A meeting or coming together in one place; a gathering and mingling; a union.—"The display was terminated by a *confluence* of the clouds."—C. Brooke Worth.

**con ge'ri es** (kon jee'ri eez). Assemblage; collection of people or parts; aggregation; mass; massed gathering.—"It must be our ambition to give humanity a sense of the comradeship which infuses our own *congeries* of national stocks."—Allan Nevins.

**con glom'er ate** (kŏn glom'ur it). A heterogeneous collection; a mass ormed of various parts; an accumulation.—"Labor is just a *conglomerate* of human beings with ordinary human cravings."—John L. Lewis.

**con'gru ous** (kong'grŏo ǔs). Consistent; harmoniously related; concordant in nature; suitable; fitting.—"This unification was *congruous* with the prevailing character of both the concerts."—Olin Downes.

**con"san guin'i ty** (kon"sang gwin'ǐ ti). Blood-relationship; relationship from a common ancestry; descent from common ancestors; hence, affinity, close kinship.—"The link that binds our two countries together is that indescribable *consanguinity* of race which causes us to have the same ideals."—Douglas MacArthur.

**con sorts'** (kŏn sorts'). Keeps company with; associates; hence, is in agreement with; harmonizes with; agrees with.—"If watered down a bit, the law of the Prophet *consorts* with a measure of agreeable living."—George N. Shuster.

**con'sue tudes** (kon'swē tūdes). Customs; habits; social intercourse or usage.—"This practice was in harmony with the *consuetudes* of the times."—Henry J. Powers.

**con"tra dis tinc'tion** (kon"truh disstingk'shŭn). Distinction or distinguishing of difference by contrast; distinction by contrary qualities.—"He was emphasizing creative ability in *contradistinction* to capability."—Hugh E. Blackstone.

**con'tu me"ly** (kon'tū mē"li). Rudeness or insult in manner or speech; haughtiness and contempt; scornful insolence.—"They heaped *contumely* on Negroes, Jews, and Catholics."—Harold L. Ickes.

**cor'us cat"ing** (kor'ŭss kāte"ing). Giving out sparkles of light; hence, flashing; glittering; brilliantly attired.—"The *coruscating* bell captain commands an army of bell-boys."—Hilary St. George Saunders.

**coun"ter vail'ing** (koun"tur vail'ing: 'ou' as in 'out'). Offsetting; opposing with equal power; counteracting; compensating. — "No *countervailing* influence would be available."—H. W. Prentis, Jr.

**coz'ened** (kuz"nd). Cheated; beguiled; deceived by some small art; defrauded by a maneuver.—"The room was lit only by a skylight so one could be *cozened* to bed without realizing it was still daytime in the garden."—Christopher Morley.

**crap'u lous** (krap'ū lŭs). Made ill by gross intemperance; intemperate in eating or drinking.—"The *crapulous* old fellow dropped at last into a restless sleep."—George F. Gahagan.

**crep'i tat"ing** (krep'ĭ tāte"ing). Crackling; rattling; making a succession of rapid snapping sounds.—"The *crepitating* clatter of the hoofs gradually died away."—Axel Munthe.

**cre pus'cule** (krē puss'kūle). Dusk; the twilight of morning or evening.— "In the deep *crepuscule*, the glow of the chains of lanterns is very like the glimmering of enormous fireflies."—Henry Fleming.

**cres'cive** (kress'iv). Growing; increasing.—"The spring rains encourage the lush and *crescive* grain."—Donald G. Cooley.

**cryp'tic** (krip'tik). Secret; having a hidden meaning; mysterious; enigmatic.—"The song was well known for one of those *cryptic* criticisms people sing when speech is forbidden."—May Lamberton Becker.

**cy'no sure** (sī'nō shōŏr). An object of interest or attraction; the center of attention.—"I started to use the crawl stroke, and found myself a *cynosure*."—Grace E. Barstow Murphy.

**de"cid u'i ty** (dē"sid ū'ĭ ti). Falling of the leaves; absence of leaves, the opposite to evergreen.—"The *deciduity* of these trees is obscured by the evergreen jungle palms and other growths."—William Beebe.

**de funct'** (dē fungkt'). Dead; extinct; lifeless; hence, not functioning.— "Back of him stood the propagandists for the *defunct* alliance between politics and crooked business."—Alben W. Barkley.

**den"e ga'tion** (den"ē gā'shŭn). Denial; refusal; disavowal; contradiction.— "They broke out in a wordy *denegation*."—Donald G. Cooley.

**den"i gra'tion** (den"i grā'shŭn). Defamation; blackening; aspersion; attack on the reputation.—"He joined in the general *denigration* of the distressful world about them."—H. G. Wells.

**de nom'i nat"ed** (dē nom'ĭ nāte"id). Entitled; named; called; given the name; designated.—"He is justly *denominated* in history's pages as 'the great.' "—Olin Downes.

**de nude'** (dē nūde'). Strip the covering from; lay bare.—"Man may, in a

measure, *denude* his heart of dreams."
—William Henry Boddy.

**de sid″er a′tum** (dē sid″ur āy′tŭm).
Something not possessed, but needed
or regarded as desirable.—"The time
has come when hemispheric solidarity is more than a *desideratum* of long-
range diplomacy."—Anne O'Hare
McCormick.

**des′ue tude** (dess′wē tūde). Cessation
of use; disuse.—"We may define
boredom as 'an uncomfortable consciousness of cerebral innocuous
*desuetude*.'"—John Ise.

**di″a lec′tic** (dī″uh lek′tik). Logical debate.—"In a world in which the
whole *dialectic* was the crushing of
democracy by force, pacifism seemed
out of place."—Michael Straight.

**di chot′o my** (dī kot′ō mi). Division
into two parts or branches; a cutting
into two subordinate parts.—"The
untimely *dichotomy* of the group
weakened the whole organization."
—Donald G. Cooley.

**dif″fer en″ti a′tion** (dif″ur en″shi āy′-
shŭn). Distinction on grounds of difference; preception of difference;
development of different characteristics.—"This *differentiation* in culture
was accented sharply."—Garrido
Torres.

**dis coun′te nance** (diss koun′tē nănce:
'ou' as in 'out'). Discourage by showing disapproval of; refuse to sanction
or encourage; look upon with disfavor.—"Those who are Puritans at
heart *discountenance* these innocent
pleasures."—John J. Green.

**dis″em bod′ied** (diss″em bod′ed).
Freed from the body.—"He felt like
some *disembodied* creature, for he
seemed to have shed all ordinary
interests."—John Buchan.

**dis′pa rate** (diss′puh rāte). Dissimilar;
that cannot be compared; different.
—"Inner time consists of seemingly
*disparate* elements: physiological time
and psychological time."—Alexis
Carrel.

**dis sem′i nat″ed** (di sem′ĭ nāte″id).
Scattered; spread; dispersed; distributed.—"The products of bacterial
action are absorbed day by day into
the blood and *disseminated* throughout
the body."—Donald A. Laird.

**dis′si dents** (diss′ĭ dĕnts). Dissenters;
those who disagree with an existing
order; those who differ in opinion.—
"Having crushed minorities and
purged *dissidents*, the totalitarian
state insists that it has achieved
unity."—Henry W. Wriston.

**doc″tri naire′** (dok″tri nair′). Theoretical; visionary; impractical; making no allowance for circumstances.
—"Their *doctrinaire* inflexibility did
not attract him."—H. G. Wells.

**du al′i ty** (dū al′ĭ ti). A twofold nature;
a state of being composed of two.—
"The great need today is the recognition of this *duality* of interest between our schools and industry."—
James Kip Finch.

**du′ress** (dū′ress). Constraint by force
or fear; compulsion; severe hardship.
—"A treaty, where it is not imposed
under *duress*, rests on moral obligations."—Henry Cabot Lodge.

**ec lec′tic** (ek lek′tik). One who practices selection from all systems or
doctrines; one who borrows freely
from many opinions and has liberal
views.—"The vacuum is filled with
the *eclectic*, the elective, the specialized."—Walter Lippmann.

**ef fete′** (e feet′). Incapable of further
production; exhausted.—"We were
told we were *effete*, worn out."—Winston Churchill.

**e″go cen′tric** (ē″gō sen′trik). Self-centered; looking at everything in relation to oneself.—"Truly satisfying
success in epochs of trial comes to
those who reject the *egocentric* viewpoint."—Harold W. Dodds.

**e′gress** (ē′gress). A place or means of
exit; a way out.—"Strikers may prevent ingress or *egress* from a place of
business."—James A. Emery.

**el″ee mos′y nar″y** (el″ē mos′i ner″i).
Charitable; pertaining to alms or
charity; gratuitous; dependent upon
charity.—"Our hospitals, orphan-
ages, and all our *eleemosynary* institutions are largely the product of our
outpoured wealth."—James E. Freeman.

**em′a nat″ing** (em′uh nāte″ing). Proceeding from a source; coming forth;
originating.—"The comet's peculiar
ities are probably caused by direct

radiation of short waves and power-ful light *emanating* from the sun."—Fred L. Whipple.

**e mas'cu lat"ed**  (ē mass'kū lāte"id). Deprived of strength; weakened.—"We held the line against proposals that would have *emasculated* the bill."—Arthur H. Vandenberg.

**e"men da'tions**  (ē"men dā'shŭnz). Critical corrections; alterations with a view to improvement; changes based on criticism.—"What was needed was a complete reworking, with many additions and a number of *emendations* and shortenings."—H. L. Mencken.

**e mer'i tus**  (e mer'i tŭs). Retired from active service or honorably discharged, but retained in an honorary position.—" 'This modern republic was founded by pilgrims who were looking for something unusual,' read the President *emeritus*."—Christopher Morley.

**em pir'i cal**  (em pir'i kăl). Based on experience or observation.—"The *empirical* and practical spirit which characterizes the English-speaking world is a great asset."—Dorothy Thompson.

**em"py re'an**  (em"pĭ rē'ăn). The sky; the highest heaven; the firmament.—"There was an Ascension in which the Saviour seemed to surge up towards the *empyrean* and yet to stand upon the air as steadily as though it were solid ground."—W. Somerset Maugham.

**en dog'e nous**  (en doj'ē nŭs). Growing from within; originating on the inside; produced on the inside of something.—"This slow process is in marked contrast to the many episodes of *endogenous* infection with toxic symptoms."—George G. Ornstein.

**eu pho'ri a**  (ū fō'ri uh). A sense of buoyancy and general happiness; a feeling of well-being.—"After three drinks a mild *euphoria* filled him and he felt no pain."—Donald G. Cooley.

**e vokes'**  (ē vōkes'). Calls forth; summons; brings out.—"A regulation which *evokes* the criticism of all responsible leaders cannot be sound."—Earl Constantine.

**ex cep'tion**  (ek sep'shŭn). Objection; disapprobation; offense; adverse reason or contrary argument; hence, to take exception or object to.—"All the members took *exception* to the proposal."—Douglas Brewster.

**ex co'ri at"ed**  (eks kō'ri āte"id). Abraded; scolded or criticized severely.—"He extolled his achievements and *excoriated* his opponents."—James W. Wadsworth.

**ex em'plar**  (eg zem'plur). A model to be copied or imitated; an ideal type or pattern.—"Islam is out of sympathy with a philosophy that elevates the ascetic into the highest *exemplar* of human conduct."—Lord Halifax.

**ex ig'u ous**  (eg zig'ū ŭs). Diminutive; small; slender; scanty.—"The white face frequented the streets beneath the *exiguous* tassel of a second-hand mortar-board cap."—H. G. Wells.

**ex ten'u ate**  (eks ten'ū āte). Underestimate; excuse the faults of; represent as less worthy of blame; depreciate.—"He does not *extenuate* neither does he gild his village."—Ludwig Lewisohn.

**ex tra'ne ous**  (eks trāy'nē ŭs). Foreign; outside; external.—"There is a tendency to ascribe all ills to some *extraneous* enemy."—Arthur Sweetser.

**fac'ile**  (fass'il). Moving or working easily; hence, expert; skilful; dexterous; fluent.—"I believe that a person can be versatile and *facile* and still have depth."—Louis Nizer.

**fan"fa ron ade'**  (fan"fuh rŏn āde'). Boasting speech; swaggering; bragging; arrogant blustering; rodomontade.—"He wondered why he had concocted this gaudy and pretending *fanfaronade*, when all that had been needed was plain speech."—Thomas Wolfe.

**far ra'go**  (fuh rah'gō). A mixture; a confused medley; a hotch-potch.—"Amid a *farrago* of reference and quotation there are long echoes of Homer."—Ludwig Lewisohn.

**fau'na**  (faw'nuh). The animals living in a certain area; the animals belonging to a special period.—"Africa embraces a tremendous range of climate, flora and *fauna*, and natural resources."—Henry S. Villard.

**fe lic"i ta'tions**  (fē liss"ĭ tā'shŭnz).

Congratulations; good wishes; wishes for happiness.—"He could hardly keep the joy out of his face, but he knew his master would resent any *felicitations*."—Lloyd C. Douglas.

**fe′line** (fē′līne). Catlike; resembling members of the cat family; sly; stealthy.—"She moved with a *feline*, effortless grace."—Stephen Vincent Benét.

**fe′ral** (feer′ăl). Untamed; not domesticated; wild; savage.—"By finding and destroying all the nests of the blind hornets they may quickly stamp out the *feral* brood."—Anne O'Hare McCormick.

**flag′el lat″ing** (flaj′ĕ lāte″ing). Scourging; beating with whips or sticks; flogging; whipping; lashing.—"They marched from town to town *flagellating* themselves with whips and rods."—Henry James Forman.

**fla gi′tious** (fluh jish′ŭs). Scandalous; shamefully wicked; extremely criminal; atrocious; of ill repute.—"They saw him pass into the interior of that *flagitious* establishment."—L. P. Jacks.

**flam boy′ant** (flam boy′ănt). Characterized by extravagance; showy; full of pompous, high-sounding phrases. —"His communiqués were deprecated as unsoldierly and *flamboyant*." —Arthur Krock.

**flo′ra** (flō′ruh). All the native plants of a country or district; the plants indigenous to a particular region.— "Dr. Schaffer's interest in the *flora* of Bavaria directed his attention to the possibility of new materials for papermaking."—Dard Hunter.

**fo′cal** (fō′kăl). Pertaining to a focus; situated at a central point of attention and principal seat of activity.— "The Soviet Union has entered into open competition, by open diplomacy, for a *focal* position as the magnet of Europe and Asia."— Dorothy Thompson.

**fo ren′sic** (fō ren′sik). Relating to or used in legal proceedings; pertaining to courts of law.—"I may not be able to ⸱ omplete my plans for the *forensic* medical institute, but I am going to see them well along."—Fiorello H. LaGuardia.

**for tu′i tous** (for tū′ĭ tŭs). Happening by chance; casual; accidental.—"We should not just sit and hope for a *fortuitous* concourse of events to create a better world."—Madame Chiang Kai-shek.

**fre net′ic** (frē net′ik). Frenzied; frantic; fanatical; violently agitated.— "This was the case in the *frenetic* oppression of the South after the Civil War."—Hugh S. Johnson.

**ful′some** (fool′sŭm). Of such an excessive number or quantity as to be disgusting; insincere in an offensive way; cloying or wearying.—"We cannot successfully counter the drive of collectivistic ideas with a phalanx of *fulsome* facts."—H. W. Prentis, Jr.

**fu′ri bund** (fū′ri bund). Full of fury; filled with rage; furious; enraged; frenzied.—"Simon Bolivar had to face the *furibund* mob."—Donald G. Cooley.

**gar′ner** (gahr′nur). Gather together; collect; store up.—"This was perhaps the major reason why he could never *garner* many votes."—George N. Shuster.

**gas″tro nom′ic** (gass″trō nom′ik). Pertaining to the art of preparing and serving very tasty food; hence, pertaining to the art of good living; like an epicure.—"His *gastronomic* interests led him to try to enrich the lives of our people with the food plants enjoyed by other nations."—Thomas Barbour.

**gen″u flect′ed** (jen″ū flekt′ed). Having knee bent, as in worship or deference. —"We watched the *genuflected* tilting approach of the deck steward with the forenoon beef tea."—Christopher Morley.

**gla′brous** (glāy′brŭs). Smooth; free from down or hair; hairless; bald.— "The *glabrous* heads of old men decorated the first row seats at the bur⸱ lesque show."—Ellery Marsh Egan.

**gra va′men** (gruh vāy′men). The essential part of a grievance; the burden of a charge or complaint.—"The *gravamen* of the Communist article was that the border lay a long way ahead of where the armies had reached."—Edwin L. James.

**gy ra′tions** (jī rā′shŭnz). Whirlings;

windings; going round in circles.—
"The confused *gyrations* of the three
groups of American extremists may
often cause them to bump into each
other."—Lawrence Hunt.

**ha bil′i ments** (huh bil′ĭ mĕnts). Clothing; dress; garb.—"In jackstraw
*habiliments* he was leaning over a gas
plate."—Gene Fowler.

**hab′i tat** (hab′ĭ tat). The region where
something naturally lives or is found.
—"Electrons were snatched from
their ordinary *habitat* in atoms."—
Karl T. Compton.

**hal′cy on** (hal′si ŭn). A fabulous bird
which was said to calm the waves at
the winter solstice; hence, calm,
peaceful.—"A transformation in our
way of life is taking place, and the
*halcyon* days are over."—Kirtley F.
Mather.

**har′bin gers** (hahr′bin jurz). Announc-
ers or forerunners of something coming; heralds.—"Hard times are ever
the *harbingers* of progress, as necessity
is the mother of invention."—George
Barton Cutten.

**het″er o ge′ne ous** (het″ur ō jee′nē ŭs).
Consisting of dissimilar elements;
miscellaneous; differing in kind and
qualities.—"I do not think we could
have chosen any man more capable
of keeping his very large *heterogeneous*
force together."—Winston Churchill.

**hi a′tus** (hī āy′tŭs). A gap or break
where some part is missing.—"Apparently there is a *hiatus* in the stat-
utes."—John H. Bright.

**his tri on′ics** (his tri on′iks). Dramatic
representation; theatrical effects;
stage or actors' display.—"It is a
story of family life, entirely free from
*histrionics*, and full of unostentatious
courage."—Amy Loveman.

**hol′o caust** (hol′ō kawst). Wholesale
destruction by fire and sword.—
"Our constitutional system was set up
to protect us from the very *holocaust*
we now face."—Harrison E. Spangler.

**ho mol′o gous** (hō mol′ō gŭs). Corresponding in structure and properties;
having a relative value or proportion.
—"The analogies may not hold when
other *homologous* series of drugs are
compared."—H. Hurst.

**hor′ta to″ry** (hor′tuh tō″ri). Given to
warning and exhorting; always advising and admonishing; making use
of powerful arguments to incite or
convince.—"I find him joyous and
romantic, as unlike as possible to the
*hortatory* personage he is commonly
supposed to have been."—L. P.
Jacks.

**id″i o syn′cra sies** (id″i ō sing′kruh siz).
Peculiarities; eccentricities.—"The
expense to business of complying with
the *idiosyncrasies* of the taxing jurisdic-
tions is very heavy."—Mark Graves.

**im bro′glio** (im brōle′yō). A troublesome complication of affairs; a difficult situation; a perplexing misunderstanding; a serious state of affairs.
—"In the Italo-Ethiopian *imbroglio*,
the first sanction invoked was a refusal of international broadcasting
privileges to Italy."—Levering Tyson.

**im″mo la′tion** (im″ō lā′shŭn). Sacrifice; offering up as victims.—"When
republics encounter set-backs, those
in power are marked for *immolation*."
—George W. Maxey.

**im pec′ca ble** (im pek′uh b'l). Not capable of doing wrong; faultless; sinless; free from error.—"We think of
Ingres whose technique in pencil was
*impeccable*."—Adrian Bury.

**im″pe cu′ni ous** (im″pē kū′ni ŭs). Habitually poor; having no money;
without funds.—"He was the *impecunious* younger son of an English Mar-
quess."—Edith Wharton.

**im pinged′** (im pinje'd′). Came into
close contact; encroached; infringed.
—"He had no communion with the
omnipotent God, and his creed rarely
*impinged* on his daily experience."—
John Buchan.

**im pon′der a bles** (im pon′dur uh b'lz).
Things incapable of being weighed or
estimated.—"The chief obstacles are
a couple of *imponderables*, British
pride and Indian suspicions."—William Philip Simms.

**in au′gu ral** (in aw′gū răl). An address by a person when he is formally
inducted into office; hence, an initial
performance; a first public appearance.—"It is unfair to judge her acting on one play, but her *inaugural*

is far from auspicious."—Howard Barnes.

**in car″cer a′tion** (in kahr″sur āy′shŭn). Imprisonment; detainment as a prisoner.—"I dealt with the economic and social situations in an article, and that was the cause of my *incarceration*."—James R. Young.

**in cho′ate** (in kō′it). Existing in an elementary stage; imperfectly developed; rudimentary.—"Imagine a world populated only by totalitarian communities producing from its *inchoate* mass a Moses or a Plato."—Nicholas Murray Butler.

**in′ci dence** (in′sĭ dĕnce). The range of influence; the extent of occurrence; the contact with; the direction of the fall.—"Despite their poverty and the high *incidence* of disease, the population has increased."—Albert A. Brandt.

**in cog′ni to** (in kog′ni tō). Unknown; under an assumed name; disguised. —"The Calif went *incognito* among the people."—Dorothy Thompson.

**in′cre ment** (in′krē mĕnt). Enlargement; increase; additions.—"The snow-ball of socialization on a national scale once started, gathers *increment*, and may easily get out of hand."—E. W. Palmer.

**in′cu bus** (in′kū bŭs). Anything that tends to weigh down or discourage; a nightmare.—"When he rids himself of the *incubus* of partisan politics his position will be augmented and he will be free."—Harrison E. Spangler.

**in″cul ca′tion** (in″kul kā′shŭn). A deep impression made on the mind by frequent repetitions.—"In science is the '*inculcation* of the veracity of thought' in a world sodden with intellectual dishonesty."—Herbert Hoover.

**in′di ces** (in′dĭ seez). Signs; indications; manifestations.—"The increasing demands upon physicians and the increasing financial embarrassment of voluntary hospitals are *indices* which cannot be ignored."—Nathan B. Van Etten.

**in″e luc′ta ble** (in″ē luk′tuh b'l). Irresistible; impossible to struggle against; not to be escaped; inevitable. —"That is the hard, *ineluctable* fact."—Samuel Hoare.

**in ept′ness** (in ept′ness). Unsuitability; inappropriateness.—"He complained bitterly about the *ineptness* and short-sightedness in the kind of planes being designed."—Alexander P. de Seversky.

**in eq′ui ties** (in ek′wĭ tiz). Injustices; unfair acts; want of fairness or equity.—"We must expect some *inequities* in Government rulings."—Ralph Starr Butler.

**in im′i cal** (in im′i kăl). Unfriendly; hostile; antagonistic.—"He was conscious of the strangeness of this cache in the snow, this midwinter refuge in a world *inimical* to man."—John Buchan.

**in noc′u ous** (i nok′ū ŭs). Having no harmful qualities; harmless; that can produce no ill effects.—"We contribute nothing save grudging lip service, and not much of that beyond a few *innocuous* platitudes."—James Rowland Angell.

**in nom′i nate** (in nom′ĭ nāte). Having no name; without names; of whom the names cannot be traced or verified.—"There are always many *innominate* dead heroes in every war." —Henry J. Powers.

**in″nu en′do** (in″ū en′dō). A suggestion or hint about a person or thing; an insinuation, usually derogatory.— "By sarcasm, *innuendo*, and direct misstatements he tries to prove that the council is not honest."—Walter Hoving.

**in quis′i tors** (in kwiz′ĭ turz). Officers of the law whose duty it is to investigate.—"They are subject to seizure by spies and *inquisitors* who haunt the land."—Herbert Hoover.

**in sem′i nat″ed** (in sem′ĭ nāte″id). Impregnated; sowed seed in; implanted. —"That small, well-organized cell of radicals *inseminated* the army with sedition."—Emory L. Fielding.

**in′te gral** (in′tē grăl). Essential to the completeness of the whole; necessary; intrinsic.—"There has been constant effort to maintain and improve the stature and dignity of the industry in which our members are an *integral* part."—W. Ray Bell.

**in″te gra′tion** (in″te grā′shŭn). The bringing together of parts into a whole; unification.—"*Integration* of British-American industry now seems pretty well along."—James S. Knowlson.

**in tel"li gent'si a** (in tel"ĭ jĕnt'si uh). The educated and intelligent classes as distinguished from the ignorant.— "We should discriminate between the flair for freedom and the disease of egocentric social insufficiency that afflicts the so-called *intelligentsia.*"— W. J. Cameron.

**in'ter im** (in'tur im). Between periods or events; intermediate; occurring during an interval.—"I bring you an *interim* report from July up to date." —Frank Knox.

**in ter"po la'tions** (in tur"pō lā'shŭnz). Unauthorized matter inserted in a score or text; new parts interposed; alterations by putting in new parts.— "The score is given a variety of *interpolations* by the singers and instrumentalists."—Howard Barnes.

**in ter'stic es** (in tur'sti sez). Chinks; crevices; cracks; crannies; narrow spaces or openings.—"The rotifers come out of the *interstices* and ascend with the pure water."—Frank J. Meyers.

**in tran'si gent** (in tran'si jĕnt). Irreconcilable; refusing to agree or compromise.—"They are an *intransigent* people."—Madame Chiang Kai-shek.

**in vi'o late** (in vī'ō lāte). Pure; unprofaned; unbroken; uninjured.—"We hope to keep *inviolate* the sacred concepts of liberty and democracy we cherish."—Henry A. Wallace.

**ir"i des'cent** (ir"ĭ dess'ĕnt). Having a many-colored appearance, like a rainbow; of changing colors.—"As an *iridescent* dream communism ranks high, but as a working society it has never reached even class B."— George Barton Cutten.

**jal"ou"sied'** (zhal"ōō"zeed'). Enclosed by Venetian blinds; covered by horizontal sloping slats, forming a kind of shutter to admit light and air and prevent anyone from seeing in.— "The *jalousied* windows were invariably on the second story."—C. Wellington Furlong.

**je june'** (jē jōōn'). Insipid; lacking interest; lifeless; dry and dull; unsatisfying.—"He borrowed the devices and mannerisms of the rather *jejune* sagas of a Swedish poet."—Ludwig Lewisohn.

**jet'ti soned** (jet'ĭ sŭnd). Thrown overboard; discarded or thrown away.— "We see Democracy *jettisoned* in a feverish quest of national security."— James P. Warburg.

**jux"ta po si'tion** (juks"tuh pō zish'ŭn). A placing close together or side by side.—"With a turn of a phrase or a *juxtaposition* of characters, she carries you below the surface to pearls of understanding."—Dorothy Canfield Fisher.

**ku'dos** (kū'doss). Renown; fame; glory; reputation.—"She hoped to become a nationally known figure, with all that meant in the way of cash and *kudos.*"—Don Marquis.

**lab"y rin'thine** (lab"ĭ rin'thin). Like a maze of intricate paths; having a confused network of passages; winding and twisting.—"A section of an ant nest reveals rows upon rows of *labyrinthine* chambers."—Theodore Kazimiroff.

**lach'ry mose** (lak'ri mōce). Tearful; given to weeping; sorrowful.—"We sometimes get too *lachrymose* on the one hand and too callous on the other."—John Chamberlain.

**lam'bent** (lam'bĕnt). Shining with soft radiance; flickering; gliding; moving with a soft, bright light.—"The gray was dissolving on the horizon, and outspread *lambent* fingers reached up into the dome from beyond a dazzling mountain."—Lloyd C. Douglas.

**lar'gesse** (lahr'jess). Gift; liberality; bounty.—"Do they realize that the *largesse* they seek must come from taxes or mortgages?"—John W. Davis.

**las'si tude** (lass'ĭ tūde). Weariness; languor; disinclination to work.— "*Lassitude*, irritability, a clinging tiredness in the mornings, these are some of the obvious signs that America needs more sleep."—Donald A. Laird.

**li ai'son** (lē āy'zŭn). Pertaining to unity of action between distant parties or companies; connecting.—"The

American Bankers Association is the coordinating and *liaison* agency in these matters."—W. L. Hemingway.

**li bi'do** (li bī'dō). Sexual desire; emotional craving; lust; a primal urge.— "When you think of Hollywood, you think of false eyelashes, *libido* by the bushel and claptrap by the ton."— Sidney Carroll.

**lit"e ra'ti** (lit"ĕ rāy'tī). Men of letters; scholars.—"It may be that *literati* who have dwelt in safe places will still be able to speak of revolution."— George N. Shuster.

**lo gis'tic** (lō jiss'tik). Pertaining to the details of moving and supplying forces engaged in battle.—"The next series of moves will call for major *logistic* effort."—John W. Greenslade.

**lu bric'i ty** (lū briss'ĭ ti). Slipperiness; hence, lasciviousness; lewdness; immodesty; indecency.—"The easy *lubricity* of her attitude was that of one of Rubens' vivid jades."—Don Marquis.

**mac'ro cosm** (mak'rō koz'm). The great world; the universe; any great whole; the whole of any department of knowledge related to man.—"There is an ancient saying, 'As the *macrocosm* so the microcosm,' as the great so the small."—Georgiana Tree West.

**mal fea'sance** (mal fee'zănce). Unlawful or wrongful action; wrong-doing; misconduct.—"Crime in the aggregate cannot exist without either *malfeasance* or nonfeasance in office."— J. Edgar Hoover.

**mal o'dor ous** (mal ō'dur ŭs). Having a very bad smell; obnoxious; ill-smelling; evil-smelling.—"The little flat was hot and stuffy, and from the road beat up a *malodorous* sultriness." —W. Somerset Maugham.

**man'sue tude** (man'swē tūde). Mildness; meekness; docility; tameness.— "When you consider their savage origin, the behavior of the islanders showed great *mansuetude*."—Ainslee Mockridge.

**ma rooned'** (muh rōōn'd'). In a state of helpless isolation; ashore on a desolate island or coast; left in an isolated spot like fugitive slaves who were called cimarron, wild, by the Spaniards.—"When *marooned* he lived for three months on nothing but sea grass and seals."—W. Langdon Kihn.

**mar'plot"** (mahr'plot"). A person who spoils or frustrates some plot or plan, by meddling or interfering.—"To save his pride, he charges some mythical *marplot* with destroying his work."—W. J. Cameron.

**ma"tri ar'chal** (mā"tri ahrk'ăl). Pertaining to a woman who is the mother and the ruler of her family and tribe; of a mother who is the head of the family and from whom all descendants are traced.—"The earliest of these family groups appear to have traced their relationship through the mother, and the society was a *matriarchal* one."—O. R. McGuire.

**mem"o ra bil'i a** (mem"ō ruh bil'i uh). Important things that should not be forgotten; things worthy of record; hence, the record of memorable things.—"Liquor, expense accounts, and shortage of cash are three important factors in this man's *memorabilia*."—Stanley Walker.

**men'di cant** (men'dĭ kănt). Practicing beggary; begging.—"The spectacle of *mendicant* governors and mayors marching on Washington for a share of the Federal alms, is deeply humiliating."—John W. Davis

**me phit'ic** (mē fit'ik). Noxious; due to a bad smell or stench; hence, of bad odor; poisonous.—"I shall never go to Delphi and ask advice of a woman dressed up as a priestess and sitting on *mephitic* vapors until her brain is poisoned."—Gertrude Atherton.

**mer cu'ri al** (mur kū'ri ăl). Resembling the god Mercury or the metal; hence, lively; volatile; clever; skilful. —"Of all the so-called learned professions, that of medicine is most *mercurial*."—Iago Galdston.

**mer"e tri'cious** (mer"ē trish'ŭs). Tawdry; artificially attractive; having false charms.—"I had written one *meretricious* full-length novel."—Noel Coward.

**met"a mor'pho ses** (met"uh mor'fō-seez). Transformations in character or circumstances; changes in character.—"The most fascinating thing in life is to watch the *metamorphoses* continually occurring in many of our more delightful personalities."—Elsa Maxwell.

**mi as′mic** (mī az′mik). Containing poisonous fumes or vapors.—"The critics fell victims to a strange malady which threw a *miasmic* fog of doubt over the minds of men."—Robert Gordon Sproul.

**mi′cro cosm** (mī krō koz′m). A little world; the world on a small scale; hence, a miniature reproduction or representation.—"The little island of Bermuda reveals in *microcosm* many of the economic and social problems of our day."—Frederick Lewis Allen.

**min′a to″ry** (min′uh tō″ri). Menacing; portending punishment or detruction; threatening.—"The nations faced one another as before, each pointing a *minatory* finger at one of its neighbors."—L. P. Jacks.

**mil′i tate** (mil′ĭ tāte). Have weight; have much influence or effect; operate.—"It seems hardly probable that they would *militate* against any possible favors by such uncivilized methods."—Harlowe R. Hoyt.

**mime** (mīme). To make fun of by imitating; to mimic; to ridicule by imitating.—"She had even gone so far as to *mime* for her sister (who was no mimic) the lady looking shocked at an untidy stocking."—Edith Wharton.

**mne mon′ic** (nē mon′ik). An aid to memory; something that is designed to assist memory; a system to improve memory.—"A *mnemonic* is a little trick that aids memory."—Norman Lewis.

**mod′i cum** (mod′ĭ kŭm). A moderate amount; a little; a small quantity.— "A *modicum* of good will would bring about our understanding."—William Philip Simms.

**moi′e ty** (moy′ĕ ti). A half; a small portion; a part.—"Even the Magna Charta referred to a *moiety* of the inhabitants, as it affected freemen only."—Edward F. McGrady.

**mon′i to″ry** (mon′ĭ tō″ri). Warning; admonishing; reminding; conveying notice of possible danger.—"The re-

former received a series of *monitory* letters."—Donald G. Cooley.

**mor′i bund** (mor′ĭ bŭnd). Dying; at its last gasp; in a dying condition.— "It would be possible for the promoters to take over an obscure or *moribund* organization."—Thomas E. Dewey.

**mulct** (mulkt). Punish by a fine; hence, penalize or deprive, often in a deceitful way.—"Quacks still confuse, *mulct*, and injure the public."—Edward L. Bernays.

**myr′mi dons** (mur′mi donz). Followers or underlings of desperate character who carry out the commands of their master without question or scruple.—"The glorious Greeks chased his *myrmidons* out of their country."— Irving T. McDonald.

**nec′ro man″cers** (nek′rō man″surz). Those who practice magic or divination by means of pretended communication with the dead; sorcerers; those who consult portents.—"They will fight to the last ditch rather than suffer defeat by a race of *necromancers*."—H. A. Burgers.

**ne′o phyte** (nee′ō fīte). A recent convert; hence, a novice or beginner.— "Being a *neophyte* in the realm of refrigeration engineering, and not knowing any better, I continued."— Willard L. Morrison.

**nes′ci ence** (nesh′i ĕnce). Absence of knowledge; complete ignorance; a state of not knowing or lack of knowledge.—"Certainly the hermetic air of that chamber gave him more complete *nescience* than anyone else."—Christopher Morley.

**nex′us** (nek′sŭs). A bond or tie between the several members of a group of series; a link or connection. —"Poverty, health, and relationship enter into the casual *nexus* which results in crime."—Paul V. McNutt.

**nim′bus** (nim′bŭs). A halo or circle of light around the heads of divinities; hence, a bright cloud of romance about a person.—"He was upon the scene in a *nimbus* of expectation."— H. G. Wells.

**norms** (normz). Rules or authoritative standards; patterns; models.— "These moral judgments never took into account whether the acts violated those *norms* dictated by the Eternal Judge."—Pius XII.

**nu'ga to"ry** (nū'guh tō"ri). Of no power or meaning; worthless; insignificant; vain; ineffectual; useless.— "All his objections were *nugatory*."— Emmet Holloway.

**ob"fus ca'tion** (ob"fuss kā'shŭn). Obscurity; darkness caused by confusion; perplexity; bewilderment; lack of clarity.—"The vision as transcribed on the canvas is incoherent, and the same *obfuscation* marks some of his other pictures."—Royal Cortissoz.

**ob"jur ga'tions** (ob"jur gā'shŭnz). Severe rebukes; scoldings; chidings.— "There has never been a close decision in a heated game without *objurgations* on the judge."—Hugh S. Johnson.

**ob"so les'cence** (ob"sō less'ĕnce). Discontinuance of use; disuse or discard because out of date; an antiquated and useless state.—"The types used in former years are now approaching *obsolescence*."—Drew Middleton.

**ob tund'ed** (ob tund'ed). Deadened; blunted; dulled.—"The intellects of the poor are often *obtunded* by worry and privation."—Charles Henry Crozier.

**ob'verse** (ob'vurse). The side facing the observer; the side turned toward one, as the side of a coin which bears the principal design; the front or chief surface; the opposite of the back side or reverse.—"England has been like a coin with an *obverse* and reverse."—H. G. Wells.

**oc clu'sion** (ŏ kloo'zhŭn). Stoppage; obstruction; a closing up of a passage.—"The baby swallowed a coin and nearly died of intestinal *occlusion*."—Axel Munthe.

**o'nus** (ō'nŭs). The burden; the responsibility; the duty.—"The *onus* is on our shoulders for protecting the settlements."—James R. Young.

**op pro'bri ous** (ŏ prō'bri ŭs). Odious; shameful; disgraceful; reproachful.— "The word 'tip' as used in horse-racing assumes an *opprobrious* character."—Peter Schmuck.

**or'dure** (or'dūre). Excrement; dung; waste matter from the bowels of animals or birds.—"The accumulation of *ordure* in a small nest might prove fatal to the young."—Alan Devoe.

**o"ri en ta'tion** (ō"ri en tā'shŭn). Determination of a position which has a certain relation to other people or places.—"Canadians have no tendency to seek a new *orientation* for their loyalties."—George A. Drew.

**os"cu la'tion** (oss"kū lā'shŭn). Kissing; salutation with a kiss.—"*Osculation* is the ancient Slav custom of Eastertide."—Albert Perry.

**o'ti ose** (ō'shi ōce). Indolent; hence, futile; useless.—"This refreshing writing stripped speech of the *otiose* and the equivocal and sought to limit expression to that of fact and sensation."—Ludwig Lewisohn.

**pab'u lum** (pab'ū lŭm). Nourishment; aliment; food; especially anything supplying mental nutriment.—"The mind, in order to endure, requires that it be fed a *pabulum* of sense."— Homer W. Smith.

**pal'li a"tive** (pal'i āy"tiv). An agent to reduce the severity; mitigation; alleviation without cure; a means to make less serious.—"Tobacco as the *palliative* and cure-all of human suffering forms a topic of curious interest."—Lawrence C. Wroth.

**pan'o ply** (pan'ō pli). The complete equipment of a warrior; full armor. —"As we gird on the *panoply* of war, it is our duty to renew our allegiance to American ideals."—H. W. Prentis, Jr.

**par"a sit'ic** (par"uh sit'ik). Like a hanger-on or sycophant; toadying; living on someone else at his expense. —"He gathered about him *parasitic* adherents of impeccable dullness."— H. G. Wells.

**par'si mo"ny** (pahr'sĭ mō"ni). Stinginess; niggardliness; scantiness.—"In his bombastic utterances he reveals a strange *parsimony* in regard to facts." —George Barton Cutten.

**pat'i na** (pat'i nuh). A film or kind of rust on old metals which is peculiar to antiques; hence, a softening on the surface; an outward appearance of mellowing.—"Social life and a disingenuous *patina* upon behaviour were reappearing in the world."—H. G. Wells.

**pau'ci ty** (paw'sĭ ti). Smallness of number; fewness; dearth.—"If I appear critical of the *paucity* of results, I do not wish to be unfair in my appraisal."—Lewis H. Brown.

**pe cu'ni ar"y** (pē kū'ni er"ĭ). Consisting of money; monetary; financial.—"The greed of individuals who try to secure *pecuniary* gain out of war is truly despicable."—James Cannon.

**pe dan'tic** (pē dan'tik). Making a needless display of learning; learned in a tedious or very dull way.—"The same *pedantic* character presents itself in the case of a number of men."—Winston Churchill.

**pe num'brae** (pē num'brē). The margins of a shadow seen in an eclipse; shaded regions between the deep shadow and the light.—"He said the surrounding *penumbrae* of the sunspots represented shoals or sand banks."—William H. Barton, Jr.

**per am"bu la'tions** (pur am"bū lā'-shŭnz). Walks through or around; walks taken to inspect or examine; walks or strolls about a district.—"Grandfather continued his *perambulations*."—Elizabeth Goudge.

**per cep'tion** (pur sep'shŭn). Knowledge obtained through the senses; awareness of persons or things; observation; the act or process of perceiving or apprehending; understanding or intuition.—"The book is written with verve and extraordinary *perception*."—Clifton Fadiman.

**per cip'i ent** (pur sip'i ĕnt). Capable of perceiving clearly and quickly; keenly perceptive and understanding; discerningly alert.—"I find it humiliating to observe that Russia has been much more *percipient* about vital European social and political forces than we have."—Dorothy Thompson.

**per fect'i ble** (pur fek'tĭ b'l). Capable of being perfected; capable of becoming perfect; that can be made complete, exact, perfect.—"The rocket plane can be said to be a *perfectible* invention."—Bradwell E. Tanis.

**per"i pa tet'ic** (per"i puh tet'ik). Mov-

ing from place to place; walking around; wandering; itinerant; traveling.—"His tail, in these *peripatetic* instances, would be used like an aerial."—Victor Wolfgang von Hagen.

**per"spi ca'cious** (pur"spi kā'shŭs). Possessing acute discernment; keen in sight; astute; having mental penetration.—" For a little one,' he said, 'you're too *perspicacious* to live.'"—Elizabeth Goudge.

**phan tas"ma go'ri a** (fan taz"muh gō'-ri uh). A changing series of things seen or imagined; a shifting scene of figures increasing and diminishing in size.—"Our great national dream of a better life for every family is not a political *phantasmagoria*."—W. J. Cameron.

**pic"a yune'** (pik"uh yōōn'). Of trifling value; petty; small.—"These greeds are *picayune* and harmless."—George Barton Cutten.

**plan'gent** (plan'jĕnt). Resounding like tolling bells; vibrating; reverberating like dashing waves; plaintive; moaning.—"This pagan poet is among the most sorrowful, the most *plangent* of all poets."—Ludwig Lewisohn.

**plen'i tude** (plen'ĭ tūde). Abundance; a plentiful amount; a completeness; a full supply.—"There had been a *plenitude* of metal music interspersed with Greek choruses."—Lloyd C. Douglas.

**pleth'o ra** (pleth'ō ruh: 'th' as in 'thin'). Superabundance; excess; excessive supply; oversupply.—"The unnaturally low rates on government securities were due to a *plethora* of funds arising from huge gold imports."—W. H. Schubart.

**po lem'ic** (pō lem'ik). Controversial argument; disputing discussion; aggressive dispute.—"The reader will find little of controversy and nothing of *polemic* in the book."—George N. Shuster.

**prag mat'ic** (prag mat'ik). Pertaining to the accomplishment of duty; philosophical; dealing with cause and effects; relating to civil affairs.—"I want youth to have practical *pragmatic* confidence in life."—Robert H. Jackson.

**pred'i cat"ed** (pred'ĭ kāte"id). Stated as belonging to something; asserted or affirmed as ascribable; founded or based.—"This readiness for sacrifice is *predicated* on their faith in the Emperor's divinity."—Warren J. Clear.

**pre"di lec'tions** (prē"di lek'shŭnz). Preferences; favorable predispositions; inclinations.—"The majority are reading into the Constitution their own personal economic *predilections*."—Harlan F. Stone.

**pref'a to"ry** (pref'uh tō"ri). Preliminary; introductory; like a preface or something preparatory.—"If our two forces succeeded in meeting, the *prefatory* havoc would be a great blow in itself."—John Myers Myers.

**pre var"i ca'tions** (prē var"ĭ kā'shŭnz). Misrepresentations; misleading statements; deviations from truth.— "They described as matters of common knowledge about business what are unblushing *prevarications*."— Thomas W. Lamont.

**pri mor'di al** (prī mor'di ăl). Primitive; of the earliest times; elemental; simple.—"In villages in Russia there are still *primordial* human joys."— Winston Churchill.

**priv'y** (priv'i). Secretly aware; participating with others in some hidden or private knowledge of something.—"I am one who does not profess to be *privy* to the intentions of posterity."— Alexander Woollcott.

**pro cliv'i ties** (prō kliv'ĭ tiz). Inclinations; propensities; tendencies; natural dispositions toward.—"He showed his familiar *proclivities* for looting."—John Cournos.

**Pro crus'te an** (prō kruss'tē ăn). Like the fabulous robber, Procrustes, who fitted his victims to a bed by stretching or mutilating them; hence, that ruthlessly and inflexibly forces someone or something to conform to an idea or system.—"The dictator, in his *Procrustean* way, tries to force all minds into his mould."—Emory L. Fielding.

**prog nos'ti cate** (prog noss'tĭ kāte). Foretell by indications; prophesy; predict from present signs.—"Women must take stock of their past, evaluate their present, and *prognosticate* their future."—Fannie Hurst.

**pro"le tar'i at** (prō"lē tair'ĭ ăt). The lower classes; wage-workers; workingmen.—"The dictatorship of the *proletariat* may mean in theory the rule of the workers."—John Haynes Holmes.

**pro pin'qui ty** (pro ping'kwĭ ti). Nearness in time or place; kinship.—"We have developed a national neighbourliness, not just the neighbourliness of *propinquity*."—Patricia Strauss.

**pro po'nents** (prō pō'nĕnts). Those who put forward propositions to be considered; advocates; proposers.— "I challenge the *proponents* of this startling scheme."—Carter Glass.

**pro tag'o nist** (prō tag'ŏ nist). The actor who played the chief part in a Greek drama; hence, an important performer or leader.—"Rachmaninoff was the incomparable *protagonist* of his own work."—Hans Kindler.

**pro'to types** (prō'tō tīpes). Primitive forms; original models; ideals.— "Maybe there are persons amongst us who would prefer to fight only with *prototypes* of American democracy."—Dorothy Thompson.

**pseu'do** (sū'dō). Sham; spurious; having a deceptive or false resemblance to the real thing.—"It was a circle of *pseudo* men of letters, where people dissected each other and remarks were quick on the wing."—André Maurois.

**pul'chri tude** (pul'krĭ tūde). Beauty; physical charm; loveliness.—"The modern eye is surfeited with *pulchritude* in Hollywood."—Fritz Busch.

**pu'ni tive** (pū'nĭ tiv). Inflicting punishment; tending to punish.—"If through unwise taxation or *punitive* legislation these productive facilities are impaired, the owners of the enterprises will not be the only sufferers." —M. S. Rukeyser.

**pur'view** (pur'vū). The extent, sphere, or scope of anything; the compass of sight; the scope of understanding.— "Every symptom of bad utilization is within the *purview* of the Bureau of Labor Utilization."—Paul V. McNutt.

**pu"sil lan'i mous ly** (pū"sĭ lan'ĭ mŭs li). In a cowardly way; faint-heartedly; timidly.—"Under no condition will we *pusillanimously* cry for peace at any price."—C. H. Woodward.

**pu'ta tive** (pū'tuh tiv). Supposed; reported to be; said to be; reputed; commonly thought of as.—"The enthusiastic co-operation of the *putative* Mrs. Johnson had greatly encouraged her triply banned husband."—Hervey Allen.

**ram"i fi ca'tion** (ram"ĭ fi kā'shŭn). A branching; hence, an outgrowth; an offshoot; a consequence.—"Another *ramification* of a governmentally priced economy is that equality of all citizens cannot exist."—Winthrop W. Aldrich.

**ram'i fy ing** (ram'ĭ fī ing). Dividing and subdividing into branch-like parts; spreading out into branches or outgrowths.—"This *ramifying* group was extending its tentacles to associate itself with revolutionary activity."—H. G. Wells.

**ra"ti oc'i na'tion** (rash"ĭ oss"ĭ nā'-shŭn). Reasoning; argument; the process of reasoning; the use of syllogisms; deduction of conclusions from statements assumed to be true. —"From these tales of imaginative science and the tales of *ratiocination* he derived his widest influence."— Ludwig Lewisohn.

**ra"tion al'e** (rash"ŭn ah'lē). A sensible, reasoning exposition of principles; underlying reasons; the logical basis of a fact.—"The newly educated western men no longer possess the *rationale* or the deposited wisdom which are the genius of the development of western civilization."— Walter Lippmann.

**re cant'ed** (rē kant'ed). Withdrew an opinion formerly maintained; disavowed a former belief; retracted or renounced a former opinion.— "Three times the Senate voted to forbid price roll-backs before it finally *recanted* by a single vote."—William L. Green.

**re"cep tiv'i ty** (re"sep tiv'ĭ ti). The state or quality of readiness to accept and receive; ability to admit and receive.—"The secret of deeper living is aloneness with God, *receptivity*, and inspired action."—William R. Robbins.

**re cid'i vists** (rē sid'ĭ vists). Confirmed criminals; those who relapse into crime again after having been freed from imprisonment.—"There was no well-defined tendency on the part of the courts to give heavier sentences to *recidivists* than to first offenders."— Paul V. McNutt.

**re"cru des'cence** (rē"krōō dess'ĕnce). A reappearance; a return; a renewing activity.—"The *recrudescence* of noblesse oblige is the chief reliance of our hopes."—Mark M. Jones.

**red'o lent** (red'ō lĕnt). Full of or diffusing a pleasant fragrance; hence, impregnated with; suggestive of the atmosphere.—"Our Chinese democracy will be *redolent* of our soil and expressive of the native genius of our people."—Madame Chiang Kaishek.

**re dound'** (rē dound': 'ou' as in 'out'). Come back as a result; make a great contribution to; accrue; conduce; have an effect, as by reaction.—"The incredible bravery of the British will *redound* to their credit."—Jack Bond.

**re gur'gi tat"ed** (rē gur'ji tāte"id). Threw up, as undigested food.— "Regularly after every bottle feeding, she *regurgitated*."—Samuel Z. Orgel.

**re ju"ve nes'cent** (rē jōō"vē ness'ent). Becoming young; renewing youthful qualities; becoming reinvigorated.— "The Party will go ahead. It is free; it is *rejuvenescent*."—H. G. Wells.

**re nas'cence** (rē nass'ĕnce). Renewal; revival; new birth; recuperation.— "When I am alone, this is my plan for *renascence*: I read Shakespeare— any play."—Franklin P. Adams.

**re quite'** (rē kwīte'). Make return for; pay back; recompense; repay.— "The wicked *requite* evil with evil."— Douglas E. Lurton.

**re sur'gence** (rē sur'jĕnce). A rising again; a revival; restoration to activity and vigor.—"I have not in mind a fresh *resurgence* of mysticism."— James Rowland Angell.

**ret"ro gres'sion** (ret"rō gresh'ŭn). Degeneration; deterioration; a backward movement; a decline.—"To safeguard ourselves against *retrogression* into another dark age is the

greatest task now confronting us."—
Madame Chiang Kai-shek.

**ris″i bil′i ty** (riz″ĭ bil′ĭ ti). A tendency
to laugh; a disposition to laughter;
a sense of what is ridiculous or laughable.—"They can wear these large
size slacks without arousing *risibility*
when they turn their backs."—Edith
Stern.

**rod″o mon tade′** (rod″ō mon tāde′).
Boastful bragging; bluster; vainglorious boasting.—"He addressed
himself to his guest with a torrent of *rodomontade*."—W. Somerset
Maugham.

**ru′bi cund** (rōō′bi kund). Reddish;
ruddy; high-colored; inclined to
redness.—"The face of this parish
priest was round and *rubicund*."—
S. L. Scanlon.

**ru″mi na′tions** (rōō″mĭ nā′shŭnz).
Continuous chewings of cud; hence,
meditations, quiet reflections; repeated considerations.—"What keeps
a naturalist everlastingly writing
about his observations and *rumina-
tions?*"—Alan Devoe.

**sac′ro sanct** (sak′rō sangkt). Sacred;
holy; peculiarly set apart or consecrated; inviolable.—"Military men
are no more *sacrosanct* than anybody
else, and the application of the force
of public opinion to them is just as
valuable as it is to others."—Wendell
L. Willkie.

**sa′pi ent ly** (sāy′pi ĕnt li). Wisely; in a
discerning or shrewd way; often used
ironically, as in an aping or artificially wise way.—"She *sapiently* explains that she refused to be carried
away by the revival of Southern
fiction."—Carl Van Vechten.

**sa ti′e ty** (suh tī′ĕ ti). A feeling of having had rather too much of some-
thing; a state of disgust caused by an
oversupply; a feeling of being fed up.
—"What has caused this sudden
*satiety* with success?"—John Buchan.

**sat′ur nine** (sat′ur nīne). Born under
the melancholy planet Saturn; hence,
gloomy; heavy; morose; grave; dull;
sullen.—" 'They come very young
these days,' he observed to the
*saturnine* editor."—Emma Bugbee.

**sed′u lous ly** (sed′ū lŭs li). Busily; un-
tiringly; industriously; assiduously;

unrelentingly; perseveringly.—"Our
enemies have *sedulously* propagated
these misapprehensions."—Carlton
J. H. Hayes.

**seis′mic** (sīze′mik). Produced by earthquakes; pertaining to earthquakes.—
"One or two sea waves of *seismic* origin had swept in along the coast."—
Roland T. Bird.

**se nes′cence** (sē ness′ĕnce). Old age;
the process of growing old; aging.—
"Natural death is the result of *senes-
cence*, of the wearing out of tissue and
organs."—Alexis Carrel.

**se qua′cious** (sē kwā′shŭs). Following
opinion in a servile way; void of independent action or judgment; compliant in a menial way; disposed to
follow.—"The slavish assistant had a
*sequacious* zeal for saying 'yes' to the
boss."—Charles Henry Crozier.

**ses′a me** (sess′uh mē). A magic word
used to gain entrance (in the Arabian
Nights stories); a password for admission.—"He seemed to see the confusion crystallizing under the spell of
a magic word. What was it, that
missing *sesame?*"—H. G. Wells.

**si′ne cure** (sī′nē kūre). A paid position
which involves few or no duties; a
very easy job; an office or position
that requires very little work and yet
is well paid.—"Maybe I don't mean
cynosure, I mean *sinecure*."—Christopher Morley.

**som′no lence** (som′nō lĕnce). Great
drowsiness; oppressive sleepiness.—
"She has lost her excess weight,
weariness, and *somnolence*."—Charles
H. Goodrich.

**so″po rif′ic** (sō″pō rif′ik). Tending to
produce sleep; causing sleep; sleepy;
lethargic.—"I don't think the slightly
*soporific* quality of the comedy was
the fault of the players."—Burton
Rascoe.

**sou′bri quet** (sōō′bri kāy). A nick-
name; a fanciful appellation.—"The
first necessity was to find out if he had
a name other than our frivolous but
convenient field *soubriquet*."—Joce-
lyn Crane.

**spate** (spāte). A heavy rainstorm;
hence, a flood or freshet; a rush of
water; an overflow.—"The usual

home-going stream was in *spate* with Christmas crowds."—Jan Struther.

**spe'cious** (spee'shŭs). Plausible; appearing right, reasonable, or desirable, but not being so; apparently fair.—"The world will not long be lulled by the *specious* fallacy of achieving a temporary and probably an artificial stability in foreign exchange on the part of a few large countries only."—Franklin Delano Roosevelt.

**spo rad'ic** (spō rad'ik). Occurring here and there; happening now and then; in single or scattered instances.—"The friction, the hitches and the local *sporadic* confusion will be aggravated."—Winston Churchill.

**ster'e o typed"** (ster'ē ō tīpe't"). Cast in type metal from a mold; hence, fixed firmly and unalterably; conventional; having no originality.—"Under intense emotional stress the behavior tends to conform to one of the several *stereotyped* patterns."—Edgar Douglas Adrian.

**strep'i tous** (strep'i tŭs). Noisy; boisterous; making a great clamor.—"The *strepitous* sounds of the city's traffic came in through the open window."—Ainslee Mockridge.

**stric'ture** (strik'chŏor). Severe criticism; unfavorable remark; adverse comment; hence, strictness; censure.—"It is a fact that the present Administration can now get around almost every written *stricture* in the Constitution."—Raymond Moley.

**stul"ti fi ca'tion** (stul"tĭ fi kā'shŭn). The act of making a fool of; a dishonoring; a disgracing.—"The conference is a *stultification* of collective bargaining."—John L. Lewis.

**sub serves'** (sŭb survz'). Serves in a subordinate manner; is useful in helping some purpose; ministers to or helps on; serves as a means to some end.—"A leaf obeys a star, a star *subserves* a leaf."—Donald Culross Peattie.

**sub ven'tion** (sub ven'shŭn). Subsidy; grants of money; giving of succor or aid in some form.—"Any system of public *subvention* can exercise an untoward effect upon public morale."—J. J. Spengler.

**su"per er"o ga'tion** (sū"pur er"ō gā'-shŭn). A meritorious act that does more than duty requires; hence, something superfluous and unnecessary.—"She is so dissociated in the public mind with ruffianly behavior as to render the further contents of the footnote a work of *supererogation.*"—Alexander Woollcott.

**su per'nal** (sū pur'năl). Heavenly; celestial; divine; ethereal.—"The light that streams upon the interior is *supernal*, fixing all it touches in a moment of eternity."—Edwin Seaver.

**sup pos"i ti'tious** (sŭ poz"i tish'ŭs). Hypothetical; supposed; assumed; tentatively surmised.—"About half of the *supposititious* two dozen are thought to remain in Louisiana."—Bayard Christy.

**sur cease'** (sur seece'). Cessation; end; stop.—"There is a crying need for public willingness to carry on the battle against crime relentlessly and without *surcease.*"—J. Edgar Hoover.

**sur"rep ti'tious** (sur"ep tish'ŭs). Secret; accomplished by stealth or improper means; clandestine; sly; stealthy.—"Though their eyes were fixed on me, I caught a *surreptitious* glance passing from one to another."—W. Somerset Maugham.

**su sur'rus** (sū sur'ŭs). A whispering sound; a sound of rustling; a low sibilant murmur.—"The *susurrus* of the little girls chewing gum abated noticeably."—Frank Sullivan.

**su'ze rain ty** (sū'zĕ rain ti). Superior and paramount authority; rule.—"Let us review what has resulted from our benevolent *suzerainty.*"—Gordon Heriot.

**syc'o phant** (sik'ō fănt). A servile flatterer; a toady; one who fawns on the wealthy or great to obtain some favor.—"Another *sycophant* moved outward as if to flank a retreat."—Christopher Morley.

**syn'the sis** (sin'thē siss: 'th' as in 'thin'). Combination of separate elements or parts into a new form.—"Culture represents a *synthesis*, a putting together of things."—Owen D. Young.

**tac'tu al** (tak'chŏo ăl). Pertaining to the organs of touch; caused by touch;

perceived by touch or feeling.—
"The things one remembered about
a house were the minute *tactual* in-
timacies, the feel of a door-handle or
the shape of the banister-rails."—
Jan Struther.

tat"ter de mal'ion (tat"ur dē māle'-
yŭn). Ragamuffin; made up of ragged
fellows; of people in rags and tatters.
—"This *tatterdemalion* throng wanted
him to be their king."—Lloyd C.
Douglas.

ten den'tious (ten den'shŭs). Having
an underlying purpose; having a special aim; calculated to help forward a
cause.—"The sayings of Benjamin
Franklin are clipped, direct, *tenden-
tious*."—Donald G. Cooley.

ten'e brous (ten'ē brŭs). Dark; gloomy;
dusky.—"The *tenebrous* shadows of
the jungle brought a mounting fear to
the Negro's heart."—Donald G.
Cooley.

ten u'i ty (ten ū'ĭ ti). Thinness; slen-
derness; slimness.—"I saw a young
man of an exceeding *tenuity* of body."
—James Matthew Barrie.

ten'u ous ness (ten'ū ŭs ness). Insignificance; weakness; flimsiness; lack of
substantiality.—"The confusion and
*tenuousness* of his social attitude is a
product of that country."—Lewis
Gannett.

ter"gi ver sa'tion (tur"ji vur sā'shŭn).
Evasion; conflicting statements;
equivocation; subterfuges; turncoat
or traitorous violations of allegiance;
desertion of a cause or of a party.—
"I have received a long letter full of
*tergiversation* and false reasons."—
L. P. Jacks.

tin"tin nab"u la'tions (tin"ti nab"ū-
lā'shŭnz). Tinkling sounds; ringing
and jingling sounds of bells.—
"Church bells were calling, *tintinnabulations* were rolling in waves over
town and country."—Edwin C. Hill.

trans mute' (trance mūte'). To change
from one form or substance into another; to alter in essence; to transform.—"By realism he means the
attempts by men of letters to find
reality in the life about them, and to
*transmute* that reality into art."—
Irwin Edman.

tu'mid (tū'mid). Swollen; bulging; inflated; distended.—"Her eyes were
inflamed and *tumid* from much crying."—Douglas E. Lurton.

u biq'ui tous (ū bik wĭ tŭs). Seeming
to be everywhere at once; omnipres-
ent; present everywhere.—"The service station had apparently been
overlooked by the *ubiquitous* scouts."
—Robert Gordon Sproul.

unc'tu ous (ungk'choo ŭs). Oily and
persuasive; unduly suave; bland;
smugly emotional; fawningly or hyp-
ocritically polite.—"So many Americans have been fed so much *unctuous*
complacency about our form of government."—Thomas Reed Powell.

un"e quiv'o cal (un"ē kwiv'ō kăl). Distinct; very clear and plain; impossible
to misunderstand or misinterpret;
not ambiguous.—"The achievement
of an orderly, *unequivocal*, and workable body of laws must be part of the
higher civilization towards which we
are striving."—Thomas C. Desmond.

vac'u ous (vak'ū ŭs). Lacking serious
occupation; empty; idle; blank; ex-
pressionless.—"Unless this be a Conference in more than name only, this
gathering will be *vacuous* and futile."
—Mortimer J. Adler.

va gar'y (vuh gair'i). A wild fancy; an
extravagant notion; a caprice.—"We
can hardly blame the public for
preferring some other economic *vagary*."—Edward A. Filene.

val"e dic to'ri an (val"ē dik tō'ri ăn).
The member of a graduating class
who delivers the farewell address:
usually the student whose rank in
scholarship is highest.—"The *valedic-
torian* is sometimes supposed to be
doomed to failure in real life."—
William Trufant Foster.

vap'id (vap'id). Insipid; inane; dull;
without life; spiritless; flat and without spirit or zest.—"You could not
ignore the *vapid* backing on the other
side of the record, but were forced to
play it through."—Jan Struther.

var'i ant (vair'i ănt). Variegated; varying; differing in form; different from
others.—"Darwin found truth and
beauty the same thing among the
*variant* primroses beneath the English
oaks."—Donald Culross Peattie.

**ve′ni al** (vee′ni ăl). Excusable; pardonable; not very wrong; easy to forgive; offending only slightly.—"The meaning of '*venial*' is easy to remember, for a *venial* sin is a 'genial' sin, or one that can be forgiven."—Jack Bond.

**ver′bi age** (vur′bi ij). Wordiness; use of more words than necessary; verbosity.—"Could we reduce the *verbiage* to a point of clarity in the English language?"—Geraldine Farrar.

**ver′dant** (vur′dănt). Green with vegetation; covered with growing plants or grass; green and fresh.—"We saw the *verdant* hills transformed into desolation."—Wallace L. Ware.

**ver″i si mil′i tude** (ver″i si mil′ĭ tūde). Appearance of truth; likelihood; realism; probability.—"For purposes of *verisimilitude* the author has found it necessary to use a good many Anglo-Saxon monosyllables."—Woolcott Gibbs.

**ver tig′i nous** (vur tij′ĭ nŭs). Turning round; whirling; hence, affected by vertigo or whirling; dizzy; giddy.— "Storm driven clouds carried him with *vertiginous* speed through the vastness of the infinite."—Axel Munthe.

**ves tig′i al** (vess tij′i ăl). Containing a vestige or slight trace of; giving a faint impression of; leaving a sign of something lost or no longer existing.— "His finest passages are those in which he speaks in terms of at least *vestigial* rhythm of things and thoughts that are common to the ages."—Ludwig Lewisohn.

**vi′a ble** (vī′uh b′l). Able to grow and develop; capable of living.—"It was a fatal mistake to have failed in the task of building up a *viable* system of political law."—George N. Shuster.

**vi tu′per at″ing** (vī tū′pur āte″ing). Defaming; finding fault abusively; berating severely; abusive; reviling. —"Hundreds of orators have been delivering *vituperating* indictments of the motion pictures."—Alexander Markey.

**vo′lant** (vō′lănt). Characterized by light, quick movements; nimble; light and rapid.—"Every motion of the première danseuse was *volant* and graceful."—Emory L. Fielding.

**zom′bi** (zom′bi). The snake deity of the voodoo rite; a corpse reanimated by a supernatural power.—"The starved Chinaman had the ghastly look of a walking *zombi*."—Tom Pennell.

## ONE-MINUTE REFRESHER

Here are ten definitions of ten difficult words selected from this chapter. In each case the initial letter and the last two letters of the word are given. See whether you can recall them and write them down in the blank spaces.

1. In a cowardly way; faint-heartedly; timidly:

p_____ly.

2. Tending to produce sleep; causing sleep; sleepy:

s_____ic.

3. Sacred; holy; peculiarly set apart or consecrated; inviolable:

s_____ct.

4. Insipid; lifeless; lacking interest; dry and dull:   j___ne.

5. Irreconcilable; refusing to agree or compromise:

i_____nt.

6. A placing close together or side by side:

j_____on.

7. Of doubtful authenticity; spurious; fabulous:

a_____al.

8. A reappearance; a return; a renewing activity:

r_____ce.

9. Very critical years or periods; times of crisis:

c_____cs.

10. Subordinate; auxiliary; secondary:       a_____ry.

*Answers:* 1. pusillanimously   2. soporific   3. sacrosanct   4. jejune   5. intransigent   6. juxtaposition   7. apocryphal   8. recrudescence   9. climaterics   10. ancillary

# CHAPTER XIX

## WHEN YOU SPECULATE ABOUT PLACE, TIME, SIZE, AND SHAPE

THE WORDS that are grouped around place and time and size and shape are naturally not all gathered together in this chapter. Some of these terms more properly belong among words of politics or power or elsewhere, but those that are presented here will give the reader a representative cross-section of this special vocabulary.

Our lives are influenced and circumscribed by atlas, calendar, clock and yard-stick, and whole battalions and divisions of helpful and fascinating words fall into these categories.

When we say that a tribe of South Sea Islanders live on an *atoll* we have given them a "place" on a coral island. Should we speak of an *antiquated* chair we are dealing with "time," for time has made the chair old. A statue that is *stupendous* is marked as to "size" and a bread-roll that is a *crescent* is defined as to "shape."

Words, of course, mean little or nothing unless they have their overalls on, so we will consider a few of these terms in real sentences as they have been used by discriminating persons with practiced skill. First a term that governs size:

"A miracle had happened: a miracle so wide in its *amplitude* that all were caught up in it."—Willa Cather.

Next, four words that deal with different phases of time or with the results of time's processes:

"The youngsters think of us as *superannuated* mummies."—W. J. Cameron.

"He insisted on putting the liberty of the people beyond the reach of *transitory* power."—Claude Bowers.

"Her earlier works seemed as though they might be built for *perpetuity*."—Ludwig Lewisohn.

"His body was showing the first pathetic signs of *decrepitude*." —Donald G. Cooley.

Two further words that express place and geography:

"All the territory our fathers bought and seized is *contiguous*."—Albert J. Beveridge.

"We mentioned a number of oceanic and *littoral* birds."—R. M. Suckley.

And one word that deals with shape:

"There were green forests, a blue, singing stream, and cliffs of *serrated* darkness."—John Buchan.

I believe once more it might be a guide to us in determining the meanings of these interesting words and in assaying their value if we were to turn back the pages of history where possible to their origins.

Our first one, "amplitude," is a word of great dignity and offers us a happy medium with which to express generous size, and it comes directly from the Latin *amplus* meaning "ample."

With "superannuated" the story is different. We have the Latin words *super* (over, beyond) and *annus* (year). So "superannuated" persons or things are those that have gone beyond their years of usefulness and should be retired.

With the word "transitory" we have *trans* for "over" and *ire*, "to go," so things that are "transitory" quickly pass over and do not last. The noun "perpetuity," Latin *per* (through) and *peto* (seek) gives us the phrase "endless search," which leads to its present meaning "a state that continues through unlimited time."

"Decrepitude," a condition caused by time, comes from the Latin *de* (away) and *crepo* (creak) so if you happen to be in a state of "decrepitude" your bones are often creaking or crackling!

In the realm of space we have "contiguous" which in Latin is *con* (together) and *tango* (touch), so the states of our nation that are "contiguous" are those that touch each other.

The Latin word *litoralis* derives from *litus* meaning "shore." "Littoral" birds then are those that inhabit the shores.

And when mountains are "serrated" it means they are "saw-edged" for *serra* is the Latin word for saw.

These words that follow will present an interesting study to you, and will be valuable additions to your vocabulary.

**ab″o rig′i nes** (ab″ō rij′ĭ neez). The original inhabitants of a country.— "The first thing the Pilgrim Fathers did was to fall upon their knees and then upon the *aborigines*."—Stewart W. McClelland.

**a but′ted** (uh but′ed). Touched at the end or side; bordered on; had a common boundary with; touched at some projecting point or side.—"There was an objectionable din from the tavern that *abutted* upon my property."— Ellery Marsh Egan.

**ac cel′er ate** (ak sel′ur āte). To increase the speed of.—"We are straining every nerve to *accelerate* our production."—Winston Churchill.

**ad ja′cent** (ă jāy′sĕnt). Adjoining; lying near or close at hand.—"It is necessary for us to command not only the reaches of ocean *adjacent* to our own shores, but the entire reach of the oceans surrounding the western continent."—Henry L. Stimson.

**ae′ons** (ē′ŏnz). Incalculable periods of time; ages.—"Women have had *aeons* of experience in bringing up good human beings."—Margaret Mead.

**al lu′vial** (ă lū′vi ăl). Composed of earth deposited by water.—"Reefs of dead shell have accumulated on the *alluvial* bottoms of the estuaries."— Sid Clark.

**am′bit** (am′bit). Boundary; sphere; circumference; scope.—"He would confine government within the *ambit* of its legitimate authority."—George W. Maxey.

**am′pli tude** (am′plĭ tūde). Extent; size; largeness; abundance; scope; fulness; great capacity.—"A miracle had happened; a miracle so wide in its *amplitude* that all were caught up in it."—Willa Cather.

**an ces′tral** (an sess′trăl). Derived from ancestors; inherited from forefathers; possessed by forebears.—"They go serenely on their way providing *ancestral* homes complete with domestic staffs."—Hilary St. George Saunders.

**an′nals** (an′ălz). A record of events in their chronological order, year by year.—"The *annals* of our sister-republics are glorious with freedom-inspiring exploits."—Harold L. Ickes.

**an″te ce′dent** (an″tē see′dĕnt). Prior; going before; previous; preceding; former.—"The author is curator of the zoological gardens of Buffalo with *antecedent* experience in other cities." —May Lamberton Becker.

**an′te dates** (an′tē dātes). Was in existence before; is of earlier date than; dates back before.—"The oldest American university *antedates* all the governments now existing in the New World."—William Bennett Munro.

**an″te di lu′vi an** (an″tē di lū′vi ăn). Belonging to a period before the flood; antiquated; very ancient.— "The *antediluvian* monuments of the Druids, though in ruins, can still be seen in England."—Henry J. Powers.

**an tic′i pate** (an tiss′ĭ pāte). Foresee; forecast.—"This conference will make recommendations. I cannot *anticipate* their views."—Herbert Hoover.

**an tip′o des** (an tip′ō deez). Anything at the opposite extreme from another.—"Collectivism is at the *antipodes* from democracy."—Thomas W. Lamont.

**an′ti quat″ed** (an′ti kwāte″id). Old-fashioned; out of date; very old.— "The men stepped into an *antiquated* railroad car at Compiegne."—Cecil Brown.

**an tiq′ui ty** (an tik′wĭ ti). Ancient times or civilizations.—"Our stock of learning transmitted from *antiquity* is the greatest trust fund this world has ever known."—Henry Noble Mac-Cracken.

**A pach′e** (ă pach′ē). An Indian of a fierce nomadic tribe in the southwest of North America.—"The *Apache* told us many interesting tales and was a clever and helpful guide."— Tom Pennell.

**a quat′ic** (uh kwat′ik). Living in, or adapted to the water; pertaining to the water; of that which grows in the water.—"The need for applied research is urgent for improved ranch and *aquatic* production."—Walter P. Taylor.

**ar cha'ic** (ahr kāy'ik). Antiquated; belonging to a former period.—"We would invite another depression were we to revert to the *archaic* tariff traditions of this Act."—Eugene P. Thomas.

**ar"chi pel'a go** (ahr"ki pel'uh gō). A sea studded with islands, or the islands collectively.—"Order must be established throughout the *archipelago* of the Pacific."—Albert J. Beveridge.

**at"mos pher'ic** (at"moss fer'ik). Belonging to the atmosphere or climatic condition; hence, pertaining to a surrounding element or influence; imparting atmosphere; providing tone and harmony.—"The painting is filled with this *atmospheric* effect and the alchemy of light."—Royal Cortissoz.

**at'olls** (at'olz). Ring-shaped coral islands nearly or quite surrounding a lagoon.—"There are small coral islands and *atolls* in the Solomons as well as the larger islands."—Ernst Mayr.

**aug ment'ed** (awg ment'ed). Increased; added to.—"The rise in wages has greatly *augmented* their purchasing power."—Sidney Hillman.

**bal lis'tics** (bă liss'tiks). The science of projectiles; the art of hurling missiles; the science of the movement of weapons thrown.—"He may be a *ballistics* metallurgist engaged in scientific research."—John Woodman Higgins.

**bay'ou** (bī'ōō). A kind of creek or sluggish inlet; an outlet or rivulet from another river.—"The higher ground is perhaps ten feet above the level of the *bayou* surfaces."—Bayard Christy.

**be queathed'** (bē kweethe'd': 'th' as in 'the'). Handed down to posterity; transmitted.—"The little lands have *bequeathed* to us their treasures."—Lorado Taft.

**bi sect'ing** (bī sekt'ing). Dividing into two equal parts; cutting into two parts, usually of equal size.—"The cemetery was unfenced and a wagon trail ran through the middle, *bisecting* the square."—Willa Cather.

**ca pa'cious** (kuh pā'shŭs). Large; roomy; able to hold or contain much; spacious; broad or wide.—"He sat in a *capacious* wicker chair in his garden, lost in thought."—H. G. Wells.

**ca pac'i ty** (kuh pass'ĭ ti). Maximum volume, output, or capability.— "These large contracts will keep us going at *capacity*."—Frederick Riebel, Jr.

**chasms** (kaz'mz). Deep gorges; yawning hollows.—"So-called impassable streams and *chasms* have been bridged."—C. M. A. Stine.

**co e'val** (kō ē'văl). Of the same date or duration; happening at the same time.—"The French and American revolutions were *coeval* events of immeasurable portent."—Ainslee Mockridge.

**co in'ci dence** (kō in'sĭ dĕnce). A concurrence of happenings without apparent connection; the chance occurrence of corresponding things at the same time.—"A good fiction plot is never solved by a simple *coincidence*." —S. L. Scanlon.

**co in"ci den'tal ly** (kō in"sĭ den'tăl i). Correspondingly; in the same way at the same time; concurrently.—"The birds and the farms of the North benefit *coincidentally* from the quiet insured by our wardens in the South." —John H. Baker.

**com men'su rate** (kŏ men'shōō rit). Proportionate; adequate; of equal extent.—"If the Government would allow business men to buy things cheap and sell them at profits *commensurate* with the demand, there would soon be expansion."—Lewis Haney.

**com mo'di ous** (kō mō'di ŭs). Spacious; roomy; affording ample accommodation; capacious; convenient.— "Larger aircraft for the same horsepower are more *commodious* and more efficient."—Grover Loening.

**com'pass** (kum'puhss). Range; scope; boundary; circumference.—"The world has shrunk to too small a *compass* to contain two mutually repugnant systems."—Irving T. McDonald.

**com"pu ta'tion** (kom"pū tā'shun). Calculation; numerical reckoning; work in arithmetic.—"Whether the *computation* should be performed by other payroll clerks should be considered."—Harry C. Gretz.

**con cen'tric** (kŏn sen'trik). Having a common center, as circles, one inside the other.—"There are two *concentric* realms—the realm of the Unknown and the realm of the Unknowable." —Alexis Carrel.

**con com'i tant** (kon kom'ĭ tănt). Occurring together; attendant.—"Our domestic war economy has not been geared to protect workers against inflation and its *concomitant* evils."— William L. Green.

**con'fines** (kon'fīne'z). Boundaries; frontiers; limits; borders.—"The report goes far beyond the *confines* of the country."—Emil Lengyel.

**con"for ma'tion** (kon"for mā'shŭn). The general structure or form; the manner in which a thing is formed; the disposition of the parts of a thing or form.—"The *conformation* of the shore at this point was rugged and rocky."—Hugh E. Blackstone.

**con junc'tive ly** (kŏn jungk'tiv li). In a way that connected or joined them; so as to make a combination or union.—"The two operations were performed *conjunctively*."—George F. Gahagan.

**con"stel la'tions** (kon"stel lā'shŭnz). Groups or clusters of stars; divisions of the heavens including a number of fixed stars.—"The zodiac was divided originally into 12 signs which then coincided approximately with 12 *constellations* of the same names." —Isabel M. Lewis.

**con tem"po ra'ne ous** (kŏn tem"pō rāy'nē ŭs). Occurring at the same time; belonging to the same period; existing at the same time; coeval.—"It's interesting, but it isn't exactly *contemporaneous*, so I think I shall go to Washington and ask some of the men there."—Stephen Vincent Benét.

**con tem'po rar"y** (kŏn tem'pō rer"i). Existing at the same time; belonging to our age or period.—"Our *contemporary* arts need not wait a hundred years before they are appreciated."— Nelson A. Rockefeller.

**con tig'u ous** (kŏn tig'ū ŭs). Adjacent; touching at the boundary.—"All the territory our fathers bought and seized is *contiguous*."—Albert J. Beveridge.

**con"ti nu'i ty** (kon"ti nū'ĭ ti). The state of continuing without interruption. —"There is no break in the *continuity* of history."—Dorothy Thompson.

**con trac'tion** (kŏn trak'shŭn). Shortening, narrowing, or reducing in size, by the parts drawing together.— "The amount of *contraction* is so small as to be questionable."—H. L. Kennedy.

**con verge'** (kŏn vurje'). To come together by gradual approach; to tend toward one point.—"In a few areas these two philosophies are beginning to *converge*."—David R. Craig.

**cos'mic** (koz'mik). Pertaining to the universe at large; of vast extent; very large.—"On a *cosmic* scale men listen to his oratory."—T. V. Smith.

**cres'cent** (kress'ĕnt). A shape like the first quarter of the moon; anything that curves or is shaped like the new moon.—"The star called the sun is risen, first a red *crescent*, then an opening eye."—Donald Culross Peattie.

**cre vasse'** (krē vass'). A deep narrow opening, especially in a glacier; a fissure or cleft; a crack or wide split. —"It was like a small tongue of glacier forced down into a *crevasse* from the ice-cap hidden behind."—Anne Morrow Lindbergh.

**cu'mu la tive** (kū'mū lā tiv). Gathering strength by repetition; steadily increasing.—"It is difficult for anyone to realize how grave is the *cumulative* effect of these restrictions on production."—Lord Halifax.

**cur'rent** (kur'ĕnt). Belonging to the present time.--"This audience of students of past and *current* affairs has clearly in mind the details of recent events."—J. W. Greenslade.

**cy'cli cal** (sī'kli kăl). Recurring in circles arranged in order of time.—"The President told us we were not having a natural *cyclical* recovery but a planned recovery."—James P. Warburg.

**de crep'i tude** (dē krep'ĭ tūde). Enfeeblement through infirmity or old age.—"The next day he started out in a state of abject *decrepitude*."— John Buchan.

**de ferred'** (dē furd'). Delayed or postponed.—"Many a boy expects to get an education on *deferred* payments in effort."—William Trufant Foster.

**de lim'it** (dē lim'it). Fix the boundaries of; determine the limits or bounds; prescribe the boundaries.—"To *delimit* this territory will require great diplomacy."—Emmet Holloway.

**del'ta** (del'tuh). Alluvial land shaped like a Greek 'd', or triangle, at the mouth of a river; a muddy or sandy tract of land at the mouth of a river. —"Myriads of wild duck winter on the great *delta* of the Santee River." —Archibald Rutledge.

**de'mar cat"ed** (dē'mahr kāte"id). Having the boundaries or limits fixed as though marked by a line.—"The mounds look like volcanic mountain peaks with a *demarcated* timber line and barren crown."—Theodore Kazimiroff.

**de mesne'** (dē māne'). A domain; the house and grounds of an owner; a region; a district; a realm of activity.— "His home *demesne* serves as a point of departure for journeyings."—John Chamberlain.

**de mot'ed** (dē mōte'id). Reduced to a lower rank or grade; put into a lower class or position.—"It isn't he who has *demoted* mankind: it is you."— Lloyd C. Douglas.

**des"ti na'tion** (dess"tǐ nā'shŭn). The place for which a person or thing sets out or is destined; a predetermined end; a goal.—"It took four days and five dreary nights to arrive at our *destination*."—Ainslee Mockridge.

**de"vi a'tions** (dē"vi āy'shŭnz). Deflections from the straight road; the acts of straying from a recognized standard.—"The higher management is in no way involved in these *deviations* from company procedures."—J. Lester Perry.

**dif fu'sion** (di fū'zhŭn). Circulation; spreading abroad; dispersion.—"The wide *diffusion* of prosperity is the fruit of true liberty."—William Allen White.

**dig'it** (dij'it). Any one of the figures 1 to 9 inclusive, and sometimes 0; any one of the ten Arabic numerals.— "The problem is, what's the smallest number of cards, each carrying one *digit*, she will need."—Christopher Morley.

**di men'sions** (dǐ men'shŭnz). Measurements; hence, size.—"The prints are reproduced in generous *dimensions*." —Royal Cortissoz.

**di min'ish** (di min'ish). Lessen; make smaller; reduce in importance; decrease; make less.—"A reasonable meat serving will *diminish* the need for other foods."—Donald G. Cooley.

**dim"i nu'tion** (dim"i nū'shŭn). Reduction; the act of diminishing; decrease.—"This *diminution* in the scale of the attack is not entirely due to the weather."—Winston Churchill.

**di min'u tive** (di min'ū tiv). Very small; tiny; of relatively small size.— "The little cart was drawn by a *diminutive* but very active pony."— Roy Chapman Andrews.

**dis"pro por'tion ate** (diss"prō pōr'-shŭn it). Out of proportion with regard to size or value or number; too many or too few compared with others.—"There are a few government agencies where they are *disproportionate*, where they are conspicuous for their numbers."—W. M. Kiplinger.

**di ur'nal** (dī ur'năl). Daily; happening every day; lasting a day.—"These adult mosquitoes are *diurnal*."—John Smart.

**di ver'gence** (dī vur'jĕnce). Deviation from a common center or point; disagreement; movement in different directions.—"If any one persists in these views there will be a *divergence*." —Lord Vansittart.

**di vis'i ble** (dǐ viz'ǐ b'l). Capable of being divided actually or mentally.— "In these days scientists find that even tiny particles are *divisible*."— Charles Henry Crozier.

**do mains'** (dō mainz'). Provinces; range; scope.—"The respective *domains* of the provisions can be defined by virtue, by reason, and by law."— Herbert Hoover.

**en dure'** (en dūre'). Continue; last; have duration; have power and ability to last a long time.—"The author is dead but her brave spirit has left a glow of light that will long *endure*."—George Matthew Adams.

**en sconced'** (en skonst'). Snuggly settled; established in a sheltered and protected place; comfortably and safely settled.—"The mice were *ensconced* in a snug ball of grass and leaves below the level of frost."—William J. Hamilton, Jr.

**en vi'rons** (en vī'rŭnz). The surrounding region; outskirts; suburbs.—"The place was like the *environs* of a town in the English Black Country."—John Buchan.

**e phem'er al** (ē fem'ur ăl). Living one day only; hence, transitory.—"We know the fate of the Roman and Persian Empires, and the *ephemeral* system established by Napoleon."—Madame Chiang Kai-shek.

**ep'i sodes** (ep'ĭ sōde'z). Incidents or stories in a literary work; separate events.—"Such *episodes* are astonishing."—Winston Churchill.

**ep'och** (ep'ok). An interval of time memorable for extraordinary events; any definite period of time.—"I would not have willed to live in an easier *epoch*."—Dorothy Thompson.

**e ro'sion** (ē rō'zhŭn). The wearing away of rocks, as by water.—"The tenants failed to prevent soil *erosion*."—Henry A. Wallace.

**es'tu ar"y** (ess'tū er"ĭ). The wide mouth of a tidal river; a place where the river meets the tide; a firth.—"There is an *estuary* and a delta where the Rhone flows into the Mediterranean."—G. K. Yeates.

**e ter'nal** (ē tur'năl). Without beginning or end; continuing without change; immutable; timeless; endless.—"Down in the deep of the woods were places of *eternal* twilight."—Caroline Dale Snedeker.

**ev"a nes'cent** (ev"uh ness'ĕnt). Passing away, or liable to pass away, gradually or imperceptibly; fleeting.—"The moral stimulation of work no longer must be forgotten in the mad chase of *evanescent* profits."—Franklin Delano Roosevelt.

**ex cres'cence** (eks kress'ĕnce). An outgrowth; hence, a protuberance; something sticking out or protruding.—"The night light was soon dimmed by a constellation of hidden bulbs as my frantic fingers found yet another metal *excrescence*."—Hilary St. George Saunders.

**ex ot'ic** (eks ot'ik). Belonging to another part of the world; foreign.—"These rare and *exotic* blooms have been cut from the American market."—Watson Davis.

**ex pan'sion** (eks pan'shŭn). Increase in size; a spreading out of activities; an expanding or enlarging; a wide extension.—"Industrialization produces an *expansion* of foreign as well as of domestic trade."—Thos. J. Watson.

**ex"pi ra'tion** (ek"spĭ rā'shŭn). End; natural termination or coming to a close of anything; the end of a period of time or an agreement.—"We shall continue to observe terms of employment as they were before the *expiration* of the former contract."—Sewell Avery.

**ex tant'** (eks tant'). Still existing; in existence; known to exist.—"There are not many copies of this work *extant*."—Dard Hunter.

**fjords** (fyordz). Long narrow arms of the sea, having high rocky banks.—"Norway, living amidst its mountains and *fjords*, we approached from the sea."—Tom Connally.

**fore gone'** (for gawn'). Arrived at in advance of evidence that could have been known beforehand; previously determined.—"That I would no longer accept their hospitality was a *foregone* conclusion."—John Myers Myers.

**gauge** (gāje). Determine by some test or measurement; estimate; measure; judge.—"We can easily *gauge* the effect of these events."—Edmund Wilson.

**gen'e sis** (jen'ē siss). The origin or beginning.—"I am analyzing the *genesis* of much of the crime that has shocked the community."—Edmund A. Walsh.

**girth** (gurth). Measurement around; circumference of a circular object.—"The tree measures twelve feet in *girth*, breast high."—Robert F. Griggs.

**hin'ter land"** (hin'tur land"). Land lying behind a definite portion of a seacoast or river shore.—"This *hinterland* of wealth, resource, and power, and these developments are the cornerstone of Soviet military strategy."—Joseph E. Davies.

**im mea′sur a bly** (im mezh′ur uh bli). In a way too great to count or measure.—"He has helped me *immeasurably* and I have a great respect for anything he says about the theater."—Katharine Cornell.

**im me′di a cy** (i mē′di uh si). Directness; freedom from any intervening medium.—"They have employed a camera with vigor and melodramatic *immediacy* in the battle scenes."—Howard Barnes.

**im″me mo′ri al** (im″mē mō′ri ăl). Reaching back beyond memory; belonging to the ancient past.—"We know that men have fought and bled for freedom since time *immemorial*."—Harold L. Ickes.

**im′mi nence** (im′ĭ nĕnce). The impending danger; the threatening evil; nearness; likelihood of happening soon.—"He warned the chancelleries of the *imminence* of war."—Max Immanuel.

**im mor′tal** (i mor′tăl). Imperishable; eternal; divine.—"*Immortal* song floated from the skies on that first Christmas Eve."—William J. Cameron.

**in cep′tion** (in sep′shŭn). Beginning; start; inauguration.—"Who has directed this program from its *inception?*"—Guy M. Gillette.

**in′ci dent** (in′sĭ dĕnt). An occurrence; a single event.—"One *incident* in particular will be vivid in my recollection to my dying day."—Anthony Eden.

**in cip′i ent** (in sip′i ĕnt). Belonging to the first stages; beginning to appear. —"I am impressed by the *incipient* industrial development which is so creditable for a country in transition from an agricultural to an industrial nation."—Wendell L. Willkie.

**in″di vis′i ble** (in″dĭ viz′ĭ b'l). Not separable into parts; incapable of being divided; not capable of disunion.— "Prosperity, like peace, is *indivisible*." —Henry Morgenthau, Jr.

**in fin′i tude** (in fin′ĭ tūde). Boundlessness; eternity; time and space without limit.—"On a day like this one has the feeling of being able to see into *infinitude*."—Bodo Wuth.

**in fin′i ty** (in fin′ĭ ti). Boundlessness; unlimited space, time, or amount; extent without end; immeasurable quantity.—"There was a solemnity about a storm of such magnitude; it gave one a feeling of *infinity*."—Willa Cather.

**in i′tial** (i nish′ăl). Belonging to the first stage; earliest; taking place at the beginning; existing at the beginning.—"They assumed not only the *initial* corruption of human nature, but were persuaded that this corruption was hopeless."—Ludwig Lewisohn.

**in′ter lude** (in′tur lūde). An intervening time; a pause in actions or events; something that fills in the time between two parts of an interrupted action.—"The family of democratic nations was much larger when we came out of the war *interlude* in 1918 than it is now."—Albert N. Williams.

**in″ter me′di ar″y** (in″tur mē′di er″i). Situated between; lying between others.—"The *intermediary* bases are needed to bring our short-range aviation within striking distance of the enemy."—Alexander P. de Seversky.

**in″ter me′di ate** (in″tur mee′di ĭt). Coming between other things; occurring between two other things or events.—"I hate these new-fangled *intermediate* meals."—Edith Wharton.

**in′ter vals** (in′tur vălz). Spaces of time between events; pauses between sessions; intervening time.—"The *intervals* between feedings should gradually be lengthened."—Ashton Chapman.

**in verse′** (in vurce′). Reversed; opposite in order; inverted.—"There seems to be an accepted dogma to the effect that the worth and honor of a citizen runs in *inverse* ratio to his competence and thrift."—Brice P. Disque.

**ir″re duc′i ble** (ir″rē dūce′ĭ b'l). Incapable of being brought from a larger to a smaller amount; not reducible. —"Part of his ration should be suspended to hold him to an *irreducible* minimum."—Cornelius P. Mundy.

**i tin′er ant** (ī tin′ur ănt). Going from place to place; traveling around.— "She has become an *itinerant* laundress, going from home to home."— John Erskine.

**i tin′er ar″y** (ī tin′ur er″i). The outline of a route; a plan of a proposed tour or trip; a route to travel.—"My planned *itinerary* had called for following the Loire up to Tours."— John Myers Myers.

**lapse** (laps). An interval of time; a gradual passing away of time.—"It is difficult after the *lapse* of a century and a half, to realize how reluctant the thirteen original states were to form a federated government."— Henry W. Taft.

**lit′to ral** (lit′ō răl). Of the shore; pertaining to land near the sea coast; belonging to a coastal region.—"We mentioned a number of oceanic and *littoral* birds."—R. M. Lockley.

**lon gev′i ty** (lon jev′ĭ ti). Length of life; long life; great age; tendency to live a long time.—"The simple formula guarantees a smoother trip along the road to *longevity*."—Peter J. Steincrohn.

**lon′gi tude** (lon′ji tūde). Distance east or west on the earth's surface, measured in degrees from a prime meridian, as Greenwich, or in time from the same meridian.—"The mystery of finding *longitude* was not solved for many years."—William H. Barton, Jr.

**mag′ni fy″ing** (mag′nĭ fī″ing). Increasing the apparent size; enlarging; exaggerating.—"He urged Congress to examine non-defense expenditures with a *magnifying* glass in an effort to achieve economies."—James S. Kemper.

**man′i fold** (man′ĭ fōld). Many, and having several uses; composed of many parts or elements; comprising various features.—"We do not attempt to arrange the *manifold* details of policies and practices."—Emory S. Land.

**mar′i time** (mar′ĭ tīme). Situated on or near the sea.—"Along our extended coasts our domestic *maritime* trade

proceeds with great regularity."— H. L. Roosevelt.

**ma tu′ti nal** (muh tū′tĭ năl). Occurring in the morning; of the morning; early.—"The priest was interrupted in his *matutinal* orisons."—Donald G. Cooley.

**mean** (meen). The middle point; a condition equally distant from two opposite extremes; an intermediate position.—"Simplicity is the *mean* between the boor and the fop."— Bradwell E. Tanis.

**meas′ur a ble** (mezh′ur uh b'l). Capable of being measured; of which the amount or degree can be found or measured.—"Then the real strength of what is intelligent and sound becomes a *measurable* entity."—Louis Adamic.

**me″di e′val** (mē″di ee′văl). Characteristic of the Middle Ages.—"If I am going to ask any worker to shed his blood, it will not be for *medieval* Abyssinia."—Aneurin Bevan.

**men′sur a ble** (men′shŏōr uh b'l). Measurable; that can be measured. —"The distance to many of the stars is *mensurable*."—Ellery Marsh Egan.

**me rid′i an** (mĕ rid′i ăn). An imaginary circle passing through the north and south poles and any given place; hence, the location of places on this line.—"Our friends range from the Arctic to the Antarctic, and there is no *meridian* where they do not live." —Irving T. McDonald.

**me′sa** (māy′suh). A high, flat table-land with steep cliffs sloping to plains below.—"To early people this *mesa* was a place of ghosts and mystery."— Virginia S. Eifert.

**met′ed** (meet′id). Assigned in proportion; given by measure.—"It is our intention that just and sure punishment shall be *meted* out to the ringleaders responsible for these organized murders."—Franklin Delano Roosevelt.

**mi′grate** (mī′grāte). Move from one country or region to another.—"The corporations can *migrate* from state to state like birds of passage."—Robert A. Taft.

**mil len′ni um** (mĭl len′i ŭm). A period of great happiness, good government, or the like.—"We need not expect the *millennium* all at once."—Elmer Davis.

**min'i miz"ing** (min'ĭ mīze"ing). Reducing to the smallest possible amount or degree.—"Sleep is the *minimizing* of wear and tear."—Donald A. Laird.

**min'i mum** (min'ĭ mŭm). The least possible amount; the smallest quantity; the lowest degree.—"We cut the weight to an absolute *minimum*."—Arthur C. Twomey.

**mo der'ni ty** (mō dur'nĭ ti). Something characteristic of the present or of modern times; something modern or belonging to recent time; up-to-date systems.—"He had worked in military kitchens varying from some that rival small hotels in *modernity* of equipment to the narrow confines of rolling field equipment."—Robert Parrish.

**mo'men tar"i ly** (mō'mĕn ter"i li). For the moment; transitorily; for a time likely to be of short duration.— "Nothing could be done against the dubious elements *momentarily* in control of the streets."—Franz Werfel.

**mon soon'** (mon sōōn'). A trade-wind; a wind that blows steadily along the Asiatic coast of the Pacific, in winter from the northeast (the dry monsoon), in summer from the southwest (the wet monsoon).—"Have the mariners of the ship nothing to answer for in steering her into a *monsoon?*"—William Bennett Munroe.

**mo raine'** (mō rāne'). Earth or stones carried along by a glacier or deposited by it.—"These kinds of topography are ground *moraine* and terminal *moraine*."—Paul MacClintock.

**mul'ti fold** (mul'ti fōld). Many times doubled; manifold; multiplied.— "We are facing the *multifold* duties that attend a reorganization."— Bruce Ellsworth.

**mul'ti ple** (mul'tĭ p'l). Consisting of more than one; manifold; numerous; many in number.—"Agents simple, double, or *multiple* could not work in more secure surroundings."—W. V. Archawski.

**nav'i ga ble** (nav'ĭ guh b'l). Fit to be sailed over; wide enough and deep enough for ships to pass through.—

"The court asserted that Congress had jurisdiction over all *navigable* waters."—Oscar L. Young.

**neth'er** (neth'ur: 'th' as in 'the'). Lower; under; situated lower down; lower grade.—"The clever ones among the *nether* group will resort to criminal activities."—G. E. Sokolsky.

**noc tur'nal** (nok tur'năl). In the night; of the night; during the night; relating to night-time.—"A sense of vindictive pursuit marred his *nocturnal* existence."—H. G. Wells.

**no mad'ic** (nō mad'ik). Wandering; roaming; unsettled.—"The *nomadic* tribes of the Hebrews were not far removed from this communistic experiment."—George Barton Cutten.

**o a'sis** (ō āy'siss). A fertile spot in a desert or waste where there is water. —"This *oasis* was like a precious meadow, a green refreshment amid waterless waste."—Thomas Mann.

**Oc'ci dent** (ok'sĭ dĕnt). The west; the Western Hemisphere.—"In frightful suffering, these people of the *Occident* now strive to regain this religious concept."—Thomas Mann.

**off'ing** (ŏff'ing). The most distant part of the sea that one can see from the shore; hence, something far away; something in the future.—"If a new trip was in the *offing*, it was much easier to keep my decks clear for action."—Roy Chapman Andrews.

**or'bit** (or'bit). The path of a heavenly body round another body; hence, a region of activity; a sphere of influence.—"His mind moved in a narrower *orbit* than the speaker's."— H. G. Wells.

**o"ri en'tal** (ō"ri en'tăl). Eastern; of the Asiatic countries east of the Mediterranean.—"Occidental and *oriental* scholars are alike in that they cannot be bribed and that they yield to no external master."—Maurice Baum.

**o'ri ent"ed** (ō'ri ĕnt"ed). Fixed the position with reference to the east; arranged so that an end is towards the east; placed in understood relation to other parts.—"These builders had *oriented* their construction so that the rooms were bisected by a line running almost due north."—Matthew W. Stirling.

**per″e gri na′tions** (per″ē gri nā′shŭnz).
Wanderings; travels; journeys from
place to place.—"Even the *peregrina-
tions* of the Vice President do not add
much to the dullness of repetition
among the Democrats."—George E.
Sokolsky.

**per en′ni al** (pur en′i ăl). A plant that
lasts year after year.—"The mint
plant is a *perennial* that is propagated
by rootstalks."—Tom L. Wheeler.

**pe riph′er y** (pĕ rif′ur i). Circumference; the bounding line of a figure;
the perimeter of a circle.—"The
formation of these lines takes place at
the *periphery* of the circle."—H.
Friedeberg.

**pe rim′e ter** (pē rim′ē tur). The boundary line of a body or any figure of
two dimensions; the distance around
any figure; hence, the outline or
bounding line.—"The film hits close
to the ultimate *perimeter* of horror in
dramatic terms."—Howard Barnes.

**per″i od′ic** (peer″i od′ik). Recurring
after a definite interval; occurring at
regular intervals.—"Congress under-
takes a *periodic* review of the operation of a great national policy."—
Cordell Hull.

**per pet′u al** (pur pet′ū ăl). Continuing
without end; incessant; ceaseless;
lasting forever; eternal.—"Her extravagance was the subject of *perpetual* arguments."—Willa Cather.

**per pet″u a′tion** (pur pet″ū āy′shŭn).
Continuation forever; carrying on;
endurance; continuity.—"We, therefore, fight for the restoration and *per-
petuation* of faith and hope throughout
the world."—Franklin Delano Roosevelt.

**per″pe tu′i ty** (pur″pē tū′ĭ ti). Endless
time; unending existence; the state of
being perpetual or existing forever.—
"Her earlier works seem as though
they might be built for *perpetuity*."—
Ludwig Lewisohn.

**phase** (fāze). Stage; a state between
plans or changes.—"The first *phase* of
our operations has been brought to a
successful conclusion."—George S.
Patton, Jr.

**pos ter′i ty** (poss ter′ĭ ti). Succeeding
generations, taken collectively; descendants.—"We owe it to our *posterity* to preserve and strengthen the
institutions of private enterprise."—
James E. Murray.

**pos′thu mous ly** (poss′tū mŭs li). After
the author's death; after death.—
"The prize for the most modest title
should be awarded *posthumously* to the
late Karel Capek."—Alpheus Smith.

**pre ced′ence** (prē seed′ĕnce). Priority
in place or time; greater importance;
a preceding or going before; first
consideration.—"Clothing for civilians sometimes takes *precedence* over
new bolts of cloth for the army."—
Gerard Swope.

**pre″con cep′tions** (prē″kŏn sep′shŭnz).
Ideas or opinions formed beforehand;
prejudices.—"Every book worth reading is a meeting place. Some would
call it a battleground: are the writer's
ideas or the reader's *preconceptions* to
survive?"—Hugh Walpole.

**pre″de ter′mined** (prē″dē tur′mĭn'd).
Decided beforehand; predestined;
decreed or settled in advance.—
"From the first it was *predetermined*
that he should go to Harvard."—
Catherine Drinker Bowen.

**pre dom′i nat″ed** (prē dom′ĭ nāte″id).
Were greater in number; were more
noticeable.—"As usual, the bills
and dunning letters *predominated*."—
Edith Wharton.

**pre″ma ture′** (prē″muh chŏŏr′). Happening or arriving before the proper
time; too early; untimely.—"There
is nothing so dangerous as a *premature*
attack."—Lord Cranborne.

**pre req′ui sites** (prē rek′wĭ zits). Necessary preceding conditions; things
that are required beforehand; antecedent conditions necessary to something that follows.—"Until we have
convinced people that our aim is a
better world, we wil be lacking in the
*prerequisites* to insure it."—Frederick
L. Schuman.

**pre′vi ous ly** (prē′vi ŭs li). At a time
before something else; at a preceding
time; at a previous time; before.—
"These same results had *previously*
been observed in rats and dogs."—
T. E. Murphy.

**pri′ma cy** (prī′muh si). The state of being supreme or first in rank or excel-
cence.—"At the end of the first World

War the United States was headed toward world *primacy* in sea power." —Frank Knox.

**pri'ma ri ly** (prī′mer ĭ li). In the first place; essentially; chiefly; principally.—"Office managers are *primarily* interested in getting the work done at minimum cost."—Harry C. Gretz.

**prim'i tive** (prim′ĭ tiv). Pertaining to the earliest stages; elementary.— "Capital cannot move a wheel without labor or labor advance beyond mere *primitive* existence without capital."—John D. Rockefeller, Jr.

**pro longed'** (prō long′d′). Extended in time; continued.—"We do not know whether the resistance will be *prolonged*."—Winston Churchill.

**prom'on to"ry** (prom′ŭn tō″ri). A headland; a high point of land extending in the sea.—"A *promontory* that thrusts its nose into the Mediterranean was our landmark."—W. Somerset Maugham.

**pro por'tion ate** (prō por′shŭn it). Corresponding; proportioned; having the same ratio; commensurate; measured by the same standard.—"An increase in our armed forces means a *proportionate* increase in the budget." —Gerard Swope.

**pro spec'tive** (prō spek′tiv). Considered for the future; of possible use in the future; viewed as probably of future promise, or value.—"I examined the *prospective* posts more carefully before attacking them."— Bennie Bengston.

**prov'ince** (prov′ince). A sphere of activity; a definite business; a department or branch of learning.—"He stepped right out of his *province* as a quiet scholarly pastor and ripped the vice area wide open."—William McDermott.

**quan'tum** (kwon′tŭm). Quantity; share; amount; portion; a unit of energy.—"There is a certain *quantum* of creative energy left in every human being that is not absorbed by the business of a workaday world."— W. Beran Wolf.

**quon'dam** (kwon′dam). Former; that was formerly; sometime; that once was.—"She turned to the household

duties of her *quondam* enthusiastic planning."—A. S. M. Hutchinson.

**quo tid'i an** (kwō tid′i ăn). Daily; of every day; occurring every day; hence, trivial; commonplace.—"He seemed happy in the monotonous repetition of his *quotidian* duties."— Bradwell E. Tanis.

**ra'di us** (rāy′di ŭs). A straight line from the center of a circle to its circumference; hence, the area enclosed within certain limits.—"The *radius* of urbanization in those days was only about two miles."—Harland Bartholomew.

**re cur'rence** (rē kur′ĕnce). Reappearance; return; repetition.—"The greatest single interest of these United States is and will be to prevent the *recurrence* of another war."— Thomas W. Lamont.

**re mote'** (rē mōte′). Located far away in time or space; far off; inaccessible; distant.—"Those *remote* moods of the spirit which carry us far from everyday life."—Leopold Stokowski.

**ret'ro spect** (ret′rō spekt). A view or contemplation of something past; a review or survey of past actions.— "Some of my pre-war life was fun and some in *retrospect* incredibly false and boring."—Chester S. Williams.

**re ver'sion** (rē vur′shŭn). A return; a going back to a former plan or condition; a falling back to a former or earlier procedure.—"Inflation and the collapse of money in ancient Rome caused a *reversion* to trade by barter."—Emmet Holloway.

**scope** (skōpe). The range of action; the extent of activity.—"The *scope* of the work will include a study of jaundice."—Raymond B. Fosdick.

**seg'ment** (seg′mĕnt). A section; a part divided from the other parts.—"It is the responsibility of all business, and not of one particular *segment*."— Daniel C. Roper.

**se man'tics** (sē man′tiks). The science which treats of the evolution of language; a branch of philology concerned with the meanings of words; the study of changes in word meanings as a language develops.—"As exercises in popular *semantics* these dialogues are excellent."—Sidney Hook.

**sem″pi ter′nal** (sem″pi tur′năl). Eternal; never-ending; everlasting.— "We looked from the earth, as from a shore, upon the *sempiternal* beauty of the stars."—Hugh E. Blackstone.

**ser′pen tine** (sur′pĕn teen). Turning one way and the other; twisting like a serpent; sinuous; curving back and forth; tortuous.—"The road winds its *serpentine* way up the mountain to the statue of Christ."—Sterling McCormick.

**ser′rat ed** (ser′āte id). Notched or toothed like a saw; having a notched edge like a saw.—"There were green forests, a blue singing stream, and cliffs of *serrated* darkness."—John Buchan.

**shoals** (shoalz). Shallow places; places where the water has little depth; sand banks; shallows.—"There were rocks and *shoals* uncharted on our map."— Richard E. Byrd.

**si″mul ta′ne ous ly** (sī″mŭl tāy′nē ŭs li). At the same time.—"These countries are *simultaneously* old and young."—Henryk Strasburger.

**slough** (slōō). A bog; a swamp; a place of deep mud or mire left by the tide. —"Hundreds of white ibis roosted nightly in willows bordering the *slough*."—Frank M. Chapman.

**sludge** (sluj). A muddy deposit on a shore or in a river bed; soft mud; slush; mire.—"Everything was redolent of salt and fish and *sludge*."— André Maurois.

**so′journ** (sō′jurn). Temporary residence; a temporary stay; abode for a time only.—"The book includes an account of the author's years in Spain as well as his *sojourn* in the United States."—George F. Whicher.

**sphere** (sfeer). A field of action; a scene of operations; a place of existence.—"The world is a *sphere* into which God sends his followers to transform the world."—Henry St. George Tucker.

**stat′ure** (stat′yŏŏr). The natural height of a man.—"He is short of *stature* and very well dressed."—Lord Beaverbrook.

**stu pen′dous** (stū pen′dŭs). Of prodig-

ious size; immense; enormous.— "Congress appropriated the *stupendous* sum of sixty-seven billion dollars."—Frank Knox.

**sub″ter ra′ne an** (sub″tur rāy′nē ăn). Under the surface of the earth; hence, hidden; concealed; secret.— "He possesses the same preoccupation with the meaning of experiences rooted in the *subterranean* channels of the past."—Rose Feld.

**suc ces′sion** (sŭk sesh′ŭn). A following one after another; a number of acts that succeed consecutively; the coming or happening of one person or thing after another; sequence.— "They presented themselves for worship, sometimes for several Sundays in *succession*."—Hervey Allen.

**suf fice′** (suh fīce′). Be sufficient; answer the purpose; be enough.—"It will not *suffice* for a few professors in our colleges to study abroad."— George F. Zook.

**sum ma′tion** (sum āy′shŭn). A total sum; an aggregate result.—"Our morality is a kind of *summation* of the wisdom and experience of our race." —Irving Langmuir.

**su″per a bun′dance** (sū″pur uh bun′dănce). A greater amount than is needed; an abounding excess; very great abundance; a supply that is much more than enough.—"The United States offers the strange and tragic contrast of *superabundance* and want."—John J. Green.

**su″per an′nu at″ed** (sū″pur an′ū āte″id). Incapacitated by age; retired on account of age; pensioned.—"The youngsters think of us as *superannuated* mummies."—W. J. Cameron.

**sus pend′ing** (sŭss pend′ing). Not using temporarily; debarring from operation; withholding for the time being.—"They are *suspending* certain rights because of the dangers confronting them."—Daniel J. Tobin.

**svelte** (svelt). Slender; lightly built; lissom; supple; lithe; of slight and supple build.—"Breathes there a woman who doesn't want a trim, *svelte* figure?"—George F. Gahagan.

**sym met′ri cal** (si met′ri kăl). Wellproportioned; having its parts wellbalanced; having regular form or arrangement; having the parts on one side corresponding to the parts on the other.—"Huge blocks of masonry shaped into an unknown pattern of *symmetrical* network supported the walls."—Axel Munthe.

**sym'me try** (sim'ē tri). Balancing of the parts to make a harmonious whole; congruity; regular and balanced correspondence of parts; regular formation.—"The leaves on the tree reflect the *symmetry* and beauty of the tree itself."—Bernard A. Brown.

**tem blors'** (tem blōrz'). Earthquakes. —"It was an architectural scheme to outwit rather than to defy the *temblors*."—Alexander Woollcott.

**tem'po ral** (tem'pō răl). Pertaining to the affairs of the present life; earthly; secular; worldly; of this life.—"God leads us through all things *temporal* so that we lose not the things eternal." —Thomas Casady.

**tem'po riz"ing** (tem'pō rīze"ing). Pursuing a policy of delay or timeserving; avoiding immediate action; working to gain time.—"It is time to end *temporizing* with the union chieftain."—Harry Flood Byrd.

**ten'ure** (ten'ūre). Right of holding; time or term during which something is held.—"He knew his job had no *tenure*."—George H. Chatfield.

**ter"mi na'tion** (tur"mĭ nā'shŭn). End; conclusion; close or ending in time or existence; act of limiting.—"War will then pass from us, not in the *termination* of this conflict only, but for ever."—A. S. M. Hutchinson.

**ter rain'** (te rāne'). A tract or region considered with reference to some special purpose; an area of ground.— "The cars bounced over the rough *terrain*."—M. W. Smith.

**ter res'tri al** (te ress'tri ăl). Belonging to the earth; living on earth or land; of the earth or land.—"The sand dune rose four feet above the water, and thus became a haven for *terrestrial* life."—C. Brooke Worth.

**thresh'old** (thresh'ōld). An entrance or starting point; a beginning or outset. —"Relief and reconstruction work will bring us only to the *threshold* of the new frontiers that will be opening."—Matthew Woll.

**to pog'ra phy** (tō pog'ruh fi). The physical features, lakes, streams, roads, hills, etc., of a region.—"It is not altogether the *topography* or geography or climate that has made the South what it is."—Irvin S. Cobb.

**to tal'i ty** (tō tal'ĭ ti). The whole number; the total mass of individuals; all the component parts.—"Each person seems to be going somewhere, the *totality* nowhere."—L. P. Jacks.

**tra di'tion** (truh dish'ŭn). A body of beliefs and usages handed down from generation to generation.—"We must accept gladly a self-discipline to which we are not by *tradition* accustomed."—James F. Byrnes.

**tran si'tion** (tran zish'ŭn). A passage or change from one place or condition to another; a passing from one stage of development to another.—"A *transition* period was marked by the passing of a civilization."—John Haynes Holmes.

**tran'si to"ry** (tran'sĭ tō"ri). Existing for a short time only; transient; not enduring; temporary.—"He insisted on putting the liberty of the people beyond the reach of *transitory* power." —Claude Bowers.

**trib'u ta"ries** (trib'ū ter"iz). Smaller streams flowing into a river or larger stream.—"Old man river, along with his *tributaries*, is threatening to dig a big hole in the food supply for this winter."—Charlie Stookey.

**trice** (trīce). An instant; a moment; a very short time.—"In a *trice* he whirled around, alert, revolver in hand."—S. L. Scanlon.

**tri par'tite** (trī pahr'tīte). Divided into three parts or divisions; threefold.— "Each *tripartite* body was to consist of representatives of labor, of management, and of the government."— Emory S. Land.

**tryst** (trist). An appointment to meet; a previously arranged meeting-place. —"The Colorado was on its way to its *tryst* with the Grand Canyon."— Virginia S. Eifert.

**ul'ti mate** (ul'ti mit). Final; last of a series; conclusive.—"There is general agreement that if war should break out there could be no *ultimate* victor." —William C. Bullitt.

un'du lat"ing (un'dū lāte"ing). Having a wavy appearance, a surface that rises and falls alternately.— "There are sharp declines and then a flattening out into *undulating* plains, marked by occasional hills and hollows."—Harold G. Moulton.

u"ni lat'er al (ū"ni lat'ur ăl). Onesided; affecting one side only.— "There must be an international court 'to avoid *unilateral* breakings of treaty terms.' "—Elmer Davis.

u"ni ver'sal (ū"ni vur'săl). Relating to the whole earth and to all human beings; including all; belonging to everyone; present everywhere.— "Freedom must be *universal* for there cannot be a world half free and half slave."—Henry A. Wallace.

ver'dure (vur'dūre). Fresh greenness; verdant vegetation; fresh growth of leaves and plants.—"In spite of its climate there is an appealing *verdure* in the Aleutians."—Olaus J. Murie.

ver'nal (vur'năl). Of the spring season; belonging to spring; appearing in spring.—"This *vernal* bird is a great musician."—William J. Calvert, Jr.

vi cin'i ty (vĭ sin'ĭ ti). Neighboring places; neighborhood.—"About five minutes ago the guns in the immediate *vicinity* were working."—Edward R. Murrow.

## ONE-MINUTE REFRESHER

One of the three words given under each numbered phrase is nearest in meaning to the underlined key word. See if you can choose the correct one. The word is similar in meaning, but not necessarily a direct synonym.

1. When incidents happen *coincidentally*, they happen:
   (a) accidentally; (b) suddenly; (c) at the same time.
2. A person who shows *decrepitude* is:
   (a) selfish; (b) old; (c) ugly.
3. When your automobile is *superannuated* it is:
   (a) out of order; (b) out of control; (c) out of date.
4. *Concomitant* evils are:
   (a) incurable; (b) accompanying; (c) following.
5. *Concentric* circles are:
   (a) one within another; (b) of the same size; (c) in sequence.
6. The *antipodes* are:
   (a) parts of speech; (b) parts of the globe opposite each other;
   (c) geographical boundaries.
7. The *ambit* of his legitimate authority would mean:
   (a) the end; (b) the beginning; (c) the bounds.
8. An *archaic* law means:
   (a) just; (b) antiquated; (c) unjust.

*Answers:* 1 — c; 2 — b; 3 — c; 4 — b; 5 — a; 6 — b; 7 — c; 8 — b.

# CHAPTER XX

## THESE WORDS HAVE MAGIC POWER

THERE ARE times in poetry and in poetic prose when words possess a meaning that transcends their common dictionary definitions. That is the beauty and magic of these strange hieroglyphics that we scribble on a piece of paper. There is a chemistry to words when they are used in a figurative sense that is not quite understandable, which touches sources of power that lie somewhere above and beyond the sensible world.

We can the better detect this peculiar quality of words if we first observe a few of them in homely and humble capacities, as they appear, say, in the title of a novel which reads: "The Rat Gnaws the Rope." Here the words are simple day-laborers. They are flat-footed and factual and each one checks accurately with its dictionary meaning.

When we turn, though, to the following quotations, we enter another world.

"The builders of the Great Wall were mental *myopics*"— Madame Chiang Kai-shek is speaking—"who saw only the expediency of temporary solutions."

And then Dr. Morris Fishbein: "The most despicable of all charlatans are the *ghouls* that prey on the bodies of cancer victims."

Both of the italicized words had the spark of the poet's idea in them to begin with, but when the poet of language plunges this spark into the oxygen of his imagination, the words become luminous and begin to burn and to flame with a new significance.

We come with this poetic treatment of words into the field of similes, metaphors, imagery, and the general wizardries of language that are the bases of all great poetry, as they are the power-plus of all great writing.

Back in our high-school days we learned that the word "metaphor" came from the two Greek words *meta*, "across," and *pherein*, "to carry"; that is, a carry-over or a transfer of meaning. We were

336

taught that a metaphor was a perception of similarities, a comparison in one word of two things from different fields of experience.

When Dr. Fishbein, therefore, speaks of the "ghouls" that prey on cancer victims, he is recognizing the similarity between the human vultures who rob dead bodies and the charlatans who prey and profit on human fears.

When Madame Chiang Kai-shek writes of "mental myopics" she shows that she is aware that people can be "short-sighted" mentally as well as optically.

This poetry of language is ever in the making, always in a state of efflorescence. The prosaic words of today are often the faded metaphors of yesterday, and if we polish the tarnish of the ages off their surfaces, the original figures of speech, lost long ago, will reappear.

Our two authors, whom we have just quoted, turned the sober and factual words "myopic" and "ghoul" into modern metaphors, but, centuries ago, these two words were metaphors in their own right. In ancient Greece "myopic" meant, literally, "shut eyes," while "ghoul" derives from "ghul," the name of an obscene spirit that robbed the graves of the primitive Arabs and fed upon the corpses.

Thus the processes of creation and re-creation go on eternally in our language.

Even our most simple words have pictures secreted in them. "Brown," at one time, meant "toad-color," and "purple" was the color of that little and ancient Latin fish, the *purpura*. The gay word "carnival" breaks up into *carnis* (flesh) and *vale* (farewell). It was the name given to the feast in Italy before Lent when the celebrants said "flesh farewell"!

If we flash these colored slides more swiftly on the screen, we find that the word "crestfallen" pictures the loser in the cockfight where the cockscomb is drooping. "Sediment" is something that "sits" on the bottom; "wheedle," in its etymology, merely means that you are wagging your tail in a beseeching fashion; and "precocious," when translated, means "cooked or ripened early or beforehand."

We Americans are prolific in the coining of figures of speech. Even our slang has the bright color of poetry in it, for slang is often language in the making.

Witness such vigorous and imaginative metaphorical creations as pay-dirt, gun-moll, ticket-scalper, high-jack, gum-shoe, boot-legger, bell-hop, tenderfoot, speak-easy. Note the power that they pack.

Now turn to the higher brackets of language. Read the parallel sentences selected from this chapter, and observe how the force of each phrase is drained away when the figure of speech is withdrawn:

| | |
|---|---|
| "The thunder of *Armageddon* rolls closer and closer."—H. W. Prentis, Jr. | *War* rolls closer and closer. |
| "Many forms of human slavery have *spawned* their power in our time."—Virgil Jordan. | Many forms of human slavery have *grown* to power in our time. |
| "We are in the *Gethsemane* of civilization."—Francis J. Spellman. | We are in *distressing days* of civilization. |
| "The future of Asia has again been thrown into the boiling *caldron* of a great war."— Edmund C. Lucas. | The future of Asia has again been *endangered* by a great war. |

The masters of language—labor leaders, industrialists, statesmen and all—are fully aware of the magic of metaphors, and they use this magic designedly to stir men's imaginations and emotions. They train themselves in this art.

Read over these sentences that they have written and spoken. You will find them exciting and stimulating. Read some of them aloud; I believe that their mere recital may spur you on to invent metaphors of your own. The practice of this creative art will do much to freshen a speech that grows too easily stale.

## These Words Have Magic Power

**a bor′tion** (uh bor′shŭn). Untimely birth; hence, a failure to develop a project; the failure of an action during its progress or development.—"The trial resulted in an *abortion* of justice."—Bruce Ellsworth.

**a bor′tive** (uh bor′tiv). Born prematurely; hence, coming to nothing; vain; useless.—"An *abortive* attempt was made to capture the city."—Roy Chapman Andrews.

**ab″ra ca dab′ra** (ab″ruh kuh dab′ruh). A cabalistic word written as a triangle, and worn as a cure; a magic formula; a jargon of conjuring words. —"We are being asked constantly to subscribe to *abracadabra* and to worship hocuspocus."—William Alfred Eddy.

**ac″co lade′** (ak″ō lāde′). A touch on the shoulder with flat of sword when knighthood is bestowed; hence, the recognition of special merit; a reward. —"That a playwright dared to treat of so much material in one play is cause for an *accolade*."—Howard Barnes.

**A chil′les** (uh kil′eez). A Greek hero whose only vulnerable spot was his heel; hence, Achilles' heel stands for the only weak or assailable spot or part.—"My *Achilles'* heel was my hands, the smallest and weakest any heavyweight champion ever had."—Gene Tunney.

**A do'nis** (uh dō'niss). A Greek youth of great beauty beloved by Venus; hence, a very beautiful young man.—"No wonder this *Adonis* had such a following of female movie fans."—Donald G. Cooley.

**ae'gis** (ē'jiss). A shield or protective armor; hence, any protecting influence or power.—"If the small nations find as much freedom and security under the *aegis* of whatever League of Nations we are to have, as they found under the *aegis* of the British Empire, I shall be content."—Edward J. Meeman.

**a'er ie** (āy'ur i). The nest of a bird of prey on a high crag; hence, a human residence perched on a height.—"High in a mighty cottonwood the boys had built themselves an *aerie.*"—Donald G. Cooley.

**Aes"cu la'pi an** (ess"kū lāy'pi ăn). Pertaining to Aesculapius, the Roman god of medicine; hence, a physician.—"Despite his lack of fancy instruments, the horse-and-buggy doctor was a faithful *Aesculapian.*"—Donald G. Cooley.

**A lad'din** (uh lad'in). The hero of a story in The Arabian Nights who summoned jinns to gratify his wishes by rubbing a magic lamp; hence, one whose commands are carried out as if by magic.—"At any moment the new *Aladdin* who has the cup in keeping may rub it and send them off on impossible errands."—Hervey Allen.

**a lem'bic** (uh lem'bik). An apparatus used in distilling; hence, a device or testing tube for purifying and transforming.—"We constantly distill new law from the customs and conditions of a fast-changing economy, in the *alembic* of history and precedent."—Paul Shipman Andrews.

**a mal'gam** (uh mal'găm). A mixture of two or more substances or things; a compound.—"Culture may be only an *amalgam;* it is better if it be a chemical combination."—Owen D. Young.

**am'a zon** (am'uh zon). One of a race of female warriors; hence, a courageous, masculine woman; a woman warrior.—"He could picture her standing in a chariot, an *amazon* queen with maimed and iron breast."—Stephen Vincent Benét.

**An"a ni'as** (an"uh nī'ăss). A follower of the apostles who was struck dead for lying; hence, a liar; one who distorts or exaggerates the truth.—"Baron Munchausen was the superb *Ananias* of his age."—Emmet Holloway.

**an'ti dote** (an'ti dōte). Anything that will remove evil effects.—"If militarism is to be destroyed, then the *antidote* is social security."—Ernest Bevin.

**a pach'e** (uh pa(h)sh'). One of a fierce tribe of North-American Indians; hence, one of a gang of lawless, and often violent, criminals or ruffians frequenting the streets of Paris.—"An accomplished actor can show meanness without slouching all over the stage like a musical comedy *apache.*"—Joseph Downing.

**A pol'lo** (uh pol'ō). The Greek god of youth and manly beauty; hence, a perfect specimen of young manhood.—"He was trained in the gymnasium till he looked like a young *Apollo.*"—Gertrude Atherton.

**Ar ca'di an** (ahr kāy'di ăn). Resembling Arcadia, the mountain district in ancient Greece whose inhabitants lived pleasant, contented lives; hence, ideally simple and contented.—"What he wanted was an English bride of ancient lineage and *Arcadian* innocence."—Edith Wharton.

**Ar'go nauts** (ahr'gō nawts). Legendary heroes who sailed with Jason in the ship Argo in search of the Golden Fleece; hence, those who brave great dangers in seeking wealth.—"The city was more varied and arresting, and there were *Argonauts* in those days."—Theodore Dreiser.

**a rid'i ty** (ă rid'ĭ ti). A state of being very dry and parched; dryness; barrenness; lack of interest or life.—"They invented new gew-gaws with which to protect themselves from the boredom of their own intellectual and cultural *aridity.*"—John Ise.

**Ar'gus-eyed"** (ahr'gŭss-īde"). Like the mythical hundred-eyed monster Argus; vigilant; sharp-sighted and watchful.—"The *Argus-eyed* captain swept the sea with his glasses, watching for hidden dangers."—Donald G. Cooley.

**Ar″ma ged′don** (ahr″muh ged′ŭn). The prophetic scene of the great battle at the end of the world; hence, a great final conflict.—"The thunder of *Armageddon* rolls closer and closer." H. W. Prentis, Jr.

**ar′ter ies** (ahr′tur iz). The tubelike vessels that carry the blood from the heart through the body; hence, channels or main highways of communications.—"The road is one of the main trade *arteries* through the province." —Roy Chapman Andrews.

**a stig′ma tism** (uh stig′muh tiz′m). A structural defect of the eye causing imperfect or indistinct vision.—"His warped and twisted point of view was a king of moral *astigmatism*."—Donald G. Cooley.

**as′tral** (ass′trăl). Like the stars; starry; connected with the stars.—"Earthbound though our bodies be, our minds can be *astral* in their roamings."—Donald G. Cooley.

**At′las** (at′lăss). A Titan forced to hold up the heavens on his head and hands; hence, a person who carries a great burden.—"Like an *Atlas* he carried all the troubles of the world upon his shoulders."—Henry J. Powers.

**at ten′u at″ed** (ă ten′yū āte″id). Weakened; enfeebled; diluted.—"Examples of dictatorship and democracy, the latter considerably *attenuated*, are to be found as governmental patterns."—George Barton Cutten.

**At′tic** (at′ik). Resembling the symmetry, refinement, and simplicity of Attica in ancient Greece; hence, classic; delicate; refined.—"The new play is blessed with *Attic* style and salty wit."—Donald G. Cooley.

**Au ge′an** (aw jee′ăn). Like the stables of Augeas, not cleaned for 30 years; hence, filthy and very hard to clean; needing hard work; difficult to solve. —"The problem of keeping these rooms in order is becoming *Augean*." —Emily Post.

**au′ra** (aw′ruh). A subtle emanation from a person or thing, surrounding it, and said to be visible to some people at times; a characteristic atmosphere.—"In spite of everything, opera continues to wear its social *aura*."—Fiorello H. LaGuardia.

**Bab″y lo′ni an** (bab″ĭ lō′ni ăn). Like the ancient city of Babylon; hence, vicious; luxuriously voluptuous; full of vice and wickedness.—"The tropical city was *Babylonian* in its corruption."—Sterling McCormick.

**bac″cha na′li a** (bak″uh nāy′li uh). A Roman festival in honor of Bacchus; hence, an orgy; a drunken revel; a riotous feast.—"There is a *bacchanalia*, for example, which has all the makings of a terpsichorean riot."— Howard Barnes.

**bal′last** (bal′uhst). A heavy substance used to stabilize a vessel; hence, that which steadies or gives stability to character or conduct; a steadying element.—"Early Puritan training gave a *ballast* to his character."— John J. Green.

**balm** (bahm). An aromatic oily substance obtained from certain trees, used to relieve pain; hence, anything that soothes or heals; a soothing influence.—"Books are *balm*, sweet dreams, and escape."—Lewis Gannett.

**ba rom′e ter** (buh rom′ē tur). An instrument for indicating atmospheric pressure, used for forecasting the weather; something that records changes.—"Money is not always a *barometer* of human motive."—Arthur Sweetser.

**bat tal′ions** (bă tal′yŭnz). Divisions of an army consisting of two or more companies, batteries, or troops; parts of an army organized to act together; hence, any forces in battle array; organized units.—"Above, on the vast, bare cliffs hung the tired *battalions* of the storm, casting shadows over uplands and ravines."—Caroline Dale Snedeker.

**bat′tened** (bat″nd). Covered with tarpaulin and secured by strips of wood; hence, securely closed against anything entering.—"The hatches of his mind are *battened* down so as never to admit any consistency."—George Barton Cutten.

**Beau" Brum'mell** (bō" brum'ĕl). A dandy; a man who pays exaggerated attention to clothes; a person who loves to dress in the latest fashion.— "Byron was a bit of a *Beau Brummell.*"—Charles Henry Crozier.

**be drag'gled** (bē drag"ld). Made wet or soiled, as by dragging.—"These women see politics as the humble and sometimes *bedraggled* handmaid of liberty."—Martha Taft.

**bludg'eon ing** (bluj'ŭn ing). Striking with a short club; hence, using violent argument or criticism.—"Neither *bludgeoning* nor cajoling will convince anyone of this truth."—Robert Gordon Sproul.

**Bo he'mi an** (bō hē'mi ăn). Unconventional; free and easy; paying no heed to social formalities.—"It is a burlesque of *Bohemian* country life in a resort district."—Henry Seidel Canby.

**boom'er ang** (bōōm'ur ang). An Australian weapon which when thrown returns to the thrower; hence, anything that reacts or recoils upon the user.—"To be effective, advertising must reflect realities, not phantoms, else it becomes a *boomerang.*"—Charles L. Kaufman.

**Brob"ding nag'i an** (brob"ding nag'i-ăn). Of the imaginary country of giants in "Gulliver's Travels"; hence, of enormous size.—"A *Brobdingnagian* marmot was sunning himself before his hole."—Eleanor Lattimore.

**browse** (brouze: 'ou' as in 'out'). Nibble at shoots or twigs; hence, read passages here and there in books at a library or in a store.—"For half an hour I would *browse* about the quiet building."—Edwin Way Teale.

**buc"ca neers'** (buk"uh neerz'). Pirates or freebooters.—"The greed of legally incorporated *buccaneers* has provided an evil example for criminals."—Edmund A. Walsh.

**buf'fet ing** (buf'et ing). Contending; striking with repeated blows.—"There is a *buffeting* of thought, although personal comments are not indulged."—James G. Harbord.

**bul'wark** (bŏŏl'wurk). A fortification; hence, any defense.—"We feel strongly that our federal system of government is an additional *bulwark* to safeguard our future freedom and liberty."—Harold E. Stassen.

**bur'geoned** (bur'jŭnd). Put forth buds; sprouted; hence, began to show signs of life.—"The bare stage *burgeoned* with the buildings, people, and small realities of life."—Marc Connelly.

**cal'dron** (kawl'drŭn). A large kettle or boiler; a heating pot.—"The future of Asia has again been thrown into the boiling *caldron* of a great war."—Edmund C. Lucas.

**Cal'va ry** (kal'vuh ri). The place where Jesus was crucified; hence, a place or time of intense suffering.—"He had ignored the sufferings of others, and now his own *Calvary* was approaching."—Ainslee Mockridge.

**ca nal'ized** (kuh nal'īze'd). Converted into separate courses or routines.— "Conflicts of interests can be *canalized* into political, constitutional, and legal channels."—William G. Carleton.

**can'kered** (kang'kurd). Eaten away, as by an ulcer or canker; infected, as with a secret evil; soured, diseased, or corrupted.—"Your thoughts were lifted out of the trouble which had *cankered* them."—A. S. M. Hutchinson.

**Cas san'dra** (kă san'druh). A Trojan prophetess doomed by Apollo to have her prophecies continually disbelieved; hence, a person whose dire predictions are not believed.—"Anyone who tells him that he cannot expect much for himself but only for the next generations, is likely to be called a calamity howler and a *Cassandra.*" —Dorothy Thompson.

**cat"a lyt'ic** (kat"uh lit'ik). Pertaining to a chemical change brought about by an agent which itself remains stable.—"Our resources are adequate, and as a *catalytic* agent we have billions of money."—Alfred P. Sloan, Jr.

**cat'a pult"ed** (kat'uh pult"ed). Hurled, as though from a bomb-throwing engine; shot forward with great force.— "If some change were made they thought failures would be eliminated, and all D students would immediately be *catapulted* into class A."—George Barton Cutten.

**cat'er waul"ing** (kat'ur wawl"ing). Uttering discordant cries like a cat; hence, quarreling noisily like cats.— "All sorts of *caterwauling* and name-calling filled the air."—William Allen White.

**ca thar'sis** (kuh thahr'siss: 'th' as in 'thin'). Purification of the emotions by drama or other arts; a cleansing outlet, purging the soul of sordid desires.—"The beauty in this talent has little commerce with earthly things, but like great tragedy effects a *catharsis* in its lovers and worshipers."—Ludwig Lewisohn.

**cav"i ar'** (kav"i ahr'). An expensive relish made from sturgeon-roe; hence, something too choice to be appreciated by the general public.— " 'You are wine and *caviar* to me!' he cried."—Thomas Wolfe.

**Cer'ber us** (sur'bur ŭs). The three-headed dog which guarded the gates of the infernal regions; hence, a watchman or guard.—"Where was her enemy the watchman? Luck was with her. *Cerberus* had his back to her, again reading his paper."—Emma Bugbee.

**chan'cer y** (chan'sur i). Litigation or lawsuits about property or other possessions; hence, a rather hopeless position.—"In his latter years poverty held Sir Walter Scott in *chancery*."—Bruce Ellsworth.

**Cha'ron** (kair'ŏn). The son of Erebus who ferried the dead over the Styx river to Hades.—"He foresaw that *Charon* and his ferry would take him on his next trip."—Bruce Ellsworth.

**chi me'ra** (kī mee'ruh). A mythical monster which breathed out flames; hence, a foolish fancy; a wild or absurd idea.—"Is world peace, then, a *chimera*, an absurd and groundless dream?"—Donald G. Cooley.

**chrys'a lis** (kriss'uh liss). The pupa of an insect enclosed in a kind of shell; hence, a case or enclosure; a person or creature in a preparatory or undeveloped stage.—"Shy little Eva broke out of her *chrysalis* and became

the life of every party."—Donald G. Cooley.

**Cim me'ri an** (si meer'i ăn). Gloomy; shrouded in darkness; like the dense, misty darkness in which the mythical Cimmerii dwelt.—"They groped their way through the *Cimmerian* windings in the cave."—Charles Henry Crozier.

**Cir'ce** (sur'sē). An island sorceress who transformed men into swine; hence, an enchantress; a bewitching and degrading person; a temptress.—"Like the character in the book, she was all *Circe* and not Penelope. There was neither beauty nor harmony where her shrines stood."—Ludwig Lewisohn.

**clar'i on** (klar'i ŭn). Loud and clear, as the sound of a trumpet.—"The thing that is uppermost in our minds is the *clarion* call of democracy."—Percy C. Magnus.

**cod'dled** (kod"ld). Treated with kindness and tenderness; pampered.—"I have *coddled* this notion for years, waiting for a chance to give it publicity."—Joseph Jastrow.

**co los'sus** (kō loss'ŭs). Anything of gigantic size like the Colossus of Rhodes.—"Russia is the new *colossus* that bestrides the continent of Europe."—Jan Christiaan Smuts.

**con'tours** (kon'tōōrz). Outlines; boundary lines, hence determining lines.— "He shaped and molded that office to the *contours* of his own heroic stature." —Wm. J. Cameron.

**Cov'en try** (kov'ĕn tri). A state of ostracism or disgrace; banishment from social intercourse; a position in which association with others is impossible as the offender is cut or generally ignored.—"She was in *Coventry*, estranged from all."—A. S. M. Hutchinson.

**Croe'sus** (kree'sŭs). A very wealthy king of Lydia; hence, a man of great wealth.—"He played the part of *Croesus* among his peers."—Franz Werfel.

**cru'ci ble** (krōō'si b'l). A melting pot; hence, a trying and purifying agency. —"Now the *crucible* of war is further crystallizing colonial nationalism."— William G. Carleton.

**crys'tal lize** (kriss'tăl īze). Assume a permanent form; form into a definite shape; take on a fixed aspect; become concrete.—"If ideas are to *crystallize* into action, they must be clothed in living words."—William A. Temple.

**cush'ion** (kŏosh'ŭn). To check easily and gradually so that the shock is scarcely felt; to soften the blow.—"It is not easy to prevent or *cushion* inflation."—Noel Sargent.

**Cy'clops** (sī'klops). One of the race of giants having only one eye.—"Admiral Nelson, the great British *Cyclops*, made history when he refused to use his one eye."—Bruce Ellsworth.

**Dam'o cles** (dam'ō kleeze). A flatterer who was seated at a royal banquet with a sword hanging by a single hair over him; hence, an imminent danger.—"This former and unknown prison sentence was a sword of *Damocles* hanging over him."—Donald G. Cooley.

**De li'lah** (dē lī'luh). Samson's mistress who betrayed him to the Philistines; hence, a temptress; a false and crafty woman.—"Cleopatra was the *Delilah* who cost Mark Antony his power."—Donald G. Cooley.

**Del'phi an** (del'fi ăn). Of the famous oracle at Delphi in ancient Greece through whose mouth Apollo gave prophecies which generally had a double meaning; hence, ambiguous; obscure.—"Could the commentator possibly be alluding to the *Delphian* prophecies of Heinrich Heine?"—Bruce Ellsworth.

**de vour'** (dē vour': 'ou' as in 'out'). Eat up; consume ravenously; prey upon; hence, absorb or engross the whole attention.—"Let not your curiosity *devour* you."—Bradwell E Tanis.

**di lute'** (di lūte'). To make weaker by adding some mixture; lessen or diminish by some addition.—"Military strategy dictates that we should not *dilute* our effective power."—Hugh S. Johnson.

**dis arms'** (diss'ahrmz). Deprives of weapons; takes away the power to harm or annoy; allays anger or suspicion.—"He *disarms* criticism by not taking himself or his ideas too seriously."—Allan Nevins.

**dis'taff** (diss'taff). The staff that holds wool or flax for hand-spinning; hence, woman's work; the females of the family, or holders of the distaff; feminine.—"That type of work is a little on the *distaff* side."—Emmet Holloway.

**doff'ing** (doff'ing). Taking off, as a hat or cape; removing; hence, putting to one side; discarding; giving up.— " 'It's no secret,' he proclaimed, *doffing* his air of mystery."—Lloyd C. Douglas.

**dom'i cile** (dom'ĭ sil). Settled place of abode; dwelling place; home.— "There is a phase of experience which we do not share with others, and therein is the *domicile* of our personal integrity."—Edmund Ezra Day.

**Don Ju'an** (don jōō'ăn). A profligate nobleman of Spain; hence, a rake; a seducer; a libertine.—"The decrepit old *Don Juan*, the sly old sinner, too worn out himself to make love still enjoyed watching others making fools of themselves."—Axel Munthe.

**Don Quix'ote** (don kwik'sot). The hero of a Spanish romance; hence, a man who is ridiculously chivalrous and impractical; an extravagantly romantic and idealistic man.—"His stories are too raw for me. I'm no sissy, but that fellow's a regular *Don Quixote*."—Willa Cather.

**dregs** (dregz). Sediments of liquids; grounds or lees; hence, the worthless remainder.—"Napoleon had drunk of the cup of power to the *dregs*."—Raymond Moley.

**dross** (dross). Refuse or impurities; waste matter.—"Only in the purifying fire of sacrifice is the *dross* of selfishness consumed."—John D. Rockefeller, Jr.

**dy'na mos** (dī'nuh mōze). Machines for converting mechanical power into electric energy in the form of current. —"Individual initiative, freedom, and opportunity for advancement are the *dynamos* of all our progress." —Bernard M. Baruch.

**ef"flo res'cence** (ef"lō ress'ĕnce). The act or time of flowering; hence, the making manifest of something beautiful.—"These people found a new way of life which was to be the *efflorescence* of many centuries of developing culture."—John Ise.

**El Do ra'do** (el dō rah'dō). A city sought by Spaniards in South America because it was said to be full of gold and other treasures; hence, a city of fabulous wealth; a golden opportunity.—"The undiscovered resources of Brazil are our new *El Dorado*."—Ellery Marsh Egan.

**e lix'ir** (ē lik'sur). A tincture or medicine; a remedy or imaginary cordial which was supposed to lengthen life indefinitely; hence, a panacea or life-giving potion.—"The book is full of a veritable *elixir* of spiritual vitality." —Dorothy Canfield Fisher.

**E ly'sian** (ē lizh'yǎn). Resembling or of Elysium, the place of perfect happiness; hence, heavenly; delightful. —"I looked over the gardens, all fragrant with the scent of *Elysian* flowers."—Axel Munthe.

**em balmed'** (em bahm'd'). Preserved or kept from decay; protected from oblivion.—"Was this organization *embalmed* or merely anesthetized pending election?"—Hugh S. Johnson.

**en shroud'** (en shroud': 'ou' as in 'out'). Cover with a shroud; hence, enwrap or cover completely; hide or conceal. —"These uncertainties envelop and *enshroud* the future."—Harold G. Moulton.

**ex hume'** (eks hūme'). Dig up what has been buried; hence, unearth; bring out into the light.—"They would certainly *exhume* from obscurity certain leaders who escaped death and prison."—Dorothy Thompson.

**fa'bi an** (fāy'bi ǎn). In the manner of the Roman general, Fabius, who used dilatory tactics; hence, tending to delay; tardy; cautious.—"In Russia, also, the tactics were said to have been *fabian*."—Hansen W. Baldwin.

**fac'ets** (fass'ets). Sides; aspects.— "There are many *facets* to war."— Harry M. Warner.

**Fal staff'i an** (fawl staff'i ǎn). Characteristic of Shakespeare's fat braggart, Sir John Falstaff; hence, jovial and boastful; like the ragged rascals of his regiment; witty and untruthful.— "Words like *Falstaffian*, Quixotic, Pickwickian, sum up cultural attitudes and segments of human experience as nothing else can."—Christian Gauss.

**Faus'ti an** (fawce'ti ǎn). Of or like Faust, the hero of Goethe's drama who sold his soul to the devil who agreed to fulfil all Faust's wishes at this great price.—"The studio exercises its rights sometimes with *Faustian* vengeance."—Douglas Gilbert.

**fe cun'di ty** (fē kun'dǐ ti). Productiveness; fruitfulness; fertility.—"The *fecundity* of thought and accomplishments in the Elizabethan period in England was comparable with the Golden Age of Pericles in Athens."— O. R. McGuire.

**fi'ber** (fī'bur). A thread-like component of a substance; that which makes up the texture; hence, the necessary character, the essential qualities.— "The youngest of these children who have never known other than our distorted time have had their moral *fiber* weakened."—Lena Madesin Phillips.

**fis'sure** (fish'ur). A cleft, crack, or split.—"We will only emerge from the abyss by uniting in a solid bloc within which no *fissure* will be tolerated."—Charles de Gaulle.

**flayed** (flāde). Stripped off the skin; hence, harshly censured; criticized severely.—"Sinners are ruthlessly *flayed* in these pages."—Iris Barry.

**forged** (forjd). Formed; shaped; fashioned; produced; made the shape of. —"Make a plan, demand a daily performance, set a date for completion, and you will have *forged* your future."—Hugh E. Blackstone.

**forged** (forjd). Moved forward slowly but steadily; moved ahead with difficulty; moved gradually forward. —"Illegal rearmament *forged* ahead." —Lord Vansittart.

**Frank'en stein** (frangk'ěn stīne). A student described in fiction as having made a monster to which he gave a kind of life power which it finally used to kill its maker; hence, a person or agency that is destroyed by something that it has created; something that ruins its maker.—"They soon found themselves powerless to control the *Frankenstein* monster thus called into being."—H. W. Prentis, Jr.

**fru i'tion** (froo ish'ŭn). Fruit-bearing; hence, the yielding of results; realization; fulfilment; attainment.—"The complete *fruition* of that policy of unselfishness has not in every case been obtained."—Franklin Delano Roosevelt.

**fused** (fūze'd). Melted or liquefied by heat; hence, united.—"By the fires of war they have become *fused* and welded into a nation."—Monroe E. Deutsch.

**gar gan'tu an** (gahr gan'choo ăn). Resembling Gargantua, the gigantic king; like a voracious giant; enormous.—"Japan's dreams of empire were modest in comparison with the *gargantuan* aspirations of Germany."—Franklin Delano Roosevelt.

**gar rot'ting** (guh rot'ing). Strangling or throttling in order to rob.—"The most tragic casualty on the home front is the *garrotting* of Milo Perkins."—Louis Ludlow.

**Geth sem'a ne** (geth sem'uh nē: 'th' as in 'thin'). The garden at the foot of the Mount of Olives, the scene of the agony of Jesus; hence, a place or time of great suffering.—"We are in the *Gethsemane* of civilization. Never before has there been anything comparable to the present misery and devastation."—Francis J. Spellman.

**ghouls** (gōolz). Persons who rob dead bodies; hence, people who act like them.—"The most despicable of all charlatans are the *ghouls* that prey on the bodies of cancer victims."—Morris Fishbein.

**Gol'go tha** (gol'gō thuh: 'th' as in 'thin'). Calvary; hence, place or time of great torment or suffering.—"His *Golgotha* was the month in prison which he wished so fervently to avoid."—Konrad Heiden.

**go li'aths** (gō lī'ăths: 'th' as in 'thin'). Giants; men or animals of enormous size, so called from Goliath, the giant whom David slew.—"The Dinosaurs ranged from these *goliaths* to compar-

atively small dragons."—Robert G. Chaffee.

**Gor'di an** (gor'di ăn). Like the difficult knot tied by Gordius and cut by Alexander the Great; hence, intricate; difficult to unravel; very complicated.—"He was all for cutting the *Gordian* knot of any difficulty instead of fiddling about with it."—H. G. Wells.

**gor'gon** (gor'gŭn). One of the three winged sisters of mythological fame who had snakes for hair and whose looks turned any beholder to stone; hence, a terribly ugly or repellent woman.—"As she glared down at me I understood what a *gorgon* was like."—John Myers Myers.

**gos'sa mer** (goss'uh mur). A film or cobweb; a very thin gauze-like fabric; something flimsy and easily broken.—"In the day when the pledged word of men becomes a *gossamer*, modern civilization will collapse."—Hugh S. Johnson.

**har'py** (hahr'pi). A mythological monster which seized dead souls; hence, a plunderer; a rapacious person; one who extorts from others.—"He understands that the picture of the business man as vulgarian and a *harpy* is more than a little out of focus."—Stanley Walker.

**he gi'ra** (hē jī'ruh). The flight of Mohammed from Mecca; hence, any similar flight or departure; an exodus.—"This tremendous Russian *hegira* was not carried out according to the blue-print."—Hugh E. Blackstone.

**her'ald** (her'ăld). An announcer; a person who brings a message; a bearer of news or tidings; a forerunner; a harbinger.—"Pity comes without a *herald* when we are far from the scenes that pity comes from."—Thomas Wolfe.

**her cu'le an** (hur kū'lē ăn). Requiring the great strength of the Greek hero, Hercules; very difficult.—"Teachers and school administrators have rallied to the *herculean* task of registering millions of American consumers."—Prentiss M. Brown.

**her met'i cal ly** (hur met'i kăl li). In a way that makes something perfectly airtight; imperviously closed against air, other fluids, or gases.—"Hermes is said to have kept his discoveries from prying eyes by putting his product into jars which were carefully sealed. From this arose the term '*hermetically* sealed.' "—Karl T. Compton.

**hi"ber na'tion** (hī"bur nā'shŭn). Passing the winter asleep, as do some animals; hence, passing the time in inactivity; in a torpid state as though asleep; period of inaction.—"Free enterprise has regained a great amount of prestige that it lost through its *hibernation* during the depression." —H. Stanley Marcus.

**hoar'y** (hōre'i). Gray or white, as from age; hence, ancient; venerable; remote or far removed from the present.—"It was a familiar melody out of the *hoary* past."—Caroline Dale Snedeker.

**Ho mer'ic** (hō mer'ik). Suggestive of the Greek epic poet Homer who described the noisy laughter of the gods; hence, irrepressible; loud and hearty. —"She is a teacher of Greek and there's something quite *Homeric* about her, a sort of bosun's voice."—Christopher Morley.

**ho ri'zon** (hō rī'z'n). The range of sight or perception; the boundary line of vision; the range of experience.—"Our *horizon* must go on expanding till it is as wide as the world's."—Allan Nevins.

**Hy'dra** (hī'druh). A mythical Greek serpent having nine heads, on which two heads grew in place of each one that was hewn off; hence, of a kind that has many forms and is very hard to overcome.—"One would have thought that the Pilgrims would have drowned the *hydra*-headed monster of intolerance in the depths of the ocean."—Stewart W. McClelland.

**ig nite'** (ig nīte'). To set on fire; to kindle.—"Only a spark is needed to *ignite* the already existing fuel of inflation."—Noel Sargent.

**im"pri ma'tur** (im"pri māy'tur). A license to print or publish; hence, approval; sanction; imprint.—"His study of the G-men's operations bears the *imprimatur* of the F.B.I. itself."— D. W. Talmadge.

**in'cu bat"ing** (in'kū bāte"ing). Hatching; hence, being produced or planned.—"Some of the refinements of living are still *incubating* in our laboratories."—Eric A. Johnston.

**in cur'sions** (in kur'shŭnz). Raids; temporary invasions; hostile entries into a territory.—"We diplomats sometimes make *incursions* into strategy, if only as amateurs."—Maxim Litvinoff.

**in gre'di ent** (in gree'di ĕnt). A component part of a mixture.—"Leadership among the people is the priceless *ingredient* of democracy."— Wendell L. Willkie.

**in oc'u late** (in ok'ū lāte). To insert under the skin; hence, to introduce into the mind; to communicate, as by infection; to impregnate or imbue; to implant.—"The ideal is to *inoculate* the students with the nobler conceptions of character and conduct."— Don Marquis.

**in sa'ti a ble** (in sāy'shi uh b'l). Not capable of being satisfied; greedy.— "War has an *insatiable* appetite for materials."—William L. Batt.

**in'su lar** (in'sū lur). Like islanders; hence, isolated; narrow-minded; not liberal; having a very limited viewpoint.—"As the narrow barrier of the Channel makes the English appear *insular* to Continental nations, so the Americans seem *insular* to Europeans."—Bertrand Russell.

**in"tra mu'ral** (in"truh mū'răl). Within the walls; hence, confined or limited to members or a group.—"On the *intramural* affairs of the nation the book is furiously polemic."—Orville Prescott.

**I sa'iah** (ī zāy'uh). A major Hebrew prophet who warned of coming judgments on the people; hence, one who is fearless in rebuking wrong.—"An *Isaiah* in a sunbonnet, wherever wrong and injustice reared their heads she was there in valiant spirit." —Edwin Way Teale.

**jad'ed** (jaid'ed). Wearied by hard service; hence, no longer keen, wanting in zest.—"The Romans recommended endive to those whose appetites were *jaded*."—Earlene M. Cornell.

**jan'is sa"ries** (jan'i zer"iz). Turkish infantrymen, often former slaves or prisoners; hence, instruments of tyranny.—"They were sore because he called them *janissaries;* that's just janitors in uniform."—Christopher Morley.

**Ja'nus** (jāy'nŭs). An ancient Roman deity having two faces; hence, two-faced or looking both ways; deceitful.—"He wants to keep this aspect of his *Janus* face pointed toward us."—Frank Kingdon.

**jaun'dice** (jawn'diss). To affect a person's judgment with prejudice; to give a disordered vision; to color with envy or prejudice.—"A bout with the newspaper at the beginning of the day is enough to *jaundice* the eye for the rest of the waking hours."—Donald Culross Peattie.

**Je'hu** (jē'hū). A king of Israel who drove at a rapid pace; hence, a fast driver; one who drives furiously.—"The driver of the jeep was a wild and reckless *Jehu*."—Bradwell E. Tanis.

**jer"e mi'ad** (jer"ē mī'ad). A lamentation resembling the lamentations of the prophet, Jeremiah; a doleful tirade; a dolorous tale; a dismal complaint.—"The tract was like some angry *jeremiad* of an ancient Hebrew prophet."—Ellery Marsh Egan.

**Jo'vi an** (jō'vi ăn). Like the god Jupiter or Jove; Jove-like; like the god of the elements.—"I sent him a colored picture of the tanks and guns, with a *Jovian* bearded face directing operations from a cloud in the top corner."—Jan Struther.

**ka tab'a sis** (kuh tab'uh siss). A going down; hence, a march back from a former position; a retreat.—"We witnessed the *katabasis* of the Germans after the battle of Stalingrad."—Henry J. Powers.

**kin'dled** (kin'd'ld). Inflamed; set on fire; aroused; stirred up.—"War has *kindled* a new spirit of sacrifice and fostered a deeper spirit of charity."—Francis J. Spellman.

**knell** (nel). The tolling of a bell giving bad news; hence, a warning sound.—

"Any paralysis of inquisitiveness will sound the death *knell* of human advance."—Owen D. Young.

**lab'y rinth** (lab'ĭ rinth). A bewildering place of intricate paths or passages; a maze; hence, a perplexity; a confusing combination.—"She had not bargained for this glimpse into the *labyrinth* of the peerage."—Edith Wharton.

**lack'ey** (lak'i). A footman; hence, a servile attendant, a menial.—"The dictator has used the free spirit, learning, as a *lackey*, a slave."—Monroe E. Deutsch.

**lat'i tude** (lat'ĭ tūde). Range or scope; freedom from limits.—"I ask the House to accord me greater *latitude* than is sometimes allowed in personal explanations."—Samuel Hoare.

**lay'man** (lay'măn). One of the laity; a man not belonging to one of the professions; hence, one who is uninitiated.—"I speak as a *layman*, but I do believe the dictator can be destroyed by international strategy."—Maxim Litvinoff.

**leav'en** (lev'ĕn). A fermenting agent, such as yeast; hence, any influence that causes changes and transformation by spreading silently but with power.—"If our homes can be truly Christian, then the influence of that spirit will assuredly spread like *leaven* through all aspects of our life."—Queen Elizabeth of England.

**leg'a cy** (leg'uh si). Bequest; something left by will or derived from an ancestor.—"The obligation to protect old age is the *legacy* from the machine age in which we live."—Alfred M. Landon.

**Le'the** (lē'thē: 'th' as in 'thin'). A river of Hades which produced forgetfulness of the past in all those who drank its waters; hence, oblivion; forgetfulness.—"He sought *Lethe* in bars and taverns, but could not drown his remorse."—Bertram M. Myers.

**le vi'a than** (lē vī'uh thăn: 'th' as in 'thin'). An enormous sea-animal; hence, something unusually huge; something of colossal size or importance.—"His eye rested on the huge pile of his manuscript and it seemed impossible that a publisher could be found who would publish this *leviathan*."—Thomas Wolfe.

**lig'a ture** (lig'uh chŏŏr). Something that binds or ties; anything that unites, as a thread to tie up blood vessels.—"Creator and receiver are eternally joined by the unbreakable *ligature* of beauty."—William J. Calvert, Jr.

**Lil"li pu'tian** (lil"i pū'shăn). Of the fictitious kingdom of Gulliver's Lilliput and its tiny inhabitants; hence, diminutive, very small.—"Only a *Lilliputian* fraction continue on for three years in order to earn master's degrees."—H. F. Harding.

**lim'bo** (lim'bō). An indefinite border region, neither heaven nor hell, where the souls of unbaptised infants and of those who lived before the Christian era are said to dwell; a place of oblivion.—"I have faith that war will be relegated to the *limbo* of things forgotten."—Cordell Hull.

**Lo thar'i o** (lō thair'i ō: 'th' as in 'thin'). A gay seducer; a rake; a libertine.—"They learned that an attendant, a rather gay *Lothario*, had shown marked attention to the girl." —Archie McFedries.

**lu'mi nar"ies** (lū'mĭ ner"iz). Bodies that give light; heavenly bodies; hence, people who are leaders; eminent people; those who shed light around them in some way.—"Minor *luminaries* never interested him when stars of the first magnitude were in view."—Edith Wharton.

**lu'mi nous** (lū'mĭ nŭs). Shining; illuminated; hence, intelligent.—"The stars proclaim in *luminous*, inerasable language the existence of God."—Francis J. Spellman.

**ma ca'bre** (muh kah'b'r). Descriptive of the dance of death in which death leads other skeletons to the grave; hence, relating to or symbolizing the power of death.—"The *macabre* tragedy of Italy is marked by so many dizzy turns and grotesque incidents that it has lost reality."—Anne O'Hare McCormick.

**mael'strom** (māle'strŏm). A whirlwind or current off the Norwegian coast; hence, any wide-spreading influence or resistless movement that is violent. —"We must take heed lest we be drawn into the *maelstrom*."—Matthew Woll.

**mar'a thon** (mar'uh thon: 'th' as in 'thin'). A foot-race, so called from Marathon, 20 miles from Athens, from whence a runner sped on foot to Athens to announce the victory over Persia; hence, an endurance contest. —"The dervishes dance themselves into an unconscious *marathon* of invocations."—William Alfred Eddy.

**ma'trix** (māy'triks). The womb; hence, the formative cells of a structure; the place or element that gives form to something within it; the material in which something originates and is formed.—"Here is a volume portraying the cultural *matrix* of his achievements."—Philip P. Wiener.

**maw** (maw). The mouth or stomach of a voracious animal; hence, appetite or jaws.—"All civilization was being devoured by the greedy *maw* of war." —Sterling McCormick.

**may'hem** (māy'hem). The act of depriving a person by violence of the use of a limb or organ; hence, any kind of mutilation; a serious injury to a person or thing that lessens its usefulness.—"The author who is abroad probably hasn't seen the *mayhem* committed by Hollywood on his books." —Douglas Gilbert.

**mec'ca** (mek'uh). Any place sought as a center of inspiration and recuperation, as Mecca, the birthplace of Mohammed.—"The farm will be a vacation *mecca* for business men."— Chester M. Davis.

**Meph"i stoph'e les** (mef"ĭ stoff'ĕ leeze) The fiend of Goethe's drama Faust; hence, a relentless fiend; a devil; a demon.—"He imagined a species of pocket *Mephistopheles*, climbing in the trees, and making horrible faces just to defy him."—Jules Romains.

**me rid'i an** (mĕ rid'i ăn). The highest point attained by the sun or any star in the sky; noonday; hence, the culmination or highest point of anything; the zenith.—"To that ambitious task he had again pledged himself in the *meridian* of manhood." —Maud Diver.

**met′a phors** (met′uh forz). Figures of speech in which a word or phrase denoting something is used for another thing to suggest likeness or analogy between the two.—"Through grammar we understand the role of ambiguity in the invention of *metaphors* for purposes of imaginative or poetical literature."—Robert M. Hutchins.

**Mı′das** (mī′dăss). A mythological king of Phrygia who was granted power to turn whatever he touched into gold; hence, wealth producing; fabulously rich.—"Indubitably she was a part of this *Midas* world."—Thomas Wolfe.

**mock** (mok). Imitating the reality; not the real thing; sham.—"The army has not had to rely on text books and *mock* warfare for its training; it has had actual warfare."—Elbert D. Thomas.

**mo guls′** (mō gulz′). Mongol conquerors of India; hence, great or very wealthy people; pretentious personages; magnates.—"Like all movie *moguls*, he knows the value of publicity."—Louis Adamic.

**Mo′loch** (mō′lok). A Semitic god to whom human sacrifices were made; hence, a system or method that requires frightful sacrifice.—"Foreigners sincerely believe that American business men are worshipers of the great god *Moloch*."—Emory L. Fielding.

**mo rass′** (mō rass′). A marsh, swamp, or quagmire; hence, a difficulty.—"Understanding and consultation may well prove the way out of the present *morass*."—Jan Christiaan Smuts.

**mo sa′ic** (mō zāy′ik). A pattern composed of many pieces of various shapes and colors.—"Like every other segment in the *mosaic* of American society, labor surely will live up to the social responsibilities that come with growth and power."—Eric A. Johnston.

**my op′ics** (mī op′iks). Nearsighted people; hence, those who cannot foresee future possibilities.—"The builders of the Great Wall were mental *myopics* who saw only the ex-

pediency of temporary solutions."—Madame Chiang Kai-shek.

**na′bobs** (nāy′bobz). Native deputies or viceroys in India; hence, men of great wealth.—"The *nabobs* have to make a show of lamenting the loss of their kingdom, but these fat old merchants would be quite upset if a revolution got started."—Lloyd C. Douglas.

**nar cot′ic** (nahr kot′ik). Any one of the substances that reduce pain and induce sleep; something that lulls to sleep.—"To dole out relief in this way is to administer a *narcotic*, a subtle destroyer of the human spirit."—Franklin Delano Roosevelt.

**neb′u lous** (neb′ū lŭs). Hazy; indistinct; having its parts confused; vague.—"Security is no abstraction too *nebulous* for definition."—John G. Winant.

**ne pen′the** (nē pen′thē: 'th' as in 'thin'). A drug which ancient peoples thought could drown pain and cause forgetfulness; hence, a potion or other agent that produces forgetfulness or oblivion.—"She used hard work as the *nepenthe* for her great sorrow."—S. L. Scanlon.

**Nes′tor** (ness′tur). An aged and wise Greek chief at the siege of Troy, renowned for his advice; hence, a wise and experienced counselor; the wisest and oldest man of a company or organization.—"They turned to Winston Churchill as the *Nestor* of England."—George F. Gahagan.

**niche** (nich). A recessed space or hollow; especially, a recess in a wall for a statue or the like.—"He has carved for himself a *niche* of fame in the industrial temple of America."—Charles E. Coughlin.

**nir va′na** (nir vah′nuh). The Buddhist state of supreme bliss or heaven in which the individual loses personal consciousness and is absorbed into the divine; hence, freedom from hatred, pain, and care; heavenly peace and happiness.—"There are times when even an occidental longs for *nirvana*."—Hugh E. Blackstone.

**oc′to pus** (ok′tō pŭs). A sea-animal having a number of arms; hence, an organized power which has far-reaching capacities for harmful action.—"You became aware on every side of this *octopus*. Its tentacles emerged now and then in international life."—Louis Bromfield.

**O lym'pi an** (ō lim'pi ăn). Pertaining to the great gods of Olympus; hence, godlike; far superior to ordinary mortals.—"Here and there a call is sounded for a leader who is not too coldly aloof, too *Olympian*."—Annie Nathan Meyer.

**om niv'o rous** (om niv'ō rŭs). Eating up everything; hence, swallowing up; devouring.—"The most *omnivorous* pitfall is pride."—Madame Chiang Kai-shek.

**o'pi ate** (ō'pi āte). A medicine inducing sleep; hence, anything that rests or soothes; a narcotic.—"They call religion the *opiate* of the people."—Fulton J. Sheen.

**os mo'sis** (os mō'siss). The tendency of fluids separated by septa or membranes to seep through and intermix; percolation or seepage; permeation; filtering through.—"Students in college get a certain culture, mostly by *osmosis*."—Ainslee Mockridge.

**os'si fied** (oss'ĭ fīde). Hardened like bone; made callous; that has become hardhearted; that has taken a very conventional or conservative form, or become callous.—"A dubious test of truth is 'to feel it in the bones,' which is generally indicative of *ossified* thought."—Edwin Grant Conklin.

**pach'y derm** (pak'ĭ durm). A hoofed and thick-skinned quadruped that does not chew the cud, such as a rhinoceros or elephant; hence, a thick-skinned or insensitive person.—"Al Capone is an amoral man with the thick skin of a *pachyderm*."—George F. Gahagan.

**pal'a din** (pal'uh din). One of the twelve peers of Charlemagne; hence a knight errant, a champion.—"We have as our leader the man who is rightly regarded as the *paladin* of the forces of liberal democracy."—Sumner Welles.

**pale** (pāle). That which is enclosed within bounds, literally or figuratively; a boundary; protection or privileges.—"Some judges infer that the primary aim of punishment is to place an offender beyond the *pale* of society for a certain time."—Lewis E. Lawes.

**pal la'di um** (pă lāy'di ŭm). The image of Pallas in the citadel of Troy on which the people depended for safety; hence, a safeguard, a protection.—"De Witt Clinton said that these schools were the *palladium* of our freedom."—William F. Russell.

**parched** (parch'd). Dried up; scorched; shriveled.—"It is our duty to cause these springs of generosity to spread their waters upon a land now *parched* from long meanness."—Rex G. Tugwell.

**pa ri'ah** (puh rī'uh). A member of a low caste in India; hence, an outcast; something despised; a person or thing socially banned.—"The editor wanted me to write a piece about the *pariah* 'Bureaucrat'."—Harold L. Ickes.

**Par nas'sus** (pahr nass'ŭs). A mountain in central Greece sacred to Apollo and the Muses; hence, the sphere of poetic or literary action, thought, or influence; the realm of poetry.—"For once the author descended from *Parnassus* and wrote plain prose."—Tom Pennell.

**Pen'te cost** (pen'tē kost). The festival of the descent of the Holy Spirit on the Apostles; hence, an out-pouring of illumination and power.—"He stared for an instant, vainly—hoping for a *Pentecost* that did not descend." —Stephen Vincent Benét.

**Per"i cle'an** (per"i klee'ăn). Pertaining to, or like, Pericles, the great Athenian statesman who swayed great crowds with his oratory; hence, possessing an unusual power to influence and persuade.—"It was evident that she wielded a *Periclean* power in her family."—Gertrude Atherton.

**pet"ri fi ca'tion** (pet"rĭ fi kā'shŭn). The state of being made hard or rigid like stone; conversion into a lifeless, stony being; fossilization; hence, inability to change or progress.—"The tragedy of the creative artist in America is his apparent *petrification* at a certain point."—Ludwig Lewisohn.

**phan'tom** (fan'tŭm). In appearance but not in reality; existing only as an apparition; unreal; having a semblance to the real thing, but not valid.—"Bureaucracy never submits even to *phantom* elections."—Henry W. Wriston.

**phar"i sa'i cal** (far"ĭ sāy'ĭ kăl). Self-righteous; observing the outward form but neglecting the spirit of religion or ethics; like a Pharisee.—"Unprincipled men will join the hypocritical and *pharisaical* chorus."—Joseph T. Robinson.

**phi lip'pics** (fĭ lip'iks). An oration denouncing Philip, king of Macedon; hence, a bitter invective or attack in strong language; an acrimonious discourse; an impassioned, censorious speech.—"He bloodied and butchered him with a series of eloquent *philippics*."—S. L. Scanlon.

**Phi lis'tines** (fĭ liss'tinz). Unenlightened warlike natives of ancient Philistia; hence, those antagonistic to art and culture; narrow-minded or prosaic people.—"Nor was this poet a child of light battling the *Philistines* in a dusty and clamorous age."—Ludwig Lewisohn.

**phoe'nix** (fee'nix). A miraculous bird, fabled to burn itself and then rise from the ashes young and beautiful; hence, a symbol of immortality.—"Humankind will survive and, like the *phoenix*, come out from the fire cleaner and stronger."—Aleš Hrdlička.

**pil'lo ry ing** (pil'ō ri ing). In olden times, placing in a frame of wood having holes for head and hands as a punishment; hence, holding up to scorn, ridicule, or abuse.—"If the leaders of Government and Labor had gone through the same *pillorying*, the result would probably have been less complimentary."—M. W. Clement.

**pin'na cle** (pin'uh k'l). A high or topmost point; a lofty peak; slender spire; a dizzy or insecure height.—"Crime has reached a *pinnacle* of appalling height."—J. Edgar Hoover.

**Pla ton'ic** (pluh ton'ik). Characteristic of the Greek philosopher, Plato; hence, of a kind that is spiritual and free from sexual feelings and desire; idealized; harmless and friendly without sensual feeling.—"Wise young girls show their *Platonic* interest in all boys."—Priscilla Wayne.

**plex'us** (plek'sŭss). An interwoven combination of parts; a network.—"That very different and most radically foreign *plexus* stretched even further south."—Theodore Dreiser.

**plumb** (plum). To sound the depth with a weight of lead or plummet; hence, to find out the depth; to fathom; to take the measure of.—"There have been more thorough and patient attempts than mine to *plumb* the murky bottoms of night's biology."—Donald Culross Peattie.

**por'tals** (por'tălz). Wide entranceways; passages for entrance.—"These children were brought to the *portals* of dishonor through the negligence of older persons."—J. Edgar Hoover.

**preg'nant** (preg'nănt). Great with child; hence, big with consequences; filled; significant; potential.—"I wish to quote a few of his wise sayings—they are *pregnant* with thought, and 'meaty.' "—George Matthew Adams.

**Pro me'theus** (prō mee'thūce: 'th' as in 'thin'). The Titan who brought fire from heaven to man and was chained to a rock and tortured continually till released by Chiron; hence, a great man who appears to be inescapably bound.—"His friend awakened him to his real mission. He unbound *Prometheus*."—Gene Fowler.

**pro'te an** (prō'tē ăn). Characteristic of Proteus, a sea god, who had the power to assume whatever shape he chose; hence, exceedingly changeable; very variable; assuming different forms.—"In this handful of earth are all life's primal characteristics: the *protean* shape always individual, the resilient feel of it in the fingers."—Donald Culross Peattie.

**pur'ga to ry** (pur'guh tō ri). An intermediate state where, according to Roman Catholic doctrine, the souls of the departed are purified if they are penitent; hence, a place or state of punishment or suffering for wrong doing.—"Out of that *purgatory* of world conflict, there emerged a profound realization that a new basis must be found for relations among nations."—Cordell Hull.

**Pyr′rhic** (pir′ik). Gained at a ruinous loss, as that of Pyrrhus over the Romans.—"The triumph may be a *Pyrrhic* one, because of the headlong greed with which Mars is rifling material stocks."—Alfred M. Landon.

**quag′mire″** (kwag′mīre″). A bog or marsh; hence, any difficult situation; a position in which one seems to be bogged down.—"We are naturally skeptical of the plans of those partisans who formerly led the nation into the *quagmire* of unarmed neutrality." —Eugene P. Thomas.

**quar′ry** (kwor′i). Prey; a beast or bird hunted; something eagerly hunted and pursued.—"The planes located the convoys and guided the submarines to their *quarry*."—Yates Stirling, Jr.

**quis′lings** (kwiz′lingz). Traitors; despicable people who are untrue to their country, so called from Quisling, the Norwegian traitor.—"The men who deny their duty, whether it be for one hour, one day, or one week are entitled to be placed in the same category as *quislings*."—J. A. Hall.

**quix ot′ic** (kwiks ot′ik). Pertaining to the hero of a Spanish romance, Don Quixote; hence, ridiculously chivalrous or romantic.—"Many people can quote from 'Don Quixote,' and they certainly would use the word *quixotic*."—Lyman Bryson.

**Rab″e lai′si an** (rab″ĕ lāy′zi ăn). Characteristic of the French humorist, Rabelais; hence, coarsely satirical; grossly humorous; employing extravagant caricature.—"The old lady was shrewd, witty, malicious, and sometimes *Rabelaisian*."—Louis Bromfield.

**ram′part** (ram′part). A bulwark or strong defense; a bulwark; a means of protection.—"We feel that we are a *rampart* for democracy."—Walter Citrine.

**ra vines′** (ruh veenz′). Deep gorges or hollows; gullies; long narrow valleys; hence, lower levels.—"The rate structure may be likened to a plateau subject to erosion, and the reductions are the *ravines* produced."—Ralph Budd.

**realms** (relmz). Kingdoms; provinces; regions; domains; spheres.—"The trouble seemed to expand to immense proportions until it lost its outlines in the *realms* of nonsense."—L. P. Jacks.

**rep til′i an** (rep til′i ăn). Resembling snakes or crawling animals; groveling; sly and treacherous like reptiles. —"Political crooks and illiterates and other *reptilian* forms of life would rather we didn't know the truth."— Sterling North.

**res′er voirs** (rez′ur vworz). Stores; reserve supplies.—"In the faculties and the students of the graduate schools of our universities the nation has had one of its greatest *reservoirs* of brain power."—George B. Pegram.

**Rhad″a man′thine** (rad″uh man′thin). Resembling Rhadamanthus, son of Zeus and one of the judges of the underworld, who was renowned for his exemplary justice; hence, strictly honest and just.—"Oliver Wendell Holmes was a great, a wise, a *Rhadamanthine* judge."—Donald G. Cooley.

**ro co′co** (rō kō′kō). Profuse decoration; hence, anything that is florid, in bad taste, or exaggerated.—"Ochlocracy is but the inchoate *rococo* of mob rule bred from unrestraint."—Madame Chiang Kai-shek.

**ro′se ate** (rō′zē āte). Rosy; hence, happy, smiling, optimistic.—"It seemed to be an ever-opening dawn of *roseate* promise."—William Allen White.

**Ru′bi con** (rōō′bi kon). The river between Italy and cisalpine Gaul which when crossed by Caesar made war with Pompey inevitable; hence, a boundary which once crossed leaves no escape from a definite course of action.—"When Martin Luther nailed the thesis on the door of the church he knew he had crossed his *Rubicon*."—Douglas E. Lurton.

**sat′el lite** (sat′ĕ līte). A secondary planet; hence, resembling a submissive or servile attendant; subordinate; dependent.—"There will be tough fighting for them and their *satellite* allies."—W. Averell Harriman.

**Sat″ur na′li a** (sat″ur nāy′li uh). A season or period of general license or revelry, like the Greek festival of Saturn.—"What are the violations of the liquor law compared to the *Saturnalia* of corruption in this country from 1921 to 1923?"—William E. Borah.

**Scrooge** (skrōōje). A character in Dickens's 'Christmas Carol' who was very miserly; hence, a mean, greedy person.—"He felt himself a *Scrooge* when he refused."—Ursula Parrott.

**Scyl'la** (sil'uh). A dangerous rock on the coast of Italy opposite the whirlpool of Charybdis off Sicily; hence, a danger that threatens on one side when there is something equally dangerous on the other side.—"It takes a lot of wisdom to steer the boat safely between the *Scylla* of indulgence and the Charybdis of denial."—Bernard Glueck.

**seared** (seerd). Scorched, scarred, or branded by a burning pain.—"From the bottom of a *seared* and stricken heart, I pray."—Douglas MacArthur.

**shack'les** (shak''lz). Fetters; implements of restraint; things or acts that prevent freedom of action.—"It means a padlock on the lips, *shackles* on the press."—James A. Farley.

**sham'bles** (sham'b'lz). Slaughterhouses; places where animals are killed for meat; hence, a scene of destruction and death.—"The Navy Yard was a blazing *shambles* after the raid."—Fletcher Pratt.

**shards** (shahrdz). Broken pieces of glass or earthenware; fragments of brittle substances; potsherds; broken remains.—"Even the *shards* of the wreckage of civilization would be memorable to piety."—Christopher Morley.

**sheath** (sheeth: 'th' as in 'thin'). A case for a sword or knife; hence, any similar covering or protection; a protective cover.—"Shapes like these wooden ships formed along its shores to be the *sheath* of its valor."—Willa Cather.

**shib'bo leth** (shib'ō leth). The Hebrew word which Jephthah's men used as a test word; hence, a pet phrase of a party; a watchword.—"Democracy

is no empty word, no mere *shibboleth*."—William O. Douglas.

**shore** (shōre). To support; to prop or hold up; to support by a prop to prevent sagging.—"Democracy has tottered and shifted many times, but so far we have been good enough engineers to *shore* it up."—Albert N. Williams.

**Shy'lock** (shī'lock). A revengeful and avaricious Jewish money-lender in Shakespeare's 'Merchant of Venice'; hence, a hard-hearted and extortionate creditor.—"This attitude gave the outside world the false impression that Uncle Sam was a wealthy old *Shylock*."—William L. Shirer.

**sib'yl** (sib'il). One of the women whom Apollo was supposed to inspire to prophesy and deliver oracles; a pagan prophetess who acted as the mouthpiece of a god in ancient times. —"As a prophetess of doom she is a modern *sibyl*."—Donald G. Cooley.

**sin'ews** (sin'ūze). Tendons; hence, strength, framework, means of strength.—"Britannia's might comes in large measure from the *sinews* of science."—Watson Davis.

**skein** (skāne). A fixed quantity of yarn, wool or thread wound in a large circle and then knotted in a kind of bunch; hence, threads of circumstances, undertakings or life which easily become mixed up or tangled.—"He reviews the tangled *skein* of Balkan politics."—Orville Prescott.

**smol'dered** (smōle'durd). Burned in a smothered way, showing little smoke and no flame.—"Experimental science *smoldered* like a fire in a deep mine, the mine of human intellect." —C. C. Furnas.

**snuffed** (snuft). Put out or extinguished, as the wick of a candle.—"The light of liberty is being *snuffed* out in one land after another."—C. M. Chester.

**Sod'om** (sod'ŭm). A city in Palestine destroyed because of the wickedness of its people; hence, a city or region of sin and impurity.—"The city of Suez became the *Sodom* of Africa.— Tom Pennell.

**so'lons** (sō'lonz). Men like the Athenian lawgiver; hence, legislators; wise men; men of great knowledge.—

"It was unlikely that the *solons* would risk offending the Emperor and the army."—Lloyd C. Douglas.

**sol'vent** (sol'vĕnt). A fluid used to dissolve substances; hence, that which will melt away differences; a solution. "Identity of ideals is the strongest possible *solvent* of racial dissimilarities."—Madame Chiang Kai-shek.

**spawned** (spawnd). Generated or produced offspring; brought forth abundantly.—"Many forms of human slavery have *spawned* their progeny of power in our time."—Virgil Jordan.

**spec'ter** (spek'tur). A phantom, ghost, or apparition.—"The *specter* of substantial increase in unemployment stalks across the land."—C. M. Chester.

**stalks** (stawks). Approaches stealthily; steals along for the purpose of killing or destroying, as a beast after its prey. —"Dark hours appear when despair *stalks* boldly."—George Matthew Adams.

**Sto'ic** (stō'ik). A member of a Greek school which taught suppression of feelings; hence, a person indifferent to pleasure or pain; one who is entirely self-controlled and represses all feeling.—"He met his end, not merely with the courage of a *Stoic*, but with the faith of a Christian."—James M. Beck.

**stra'tum** (strāy'tŭm). A layer; one of several layers or thicknesses placed one upon another; hence, a social grade.—"Dreams of empire had not yet permeated below the upper *stratum* of officialdom."—Roy Chapman Andrews.

**Styg'i an** (stij'i ăn). Pertaining to the river Styx in the lower regions; hence, very gloomy; like the nether world; dark.—"A weak bark sounded from the end of the *Stygian* corridor of the boardinghouse."—Gene Fowler.

**sty'mied** (stī'mid). Unable to putt on a golf green because the opponent's ball lies between the player's ball and the hole; hence, impeded; hindered by an obstacle.—"I had come to do a job and was *stymied* by circumstances."—Roy Chapman Andrews.

**Syb"a rit'ic** (sib"uh rit'ik). Given to luxury; voluptuous; luxurious; so called from Sybarites of Greece who loved luxury.—"The final fall of the Roman Empire was due to the *Sybaritic* and effete practices indulged in by the Roman people."—Madame Chiang Kai-shek.

**tan'gent** (tan'jĕnt). A meeting along a line without further intersection; hence, a sudden or abrupt change of course or direction.—"Our pursuers halted a little beyond, where the *tangent* the riders had taken led to a meeting."—John Myers Myers.

**Tan'ta lus** (tan'tuh lŭs). A son of Zeus who was punished by being placed in water up to his chin, with fruit hanging just above him, and both receding whenever he tried to quench his thirst.—"He was *Tantalus*, lost in the desert and tortured by the receding mirage of an oasis."—Douglas Brewster.

**Thes'pi an** (thess'pi ăn). An actor, so called from Thespis, the inventor of Greek tragedy.—"He remembers talking with an old amateur *Thespian* who had seen the prominent actor." —F. Gordon Roe.

**ti tan'ic** (tī tan'ik). Gigantic; of enormous size and power, like the Titans. —"We are giving everything we have in contributing our part in this *titanic* fight."—Madame Chiang Kai-shek.

**ti'tans** (tī'tănz). People of gigantic size; hence, those who have great power. —"To see these *titans* of business at play was a revelation and a privilege."—Roy Chapman Andrews.

**toils** (toylz). Nets to trap game; hence, traps or snares.—"He was caught in the *toils* of illicit love and ambition." —George N. Shuster.

**toll** (tōle). Payment collected for some service; a fixed compensation for something; that which is exacted in this way; hence, number of casualties.—"Careless use of anesthetics is largely responsible for America's tragic maternal mortality *toll*."— J. D. Ratcliff.

**tor'rid** (tor'id). Very hot; burning; of the tropical regions where it is always hot; hence, heated, fiery.—"He lives and labors in the *torrid* zone of controversy."—Robert Humphreys.

**Tro'jan** (trō'jăn). A native of ancient

Troy; hence, one who suffers courageously; a person who endures bravely and pluckily.—"The small lad took his beating like a *Trojan*."—Jack Bond.

**ty coon′** (tī kōōn′). The shogun; the title of the former hereditary commander-in-chief of the Japanese army; hence, a very rich and powerful industrialist or one of high rank.—"To every boy has been held out the real possibility of becoming a business *tycoon*."—Wilfred L. White.

**Val hal′la** (val hal′uh). The hall where Odin received the souls of heroes slain in battle; hence, the abode of dead heroes; the Temple of Fame.—"Among these superhuman creatures, come down from *Valhalla*, she is a little crushed."—André Maurois.

**vein** (vāne). A particular character; a distinctive tendency; a specific mood or cast of mind.—"The other stories, in a more straightforward storytelling *vein*, are charming."—Barbara Woollcott.

**ve neer′** (vĕ neer′). A thin layer of wood upon a commoner surface; hence, mere outward show.—"We must remove the *veneer* to uncover the future course."—L. J. Dickinson.

**vol′a tile** (vol′uh til). Evaporating or turning to vapor readily; hence, changeable; fickle.—"Americans feel the need of protection against *volatile* majorities."—Erwin D. Canham.

**vor′tex** (vor′teks). A whirlpool; a whirling motion sucking bodies or masses toward its center.—"The budget for the next fiscal year is the grim proof of the financial *vortex* into which we are being drawn."—Alfred M. Landon.

**war′rens** (wawr′ĕnz). Tenement houses which are so crowded that they resemble the breeding places of rabbits; thickly populated districts.—"You will find only filth and poverty among the *warrens* of the East Side."—Tom Pennell.

**wraiths** (rāyths: 'th' as in 'thin'). Phantoms of living people supposed to be sometimes seen just before they die; apparitions; specters.—"You can't write fiction about the *wraiths* of your imagination."—Emma Bugbee.

## ONE-MINUTE REFRESHER

These words have all been used as metaphors in the chapter you have just completed. Try to introduce each one of them as a figure of speech into a sentence of your own construction.

| | | |
|---|---|---|
| 1. ignite | 4. barometer | 7. specter |
| 2. shackles | 5. dross | 8. opiate |
| 3. lackey | 6. Saturnalia | 9. hydra-headed |

1._____

2._____

3._____

4._____

5._____

6._____

7._____

8._____

9._____

*Examples:*
1. One small spark will *ignite* a new revolution.
2. The peons are throwing off the *shackles* of ignorance.
3. A university should not be a *lackey* to wealth.
4. It is high time that we read the *barometer* of public opinion.
5. Sacrifice and suffering often burn away the *dross* of selfishness.
6. The late 1920's led to a *Saturnalia* of immoral luxuries.
7. The minds of the poor are always haunted by the *specter* of possible sickness.
8. Napoleon called religion the *opiate* of the masses.
9. We are always battling against the *hydra-headed* monster of crime.

# CHAPTER XXI

## WHEN YOU DISCUSS RELIGION AND ETHICS

In the field of religion the words themselves, words of faith, hope, charity, peace, forgiveness, and divine mercy, with all of their multitudinous connotations, are capable of bringing a measure of spiritual comfort and even of physical healing to troubled people by their very recital. We are again crossing the threshold that leads to word magic.

It is hardly necessary to attend to the meanings of the Lord's Prayer, or the Beatitudes, or the Psalms, or the sayings of St. Paul to receive at least a measure of benefit from them.

"The Lord is my Shepherd, I shall not want."

"Blessed are the merciful for they shall obtain mercy."

"For now we see through a glass darkly: but then we shall see face to face. Now I know in part, but then I shall know even as also I am known."

"Though I walk through the valley of the shadow of death, I will fear no evil."

The sounds of these words, themselves, carry a miraculous message.

The power of religious words, when they stand as an expression of a great philosophy, is beyond compute. The spoken words of Jesus Christ have set church spires in a thousand, thousand valleys and upon a thousand, thousand hills. The written words of Confucius control the lives of nearly a quarter of the people on the earth. It was the founder of Confucianism who said: "Without knowing the force of words it is impossible to know men." And it was the apostle St. John who wrote: "In the beginning was the word, and the word was with God, and the word was God."

Many of the words that surround religion and ethics have, most understandably, a fascinating etymology behind them, that can often throw a new light on their present-day meanings. And in all discussions of religion it is of extreme importance to know these

meanings and to get the terminology as clear as possible, because
we are again exposed to Ghost Words: to such vague abstractions as
"good," "evil," "honesty," "faith," and "truth." The Biblical
Pilot proposed a pertinent question when he asked: "What is
truth?"

Etymology can help us to some extent in understanding the
meanings of the words connected with religion, morals, and ethics.
For instance, do you recognize the root *lig* in "re*lig*ion"? You will
remember that we discussed it in Chapter XIII, and that it meant
to "tie together" and occurred in such words as ob*liga*tion, *liga*ture
and other terms that have the meaning of "tie" or "bind" within
them.

This identical root occurs in re*lig*ion, and "religion" derives
from the Latin word *religare* which itself means "to bind."

If we are "religious," therefore, we are "bound" to certain
ethical and moral codes. We can no longer act with the same freedom. We are under the restraint of such commandments as:
"Thou shalt not kill," and "Thou shalt not steal"; and, quite
logically, the nearest synonym to "religion" is the word "taboo" of
the South Seas, a word that covers all of those objects and acts
that are set apart as sacred by the religious customs of the natives
or that are forbidden by tradition and social usage.

By our interpretation of the word "religion" we are not only
"bound" *not* to do certain things; we are "bound" to *do* certain
other things. We must follow such a command as: "Thou shalt love
thy God with all thy soul and all thy heart and all thy might, and
thy neighbor as thyself."

Historically, then, religion is a codified system of laws issued
by a divine being for the regulation and conduct of our lives.

There are a multitude of fascinating word-histories in the
general world of religion and ethics.

For instance, there are the two common words, "atheist," from
the Greek (*a*, not, + *theos*, god) "there is no god"; and "agnostic,"
also Greek, (*a*, not, + *gignoskein*, know), "I don't know whether
there is a god or not."

Then there are the two somewhat amusing ones: "orthodoxy,"
again from the Greek (*orthos*, right, + *doxa*, opinion) and heterodoxy (*heteros*, other, + *doxa*, opinion). That is, *your* religion is
"orthodox" and right, but the other person's religion is "hetero-
dox" and wrong!

Again in our religions we always have the "iconoclasts" among
us; those who destroy our images or idols and break down our faith,

and this meaning is almost a literal translation of the Greek words *eikon*, image, and *klastes*, a breaker. The "iconoclast," therefore, is a breaker of images.

In ancient Greece the word *hairein* meant to take or choose, so when the "heretic" practices "heresy" he abandons his own faith and "takes" or "chooses" another.

The Latin word *alter* means "other" in English and gives us the "*alt*ruistic" person or the "*alt*ruist" who is not interested in himself but in the welfare of "others."

We have all heard of the "contrite" man, the man whose heart is filled with "contrition" for his misdeeds. Here we have the Latin *con* (with) and *terere* (rub) and this indicates that the guilty man's conscience is "rubbing" him with his sins until it hurts!

And lastly, for the purpose of this brief etymological survey, we have the over-all term "theology" from our now familiar root *theos* (god) plus *logos* (word). A "theologian," then, is "one who speaks of God." Or, in our more modern interpretation, a scholar who has studied the subject of God and religion profoundly and so can speak with authority.

The history of the Christian religion provides an astounding example of the power of words.

In the beginning of the fourth century A.D. a bitter dispute had arisen in the church between a presbyter called Arius and another Alexandrian cleric, Athanasius. The followers of Arius claimed that Christ, since he had been created by the Father, could not be held equal to the Father or coeternal with Him; that he was made of a "like substance" but not of the "same substance." The Athanasians claimed that Christ was equal to the Father and coeternal with Him, and was formed of the "same substance." On these two Greek words, *homoousios* ("of the same substance"), and *homoiousios* ("of like substance") with only an iota (and *iota* is the Greek word for the letter "i" in our alphabet) of difference between them, the early Christian Church was rent apart for many years and almost wrecked. Such is the unbelievable power of the meanings of words.

It is of high importance therefore that we should employ religious words well and with as sure a knowledge of their meanings as we can acquire; otherwise we shall be confused in our discussions and in our readings on these subjects. The words that are included here will give you excellent practice.

**ab″so lu′tion** (ab″sō lū′shŭn). An absolving or freeing from guilt and punishment; forgiveness; the act of a priest releasing penitents from consequences of sin; remission of penance. —"After he had pronounced the words of *absolution* the penitent had risen."—Helen C. White.

**ab solv′ing** (ăb solv′ing). Acquitting; exonerating; exculpating; freeing from blame or guilt.—"He couldn't help that, she realized, *absolving* him grudgingly."—Anne Morrow Lindbergh.

**ad mon′ish ment** (ăd mon′ish mĕnt). A gentle and kindly reproof; a warning or exhortation; a reproof that includes counsel against some fault.— "One hand lay upon the knee while the other was lifted as though in calm *admonishment*."—Pearl S. Buck.

**ad″mo ni′tions** (ad″mō nish′ŭnz). Gentle reproofs; warnings; advice against wrong-doing.—"I will burden you with no further advice, no *admonitions*."—Henry H. Arnold.

**af fla′tus** (ă flāy′tŭs). An overpowering impulse; a divine or supernatural communication; an inspiration.— "Something happened, some sort of *afflatus*, and his mind took on a new power and energy."—H. G. Wells.

**ag nos′tic** (ag noss′tik). One who holds the theory that God is unknown or unknowable; one who professes ignorance, especially about the human soul and God.—"The moral *agnostic* is for the most part either an egocentric sensualist or a moral craven."—James Rowland Angell.

**al′mon er** (al′mŭn ur). One who distributes gifts to those in need.—"Our Saviour becomes the *almoner* of grace and of the bread of life for those souls who love Him."—Pius XII.

**al′tru ism** (al′trōō iz′m). Disinterested benevolence; devotion to the interests of others.—"As a citizen of some other republic I might have found it difficult to believe fully in the *altruism* of the richest American republic."—Franklin Delano Roosevelt.

**am′u lets** (am′ū lets). Small objects worn to protect from harm; charms worn as protection against ill luck.— "*Amulets* of all kinds were popular and special emblems were worn to give the wearer confidence."—S. Bernard Wortis.

**an′cho rite** (ang′kō rīte). A hermit; a recluse; a person who lives in seclusion; one who has renounced the world in order to meditate alone on religious matters.—"The *anchorite* gave no sign of his knowledge."—J. Rodger Darling.

**a noint′ed** (uh noynt′ed). Consecrated; made sacred.—"Legislators are often appointed; they are never *anointed*." —George W. Maxey.

**A poc′a lypse** (uh pok′uh lips). The last book of the New Testament; the Revelation of St. John the Divine; a prophetic revelation.—"Theosophy, metempsychosis, and the *Apocalypse* all seem to have played a part in the inspiration of these water colors."— Howard Devree.

**a pol″o get′ics** (uh pol″ō jet′iks). That department of religious doctrines which deals with the defensive facts and proofs of Christianity; hence, defensive proofs.—"I believe capitalism has no need for mealy-mouthed *apologetics*."—Eric A. Johnston.

**a pos′ta sy** (uh poss′tuh si). Desertion of one's faith or religion.—"We fear because our false freedom and *apostasy* from God have caught up with us."—Fulton J. Sheen.

**a pos′tle** (uh poss″l). One of the twelve men chosen by Jesus to go forth and spread his teachings; hence, a leader of a cause; an advocate of a belief or doctrine.—"Francis Willard was an early *apostle* of woman's rights."— Paul Anderson.

**a poth″e o′sis** (uh poth″ē ō′siss: 'th' as in 'thin'). An exaltation or raising in rank to divine honors.—"To put the Kingdom of God above nationalism would not be the denial of patriotism but its *apotheosis*."—Harry Emerson Fosdick.

**as cet′i cism** (ă set′ĭ siz′m). Extreme self-denying belief and conduct.—

"Years ago men regarded the body as vile and of no account. Today such *asceticism* is deemed erroneous."—Edward J. Meeman.

**a"the is'tic** (āy"thē iss'tik: 'th' as in 'thin'). Disbelieving in the existence of God.—"The way Shaw believes in himself is very refreshing in these *atheistic* days when so many believe in no God at all."—Israel Zangwill.

**a tone'** (uh tōne'). Make amends for; make reparation or give satisfaction for the wrong or injury; expiate.—"We must *atone* for those frustrated and disillusioned years, and quickly."—Raymond Massey.

**au're ole** (aw'rē ōle). A halo; a circle of light or glory around the head of a sanctified person; hence, a crown of glory or victory.—"He pleads against that divorce, and for this possessiveness gets his private *aureole*."—Ludwig Lewisohn.

**aus'pices** (aws'pi siz). Protection; favoring influences or guidance.—"Recently a book has been turned out under apparently innocent *auspices*, whose real source has now been betrayed."—Westbrook Pegler.

**bac chan'tes** (buh kan'teez). Devotees of Bacchus; priests or priestesses of the wine god; attendants of Bacchus.—"The ruined fresco with its dancing fawns and the flower-crowned *bacchantes* once adorned the walls of his palace."—Axel Munthe.

**base'ness** (bāce'ness). Mean or low character; despicable conduct; low moral quality; ignoble trait or act.—"She lectured me soundly on the *baseness* of ingratitude."—A. J. Cronin.

**be at'i tudes** (bē at'ĭ tūdes). Special blessings or felicity.—"Many American citizens are weary and chary of political *beatitudes*."—Lawrence Hunt.

**ben"e dic'tion** (ben"ē dik'shŭn). Blessing.—"My *benediction* go with you."—Pius XII.

**blas'phe my** (blass'fē mi). Irreverent speech; speaking evil of God or sacred things; contempt for God; the use of profane language.—"He is a religious zealot, struggling with what he regards as the *blasphemy* of the new religion."—Henry Seidel Canby.

**bodes** (bōde'z). Predicts or presages; foreshadows.—"You are a living example of the toughness of China which *bodes* ill for her enemies."—Leonard H. Leach.

**cairn** (kairn). A mound of stones set up for a memorial; a pile or pyramid of rough stones heaped up as a landmark or sepulcher.—"Upon the rugged slope stood a *cairn* of stone."—Caroline Dale Snedeker.

**cant** (kant). The language peculiar to a class or profession; insincere statements about religion or morals; phrases implying piety but having no real meaning.—"He reproaches himself for his acquiescence in the development of this *cant*."—H. G. Wells.

**car'nal** (kahr'năl). Of the body; bodily, not spiritual; sensual; fleshly; worldly.—"The *carnal* mind is an expression which we owe to Paul."—Emmet Fox.

**cat'e chiz"ing** (kat'ē kīze"ing). Teaching by means of questions and answers; instructing in elementary principles or religious truths; questioning fully and carefully.—"He was busy *catechizing* her."—André Maurois.

**cau sa'tion** (kaw zā'shŭn). Causing or producing an effect; causality; power or agency that causes or produces.—"The law of *causation* is that every event must have an appropriate and adequate cause."—Emory L. Fielding.

**ce les'tial** (sē less'chăl). Heavenly; divine; pertaining to what is good and beautiful.—"He would tolerate no spiritual advisers except those duly appointed by mundane authority to ration their *celestial* nonsense to the troops."—Hervey Allen.

**cere'ments** (seer'mĕnts). Shrouds or wrappings for the dead; cloths or garments in which bodies are wrapped for burial.—"The *cerements* were his wife's sheets with her monogram interwoven with the symbol of Shiva."—Louis Bromfield.

**chal'ice** (chal'iss). A goblet or drinking cup, especially the cup consecrated for use at the Lord's Supper.—"He held the *chalice* in his hands at early morning Mass."—Helen C. White.

**chas'ten ing** (chāce"n ing). Disciplining by pain or sorrow; purifying.— "They can derive what satisfaction they like from this *chastening* thought." —Oliver Lyttelton.

**chas'tise ment** (chass'tiz mĕnt). The infliction of punishment.—"Shall the Cross be imposed by *chastisement*, or shall it be freely accepted by penance?"—Fulton J. Sheen.

**clair voy'ant** (klair voy'ănt). Having intuitive sagacity or perception; having discernment of things not materially visible.—"One would have to be *clairvoyant* or an astrologer, to do justice to a subject which lies 90 percent in the future."—James P. Warburg.

**cler'ic** (kler'ik). A clergyman; a minister; a pastor.—"It's the story of a mind which was, he says, a born *cleric* or poet."—Christopher Morley.

**com mem'o ra"tive** (kŏ mem'ō rā"- tiv). Designed to keep in remembrance; in celebration of; in memory of.—"These occasions of the holy festival were *commemorative* of an ancient flight from bondage."—Lloyd C. Douglas.

**con dign'** (kŏn dīne'). Well deserved; merited.—"We will never cease to strike until these crimes have been brought to *condign* and exemplary justice."—Winston Churchill.

**con duct'** (kŏn dukt'). Behave; act; direct; comport or carry (yourself).— "Always *conduct* yourself as a gentleman, please."—Jack Bond.

**con'jured** (kun'jurd). Summoned up as if by magic; evoked; made to appear; produced.—"It was as grotesque an art education as could be *conjured* up for such a man."—Ernest W. Watson.

**con niv'ing** (kŏ nīve'ing). Being in collusion with; encouraging or assenting to a wrong by silence or feigned ignorance.—"Ambition, personal *conniving*, and business-as-usual have been permitted to spike the guns of national security."—Harry S. Truman.

**con"se cra'tion** (kon"sē krā'shŭn). Dedication to sacred uses with appointed ceremonies.—"This is a day of national *consecration*."—Franklin Delano Roosevelt.

**con'trite ly** (kon'trīte̦ li). Penitently; expressing deep regret; in a way that showed real sorrow; repentantly.— " 'I am sorry,' he murmured, *contritely*."—Lloyd C. Douglas.

**con tri'tion** (kŏn trish'ŭn). Sincere sorrow for wrongdoing; deep penitence. —"*Contrition* of heart should be accompanied by an act of faith."— Henry M. Wriston.

**cor rec'tive** (kŏ rek'tiv). Tending to correct or punish; serving to counteract something wrong; adapted to reform and improve.—"He was resentful of the *corrective* measures taken by his muscular parent."—Charles B. Driscoll.

**coun'sel or** (koun'sĕ lur: 'ou' as in 'out'). Adviser; one who gives counsel and help; a person to whom one comes for guidance; a consultant.— "A very important part of the job of a chaplain is being a big brother and *counselor*."—Barnett R. Brickner.

**cre'dence** (kree'dĕnce). Belief; confidence founded on evidence; acceptance as true.—"*Credence* cannot always be given to stories of strange things seen."—S. N. F. Sanford.

**cred"i bil'i ty** (kred"ĭ bil'ĭ ti). Trustworthiness; reliance on the truth of something.—"Every morning we meet in a staff conference to weigh the *credibility* of rumors."—Ralph M. Ingersoll.

**cre'do** (kree'dō). A creed; a religious belief; a confession of faith; a statement or summary of religious belief. —"We must have a positive *credo*, a clear, consistent faith."—Ayn Rand.

**creed** (kreed). Doctrine; tenets; principles of faith.—"Costa Rica is the heart of this continent that has the same *creed* of democracy and of liberty."—Henry A. Wallace.

**de based'** (dē bāce'd'). Lowered in character; degraded.—"They were exploited without stint by corporate industry, and socially *debased*."— John L. Lewis.

**de bauch'ing** (dē bawch'ing). Corrupting; vitiating; perverting; depraving.—"They have brutalized eighty millions, *debauching* their thoughts by *debauching* their words, poisoning the very food of their minds."—Robert G. Sproul.

**de ca′dent** (dē kāy′dĕnt). Characterized by deterioration or decline; falling into ruin or decay; deteriorating. —"A *decadent* aristocracy and a medieval school system could not dampen the quiet and charm of the city."—Orville Prescott.

**ded′i cat″ed** (ded′ĭ kāte″id). Set apart for sacred uses or duties; consecrated; hence, set apart for a special occasion.—"Labor Day is *dedicated* to the working people of America."—Frances Perkins.

**de gen′er ate** (dē jen′ur āte). Deteriorate; become inferior, or of a lower type; become degraded.—"Democratic ferment may *degenerate* into chaos."—Wendell L. Willkie.

**de′i fy** (dee′ĭ fī). Make a god of; worship as a god; regard as a god; make godlike.—"This urge to *deify* would create for itself local dissentient figures."—H. G. Wells.

**de′i ties** (dee′ĭ tiz). Gods or goddesses; beings who are considered divine.— "Time was when your Roman *deities* were regarded with some respect."— Lloyd C. Douglas.

**de meaned′** (dē meen′d′). Degraded; lowered in dignity.—"Many will regret that the office revered for generations should have been *demeaned* by grasping at political advantage." —L. J. Dickinson.

**de mor′al iz″ing** (dē mor′ăl īze″ing). Corrupting; disheartening.—"There is nothing more *demoralizing* than sudden, overwhelming disillusionment."—Dorothy Thompson.

**de nom′i na′tions** (dē nom″ĭ′nă′shŭnz). Bodies of Christians having distinguishing names and tenets; religious sects.—"What a demonstration we could give the world if we would heal the breach within our own *denominations*."—Henry Sloane Coffin.

**de praved′** (dē prāvd′). Perverted; evil; immoral; wicked; vicious; corrupt.—"However *depraved* the majority may be, summary condemnation only makes them worse."—Thomas Mann.

**de prav′i ty** (dē prav′ĭ ti). Wickedness; corruption; viciousness; defilement.

—"It suggests a *depravity* below the human level."—Anne O'Hare McCormick.

**der′vish es** (dur′vish ez). Members of certain fanatical tribes of Upper Egypt; Mohammedan mendicant friars or religious enthusiasts.—"The whirling *dervishes* intone the ninety-nine names of Allah."—William Alfred Eddy.

**des′e crat″ed** (dess′ē krāte″id). Diverted from a sacred to a common use; profaned.—"They *desecrated* a house of worship."—Thomas E. Dewey.

**de te′ri o rate** (dē tee′ri ō rāte). Become degraded; degenerate; become impaired or weakened.—"You can lose your talents by letting them *deteriorate*."—Karl T. Compton.

**dev″o tees′** (dev″ō teeze′). Religious fanatics; zealots; persons fervently devoted to religious ceremonies; votaries.—"He could see the two *devotees* leaving the altar hand in hand for the journey."—Caroline Dale Snedeker.

**de vout′** (dē vout′: 'ou' as in 'out'). Religious; pious; devoted to religious services; reverend.—"She was an austere, *devout* woman."—A. J. Cronin.

**dis″en chant′ment** (diss″en chant′-mĕnt). Freedom from a magic spell or charm; disillusionment; freedom from delusion.—"Such an approach is a quick route to *disenchantment*, and perhaps, disillusion and divorce."— Margery Wilson.

**dis hon′or** (diss on′ur). Disgrace; shame; degradation; loss of a good name or reputation; deprivation of dignity and standing.—"To face *dishonor* among your friends is a bitter experience."—John J. Green.

**dis″pen sa′tion** (diss″pen sā′shŭn). A special exemption from an obligation; a special permission to pay no attention to some rule; a specific arrangement.—"He had asked her if teachers had a *dispensation* for encouraging the absurdities of the children."—Helen C. White.

**div″i na′tion** (div″ĭ nā′shŭn). Instinctive power of forecasting or divining; insight into the unknown; skill in foretelling or foreseeing.—"I had not enough gift of *divination* to realize in advance how inexpressibly consoling every aspect of the house would be."—Alexander Woollcott.

**di vine′** (dĭ vīne′). Perceive through intuition; foretell by divination or magic; hence, find out by deduction; presage or predict.—"The idealists tried to *divine* the trend of modern social development."—George N. Shuster.

**di vin′i ty** (dĭ vin′ĭ ti). The character of being divine, or having the nature of God; the likeness to God; the godhead or divine nature; possession of godlike powers.—"The Christmas story sets forth the *divinity*, the priceless character, of that babe."—Paul Austin Wolfe.

**doc′tri nal** (dok′trĭ năl). Containing a doctrine or principle of faith; pertaining to tenets or teachings; instructive.—"The pastors preached sermons several times a year accentuating *doctrinal* points of difference."—Don Marquis.

**doc′trine** (dok′trin). A working principle set forth for acceptance; a belief or precept held as true; a teaching or dogma; that which is taught; a tenet.—"Recognition does not imply approval of the form, personnel or *doctrine* of a government."—Richard Pattee.

**dox ol′o gy** (doks ol′ō ji). A hymn of praise to God, especially the "Gloria in Excelsis"; chants, stanzas, or psalms that give praise to God.—"Springtime is Nature's *doxology*."—George Matthew Adams.

**dry′ads** (drī′adz). Wood-nymphs; semi-divine maidens or lesser goddesses inhabiting trees and living only during the life of the tree.—"The boy was not without his prayer to the shy *dryads* that almost visibly haunted the place."—Caroline Dale Snedeker.

**ec cle″si as′tics** (e klee″zi ass′tiks). Clerics; churchmen; priests.—"Irish scholarship was kept alive in the colleges for Irish *ecclesiastics* on the Continent."—Eamon de Valera.

**ef′fi gy** (ef′ĭ ji). Image; sculptured representation of a person; a stuffed figure; a portrait; a carved likeness.—

"The early Christians refused to burn incense before the *effigy* of Caesar."—H. G. Wells.

**em′blem** (em′blĕm). A symbol or figurative representation; a distinctive badge.—"The *emblem* on Japan's flag looks to me like an inflated balloon, ready to burst."—Monroe E. Deutsch.

**en chant′ed** (en chant′ed). Charmed; laid under a spell or enchantment; bewitched; under the influence of unseen forces.—"He did not wish to be a stranger to that alien, *enchanted* ground."—Stephen Vincent Benét.

**en croach′ments** (en krōch′mĕnts). Gradual intrusions; invasions; advances beyond recognized limits.—"We have fought since time began against the *encroachments* upon liberty."—Richard Llewellyn.

**en shrines′** (en shrīne′z′). Places in a shrine or sacred place; hence, keeps sacred; cherishes as holy.—"Faith in immortality is in the very air we breathe; our literature *enshrines* it."—Harry Emerson Fosdick.

**en′ti ties** (en′tĭ tiz). Beings or things that really exist and have distinguishing marks or characteristics.—"The States and the Federal Government, both as sovereign *entities*, must be preserved."—Herbert R. O'Conor.

**ep″i cu re′an ism** (ep″i kū rē′ăn iz′m). Indulgence in the pleasures of the table; the search for pleasure, as the chief good.—"The most influential part of the urban population is softened with *epicureanism*."—Will Durant.

**es′ti ma ble** (ess′tĭ muh b′l). Worthy of esteem; valuable; that deserve respect and regard; worthy of a high opinion.—"The intentions were *estimable*, but the results were disastrous beyond belief."—Tom Pennell.

**eth′ics** (eth′iks: 'th' as in 'thin'). The basic principles of right action; moral science; the science of human duty.—"By Christian *ethics* I mean no mere ordinary humane decency, but the demands of Jesus that we love our enemies."—Harry Emerson Fosdick.

**e van′gel ist** (ē van′jel ist). A missionary or traveling preacher of the gospel.—"Charlemagne was an *evan-*

*gelist*, but his evangelizing medium was a good, sharp saber."—Ennis P. Whitley.

**ex′or cised** (ek′sor sīze′d). Cast out, as something evil; expelled by prayer.— "Many believed that the spirit of war might be *exorcised* by resolutions and declarations."—Maxim Litvinoff.

**ex′pi ates** (eks′pi ātes). Atones for; makes reparation for; pays the penalty for; makes amends for.—"He explains the moral torment in which men find themselves and *expiates* it for them."—Ludwig Lewisohn.

**ex″pi a′tion** (eks″pi āy′shŭn). The active means of making reparation for an offense or sin; atonement; payment in penalty for wrong-doing.— "Excluding convicts from their fellow men is but a logical consequence of the necessity for *expiation*."—Madame Chiang Kai-shek.

**fa kir's′** (fāy keerz′). Of a Mohammedan ascetic or religious devotee who practices self-torture; of a religious wonder-worker; belonging to a dervish or yogi.—"His couch is the nearest thing to a *fakir's* bed of nails that I have ever felt."—Bennett Cerf.

**fal″li bil′i ty** (fal″ĭ bil′ĭ ti). Liability to err or be inaccurate.—"Mistakes are bound to be made—not mistakes of intent, but mistakes due to the *fallibility* of human judgment."—Ralph Starr Butler.

**fal′si fy** (fawl′sĭ fī). Represent falsely; change from the correct standard; make deceptive; make delusive; pervert.—"We *falsify* the real character of the problems and miss the real solutions."—Jan Christiaan Smuts.

**fa nat′ics** (fuh nat′iks). People who are over-enthusiastic, especially about religion; those who are unreasonably zealous about their beliefs or feelings; people actuated by zeal beyond reason.—"*Fanatics* make life unbearable."—Donald Culross Peattie.

**fa′tal ism** (fāy′tăl iz′m). The doctrine that all events are determined beforehand and hence inevitable; the belief that every event is predetermined by an unalterable decree, and that destiny or fate cannot be changed.— "His voice held that indolent *fatalism* that had so often deceived them by its languid pride."—Stephen Vincent Benét.

**fate′ful** (fāte′fool). Ominous; prophetic; controlled by fate; hence, fraught with destiny; decisive; important; fatal.—"The autumn of that *fateful* year was lovely in New York." —Louis Adamic.

**fe′tish** (fee′tish). An object of devotion or blind affection; something supposed to have magic powers of protection.—"One of the merits of the British Commonwealth is its refusal to make a *fetish* of federalism."— Eduard Beneš.

**fi′nite** (fī′nīte). Subject to bounds or limitations; limited; subject to or limited by conditions that affect human life.—"God is infinite in His power. Man *finite*."—Sterling McCormick.

**fore bod′ings** (fōre bōde′ings). Apprehensions of coming danger or misfortune; presentiments of evil.— "Whether or not there is any solid basis for such gloomy *forebodings*, the people and their leaders will not accept a policy of inaction."— Harold G. Moulton.

**fore″or dained′** (fōre″or daind′). Predestinated; appointed beforehand; determined or ordained beforehand. —"Individualists rebel against the idea that things are *foreordained*." —Bertram M. Myers.

**fore′sight** (fōre′sīte). Thought for the future; power of knowing beforehand; prudence; prudent care for the future.—"She has much more *foresight* than I in our personal affairs." —Roy Chapman Andrews.

**fraud′u lent ly** (frawd′u lent li). In a deceptive way; deceitfully; deceptively; dishonestly; in a way that uses an artifice to trick or deceive.— "The spring rains had *fraudently* invited an occasional tuft of vegetation to believe it had a chance of survival."—Lloyd C. Douglas.

**ge′nie** (jee′ni). A spirit that could be called up by magic.—"The *genie* and Aladdin were flying on the magic carpet."—Gloria Chandler.

**hal′lowed** (hal′ōde). Blessed; made holy by deeds or associations.—"He who enters a university walks on *hal-*

*lowed* ground."—James Bryant Conant.

**he'don ism** (hē'dŏn iz'm). The doctrine of certain ancient Greek philosophers that pleasure is the only or chief good in life; self-indulgence; living for pleasure.—"The professors push a lot of philosophy at you and you write down pragmatism, *hedonism*, agnosticism, rationalism."—Christopher Morley.

**her'e sy** (her'ĕ si). A view or belief at variance with the recognized opinion, doctrine, or tenets of a church or party.—"Some of the enlightened doctrines of government the Old Guard leaders of former years considered nothing short of political *heresy*."—James A. Farley.

**her'e tic** (her'ĕ tik). A person who holds a belief contrary to the fundamental doctrines of his church; one who rejects the tenets of his church and helps to promote schism.—"Men differed as to whether he was charlatan, *heretic*, or saint."—George N. Shuster.

**her'mit age** (hur'mĭ tij). The cell or abode of a hermit; the home of a person who retires from the world for religious reasons; the solitary retreat of a recluse or anchorite.—"Men in other ages have taken refuge in some monastery or *hermitage* either of the soul or of the body or of both."—Ludwig Lewisohn.

**het'er o dox"y** (het'ur ō dok"si). Disagreement with commonly accepted doctrines in religion; the opposite of orthodoxy; refusal to accept an acknowledged standard or opinion.—"He blazed new trails in half a dozen different directions at a time when such *heterodoxy* was regarded as extreme radicalism."—Virginia Dabney.

**hi'er ar"chy** (hī'ur ahr"ki). A body of ecclesiastical rulers; all the clergy; a governing body.—"Cardinal Hinsley will serve as a lasting inspiration to the *hierarchy*, the clergy, and the faithful."—Richard Downey.

**i'con** (ī'kon). An image or likeness; a statue or painting of some holy person venerated or regarded as sacred. —" 'My grandfather,' she said, 'still keeps an *icon* in a corner of the room and burns a bit of candle in front of it.' "—Mazo de la Roche.

**i con'o clasts** (ī kon'ō klasts). Image-breakers; those who assail religious beliefs; those who oppose the use of icons or images.—"From these *iconoclasts* spring the germs of new life."—Charles Seymour.

**i de"al is'tic** (ī dē"ăl iss'tik). Devoted to high ideals or perfection; pertaining to one's highest conception; relating to a perfect type.—"None but a Greek could give to a conception so *idealistic* a devotion."—Caroline Dale Snedeker.

**ill'-starred'** (il' stahrd'). Born under an evil star; unlucky; unfortunate, as though under the influence of an evil star.—"The word 'disastrous' in the Latin literally means '*ill-starred*.' "—Jack Bond.

**im'ma nence** (im'uh nĕnce). Indwelling; permanent abiding within; the indwelling presence of God in man and in the world.—"The boy heard very little about the supreme *immanence*, and his mother had a delicacy about mentioning God."—H. G. Wells.

**im pi'e ty** (im pī'ĕ ti). Ungodliness; wickedness; irreverence toward God or sacred things; lack of natural respect or affection.—"Why did God sometimes allow George Byron his desire for cruelty and *impiety*?"—André Maurois.

**in"can ta'tions** (in"kan tā'shŭnz). Recitals of magical words of enchantment; magic spells.—"Treatments for these diseases ranged from freezing or heating to the employment of amulets and *incantations*."—John F. O'Ryan.

**in car'nate** (in kahr'nāte). Embodied in flesh; personified.—"The Japanese know that their Emperor is the Son of Heaven, the Supreme Being, an *incarnate* god."—Warren J. Clear.

**in fal'li ble** (in fal'ĭ b'l). Perfect; exempt from liability to error; unerring; incapable of making mistakes.— "The administration is far from being *infallible*."—Norman Thomas.

**in'fa my** (in'fuh mi). Depravity; entire lack of honor and reputation;

disgrace or evil fame.—"He is always cast in parts of hardened *infamy*, despite his hanker to go straight."—Lucius Beebe.

**in'fi dels** (in'fĭ dĕlz). Non-Christians; unbelievers; disbelievers; those who do not belong to the true faith or believe in religion.—"He dared to think with the most atrocious boldness of matters which even *infidels* hitherto treated with respect."—H. G. Wells.

**in i'ti ate** (i nish'i āte). One who has been admitted into a secret society; one who had already been instructed in the principles of a group or organization.—"She was grateful to them for treating her as an *initiate*, for showing her the manuscripts."—André Maurois.

**in"spi ra'tion al** (in"spĭ rā'shŭn ăl). Moved by or filled with the desire to uplift thought to the highest and best; inspired; imparting elevating, creative, or spiritual influence or ideas.—"Nearly all the articles he wrote in later years were *inspirational*."—S. L. Scanlon.

**in"ter ces'sor** (in"tur sess'ur). A person who intercedes or pleads for another; one who asks a favor from one person to another.—"He is a wise and tactful man. Let him be your *intercessor*." —George F. Gahagan.

**in"tu i'tion** (in"tū ish'ŭn). Instinctive knowledge; insight; apprehension without the aid of reason.—"When Pythagorous guessed that the earth circled the sun, it was a surprising leap of *intuition*."—Harry Emerson Fosdick.

**in voke'** (in vōke'). Call on for aid; summon, as by means of sorcery; call forth by conjuring; petition or appeal for support.—"The theater is very much alive when it can *invoke* such a range of sorcery as you will find here."—Howard Barnes.

**kis'met** (kiz'met). Fate; destiny; appointed lot or fortune.—"Most of the men believed in *kismet* and in the utter futility of trying to change it." —Hugh E. Blackstone.

**li cen'tious** (lī sen'shŭs). Exceeding the limits of propriety; wanton; lawless; evil; unrestrained; indecent.—

"Your personality can degenerate through *licentious* practices."—Karl T. Compton.

**la'i ty** (lāy'ĭ ti). The people, as distinguished from the clergy; laymen; those not belonging to a professional class.—"It was only natural that his rather unwelcome news should not be received by the *laity* with a burst of glee."—Hervey Allen.

**li ba'tions** (lī bā'shŭnz). Wines or other liquids poured out in honor of a god; drink-offerings; the pouring out of such liquids in sacrifice to a god.—" 'My father offered *libations* to the gods on their feast days.' "—Lloyd C. Douglas.

**load'stone"** (lōde'stōne"). A magnetic oxide of iron; hence, something that acts as a magnet and attracts irresistibly.—"Like a *loadstone*, the house at the foot of the lake drew her."—Mazo de la Roche.

**Log'os** (log'oss). The divine creative word; Jesus Christ; the second person of the Trinity; the rational principle in the universe.—"He manages to explain dimly the pantheistic sense of '*Logos*,' Universal Mind."—P. J. Searles.

**mar'tyr dom** (mahr'tur dŭm). The punishment of death because of one's religious faith or adherence to a cause; torture or persecution.—"It was the day of the *martyrdom* of a prophet."—Stephen S. Wise.

**ma te"ri al is'tic** (muh teer"i ăl iss'tik). Having an undue regard for the necessities and comforts of life; thinking only of material well-being; giving great importance to material interests.—"His *materialistic* mind visualized the thousands of dollars their carcasses would bring."—Roy Chapman Andrews.

**Mes si'ah** (mĕ sī'uh). The Anointed One; the promised king and deliverer of the Jews; hence, a deliverer or liberator of oppressed peoples.—"One day, a *Messiah* shall arise and reign." —Lloyd C. Douglas.

**met"a phys'i cal** (met"uh fiz'i kăl). Pertaining to mental science; about real being or the essential nature of things; of subtle thought and expression.—"Much of the art of the present day is *metaphysical* instead of the expression of an emotion."—Carl Milles.

**min"a ret'** (min"uh ret'). A slender, high tower attached to a mosque and built of several stories, each surrounded by a balcony, from which the muezzin sounds the summons to prayer to Mohammedans.—"He can give the call to prayer from the *minaret*."—William Alfred Eddy.

**mis trust'** (miss trust'). Want of trust; lack of confidence; doubt; suspicion. —"Fear, hatred, and *mistrust* is there among them."—Thomas Wolfe.

**mo nas'tic** (mō nass'tik). Like a monastery; resembling the strict religious life of monks and nuns; as stern as the fixed rules governing people under religious vows.—"He enforced upon his family an austerity so rigid that it became almost *monastic* in quality." —Don Marquis.

**mor'al ize** (mor'ăl īze). To explain with reference to right and wrong; to discuss from an ethical standpoint; to make moral reflections.—"This is no time to *moralize* upon the follies of these countries."—Winston Churchill.

**mum'mer ies** (mum'ur iz). Ridiculous ceremonies; useless or silly shows; hypocritical acts; pretentious rites.— "He had been invited to the villa to perform *mummeries* over the Greek, who had been wounded."—Lloyd C. Douglas.

**mun'dane** (mun'dāne). Worldly; pertaining to earthly things; earthly.— "*Mundane* things have meant much to me."—Madame Chiang Kai-shek.

**myth'i cal** (mith'i kăl: 'th' as in 'thin'). Of the nature of a myth or invented story; not real; imaginary; made-up or legendary; fabulous.—"His stories centered about frontier days or about the doings of a *mythical* 'Mr. Bump.'" —Edwin Way Teale.

**ob liq'ui ty** (ŏb lik'wĭ ti). Crooked conduct; deviation from that which is moral and right; indirectness of sound thinking or upright behavior; deceit.—"The whole affair was tainted with moral *obliquity*."—John J. Green.

**o'men** (ō'mĕn). A sign which is believed to foretell good or bad fortune; a presage; a forecast.—"The next morning, like a good *omen* for the New Year, the weather was bright and clear."—George W. Humbrecht.

**om"ni pre'sence** (om"ni prez'ĕnce). The quality of being present everywhere at the same time; ubiquity; all-inclusive presence.—"Certain facts were the buttresses of his faith, and the chief of them was the omnipotence and *omnipresence* of God."— John Buchan.

**or'a cle** (or'uh k'l). The shrine of Apollo at Delphi where prophecies were made and questions answered by the priests; hence, a high authority.—"The motion picture is the modern *oracle* and has a lasting effect on the trend of the times."—Alexander Markey.

**o rac'u lar** (ō rak'ū lur). Very wise; like an oracle; prophetic.—"They found something *oracular* and decisive in his penetrating detestations." —H. G. Wells.

**or dained'** (or daind'). Predestined; officially decreed; ordered; destined; prescribed by fate.—"Perhaps it had been *ordained* that he was not to die, but only to make a close acquaintance with death."—L. P. Jacks.

**or'i sons** (or'i zŭnz). Prayers; words appropriate to prayer.—"Three hundred years earlier, the choir of monks had chanted their *orisons* to Our Lady."—André Maurois.

**or'tho dox"y** (or'thō dok"si: 'th' as in 'thin'). Belief in established doctrine; agreement with accepted standards. —"Liberty is the only *orthodoxy* within the limits of which art may express itself and flourish."—Arturo Toscanini.

**pa'gan** (pāy'găn). Irreligious; heathen; neither Christian, Mohammedan, nor Jewish.—"He turned an inquiring gaze upon his *pagan* guest."— Lloyd C. Douglas.

**pan'the ism** (pan'thē iz'm: 'th' as in 'thin'). The doctrine that the universe is God; the worship of all gods. —"Here in this opera are his folklore, his *pantheism*, and his poetic fancy." —Olin Downes.

**pas'tor al** (pass'tō răl).    Pertaining

to a minister or pastor and his work; pertaining to the care of souls.— "The Bishop of Berlin reviewed those matters in a *pastoral* letter to the faithful of his diocese."—Lord Halifax.

**pay'nim** (pāy'nim). Pagan; non-Christian; Mohammedan; infidel.— "Roland clave *paynim* skulls without understanding the mechanism of muscles."—Donald Culross Peattie.

**pen'ance** (pen'ănce). The performance of some act as an expression of sorrow for sin; a disciplinary punishment.— "Europe knew obedience to authority, self-discipline, and *penance*."— Fulton J. Sheen.

**pen'i tent** (pen'ĭ tĕnt). Repentant; expressing sorrow for wrong-doing; contrite.—"She lifted a *penitent* countenance to her governess."—Edith Wharton.

**per fec'tion ism** (pur fek'shŭn iz'm). The theory that moral perfection can be attained on earth; the doctrine that man's ideal nature is the greatest moral end; the belief that man can be perfect here on earth.—"*Perfectionism* on the part of a housewife can ruin marital happiness."— Malcom Babbitt.

**per ver'sion** (pur vur'shŭn). Distortion; misrepresentation; malformation; a change to an abnormal condition.—"The totalitarian state is a *perversion* and a monstrosity."— Robert Maynard Hutchins.

**pe ti'tion** (pē tish'ŭn). A solemn request; a formal supplication; a prayer; an entreaty or asking.—"He composed a litany in which refreshment and chill alike found their humble part in thanksgiving and in *petition*."—Helen C. White.

**phan tas'mal** (fan taz'măl). Like a phantasm or ghost; illusive; fanciful; like a thing imagined or a strange fancy; unreal; having an immaterial semblance.—"Treat these people as *phantasmal*, incapable of knowing what they do."—L. P. Jacks.

**phil''o soph'ic** (fil''ō soff'ik). Reasonable; calm; thoughtful; serene; wise, as one who has practical wisdom.—"The men soon became friendly and *philosophic*, and forgot all about the rush job next door."— Gene Fowler.

**pi'e tism** (pī'ĕ tiz'm). Exaggerated religious devoutness tinged with mysticism; affected devotion to religion. —"He became a devotee to a certain mystic *pietism* which guided his acts." —Henry Cabot Lodge.

**pil'fer ing** (pil'fur ing). Making petty thefts; stealing things of little value; stealing in small quantities.— "Through this political *pilfering*, Americans have become accustomed to petty graft."—Brice P. Disque.

**pol'y the ism** (pol'i thē iz'm: 'th' as in 'thin'). The belief in many gods; the worship of many gods; the doctrine that there are more gods than one.— "*Polytheism* is a belief in many gods. Pantheism is the doctrine that the universe, taken as a whole, is God." —Ainslee Mockridge.

**pon tif'i cal** (pon tiff'i kăl). Papal or episcopal; pertaining to the Pope.— "Within the limits of Rome are numerous *pontifical* institutes."— Pius XII.

**por'tents** (por'tents). Forewarnings of evil to come; signs of coming events. —"There were already *portents* in the early and middle twenties that all was not well with the national economy."—Sidney Hillman.

**pre des''ti na'tion** (prē dess''tĭ nā'shŭn). Ordaining beforehand; the decreeing of all things beforehand by God; the purpose of God respecting men and events.—"Some regarded the wife's rescue and the husband's reform as *predestination*."—Don Wharton.

**pre dic'tions** (prē dik'shŭnz). Prophecies; forecasts; foretellings; prognostications about the future.—"After that war glamorous *predictions* were made for the future."—Eric A. Johnston.

**pre mon'i to''ry** (prē mon'ĭ tō'ri). Giving or containing an actual warning of something yet to occur.—"The *premonitory* symptoms of despotism are upon us."—Hugo L. Black.

**pre'sci ent** (prē'shi ĕnt). Having foreknowledge; foreseeing or knowing beforehand; having knowledge about future events.—"His demands upon

Congress were replete with *prescient* pleadings to prepare against a day of peril."—Arthur H. Vandenberg.

**pre″ter nat′u ral ly** (prē″tur nat′yŏŏ-răl i). Strangely and abnormally; inexplicably; in a way beyond or outside the ordinary course of things; in a way that exceeds the natural.—"A paralysis of the will held me, though my senses seemed *preternaturally* acute."—Samuel Hopkins Adams.

**prin′ci ple** (prin′sĭ p'l). A rule of right action, conscientiously adopted; loyalty to a law of conduct.—"The best way to test a *principle* is to apply it to a set of facts."—Neville Miller.

**pro phet′ic** (prō fet′ik). Giving foreknowledge of coming events; predictive; giving warning of the future; interpretative.—"He is *prophetic* of the very phraseology of certain patriotic organizations that flourished much later."—Ludwig Lewisohn.

**pros′e lyt iz″ing** (pross′ĕ lit īze″ing). Winning over or converting to a different religion, sect, or party; making converts.—"Hinduism was seeking a defensive armor against the *proselytizing* enemy within the gates."—Lord Halifax.

**psy′chic** (sī′kik). Pertaining to forces that are outside the realm of physical law; non-physical; mental; of occult mental processes.—"She is a medium whose honesty and attitude toward her own powers have contributed valuable evidence to the modern study of *psychic* phenomena."—Thomas Sugrue.

**pu″ri tan′i cal** (pū″rĭ tan′i kăl). Resembling the Puritans and their doctrines; extremely strict; rigidly scrupulous in religion or morals.—"He became estranged from all the hard-bitten and *puritanical* members of the clan."—Thomas Wolfe.

**pyre** (pīre). A heap of combustibles arranged for burning a dead body, often part of the ceremony of funerals in eastern lands.— The wood of the *pyre* of Jeanne d'Arc lighted here becomes the torch of France."—William C. Bullitt.

**qualm** (kwahm). A twinge of conscience; a sensation of misgiving; an uneasy scruple or hesitation.—"I felt a certain *qualm* of nervousness."—Lord Cecil.

**re′al ism** (rē′ăl iz′m). The doctrine that the material world exists independently of our consciousness of it; the opposite of idealism; preoccupation with facts and life as it really is. —"Her grim *realism* made short work of the phantoms."—Edith Wharton.

**re demp′tion** (rē demp′shŭn). Deliverance; recovery of something lost; rescue; salvation; recovery from captivity or liability.—"He had been so ecstatic over his release from the bondage of melancholia that he was in no mood to examine the nature of his *redemption*."—Lloyd C. Douglas.

**re gen″er a′tion** (rē jen″ur āy′shŭn). Spiritual renewal; rebirth of spiritual life and character; improvement in moral condition.—"I believe in America's power of *regeneration*."—Fulton J. Sheen.

**re″in car na′tion** (rē″in kahr nā′shŭn). The rebirth of a soul into a new body; re-embodiment in human form.—"I am not much of a mystic and have no special belief in *reincarnation*."—Louis Bromfield.

**rel′i quar″y** (rel′i kwer″i). A coffer or shrine for keeping relics; a small casket or other repository in which relics are exhibited.—"This creation of the Weingarten atelier, constructed for use as a *reliquary*, is widely known as a splendid specimen."—Lawrence C. Wroth.

**re pent′ant** (rē pen′tănt). Penitent; expressing sorrow for wrong-doing; feeling regret or contrition; showing repentance.—"He lived to a *repentant* and serene old age."—J. Donald Adams.

**rep″u ta′tion** (rep″ū tā′shŭn). What people say and think about the character of someone or something; estimation in which something is held; character according to the opinion of others.—"The town had the *reputation* of being the hardest drinking port in the Far East."—Roy Chapman Andrews.

**res″ur rec′tion** (rez″uh rek′shŭn). Rising again to new life and spiritual understanding; renewal; restoration. —"Somewhere there must be a perpetual song of *resurrection*."—Henry A. Wallace.

**rev″e la′tion** (rev″e lā′shŭn). The process of revealing or giving knowledge of; the act of making known or disclosing secrets.—"God leads us through the *revelation* of nature."—Thomas Casady.

**re vere′** (rē veer′). Respect deeply; honor; regard with deference; esteem. —"I had learned to *revere* carving as one of the higher arts."—Irvin S. Cobb.

**rev′er ent** (rev′ur ĕnt). Impressed with or feeling profound respect, awe, and affection; deeply respectful; expressing reverence.—"The only words worthy of Jeanne d'Arc are those spoken in *reverent* silence."—William C. Bullitt.

**rit′u al** (rit′yŏŏ ăl). The prescribed form of a religious ceremony; a book of rites and observances; the rites and ceremonies themselves.—"The Puritans tried to purify the *ritual* and worship and faith of the church."—Daniel L. Marsh.

**sac′ri lege** (sak′rĭ lej). An action profaning something sacred; the violation of anything sacred; desecration; profanation.—"Affixing fasces to the entrances of the mosques was a *sacrilege* in a religion which forbids idols and images."—Hiram Blauvelt.

**sac″ri le′gious** (sak″rĭ lē′jŭs). Involving desecration; injurious or disrespectful to something sacred; impious.—"One of the girls came up to me afterward and said the problem was *sacrilegious*."—Christopher Morley.

**sanc′ti fied** (sangk′tĭ fīde). Hallowed; made holy; set apart as sacred; consecrated; given a sacred character to. —"The Acropolis for all its fame was little better than a barren rock, *sanctified* only by its history."—Gertrude Atherton.

**sanc″ti mo′ni ous** (sangk″tĭ mō′ni ŭs). Putting on an appearance of holiness; making a hypocritical pretense of saintliness; simulating piety.—"The official made the remark with a shake of the head and a *sanctimonious* smirk."—Roy Chapman Andrews.

**sanc′ti ty** (sangk′tĭ ti). Holiness; sacredness; inviolability; sacred and binding obligations.—"We declared war to defend the *sanctity* of treaties."—Anthony Eden.

**sanc′tu ar″y** (sangk′tū er″i). A building or space devoted to sacred use; a consecrated and holy spot.—"You shall see your workshop changed into the *sanctuary* of Nazareth."—Pius XII.

**sanc′tum** (sangk′tŭm). A holy place; hence, a place of privacy; a place of retreat.—"If nothing happened in the court, they entered the *sanctum* where I lived."—Roy Chapman Andrews.

**sat′yrs** (sāt′urz). Woodland deities, having goat-like ears and budding horns; merry but wanton wood creatures, part man and part beast.— "What leaping of *satyrs* clad in rough goat-skin; what music of wild pipes!" —Caroline Dale Snedeker.

**scourge** (skurje). A whip for inflicting punishment; hence, any severe punishment or affliction.—"War was considered a calamity, a *scourge* sent by God."—Fulton J. Sheen.

**scru′ples** (skrōō′p'lz). Doubts about questions of right action; uncertainties about what should be done; feelings of uneasiness or hesitation about what is right to do.—" 'I suppose these girls haven't any *scruples*,' he remarked carelessly."—Willa Cather.

**scru′pu lous ly** (skrōō′pū lŭs li). Very carefully and exactly; conscientiously.—"The union has *scrupulously* followed the terms of its agreement." —Myron C. Taylor.

**sec tar′i an** (sek tair′i ăn). Characteristic of a particular sect; denominational; bigoted; like parties, factions, or religious bodies which are narrow-minded.—"Let's take a broad, rather than a *sectarian* point of view."—Bertram M. Myers.

**sec′u lar** (sek′ū lur). Worldly; of or pertaining to temporal things; of this world or the present life.—"Many influences, religious as well as *secular*, are at work in Hindu society for the uplift of the depressed classes."—Lord Halifax.

**seers** (seerz). Prophets; those who foresee events.—"We in Washington, are no more *seers* and prophets than the men in Wall Street."—Ganson Purcell.

**se raph'ic** (sē raff'ik). Angelic; resembling an angel of the highest order; like the seraphs or seraphim.—"In *seraphic* innocence he did not realize that the banner was occasionally demagogic."—William Allen White.

**shriv'en** (shriv'ĕn). Pardoned of the sins confessed; having received absolution after confession.—"I haven't much longer time to tell anything, but I'll go, *shriven* of that secret."—Samuel Hopkins Adams.

**skep'ti cism** (skep'tĭ siz'm). A doubting and incredulous state of mind; doubt of possible success.—"Offensive operations have been replaced by the uncertainty and *skepticism* of defensive action."—Eduard Beneš.

**skul dug'ger y** (skul dug'ur i). Trickery; deception; secret wickedness.—"Are we going to stand the same political *skulduggery*, waste, and inefficiency in war as we have stood in peace?"—Lewis Haney.

**sol'ace** (sol'ĭss). Comfort in grief, trouble, or calamity; consolation.—"The Church of the Air has brought spiritual *solace* to thousands of souls."—Francis J. Spellman.

**sor'cer ess** (sor'sur ess). A witch; a woman who practices witchcraft or sorcery; a woman who practices magic.—"Tonight I shall be the *sorceress*, the sinner, the saint."—André Maurois.

**spir'i tu al** (spir'i choŏ ǎl). Of or pertaining to God, his Spirit, or his law, or to the soul as acted upon by the Holy Spirit; religious; unworldly; of the soul or spirit.—"It is on the strength of our *spiritual* life that the right rebuilding of our national life depends."—Queen Elizabeth of England.

**sto'i cism** (stō'ĭ siz'm). An indifference to pleasure and pain; impassivity; controlled endurance; austere control of the passions.—"Sometimes you saw an untaught *stoicism* which was profoundly moving."—W. Somerset Maugham.

**sub jec'tive** (sŭb jek'tiv). Existing in mind; imaginary; belonging to consciousness; determined by the mind.—"The Bible uses concrete things to express inner, *subjective*, or abstract ideas."—Emmet Fox.

**sub'li ma"tion** (sub'lĭ mā'shŭn). The process of refining and purifying; the direction of psychic energy of sexual desire into higher channels of creative expression.—"One can see the possibility of a sensitive spirit driven mad, despite attempts at *sublimation*, by the unbearable dullness of life."—Ludwig Lewisohn.

**tal'is man** (tal'iss mǎn). A charm; a ring, stone, or other object supposed to have power to protect or cure; an amulet.—"The crews of medieval vessels would not venture beyond sight of land without their agate *talisman*."—Hobart E. Stocking.

**tem'per ate ly** (tem'pur ĭt li). Moderately; free from extremes or excesses; self-restrainedly; mildly.—"His life now passed more evenly, more *temperately* than it had done before."—Thomas Wolfe.

**ten'et** (ten'et). An opinion, principle, dogma, or doctrine that a person believes or maintains as true.—"The *tenet* of autocracy is that man must be guided or controlled."—George W. Maxey.

**the ol'o gy** (thē ol'ō ji: 'th' as in 'thin'). The branch of religious science that treats of God and His relations to all His creation; the study of religious truth; knowledge of God.—"The ultimate conclusions of metaphysics comprise a natural *theology*."—Mortimer J. Adler.

**tra di'tion al** (truh dish'ŭn ǎl). Handed down through generations, especially by word of mouth; customary; according to oral transmission of beliefs or customs.—"The *traditional* forecast is of wider scope, prefiguring a king."—Lloyd C. Douglas.

**trans fig"u ra'tion** (trance fig"yoŏ rā'shŭn). A change of form or appearance; a metamorphosis; a change to an ideal or exalted state.—"They try to make him out a melancholy young poet with his mind chiefly on death and *transfiguration*."—Lincoln Colcord.

**un con'scion a ble** (un kon'shŭn uh-b'l). Unreasonable; going beyond customary bounds or limits; not governed by conscience or sense.—"She was taking an *unconscionable* time about it."—Louis Bromfield.

**un're gen"er ate** (un're̅ jen"ur it). Remaining unreconciled to God; at enemity with the higher spiritual nature; not renewed in heart.—"These officers were the most *unregenerate* of all and some of them were also the biggest liars."—Leland Stowe.

**un scru'pu lous** (un skro͞o'pū lŭs). Unprincipled; not conscientious; paying no attention to right and wrong.—"Practices of the *unscrupulous* money changers stand indicted in the court of public opinion."—Franklin D. Roosevelt.

**u til"i tar'i ans** (ū til"ĭ tair'i ănz). Those who believe that conduct should be determined by the usefulness of actions; those who followed the theory that the greatest good for the greatest number should be the guide and aim of all actions.—"The *utilitarians* brushed aside the ancient verities of both radical and conservative thought."—O. R. McGuire.

**ven"er a'tion** (ven"ur āy'shŭn). Reverence; respect that is filled with admiration and deference.—"Our institutions will not be preserved by *veneration* of what is old, if that is simply expressed in the formal ritual of a shrine."—Charles Evans Hughes.

**ver'i ties** (ver'ĭ tiz). True statements; facts; realities; truths.—"Its philosophy has been founded on the simple *verities* of life."—Myron C. Taylor.

**ves'pers** (vess'purz). The last but one of the canonical hours of the breviary of Roman Catholics; a late afternoon or evening service.—"Atop a native chapel, an old train bell clanged a summons to *vespers*."—J. P. Rich.

**vo'ta ry** (vō'tuh ri). A devotee; a person devoted to something; a loyal adherent or worshipper.—"I have been already held up as the *votary* of licentiousness."—André Maurois.

**vo'tive** (vō'tiv). Given in fulfillment of a vow; dedicated by a promise; consecrated by a vow.—"Jade was used for *votive* offerings centuries before the Christian era."—Martin Ehrmann.

## ONE-MINUTE REFRESHER

Each phrase below describes a word in this chapter. See if you can recall the word and write it in the proper blank space.

1. This word stands for a principle or doctrine that a person holds to in the belief that it is true.

    t___t.

2. These people are somewhat materialistic and they think that their conduct should be determined by the usefulness of actions.

    u_____ns.

3. This adjective is used to describe a quality or a divinity that is embodied in human form.

    i_____te.

4. A verb, past tense, that is used in connection with the casting out of evil, often by prayer.

    e_____ed.

5. A noun that indicates an exaltation or a raising in rank to practically divine honors.

    a_____is.

6. The desertion of one's faith or religion.

    a_____sy.

7. The payment in penalty for wrong-doing.

    e_____on.

8. An adjective that means worldly; earthly.

    m____ne.

*Answers:* 1. tenet; 2. utilitarians; 3. incarnate; 4. exorcised; 5. apotheosis; 6. apostasy; 7. expiation; 8. mundane.

# CHAPTER XXII

## WORDS WE SOMETIMES NEGLECT

A LARGE NUMBER of words that we know well and are perfectly familiar with are apt to slip through the fingers of our minds and fall into disuse.

I would like to recall some of these words so that the reader will be tempted to put them back to work again, for while it may be slightly difficult to gain a mastery over new words that are complete strangers, surely nothing could be easier than to take words that are already old acquaintances and turn them into intimate friends.

There is a simple beauty to such familiar verbs as *foster*, *forbear*, *espouse*, and to such plain nouns as *guise*, *gravity*, *penury*, *import*, *subsistence*. Why not re-examine them, sharpen your mind as to their meanings, observe how they are used in sentences by the experts, and then readopt them for your own everyday purposes.

It would be greatly to our advantage if all of us were to take inventory of our vocabularies in this way from time to time. We could then on these occasions substitute new words for those favorite ones of ours that we have worn thin with much handling. If we are willing to become temporarily self-conscious about our speech, we shall uncover many verbal tools in our word-chests that we have blunted by over-use.

In our general conversation we so often say "he *got* success" when once in a while "he *attained* success" would give a fresh turn to the subject. Again, while it is perfectly proper to say "he can *make mistakes*," such a statement as "he is *fallible*" also has its place. Once more, there is a pleasing variety in using such phrases as "the *gravity* of the disease" instead of "the *seriousness* of the disease," and "I made a sharp *retort*" instead of "I made a sharp *answer*."

You can freshen up your vocabulary in so many ways. A study of the vocabularies of the political columnists that appear in your daily paper will help immensely. You may uncover a writer, we'll say, who has a hard-hitting, muscular style, or, on the other hand, a modernist with a vernacular as fresh as the day after tomorrow. You may locate a painstaking stylist who works with a thesaurus by his side, or a writer who is a master of emotional words. Still another may offer you an example of that intellectual type of vocabulary that applies to the cold and measured processes of reasoning. Our newspapers command a whole army of disciplined political columnists and editorial commentators, and in their sentences and paragraphs you will see that many familiar words can be used in a new sense, and you will come across new words that you will wish to look up and to remember. And all this time you will be developing an eager enthusiasm for the enthralling subject of words.

Another suggestion, and one that will help call back into service a group of words that you may have long since discarded as being too threadbare because you may be accustomed to use them in only one or two of their more usual senses. You will hear a person employ the jejune phrase: "I can't *bear* that man." We forget the many facets that such a prosaic word as "bear" can have, and several of them may have a value for us. We can "bear up" in time of trouble or "bear down" on a difficult job. We can "bear" a burden or "bear" a good reputation. We can "bear" in mind or "bear" the costs or "bear with" a tiresome bore. A woman can "bear" a child, or "bear" pain, or "bear" herself with dignity. We can "bear" to the right or we can bring pressure to "bear" on a problem. Facts will "bear" on a question, guns will "bear" on a beach, and statistics will "bear out" a person's contention.

Some words are terrific breeders, and there are thousands of them, too common to be included in this book, that have given birth to an astonishing number of meanings. Such simple words as "hand," "make," "service," "strike," and "turn" have more than twenty meanings apiece. As a verbal setting-up exercise, see whether you can think of at least ten different meanings to each one.

The word "address" is another example of the fertility of our language. You write your speech or "address" and then you "address" the meeting. You can "address" a letter or you may "address" your remarks to a friend. When you court a girl, you are said to "address" her or pay your "addresses" to her, or you can "address" your energies to your job, or merely "address" a golf ball. You can handle an unruly mob with skill and "address," particularly if it can be said of you that you had a dignified bearing and "address" at the time.

We all suffer from lazy vocabularies, and early in life we get into as many comfortable ruts as we can. The beautiful part of it is that, if we succeed in getting out of our word ruts, it will help us get out of other ruts. The illustrative sentences that are presented in this division should be an aid to this end.

## WORDS WE SOMETIMES NEGLECT

**a bide'** (uh bīde'). Remain; dwell; stay; continue.—"They were singing the well-known hymn, '*Abide* with Me.' "—Ellery Marsh Egan.

**a bode'** (uh bōde'). A place to live in; a dwelling; a home; a dwelling-place.—"The castle was gloomy and dilapidated, the *abode* of owls and bats."—Henry J. Powers.

**ab stain'** (ăb stain'). To refrain voluntarily; to hold back from.—"We, in Canada, were free to make war or to *abstain* from making war."—W. L. Mackenzie King.

**ac cost'ed** (ă kost'ed). Came up and spoke to; approached with a remark; greeted; addressed.—"They waylaid him in the corridors and *accosted* him in the reading-room."—H. G. Wells.

**ac count'a ble** (ă koun'tuh b'l: 'ou' as in 'out'). Responsible; answerable; liable to be called to account.—"God holds men *accountable* for their acts in relation to government."—J. Reuben Clark, Jr.

**ac cu'sa to"ry** (ă kū'zuh tō"ri). Of the nature of an accusation or charge; implying a charge of wrong-doing or offense; accusing.—"The words were unobjectionable but the tone was *accusatory*."—Donald G. Cooley.

**a chieved'** (uh cheev'd'). Accomplished by perseverance and skill; attained an object; carried something through to a successful conclusion; gained as the reward of exertion or valor.—"He had *achieved* a high point of intensity by imposing on life his personal dream."—Edmund Wilson.

**ac'me** (ak'mē). Highest point; summit; hence, climax; culmination; point of perfection.—"Suppression as a fine art has reached its *acme* in Japan."—Sterling North.

**ac quis'i tive** (ă kwiz'ĭ tiv). Able to ob-tain or gain; inclined to get as one's own; anxious to acquire; hence, grasping, greedy, avid.—"Suppose the strong, just men refused to take action against the *acquisitive*, unjust men."—Richard E. Byrd.

**ad dled** (ad"ld). Made rotten, empty, as eggs; hence, muddled; confused; made unsound or worthless.—"His moments of success in certain literary coteries completely *addled* his feeble understanding."—Ludwig Lewisohn.

**ad dress'** (ă dress'). To devote; to apply; to turn the attention of.—"They began to *address* themselves to the task of beating these powers at their own game."—Aldous Huxley.

**ad'e quate** (ad'ē kwit). Fully sufficient for some special requirement; enough to satisfy some need; suitable to some occasion; equal to what is required. —"I have discovered that misunderstandings arise between men largely because of the failure of *adequate* expression."—Owen D. Young.

**ad heres'** (ad heerz'). Sticks fast; clings to; holds firmly to.—"There is no official statement that she *adheres* to the line drawn in her bargain."—Edwin L. James.

**a dorn'ment** (uh dorn'měnt). A decoration; an ornament; something that adds beauty, or embellishes; an addition that enriches or bedecks.—"Beauty is still acknowledged as a necessity of human life and not as a mere *adornment* whose presence or absence makes no vital difference."—L. P. Jacks.

**ad'vo cate** (ad'vō kāte). Speak in favor of; plead for or defend.—"The Rockefeller Foundation does not *advocate* any doctrine or theory."—Raymond B. Fosdick.

**af fray'** (ă frāy'). A noisy quarrel; a

**brawl**; a public fight.—"A score of men laid to with bludgeons, and not a single rioter emerged unwounded from the *affray*."—Donald G. Cooley.

**al'ien at"ed** (āle'yĕn āte"id). Estranged; separated, as though foreign or an alien; made a stranger; excluded from confidence or attachment.—"I felt *alienated* by his failure to share my prejudices."—Alexander Woollcott.

**al'lo cate** (al'ō kāte). Distribute; allot; assign to others.—"Let me *allocate* and apportion responsibilities which he cannot discharge himself."—Winston Churchill.

**am'bling** (am'bling). Walking with an easy gait; moving with an easy pace; going along with a careless, swaying motion.—"He turned and started *ambling* slowly back toward the barracks."—Lloyd C. Douglas.

**am"pli fi ca'tion** (am"plĭ fĭ kā'shŭn). Enlargement; extension; elaboration; addition.—"These points require *amplification*, but here is the rock-bottom minimum for security."—Lord Vansittart.

**a nom'a lous** (uh nom'uh lŭs). Unusual; abnormal; irregular; exceptional; deviating from the common rule.—"His friends regarded his position as *anomalous* and compromising."—L. P. Jacks.

**ap'er ture** (ap'ur chŏor). An opening; hole; slit; gap.—"Fingers made holes through the paper screens and a curious eye gleamed at every *aperture*."—Roy Chapman Andrews.

**ap"per tain'ing** (ap"ur tain'ing). Belonging as a part or right; pertaining; relating; being appropriate to.—"He was voted to the chair as the greatest Master of them all in things *appertaining* to the Sportsmanship of the Spirit."—L. P. Jacks.

**ap"pre hend'** (ap"rē hend'). Understand; grasp; comprehend; become aware of; perceive by the senses or mentally.—"At first he did not *apprehend* this clearly, but the perception of it seeped into his mind."—H. G. Wells.

**a thwart'** (uh thwort'). Across the course of.—"Hundreds of potential but undreamed-of landing fields directly *athwart* our trade routes were left to await the Japanese."—J. W. Greenslade.

**at tain'ment** (ă tain'mĕnt). Accomplishment; achievement.—"The Royal Air Force constitutes one of the most magnificent bodies of men and scientific *attainment* that exist in the whole field of modern military progress."—Winston Churchill.

**at'tri butes** (at'ri būtes). Characteristics; qualities.—"From the start I invested him with all the *attributes* of heroism."—Alexander P. de Seversky.

**at tune'** (ă tūne'). Bring into tune with; harmonize; adjust.—"My mission has been to *attune* the policies of the corporation to the national policies."—Myron C. Taylor.

**ban'ter ing** (ban'tur ing). Chaffing; joking; making fun of; good-humored teasing; ridiculing.—"He looked at me with genuine interest, and his *bantering* manner fell like a bullfighter's cape."—Gene Fowler.

**bas'al** (bāce'ăl). Forming the base; fundamental; basic; hence, needed in order to maintain the lowest level of vitality.—"The lung-fish were accorded the soothing privilege of having their *basal* metabolism taken every day."—Alexander Woollcott.

**bask'ing** (bask'ing). Warming oneself, as in the sun; lying exposed to the sunshine; enjoying the genial heat of the sun.—"The sea otter lives almost wholly in the water, with occasional interludes of sun *basking* on the rocks."—Alan Devoe.

**be get'** (bē get'). Generate; bring into existence; produce.—"Faith and hope *beget* charity."—Francis J. Spellman.

**be grudge'** (bē gruj'). Grumble about; grudge; be unwilling to supply.—"Not one of us should *begrudge* anything we are called upon to do to aid in this great cause."—Monroe E. Deutsch.

**be guile'** (bē gīle'). Amuse; charm; entertain; divert the attention to pleasant thoughts.—"In the Victorian Era novelists used flowery phrases to *beguile* the reader."—William A. Temple.

**be lied'** (bē līde'). Given the lie to; shown to be wrong.—"American business has come into its own, and *belied* those critics who questioned its virility."—Irving S. Olds.

**bent** (bent). Inclination; a fixed tendency; propensity in a particular direction.—"Though he had a natural *bent* for the work, he would probably never have chosen it."—Edith Wharton.

**be stir'** (bē stur'). Stir up or rouse to action; exert; incite to move quickly or briskly.—"The revels are ended and the guests *bestir* themselves to depart."—L. P. Jacks.

**be to'kens** (bē tō'kĕnz). Is a sign of; gives evidence of.—"A creeping paralysis sets in that *betokens* the end of growth."—John W. Davis.

**bev'y** (bev'i). A small group; a company; a gathering of people.—"To be on the safe side, it took a *bevy* of lawyers."—Josiah Stamp.

**bi'as** (bī'ŭs). Mental prejudice; decided tendency or inclination.—"The fault-finding was based not on information but on *bias*."—Sidney Hillman.

**bib'u lous** (bib'ū lŭs). Fond of drinking; tippling; addicted to drinking.— "I have memories of Rip Van Winkle, the *bibulous* Dutch settler of story-book fame."—Wallace L. Ware.

**bi zarre'** (bi zahr'). Odd; strange; fantastic; of queer, fanciful shape.— "The story of quackery is a series of *bizarre* pictures."—Morris Fishbein.

**blan'dish ments** (blan'dish mĕnts). Soothing or flattering speeches or actions.—"We have many honorable Congressmen who resist the *blandishments* of patronage."—John Chamberlain.

**bo'gus** (bō'gŭss). Sham; counterfeit; made-up; fictitious; not of true origin.—"They have regarded the doctrine of the divine right of kings as *bogus* and antique."—Rebecca West.

**brack'ish** (brak'ish). Somewhat salty; partly salt and partly fresh; saltish.— "In the salt or *brackish* tidal mud, only mangroves are able to hold their own."—William Beebe.

**brash** (brash). Quick-tempered; saucy; pert; impudent.—"*Brash* and ignorant children despise the yesterdays of which they know so little."— Robert I. Gannon.

**brig'ands** (brig'ăndz). Bandits; robbers who live by plundering travelers; outlaws who become robbers.— "At last the *brigands* found what they wanted and disappeared into the mountains."—Roy Chapman Andrews.

**broached** (brōcht—ch as in coach). Introduced; mentioned for the first time; began to talk about.—"As they sat together looking out upon the tennis courts he *broached* the subject."—H. G. Wells.

**brooks** (brŏŏks). Tolerates; endures; puts up with; allows.—"In the fascist regime, the will of the state is supreme; it *brooks* no opposition, no questioning."—Edmund Ezra Day.

**broth'els** (broth"lz: 'th' as in 'the'). Houses of prostitution; houses of ill reputation.—"The atrocities that they commit include arson, looting, and the constitution of *brothels* and gambling houses." — Generalissimo Chiang Kai-shek.

**bu col'ic** (bū kol'ik). Rustic; rural; of shepherds; countrified.—"There is a kind of innocence, a kind of *bucolic* ignorance about so many of them."— Louis Bromfield.

**buoy'an cy** (boy'ăn si). Power to keep afloat.—"When you let the air out, you begin to lose your *buoyancy* and sink."—Vincent Palmer.

**cal'i ber** (kal'ĭ bur). Degree of individual capacity or power; quality; ability.—"I am impressed with the *caliber* of the men going through the school."—Harold E. Stassen.

**ca price'** (kuh preece'). A sudden change of mood; a whim; a fancy; a notion; a change of action without reason.—"I let pure *caprice* dictate where my legs shall carry me."— Roy L. Abbott.

**cath'o lic** (kath'ō lik: 'th' as in 'thin'). Universal; general; broad-minded; all-inclusive.—"Churchill loved his world with the *catholic* appetite of the artist of life."—Dorothy Thompson.

**cher'ish** (cher'ish). Hold closely to; hold dear; value.—"Working people *cherish* freedom as a priceless possession."—William L. Green.

**clam′ber** (klam′bŭr). Scramble up by using both hands and feet; climb with difficulty; to climb on all fours.— "The red beast horned the tree-bark into grooves, and snorting tried to *clamber* with his hooves."—John Masefield.

**clar′i fy″ing** (klar′ĭ fī″ing). Freeing from impurities; making clear.— "The confused state of our minds calls for the *clarifying* of general principles."—Karl M. Chworowsky.

**clar′i ty** (klar′ĭ ti). Clearness; lucidity. —"The very narrowness of the frame in which the terrific action is crowded gives the picture an unequalled *clarity*."—Anne O'Hare McCormick.

**clat′tered** (klat′urd). Moved with a rattling noise or commotion; moved making a confused sound as though plates were striking together.—"It was this narrow street through which Becket's murderers *clattered*."—May Lamberton Becker.

**cleav′ing** (kleev′ing). Sticking fast to; adhering to; causing to cling to.— "A spasm of terror came over her, *cleaving* her tongue to the roof of her mouth."—Joel Townsley Rogers.

**cloaked** (klōke′t). Disguised; hidden; concealed; simulated; made to appear like something else.—"Every word might be an insult meriting his resentment, meriting it none the less because it was masked and *cloaked*." —H. G. Wells.

**cloy′ing** (kloy′ing). Surfeiting; satiating; wearying by an excess.—"There is a famine and he goes about hawking expensive and soon *cloying* sweets."—Ludwig Lewisohn.

**cog′ni zance** (kog′ni zănce). Recognition; perception; hence, heed; notice. —"A point has been reached where the people of the Americas must take *cognizance* of the growing ill-will."— Franklin Delano Roosevelt.

**co he′sion** (kō hee′zhŭn). Union; the state of sticking together for a common principle or purpose.—"We had a wholly wrong idea of the *cohesion*, industrial capacity, and military power of Russia."—Robert H. Jackson.

**com po′nent** (kŏm pō′nĕnt). Forming an ingredient; composing; constituent; forming a part or element.— "There is a universality of interests upon this earth. We are all a *component* part of the whole."—George Matthew Adams.

**com ports′** (kŏm portz′). Carries; bears; conducts; behaves.—"It can be said that the Duke always *comports* himself with dignity."—George F. Gahagan.

**com prise′** (kŏm prīze′). Make up; constitute; form; are the component parts of.—"Several thousand American troups *comprise* the vigorous garrison of the island."—John Gunther.

**con′cept** (kon′sept). An abstract general idea; a thought; an idea.— "Bolivar created the *concept* of Pan-American democracy."—Henry A. Wallace.

**con cep′tion** (kŏn sep′shŭn). A thought; an original idea; a plan in the mind; an image; a mental picture.—"The piecing of the life-story together becomes fascinating because it is directed by a definite *conception*." —Edmund Wilson.

**con coct′ed** (kon kokt′ed). Prepared by mixing ingredients.—"Johnny *concocted* a dish of his own for the sick man, for he made a kind of broth from willow grouse."—John Buchan.

**con′cord** (kon′kord). Agreement; harmony; accord; unity of feeling or interest.—"A fortunate *concord* developed among the South American Republics."—Tom Pennell.

**con di′tioned** (kŏn dish′ŭnd). Brought to this state or condition; limited by circumstances; placed in these relations.—"They have been *conditioned* by centuries of false indoctrination, mad philosophy and mystical paganism."—Louis Nizer.

**con doned′** (kŏn dōne′d′). Pardoned; forgiven; treated as overlooked.— "These deviations were not permitted or *condoned* by officials."— J. Lester Perry.

**con fed′er ate** (kŏn fed′ur it). Accomplice; associate; ally; one who joins with others in some plan or plot.— "They caught the thief but his *confederate* is still at large."—Bruce Ellsworth.

**con ferred'** (kŏn furd'). Bestowed; granted as a gift.—"In 1928 Yale University *conferred* the degree of Doctor of Laws upon him."—Malcom Babbitt.

**con front'** (kŏn frunt'). Stand face to face with.—"We shall both *confront* the task of demobilization."—Sumner Welles.

**con strained'** (kŏn strain'd'). Compelled or urged.—"Let us, *constrained* by the love of Christ, seek to make America more truly Christian."—Henry St. George Tucker.

**con straint'** (kon straint'). Restraint; repression or embarrassment; hence, strained or unnatural behavior.—"A disturbing *constraint* on his part, an involuntary shrinking from contact, constituted a baffling situation."—Lloyd C. Douglas.

**con'tem plat"ed** (kon'tĕm plāte"id). Looked at attentively; considered thoroughly.—"The ultimate reestablishment of equilibrium in the international exchanges should also be *contemplated*."—Franklin Delano Roosevelt.

**con ten'tion** (kŏn ten'shŭn). A statement in support of an argument.—"Every department makes the same *contention*."—Joseph E. Kinsley.

**con tin'gen cies** (kŏn tin'jĕn siz). Possible events or conditions; future hazards.—"The desire to possess a gold reserve against unforeseen *contingencies* is likely to remain."—Lord Keynes.

**con tin'gent** (kŏn tin'jĕnt). Conditional; dependent on something uncertain; accidental; possible; chance; uncertain; probable.—"Risk may itself become an object of desire apart from any *contingent* prospect of gain."—L. P. Jacks.

**con trib'u to"ry** (kŏn trib'ū tō"ri). Supplying as part of something; sharing in bringing about a result; helping or contributing in effecting an end.—"These suggestions contemplate the extension of our present system into one national *contributory* insurance system."—Arthur J. Altmeyer.

**con trive'** (kŏn trīve'). Plan ingeniously; devise; bring about.—"I shall *contrive* frequent interruptions,

frictions, delays, in the smooth-flowing chain of habitual action."—Henry C. Link.

**con'tro vert"ed** (kon'trō vurt"ed). Contradicted; opposed; tried to disprove; argued against.—"The research of the psychiatrists *controverted* all of Jack's theories about children."—George F. Gahagan.

**con'ver sant** (kon'vur sănt). Intimately acquainted; familiar with, from previous knowledge.—"It has a backbone of civil servants who are *conversant* with the work with which the Ministry is occupied."—W. Somerset Maugham.

**co'pi ous** (kō'pi ŭs). Plenteous; abundant; ample.—"They welcomed the broad and *copious* flow of the latest weapons of all kinds."—Winston Churchill.

**coun'ter** (koun'tur: 'ou' as in 'out'). Contrary; opposed; in opposition; adverse.—"What he proposed ran *counter* to every prejudice that constitutes the modern frame of mind."—Mortimer J. Adler.

**cri te'ri on** (krī tē'ri ŭn). A standard by which to determine the correctness of a judgment or conclusion.—"This week in June cannot be taken as a *criterion* but it is the best ever."—Winston Churchill.

**crux** (kruks). The pivotal point; the critical point.—"The *crux* of the whole matter is that money alone will not make jobs."—Philip B. Fleming.

**cudg'el** (kuj'ĕl). A short thick stick or club used as a weapon.—"This *cudgel* was hardly more than a symbol of the authority vested in the overseers."—Thomas Mann.

**culled** (kuld). Selected; picked out from among others; chose.—"I *culled* the sentence from an article in a leading magazine."—H. W. Prentis, Jr.

**cun'ning** (kun'ing). Skill; dexterity; knowledge combined with skill.—"Association with the great painter had given vision to his eyes and *cunning* to his hands."—Ellen Lewis Buell.

**cur'ry** (kur'i). To seek by subservience or flattery; to seek favors by servile praise.—"For a while the clever way to win an election was to *curry* favor with gallant sons of the Bill of Rights."—Robert I. Gannon.

**cur′so ry** (kur′sō ri). Rapid and superficial; hasty.—"You can ask your doctor to make a *cursory* examination of your eyes as a part of his routine physical examination."—Harry S. Gradle.

**cus to′di ans** (kuss tō′di ănz). Guardians; caretakers.—"Women were the earliest *custodians* of the urge to foster life and protect the hopeless."—Jane Addams.

**dal′ly** (dal′i). Trifle away time; loiter; waste time.—"People who *dally* with comfort and the laziness which it engenders, are not the people with whom God cooperates."—George Barton Cutten.

**dank** (dangk). Unpleasantly damp or moist; disagreeably wet; humid.—"There were hours in his life like sunlit meadows after the *dank* chambers in the charnel-house of Poe."—Ludwig Lewisohn.

**de bouched′** (dē bōōsh′d′). Emerged; opened out; issued from a confined place into open ground.—"I rode along a road bordered by cottages to where it *debouched* into a wide square."—Roy Chapman Andrews.

**de cern′** (dē surn′). Discern clearly; adjudge.—"It is difficult for us who are uninitiated to *decern* the reason for the move."—Emmet Holloway.

**dec″li na′tion** (dek″lĭ nā′shŭn). A polite refusal; non-acceptance.—"The senator disliked the proffered responsibility and sent in his *declination*."—Sterling McCormick.

**de cliv′i ty** (dē klĭv′ĭ ti). The surface of a hill or mountain that descends gradually; a downward slope; a descent.—"They started down the steep *declivity*."—Edith Wharton.

**de coct′ed** (dē cokt′ed). Boiled down something in order to obtain an essence; prepared by steeping or boiling in hot water; concocted.—"The chef *decocted* a strange and tasteless kind of soup."—Malcom Babbitt.

**deems** (deemz). Thinks; considers; believes; judges.—"The Arab desires to shape his corner of the earth as he *deems* best."—George N. Shuster.

**de mer′its** (dē mer′its). Faults; things worthy of blame.—"Time will not permit me to elaborate on the merits or *demerits* of these appropriations."—Fred A. Hartley, Jr.

**de murred′** (dē murd′). Offered objections; objected; taken exception.—"Never once have our union executives *demurred* at any reasonable sacrifice."—Walter Citrine.

**den′i zens** (den′ĭ zĕnz). Inhabitants; occupants; those who make their home in that locality.—"Passing to and fro from his concerns, he faced the *denizens* of Our Square."—Samuel Hopkins Adams.

**de plete′** (dē pleet′). Reduce, lessen or exhaust (our strength).—"Many of us are afraid that this expenditure of passion will drain away energy, *deplete* us for our own tasks."—Bruce Barton.

**de rid′ed** (dē rīde′id). Mocked; ridiculed; laughed at contemptuously; made fun of.—"Nowhere else was she more violently belauded or more savagely *derided*."—Hilary St. George Saunders.

**de ri′sion** (dē rizh′ŭn). Contemptuous laughter; scornful or mocking ridicule; mockery; jeering scorn.—"There was a look of *derision* on the face of the head waiter."—Henry J. Powers.

**des cried′** (dē skrīde′). Discovered by observing, as something at a distance; caught sight of; was able to detect or make out; discerned.—"The workers could be *descried* through the window."—Alexander Woollcott.

**de spite′** (dē spīte′). In spite of; notwithstanding.—"*Despite* many losses we have now a stronger, larger fleet."—Frank Knox.

**des′ul to″ry** (dess′ŭl tō″ri). Unmethodical; irregular; passing from one thing to another; aimless; without order.—"The technique had been going on in a *desultory* and amateurish manner for over a century."—F. Gordon Roe.

**de tach′ment** (dē tach′mĕnt). Aloofness; dissociation from worldly interests; indifference to the opinions of others; unconcern.—"The author looks upon the world with serene *detachment*."—Orville Prescott.

**de'vi ates** (dee'vi ātes). Turns aside from; strays from; departs from; digresses from; differs from.—"The less the biographer's temperament *deviates* the natural colors of the re-created figure of his hero, the greater the achievement."—J. Donald Adams.

**de vise'** (dē vīze'). To form plans; to invent; to contrive.—"It is up to every motorist to *devise* ways of saving miles."—Prentiss M. Brown.

**dil'i gence** (dil'ĭ jĕnce). Industry; persevering application; assiduous attention; giving proper heed and working hard; persistent effort.—"An old Arabic proverb states a great truth. '*Diligence* is a great teacher.' "—S. L. Scanlon.

**dint** (dint). A mark made by pressure or a blow; a dent; hence, force; means.—"By *dint* of her mother's brains, personality, talent, and know-how, the offers began to come in."—Sidney Carroll.

**dis'a buse'** (diss"uh būze'). To disillusion; to undeceive; to rid of a false impression; to set right.—"It is so difficult to *disabuse* those who have followed this teaching so long."—Donald G. Cooley.

**dis"ar range'ment** (diss"ă rānje'mĕnt). Disorder; disorganization; disturbance owing to everything being out of place; change of due arrangement; displacement.—"The room was in a state of *disarrangement*."—Ellery Marsh Egan.

**dis"ar ray'** (diss"ă rāy'). Disorder; confusion; a disturbed, disorganized condition or state.—"All his mental processes had been thrown into *disarray*."—Lloyd C. Douglas.

**dis claim'ing** (diss klāme'ing). Repudiating; disavowing any connection with; disowning; denying having anything to do with.—"Nine out of ten. registrants, while *disclaiming* prejudice, prefer someone of their own faith."—Jess Stearn.

**dis com'fi ture** (diss kum'fi chŏor). Frustration; defeat; a baffled state; a feeling of having been thwarted in some purpose.—"We returned to the Club to drown our *discomfiture* in more champagne."—Roy Chapman Andrews.

**dis"com mode'** (diss"kŏ mōde'). Cause inconvenience or trouble; incommode; annoy; put out; disturb arrangements.—"It's a splendid arrangement if it doesn't *discommode* you."—Douglas E. Lurton.

**dis"con cert'** (diss"kŏn surt'). Upset; discompose; confuse; disturb; embarrass; abash; destroy the self-possession of.—"The atmosphere of the university itself seemed particularly designed to *disconcert* the son of the innkeeper."—Jules Romains.

**dis fa'vor** (diss fāy'vur). Disapproval; dislike; lack of favor.—"She eyed most of these ladies with a melancholy *disfavor*."—Edith Wharton.

**dis in'ter est ed** (diss in'tur ess ted). Free from self-interest or selfish motives; impartial; not biased by consideration of personal advantage.—"To say that he was *disinterested* in the project is to put it mildly."—John J. Green.

**dis qual"i fi ca'tion** (diss kwol"ĭ fi kā'shŭn). Incapacity; unfitness; deprivation of power or rights; disability; a pronouncement of unfitness owing to lack of some quality.—"These critics added to ignorance a more pernicious *disqualification*."—Joseph Wood Krutch.

**dis qui'et ing** (diss kwī'ĕt ing). Disturbing; causing uneasiness.—"The management of our food controls is *disquieting*."—Leonard P. Ayres.

**dis"re gard'ed** (diss"rē gahrd'ed). Overlooked; slighted, as unworthy of notice; unheeded.—"We read that the sanctity of treaties between nations is *disregarded*."—Franklin Delano Roosevelt.

**dis sev'ered** (di sev'urd). Severed or cut off completely; separated from; disunited; disjoined.—"It was most fortunate that he had *dissevered* all possible connections with the company."—Charles Henry Crozier.

**dis sim'u la'tion** (dis sim"ū lā'shŭn). Pretense; feigning; deceit; hypocrisy; deception.—"She was too emotional for a game based on *dissimulation* and

no match for such seasoned players."
—Edith Wharton.

**di ver′si fied** (dĭ vur′sĭ fīde). Made up of various kinds or forms; distributed among different kinds; varied; composed of unlike or various types.— "He staffed his bank with men experienced in every department of this *diversified* farming program."— J. P. McEvoy.

**dole′ful** (dōle′fool). Melancholy; sad; dismal; dreary; mournful; rueful.— "The Colonel said in a *doleful* voice that he was much disappointed."— Roy Chapman Andrews.

**droll** (drōle). Funny; comical; ludicrous; humorous; amusing; calling forth laughter; queer; odd.—"He had a *droll* expression which the eyeglasses enhanced and his long legs completed."—Robert Dean Frisbie.

**drone** (drōne). A dull, humming sound, as of bees; a low and monotonous buzzing sound.—"The *drone* of saws started cutting the lumber."— Stewart H. Holbrook.

**dwell** (dwel). Linger; pause; think for a long time; center thought continuously.—"Why *dwell* on things that can't be helped?"—S. L. Scanlon.

**ed′i ble** (ed′ĭ b'l). Fit to be eaten and suitable for food; eatable.—"Dr. Carver proved that most of the weeds that line our roadways are actually *edible* and rich in vitamin value."— George Matthew Adams.

**ee′rie** (ee′ri). Weird; strange; inspiring fear; awesome; uncanny.—"An *eerie* whistle came from the nose of the sloth."—V. Wolfgang von Hagen.

**ef fect′** (ĕ fekt′). Purport; meaning; import; intent; seeming to imply.— "He said something in his letter to this *effect*."—Donald G. Cooley.

**e lab″o ra′tion** (ē lab″ō rā′shŭn). Painstaking and careful development of details.—"That is a great step forward which only requires *elaboration* to become a real Magna Charta of nations."—Jan Christiaan Smuts.

**e lic′it ed** (ē liss′it ed). Drew forth; called forth or evoked.—"The spectacle of a free people setting up this tribunal, justly *elicited* the admiration of the world."—Henry Breckinridge.

**em bod′i ment** (em bod′i mĕnt). That which gives a body to; hence, a concrete expression.—"He is the *embodiment* of warmth and spontaneity."— Madame Chiang Kai-shek.

**em′i nence** (em′i nĕnce). An exalted position or condition; a high rank in affairs; a lofty or elevated place among associates; elevation above others.—"Never again would he be so glorious, so revered. But the *eminence* had not lasted."—Elizabeth Goudge.

**em′u late** (em′ū lāte). Strive to equal or surpass.—"If we are called upon to endure what they have suffered, we shall *emulate* their courage."— Winston Churchill.

**en com′pass** (en kum′puhss). To put a ring about; to enclose or embrace.— "My mind raced to *encompass* the remoter contingencies."—Burton Rascoe.

**en count′ered** (en koun′turd: 'ou' as 'out'). Come upon; met unexpectedly; met face to face.—"Many practical problems have been *encountered*." —David Sarnoff.

**en cum′ber ing** (en kum′bur ing). Obstructing or hindering in action or movement; burdening with difficulties.—"We must discard *encumbering* practices and procedures."—Ralph Starr Butler.

**en dow′ment** (en dou′mĕnt: 'ou' as in 'out'). Any natural gift.—"Children may lack some intellectual development but their emotional *endowment* is far more tender."—Merrill Moore.

**en due′** (en dū′). Endow; furnish; invest; clothe; bestow powers or qualities upon.—"Who else but a lover would *endue* her with these charms?" —Donald G. Cooley.

**en liv′ened** (en līve″nd). Animated; given life and vigor; stimulated; given renewed vivacity; made more active.—"All the services which make for distribution are *enlivened* when industries are in full production."— Fred I. Kent.

**en tailed′** (en tail′d′). Necessitated; involved as a result.—"Delay would have *entailed* considerable curtailment of our operations."—Winston Churchill.

**en tic′ing ly** (en tīce′ing li). Temptingly; alluringly; attractively; invitingly.—"The shaded windows of other rooms seemed to beckon *enticingly*."—Roy Chapman Andrews.

**en trenched'** (en trencht'). Protected, as by a trench; fortified by protection.—"We have invited battle. We have earned the hatred of *entrenched* greed."—Franklin Delano Roosevelt.

**e nu'mer ates** (ē nū'mur ātes). Names one by one.—"He *enumerates* these various features of our present system as its characteristic evils."—Thos. Reed Powell.

**en vel'oped** (en vel'ŭpt). Enclosed, as in a wrapper; surrounded, as though wrapped up in; covered over.—"I was *enveloped* in a strange intense moonlight blue."—Roy Chapman Andrews.

**e ques'tri an** (ē kwess'tri ăn). Of horses or horsemanship; of a rider on horseback.—"The two *equestrian* portraits are by George Stubbs."—John Hanbury-Williams.

**er'rant** (er'ănt). Wandering; roving; erratic; mistaken.—"They found solace in his motives, however *errant* his search."—Robert Humphreys.

**er ro'ne ous** (e rō'nē ŭs). Marked by error; mistaken; incorrect.—"The assumption that all officers have combat knowledge is *erroneous*."—Robert P. Patterson.

**es pous'es** (ess pouz'iz: 'ou' as in 'out'). Assumes an interest in; takes upon itself the defense of.—"Unless the United States *espouses*, and promptly urges, a project of world organization, none such will reach fruition."—Owen J. Roberts.

**es say'** (e sāy'). Attempt; try; endeavor; make an effort.—"She recognized before long that she could not *essay* to convert him to the cause without rousing his suspicions."—Gertrude Atherton.

**es teem'** (ess teem'). Value or think highly of; appreciate the worth of; prize; regard as having excellence.—"In order that we may understand and *esteem* each other, we need to work together."—Fernando Carbajal.

**e vac'u at"ed** (ē vak'ū āte"ed). Moved away from a danger zone; withdrawn.—"A large part of the civil population has been *evacuated*."—Winston Churchill.

**ex empt'** (eg zempt'). Free; excused; granted immunity.—"Letters mailed to interned civilians are *exempt* from postal charges."—Albert Goldman.

**ex em'pli'fied** (eg zem'plĭ fīde). Illustrated; showed as an example.—"The meeting *exemplified* the kind of cooperation that must be practised."—Thomas E. Dewey.

**ex pe'di ent** (eks pee'di ĕnt). Something that furthers or promotes a desired end; a means used in an emergency; a device.—"The President's proposal is neither a permanent reform nor a temporary *expedient*."—Burton K. Wheeler.

**ex pound'ed** (eks pound'ed: 'ou' as in 'out'). Explained; interpreted; elucidated.—"Only those doctrines which this government approves may be *expounded*."—Robert M. Hutchins.

**fa cil'i ty** (fuh sil'ĭ ti). Ease in doing something; dexterity; readiness owing to skill.—"Some are born inarticulate. Others have an unusual *facility* for self-expression."—Emory L. Fielding.

**fac'tu al** (fak'chŏŏ ăl). Containing facts; literal and exact; genuine.—"There has been absolutely no *factual* evidence to support the statements."—Ralph M. Ingersoll.

**fal'low** (fal'ō). Left neglected or unseeded after being plowed.—"There is enough land lying uncultivated and *fallow* to support all human beings on the earth."—Louis Ludlow.

**fan'ci er** (fan'si ur). A person who breeds or sells birds or animals especially for their good points; an amateur interested in some special animals or objects.—"Personally, I am a *fancier* of dogs."—Hugh E. Blackstone.

**fash'ion** (fash'ŭn). To give shape or form to; to make; to mold; to frame.—"What a Mind it took to *fashion* this earth!"—George Matthew Adams.

**fath'om** (fath'ŭm: 'th' as in 'the'). To find the depth by sounding; hence, get to the bottom of; comprehend; understand.—"I've never been able to *fathom* Indians."—Louis Bromfield.

**fes tooned'** (fess tōōn'd'). Decorated, as with a garland or wreath; adorned as for a festival.—"The sides of the nest were *festooned* with moss."—Bennie Bengston.

**fig'ment** (fig'mĕnt). Something imaginged or feigned; an invention.—"This statement is not a *figment* of the imagination: it is based on practical experience."—Joseph C. Grew.

**fil'lip** (fil'ĭp). A stimulus; something that revives or arouses; something that excites ambition or supplies an impulse.—"She would have found life unendurable without the little *fillip* of confidence which the relationship provided."—Louis Bromfield.

**fir'ma ment** (fur muh mĕnt). The heavens; the sky; the expanse of heaven.—"His sacrifice has enriched all human values, and his memory is celebrated by another star in the *firmament* of human freedom."—George Matthew Adams.

**fit'ful** (fit'fōōl). Spasmodic; restless; occurring irregularly.—"We see in *fitful* dreams the better world of our hopes."—Henry Sloane Coffin.

**flagged** (flagg'd). Grown languid; become tired; halted.—"We have never looked back, never *flagged*, never flinched."—Winston Churchill.

**flecked** (fleckt). Spotted; streaked; marked with specks or small spots; dappled.—"The mountain slopes were dark with spruce and *flecked* with golden, russet birches and rowans."—Sigrid Undset.

**flux** (fluks). Continuous flowing or movement.—"The central quest has been to find stability in the midst of *flux*."—William J. Cameron.

**fo'cus** (fō'kŭs). Bring to a central point; hence, concentrate.—"The office manager must *focus* his attention on how to get more out of his machine and his men."—F. W. Stein.

**for bear'** (for bāre'). To refrain or abstain from; to hold back.—"I might speak with more emphasis on this point, but it is prudent to *forbear*."—Winston Churchill.

**fore go'** (fōre gō'). Give up; refrain from enjoying.—"We will *forego* food

from abroad if the ships are needed."—William Maxwell Aitken.

**for fend'** (for fend'). Ward off; prevent; avert; keep off; forbid.—"*Forfend!* else strange and terrible things will devour us all."—Theodore Dreiser.

**forte** (fort). One's strong point; something that one does or manifests really well; that which one does most readily or in which one excels.—"Modesty is not my *forte*."—Bertram M. Myers.

**fos'ter** (foss'tur). To help; to promote the growth.—"The political attitude of the League tended to *foster* rather than prevent the rise of gangsterism."—J. W. Greenslade.

**fraught** (frawt). Laden; filled; loaded; stored; full of; attended with.—"It might be *fraught* with disastrous consequences to the personality of the nurse and of others."—L. P. Jacks.

**frays** (frāyz). Fights; noisy quarrels; brawls; altercations.—"He continued to roam among his people and to probe into their *frays* with a peculiar air of authority."—Thomas Mann.

**fre quent'** (frē kwent'). To go to frequently; to visit habitually; to be often in.—"I was thinking of those barrooms which had existed before it was customary for women to *frequent* them."—John P. Marquand.

**fru gal'i ty** (frōō gal'ĭ ti). Strict economy; thrift.—"The industry, *frugality*, piety, and ingrained dignity of the Quebec population are well depicted."—Allan Nevins.

**func'tion** (fungk'shŭn). Appropriate or assigned duty or business; special work or purpose; occupation.—"The proper *function* of government is to help people to help themselves."—Lewis H. Brown.

**fur'nished** (fur'nisht). Provided or supplied with whatever is necessary; given a supply of.—"Every single one of the trees, plants and flowers must be *furnished* its special chemical mixture from the ground to keep it in health."—George Matthew Adams.

**fur'thered** (fur'thurd: 'th' as in 'the'). Helped forward; promoted; advanced; aided.—"The investment of foreign capital *furthered* the devel-

opment of our national resources."—
Thomas J. Watson.

**fur′tive** (fur′tiv). Stealthy; secret; illusive; sly.—"Somewhere in Washington a *furtive* little group of men are craftily erecting agency after agency."—Wayne Coy.

**gain″said′** (gain″sed′). Contradicted; denied; disputed.—"That their philosophy has succeeded in raising up a powerful State cannot be *gainsaid*." —O. R. McGuire.

**gar′nished** (gar′nisht). Embellished; surrounded with additions; adorned; decorated; furbished; bedecked.— "His caution is heavily *garnished* with curiosity."—Victor Wolfgang von Hagen.

**gird′ing** (gurd′ing). Equipping; clothing, as with power; endowing with capacity; preparing or bracing.— "Every time a youngster acts boldly and decisively he is *girding* himself anew with confidence and courage." —Charles F. Kettering.

**gran′deur** (gran′dūre). Magnificence; greatness; sublimity; nobility; dignity.—"The narrative as a whole has verve and simple *grandeur*."—George N. Shuster.

**graph i cal ly** (graff′i kăl li). In an illustrative or pictorial way; by means of diagrams or graphs.—"The areas over which overlapping of teeth occur are shown *graphically*."—A. W. Harris.

**grav′i ty** (grav′ĭ ti). Importance; seriousness; enormity.—"The *gravity* of the crash that followed in this country should not be minimized."— Lewis H. Brown.

**groom′ing** (grōōm′ing). Making oneself tidy or smart; giving care to one's appearance; smartening up.— "Her father was still, as they would say, *grooming* for the conflict."— Franz Werfel.

**guile** (gīle). Craftiness; deceitful trickery; cunning treachery; artifice; deception to gain an advantage.—"She saw through *guile* as through a windowpane."—Edwin Way Teale.

**guile′less ly** (gīle′less li). Frankly; candidly; innocently.—"The author is *guilelessly* ignorant of his responsibility."—Dorothy Canfield Fisher.

**guise** (gīze). External appearance; manner or dress; hence, semblance; assumed or disguised appearance. —"Her agents were distributed throughout our territory in the *guise* of diplomatic representatives."— Haile Selassie.

**hab″it a bil′i ty** (hab″ĭ tuh bil′ĭ ti). Fitness as a place of abode; capability of being used as dwelling-places; fitness to live in.—"They did not design their ships to keep at sea for long periods, and *habitability* was not considered a necessity."—C. S. Forester.

**har′bored** (hahr′burd). Entertained in the mind; given shelter to; indulged or yielded to, as thoughts or feelings. —"He had *harbored* an especial aversion to me."—John P. Marquand.

**hi lar′i ty** (hi lar′ĭ ti). Noisy mirth; boisterous gaiety; joviality.—"The mood of good-natured *hilarity* had been characteristic of him since he arrived."—Hendrik Willem Van Loon.

**hom′age** (hom′ij). Respect and deference.—"Generations to come will pay *homage* to these allies who have caused freedom's holy light to shine." Louis H. Brereton.

**hom′i ly** (hom′ĭ li). An exhortation or admonition; a sermon.—"The reason for this *homily* is that I am confronted by public men who ask why I am opposed to them."—Frank Kingdon.

**ig no′ble** (ig nō′b'l). Not noble; mean or base; dishonorable; degraded in character; unworthy.—"A visitor from another planet listening to these arguments would conclude that we are a money-getting, *ignoble* people."—James B. Conant.

**ilk** (ilk). Those of the same name or family or estate; hence, often misused to mean kind or class.—"The bishop of Exeter and his *ilk* seemed unnecessary and far away."—Hervey Allen.

**im bib′ing** (im bībe′ing). Receiving and absorbing into the mind or character; drinking in and retaining.— "They are *imbibing* conduct patterns based on your words and your examples."—Irving T. McDonald.

**im′i ta″tive** (im′ĭ tāy″tiv). Inclined to

copy or imitate; given to copying what others make and do.—"The Japanese race has long been thought of as *imitative*."—Bertram M. Myers.

**im mac′u late ly** (i mak′ū lit li). Spotlessly; stainlessly.—"She kept a three-story house *immaculately* clean from top to bottom."—Dale Carnegie.

**im″ma te′ri al** (im″muh teer′i ăl). Unimportant; irrelevant; without bearing; of no great consequence.— "Whether the men acted through misunderstanding or as the agents of the enemy powers is *immaterial*."— Philip Murray.

**im″ma ture′** (im″uh tūre′). Not full-grown; undeveloped; youthful.—"I saw an adult and an *immature* kite." —Hugh Birckhead.

**im′mi nent** (im′ĭ nĕnt). Liable to happen at once; impending.—"We have little left to do except prepare for the *imminent* surrender of the enemy."— William O. Douglas.

**im mo′bi lized** (im mō′bĭ līze'd). Rendered unable to move; made incapable of movement.—"He was carried out on a stretcher, *immobilized* by his ailment."—Charles B. Driscoll.

**im mu′ni ty** (i mū′nĭ ti). Freedom or exemption from harm or penalty.— "The dreamiest of all our dreamers have been those who told us that *immunity* from risks lay in attempted secession from the planet."—W. W. Waymack.

**im pal′pa ble** (im pal′puh b'l). Intangible; that cannot be felt; that cannot be grasped mentally; not easily perceived; not palpable.—"Hints of disillusionment, *impalpable* but cumulative, gathered in his consciousness."—H. G. Wells.

**im part′** (im pahrt′). To share with another; hence, to make known by words or signs; to communicate; to reveal; to give.—"The Bible uses parables to *impart* its teaching."— Emmet Fox.

**im pede′** (im peed′). Hinder; obstruct; limit.—"The situation will *impede* and in some degree prevent the larger development."—David E. Lilienthal.

**im ped′i ment** (im ped′ĭ mĕnt). Hindrance; obstruction; obstacle; inter-

ruption.—"The training can proceed without any distraction or *impediment*."—Winston Churchill.

**im per′vi ous** (im pur′vi ŭs). Impenetrable; impermeable; permitting no entry; not letting ideas enter; deaf to. —"He says that what people are told in these mass meetings will remain ineradicable, and *impervious* to every reasonable explanation."—George V. Denny.

**im plant′ing** (im plant′ing). Planting deeply and firmly; hence, instilling; inserting; inculcating; impressing by repetition.—"She knew that part of her textbook about *implanting* one idea for another."—Virginia Dale.

**im′pli cat″ed** (im′plĭ kāte″id). Involved or concerned in; connected with; entangled.—"They are irretrievably *implicated* in the crimes."— Walter Lippmann.

**im′port** (im′port). Meaning; significance; importance; purport.— "These judgments, when they are soundly made, are of universal *import*."—Robert I. Gannon.

**im pov′er ished** (im pov′ur isht). Reduced to poverty.—"Farmers were *impoverished* by abundance, while at the same time millions of consumers were hungry."—Henry A. Wallace.

**im prov′i dent** (im prov′ĭ dĕnt). Lacking thrift or foresight; thriftless; failing to provide for the future.—"We should stop this policy of purchasing gold and silver from abroad at *improvident* prices."—George N. Peck.

**im pu′ni ty** (im pū′nĭ ti). Freedom from punishment or from injurious consequences.—"Such an amendment would encourage other nations to believe that they could violate American rights with *impunity*."— Franklin Delano Roosevelt.

**in ac′tion** (in ak′shŭn). Idleness; absence of action or work; inactivity.— "One thing that Karl could not stand was a long period of *inaction*." —George F. Gahagan.

**in″ad ver′tent** (in″ŭd vur′tĕnt). Inattentive; without giving special heed; careless; unintentional.—"I caught an *inadvertent* glimpse of my husband."—Nina Wilcox Putnam.

**in ane′ly** (in ain′li). Pointlessly; fool-

ishly; in a silly way; senselessly.—
"The rain would wash some of the
blood off, he thought, *inanely*."—
Stephen Vincent Benét.

**in'ci dent** (in'sǐ děnt). Apt to occur;
liable to happen; hence, usually attending or belonging as a subordinate
feature.—"These problems have been
*incident* to our transition from a
peacetime to a war economy."—
Paul G. Hoffman.

**in clem'ent** (in klem'ent). Severe;
stormy; harsh; rigorous; not clement
or mild.—"This was the family
gathering-place when the sun was hot
or the weather *inclement*."—Gertrude Atherton.

**in″com mu′ni ca ble** (in″kǒ mū′nǐ kuh-
b'l). Not capable of being imparted;
that cannot be shared with others;
not capable of being transmitted or
passed on to others.—"He felt the
queer *incommunicable* joy of the vivid
phrase that turns the statement of a
horrid fact to beauty."—H. G. Wells.

**in cum'bent** (in kum'běnt). Resting
upon one, as a moral obligation;
obligatory; pressing as a duty.—"It
is *incumbent* upon us to give the best
that is in us."—John D. Rockefeller, Jr.

**in del'i cate** (in del'ǐ kit). Improper;
immodest; unrefined; offensive to
propriety; lacking refinement and
good manners.—"These new fashions
make all dances seem rather *indelicate*."—Edith Wharton.

**in″di ca′tions** (in″di kā′shǔnz). Signs;
manifestations.—"All *indications* are
pointing to a stepping up of the offensive."—Merrill Decker.

**in dic′a tive** (in dik′uh tiv). Giving intimation or hint; making known;
pointing out; suggesting; giving
knowledge of or being a sign of
(something not seen).—"Her questions were *indicative* of idle-minded-
ness."—Channing Pollock.

**in dig′e nous** (in dij′ē nŭs). Originating in a special place; native.—"This
country has invented a type of building unique and *indigenous*—the sky-
scraper."—Dorothy Thompson.

**in″dis cern′i ble** (in″di zur′nǐ b'l). Imperceptible; indistinguishable; im-
perceivable; not clearly seen or rec-

ognized.—"In a matter of seconds
the plane was almost *indiscernible* in
the skies."—Donald G. Cooley.

**in'do lent** (in'dō lěnt). Disliking work;
idle; lazy; averse to exertion; habitually inactive.—"The hot sun made
us golden brown and *indolent*."—
Elinor Graham.

**in du′bi ta bly** (in dū′bǐ tuh bli). Unquestionably; undeniably.—"*Indubitably* the highest kind of government
is maintained through self-government."—Madame Chiang Kai-shek.

**in ev′i ta bly** (in ev′ǐ tuh bli). Un-
avoidably; unpreventably.—"Cut-
throat competition is *inevitably* expensive and wasteful."—Lord Cranborne.

**in″fer en′tial** (in″fur en′shǎl). Capable of being inferred or deduced by
passing from a belief to a judgment;
able to be reached by reasoning; implied from something else.—"This
meaning was not directly expressed,
but *inferential*."—Donald G. Cooley.

**in flat′ed** (in flāte′id). Puffed up;
swelled out; dilated; expanded;
elated; unduly increased or magnified.—"Benito Mussolini will go
down into history as an acute case of
*inflated* ego."—Ellery Marsh Egan.

**ink′ling** (ingk′ling). A slight intimation; a faint notion or idea.—"To
those of us who have the slightest
*inkling* of economics the maxim
sounds laughable."—Madame Chiang Kai-shek.

**in op′er a ble** (in op′ur uh b'l). Not
operable or able to perform the
work; in an unusable state; not able
to be put in motion and used for
work.—"One stupid mistake had
made the machine *inoperable*."—Jack
Bond.

**in or′di nate** (in or′di nit). Not restrained by rules; immoderate; unreasonable; excessive.—"Economic
strife, resulting from *inordinate* trade
barriers, is a fruitful source of political animosity."—Franklin Delano
Roosevelt.

**in sen′si ble** (in sen′sǐ b'l). Unable to
feel; unconscious; unaware; lacking
sensitiveness; indifferent; not sensitive; unimpressed.—"He had mag-
netism, a personal charm to which

few were *insensible*."—Herbert Ravenel Sass.

**in sol'u ble** (in sol'ū b'l). That cannot be explained or solved.—"The love of God and man is the final answer to all the *insoluble* questions of all the ages."—Jan Christiaan Smuts.

**in"sta bil'i ty** (in"stuh bil'ĭ ti). Lack of firmness; insecurity; unsteadiness; inconstancy; fickleness.—"War, revolution, famine and pestilence cause emotional *instability*."—Orville Prescott.

**in stall'** (in stawl'). To place in position for use; to fix in place for service.—"There would be no plumbing or piping to *install* in the house."—Norman Bel Geddes.

**in stilled'** (in stild'). Poured in drop by drop; hence, implanted gradually; inculcated; filled little by little.—"Political slogans have been revived and *instilled* with new meaning."—Maxim Litvinoff.

**in'ter lop"ers** (in'tur lōpe"urs). Those who thrust themselves into a place without any right; intruders.—"The peasants of Norway look upon the townsfolk of the coasts as *interlopers*."—Percy Aldridge Grainger.

**in"ter posed'** (in"tur pōze'd'). Interfered in order to help; intervened; put forth authority to prevent a result.—"When the drunken brute of a teamster flayed the horse, he quickly *interposed*."—Samuel Hopkins Adams.

**in"ter spersed'** (in"tur spurst'). Distributed or scattered between other people or things; diversified here and there.—"The workers in the factories are now thickly *interspersed* with women."—Anne O'Hare McCormick.

**in trac'ta ble** (in trak'tuh b'l). Unruly; refractory; difficult to manage; passively resistant.—"The minds of these men are tools fit for working those most *intractable* materials—ideas."—Paul Shipman Andrews.

**in vest'ed** (in vest'ed). Endowed, or surrounded; bestowed upon; endued.—"From the start I *invested* him with all the attributes of heroism."—Alexander P. Seversky.

**in vid'i ous** (in vid'i ŭs). Unjustly discriminating; malicious; likely to cause ill-will or to offend.—"The Prime Minister dwelt on the *invidious* effect of such powers upon individual firms."—Winston Churchill.

**in volved'** (in volve'd'). Drawn into entanglement, literally or figuratively; embroiled; entangled.—"I am not *involved* in the coat dispute."—Donald M. Nelson.

**irk** (urk). Vex; fatigue; annoy; trouble.—"Oftentimes it is not the major problems of existence that *irk* a man's soul."—Madame Chiang Kai-shek.

**ir"re spec'tive** (ir"rē spek'tiv). Regardless; lacking relation; independent of.—"Political management, *irrespective* of degree, can have no other result than lowering the ceiling of industry's ability to contribute toward human progress."—Alfred P. Sloan.

**japes** (jāpes). Jibes; jests; tricks.—"The comedian saved the play from the tedious reiterations of antique *japes*."—Howard Barnes.

**joc'u lar** (jok'ū lur). Funny; said as a joke; droll; humorous.—"Even the name pumpkin is *jocular*, a word to be rhymed with bumpkin."—Earlene M. Cornell.

**ken** (ken). The range of sight; the range of knowledge; cognizance.—"They had perhaps strayed into the *ken* of another planet."—Anne Morrow Lindbergh.

**kin'dred** (kin'drĕd). Of like character; related; akin.—"In all these and *kindred* matters the Chinese and the Indian are moulded in the same pattern."—Shanmukham Chetty.

**la ment'** (luh ment'). Expression of grief or sorrow; lamentation; mourning; songs of grief; a dirge; weeping.—"They celebrated his death with fasting and *lament*."—Caroline Dale Snedeker.

**laps'es** (laps'iz). Slight errors; mistakes; momentary forgetfulness; careless slips or mistakes in conduct.—"He cannot help lecturing his comrades on their *lapses* of manners and taste."—Edmund Wilson.

**laud'a ble** (lawd'uh b'l). Praiseworthy; commendable; worthy of approval.—"The house had the best of taste and a simple and *laudable* architecture."—Sinclair Lewis.

**lean** (leen). Unproductive; thin; poor; attended by want.—"In the *lean* weeks they ate salted fish and the leaves of trees."—Florence Haxton Bullock.

**lis'some** (liss'ŭm). Supple; lithe; pliant; flexible; hence, agile.—"I never saw you so *lissome* and elastic."—E. F. Benson.

**lithe** (līthe: 'th' as in 'the'). Limber; tractable; adaptable; compliant.— "We congratulate all our leaders, and all their *lithe*, active, ardent men."— Winston Churchill.

**lunge** (lunje). A sudden plunge forward; an abrupt forward movement; a leap; a forward lurch.—"He dropped his paddle and made a *lunge* to recover it."—Roy Chapman Andrews.

**lurk'ing** (lurk'ing). Lying concealed; hidden; waiting out of sight; moving about secretly, as if waiting to attack. —"The sea is dark and terrifying enough without the *lurking* things." —John Steinbeck.

**maj'es ty** (maj'ess ti). Grandeur; stateliness of aspect; impressive dignity; sublimity.—"He is excited about the color of the sea, and the beauty and *majesty* of the scene."—Lincoln Colcord.

**mal'le a ble** (mal'e uh b'l). Easily led; ductile; susceptible to pressure.— "The American public is very *malleable*, very receptive."—Morton Freud.

**mal treat'ed** (mal treet'ed). Badly treated; abused; ill-used; roughly handled.—"He has been the chief ruler since these *maltreated* people were seized."—Oswald Garrison Villard.

**man″i fes ta'tion** (man″ĭ fess tā'shŭn). Something that is clearly evident or apparent to the eye or mind; showing; acts or signs that show clearly; collective actions that reveal or make plain special tendencies.—"The business underwent a rapid transformation, both as to its inner character and as to its outward *manifestation*." —L. P. Jacks.

**mask'ing** (mask'ing). Covering the face, as with a mask; hence, disguising; hiding; concealing; veiling.— "Spring came late that year with an austerity of beauty as if nature were mercifully *masking* the splendor of the June that so many would never see."—Helen C. White.

**mas'ti cate** (mass'tĭ kāte). Chew; crush or grind as with the teeth so as to prepare for swallowing; reduce to pulp.—"They have bitten off more than they can chew, more than any single state can *masticate*."—George Fielding Eliot.

**ma te'ri al ize** (muh tee'ri ăl īze). To take substantial form; to become a fact; to be realized.—"The promised invasion of England failed to *materialize*."—William L. Shirer.

**me an'der** (mē an'dur). To wind about; to wander without a goal or object; to wind and turn in a course. —"Shall that stream be allowed to *meander* aimlessly through swamps and sands?"—George D. Aiken.

**me'di o″cre** (mee'di ō″kur). Ordinary; of moderate capacity or ability.— "More *mediocre* women will find a better chance against *mediocre* men." —Mildred H. McAfee.

**me″di oc'ri ty** (mē″di ok'rĭ ti). A moderate or intermediate state; an average or ordinary quality or state; hence, a middle position neither high nor low.—"Madison Avenue then stood for a decent *mediocrity*."—Edith Wharton.

**me'di um** (mee'di ŭm). Something through which an action or service is accomplished.—"News is not only the conveyor of information, it is also the chief *medium* of global education." —Carl W. Ackerman.

**mel'low** (mel'ō). Softened by experience; made wise by age; companionable; mature.—"This is a contemplative, intellectualized, discursive, *mellow* book." — Orville Prescott.

**men'tor** (men'tur). An adviser or monitor; a wise and trusted guide; an experienced counselor; a guiding influence.—"The supreme *mentor* of the people in all questions relating to national policy was the State."—Raymond H. Geist.

**met″ro pol'i tan** (met″rō pol'ĭ tăn). Pertaining to the chief or most important city of a state or country.—

"The back-country roads are the lifeline of our great *metroplitan* areas." —Charles M. Upham.

**mis cal'cu lat"ed** (miss kal'kū lāte"id). Reckoned erroneously; computed incorrectly; calculated wrongly; put a false estimate on.—"He had *miscalculated* personalities."—Virginia Dale.

**mis'cel la"ny** (miss'ĕ lāy"ni). A mixture of things of various kinds; a miscellaneous collection; a medley.—"A *miscellany* of lights, electric lights of all sorts, added strange shadows to the ruins."—H. G. Wells.

**mis"con strued'** (miss"kŏn strood'). Misinterpreted; misunderstood.— "The Army said that the visual all-clear would be *misconstrued*."—Fiorello H. LaGuardia.

**mis prized'** (miss prīze'd'). Undervalued; despised; misunderstood; scorned.—"She wanted to tell them that their love would be *misprized*."— Thomas Wolfe.

**moot'ed** (moot'ed). Argued for and against; debated.—"The question has been *mooted* over the radio in the last few days."—William E. Borah.

**mulled** (mul'd). Pondered; worked over mentally; ruminated.—"It is not a question to be *mulled* over at leisure, but a thing on which the possibility of victory depends."—Maxim M. Litvinoff.

**mu'ti nous** (mū'tĭ nŭs). Rebellious; seditious; disposed to stir up mutiny or insurrection against authority.— "She had learned to pour the warmth of her own determination upon them until from great *mutinous* silent beasts they turned to obedience again."— Pearl S. Buck.

**ne ces'si tate** (nē sess'ĭ tāte). Make necessary; render unavoidable or inevitable; make indispensable; force or compel.—"That last leak will *necessitate* the re-papering of the whole room."—Ainslee Mockridge.

**neg'li gence** (neg'lĭ jĕnce). Neglect; lack of proper care; want of attention; carelessness.—"Investigation showed that the wreck was due to the *negligence* of the engineer."—Ainslee Mockridge.

**neg'li gi ble** (neg'lĭ jĭ b'l). Trivial; that may be disregarded; that can be neglected.—"There was another and be no means *negligible* factor to persuade me."—Marc Connelly.

**net'tled** (net"ld). Vexed; irritated; provoked; stung, as by a nettle.— "Slightly *nettled*, he asked why the organization should risk the names." —Franz Werfel.

**neu'tral ize** (nū'trăl īze). To make of no effect; to destroy the effect of.— "Suspicion served to *neutralize* much of what the government was trying to do."—Lewis H. Brown.

**nil** (nil). Nothing; no amount.— "Without proper tuning and regulating, the value of even the best piano is reduced to *nil*."—Theodore E. Steinway.

**non'cha lant** (non'shuh lănt). Jauntily indifferent or unconcerned; without enthusiasm or interest; casual.—"If we grow soft, smug, and *nonchalant*, we may lose our birthright."—Ennis P. Whitley.

**non"-com mit'tal** (non"-kŏ mit'ăl). Of a character that neither consents nor dissents, refusing to say yes or no.— "Being *non-committal* and never admitting error is called politics."— Hugh S. Johnson.

**non'plused** (non'plust). Disconcerted; taken aback; brought to a mental standstill; puzzled; in a quandary.— "They were *nonplused*: strange women were not in the habit of flying into this airport."—Grace E. Barstow Murphy.

**ob liv'i ous** (ob liv'i ŭs). Not noticing; unmindful.—"They were walking through the lobbies *oblivious* of the criticisms they heard."—Winston Churchill.

**ob'so lete** (ob'sō leet). Out of date; discarded; no longer in use.—"The dictating machine cylinders of today may become *obsolete* when this recording wire becomes available."—Stanley S. Jacobs.

**of'fic es** (off'iss ez). Services; acts of kindness or attention; things done for others whether helpful or harmful; tasks or duties.—"I decided to lend my good *offices* to the cause."— Emory L. Fielding.

**on'set** (on'set). Attack; assault; onslaught; impetuous assailment.—"A gnawing fire of despair in her heart, she plunged blindly against the *onset* of a furious March wind."—Samuel Hopkins Adams.

**op'u lence** (op'ū lĕnce). Wealth; affluence; riches; abundance.—"The only poverty from which a nation suffers in war is poverty resulting from the excesses of *opulence*."—Thurman W. Arnold.

**os ten'si bly** (oss ten'si bli). Seemingly; apparently; professedly.—"Further increase in wages will invite disaster that will wash away far more than the monetary stimulation of *ostensibly* higher wages."—Jacob Aronson.

**out weighed'** (owt wāde'). Exceeded in weight; surpassed in value; exceeded in importance.—"They find that the importance of their original plan is alarmingly *outweighed* by invasions of their freedom."—Westbrook Pegler.

**o"ver wrought'** (ō"vur rawt'). Overstrained; worn out or exhausted by overwork; overexcited; suffering a reaction from excessive work or excitement.—"He was nervous, ashamed, *overwrought*."—Lloyd C. Douglas.

**pal'at a ble** (pal'ĭt uh b'l). Agreeable to the taste and appetite; pleasing as a food; acceptable for a meal.—"The new rayon will wash perfectly and will not be *palatable* to moths."—Francis Westbrook, Jr.

**palled** (pawld). Became dull; became satiated; became tiresome; ceased to please.—"His repertoire was wide enough so that his popularity never *palled*."—Carlos Baker.

**pal'lid** (pal'id). Pale; wan; feeble in color; lacking color.—"The men tear the skin off in great strips and the hog emerges, naked and *pallid*, ready for dismemberment."—Hilary St. George Saunders.

**pal'pa bly** (pal'puh bli). Obviously; evidently.—"The reasons they give are *palpably* false."—Walter Lippmann.

**pal'pi tat"ed** (pal'pĭ tāte"id). Beat rapidly; throbbed; quivered; pulsated.—"Unfamiliar scenes and faces always *palpitated* in her long afterward."—Edith Wharton.

**pal'try** (pawl'tri). Having little or no worth or value; insignificant, small.—"All of them together raised only a *paltry* sum."—Arthur Sweetser.

**par'a pet** (par'uh pet). A rampart or breastwork; a low wall surrounding a balcony or at the edge of a roof or terrace.—"Sailors were standing by the *parapet* overlooking the Marina."—Axel Munthe.

**par'ry** (par'i). To ward off, as a blow; to evade a thrust; to turn something aside; to avoid a weapon or question.—"He had learned to dodge or *parry* the strokes of village critics."—Franz Werfel.

**par takes'** (pahr tākes'). Receives a share; has a part in; possesses somewhat of the nature, properties, or character.—"All nature is pervaded by wisdom and even a wasp or a frog *partakes* of it."—Alan Devoe.

**pat'ent** (pāy'tĕnt). Open; not hidden; evident; obvious.—"It was a self-conscious effort that did not achieve its *patent* purpose."—Stewart Holbrook.

**peers** (peerz). Those of equal rank; people of equal social rank or position.—"She lifted her face from the papers and began to talk with a knot of her *peers*."—Hilary St. George Saunders.

**pend'ent** (pen'dĕnt). Suspended; hanging; drooping downwards.—"A limp Roman banner was identified, *pendent* from an oblique pole."—Lloyd C. Douglas.

**pen'du lous** (pen'dū lŭs). Hanging; suspended; swinging; pendent.—"Great bunches of blossoms, heavy and *pendulous* as grapes, filled the world with scent."—Elizabeth Goudge.

**pent** (pent). Closely confined; penned or shut in; shut up inside something.—"Suddenly her *pent* up feelings burst out in a torrent of tears."—Emmet Holloway.

**pen'u ry** (pen'ū ri). Extreme poverty or want; indigence; destitution.—"Until true liberalism is resurrected we probably will languish in *penury* and woe."—Mark M. Jones.

**per func'to ry** (pur fungk'tō ri). Mechanical and without interest; superficial; indifferent.—"Our philosophers have consulted with businesses and trades in no more than a *perfunctory* manner, if at all."—David R. Craig.

**per′son ag″es** (pur′sŭn ij″iz). Persons of rank or importance; distinguished people.—"She made a vivid impression upon the most fashionable *personages*."—Louis Bromfield.

**per vades′** (pur vāde′z′). Spreads through every part; permeates; is widely diffused.—"Dictatorial and suave, their government *pervades* all public and private life."—Joseph C. Grew.

**phi lan′der ing** (fi lan′dur ing). Making love; flirting; playing at courtship; dangling or trifling in lovemaking.—"The story concerns two former mistresses of a *philandering* playwright."—Austin Wright.

**pine** (pīne). Waste away with grief or longing; grieve secretly; languish; grow thin and weak.—"The poor dog began to *pine* away during his master's absence."—Bradwell E. Tanis.

**piv′ot ing** (piv′ŭt ing). Turning around, as on a pin or shaft; turning around, as on a hinge.—"He took in his surroundings with a *pivoting* head and cautious eye."—William J. Calvert, Jr.

**por tend′ed** (por tend′ed). Gave a warning of; foretold; presaged; indicated by signs.—"His glowering looks *portended* trouble."—Ellery Marsh Egan.

**pos′tu lat″ed** (poss′tū lāte″id). Assumed or affirmed without proof as self-evident or already known; claimed as true.—"The belief in personal liberty was *postulated* on two corollaries."—William J. Donovan.

**po′ta ble** (pō′tuh b'l). Suitable for drinking; hence, liquid.—"He was reduced to this *potable* lava which seared the throat and was only fit for a hostelry in inferno."—Hervey Allen.

**pre sen′ti ment** (prē zen′tĭ mĕnt). Premonition; foreboding; prophetic feeling or impression that something was about to happen.—"They had a faint, far-off *presentiment* of impending disaster."—Bradwell E. Tanis.

**pres tige′** (press teezh′). Reputation; importance based on past achievements; renown; commanding position.—"I perceived that the *prestige* of my own army was involved."—Warren J. Clear.

**pre sump′tion** (prē zump′shŭn). Conclusion based on probable but not conclusive evidence; inference from facts; probable evidence.—"He is misguided, of course, but my *presumption* is that his motives are honest."—Emory L. Fielding.

**pre″sup pose′** (prē″sŭ pōze′). Suppose beforehand; imply as an antecedent condition; take for granted.—"Who are we to *presuppose*, or prejudge?"—George Matthew Adams.

**pre′text** (prē′text). A fictitious reason or motive; an excuse.—"These groups encourage a systematic organization under the sham *pretext* of local interests."—John L. Lewis.

**prev′a lent** (prev′uh lĕnt). Of wide extent or frequent occurrence; common.—"A type of military education became more *prevalent* as a reaction to defeat by Napoleon."—Henry A. Wallace.

**prob″lem at′i cal** (prob″lĕm at′i kăl). Puzzling and difficult to answer; involving a problem; uncertain.—"It is *problematical* to what degree our arrangements will permit us to extend these projects."—Henry S. Villard.

**pro fuse′** (prō fūce′). Bountiful; very abundant; pouring forth freely; copious; overflowing.—"His plane wabbled as he broke into a *profuse* perspiration."—Allan R. Bosworth.

**pro sa′ic** (prō zāy′ik). Unimaginative; commonplace; matter-of-fact; humdrum; ordinary.—"The patriotic urge will be replaced by the less *prosaic* incentive to earn a profit."—Emil Schram.

**pro tu′ber ant** (prō tū′bur ănt). Bulging out; prominent; swelling out; sticking out.—"He was a small, bald fellow of about 70 with *protuberant* black eyes."—Gene Fowler.

**prox im′i ty** (proks im′ĭ ti). The state of being near or next; nearness.—"*Proximity* to the sun affects the luminosity of comets."—Fred L. Whipple.

**pul'sat ing** (pul'sāte ing). Beating; throbbing; vibrating; quivering.—"I saw thousands of luminous stars and planets, all *pulsating* with life and light."—Axel Munthe.

**pur ports'** (pur ports'). Gives an impression of; appears to be; professes to be; implies.—"It *purports* to be an agreement between the two countries."—H. N. MacCracken.

**pur su'ant** (pur sū'ănt). Done in accordance with; conformable; carrying out or following.—"The members shall receive expenses for duties actually engaged in *pursuant* to this order."—Franklin Delano Roosevelt.

**quaff** (kwa(h)ff). Drink deeply; drink freely; drink in big drafts and with relish.—"In an old-fashioned way there is something satisfying in the phrase, 'I will *quaff* my ale.'"—Ainslee Mockridge.

**quelled** (kweld). Subdued; calmed; mollified; quieted; pacified; suppressed; overpowered.—"The coolies were soon *quelled* and we started out."—Eric Sevareid.

**quib'bling** (kwib'ling). Evading the truth; prevaricating; equivocating; evading the point.—"It is imperative to cease wasteful *quibbling*."—Joseph T. Robinson.

**quick'en** (kwik'ĕn). Make rapid or quick; accelerate; hasten; move more quickly; increase the speed of.—"If you will *quicken* your pace ever so little we shall still be there on time."—S. L. Scanlon.

**qui'e tude** (kwī ĕ tūde). Tranquillity; quietness; calmness; stillness; state of rest or repose.—"I have stood in an entire room of Raeburns at the Huntington Gallery and become lost, as E. V. Lucas once said, 'in the *quietude* of the paint.'"—George Matthew Adams.

**ra'di ance** (rāy'di ănce). Brightness; effulgence; brilliancy; beams of light.—"I gazed at the myriad twinkling lights and beyond them at a faint, far-off *radiance* which had been a gilded glory."—Hilary St. George Saunders.

**rai'ment** (rāy'mĕnt). Wearing-apparel; vesture; garment; clothing.—"We all remember that Joseph's *raiment*

was of many and variegated colors."—George F. Gahagan.

**re"af firmed'** (rē"ă furm'd'). Asserted again in order to strengthen; established again so as to confirm.—"He *reaffirmed* his place as one of the great clowns of this era."—John K. Hutchens.

**re"al i za'tion** (rē"ăl i zā'shŭn). A making real of something imagined; perception as a reality; understanding; vivid conception.—"It is perhaps fortunate that we have so little *realization* of what lies ahead of us."—Donald G. Cooley.

**re"ca pit'u lat ing** (rē"kuh pit'ū lāte-ing). Repeating the chief points; summing up the main points; reviewing briefly.—"What was the use of *recapitulating* these points when she was no longer the same girl."—Edith Wharton.

**re cip'ro cat"ed** (rē sip'rō kāte"id). Made a return in the same kind; returned an equivalent; repaid in a corresponding way.—"He was unrestrained in his affection for animals and birds, and they *reciprocated* in kind."—Gene Fowler.

**re dun'dant** (rē dun'dănt). Superfluous; superabundant; more than is necessary.—"Youth has its irrepressible enthusiasms and its *redundant* vigor."—George B. Cutten.

**re flec'tions** (rē flek'shŭnz). Reproaches; causes of blame; statements or thoughts of censure; imputations; acts or ideas that shed discredit on behavior.—"I had the affrontery to ask him if he felt this cast any *reflections* on his own skill and devotion as a parent."—Alexander Woollcott.

**re fur'bish ing** (rē fur'bish ing). Freshening up; polishing and brightening; putting in order.—"The dealers have been *refurbishing* second-hand pianos."—Theodore E. Steinway.

**re ga'li a** (rē gāy'li uh). The emblems or symbols of royalty; hence, the insignia of office; the special dress for some function or event.—"I'll be done with after-dinner speaking forever, so why despatch me hence in the *regalia* of the craft?"—Irvin S. Cobb.

**re gal'ing** (rē gāle'ing). Entertaining royally or sumptuously; diverting pleasantly; refreshing delightfully; feasting.—"He enjoyed *regaling* himself with terrific tales of his forebears, the cateran chiefs who had plundered these glens."—André Maurois.

**re"im burse'** (rē"im burse'). Pay back as an equivalent for what has been spent or lost; repay.—"How can our shipmen *reimburse* Sweden for John Ericsson?"—Harold Fields.

**re"in state'** (rē"in stāte'). Restore to a former state or position; put back again into its former place or standing.—"We must *reinstate* the philosophy which achieved our success in the past."—William A. Hanley.

**rel'e gat"ed** (rel'e gāte"id). Consigned; put back; banished; removed.—"We see dictatorships under which woman is being *relegated* to the place she had in the Middle Ages."—David Sarnoff.

**rel'e van cy** (rel'ē văn si). Applicability; obvious relation; connection with the matter.—"What is the *relevancy* of these plans to our actual needs?"—Winston Churchill.

**re nounced'** (rē nounst': 'ou' as in 'out'). Gave up entirely and formally; abandoned; disclaimed in a speech or proclamation.—"He publicly *renounced* imperialist ambitions."—Leland Stowe.

**re past'** (rē past'). A meal; food prepared or eaten at a meal.—"The *repast* she had prepared for him did not seem to justify his ingratitude."—H. G. Wells.

**re plete'** (rē pleet'). Filled to the uttermost; completely filled; abundantly supplied.—"This book is *replete* with the details on just how the men advanced."—Cecil Brown.

**req'ui site** (rek'wĭ zit). Required by the nature of things; necessary.—"If Congress would legislate the *requisite* authority to such an office, much good would be accomplished."—James E. Murray.

**ret'i cence** (ret'ĭ sĕnce). The habit of being reserved in speech and saying very little; a disposition to keep silent; secretiveness.—"We do claim and exercise the right to debate whether the question is a matter of security or only of the habitual *reticence* of the navy."—Elmer Davis.

**ret'i nue** (ret'i nū). A body of attendants or retainers; an escort; a suite or train of persons in attendance on a distinguished man or woman.—"Many a general had such a *retinue*, but to the simple people these could only belong to the king."—Caroline Dale Snedeker.

**re tract'** (rē trakt'). To disavow; take back; declare false; withdraw.—"All this is quite true, I have nothing to *retract*."—Axel Munthe.

**rife** (rīfe). Prevalent; common; numerous; plentiful; current.—"The stories of midnight revels were still *rife* when I first went there."—Roy Chapman Andrews.

**rue** (rōō). Repent of; regret; be sorry for; suffer remorse for; lament over. —"He will *rue* that one act all the rest of his days."—Hugh E. Blackstone.

**rug'ged** (rug'ĕd). Robust; sturdy; strong; vigorous; harsh; stern.—"A few *rugged* individualists will engage a high-priced lawyer, who never saw the inside of a factory, to blast the proposal as unconstitutional."—Austin M. Fisher.

**sa gac'i ty** (suh gass'ĭ ti). Discernment and judgment; shrewdness; mental keenness; perspicacity.—"They could neither rise to Johnson's rich melancholy nor to his human *sagacity*."—Ludwig Lewisohn.

**san'guine** (sang'gwin). Hopeful; confident; optimistic; hopefully cheerful. —"This is not a time for us to indulge in *sanguine* predictions."—Winston Churchill.

**saun'tered** (sawn'turd). Walked in a leisurely and aimless way; strolled idly; walked along slowly.—"Her hand sought his and they *sauntered* across the courtyard."—Pearl S. Buck.

**scru'ti nize** (skrōō'tĭ nīze). Observe carefully in every detail; examine very closely.—"*Scrutinize* every report that comes to your desk."—J. C. Staehle.

**se cured'** (sē kūre'd'). Acquired; obtained; procured; gained by effort.—

"His release from the Navy was *secured*."—Richard W. Abbott.

**sem'blance** (sem'blănce). Outward appearance; look; similarity; resemblance.—"There are areas of block upon block where there is not even a *semblance* of the structures that had been there—only débris."—Paul H. Appleby.

**sheer** (sheer). Perpendicular; straight up and down; ascending vertically; steep.—"I used to look up and up along the *sheer* rise of the great bole of the immense white oak."—Edwin Way Teale.

**shunned** (shund). Kept away from; deliberately avoided; kept clear of; evaded.—"Serf and farmer alike *shunned* the blackened ruins after nightfall."—Helen C. White.

**sig'nal ized** (sig'năl īze'd). Made stand out; pointed out carefully; showed distinctly; made noteworthy.—"The landing of the planes *signalized* the complete unity of the effort."—W. H. Lawrence.

**si mil'i tude** (si mil'ĭ tūde). Similarity; semblance; likeness; that which is similar or resembles.—"In his garden he found the *similitude* of that peace that ought to obtain among God's creatures."—Ludwig Lewisohn.

**sim'u lat"ed** (sim'ū lāte"id). Feigned or pretended; having the appearance or form of, without the reality; not real, but looking as though it were.—"He charged up a hill to take a *simulated* enemy."—Warren J. Clear.

**sin'is ter** (sin'iss tur). Boding disaster and, therefore, adverse or harmful; disastrous; ominous.—"What is funny in one country is sometimes *sinister* in another."—Cedric Hardwicke.

**so bri'e ty** (sō brī'ĕ tï). Temperance; moderateness in temper and conduct; seriousness; moderation.—"If we can muster the *sobriety* and intelligent industry, I believe we can create a century of progress."—George N. Shuster.

**so lem'ni ty** (sō lem'nĭ tï). Seriousness and dignity; solemn feeling; impressive reverence.—"The deep history of the Cathedral of Notre Dame and the dark shadows of the interior al-ways produce a mood of *solemnity*."—Emmet Holloway.

**so lic'i tous ly** (sō liss'ĭ tŭs li). Full of anxiety or concern; anxiously and attentively; thoughtfully.—"General Mitchell thereafter never saw or phoned me without inquiring *solicitously* after my dog."—Alexander P. de Seversky.

**sol'i tude** (sol'ĭ tūde). A state of being alone or in seclusion; being alone; loneliness; seclusion.—"Henry Thoreau believed rich dividends could be derived from *solitude*."—Charles Henry Crozier.

**sol'u ble** (sol'ū b'l). That can be solved or worked out, as a problem; able to be explained and cleared up; for which an answer can be found.—"Only a naïve people could believe that the Negro question is *soluble* in the sense that a final solution can be found."—David L. Cohn.

**spars'er** (spahrce'ur). More thinly diffused; scattered at greater distances apart; more scanty.—"Passing eastward, the islands become *sparser*."—E. S. C. Smith.

**spent** (spent). Exhausted; worn out with fatigue; used up; deprived of force; tired out.—"He held the *spent* and panting animal in his arms as if it were an ailing child."—Gene Fowler.

**spon ta'ne ous ly** (spon tāy'nē ŭs li). Freely, without premeditation; instinctively; naturally; from an inner urge.—"The virtues upon which human freedom depends do not grow *spontaneously* in the soil of human nature."—Henry St. George Tucker.

**spor'tive** (spor'tiv). Playful; frolicsome; merry; vivacious.—"The March wind was *sportive* and scented with new growth."—Mazo de la Roche.

**stark** (stahrk). Stubborn; inflexible; unadorned; obdurate; bare.—"Not one word of comment is required; the *stark* facts speak for themselves."—Monroe E. Deutsch.

**stim'u late** (stim'ū lāte). Rouse to action; spur on; increase activity by a stimulus or incentive.—"These schools will *stimulate* the quick to learn and speed them along."—Walter Adams.

**sub sist'** (sŭb sist'). Remain in existence; continue to live; exist; keep alive.—"We could make you *subsist* on thin toast and lettuce salad if we wanted to starve you into subservience."—Sylvia F. Porter.

**sub sis'tence** (sŭb siss'tĕnce). Necessary supplies for maintaining life; means of support; livelihood.—"Our task is to see that those in the lower rungs are not ground down below the margin of *subsistence*."—James F. Byrnes.

**suc cinct'ly** (suk singkt'li). Tersely; concisely; in few words.—"I wish we had a grand phrase such as 'Lafayette, we are here,' that would tell us *succinctly* the story of the occupation of North Africa."—Dwight D. Eisenhower.

**suf fused'** (suh fūze'd'). Overspread; gradually spread over the surface, coloring or tinting it.—"The slanting rays of the early morning sun *suffused* the high prairie with a soft light."—Edwin H. Colbert.

**sug gest"i bil'i ty** (sŭg jess"tĭ bil'ĭ ti). Susceptibility to suggestion; readiness to believe or comply.—"There are drugs that enormously increase the individual's *suggestibility*."—Aldous Huxley.

**sun'dry** (sun'dri). Various; several; miscellaneous; of different kinds that cannot be classified.—"We handle all types of cases involving strikes, controversies, and *sundry* disputes."—John R. Steelman.

**su"per im posed'** (sū"pur im pōze'd'). Placed upon something else; imposed or added on top of something, over and above.—"*Superimposed* upon these specific demands is the additional demand for consumer goods."—Alfred P. Sloan, Jr.

**su"per nu'mer ar"y** (sū"pur nū'mur er"i). Beyond a fixed number; extra; superfluous; more than usual.—"He was a sort of *supernumerary* in an accounting department."—Ursula Parrott.

**sup"po si'tions** (sup"ō zish'ŭnz). Things thought or imagined to be true; assumptions; theories; conjectures; thoughts that are surmised; hypoth-eses.—"I deal in facts, not *suppositions*."—Henry J. Powers.

**swathed** (swāthe'd: 'th' as in 'the'). Wrapped around as with a blanket; enveloped; enclosed; covered over.—"The place was *swathed* in folds of funereal mist shot with watery sunshine."—Edith Wharton.

**tac'it ly** (tass'it li). By silent acquiescence; in a way that implies something without speaking; silently.—"We did not speak of it publicly and we *tacitly* agreed to make no mention of it."—M. L. Brittain.

**tac'ti cal** (tak'ti kăl). Pertaining to clever maneuvering; strategic; using skilful methods.—"There has been no change in our *tactical* doctrines."—David G. Barr.

**tang** (tang). A penetrating flavor; a sharp taste; a strong, specific flavor; an odor; hence, a characteristic or distinct quality or property.—"The homespun narrative communicated somehow the very tone and taste and *tang* of American life."—Ludwig Lewisohn.

**tan'ta mount** (tan'tuh mount: 'ou' as in 'out'). Equivalent in effect or meaning.—"One nation's will to live must never be *tantamount* to the death sentence for another."—Elmer Davis.

**tar'nish** (tahr'nish). Sully; smirch; dull the brightness of; dim the purity of; destroy the luster of.—"An evil sophistication seeks once more to *tarnish* the doctrine of the natural and inherent rights of man."—Ludwig Lewisohn.

**te'di um** (tee'di ŭm). Monotony; wearisomeness; tediousness; dullness; tiresomeness.—"The boys have a way of relieving the *tedium* by horse-play."—Brooks Atkinson.

**tem'per** (tem'pur). To moderate; to reduce the intensity; to mitigate by blending.—"My reward will be that I shall have done something to help to *temper* justice with mercy."—Clarence S. Darrow.

**ten'a ble** (ten'uh b'l). Capable of being held, maintained, or defended.—"They justified their support on the ground, completely *tenable*, that the bill could go counter to the Constitution."—Mark Sullivan.

**ten'ta tive"ly** (ten'tuh tiv"li). Provisionally; experimentally; for possible test or trial.—"Proposals were *tentatively* suggested for the improvement of the status of silver."—-Franklin Delano Roosevelt.

**trav'ers ing** (trav'urce ing). Passing across; passing through; traveling over.—"After *traversing* 15 miles I was fully prepared to believe that the street was 48 miles long."—Hilary St. George Saunders.

**trench'ant** (trench'ănt). Vigorous; keen; effective; sharp and clear.— "The final act, with its *trenchant* observations on the current scene, would have sufficed by itself to have made this a glowing play."—Howard Barnes.

**trite** (trīte). Commonplace; hackneyed; stereotyped; worn out by continual use.—"I am confident that you do not consider it merely a *trite* phrase when I tell you that I am truly glad to greet you."—Franklin Delano Roosevelt.

**truc'u lent** (truk'ū lĕnt). Harsh; of savage character; fierce; cruel.—"It is impossible to create a brotherhood out of hostile, *truculent*, aggressive competitors."—Dorothy Thompson.

**ul te'ri or** (ul teer'i ur). Undisclosed; lying beyond what appears on the surface; more remote; hidden.— "The United States Steel Corporation has often been used as a whipping-boy by persons having *ulterior* purposes."—Eugene S. Grace.

**um'brage** (um'brij). Offense; a sense of injury or resentment; a feeling that one has been slighted or injured. —"The indignant Mother Superior took *umbrage* when her charge referred to the mystery as spontaneous combustion."—Alexander Woollcott.

**un"fre quent'ed** (un"frē kwen'ted). Seldom visited; rarely resorted to by people; not frequently visited; to which people seldom came.—"It was one of those *unfrequented* towns in England with sedate, slow-breathing squares."—Donald G. Cooley.

**u'ni fy"ing** (ū'nǐ fī"ing). Uniting; forming into one; consolidating; making uniform.—"He overlooks the significant influences which literary masterpieces exert in *unifying* the language."—Christian Gauss.

**un"im ag'i na ble** (un"i maj'ǐ nuh b'l). Inconceivable; not capable of being imagined; of which no idea can be formed.—"He had ever a sense of the significance of belonging to some *unimaginable* whole."—Henry Steele Commager.

**un"re mit'ting ly** (un"rē mit'ing li). Incessantly; perseveringly; without stopping.—"A long period of reconstruction faced the British trader who worked *unremittingly* to lay the foundation."—Lord Halifax.

**un"re quit'ed** (un"rē kwīte'id). Unrepaid; not compensated for; for which no return has been made.—"The situation comes down to fears, misunderstandings, and demands *unrequited*."—George E. Sokolsky.

**un slaked'** (un slaikt'). Unquenched; unallayed; unappeased; unsatisfied. —"His thirst for glory was still *unslaked*."—Drew Middleton.

**un think'ing** (un thingk'ing). Thoughtless; careless; inconsiderate; heedless.—"They sang the praises of the Almighty One with innocent, *unthinking* hearts."—Hervey Allen.

**un to'ward** (un tōrd'). Inconvenient; unfavorable; unfortunate; annoying; vexatious.—"It was inconceivable that anything *untoward* could happen to her."—John P. Marquand.

**un tram'meled** (un tram'ld). Without embarrassment from hindrances or limitations; unburdened; unimpeded. —"Our people will resume the American way of life, *untrammeled* by the arrogant processes of dictatorship."—Thomas E. Dewey.

**un wit'ting ly** (un wit'ing li). Unknowingly; unconsciously; unintentionally.—"American citizens, *unwittingly* in most cases, are abetting the work of enemy agents."—Franklin Delano Roosevelt.

**ur bane'ly** (ur bāne'li). In a refined manner; politely; courteously; suavely; graciously; affably.—"It is exceedingly interesting and *urbanely* well-written."—Orville Prescott.

**vent** (vent). Audible or public expression; utterance; free and unchecked expression.—"Some of those who were dissatisfied with the decision gave *vent* to violent criticism."—Edward R. Burke.

**verve** (vurve). Enthusiasm; keen imagination; vivacious spirit; talent.—"You must find the way without impairing the *verve* of those who lead."—Owen D. Young.

**vest** (vest). Furnish with authority; endow; put in the possession or under the control of.—"The Constitution was so framed as to *vest* in the Congress the entire war-making power."—Robert Marion La Follette.

**ves'tig es** (vess'tij iz). Visible traces or signs; tracks; evidences.—"They are discussing a scheme to do away with the last remaining *vestiges* of international law."—Walter Lippmann.

**vet'er an** (vet'ur ăn). Grown old in service and experience; having had long practice.—"What chance did they stand against such *veteran* eulogy experts?"—Charles B. Driscoll.

**vi'ands** (vī'ăndz). Articles of food; victuals; things to live on.—"He sprinkles what seems to be sugar, but is actually salt, on the *viands*."—Henry Seidel Canby.

**vi car'i ous** (vī kair'i ŭs). Performed by substitution; done in place of another; taking the place of another.—"A publisher gets a *vicarious* thrill out of discovering a new writer."—Harry Hansen.

**vied** (vīde). Put forth great effort to outdo others; strove for superiority; competed.—"Bungling and waste were due to the agencies which *vied* with each other for a place in the spending sun."—Hugh Butler.

**vir'tu al ly** (vur'chŏŏ ăl li). Practically; essentially.—"Radiophotos of the conference were published in *virtually* all cities in Turkey."—George J. Hummel.

**void** (voyd). Empty; destitute; devoid; free from; lacking.—"It is amazing how anyone could live and still be so completely *void* of common sense."—Charles Henry Crozier.

**vo li'tion** (vō lish'ŭn). Power of willing; choice; determination; decision.—"'That's entirely at your own *volition*, sir,' said the reception clerk briskly."—Stephen Vincent Benét.

**wane** (wāne). Gradually decline; diminish in size and power; grow dim or faint.—"If pride or restricted horizon tethers us to our own particular project, our influence will *wane*."—Amos L. Peaslee.

**wan'ness** (wŏn'ness). Worn and tired look or feeling; sickliness; pallidity; exhausted appearance.—"There is a hard pathos about him, the *wanness* of a stripped, unblossoming tree against a gray sky."—Ludwig Lewisohn.

**war'rant** (wawr'ănt). To give good or sufficient reason; to promise or guarantee against loss; to justify; to furnish sufficient grounds.—"Enough good was accomplished to *warrant* a continuation of the fight."—Hendrik Willem Van Loon.

**weath'ers** (weth'urz: 'th' as in 'the'). Passes safely through a storm; survives, as a trial or adversity; bears up against hardships.—"She *weathers* the pangs of displacement manfully."—Florence Haxton Bullock.

**well'ing** (wel'ing). Springing up as a fountain; issuing forth, as from a well; pouring forth, as water from a spring.—"The truant thought stabs as a truth through the *welling* sentiment within you."—Margery Wilson.

**wel'ter** (wel'tur). A rolling motion; hence, a commotion; confusion.—"Deeply hidden, in the *welter* of casual news about warfare, the morale of these struggling people was not then understood."—C. T. Feng.

**whorls** (hwurlz). Coils; turns of a spiral; volutions or turns of a shell.—"The *whorls* of the sea-shell had delicate tints of faint blue and ivory."—Donald G. Cooley.

**wont** (wunt). Accustomed; in the habit of; used to.—"He suddenly remembered that in Spartan streets noble virgins were *wont* to go unveiled."—Caroline Dale Snedeker.

**wreak'ing** (reek'ing). Inflicting, as vengeance; working off or giving rein to; exacting.—"If this flood is not diverted into ordered channels, it will seek its level, *wreaking* along the way a toll of confusion."—Haraden Pratt.

## One-Minute Refresher

While the words that we have reviewed are, for the most part, familiar, our ideas about their meanings can get hazy through neglect and disuse. Test yourself on this brief brush-up review.

Nine words are listed. Opposite each word are three words or phrases. Underline the word or phrase that is *nearest* in meaning to the key word and then check yourself against the answers.

1. *urbanely*—(a) happily (b) politely (c) awkwardly
2. *cursory*—(a) cruel (b) rapid (c) profane
3. *beguile*—(a) out-smart (b) dissipate (c) amuse
4. *constrained*—(a) compelled (b) erected (c) contaminated
5. *ulterior*—(a) undisclosed (b) inside (c) artistic
6. *demurred*—(a) insulted (b) objected (c) demoted
7. *import*—(a) deportment (b) importance (c) confidence
8. *sanguine*—(a) bloody (b) profitable (c) hopeful
9. *conversant*—(a) near-by (b) familiar with (c) talkative

*Answers:* 1 — b; 2 — b; 3 — c; 4 — a; 5 — a; 6 — b; 7 — b; 8 — c; 9 — b.

# CHAPTER XXIII

## WHEN YOU CONSIDER LITERATURE AND
## THE ARTS

WORDS ARE in their finest service when they are being used in the discussion of the arts. And each art has its special vocabulary. We have the *allegro, podium* and *cadenza* of music; the *choreography* of the dance; the *pigments* for painting; the *ceramics* of pottery; the *dramaturgy* of the stage; the *baroque* of architecture.

Don't try too hard to add these words to your working vocabulary unless you are sincerely interested in some form of the arts, or unless you believe you may become interested. Without interest you will forget the words as soon as you learn them. On the other hand, if you study to *learn* this vocabulary the very process may encourage you to *become* interested.

After all it is a pleasant thing and quite flattering to one's ego to know what Guy Maier means when he says: "with Chopin the *coloratura* often constitutes the very substance of his music," or when he adds that "the composer is unexcelled in mixing *consonance* with *dissonance*." It is satisfying to understand Franklin P. Adams when he remarks on "variety shows that are full of *bathos*," or Fairfield Osborne when he states that "Education has many facets. With this *aphorism* as a cue, we are making a number of experiments." It cannot help but create a certain confidence to be able to understand Wheeler McMillen when he writes that "Asia will send us *ceramics*," and T. P. Grieg, when he discusses the Persian carpet with its "branches of flowers and *arabesque* foliage."

There are delicate distinctions of meaning between words within the arts. As a simple instance of this we have the six verbs *depict, delineate, portray, illustrate, sketch,* and *describe*. Before you read any further, you might find it an interesting exercise to see whether you could determine the shaded differences in meaning between these words.

All of these terms, with the exception of "describe," are used in

connection with either painting, writing, or speaking, and to learn
about them it will be helpful to consider their derivations (Latin
*de*, from; *rivus*, stream) or "the streams from which they flow."

"Depict," from the Latin *de* (down) and *pingo* (paint), means to
describe or represent vividly.

"Delineate," *linea* (line), is to draw or to describe in outline,
as, "He *delineated* a pattern—or a man's features."

"Portray" *pro* (forth), *trahere* (draw), is to make a natural picture or painting of, or to describe in words.

"Illustrate," *lustrum* (light) is, roughly, to provide pictures for
a book or magazine story, or to explain by means of examples.

"Sketch"—the Latin *schedius* (made suddenly)—is to draw or
paint hastily, or to describe hurriedly and briefly.

"Describe," from the Latin *de* (fully), *scribo* (write), applies only
to writing and speaking, and means to give the characteristics of,
as in words and signs, so that another may form a mental picture.

Increasing your vocabulary in the specialized field of the arts
will be immensely stimulating to you. It will broaden your horizons,
fire your imagination, sharpen your wits, and will intensify your
enthusiasm for all the departments of the mind, and of life itself.
And, truly, when you use words of distinction correctly and pleasingly, when you use words of beauty and originality, aflame with
power, it marks you as a person of distinction and intelligence. To
give the impression of culture and education to those whom you
meet is not only soul-satisfying, it will be invaluable to you in any
career you may choose. Social doors and business doors will swing
wide to you, for the solid fact is that people who talk well go places.

In this vocabulary-building your daily conversation can be a
great help. Why not plan to make it so?

Try having a new couple in for dinner some night. Preferably
people you don't know too well. This will be a challenge to your
conversational powers. You ought to be able to unearth two dinner
guests from among your acquaintances who are versed in one of
the arts. Think up a few conversational subjects ahead of time.
Read a theatrical critique, a musical column, a book review. Conduct a brief mental rehearsal in advance. You are planning to make
an impression on the people you are about to meet. Why not make
as good a one as possible? These folks will be your salesmen from
then on. Or your detractors.

Bear in mind that conversation is like a game of tennis. Always
give your opponent a ball to hit back. And remember, too, that an
eloquent conversation will depend much on your sympathy, your

kindness, and your consideration for the thoughts and feelings of your fellow man, and it will increase your genuine, unselfish interest in the other person.

When you first read over the words that surround the arts, you may fear that you would sound stilted if you tried to use them. That could easily be true. You must always speak your listener's language and fit your words to his terminal facilities. Of course we don't use difficult or literary or arty words in ordinary, colloquial conversation. That would be stupid. We are all actors and each day we fill many parts and each part demands a different script. We naturally would not employ the same vocabulary in conversing with the ignorant that we use with the cultured.

The important thing is to have these words at our command to think with, to read with and to understand with. And we may be surprised to find that, as our vocabulary improves, the intellectual level of our friendships will improve also.

There are not too many words that concern themselves with literature and the arts. Those that are set before you in the lists that follow do not present too formidable a task. And if you learn to know them and become comfortable with them and happy in their use, you will be able to share in conversation when it is at its cultured best.

While we are considering the vocabulary of literature, it might be profitable and enlightening to touch upon the theory of words themselves and to examine the professional terminology of the very language that we are using in this chapter. For language, in some of its phases, approximates a science.

In these days we are exposed to such impressive terms as *philology, semantics, linguistics, phonetics, etymology*, and these words are sometimes used in careless fashion and almost interchangeably. A paragraph or so may clarify the matter for some.

The over-riding subject of *philology*, or *linguistics* as it is now preferably called, is the study of all phases of languages. The scholar, in this field, is a philologist and is a specialist in the subject of linguistics.

*Etymology* is the history of words, a study of their origins, showing the sources and the development in forms and meanings. The etymologist knows the derivations of words and the stories that lie behind them: such stories, for instance, as we have told in this chapter.

In *phonetics* we are dealing with the science of speech sounds which, of course, includes the pronunciations of words. This can be contrasted with *semantics* which is the science of the meanings of words, although, at the moment, *semantics* should be called an exploration rather than a science. And it is an exploration that can so swiftly carry one into the deeper waters of the theory of the meaning of meanings. Among other things *semantics* makes one face the primitive question of "What is a word?" And that question opens up a whole world of mysteries.

What, to propose the problem, is the word "describe" that we have mentioned in this chapter? Is it the black marks that are printed on this page? Is it a "verb"? Something I have just said out loud? The sound you heard? Is it a "word"? Or is it only an idea in your mind? In my mind? In several peoples' minds? Is it something you say to yourself? Has it many meanings? Or is it simply a "meaning"?

It is better to leave this subject before our heads start to swim. For swim they will. The meaning of meanings will soon lead us into highly disturbing speculations that have no legitimate place in a practical book of vocabulary building.

The theories of language can be fascinating to those who care to study them. In similar fashion the theory of *ballistics* is interesting. But we can shoot a gun and play billiards as the experts do without knowing anything about *ballistics*. And it is comforting, also, to realize that we can use words effectively without concerning ourselves with the nebulous abstractions that surround them.

In the event that the reader should choose to go further with the subject of *semantics* two of the simplest and most engaging books about it are *The Tyranny of Words* by Stuart Chase and *Language in Action* by S. I. Hayakawa.

It is easy to see how, with words, we are soon sailing to the farthest shores of the universe.

**ab'stract** (ab'strakt). A summary; an epitome; a synopsis of the essential facts.—"Their knowledge came from a book that is now known only in the form of a condensed *abstract*."— Willy Ley.

**ab struse'** (ab strōōce'). Hard to understand; mysterious; obscure; complex; difficult to get the meaning of.— "Only a limited circle can appreciate his *abstruse* philosophical writings."— Orville Prescott.

**ac"cep ta'tions** (ak"sep tā'shŭnz). The meanings that are generally accepted or understood; the general interpretations of a word or expression.— "There are so many *acceptations* to the word 'knowledge.'"—Malcom Babbitt.

**a da'gio** (uh dah'jō). Slow; slower than andante but quicker than largo; in a leisurely tempo.—"The *adagio* movement gave the perspiring musicians a breathing space."—S. L. Scanlon.

**aes'thete** (ess'theet: 'th' as in 'thin'). A person who has fine taste and artistic culture; a votary of art; one who has a very keen appreciation of the beautiful.—"An *aesthete* lives his life in slow-motion, and marriage means too abrupt a decision."—André Maurois.

**aes thet'ic** (es thet'ik: 'th' as in 'thin'). Artistic; pertaining to beauty, taste, or the fine arts.—"The main purpose in collecting should be to satisfy your own *aesthetic* needs."—Sam A. Lewisohn.

**al'a bas"ter** (al'uh bass"tur). A white translucent mineral somewhat like marble.—"We discovered it was an *alabaster* pillar turned as accurately as on a modern lathe."— Peter W. Ranier.

**al"le gor'i cal** (al"ē gor'i kăl). Figurative; symbolic; teaching or explaining by similes or metaphors.—"To the Middle Ages the *allegorical* interpretation of the world was a science that occupied many minds."—E. K. Rand.

**al le'gro** (ah lāy'grō). Brisk; lively; gay; a movement or piece of music in allegro tempo; a quick movement.— "In the *Allegro* of the Quartet in B flat major sound seemed to pass into the light flutter of wings."—Douglas Brewster.

**am'phi the"a ter** (am'fi thē"uh tur: 'th' as in 'thin'). A circular or oval structure or building built around an open space or arena, and having tiers of seats sloping upward and outward all around; any similar structure.— "We went hopefully to the jungle *amphitheater* and sat down to wait."— George T. Fielding III.

**al lit"er a'tion** (ă lit"ur āy'shŭn). The use of a number of successive words which begin with the same sound or letter.—"'Wedding-cake or workbasket, what will be will be.' There she goes again, she thought. Rhythm and *alliteration:* the phrase-makers always get the last word."—Jan Struther.

**an'a gram** (an'uh gram). Another word or phrase made by transposing letters or words in a different word or phrase.—"He issued these pieces under an assumed name which was his own *anagram*."—Olin Downes.

**a nal'y sis** (uh nal'ĭ siss). An examination of the separate parts of anything; a logical synopsis.—"Mr. Hoover made a striking *analysis* of the situation."—J. A. McConnell.

**an"a lyt'i cal ly** (an"uh lit'i kăl li). By separating things into their composite parts and examining each part; by minute and careful inspection of all parts.—"Wild creatures do not reflect, form concepts, or reason *analytically*."—Alan Devoe.

**an dan'te** (an dan'tē). Moderately slow, but flowing; music in andante time; a rather slow movement or piece.—"The *andante* movement was applauded loudly."—Douglas Brewster.

**an"no ta'tion** (an"ō tā'shŭn). An explanatory note; a critical comment; a comment; criticism.—"Critics sooner or later have their say and the rivers of *annotation* dribble off."—Clifton Fadiman.

**a nom'a lies** (uh nom'uh liz). Irregularities; deviations from rules; abnormal forms or types.—"If freight is meant for a ship, you call it cargo; if it goes in a car, you call it shipment. What can science do with such *anomalies?*"—Christopher Morley.

**an thol'o gy** (an thol'ō ji: 'th' as in 'thin'). A collection of choice selections of prose or poetry.—"The Library has included one *anthology.*"—Bennett Cerf.

**an″ti cli'max** (an″ti klī'maks). An event or act that descends from something lofty to something unimportant or trivial; something much less important than what preceded it.—"She did not want to face all these people at the party; it would have been an *anticlimax.*"—Elizabeth Goudge.

**ap'o logue** (ap'ō log). A fable; a short fictitious story containing a moral; an allegorical tale which teaches a lesson.—"The story is more varied in scene and more richly peopled. It is less *apologue* and more story."—Ludwig Lewisohn.

**a pos'tro phe** (uh poss'trō fē): A speech or address to a dead or absent person; a speech or poem addressed to an imaginary person or object.—"He reached the climax of his father's ode with an *apostrophe* to our Prince."—Lloyd C. Douglas.

**ap″pel la'tion** (ap″ĕ lā'shŭn). A name or title.—"People from the occupied countries at war with the Axis are often spoken of as exiles, but this is a mistaken *appellation.*"—H. J. Van Mook.

**apt'ness** (apt'ness). Ability; special fitness; suitability; appropriateness; readiness.—"The story is written with *aptness* and facility of phrase."—Joan Vatsek.

**ar″a besque'** (ar″uh besk'). An ornamentation consisting of interlaced lines and curves; fanciful intertwining of animal and plant forms.—"The Persian carpet had branches of flowers and *arabesque* foliage on a red ground."—T. P. Grieg.

**ar cades'** (ahr kāde'z'). Long arched galleries; passageways with arched roofs; series of arches with supporting columns.—"I want columns of priceless marble, supporting loggias and *arcades.*"—Axel Munthe.

**ar'chives** (ahr'kīve'z). Places for keeping public records or documents.—"An established price not sufficient to permit production is just a statistic for the *archives.*"—David R. Craig.

**a'ri as** (ahr'ri uhz). Songs, airs, or melodies for a single voice; melodies that are sung as solos in operas and cantatas.—"They were invited to prepare a condensed pre-view of *arias* from the coming broadcast."—Milton J. Cross.

**ar peg'gios** (ahr pej'yōze). The sounding of the notes of chords in succession instead of together; chords thus played.—"Ample study of scales, *arpeggios,* and octaves should not be omitted."—Ann Chenée.

**ar tic″u la'tion** (ahr tik″ū lā'shŭn). Distinct utterance; clear enunciation; clear expression.—"The *articulation* of American public opinion is a powerful and constructive factor in our dealings with foreign governments."—Sumner Welles.

**art'ist ry** (ahr'tiss tri). Artistic workmanship; skilful ability; the artistic quality of genius.—"The story is developed with depth of feeling and complete *artistry.*"—Lisle Bell.

**a side'** (uh sīde'). Words spoken to one side which are not supposed to be heard by anyone but the person addressed; a remark made in this way.—"The factitious *aside* is no longer a part of the modern play."—Ellery Marsh Egan.

**ax″i o mat'ic** (ak″si ō mat'ik). Self-evident; needing no proof.—"It has long since become *axiomatic* that international trade cannot be a one-way affair."—Cordell Hull.

**bal″us trad'ed** (bal″ŭs trāde'id). Having a kind of hand-rail supported by small pillars; having rows of upright supports or balusters topped by a rail.—"The waterfront was beautified by a *balustraded* promenade."—C. Wellington Furlong.

**bar'ca role** (bahr'kuh rōle). A popular melody sung by boatmen in Venice;

music that imitates the songs of these gondoliers.—"Over the water came the soft-voiced *barcarole* of a Venetian boatman."—Henry J. Powers.

**ba roque′** (buh rōke′). A fantastic style of architecture common in the beginning of the 18th century; rococo; grotesque; characterized by contorted forms.—"Its cathedral is of neo-classic design mixed with *baroque*."—G. Jones Odriozola.

**ba sil′i cas** (buh sil′i kuhz). Early Christian churches rectangular in form; especially, the seven churches built by Constantine.—"Rome is filled with innumerable sanctuaries, without counting our magnificent patriarchal *basilicas*."—Pius XII.

**ba′thos** (bā′thoss: 'th' as in 'thin'). False pathos; a ridiculous descent from the lofty to the commonplace; a rendering inferior to the occasion. —"The music of these variety shows was full of *bathos*."—Franklin P. Adams.

**bib″li og′ra phies** (bib″li og′ruh fiz). Histories or descriptions of books; lists of books on a particular subject; lists of the works of an author; studies of editions of books.—"The list is made up of monographs, catalogues, reprints and *bibliographies*."—Lawrence C. Wroth.

**bib′li o phile** (bib′li ō fīle). A person who loves books; a book-fancier; one who loves the general make-up of a book.—"They shopped for birds or berries as a *bibliophile* would scrutinize first editions."—Christopher Morley.

**bi lin′gual** (bī ling′gwăl). Using two languages; speaking or expressing oneself in two languages.—"Over and over rolled the combatants filling the air with *bilingual* fury."—Samuel Hopkins Adams.

**bi″o graph′i cal** (bī″ō graff′i kăl). Pertaining to a written account of a person's life.—"Purposeful reading of *biographical* material helps us to diagnose ourselves."—Walton E. Cole.

**bla′zoned** (blāy′z'nd). Painted heraldically; inscribed or depicted in colors; emblazoned, as a coat of arms.—"At the top of the card is *blazoned* the crest of the family."—Samuel Hopkins Adams.

**brev′i ty** (brev′ĭ ti). Briefness; condensation into a few words.—"For the sake of *brevity*, I shall present the quotations together."—Robert Marion La Follette.

**bro chure′** (brō shūre′). A pamphlet; a stitched booklet.—"Perhaps you have not had such concrete evidence, in pictures, of the war uses of plywood as are shown in this *brochure*."—W. R. Difford.

**buf foon′er y** (buh foon′ur i). Undignified drollery or coarse jokes; tricks and pranks of a clown.—"All these actions were mixed with true features of Italian *buffoonery* and burlesque."—Sigmund Neumann.

**bur lesqu′ing** (bur lesk′ing). Caricaturing; mocking; making ludicrous; giving a comical imitation.— "'What's the world coming to?' he added, *burlesquing* one of their favorite sayings."—Christopher Morley.

**ca′denc es** (kāy′děn siz). Intonations and inflections in the speaking voice. —"Thanksgiving recalls remembered *cadences* of loved voices."—Edwin C. Hill.

**ca den′za** (kuh den′zuh). A musical flourish or embellishment for a voice or instrument in an aria or other composition.—"He had a painful experience with a soloist who began his *cadenza* bravely enough but soon got into difficulty."—Bennett Cerf.

**cal lig′ra phy** (kă lig′ruh fi). Handwriting in general; beautiful penmanship.—"From Damascus steel to *calligraphy* we are indebted to the peoples who inhabited the Near East."—P. J. Searles.

**cam′ou flage** (kam′ŏŏ flahzh). A disguise used to give a false appearance to something in order to protect it from an enemy; striped or other painting of various colors used as a disguise.—"The covers of the brief volume are bound with shelter tent duck printed in *camouflage* pattern." —W. Ray Bell.

**ca nard′** (kuh nahrd′). A sensational story or report; a newspaper hoax; an absurd story to deceive the public. —"A base *canard* was circulated which particularly enraged him."—Lucius Beebe.

**can ta′tas** (kăn tah′tuhz). Choral compositions for chorus, solos, and orchestra in the style of oratorio, or sacred drama set to music.—"The *cantatas* of Bach were specifically intended for the church."—Albert Stoessel.

**can′tos** (kan′tōze). The main divisions of a long poem, similar to the chapters in prose writings.—"Byron published the first two *cantos* of 'Childe Harold' at twenty-four."—George B. Cutten.

**car′i ca ture** (kar′i kuh chŏŏr). Distortion; a grotesque exaggeration of peculiarities.—"We were prepared to start from ruin, but we did not know that we would have to start from lower still, from the *caricature* of the country we loved."—Eve Curie.

**car′il lon** (kăr′i lon). A set of fixed bells that can be rung either by hand or mechanically; a chime of bells; tunes played on a set of bells; a peal from a carillon.—"The organ chimes and the *carillon* can be played between classes."—Dwayne Orton.

**car tog′ra phy** (kahr tog′ruh fi). The art of drawing and compiling maps and charts.—"The course of instruction for pilots included adjustments of instruments and *cartography*."—William H. Barton, Jr.

**cas′tel lat″ed** (kass′tĕ lāte″id). Having battlements; built like a castle with turrets; having indented parapets.—"*Castellated* church towers carried the fires to greater heights."—T. H. J. Underdown.

**cat′a combs** (kat′uh kōme′z). Long underground galleries having excavations for tombs in the sides; subterranean passages or chambers containing recesses for burials.—"For three hundred years the early Christians sought the refuge of the *catacombs*."—John P. McGoorty.

**ca vort′** (kuh vort′). Prance about; curvet, or give a light leap, as a horse; caper.—"Dinosaurs and flying reptiles *cavort* across the magic screen."—Hebe Bulley.

**ce ram′ics** (sē ram′iks). The art of modeling and baking in clay; pot-tery.—"Asia may send radios, *ceramics*, textiles, and other products of the cheap labor of the Orient."—Wheeler McMillen.

**ce ru′le an** (sē rōō′lē ăn). Sky-blue; azure; of a deep clear blue color.—"The *cerulean* blue of the deeper water was flecked with white."—Frederick Lewis Allen.

**cha″lets′** (sha″lāyz′). Swiss cottages or herdsmen's hut; any wooden houses built in this style.—"The lure of salt is often placed for the mountain goats at certain *chalets*."—Henry P. Zuidema.

**chi a″ro scu′ro** (ki ah″rō skū′rō). The treatment or distribution of lights and shades in a picture; light and shade in scenes in nature.—"The sharp eyes of our Indian guide could descry the sloth from the *chiaroscuro* of the jungle."—V. Wolfgang von Hagen.

**chi rog′ra phy** (kī rog′ruh fi). Handwriting; style or character or handwriting.—"We soon found that her conundrum was as indecipherable as her *chirography*."—Emory L. Fielding.

**chor″e og′ra phy** (kor″ē og′ruh fi). The art of arranging ballets or dances; designing and arranging elaborate dances.—"His bull-fight dance is a striking bit of *choreography*."—Howard Barnes.

**cho rog′ra phy** (kō rog′ruh fi). The art of describing a region; the charting or making maps of a particular district or region; the physical features of a region.—"Aerial *chorography* has almost reached the stage of miracles."—Douglas Brewster.

**chro mat′ic** (krō mat′ik). Colorful; having many bright colors.—"The slide showed a highly *chromatic* version of the outer cover of the song sheet."—Franklin P. Adams.

**cite** (sīte). To quote; to refer to specifically; to mention as an illustration.—"Only one voter in eight is familiar enough with the report to *cite* any point."—George Gallup.

**clas′sic** (klass′ik). Belonging to the first class or rank; standard.—"The African victory is a *classic* example of military art."—Clement Attlee.

**clas′si cal** (klass′i kăl). Similar to the

ancient Greek and Roman classics; modeled after the best forms of ancient art and literature.—"He resembles the *classical* picture of a jealous husband, as presented by Tolstoy."—Marjorie Farber.

**clas′sics** ((klass′iks). Masterpieces; the literature of ancient Greece and Rome; works of acknowledged excellence.—"Only the *classics*, when loved and intimately known, can supply this rich culture."—William Mather Lewis.

**col″o ra tu′ra**    (kul″ur uh tū′ruh). Trills, runs, and other embellishments in music; florid and brilliant passages giving added color to the music.—"With Chopin the *coloratura* often constitutes the very substance of the music."—Guy Maier.

**com′men tar″y** (kom′ĕn ter″i). A series of comments; an explanatory treatise; an exposition; something serving as an illustration.—"Women have done some of the best social *commentary* in our fiction."—J. Donald Adams.

**com pen′di um** (kŏm pen′di ŭm). A brief, inclusive summary of an extensive subject or system; an abridgment; an epitome.—"There could not be a greater mistake than to look upon the Bible as an out-of-date *compendium* of conventional religion." Emmet Fox.

**com piled′** (kŏm pīle′d′). Gathered or made up of material or accounts from other documents.—"The March figures have not yet been *compiled*."— R. G. A. Van Der Woude.

**com″po si′tion** (kom″pō zish′ŭn). The art or process of combining the parts of a work of art to produce the best effect; the art of the arrangement of parts to form a harmonious whole.— "One of the first things that must be learned by the amateur photographer is the art of *composition*."—Donald G. Cooley.

**con cord′ance** (kon kor′dănce). An alphabetical index or list of the principal words in a book, giving references to the passages in which they occur. —"A good *concordance* of the Bible is a very real aid to religious study."— Donald G. Cooley.

**con″no ta′tion** (kon″ō tā′shŭn). The inclusion of implied additional meanings in some word or statement.— "We in Britain use the word empire in quite a different *connotation* from its meaning over here."—Michael Coleman.

**con ser′va to″ries** (kŏn sur′vuh tō″riz). Schools of music and art.—"For vocal training our own country has excellent *conservatories*."—Nelson Eddy.

**con′so nant** (kon′sō nănt). Consistent; in agreement or harmony.—"The terms of the agreement are fully *consonant* with the social objectives that we cherish."—Franklin Delano Roosevelt.

**con′text** (kon′text). The part of a discourse or writing which is connected with the words or passage quoted and therefore helps to explain the meaning of the quotation.—"In England we have a law that in a statute the masculine shall include the feminine unless the *context* otherwise requires." —Sir Gerald Campbell.

**co nun′drum** (kō nun′drŭm). A riddle; a perplexing question.—"Whether or not we can rely on that country is a *conundrum* about which you may argue."—George N. Shuster.

**cor′ol lar″y** (kor′ŏ ler″i). Something that follows so obviously from another that it requires little or no proof.—"Freedom has a *corollary*. Its *corollary* is responsibility."—Dorothy Thompson.

**cor′re lat″ed** (kor′ē lāte″id). Related by connection or correspondence; connected in such a way that one really implies the other.—"These four points are all essential, all *correlated*."—Dorothy Kenyon.

**couched** (kouch′d: 'ou' as in 'out'). Expressed; concealed in the form of words.—"We have received messages *couched* in the most moving terms."— Winston Churchill.

**crab′bed** (krab′ed). Perplexing; abstruse; hard to read; hard to understand; difficult; intricate.—"This verse is cold and *crabbed* in the second-rate mid-seventeenth-century manner."—Ludwig Lewisohn.

**cren′el at″ed** (kren′ĕ lāte″id). Fortified or decorated with battlements; hence, having indented parapets along the top; having loopholes cut through.—"I walked along the summits of the gray old walls and peered through the *crenelated* battlements." —Roy Chapman Andrews.

**cri tique'** (kri teek'). A critical essay; a critical review of a piece of literature.—"They give us a thoroughgoing *critique* of the weaknesses in the earlier attempts to create an international language."—Christian Gauss.

**cu'bi cles** (kū'bi k'lz). Partly enclosed sections of dormitories; sleeping places partitioned off from the main room.—"The ultra-violet screen method is often installed across corridors or *cubicles* in hospitals to control the circulation of bacteria."— Alexander Hollaender.

**cue** (kū). A signal; a hint or suggestion as to what should be done.— "Politicians, then as now, were taking their *cue* from popular passions." —Robert I. Gannon.

**cu ra'tors** (kū rāy'turz). Persons having charge of a library or museum; custodians of exhibitions.—"The *curators* of public libraries have had as their goal to increase the number of books of literary quality read by citizens."—Dorothy Canfield Fisher.

**da'is** (dāy'iss). A platform above the level of a large room or auditorium for seats of honor; a raised platform or stage for speakers in a hall or room.—"On a raised *dais*, nine tall black-leather chairs faced the chamber."—Catherine Drinker Bowen.

**de ci'phered** (dē sī'furd). Translated from cipher or secret characters into ordinary words; interpreted by the use of a key; changed into intelligible terms.—"The air was so full of conflicting radio waves that no messages could be *deciphered*."—Roy Chapman Andrews.

**de claim'ing** (dē klaim'ing). Haranguing; speaking like an orator; making formal speeches; reciting in a rhetorical style.—"The house re-echoed with his over-strained voice, *declaiming* his own orations."—Willa Cather.

**de faced'** (dē fāyst'). Marred the face of; disfigured the surface of.—"By stealth in the night it was *defaced* by obscene writing."—Thomas E. Dewey.

**de fin'i tive** (dē fin'i tiv). Sharply defined; conclusive; complete; fully developed.—"The produce of his pen is enshrined in an edition as nearly *definitive* as skill and knowledge can make it."—Lawrence C. Wroth.

**de lete'** (dē leet'). To erase; to cancel; to take out.—"I often suspect the censor has done his best to *delete* the overtones and undertones which give significance to the news."—Ralph M. Ingersoll.

**de lin'e at"ed** (dē lin'ē āte"id). Portrayed or pictured; drawn in outline or traced out.—"The newest screens project an image that is sharply *delineated*."—Ralph R. Beal.

**de liv'er y** (dē liv'ur i). Manner of speaking; mode of utterance; way of sounding words.—"The President has a magnificent *delivery* over the radio."—Donald G. Cooley.

**de pict'ing** (dē pikt'ing). Portraying; picturing; representing vividly.— "Like all the Dutch school he delights in *depicting* the ordinary objects of everyday life."—Edwin Seaver.

**des cant ing** (dess kant'ing). Discoursing at length; holding forth.— "Robespierre bathed France in blood while *descanting* voluminously on natural virtues."—Edmund A. Walsh.

**di'a lects** (dī'uh lekts). Modes of speech peculiar to a particular class of people or to a region.—"In India there are no less than 222 distinct languages and countless *dialects*."—S. Stanwood Menken.

**di'a logue** (dī'uh log). A conversational discussion in which two or more persons take part.—"The director called in a continuity writer who consulted a *dialogue* writer."— Alexander Markey.

**dic'tion** (dik'shŭn). Choice and use of words; language; expression; style; phraseology; enunciation; way of speaking.—"His eloquence was in the power of his thought and the smoothness of his *diction*."—David Lawrence.

**di lat'ed** (dī lāte'id). Written or spoken diffusely or in detail; enlarged; expatiated.—"They have *dilated* upon the evils of compulsion."—Winston Churchill.

**dirge** (durje). A song, tune, lament, or other musical composition expressing grief or mourning; a psalm, hymn, or . requiem mass sung at a funeral.— "It was the *dirge* to which they marched home after the battle."— Alvin C. White.

**dis cord'ant ly** (diss kor'dănt li). Out of harmony; harshly; clashingly; dissonantly; inharmoniously; jarringly.—"The triumphal music was blaring *discordantly* from a dozen gaudily decorated equipages."— Lloyd C. Douglas.

**dis"qui si'tions** (diss"kwĭ zish'ŭnz). Formal discussions; systematic discourses; dissertations; elaborate enquiries; long and formal essays.— "They are at a loss for a subject for their Saturday and Sunday *disquisitions*."—George Jean Nathan.

**dis"ser ta'tion** (diss"ur tā'shŭn). An extended treatise or discourse.— "John Ray, of England, prepared a *dissertation* on mint which may have been the forerunner of our distillation process."—Tom L. Wheeler.

**dis'so nance** (diss'ō nănce). Discord; a discordant mingling of sounds; tones that are not in harmony sounded together.—"Chopin is unexcelled in mixing consonance with *dissonance*." —Guy Maier.

**di'vas** (dē'vuhz). Prima donnas; principal women singers in an opera; chief soloists.—"One was able to see a shining galaxy of players, *divas*, ballerinas and theatrical favorites." —Frank Crowninshield.

**dog'ger el** (dog'ur ĕl). Irregular or trivial verse; loose, undignified rhymes that are ill-made.—"The early verse is nearly all *doggerel*."— Ludwig Lewisohn.

**dra'ma** (drah'muh). A composition to be acted on a stage; a play or representation of something.—"What is going on in our lives is not a *drama* on the stage, but a *drama* in real life." —Albert W. Hawkes.

**dram'a tur"gy** (dram'uh tur"ji). The art of making dramas; the art of composing theatrical representations and placing them properly on the stage. —"The play might have been a success had its author remembered a cardinal tenet of *dramaturgy*."— George Jean Nathan.

**dul'cet** (dul'set). Sweet to the taste or ear; hence, mentally pleasing; soothing; pleasing to the sight.—"There are handsome pastels and a *dulcet* and imaginative landscape."—Carlyle Burrows.

**ed'i fice** (ed'ĭ fiss). An important structure; a large building.—"The impression which the majesty of the *edifice* has given to the worshipers is wonderful to see."—William T. Manning.

**el'e gies** (el'ē jiz). Poems of mourning for the dead; sorrowful, meditative poems; lyric verses written in the meter suited to laments.—"He was conscious that the world was fed up with *elegies* and meditations upon mossy tombstones."—Donald Culross Peattie.

**e lide'** (ē līde'). Omit a vowel or syllable in pronunciation; suppress a vowel for the sake of euphony or meter.—"We didn't know how to read hexameter so that it sounded like poetry, but the Commandant showed us how to *elide*."—Christopher Morley.

**e li'sion** (ē lizh'ŭn). The striking out or eliding of a vowel or part of a word; the suppression of a vowel or syllable in pronunciation.—"Poets generally prefer to use an *elision* when possible and write 'e'er' for 'ever.' "—George F. Gahagan.

**el lip'sis** (e lip'siss). The omission of one or more words which are needed to complete the grammatical construction of a sentence.—"An *ellipsis* in which the verb is implied but not actually expressed occurs chiefly in poetry."—Donald G. Cooley.

**e lu"ci da'tion** (ē lū"si dā'shŭn). The act of throwing light upon something to clear it up; making clear; interpretation; explanation.—"The importance of the problem will perhaps justify our efforts at its *elucidation*."— John Ise.

**em"blem at'ic** (em"blĕ mat'ik). Symbolic; serving as a type or representation; signifying; typical.—"The crown has always been *emblematic* of royalty."—Sterling McCormick.

**em bossed′** (em bost′). Represented in relief on a surface so as to stand out; ornamented with raised figures or words.—"This pronouncement of our fathers, 'In God we trust,' is *embossed* on our coins."—Albert W. Hawkes.

**em′i nent** (em′ĭ nĕnt). Distinguished; notable; above others in position or talents; noted; celebrated.—"You are secure and respected and rather *eminent*."—John Buchan.

**en co′mi um** (en kō′mi ŭm). A formal expression of praise; a eulogy.—" 'I never heard him say a harsh word against anybody' is an *encomium* I have often heard."—Frank Kingdon.

**en cy″clo pe′di a** (en sī″klō pee′di uh). A work containing information on all subjects; a compendium of knowledge.—"I will not ask you to listen to a complete *encyclopedia* of our blunders."—David R. Craig.

**e nig′ma** (ē nig′muh). A riddle; a puzzle; something of which the meaning cannot be explained.— "That Indians should celebrate the feast is part of the *enigma* of South America."—Edith Guevara.

**ep″i gram mat′ic** (ep″ĭ gră mat′ik). Expressive of a witty thought in few words; pithy; short and to the point; ingeniously expressed.—" 'A hedge may save you from falling into a ditch.' How *epigrammatic!*" E. F. Benson.

**ep′i grams** (ep′ĭ gramz). Pithy or witty thoughts cleverly expressed in a short poem or saying.—"Humor of the intellect, such as *epigrams*, puns, and satire, was not understood by the younger students."—Winifred H. Nash.

**ep′i graph** (ep′i graff). A superscription; a pertinent motto prefixed to a book.—"We referred to the famous *epigraph* that is engraved over the entrance to the Post Office Building."—Charles Henry Crozier.

**ep′i logue** (ep′ĭ log). A concluding speech; a conclusion to a book or literary work.—"From this compendium, with an *epilogue* by Prince

Cesi, the extract of the great work was finally printed in Rome."—Victor W. von Hagen.

**e pis′to lar″y** (ē piss′tō ler″i). Carried on by epistles or letters; suitable to correspondence by letters; pertaining to letters.—"It was his *epistolary* habits that finally put the noose round his neck."—Alexander Woollcott.

**ep′i taph** (ep′ĭ taff). An inscription on a tomb or monument; a sentiment or motto written as if for inscription on a monument; an epigraph.—"There are too many lost territories marked with the *epitaph* 'Too late, too late.' " —Walter D. Fuller.

**ep′i thets** (ep′ĭ thets: 'th' as in 'thin'). Phrases or words used as adjectives to describe some quality.—"There is an urgent need for clear-thinking study, without slogans or *epithets*."—Thomas E. Dewey.

**e pit′o me** (ē pit′ō mē). A concise summary; a condensed account; an abstract, as of a book.—"An excellent *epitome* of his work in more concentrated form exists in the novelette."—Ludwig Lewisohn.

**er ra′ta** (e rāy′tuh). Mistakes made by a writer; printer's errors; lists of these errors attached to a book.— "One of the crucifixions of writing a book is the obligation to correct the *errata*."—Donald G. Cooley.

**es cutch′eon** (ess kuch′ŭn). A shield on which a coat of arms is displayed; the heraldic shield or surface on which armorial bearings are emblazoned.—"A ruined young nobleman marries to regild his *escutcheon*." —André Maurois.

**es″pla nades′** (ess″pluh nāde′z′). Level open spaces along a water front used for promenading or driving; promenades; public walks or drives along a shore.—"The city had taken pride in placing these statues in its most beautiful squares and *esplanades*."— Rebecca West.

**et″y mol′o gy** (et″ĭ mol′ō ji). A study of the origin or derivation and history of a word; the branch of philology concerned with word meanings; that branch of grammar that deals with the inflections of words.—"Every time they captured a village he learned some new *etymology*, and that campaign started him on philology."—Christopher Morley.

**eu′lo gy** (ū′lō ji). High praise; an oration in praise of the life or character of someone; an enconium; a panegyric.—"John Tyndall, no friend of the church, pronounced a *eulogy* of Michael Faraday."—Edwin Grant Conklin.

**eu′phe misms** (ū′fē miz′mz). Mild or agreeable expressions for disagreeable things.—"Some people still search in the dictionary for *euphemisms* and evasions of the word 'capitalism.' "—Eric A. Johnston.

**eu′phu ism** (ū′fū iz′m). A high-flown, artificial style of the Elizabethan age which was marked by similes, alliteration and elegance; an affected style of writing; affected elegance.—"The style of Woollcott is often touched by *euphuism*."—Donald G. Cooley.

**eu ryth′mic** (ū rith′mik : 'th' as in 'the'). Of harmonious movement; marked by good rhythm; rhythmically and harmoniously correlated.—"The work of the ballet was gracious and *eurythmic*."—Charles Henry Crozier.

**ex cep′tion** (ek sep′shŭn). Something that is different from the rule; the thing that does not follow the rule or is excepted from it.—"As the old McGuffey reader says, 'The *exception* proves the rule.' "—Bertram M. Myers.

**ex′cerpts** (ek′surpts). Extracts from written or printed matter.—"Throughout the past hour *excerpts* from editorials have been pouring into this News Room."—Bob Trout.

**ex clam′a to″ry** (eks klam′uh tō″ri). Containing abrupt passionate outcries; using sharp, short utterances of strong feeling; expressing emphatic or sudden emotion.—"The startling talk of the lecturer was punctuated by *exclamatory* remarks from the audience."—Sterling McCormick.

**ex″hor ta′tion** (eg″zor tā′shŭn). An attempt to arouse or incite by an appeal or admonition.—"The Sermon on the Mount is a very moving *exhortation*."—George Bernard Shaw.

**ex tem″po ra′ne ous ly** (eks tem″pō-rā′nē ŭs li). In an unpremeditated way; without notes or special preparation.—"Perhaps you will not expect over much of me in speaking to you *extemporaneously*."—Madame Chiang Kai-shek.

**ex tem′po re** (eks tem′pō rē). Without the use of manuscript or notes; extemporary; without special preparation.—"Woodrow Wilson's *extempore* speeches were among the best I have ever heard."—Donald G. Cooley.

**ex tem′por ize** (eks tem′pō rīze). Speak without previous study of a subject; speak offhand without premeditation; improvise.—"This is as far as I have ever gone in this problem. From now on I'll have to extemporize."—Donald G. Cooley.

**fa″cade′** (fa″sahd′). The front or chief face of a building.—"The words are engraved in stone across the *facade* of the building."—Watson Davis.

**fal set′to** (fawl set′ō). Uttered in a voice which is higher than the natural voice; artificial in tone; shrill; in an unnaturally high-pitched voice.—"It was the poor old general; she recognized his *falsetto* screech."—Joel Townsley Rogers.

**fan′ci ful** (fan′si fŏŏl). Whimsical; given to fancies or led by them; imaginary; capricious.—"Your ideas are charming, but very *fanciful*."—Emmet Holloway.

**fan tas′tic** (fan tass′tik). Capricious; extremely fanciful; grotesque; eccentric.—"Fatalistic and *fantastic*, the Arab is fanatical too."—Clarence W. Sorensen.

**fan′ta sy** (fan′tuh si). A product of the imagination; a fanciful or odd notion or idea of something; a fancy.—"There is a very thin line between truth and *fantasy* for those who are truly young."—Ellen Lewis Buell.

**flor′id** (flor′id). Embellished with runs, trills, and other ornamentations; having many trifling ornamental phrases or passages in the composition.—"Mozart and Chopin stand out for their mastery of this *florid* style."—Guy Maier.

**for′te** (for′tāy). (Played) loudly and powerfully.—"Few effects in a string orchestra are more striking than a *forte* attack that has perfect precision."—Harold Berkley.

**fus′tian** (fuss′chăn). Bombast; pompous language; cheap, but highsounding, phrases; pretentious eloquence.—"His *fustian* was absurd and inconsistent, but it was not contemptible."—H. G. Wells.

**ger mane′** (jur māne′). Closely allied; pertinent; relevant; in close relationship.—"The negro problem is certainly *germane* to the general subject of ethnology."—S. L. Scanlon.

**ges ta′tion** (jess tā′shŭn). Pregnancy; hence, carrying or holding an idea or a subject during a formative interval until it is ready to be expressed in some concrete form.—"During this period of *gestation* the processes of condensation and of heightening take place."—Ludwig Lewisohn.

**glos′sa ry** (gloss′uh ri). A vocabulary of the words in a book; a list of meanings of difficult words; an explanatory list of obsolete or obscure words.—"Written directly for highschool students, its language is so utterly their own that in five years the book will need a *glossary*."—May Lamberton Becker.

**Goth′ic** (goth′ik). In the pointed-arch style of medieval architecture characterized by slender piers, vaulting, and a joint instead of a keystone at the point of the arch.—"The room was in a part of the old abbey which had been restored, and it had a *Gothic* window."—W. Somerset Maugham.

**gro tesque′** (grō tesk′). Fantastic; bizarre; ludicrously odd; distorted.— "The comedy theaters were crowded with people from Harrigan & Hart's down to the *grotesque* comedians like Weber & Fields."—Booth Tarkington.

**gut′tur als** (gut′ur ălz). Sounds produced in the throat.—"Distorted vowel sounds and inserted *gutturals* are horrible."—Frank H. Vizetelly.

**har mon′ics** (hahr mon′iks). The science of musical sounds and acoustics; harmonious tones.—"The language of the author has no structure and no *harmonics*."—Edmund Wilson.

**Hel len′ic** (he len′ik). Grecian; of the classical Greek period.—"I shall turn my wondrous *Hellenic* goddess into a Victorian mother."—E. F. Benson.

**hi″er o glyph′ics** (hī″ur ō gliff′iks). Picture-writing; characters or symbols used in ancient writings, especially Egyptian.—"All primitive languages were based on *hieroglyphics*." —Alexander Markey.

**hy per′bo les** (hī pur′bō leez). Exaggerations; extravagant overstatements.—"An unknown actor in an all-star cast would not stand much chance of sending the critics into *hyperboles* of praise."—Noel Coward.

**id″i o mat′ic** (id″i ō mat′ik). Peculiar to idiom; characteristic of terms of expression of a particular people; using phrases whose meaning cannot be understood from component parts. —"English is primarily an *idiomatic* language."—Daniel P. Eginton.

**i′dyll** (ī′dĭl). A short descriptive poem; a short narrative of country or pastoral life; a picturesque tale of chivalry.—"A tender love *idyll* is woven into an interesting novel."— Amy Loveman.

**il lu″mi na′ti** (i lū″mĭ nah′ti). Persons having or claiming to have remarkable discernment; those who possess special enlightenment or illumination, intellectual or spiritual.—"These great *illuminati* seemed to live in a kind of golden colony that now seemed miraculously near."— Thomas Wolfe.

**il lu″mi na′tion** (i lū″mĭ nā′shŭn). Mental enlightenment; making clear; throwing light on a subject; elucidation.—"Creation of character, honest reflection, and *illumination* of life are the fundamentals of serious fiction." —J. Donald Adams.

**il lus′tra tive** (i luss′truh tiv). Serving as an explanation; tending to make clear; tending to elucidate or adorn. —"In these paintings a kind of urgent *illustrative* quality makes itself felt."— Howard Devree.

**im′age ry** (im′ij ri). Figurative description; mental images produced by figurative language; descriptions that help to form mental pictures.-- "Beneath the poetic *imagery* of the

Bible words lies a scientific truth."—
E. M. Forster.

**im per′son a″tor** (im pur′sŭn āte″ur).
One who assumes the character of
another; one who plays the part of
another; a person who represents in
bodily form, or personifies.—"I know
this is the genuine message. It was
sent by a well-known female *imper-
sonator*."—Gene Fowler.

**im″pre sa′ri o** (im″prā sah′ri ō). One
who manages, conducts, or is responsible for an opera company or musical performance.—"The Board will
hire an *impresario* for the music center."—Fiorello H. LaGuardia.

**im pres′sion ism** (im presh′ŭn iz′m). A
form of realism or fidelity to nature
and real life which aims to produce
the force of the first impression nature
makes on the artist's vision, and
convey a vivid sensation of light and
movement.—"The exhibition is significant of the impact of *impressionism*
upon still-life painting in France."—
Royal Cortissoz.

**im′pro vis″ing** (im′prō vīze″ing).
Making up offhand; extemporizing;
composing or reciting on the spur of
the moment; speaking without previous study or preparation; making
up as he went along.—"He would sit
for hours holding his small daughter
on his knee, *improvising* fabulous
stories of the deeds of a mysterious
people."—Gene Fowler.

**in″ar tis′tic** (in″ahr tiss′tik). Lacking
taste; not according to the fine arts;
not tastefully executed.—"Their condition was no doubt connected in the
*inartistic* way of science with characters in Greek mythology."—John P.
Marquand.

**in cor′po rate** (in kor′pō rāte). Introduce into something already formed;
make a part of something else; combine or include to make a whole;
unite into a body.—"It will not be
too hard to *incorporate* that new chapter in the novel."—Ainslee Mockridge.

**in″de fin′a ble** (in″dē fīne″uh b'l). That
cannot be exactly described or defined; evanescent; that cannot be
outlined.—"There is something *indefinable* about Brooklyn that makes
it different from New York."—Betty
Smith.

**in flec′tion** (in flek′shŭn). Change of
pitch in the voice; a modulation of
tone in speaking.—"We were made
to recite some passage in unison with
identical *inflection*."—Gretchen Finletter.

**in tagl′io** (in ta(h)l′yō). A sunken design; a figure cut in or incised below
the surface of some material; a gem
with incised carving.—"Wood cuts
and wood engraving belong in a relief group distinct from the *intaglio*
groups."—Norman Kent.

**in″ter rog′a to″ry** (in″tĕ rog′uh tō″ri).
Expressing a question; implying a
question; asking questions.—"We
should not be declaratory but *interrogatory* in these investigations."—
Thomas I. Parkinson.

**in″to na′tion** (in″tō nā′shŭn). The
modulation of the voice in speaking;
the rise and fall of the voice when
speaking; the manner of uttering
words.—"A desired effect can be
produced by gesture, *intonation*, and
dramatic sincerity."—Paul F. Cadman.

**i ron′ic** (ī ron′ik). Using words to
mean the opposite of what they
usually express; covertly sarcastic.—
"His style is only mildly *ironic*."—
Harry Hansen.

**i′ro ny** (ī′rō ni). The use of words to
signify the opposite of what they
usually mean; satire; sarcasm; ridicule under the guise of praise.—"He
made the speech in a spirit of contemptuous *irony*."—H. G. Wells.

**jar′gon** (jahr′gŏn). Confused or unintelligible speech; hence, a technical
speech or dialect used only by a
special sect or profession.—"Medical
schools and hospitals use generaliza-
tions and medical *jargon*."—Edward
L. Bernays.

**joust** (just). A fight on horseback; a
tilting match between knights; a
combat between two mounted knights
armed with blunt lances.—"The
knights are mounted on chargers
ready for the *joust*."—John Woodman Higgins.

**lam poons′** (lam pōōnz′). Satirical
writings that are abusive; writings

that bring a person into ridicule or contempt; squibs; scurrilous satires. —"In satires and *lampoons* he belabored the Federalists and took the part of the people."—Ludwig Lewisohn.

**lar'go** (lahr'gō). A piece of music, or movement, in a very slow and stately tempo.—"The strains of Handel's *Largo* soothed and comforted her."—Douglas Brewster.

**leg'end ar"y** (lej'ĕn der"i). Traditional; pertaining to myths or fables. —"Men whose names and deeds are now *legendary* come and go as they lived."—F. I. Brock.

**lex"i cog'ra phers** (lek"si kog'ruh furz). Authors of dictionaries or lexicons; compilers of dictionaries; writers of lexicons.—"It has been my privilege to associate with several *lexicographers* —men who make dictionaries."— Daniel P. Eginton.

**lex'i con** (lek'si kŏn). A dictionary; a book containing an alphabetical list of the words of a language and the meaning of each.—"Famine is a word that has not yet appeared in the *lexicon* of our history."—W. J. Cameron.

**li bret'tist** (li bret'ist). A writer of books containing the words of operas.—"Gilbert, the *librettist*, said he couldn't carry a tune."—Franklin P. Adams.

**lilt'ing** (lilt'ing). Gay and lively, as though tripping along; merry and with a swing; cheerfully rhythmic.— "The *lilting* measures embodied their own people. They were their soul."— William Addleman Ganoe.

**limned** (limd). Portrayed; delineated; drawn or painted as a picture.—"He is an unabashed admirer of the man whose public career he has *limned* in the book."—Virginia Dabney.

**lin'guist** (ling'gwist). An adept in languages; one who is skilled in a number of living languages.—"Not every student can be a *linguist* or a poet."— Edwin G. Conklin.

**lin guis'tic** (ling gwiss'tik). Pertaining to language; hence, full of long and difficult-to-understand phrases.—"It is up to us to make sure this *linguistic*

and complicated form is never issued again."—Sylvia F. Porter.

**lu'cent** (lū'sĕnt). Clear; transparent; luminous; showing radiance.—"They had struck the city's stony heart and brought forth *lucent* water."— Thomas Wolfe.

**lu"cu bra'tions** (lū"kū brā'shŭnz). Deep or earnest studies; laborious or elaborate literary works.—"Such a fellow may pass where the standard of erudite information is governed by those *lucubrations*."—Thomas Wolfe.

**lus'ter** (lus'tur). Natural sheen; gloss; brightness; brilliance; the glow of reflected light.—"Minerals have two general types of *luster*, metallic and non-metallic."—Eunice Robinson.

**ly'ric** (lir'ik). Adapted for singing; suited for singing; expressed in song. —"America has discovered the *lyric* theater is an abiding outlet for laughter and tears."—Ronald F. Eyer.

**ma e'stro** (mī'strō). A master in an art, especially music; a great composer; a great teacher or conductor. —"I told the *maestro* that I could at least go home and say I had seen Rome and rehearsed with Toscanini."—Giovanni Martinelli.

**med'ley** (med'li). A mixture; a composition of different parts; a mingled and confused sound; a sound made up of parts which do not belong together.—"The singing insects filled the air with a *medley* of shrill vibrations."—Roy Chapman Andrews.

**mel lif'lu ous** (mĕ lif'lŏŏ ŭs). Flowing smoothly like honey; dulcet.—"He had a *mellifluous* baritone speaking voice."—William Allen White.

**me lod'ic** (mē lod'ik). Melodious; containing melody.—"Ireland's music is characterized by variety of *melodic* content."—Eamon de Valera.

**mem'oir** (mem'wahr). A record of events written from personal knowledge of them; an account of personal experiences; reminiscences of a person; a biography.—"The style of the book is that of an Edwardian *memoir* by an admiring friend."—May Lamberton Becker.

**mez'za nine** (mez'uh neen). A low story or floor between two more important ones; the floor between the ground floor and the one above it.— "The whole *mezzanine* was given over to the bridge games that evening."— Henry J. Powers.

**mod′u lat″ed** (mod′ū lāte″id). Softened; adjusted; regulated; toned down; tuned to a certain pitch.— "Say some well-chosen words in a *modulated* voice of low tone."—A. H. Dente.

**mu″si cale′** (mū″zi kahl′). An informal concert; a private recital; a social gathering in which music is the chief entertainment.—"The composer discussed politics and his mother and her friend chatted about a *musicale*." —Emma Bugbee.

**mut′ed** (mūte′id). Muffled; deadened; having the sound softened; in a low tone.—"The radio was on as usual next door—*muted* and throbbing."— Stephen Vincent Benét.

**my thol′o gy** (mi thol′ō ji; 'th' as in 'thin'). The myths, legends, and popular fables of a race of people.— "Wagner's Nibelungenlied was put together out of several legends which belonged originally to Norse *mythology*."—Deems Taylor.

**nar ra′tor** (na rāy′tur). One who tells a story; a person who narrates or relates something; one who gives an account of something.—"Apparently the story bored him as he abruptly turned his back on the *narrator*."— Roy Chapman Andrews.

**nar′ra tive** (nar′uh tiv). Story-telling; in the form of a story; narrated; related or recited as a tale.—"The job ahead of me was to write the *narrative* volume of the expedition's reports." —Roy Chapman Andrews.

**ob″bli ga′to** (ob″li gah′tō). A musical accompaniment of some sort; an instrumental accompaniment to a song or recitation.—"You'll soon be getting a nice little *obbligato* from the ship herself as the fog thickens."— Christopher Morley.

**ob″jec tiv′i ty** (ob″jek tiv′ĭ ti). Stressing or placing emphasis on the nature of reality; treating people and events as self-existent and external apart from thought or feeling about them. —"He has written with perspective

and *objectivity* about this cross-section of society."—Orville Prescott.

**ob lique′** (ŏb leek′). Slanting; neither perpendicular nor horizontal; inclined; at an angle.—"*Oblique* photographs are not extensively used in precise mapping operations."—Bradford Washburn.

**om′ni bus** (om′ni buss). Covering a collection of things; containing a number of reprints or writings; providing many works or items; serving several objects at once.—"He uses the *omnibus* volume of stories and verse as a peg for his remarks."— J. Donald Adams.

**on″o mat″o poe′ia** (on″ō mat″ō pē′-yuh). The formation of words in imitation of natural sounds; imitative words.—" 'It's literary,' he defended. 'It's in Virgil, what uncle calls *onomatopoeia*.' "—Christopher Morley.

**o″pal es′cent** (ō″păl ess′ĕnt). Reflecting iridescent colors, as in an opal; milky white and exhibiting a rainbow-like display of colors.—"Precision is a beam that will pierce through this precious *opalescent* light."— Donald Culross Peattie.

**o′pus** (ō′pŭss). A musical composition; a literary work; a musical drama.— "Nothing much does happen in the amiable little *opus* which meandered last night into the Music Box Theatre."—Robert Garland.

**o′ral** (ō′răl). Consisting of spoken words; uttered by word of mouth; verbal.—"A contract can be *oral* or written."—Samuel W. Reyburn.

**or″a to′ri o** (or″uh tō′ri ō). A sacred composition for solos and choruses and orchestra; a religious story set to music and performed without scenery, costumes, or action.—"These ventures into the *oratorio* field are, perhaps, the highlights of my career." —T. Tertius Noble.

**or′a to″ry** (or′uh tō″ri). The art of speaking eloquently in public; skill in speaking effectively; rhetorical language.—"He gave a great deal of time to the practice of elocution and *oratory*."—Willa Cather.

**or nate′** (or nāte′). Elaborately adorned; much ornamented; decorated.—"The furniture in these cottages is hard in the literal sense of the word and not particularly *ornate*."—Maurice Hindus.

**or'tho e"pists** (or'thō ē"pists: 'th' as in 'thin'). Those who pronounce words correctly; authorities on pronunciation.—"I'm having a good time with my lecture for *orthoepists* on Given Names as a Social and Cultural Index."—Christopher Morley.

**or thog'ra phy** (or thog'ruh fi: 'th' as in 'thin'). Correct spelling; the art and study of spelling correctly or according to usage.—"*Orthography* is at once the art of writing words and the science of spelling."—Emory L. Fielding.

**o'ver tones"** (ō'vur tōnes"). Fainter, higher tones heard above the fundamental tones; hence, rich suggestions that add to original meanings; a lavish supply of connotation.—"She has bridged the years with flashbacks and occasional elusive *overtones*."—Howard Barnes.

**pae'an** (pee'ăn). A song of joy or exultation; a hymn of praise.—"The bell sent forth a *paean* of triumph."—James M. Beck.

**pag'eant ry** (paj'ĕnt ri). Pomp; ceremonial display; splendid celebrations; gorgeous processions.—"The Queen was emerging from widowhood into the gorgeous *pageantry* of a world-wide empire."—P. W. Wilson.

**pan"e gyr'ics** (pan"ē jir'iks). Elaborate eulogies; orations expressing great praise.—"When panaceas are offered on one side, only to be answered by *panegyrics* on the other, the argument lacks in conclusiveness."—John W. Davis.

**pan'to mime** (pan'tō mīme). A play in which the actors express themselves by gestures and postures without speaking; a dumb-show; a dramatic production by actors who use little or no dialogue.—"The story takes new forms in *pantomime* productions, but the outline is preserved."—May Lamberton Becker.

**par'a ble** (par'uh b'l). A short fictitious story which contains a spiritual truth; a tale that teaches a moral lesson; an allegory; a narrative which makes use of comparisons or types to convey a meaning.—"The book is story and *parable*, moral history and its interpretation."—Ludwig Lewisohn.

**par'a digms** (par'uh dimz). Patterns; models; hence, examples of declensions and conjugations.—" 'You cannot appreciate any language which has scientific rules and *paradigms*.' "—Christopher Morley.

**par'a dox** (par'uh doks). A statement or condition that is seemingly absurd and contradictory, but which may be true.—"The *paradox* of starvation in the midst of plenty."—Sidney Hillman.

**par'a phras es** (par'uh frāze iz). Free translations of passages or works; restatements in other words.—"They adopted as slogans *paraphrases* of our most precious principles."—Rex G. Tugwell.

**par"en thet'i cal ly** (par"ĕn thet'i kăl i: 'th' as in 'thin'). By inserting a word or phrase as an explanation or comment.—"We must admit *parenthetically* that a good thing can be pushed too far."—Winifred H. Nash.

**par'lance** (pahr'lănce). Mode of speech; language.—"In football *parlance*, a triple threat player is one who can run, pass, or kick."—Sherman Minton.

**par'o dies** (par'ō diz). Burlesque compositions imitating serious work; caricatures; mimicking or comic imitations.—"We all do trifles; our hasty sketches are but *parodies* and arrangements."—Lorado Taft.

**par tic'u lar ize** (per tik'ū lur īze). Mention in detail; state individually; enumerate the particulars or details. —"Let me *particularize* my objections to the present methods of education."—Hugh E. Blackstone.

**pas tiche'** (pass teesh'). A work made up of fragments and often imitating other writings; a medley caricaturing previous work; a literary patchwork using the style of some well-known author.—"Was this all that had come out of two years of travel and adventure? A chilly *pastiche*, some labored jesting, no freshening of form or of thought?"—André Maurois.

**per″o ra′tion** (per″ō rā′shŭn). The concluding part of a speech or oration.—"He closed his *peroration* with a stirring question."—H. W. Prentis, Jr.

**per′si flage** (pur′si flahzh). Raillery; banter; light, flippant talk.—"They demand adult judgment rather than *persiflage*."—Wayne Coy.

**per son″i fi ca′tion** (pur son″ĭ fi kā′shŭn). Embodiment; a person seen as a striking example; a representation; a typical exemplification; a personifying.—"The actress was the *personification* of all the graces that attend a lovely woman."—George F. Gahagan.

**per son′i fied** (pur son′ĭ fīde). Attributed human qualities to; symbolized something by conceiving of it as a person; regarded as a person.—"Many races *personified* the sun and worshiped it as a god."—William H. Barton, Jr.

**per″spi cu′i ty** (pur″spi kū′ĭ ti). Clearness in expression; lucidity; the art of expressing ideas so that they are easily understood.—"He quotes Ben Jonson approvingly to the effect that *perspicuity* is the chief virtue of a style."—Samuel C. Chew.

**pe rus′al** (pē rōōz′ăl). The act of reading attentively; a careful reading; perusing thoroughly or critically.— "It was like looking at the index of a book, with no time for *perusal* of a single chapter."—Grace E. Barstow Murphy.

**phi lol′o gist** (fi lol′ō jist). One who studies language in connection with history and literature.—"The Irish language is, from the point of view of the *philologist*, one of the most interesting in Europe."—Eamon de Valera.

**pho net′ics** (fō net′iks). The science of sounds made in speaking and the study of the formation of these sounds by the vocal organs.—"A short time ago I knew these friends as specialists in English *phonetics*."— H. F. Harding.

**pho″to gen′ic** (fō″tō jen′ik). Producing or throwing out light; phosphorescent; hence, highly suitable for beautiful photographs.—"It took her three years to decide that a *photogenic* football star would make a desirable husband."—Lisle Bell.

**phra″se ol′o gy** (frā″zē ol′ō ji). Diction; choice and arrangement of words and phrases; language chosen to express oneself.—"All of the learned *phraseology* on the subject can be boiled down to this: Trade consists in swapping things that we have for things that we want."—Harry L. Hopkins.

**phys″i og′no my** (fiz″i og′nō mi). Features; external aspect; hence, outward appearance revealing the inner character.—"None questioned the sincerity, the force, and the striking *physiognomy* of the composition."— Olin Downes.

**pi″a nis′si mo** (pē″uh niss′i mō). Very softly; extremely soft; a musical direction to play a passage very softly.—"*Pianissimo* will be ineffective until weight and firmness in the finger tips can be retained."—Ann Chenée.

**pic″a resque′** (pik″uh resk′). Portrayal of rascals; a style of literature having a picaroon or rogue as a hero.— "The romantic movement was too imminent for either the *picaresque* or the eighteenth-century sentimental to prevail."—Ludwig Lewisohn.

**pic″tur esque′** (pik″chŏor esk′). Interesting, unusual, or quaint enough to make a striking picture; expressing a peculiar kind of beauty suitable for a picture; representing pleasing scenes or thoughts.—"Seoul, the *picturesque* capital of Korea, is a fascinating place in which to bargain for amber."—Harriet Geithmann.

**pig′ments** (pig′mĕnts). Coloring materials for making paint.—"A man may be able to analyze all the *pigments* of a painting, but is no nearer for that to explaining why a picture is a masterpiece."—Lord Halifax.

**pla′gi a rism** (plāy′ji uh riz′m). The act of appropriating and claiming as one's own the artistic or literary work of another.—"In selecting this title, I am not guilty of *plagiarism*."— Carl A. Hatch.

**plas′tic** (plass′tik). Capable of being molded; pliable; impressionable.—

"He might not even watch the vivid face as *plastic* as the material which her hands patted and kneaded."— Samuel Hopkins Adams.

**plat'i tudes** (plat'ĭ tūde'z). Dull, flat, or commonplace statements.— "Americans cannot eat or live on *platitudes* or musical phrases."— John L. Lewis.

**plat"i tu'di nous** (plat"ĭ tū'dĭ nŭs). Dull; trite; commonplace; resembling a platitude; flat.—"Under the prosperous and *platitudinous* farmland lie the great tree fern fossils in the coal mines."—Donald Culross Peattie.

**pleas'an tries** (plez'ăn triz). Amusing or playful remarks; humorous or jesting comments.—"I do not believe that you expect easy *pleasantries* from me today."—George V. Denny.

**po'di um** (pō'di ŭm). A raised platform round the arena of an amphitheater; a dais or platform for orchestra and conductor in an auditorium. —"To watch from the guard's van is like being on the *podium* when the conductor ignites an orchestra with his wand."—Christopher Morley.

**pol'y glot** (pol'ĭ glot). Expressed in several languages; written or printed in many languages.—"I will not bore you with even a partial list of the *polyglot* leaflets that come to my desk."—William Alfred Eddy.

**por nog'ra phy** (por nog'ruh fĭ). Licentious literature; obscene writings; a description of obscene subjects.— "Many papers were little more than personal gossip and photographic *pornography*."—H. G. Wells.

**port fo'li o** (port fō'li ō). A portable case for holding drawings and papers. —"This second *portfolio* of drawings represents an effort to bring collections into a more usable form."— Francis Henry Taylor.

**por tray'al** (por trāy'ăl). A natural and vivid representation, picture, or description.—"The *portrayal* of human character is set forth in the Bible in deathless lines."—James J. Davis.

**pre'am"ble** (prē'am"b'l). The introductory part of a writing or speech; a statement explaining what follows.

—"It is worth our while to read and reread the *preamble* of the constitution."—Franklin Delano Roosevelt.

**pre"ci os'i ty** (presh"i oss'ĭ ti). An affected or fastidious refinement in use of words; an overnice or ultra-fine distinction in language.—"There has been too much *preciosity* about folklore."—Stewart Holbrook.

**pref'aced** (pref'ist). Gave an introduction to; introduced; opened by first giving some preliminary words; led up to; commenced with a preface or introduction.—"The lecturer *prefaced* his serious remarks with a few pleasantries."—Bertram M. Myers.

**pre mière'** (prē mi air'). The first public presentation of a play; the first performance of an opera or other music.—"Of the violin concerts much was said following the New York *première* two nights previous."— Olin Downes.

**pro lix'** (prō liks'). Tediously long and verbose; too long; long-winded; lengthy; wordy; unduly prolonged. —"Even his kindest critics will admit that the style of Thomas Wolfe is *prolix*."—Henry J. Powers.

**pu ris'tic** (pū riss'tik). Overparticular about purity in language; insistent on purity of diction; finically strict about nicety in the use of words.— "His political and *puristic* philosophy was that of Brandeis rather than of Brewer."—Henry Steele Commager.

**quaint** (kwaint). Pleasingly old-fashioned; strange but interesting because recalling former customs and fashions; odd or unusual.—"The play has a *quaint* saltiness and piquancy."—Burton Rascoe.

**qual'i fy** (kwol'ĭ fĭ). To modify; to make less strong; to limit; to restrict; to moderate; to change somewhat.— "The man found it necessary to *qualify* his blunt statement."—Donald G. Cooley.

**rac'y** (rāce'ĭ). Spirited; full of zest; having a distinctive native quality; spicy; hence, sometimes slightly suggestive.—"The story is *racy*, crammed with folk-stuff, and immensely funny."—Dorothy Canfield.

**rail'ler y** (rāle'ur i). Good-tempered jesting; good-humored ridicule; bantering speech; quizzical teasing; a satirical or witty jest.—"He acknowledged the *raillery* with a grin."—Lloyd C. Douglas.

**rant′ing** (rant′ing). Speaking loudly and violently; raving; talking wildly; using extravagant language.—"Her *ranting*, melodramatic voice ceased to come off the air waves."—William L. Shirer.

**re′al ist** (ree′ăl ist). An artist or writer who faithfully depicts nature and real life; one who is devoted to what is real and practical rather than to imaginary ideals and theories.—"As a *realist*, the author had no superiors among those using our language as a vehicle for the expression of thought."—Irvin S. Cobb.

**re″al is′tic** (rē″ăl iss′tik). True to nature; lifelike; representing things, people, and actions as they really are.—"The film gives a vivid and *realistic* picture of the battles."—Winston Churchill.

**re fine′ment** (rē fīne′měnt). A subtlety; fine distinction; a fastidiousness or nice distinction or discrimination.—"There was a certain over-*refinement* in his reasoning."—Donald G. Cooley.

**re it″er a′tion** (rē it″ur āy′shŭn). Repetition of words or phrases, usually with some slight change.—"The myriad banners, the endless marching and playing of bands, the *reiteration* of slogans, all encouraged them."—Ivy Lee.

**rel′ic** (rel′ik). A portion of that which has vanished; a memento; hence, a survival.—"A really close relationship was inconceivable between a child of the Third Reich and a *relic* of the past."—Bruno Frank.

**ren″ais sance′** (ren″e sahnce′). Revival; new birth; especially the movement marked by the revival of literature and art in Europe in the 14th to 16th centuries.—"Without Moslem influence there would have been no medievalism or *renaissance* in the West."—P. J. Searles.

**rep″ar tee′** (rep″ahr tee′). Clever and witty replies; skilful retorts; apt or smart rejoinders.—"Their conversation was heightened by *repartee* culled from lines in 'Alice in Wonderland.' "—Rose Feld.

**rep′er to″ry** (rep′ur tō″ri). Pertaining to the list of plays, or the like, that the company or any of its members are prepared to play; hence, possessing a repertoire, ready store, or collection.—"I am in favor of a civic *repertory* group to offer plays at the Center."—Fiorello H. LaGuardia.

**rep″e ti′tious** (rep″ē tish′ŭs). Containing useless repetition; that repeat tediously.—"Most of the new pages of the book consist of *repetitious* additions."—Lewis Gannett.

**rep′li cas** (rep′li kuhz). Copies; reproductions; exact copies or facsimiles; duplicates.—"I have sample *replicas* that show all the formative steps."—Vincent J. Schaefer.

**rep″re sent′a tive** (rep″rē zen′tuh tiv). Typical; qualified to represent or depict; able to portray; that present a model or type.—"The paintings of Leonardo da Vinci are *representative* of the best art of the Italian Renaissance."—Charles Henry Crozier.

**res′o nance** (rez′ō nănce). The resounding quality; the enrichment and intensification of a musical tone; an increasing and prolonging of sound.—"The tonal focus, or *resonance*, he can draw from his choir will liven up the deadest acoustics."—T. Tertius Noble.

**rhap′so dists** (rap′sō dists). Those who recite epic poems professionally; people who write or speak with extravagant enthusiasm.—"The evidence had been pawed over by the phlegmatic and the fiery, by *rhapsodists* and cynics."—Willa Cather.

**rhap′so dy** (rap′sō di). An instrumental composition of irregular form, wild and emotional, and often containing national melodies.—"Gershwin proved that jazz rhythms, colors, and harmonies can be successfully transposed into the *rhapsody*, the concerto, and the opera."—Raymond Scott.

**rhet′o ric** (ret′ō rik). Exaggerated display in the use of language; the use of artificially elegant phrases.—"Maybe we shall do some frank, forthright talk across the Atlantic instead of *rhetoric*."—Edward R. Morrow.

**rhe tor'i cal** (rē tor'i kǎl). Placing emphasis on style rather than on the underlying thought; oratorical; making a display of words; using words for effect instead of information.— "The French are tempted to manufacture *rhetorical* literature at all times."—Edmund Wilson.

**rhyth'mic** (rith'mik: 'th' as in 'the'). Marked by a regular rise and fall of sound; having a regular repetition of beats or accents.—"There was no sound but the *rhythmic* thud of the engines."—Elizabeth Fowler.

**role** (rōle). The part or character taken by an actor; hence, a part or character assumed or played in real life.— "She plays the *role* of a seeress."— Howard Barnes.

**Ro"man esque'** (rō"mǎn esk'). Of a style of architecture prevalent in Italy and western Europe before the Gothic, and characterized by the round arch and vault, arcades and ornamentation.—"*Romanesque* architecture was the prevailing western style from the 5th to the 12th century."— Donald G. Cooley.

**ros'trum** (ross'trŭm). An orator's platform; a stage or raised platform for a speaker.—"He ran lightly up the steps of the *rostrum*."—William Allen White.

**rote** (rōte). A mechanical repetition of words or phrases without thought of the meaning; unintelligent memorizing; saying things over without paying much attention to the sense.— "This, the obedient mind repeats by *rote*, is in reality one of the less brilliant of the stars."—Donald Culross Peattie.

**sat'i rist** (sat'ĭ rist). A writer of sarcasm, irony, or keen wit.—"Dean Swift is perhaps the greatest *satirist* in the English language."—Eamon de Valera.

**screed** (skreed). A tirade; a prolonged harangue; a long tiresome discourse. —"The speech that began so innocently turned into a violent *screed*."— Douglas Brewster.

**sib'i lant** (sib'ĭ lǎnt). A letter of the alphabet which is uttered with a hissing sound; a hissing sound.—"Although it hasn't a *sibilant* in it, the word 'Bureaucrat' is rolled hissingly on the tongue."—Harold L. Ickes.

**sil"hou et'ted** (sil"ōō et'id). Outlined in shadow; formed by a dark image outlined against a lighter background.—"I saw three buzzards *silhouetted* against a cloudless sky."— Frank M. Chapman.

**sim'i le** (sim'ĭ lē). A rhetorical figure of speech expressing comparison by the use of the words 'like' or 'as'.—"The *simile* is not perfect, so I'll change it to a metaphor."—Thomas Roy Jones.

**sol'e cisms** (sol'ē siz'mz). Violations of grammatical rules; mistakes in the use of words or idioms; blunders in speech or language.—"He is capable of sudden *solecisms* of style."—Ludwig Lewisohn.

**stac ca'to** (stuh kah'tō). Played in an abrupt, disconnected manner.— "Our sirens are too big for the nice little *staccato* notes we're supposed to sound."—Fiorello H. LaGuardia.

**sten'cil** (sten'sĭl). A thin sheet or plate in which a pattern is cut and through which the design is transferred to a surface below by painting over the metal sheet or plate; hence, a reproduction.—"It is a faintly incredible *stencil* copy of movie classics of the grade below B."—Lewis Nichols.

**stilt'ed** (stil'ted). Raised up or elevated on stilts or poles; hence, pompous; dignified and stiff; very formal; bombastic.—"These odds and ends of facts do not compensate for long stretches of *stilted* prose."—Philip W. Wagner.

**stip'pled** (stip"ld). Painted by small dots or splotches of a darker tint than the background; applied in light touches of another shade; hence, blotched; dotted.—"There was a pushing and a tugging in the *stippled* mass of bodies below."—Helen C. White.

**stud'ded** (stud'ded). Supplied with studs; adorned with ornaments or supports that project; covered with knobs or pieces that stick out.—"The approaches to the vault are *studded* with sudden death for the unwary stranger."—Jay Nelson Tuck.

**sur re′al ist** (sū rē′ăl ist). In which images present themselves to the mind without order as in a vision, or as the expression of something in the subconscious.—"The horrors of this railroad are such that the men who train on it feel that they are in some *surrealist* dream."—Bertram Fowler.

**sym po′si um** (sim pō′zi ŭm). A collection of comments, opinions, or short essays brought together.—"A *symposium* of opinions was contributed by average American citizens of all classes."—Ruth Alexander.

**syn′co pat″ed** (sin′kō pāte″id). Contracted, by displacing the usual accent; containing a new accent; that shifted an accent or emphasis.—"The young ᴍan cleared his throat, producing a small, *syncopated* noise." Dorothy Parker.

**syn″co pa′tions** (sin″kō pā′shŭnz). Rhythms, such as ragtime, in which the regular metrical accent is displaced or shifted.—"The music of his band differs little from the brassy *syncopations* of the early jazz era."—John Ferris.

**syn op′sis** (sin op′siss). A general view, as of some subject, book, or law; a summary; an abstract; a condensed account or statement.—"At that dinner you gave an admirable *synopsis* of the nature of our future planning."—Thomas W. Lamont.

**tau tol′o gies** (taw tol′ō jiz). Unnecessary repetitions of meaning; needless repetitions in words or in sense; useless words expressing an idea already given.—"The writing, though fluent, is full of repetitions and *tautologies*."—Edmund Wilson.

**ter″mi nol′o gy** (tur″mi nol′ō ji). The technical or special terms or phrases used in a business or science paper; mode of expression.—"The *terminology* of the bill is so ambiguous that public misconceptions have already arisen."—Franklin Delano Roosevelt.

**tes′sel lat″ed** (tess′ē lāte″id). Adorned with mosaics; formed of small square blocks; decorated with inlaid checkered work; made up of small square pieces of different colors or design.—"Everything in this immense peristyle dwarfed her. Here on this expanse of *tessellated* tiling she always felt insignificant."—Lloyd C. Douglas.

**theme** (theem). A subject of discourse; a topic to be discussed.—"It is fitting to speak upon this *theme* of the fraternal association of Britain and the United States."—Winston Churchill.

**the sau′rus** (thē saw′rŭs: 'th' as in 'thin'). A place where treasure is stored; hence, a repository of knowledge or words; a dictionary; a lexicon; a cyclopedia.—"The fat volume, with a few pictures inserted, had been turned over to her as her private *theasaurus*."—Christopher Morley.

**the′ses** (thē′seez: 'th' as in 'thin'). Essays or dissertations on particular subjects; propositions or statements put forth for argument or to be proved.—"Luther nailed his *theses* on the chapel door at Wittenberg."—H. W. Prentis, Jr.

**tim′bre** (tim′bur). The special peculiarity of a musical tone; the distinctive character or quality of a tone, as distinguished from intensity and pitch.—"It is the natural *timbre* of the contralto voice that gives it its character."—Hertha Glaz.

**top′i cal** (top′i kăl). Belonging to a special subject or place; referring to matters of present-day interest.—"There is not a single *topical* reference or allusion in the entire script."—Lucius Beebe.

**trac′er y** (trāce′ur i). Ornamental stonework formed of branching lines; decorative designs or carving.—"In architecture, every part of the *tracery* and sculpture enrich the whole."—Madame Chiang Kai-shek.

**trans lu′cent** (trance lū′sĕnt). Shining through; letting light through but only partly transparent.—"The grey-green color of most lichens is due to a thin layer of *translucent* white fungus covering the green alga beneath."—Charles E. Mohr.

**trans pos′ing** (trance pōze′ing). Changing from audible to written music; transforming from bird sounds to human sounds; rendering in changed form.—"*Transposing* a bird's song to our musical scale is always an approximation."—William J. Calvert, Jr.

**trav′es ty** (trav′ĕss ti). A burlesque or caricature; a parody; an absurd distortion.—"To brand him would be an outrage against the Bill of Rights and a *travesty* on democracy."—Harold L. Ickes.

**trea′tise** (tree′tiz). An elaborate presentation of a subject, often in a literary style; a formal and systematic written discourse on some subject; a methodical account of facts and conclusions.—"Dr. Schaffer's work is the earliest *treatise* in the Occident on the use of various plant fibers for papermaking."—Dard Hunter.

**triv′i a** (triv′i uh). Trifles; things that are unimportant; trivial, commonplace matters.—"The book is filled with the rich stuff of experience culled from the *trivia* of daily life."—Rose Feld.

**ty pog′ra phy** (tī pog′ruh fi). The appearance of the printed matter; the arrangement of the type.—"This credulous attitude trusts in the printed word because the *typography* or the book-binding is appealing."—James Duane Squires.

**un″in tel′li gi ble** (un″in tel′ĭ jĭ b′l). That cannot be understood; incomprehensible; not capable of being apprehended by the intelligence.—"To my benighted mind so much of Browning's poetry is *unintelligible*."—Hugh E. Blackstone.

**un prin′ci pled** (un prin′sĭ p'ld). Without moral principles or rules of conduct; lacking conscientious scruples; perfidious; bad.—"He left his dearly beloved bottles and his *unprincipled* life and was gathered to his fathers."—Emmet Holloway.

**un writ′ten** (un rit′′n). Not written; understood and taken for granted, although not written down; traditional; assumed.—"These aberrations are inescapable in a society that is kept going by *unwritten* and unwritable laws affecting the races."—David L. Cohn.

**ut′ter ance** (ut′ur ănce). Spoken words; that which is uttered or spoken; expression in words; vocal remarks.—"Only in time of stress is freedom of *utterance* in danger."—William Allen White.

**ver ba′tim** (vur bāy′tim). In the exact words; word for word.—"I am going to read the news dispatch *verbatim*." Joseph T. Robinson.

**ver nac′u lar** (vur nak′ū lur). The language of a particular locality; one's mother tongue; native language; the language of a class or profession.—"His vocabulary is the common *vernacular* of the modern man—a bit slangy, but always clear."—William Allen White.

**vi gnettes′** (vin yets′). Character sketches; illustrations or word pictures that shade off into the surrounding background of a story.—"The author gives a picture of idealistic enterprise and many *vignettes* of persons."—Ernestine Evans.

**vir″tu os′i ty** (vur″tū oss′ĭ ti). Technical mastery of an art; technical skill in music or drama.—"She brought to the play a *virtuosity* which was apparent in a hundred ways."—Austin Wright.

**vogue** (vōg). A prevalent way or fashion; popularity; a style in favor at the time.—"History novels and biography are having a considerable *vogue*."—John T. Frederick.

**way′ward** (wāy′wurd). Insisting on taking one's own way; wilful; froward; disobedient; intractable.—"The wild and *wayward* girl often becomes a prim and strict mother."—Bradwell E. Tanis.

**wit′ti cisms** (wit′ĭ siz′mz). Clever, witty sayings; jests; humorous remarks.—"Though she often speaks about the weather in joking terms, these *witticisms* are not taken lightly."—Mark A. Schubart.

### ONE-MINUTE REFRESHER

One of the words in this list can be used in place of the italicized words in each of the following sentences.

a. descanting    c. pantomime    e. arpeggios    g. impresario
b encomium    d. cartography    f. timbre    h. delineated

1. It is the natural *and distinctive character or quality of tone* of the contralto voice that gives it its character.
2. The play is done in *that type of acting where the performers express themselves by gestures and postures without speaking.*
3. Hitler bathed Germany in blood while *discoursing at length* on the great new order.
4. The new television sets project a picture that is sharply *portrayed or pictured.*
5. The student should have ample study in *the sounding of the notes of chords in succession instead of together.*
6. There is a high art in *the drawing and compiling of maps and charts.*
7. The speaker delivered a *formal and eulogistic address* about the dead hero.
8. The Metropolitan is planning to hire a new *man to manage the musical enterprises.*

*Answers:* 1 — f; 2 — c; 3 — a; 4 — h; 5 — e; 6 — d; 7 — b; 8 — g.

# CHAPTER XXIV

## THE ROAD TO VOCABULARY POWER
## AND CULTURE

IF YOU have planned to make the five thousand and more words in this volume your property; if you have determined to train them to serve you; to work for you as willing slaves, you will not be able to accomplish this in a mattter of a few days or weeks. There is no short course to word mastery. Our language is so prodigal in the riches that it offers that the acquisition of a vocabulary of power and culture is an exciting and an unending process.

There is a warning, though, that I wish to sound for the benefit of the overambitious who are apt to want to get word rich too quickly.

The wise way to make steady progress in vocabulary building, as I said in the introduction, is to develop the habit of devoting a few minutes daily to this matter like a woman does to her knitting, and I want to show you what an enormous amount can be accomplished by brief but regular intervals of application.

Suppose, from this point on, you were to limit your total reading time to only fifteen minutes a day. There is hardly any life so full that it could not spare this absurdly small bit of time. Yet only fifteen minutes a day for 365 days allows for 5,475 minutes of reading time a year. And if you are average you will read at a speed of 300 words a minute, which is slower than a really competent reader. Simple multiplication will prove to you that, by the end of twelve months, you will have covered 1,642,500 words, or the contents of the amazing number of twenty-three standard books of average length!

So you will best accomplish your purpose in any self-development program if you will set aside a stated fifteen or twenty minutes a day for your study. But be sure you plan this as an every day proposition. You are forming a lifetime habit, and, as William James, the father of modern psychology said, when you are forming a new habit *never allow a single exception*. This is the great secret of accomplishment in any undertaking. If you will adopt this practice it will not only bring you to a mastery of language; it will lead to a more efficient reorganization of your whole career. Create the right working habits and these habits will take care of you completely.

If you are surrounded by young people, or if you have children in your family, this word program takes on a double significance. As you are well aware your children imitate you, your deficiencies, and your virtues. If you have a good vocabulary they will develop a good vocabulary. If you embark on a serious word-program, if you discuss it with them and tell them of its value, they will soon become intrigued with the whole subject. Enthusiasm is contagious. Outside of character-building itself, there is hardly any contribution you can make to the lifelong welfare of children that will be as valuable as the habit of constantly increasing their vocabularies.

Of course, the benefits of vocabulary building are in no way restricted to youth. Age is no handicap to this study whatsoever. Modern psychology has proved that, unlike the flesh, the mind never grows old. The ability to think and to decide, the capacity to learn, the genius to imagine and to create, are yours to the end of your years. Whatever your age your mind is as young as it ever was if you have employed it wisely. The mental speed is less, but not the power. If you are along in years it simply means that you should select the subjects that you wish to study with a little more care, and that you should spend more time on them. That is, you should over-learn.

Age becomes an asset if you have developed a masterful vocabulary. Elderly men or women of wisdom who are virtuosos in conversation can command any group. This skill is almost more important for age than it is for youth. We expect so little of the young, so much of the mature in years.

Among other things, this work with words will bring a certain type of happiness to you that you may never have had before. We are all endowed with a surplus of creative energy that is not wholly taken up by our normal day's occupation, and we shall find ourselves so much better contented and we shall experience such a deep satisfaction if we will use this energy well in some form of self-advancement.

Of course, there is no rule that limits you to only fifteen minutes a day of study. Devote half an hour or an hour to the subject if you conveniently can. The only danger of a much longer period is that it may prove to be a burden.

Naturally the harder you work on any project, the swifter the progress. It was the great genius Michelangelo who said: "If people knew how hard I worked to gain my mastery, it wouldn't seem wonderful at all." And it was the French novelist Dumas who wrote: "Infatuated, half through conceit, half through love of my art, I achieve the impossible, working as none else ever works."

Effort is so vitally important to accomplishment in any field. Those who possess the habit of sustained effort, or those who cultivate this habit, will find that they possess one of the rarest qualities in the world. A business survey, recently made, has proved that more than twice as many salesmen are fired for lack of *effort* as for lack of ability, dishonesty, sickness, drinking, and gambling combined.

If you will apply effort to the study of words you will find that your progress will be amazing, and you will soon discover that you will have taken up the most delightful and valuable pastime that there is. You will begin to understand that great leaders are great leaders because, through their command of vocabulary power and culture, they are able to make others see and feel what they see and feel. Gain this power for yourself, then, from this book, and you will have at your service the greatest force ever put into the hands of mankind.

# CHAPTER XXV

## THE MASTER ENGLISH VOCABULARY TEST

You have probably already taken the "15-Minute Vocabulary Test" that was presented in Chapter II. If so you will find it completely adequate for every practical purpose of vocabulary measurement.

The Master English Vocabulary Test that is printed on the following pages was the original base for the shorter test, and will require two and a half to three and a half hours for the average person to complete. A serious student may find it interesting to take both tests and cross-check the results. In a few cases the discrepancies between the two tests have run to 7 per cent and over.

It is naturally impossible to make a test of 125 words quite as accurate as the authoritative Master Test of 1,251 words. And yet, astonishing as it may seem, *the average variation between the results of the three and a half hour test and the brief 15-Minute Test is under 3 ½ per cent.*

The story of years of experimentation, of trial and error, of checking and rechecking that has led up to these total basic vocabulary tests is a long and complicated one. I will set down only a very few of the general principles that are involved.

For the practical purposes of simplification and usability this test has been focused upon what we shall call, for lack of a better name, the "basic" words of the English language. These "basic" words are those terms that are printed in bold-faced type and that extend into the left-hand margin of each of the three columns appearing on the 2,757 pages of the 1940 edition of the Funk & Wagnalls Unabridged Standard Dictionary.

Before making the final selection of words for this test, I subtracted from the total list all prefixes such as "pre" and "un," the many suffixes such as "en" and "ing," all abbreviations, Greek and Latin combining forms, obsolete and archaic terms, as either not ranking as "words" in the generally accepted sense of the term, or

430

as being the now dead and almost useless bodies of one-time living words.

The principles underlying a total vocabulary test of this type have been developed and used for years in the field of science, where it was long ago discovered that the measurements of minute samples of very extensive material will give results which are almost as accurate as the total material itself.

This same sampling method is accepted for vocabulary testing by Dr. Robert H. Seashore, of Northwestern University, and by other scholars in the field of philology, and it has been proved that the results of a test based on a sharply limited list of words chosen from a dictionary according to a scientific plan will be almost as accurate as a test based on the *total vocabulary contents of the Unabridged Dictionary itself.*

The multiple-choice method that I have used to determine your knowledge of a word is the one that is generally employed and commonly acknowledged as adequate. It is considered that a word is a part of your vocabulary if you know one of its meanings.

The directions on page 8, for the 15-MINUTE TEST will apply to the MASTER ENGLISH VOCABULARY TEST.

## THE MASTER ENGLISH VOCABULARY TEST

1. aardvark    a. a worker in Norway   b. a Danish boat   c. an ant-eating animal   d. a kind of goat
2. Abbadona    a. a Welsh mountain   b. a fallen angel   c. a river   d. a Spanish title
3. Abderite    a. a Moslem   b. the armor-bearer of Hercules   c. a reputed stupid   d. a native of Sidon
4. aboard    a. astir   b. in a foreign country   c. upon a boat   d. on top
5. Absolute    a. son of David   b. a city   c. a mountain   d. the perfect Being
6. abusive    a. busy   b. insolent   c. useful   d. overgrown
7. Accad    a. a proclamation   b. an ancient language   c. a touch conferring knighthood   d. a tribe
8. acclimation    a. a shout of approval   b. adaptation to a new climate   c. the highest point   d. a long slope
9. Acerates    a. a hero   b. milkweed   c. a town   d. ants
10. achromatic    a. a musical scale   b. containing chromic acid   c. colorless   d. relating to time measurement
11. Acotylea    a. small plants   b. worms   c. parts of seeds   d. frogs
12. acropetal    a. of pollen   b. yielding a good crop   c. without petals   d. growing from the base
13. action    a. laziness   b. a trespass   c. operation   d. indolence
14. adamite    a. zinc arsenate   b. a semi-precious stone   c. a kind of marble   d. a meteor
15. adherent    a. audible sound   b. belonging to an heir   c. a follower   d. detestable
16. adlea    a. a large meadow   b. a coin   c. freely   d. easily
17. Adoraim    a. a man's name   b. a city of Judah   c. a Turkish town   d. a Roman
18. advise    a. to cut   b. to see   c. to counsel   d. to finish
19. aerobia    a. ague   b. fear of the air   c. an air hole   d. bacteria
20. affection    a. the act of influencing   b. the consideration of disease   c. a pledge   d. an assertion
21. African    a. a cape   b. a boy's name   c. a negro   d. a noble
22. agamoid    a. an ape   b. a lizard   c. a swelling   d. an antelope

23. agglutinogen  a. a mineral  b. a surplus  c. an essential part of bacteria  d. a glutton
24. ago  a. last  b. sunny  c. in the past  d. because
25. agronomics  a. athletics  b. puzzles  c. soil management  d. relating to growth
26. Aillinn  a. a chemical  b. a legendary maid  c. an Irish town  d. a river
27. Aititaki  a. an Indian tribe  b. a Japanese  c. an island  d. a Samoan hut
28. alarm  a. a mineral  b. a gateway  c. a sample  d. a strong emotion
29. alburnitas  a. a chemical  b. natives  c. children with white hair  d. a disease of trees
30. aldose  a. sugar  b. salt  c. a prescription  d. a certain amount
31. Alfarabius  a. a tree  b. a philosopher  c. fungus  d. a newt
32. alike  a. ugly  b. new  c. having resemblance  d. pleasant
33. alla  a. after  b. away from  c. near  d. in the manner of
34. alliteral  a. having a good memory  b. marked by successive use of the same letter  c. near the shore  d. literary
35. allseed  a. a tree  b. a festival  c. a small weed  4. a Mexican fruit
36. aloin  a. a kind of pig  b. solitary  c. far away  d. a bitter compound
37. Altamont  a. a mountain  b. an isthmus  c. a town in Illinois  d. a Greek heroine
38. aluminum  a. a bird  b. a metallic element  c. a flame  d. a college graduate
39. Amati  a. a pope  b. a star  c. a king  d. a violin maker
40. ambulacrum  a. a sacred vessel  b. part of a wing  c. sucker of a parasite  d. an echo
41. American  a. of Asia  b. of Austria  c. pertaining to the U.S.A.  d. African
42. amicable  a. easy to read  b. far away  c. containing mica  d. showing good will
43. amnesty  a. an act of pardon  b. a bad temper  c. a puzzle  d. a collection
44. amphigonium  a. a red flower  b. a drug  c. a mineral  d. an organ in a plant
45. amuse  a. to soften  b. to change  c. to entertain  d. to use
46. analphabet  a. considerate  b. proud  c. illiterate  d. yearly
47. anchor  a. a nautical implement  b. a reply  c. a hermit  d. a vehicle
48. androgynous  a. difficult  b. orange-red  c. uniting characters of both sexes  d. of the oldest family
49. angelique  a. a tree  b. a prayer  c. a sharp turn  d. a table
50. Anhalonium  a. a man's name  b. a town in Sicily  c. a genus of plants  d. a genus of snakes
51. Anjar  a. a title  b. a French province  c. a district in India  d. a Chinese city
52. annulus  a. a canceled decree  b. a ring-like body  c. a record  d. a diary
53. answer  a. a large tub  b. a handle  c. a goose  d. a reply
54. antepost  a. a hitching post  b. express mail  c. a totem pole  d. a horse-racing term
55. Anthropoidea  a. insects  b. apes  c. worms  d. fish
56. antidorcas  a. a poison  b. an enemy  c. a disturber  d. an animal
57. antipepsin  a. a structure  b. a tissue  c. a contrary agent  d. a drone
58. Antonio  a. a Roman emperor  b. a Greek seer  c. a boy's name  d. a ruined town
59. ape  a. a gorilla  b. a drink  c. an insect  d. a bull
60. apishamore  a. an Indian squaw  b. a saddle blanket  c. a song  d. a silly trick
61. aponeurosis  a. a hair  b. a blood vessel  c. a tissue  d. a disease
62. apparition  a. to belong to  b. a separation  c. a ghost  d. to adjust
63. apple  a. a fruit  b. a table  c. a mineral  d. a letter
64. approach  a. to whistle  b. to go away  c. to steal  d. to come near
65. aptitude  a. natural ability  b. laziness  c. quick approval  d. censure
66. Araliaceae  a. a family of plants  b. small insects  c. a French school  4. Burmese natives
67. arc formeret  a. a right angle  b. a wall-arch  c. an ant  d. a circle
68. Archichlamydeae  a. islands  b. sea-urchins  c. a class of mammals  d. flowering plants
69. arcuate  a. clear  b. arched  c. sharp-pointed  d. smooth
70. Argidae  a. South American fish  b. herbs  c. Greek islands  d. a family of mites
71. aristotype  a. a bristle  b. a large type  c. an aristocrat  d. a print
72. armory  a. chivalry  b. heraldry  c. an arsenal  d. a plot
73. arrear  a. a career  b. to rent  c. erect  d. something overdue
74. art  a. energy  b. skill  c. weariness  d. unfitness
75. artificer  a. an animal  b. gristle  c. a mechanic  d. a thistle
76. asea  a. at sea  b. of salt  c. a gnome  d. an alloy
77. Asnah  a. a Malay fowl  b. a biblical name  c. a hill  d. a cape
78. assai  a. partly  b. very  c. enough  d. aside
79. assignee  a. lender  b. borrower  c. devotee  d. trustee
80. assurance  a. a pledge  b. a bait  c. timidity  d. rancor
81. astriction  a. the power to foretell  b. heresy  c. the act of binding  d. terror
82. Athena  a. an Anglo-Saxon king  b. the daughter of Zeus  c. a marsh  d. a bishop
83. atomization  a. an ancient philosophy  b. separation into atoms  c. atonement  d. negation
84. Attalid  a. a seaport  b. a Greek general  c. a goddess  d. one of a line of kings

85. attraction        a. puffiness  b. dislike  c. fascination  d. posture
86. Auge              a. a mythical princess  b. of Augeas  c. a Sanscrit scholar  d. a French poet
87. aurichalcite      a. a puncture  b. a carbonate  c. having ears  d. golden
88. authentic         a. severe  b. reliable  c. favorable  d. unsuitable
89. autochthonously   a. independently  b. easily  c. usually  d. indigenously
90. auxiliary         a. exaggeration  b. a bone  c. helper  d. deceiver
91. avidya            a. ignorance  b. greed  c. anxiety  d. nervousness
92. axe               a. a session  b. an auk  c. an axiom  d. a tool
93. Azamgarh          a. Aztec language  b. an Indian district  c. a naturalist  d. a biblical name
94. babbitt           a. to control  b. to confess  c. to line with a metal  d. to unearth
95. back              a. to darken  b. to amuse  c. to lead  d. to reverse the action of
96. bacterioid        a. silvery  b. gloomy  c. allied to microbes  d. rod-shaped
97. bagong            a. a bachelor  b. a flirt  c. an official  d. sea-food
98. Balaustion        a. a genus of shrubs  b. a musician  c. a town  d. a citadel
99. ballast           a. a denial  b. well-earned rest  c. material to secure stability  d. a trade
100. baluster         a. a tiny star  b. a small pillar  c. a great noise  d. a bright light
101. bandonion        a. a giant  b. a bamboo  c. a broad band  d. a concertina
102. Bannaia          a. a man's name  b. a river  c. tropical trees  d. a salutation
103. barbate          a. enclosed  b. cooked  c. frozen  d. bearded
104. barkevikite      a. an airplane  b. a Danish goat  c. a suicide  d. a mineral
105. barrack          a. a rack  b. a sword  c. a cake  d. a building for soldiers
106. baryecola        a. an excuse  b. an impediment  c. a drink  d. a bean
107. basilic          a. a sweet herb  b. an instrument  c. a serpent  d. a portico
108. bastard          a. an illegitimate child  b. a sanctuary  c. a fiber  d. a dessert
109. batling          a. a fagot  b. fighting  c. reversing  d. a small bat
110. battle           a. concord  b. combat  c. tangerine  d. a fort
111. bayonet          a. a muddy inlet  b. a small bay  c. a weapon  d. a sack
112. bear             a. a base  b. an animal  c. a stick  d. an omen
113. bed              a. a sentinel  b. a couch  c. an apology  d. a rake
114. befit            a. make angry  b. lure  c. appraise  d. be worthy of
115. being            a. hatred  b. gloss  c. existence  d. junction
116. belladonna       a. a porcelain  b. a quarrel  c. an erect herb  d. a sham
117. Beltane          a. a Norse hero  b. old May-day  c. a king  d. a French town
118. Bennettitaceae   a. appetizers  b. fossil plants  c. monks  d. blessings
119. Bergelmer        a. a giant  b. an inland sea  c. a game  d. a town clerk
120. beshrew          a. consecrate  b. curse  c. scatter  d. honor
121. betol            a. work hard  b. arrive  c. a vine  d. a chemical compound
122. Bible            a. a river  b. a town  c. the Scriptures  d. a high tower
123. bifilar          a. babbling  b. bulging  c. toothed  d. having two threads
124. bilobite         a. a library  b. an organic mark  c. a great reader  d. a granite
125. biopsychic       a. of great value  b. of phenomena of mind and life  c. of double value  d. of events
126. bishop           a. a thick soup  b. to make a spiritual overseer of  c. a section of a leaf  d. a fine lace
127. black            a. essential  b. without light  c. promising  d. eager
128. blackwood        a. timber  b. a biting fly  c. an oil  d. a dolt
129. blast            a. a rush of air  b. a block  c. a shrine  d. a shark
130. blind            a. to admire  b. to beseech  c. to announce  d. to deprive of sight
131. blocking         a. a bubble  b. widening  c. blinking  d. blocks
132. blow             a. to accustom  b. to drive by air  c. to inhale  d. to whiten
133. bluff            a. a sloth  b. a bold manner  c. a taint  d. a sprig of holly
134. bob              a. a moat  b. a float  c. a boat  d. a goat
135. Bogardus         a. a fish  b. a park  c. a protector  d. an inventor
136. Bollinger        a. a county  b. a title  c. bulrushes  d. seals
137. Bonavista        a. king of Crete  b. a hero  c. Duke of Savoy  d. a seaport
138. Boniface         a. small shrubs  b. Napoleon  c. a name  d. silkworms
139. bookkeeping      a. bruising  b. recording accounts  c. asking leave  d. preaching
140. border           a. a tool  b. an edge  c. a person who boards  d. a rustic dance
141. boss             a. to serve  b. to repeat  c. to stare  d. to emboss
142. bottle           a. an extreme  b. a fight  c. a base  d. a glass vessel
143. bounty           a. power  b. generosity  c. frivolity  d. gaiety
144. bower-plant      a. a kitchen  b. a shrub  c. a factory  d. a machine
145. boycott          a. refusal to deal with  b. the right to continue  c. the love of a son  d. a small bed
146. brain            a. an outer husk  b. nerve tissue  c. to mark  d. to mate
147. brant            a. a long walk  b. a quick step  c. a small donkey  d. a wild goose
148. breakhorn        a. a quarrel  b. a duck  c. a trombone  d. an antler
149. Bremen           a. a queen  b. a seaport  c. a god  d. a monster

150. Bridgnorth    a. a prison   b. a title   c. a palace   **d. a borough in England**
151. bristle    **a. a stiff hair**   b. a great noise   c. a breast-bone   d. a pad
152. broiler    a. a carriage   **b. a utensil**   c. a vestment   d. an essential
153. brown    **a. a color**   b. a reward   c. a reign   d. a regent
154. Bryum    a. a village   **b. a kind of moss**   c. a scientist   d. a dandy
155. buckling    a. smoothing   **b. crumpling**   c. an aperture   d. a signal
156. built    a. wandered   **b. erected**   c. erased   d. learned
157. bullhead    a. a billow   **b. a catfish**   c. a bellow   d. a brace
158. bung    a. merry   b. a rough bed   c. a rabbit   **d. to close up**
159. bureau    a. a warrior   b. a wheelbarrow   c. a storm   **d. a chest of drawers**
160. Burnet    a. a jewel   b. a Scotch minister   c. a canal   d. an Indian
161. bushel    a. two pints   **b. four pecks**   c. a copse   d. a corpse
162. butt    a. a trickle   b. a pointed tip   **c. the thicker end**   d. a stag
163. Buzfuz    a. a treasurer   b. a cape   **c. a man's name**   d. a mountain
164. Bzura    a. fruits   b. cockchafers   **c. a Polish river**   d. a prodigy
165. cable    a. to regulate   **b. a heavy rope**   c. to dispute   d. a cactus
166. cadence    a. a beetle   **b. rhythm**   c. patience   d. speed
167. Cainan    a. part of Palestine   b. of Cain   c. snakeroot   **d. a son of Enos**
168. calculous    **a. stony**   b. a silkworm   c. kicking   d. a rim
169. calico    **a. made of cotton cloth**   b. a heavy boot   c. a jar   d. a sword
170. Callista    a. a composer   b. shrubs   **c. a novel**   d. an opera
171. calycinar    a. a vault   **b. a botanical term**   c. slander   d. hidden
172. Campanales    **a. botanical species**   b. two-edged swords   c. bell-towers   d. bivouacs
173. canal    a. appetite   **b. a waterway**   c. slaughter   d. a cheese
174. Candon    a. a king   b. a queen   c. a prince   **d. a town**
175. canon    **a. a law**   b. a gun   c. a ride   d. a theater
176. cap    a. a melody   b. a cross   c. an illusion   **d. a head-covering**
177. capitalism    a. envy   b. abuse   **c. concentration of wealth**   d. distribution of badges
178. Captain Cuttle    a. a soldier   b. a thief   c. a fisherman   **d. a sailor**
179. caraway    a. a poisonous snake   b. a ship   **c. a kind of parsley**   d. a caravan
180. card    a. a coal   b. a rifle   c. a blue monkey   **d. a piece of cardboard**
181. carlick    a. a weed   b. a load   **c. a tuft of hair**   d. an axle
182. caroubin    a. a carriage   **b. a starchy substance**   c. a revel   d. a gland
183. Carrick-on-Suir    **a. an Irish town**   b. a French village   c. a Welsh county   d. an Italian lake
184. cartoon    a. a carriage   **b. a caricature**   c. a canopy   d. a canoe
185. case    a. a picture   **b. the state of things**   c. a fork   d. an intrusion
186. Cassiduloidea    a. sea-gulls   **b. sea-urchins**   c. sea-kale   d. sea-fleas
187. cat    a. a measure   **b. an animal**   c. a file   d. a chain
188. cataract    a. a sword   b. a powder   **c. a great waterfall**   d. a parrot
189. cater    a. arouse envy   b. lose heart   **c. provide food**   d. grit teeth
190. Catostomi    a. apples   **b. fishes**   c. love-birds   d. catkins
191. causeless    a. fearless   b. toothless   c. colorless   **d. groundless**
192. cedar    a. a monkey   b. a sower   c. one who yields   **d. a kind of pine**
193. Celleporidae    a. celery   b. celebrities   **c. marine animals**   d. gems
194. center    a. perimeter   b. surface   **c. middle**   d. plane
195. cephalin    a. a cloak   b. an urn   c. a scepter   **d. a fatty substance**
196. cervantite    a. a creeper   b. a sausage   c. a large tusk   **d. a compound of oxygen**
197. chafer    a. a scare-crow   **b. a beetle**   c. a joker   d. a whisker
198. chalcolamprite    **a. a chemical compound**   b. an attendant   c. a bat   d. a perennial herb
199. chancellor    a. a treasury   **b. an important official**   c. a sexton   d. a part of a church
200. chap    a. a metal plate   b. a chapel   **c. a fellow**   d. a feud
201. charity    a. a crowd   **b. benevolence**   c. speed   d. hatred
202. chastisement    a. position   b. permission   c. parapet   **d. punishment**
203. check    **a. restraint**   b. a continuance   c. freedom   d. fraud
204. chelifer    a. a lyre   b. a druggist   **c. a false scorpion**   d. a slave
205. cherry    a. to convey   b. cautious   c. gay   **d. a fruit**
206. chevaline    **a. of horse-meat**   b. courteous   c. a wig   d. a knight
207. chiefry    a. a turtle   b. a flaw   c. a prize   **d. tribute**
208. chimopelagic    a. of a bishop   **b. emerging in winter**   c. of chimes   d. blooming early
209. chippy    **a. chapped**   b. meaty   c. fat   d. brisk
210. chloral    a. a song   b. a cloak   **c. an oily compound**   d. a green bird
211. choke    a. a partner   b. a water-hen   **c. to strangle**   d. angry
212. chorok    **a. a mink**   b. a bear   c. a lion   d. a rat
213. chromatic    **a. of signs**   b. of color   c. of rope   d. of fire
214. chrysolite    a. a chrysalis   b. a bruise   **c. a chemical compound**   d. a blister
215. church    a. a whimper   b. a cyst   **c. a temple**   d. a miser
216. ciliary    a. of columns   **b. of eyelashes**   c. of milk   d. of goats' hair
217. Circassian    a. of herbs   b. of Circe   **c. of Circassia**   d. of Circars
218. circumference    a. wealth   b. influence   **c. a flowing round**   d. an accent
219. cistophorus    **a. a silver coin**   b. a prehistoric animal   c. a fossil   d. unhealthy

| | | |
|---|---|---|
| 220. | claim | a. demand  b. clog  c. clap  d. deny |
| 221. | Clark | a. a Greek hero  b. a surname  c. a Clarist  d. a play |
| 222. | clausilium | a. a lid  b. a spout  c. a handle  d. a strainer |
| 223. | clear | a. to clarify  b. to clamor  c. to obscure  d. to soil |
| 224. | clerisy | a. tyrants  b. buyers  c. intellectuals  d. monks |
| 225. | clinkered | a. of no account  b. of melted coal  c. washed  d. returned |
| 226. | clonic | a. tonic  b. spasmodic  c. colonic  d. graphic |
| 227. | clover | a. a plover  b. a plant  c. tin-foil  d. a platter |
| 228. | coal | a. an animal  b. a beetle  c. a mineral  d. a flower |
| 229. | cobweb | a. to sew evenly  b. to cover with network  c. to wrangle  d. to open |
| 230. | cockerel | a. a young cock  b. a conceited person  c. a feather  d. a rosette |
| 231. | codify | a. regain  b. systematize  c. coddle  d. clear |
| 232. | cognition | a. defense  b. indifference  c. knowledge  d. spite |
| 233. | coin | a. accidental  b. coy  c. metal money  d. a guest |
| 234. | cold | a. eagerness  b. chilliness  c. weakness  d. stillness |
| 235. | collectivism | a. socialism  b. fatalism  c. catechism  d. Druidism |
| 236. | colony | a. a coin  b. a sermon  c. a settlement  d. a pillar |
| 237. | coltish | a. frisky  b. frank  c. feasible  d. false |
| 238. | comb | a. a sphere  b. a tripod  c. a toothed strip  d. a furnace |
| 239. | comfort | a. a rich region  b. a state of ease  c. an omen  d. a penalty |
| 240. | Commiphora | a. agents  b. a town  c. a group of shrubs  d. a comedy |
| 241. | communicate | a. depart  b. impart  c. comfort  d. distort |
| 242. | compass | a. scope  b. script  c. scroll  d. scrawl |
| 243. | compose | a. augment  b. make up  c. take down  d. water |
| 244. | concealment | a. hating  b. hiding  c. heeding  d. hastening |
| 245. | conclave | a. incurved  b. a council  c. bulging out  d. a mold |
| 246. | condense | a. prevail  b. yield  c. compress  d. contribute |
| 247. | cone | a. a solid figure  b. a negro  c. a stick  d. a wedge |
| 248. | conflagration | a. a tub  b. a relic  c. a burning  d. a sweet smell |
| 249. | Congregationalist | a. a Romanist  b. a Jesuit  c. an Independent  d. a member of a French school |
| 250. | connate | a. wicked  b. dissipated  c. knowing  d. inborn |
| 251. | consciousness | a. awareness  b. nakedness  c. fewness  d. dullness |
| 252. | consociation | a. dedication  b. union  c. renunciation  d. appreciation |
| 253. | consternation | a. a departure  b. a fire  c. a group of stars  d. sudden fear |
| 254. | consumption | a. presumption  b. contemplation  c. exertion  d. gradual destruction |
| 255. | continuance | a. duration  b. selfishness  c. silence  d. seclusion |
| 256. | contrariwise | a. uniformly  b. likewise  c. fairly  d. conversely |
| 257. | convention | a. recovery  b. a firm belief  c. a meeting  d. fitness |
| 258. | convoke | a. advance  b. summon  c. feast  d. prolong |
| 259. | Copelatae | a. whales  b. sharks  c. a section of tunicates  d. a genus of spurge |
| 260. | cora | a. a duplicate  b. an antelope  c. a subtraction  d. a glaze |
| 261. | core | a. a trouble  b. a piston  c. a heart  d. a duty |
| 262. | corn | a. straw  b. paper  c. grain  d. pulp |
| 263. | coronade | a. a tiara  b. a line of pillars  c. a play  d. a sword flourish |
| 264. | correct | a. gather  b. select  c. join together  d. make right |
| 265. | coruco | a. a battle  b. an insect  c. a dome  d. a wine |
| 266. | costal | a. of price  b. of a rib  c. of a coast  d. of a pet |
| 267. | cotyle | a. triangular sails  b. a cup-like part  c. a quince  d. a ridge |
| 268. | counter | a. apologetic  b. to the point  c. contrary  d. windy |
| 269. | country | a. a lance  b. a lyric  c. a land  d. a lagoon |
| 270. | courtesy | a. graciousness  b. fantasy  c. famine  d. hatred |
| 271. | coward | a. a carton  b. a hero  c. a shelter  d. a craven |
| 272. | cracker | a. a blackbird  b. a firework  c. a mender  d. a locust |
| 273. | cranidium | a. a lobe of the ear  b. a part of the face  c. a heron  d. a fungus |
| 274. | crannog | a. a javelin  b. a decimal  c. a drink  d. a lake dwelling |
| 275. | creatin | a. folding  b. making  c. a white compound  d. a Serbian warrior |
| 276. | creole | a. tiny  b. a bribe  c. of the West Indies  d. of Creon |
| 277. | cricket | a. a table  b. an insect  c. a muffin  d. a clamp |
| 278. | critic | a. loose  b. uncertain  c. general  d. fault-finding |
| 279. | cropping | a. easing  b. baking  c. cutting off  d. upholding |
| 280. | crossed | a. mounted  b. marked crosswise  c. waked  d. waited |
| 281. | crown | a. circlet  b. square  c. cavern  d. rapier |
| 282. | crusocreatinin | a. a crab  b. an eel  c. an alkaloid  d. a protein |
| 283. | cubicovariant | a. cubiform  b. a quantic  c. private  d. a cubit |
| 284. | Cullen | a. a prelate  b. a prison  c. a palace  d. a pilot |
| 285. | Cuna | a. a witch  b. a hill in Russia  c. an Indian  d. birthplace of Judas |
| 286. | curb | a. a total  b. a delight  c. a bridle-strap  d. a duty |
| 287. | current | a. a lawyer  b. a knave  c. a stream  d. a berry |
| 288. | Cush | a. a lake  b. a bay  c. a son of Ham  d. Aaron's sister |
| 289. | cuttanee | a. a fabric  b. a white enamel  c. a cutter  d. a retort |

290. cyclic            a. mystic  b. of recent date   c. of recurring periods   d. corrosive
291. cymene            a. a goddess  b. a sect   c. an oily compound   d. a love potion
292. cysticercoid      a. of a debt  b. of a scene   c. of a worm   d. of a preacher
293. dactyl            a. an iron weight  b. a glove   c. a gimlet   d. a three-syllable measure
294. Dal-Elf           a. a mountain  b. a town   c. a river   d. a lake
295. damson            a. a dagger  b. a petrel   c. a stupor   d. a small plum
296. Darbhanga         a. a district  b. an Indian   c. a prelate   d. a dictator
297. day               a. a horn  b. sunlight hours   c. hot springs   d. a bird
298. deaf              a. lively  b. unable to hear   c. clever   d. chosen
299. debility          a. languor  b. splendor   c. ardor   d. glamor
300. decentralization  a. solution  b. distribution   c. contribution   d. abolition
301. declinatory       a. of a clinic  b. of refusal   c. of right   d. of service
302. decussate         a. crossed  b. parallel   c. striped   d. very fat
303. definite          a. filmy  b. fluid   c. having precise limits   d. without fins
304. degree            a. a grade  b. a grove   c. a grudge   d. gruel
305. deletion          a. exposure  b. erasure   c. compulsion   d. composure
306. Delray            a. an island  b. a woman's name   c. a village   d. Samson's wife
307. demiseason        a. a semitone  b. between seasons   c. half-cooked   d. a mongrel
308. denomination      a. essaying  b. spoiling   c. naming   d. mining
309. departure         a. going away  b. looking forward   c. a forfeit   d. despair
310. depressor         a. an impostor  b. a stimulant   c. a plaster   d. an oppressor
311. derogation        a. drying  b. meaning   c. detraction   d. distraction
312. designate         a. identify by name  b. sign by deputy   c. discern   d. exile
313. desquamate        a. to equal  b. to appertain   c. to scale off   d. to decimate
314. determinism       a. destination  b. a theory of motives   c. a display of valor   d. dislocation
315. devil             a. twice  b. vapor   c. Satan   d. a mistress
316. dextrin           a. a war horse  b. skilful   c. a brownish compound   d. six-oared
317. diamond           a. a cup  b. a gem-stone   c. a dye   d. a treatise
318. diastole          a. lung depression  b. heart expansion   c. headache   d. wide-awake
319. dicker            a. haggle  b. compose   c. a shirt-front   d. handy
320. die               a. a jingle  b. a cooper   c. a cube   d. a musical instrument
321. diffluent         a. flowing away  b. reserved   c. unlike   d. extended
322. diisopropyl       a. a weight  b. two radicals of a compound   c. the dilation of an organ   d. asthma
323. Dinocharidae      a. monkeys  b. minute animals   c. wild dogs   d. porcupines
324. diphyodont        a. having two fins  b. growing two sets of teeth   c. having two petals   d. union of two vowels
325. dipyre            a. two-winged  b. a substitute   c. a chemical compound   d. a void
326. disapprobation    a. disillusion  b. inconsequence   c. upkeep   d. dissatisfaction
327. discoidal         a. coiled  b. unearthed   c. disk-shaped   d. ill-mated
328. disencumber       a. sweeten  b. disburden   c. go ashore   d. disdain
329. disjuncture       a. contamination  b. separation   c. distinction   d. friction
330. dispensatory      a. of receiving  b. of dealing out   c. of forgiving   d. of recovering
331. disruption        a. growth  b. shaking   c. extravagance   d. bursting apart
332. distasteful       a. flabby  b. hand-spun   c. displeasing   d. remote
333. disturb           a. predict  b. indorse   c. disquiet   d. distribute
334. division          a. combination  b. severance   c. clearness   d. collision
335. doctor            a. arrive in port  b. cut a mane   c. treat medically   d. sulk
336. dogmatism         a. groveling  b. indiscretion   c. arrogant assertion   d. ignorance
337. dominical         a. suicidal  b. a church   c. domed   d. a schoolmaster
338. doorway           a. a turret  b. an entrance   c. a mirror   d. a quilt
339. dot               a. a section  b. a speck   c. a plane   d. a species
340. Douglas           a. an opera  b. a Scottish warrior   c. a county in New York state   d. an Irish critic
341. drag              a. a sketch  b. a grapple   c. a psalm   d. a shield
342. dread             a. transport  b. expect   c. fear   d. dissect
343. driddle           a. to delay  b. saliva   c. to waste time   d. a small piece
344. drop              a. interpret  b. let fall   c. mount   d. aspire
345. Drummondville     a. a town  b. a desert   c. a lake   d. an island
346. Duchesne          a. a goddess  b. a great historian   c. a legend   d. a fine textile
347. duke              a. a landmark  b. a peer   c. a benediction   d. dusk
348. duodecimo         a. a kind of type  b. a reproduction   c. a book-size   d. a debtor
349. dust              a. a cluster  b. swarthiness   c. buckskin   d. powdered matter
350. dye               a. an explosion  b. victuals   c. coloring-matter   d. a support
351. dysthanasia       a. bankruptcy  b. death   c. competence   d. capacity
352. early             a. at the top  b. near the beginning   c. beside   d. afterward
353. eastern           a. on the left  b. oriental   c. occidental   d. of the sunset
354. Eccles-hill       a. a town  b. a canonical book   c. a mountain   d. a peninsula
355. ecliptic          a. a laxative  b. having the same center   c. apparent path of the sun   d. choosing

356. edder — a. unsound  b. older  c. to bind  d. Scandinavian literature
357. education — a. nearness  b. systematic instruction  c. introduction  d. cancellation
358. effusion — a. an outpouring  b. confusion  c. a withdrawal  d. a clearance
359. Ehime — a. a Bible name  b. a prefecture  c. a critic  d. a naturalist
360. eland — a. an antelope  b. a chick-beetle  c. an isle  d. a kite
361. electoral — a. electrical  b. select  c. of electrum  d. of electors
362. elegy — a. a caricature  b. a funeral song  c. a harangue  d. a riddle
363. Elienai — a. a genus of shrubs  b. a man's name  c. places  d. foreigners
364. Elohim — a. paradise  b. God  c. a town in Egypt  d. a mountain
365. emboldened — a. despised  b. encouraged  c. enfeebled  d. assigned
366. emeritus — a. derivative  b. embryo  c. honorably retired  d. swollen
367. emphasis — a. escutcheon  b. stress  c. a tumor  d. candor
368. enceinte — a. present  b. prostrate  c. precise  d. pregnant
369. end — a. a demon  b. a start  c. a terminus  d. a cowl
370. endotheliolysin — a. a restorative  b. a sedative  c. an antitoxin  d. a poison
371. engine — a. a machine  b. a motive  c. a mishap  d. a maple
372. engross — a. copy legibly  b. withstand  c. differ  d. verify
373. enricht — a. wrote  b. liable  c. made rich  d. severed ties
374. entrust — a. implore  b. confide  c. ravish  d. entwine
375. Epanomeria — a. a town  b. Caledonia  c. grubs  d. plants
376. epicicle — a. a barnacle  b. a small circle  c. an icicle  d. a barrage
377. Epimachus — a. Pandora's husband  b. an oscine bird  c. a genus of herbs  d. a Greek poet
378. epistle — a. an attribute  b. a poultice  c. a curve  d. a letter
379. equality — a. rank  b. ruin  c. uniformity of value  d. superiority
380. erd — a. a mistake  b. earth  c. gloom  d. an ant
381. ermine — a. a weasel  b. a boulder  c. a hermit  d. a gallant
382. erysipelas — a. a factor  b. a contribution  c. a prank  d. a disease
383. Aesculapian — a. of a parent  b. secret  c. medicinal  d. of a mountain
384. essential — a. impotent  b. basal  c. reasonable  d. unusual
385. estreat — a. an exact copy  b. a spendthrift  c. a fencing thrust  d. esteem
386. ethnic — a. of stars  b. of human races  c. of routes  d. of conduct
387. eucrasite — a. a candle-fish  b. cocain  c. a compound  d. the pyx
388. euphony — a. a powder  b. a cavern  c. sneers  d. a pleasing sound
389. eutrophy — a. tranquillity  b. healthy nutrition  c. hard work  d. seclusion
390. eventuation — a. calmness  b. issue  c. dislike  d. a contest
391. evolution — a. accuracy  b. development  c. estimation  d. trial
392. excellent — a. current  b. defective  c. rash  d. first-class
393. executory — a. administrative  b. distributive  c. contributive  d. inactive
394. exit — a. a display  b. a way out  c. an entity  d. an entrance
395. expansion — a. repentance  b. insistence  c. restriction  d. enlargement
396. expletive — a. an oath  b. an outlay  c. precise  d. angry
397. express — a. to expunge  b. to release  c. to confuse  d. to utter
398. extinguish — a. to adjoin  b. thicken  c. quench  d. exalt
399. exultation — a. explanation  b. misery  c. discharge  d. rapture
400. Ezzolied — a. an opera  b. a war song  c. a dirge  d. a life of Christ
401. facie — a. bold  b. funny  c. true  d. spacious
402. fair — a. a swoon  b. skeptic  c. an exhibition  d. a rogue
403. fall — a. intreat  b. drop  c. contain  d. soar
404. famine — a. sudden fear  b. extreme scarcity  c. a falcon  d. a faculty
405. fantasy — a. a freckle  b. a gland  c. a ballast  d. a mental caprice
406. farthingale — a. a bird  b. a hoodoo  c. a hoop skirt  d. a coin
407. father — a. more distant  b. to beget  c. to beset  d. to line
408. favor — a. credulity  b. hostility  c. respectability  d. good will
409. Fechner — a. a French actor  b. a deity  c. a seaport  d. a scientist
410. felicitate — a. to disgust  b. to agitate  c. to congratulate  d. to urge
411. fence — a. gentian  b. a rodent  c. a railing  d. a sedge
412. fern — a. a fiction  b. a farmer  c. near  d. a flowerless plant
413. fetish — a. a fetter  b. a Turkish cap  c. hungry  d. an object of worship
414. fibrolamellar — a. of legs  b. a mass of flakes  c. a group of cells  d. like a hunchback
415. field — a. a harbor  b. a piece of ground  c. a bond  d. a kick
416. figure — a. a shape  b. a fife  c. a thrush  d. a warrior
417. fill — a. annoy  b. make full  c. testify  d. void
418. fine — a. excellent  b. a temple  c. coarse  d. to augment
419. fir — a. an oak  b. a pine  c. a skin  d. an iron
420. Firenze — a. an opera  b. a girl's name  c. a province of Italy  d. a violinist
421. fish — a. a bustle  b. a hyena  c. a space  d. an aquatic animal
422. Fitzmaurice — a. a king  b. an aviator  c. a canal  d. a dukedom
423. flaggy — a. of a lash  b. like flagstone  c. limp  d. fluid
424. flash — a. sidewise  b. an edge  c. to recall  d. to appear suddenly
425. flavin — a. boasting  b. pondweed  c. a dyestuff  d. an eel

426. fleur-de-lis     a. feather   b. iris   c. cricket   d. flicker
427. flitting     a. combining   b. easing   c. exhorting   d. darting
428. flour     a. ground wheat   b. a fiber   c. to scoff   d. a bloom
429. flume     a. a gable   b. a failure   c. a quill   d. a conduit
430. fly     a. decide   b. move in the air   c. torture   d. dawdle
431. fog     a. to clear   b. a lap   c. a thick mist   d. a mirror
432. foot     a. a ceremony   b. a part of a limb   c. a reply   d. an enigma
433. Forbes     a. a surname   b. a mountain   c. an island   d. a town
434. forehead     a. style   b. brow   c. to overpower   d. to advance
435. forfeiture     a. a juncture   b. a penalty   c. a surprise   d. a tilt
436. form     a. a gong   b. a tissue   c. a shape   d. a falcon
437. forrow     a. second-class   b. staunch   c. not pregnant   d. held firm
438. fossa     a. disgust   b. a forester   c. a ditch   d. musty
439. Fouquier-Tinville     a. a small town   b. a lawyer   c. a French race-course   d. a spa
440. Fox River     a. a glacier   b. a river in Wisconsin   c. a hunter   d. a magician
441. Franklinian     a. of Frank   b. Frankish   c. of frankincense   d. of Benjamin Franklin
442. freezing     a. a ration   b. turning to ice   c. distillation   d. distortion
443. friar     a. an ally   b. a mendicant brother   c. a cook   d. a wheel
444. Frimaire     a. a goddess   b. Friesland   c. the third month   d. a botanist
445. frontal     a. a bone   b. a muscle   c. a cell   d. a tissue
446. fruition     a. dimension   b. fulfilment   c. a crash   d. depth
447. full     a. filled   b. deducted   c. blended   d. stern
448. funnel     a. a cord   b. a herb   c. a hurricane   d. a conical vessel
449. furrow     a. a spring   b. a trench   c. rage   d. a ruin
450. gablock     a. magic   b. a hook   c. a buttress   d. a symbol
451. gain     a. state   b. acquire   c. split   d. spike
452. galley     a. a gait   b. prowess   c. a vessel   d. lace
453. Galveston     a. a whirlpool   b. a competitor   c. a county   d. a drama
454. gangion     a. a fish line   b. a yawn   c. a wrangle   d. a knob
455. Garfield, Mount     a. a town   b. a gulf   c. a peak   d. an estate
456. Gastrura     a. silkworms   b. crustaceans   c. eels   d. sharks
457. gear     a. a bend   b. a mallet   c. moving points   d. a cherry
458. gemmicule     a. a double ring   b. part of an embryo   c. a twin   d. a flaw
459. genevrette     a. an insult   b. a wine   c. a child   d. a process
460. geochemical     a. of knees   b. of humor   c. of styles   d. of geology and chemistry
461. Georgian     a. of chants   b. of an English period   c. of a giant   d. of Gaul
462. get     a. procure   b. plant   c. abandon   d. jump
463. giddy     a. resist   b. to swear   c. a trout   d. to make dizzy
464. gill-intestine     a. a leech   b. a servant   c. an organ   d. a flute
465. girder     a. a beam   b. a basket   c. a grant   d. to tie up
466. glacier     a. a starer   b. a field of ice   c. a glass fitter   d. a dessert
467. glass     a. a skull   b. a marsh   c. a mixture of silica   d. a catfish
468. glorious     a. murky   b. mysterious   c. resplendent   d. coiled
469. glue     a. a straw   b. a gurgle   c. a gulp   d. a sticky substance
470. gnaw     a. grow angry   b. to drink   c. to bite persistently   d. to gnash
471. gobble     a. to plow   b. to carry   c. to eat hurriedly   d. to fine
472. gold     a. a waffle   b. a stack   c. a curlew   d. a metallic element
473. gomashta     a. a bitter tonic   b. a freight-car   c. a native clerk   d. a stream
474. good     a. gold   b. a ghoul   c. a quill   d. moral well-being
475. gorget     a. a shrub   b. armor   c. to smear   d. to bungle
476. gouloge     a. a pitchfork   b. a system   c. a thread   d. rubbers
477. grace     a. a mast   b. a toga   c. a garden daisy   d. a pleasing quality
478. grafting     a. repelling   b. inserting a scion   c. arching   d. designing
479. granite     a. peaked   b. sheltered   c. a jewel   d. igneous rock
480. graphite     a. a grain   b. a spear   c. a carbon   d. an anchor
481. grate     a. a burden   b. freely   c. a frame of bars   d. an accent
482. graywacke     a. rock   b. oil   c. fish   d. fowl
483. green     a. a flavor   b. a contour   c. a color   d. a favor
484. Gregory     a. a seaport   b. a German writer   c. a pope   d. a clown
485. grinder     a. a screen   b. a molar   c. a snare   d. a grimace
486. gromatics     a. vaulting   b. play-writing   c. mohair   d. land-surveying
487. groundage     a. arrival   b. dregs   c. a toll   d. a piece of land
488. grum     a. suitable   b. sane   c. sullen   d. sudden
489. guard     a. a protector   b. a resin   c. a mallow   d. a fish
490. guide     a. a surmise   b. a conductor   c. a cure   d. a reward
491. gullet     a. a food-passage   b. a sneer   c. a tram-rail   d. a sewer
492. gun     a. an auk   b. a measure   c. a firearm   d. a sack
493. gutter     a. to taste   b. gutta-percha   c. to groove   d. the throat
494. gyve     a. an angle   b. a wheel   c. a child   d. a shackle
495. hackbolt     a. a sea-bird   b. a halter   c. a weapon   d. a tool
496. haith     a. to go on   b. to beware   c. by my faith   d. on the house

| | |
|---|---|
| 497. halfling | a. a coupling  b. a starling  c. a hireling  d. a stripling |
| 498. halobios | a. sea-salts  b. sea flora and fauna  c. circles of light  d. feasts |
| 499. hammer | a. a shed  b. to beat hard  c. to hinder  d. to indulge |
| 500. hand | a. a wish  b. an insect  c. a mouse  d. part of a limb |
| 501. Hansa | a. a god  b. a demon  c. a fabulous bird  d. a boy's name |
| 502. hard | a. fluid  b. firm  c. genial  d. penetrable |
| 503. harlequin | a. musical  b. leaking  c. a clown  d. an instrument |
| 504. Harper | a. a Median officer  b. an English novelist  c. a mountain  d. a publisher |
| 505. hash | a. to mince  b. harsh  c. to treat  d. tilted |
| 506. haul | a. a user  b. to enhance  c. high  d. to pull |
| 507. hawk-eagle | a. a snare  b. a nickname  c. a falcon  d. a dandelion |
| 508. head | a. a venture  b. a chief  c. five-sided  d. to the rear |
| 509. heart | a. a wound  b. a hollow organ  c. a red deer  d. a fireplace |
| 510. heaven | a. something hoisted  b. tightness  c. supreme happiness  d. weight |
| 511. hedge | a. a candidate  b. a dolt  c. a powder  d. a fence of bushes |
| 512. heir | a. before  b. atmosphere  c. an inheritor  d. a filament |
| 513. Hellanodic | a. a judge  b. a historian  c. a poet  d. a lord of Tyre |
| 514. hemaphein | a. a calendar  b. a tumor  c. paralysis  d. a coloring substance |
| 515. hent | a. a ghost  b. a furrow  c. a wizard  d. a heat-unit |
| 516. hereditability | a. of spires  b. descendibility to heirs  c. hersey  d. irritability |
| 517. Hermon | a. a mountain  b. Hestia  c. Hermes  d. a romance |
| 518. Hesperides | a. mythical sisters  b. butterflies  c. herbs  d. herrings |
| 519. heterophemy | a. asphyxia  b. amnesia  c. deafness  d. partial aphasia |
| 520. hextetrahedron | a. of six atoms  b. a crystal form  c. a radical  d. a tetrarch |
| 521. hieroglyphic | a. a slave  b. symbolical  c. of rulers  d. a medicine |
| 522. Hilgard | a. a poem  b. a mountain  c. a saint  d. a king |
| 523. hip | a. to suggest  b. a hind  c. part of the body  d. to neigh |
| 524. Hispaniola | a. a Spanish fish  b. Haiti  c. Spain  d. Iberia |
| 525. hobnob | a. a gait  b. a heavy nail  c. to chat socially  d. an imp |
| 526. hoggins | a. footless stockings  b. sifted gravel  c. casks  d. cliffs |
| 527. holiday | a. a duplication  b. a dislocation  c. a vocation  d. a vacation |
| 528. Holothuridea | a. festivals  b. lobsters  c. sea-slugs  d. swine |
| 529. homicide | a. an admonition  b. maize  c. birth  d. a person who kills another |
| 530. homotaxis | a. namesakes  b. the same category  c. small taxis  d. not taxable |
| 531. honorary | a. an extra fee  b. urban  c. difficult  d. held as an honor |
| 532. hop | a. a chance  b. short spring  c. a circle  d. a whoop |
| 533. horn | a. a danger  b. a hard growth  c. a view  d. an eyelid |
| 534. horse | a. a larva  b. a pedagog  c. a mammal  d. a mammoth |
| 535. hot | a. a jar  b. seeming  c. having heat  d. to jolt |
| 536. house | a. a variety  b. a dwelling-place  c. a window  d. a trial |
| 537. Hrolf | a. a translator  b. an inventor  c. Rollo  d. Howth |
| 538. humble | a. arrogant  b. truthful  c. lowly  d. lofty |
| 539. hunchback | a. a new idea  b. a humpback  c. a return  d. a respite |
| 540. hurry | a. haste  b. applause  c. a growl  d. a nook |
| 541. Hyalite Peak | a. a peninsula  b. a mountain  c. a cape  d. a volcano |
| 542. hydrocamphene | a. a retort  b. a pure carbon  c. a camel  d. a chemical compound |
| 543. Hydrophora | a. aquaplanes  b. airplanes  c. jelly-fish  d. flowers |
| 544. hymar | a. an Arab cloak  b. a star  c. a cavity  d. wild ass |
| 545. hypercryalgesia | a. interchange  b. sensitivity  c. criticism  d. extract |
| 546. hypocentrum | a. in the jaws  b. part of vertebra  c. under the tongue  d. at the center |
| 547. hypothec | a. a pedestal  b. a plan  c. a pledge  d. a column |
| 548. ice | a. steam  b. frozen water  c. land  d. sky |
| 549. iconomatic | a. a method of writing  b. heathen  c. frugal  d. of a roving nature |
| 550. ideally | a. substantially  b. organically  c. perfectly  d. actually |
| 551. idryl | a. of a vine  b. a prince  c. a complex compound  d. a daisy |
| 552. Iliad | a. a district  b. Troy  c. Icarus  d. an epic poem |
| 553. illure | a. to trick  b. to entice  c. sullied  d. unreadable |
| 554. imbecility | a. conviction  b. protection  c. feebleness of mind  d. incentive |
| 555. immortal | a. undying  b. embodied  c. transient  d. mutable |
| 556. impenetrable | a. overbearing  b. impervious  c. impartial  d. fluid |
| 557. implement | a. a tool  b. growth  c. energy  d. a cylinder |
| 558. impression | a. a clan  b. an imprint  c. a scaffold  d. an impost |
| 559. in | a. above  b. off  c. inclusion within  d. outside |
| 560. Inca | a. a war-chief  b. a Japanese measure  c. an Arab tribe  d. a corporation |
| 561. incisive | a. decisive  b. inside  c. cutting  d. inclusive |
| 562. incongruity | a. harmony  b. devotion  c. elegance  d. unsuitableness |
| 563. incubus | a. a hatching apparatus  b. an indent  c. a load  d. a moss |
| 564. indeterminism | a. a blank  b. a counterpart  c. an indication  d. a doctrine |
| 565. indict | a. point out  b. compose  c. exert  d. accuse |

566. Indo-Aryan      a. a Greek   b. a family branch   c. a Jain   d. a Jew
567. indulgence      a. application   b. excess   c. exemption   d. compliance
568. inextricable    a. inevitable   b. unessential   c. unarmed   d. inescapable
569. infinite        a. undecided   b. a boundless quantity   c. a limit   d. unable
570. ingress         a. access   b. exit   c. discourtesy   d. attention
571. injunction      a. a join   b. a manor   c. a mandate   d. an intrusion
572. innocent        a. infected   b. criminal   c. without scent   d. sinless
573. inring          a. inrush   b. a bee   c. a curling term   d. entered
574. inspiration     a. inhalation   b. publication   c. dictation   d. rotation
575. insufferable    a. teachable   b. intolerable   c. elemental   d. vital
576. integument      a. an envelope   b. a variable   c. an average   d. a design
577. interactive     a. rare   b. biased   c. reciprocally effective   d. estranged
578. interference    a. tiring   b. forsaking   c. meddling   d. amusing
579. internal        a. foreign   b. perpetual   c. disused   d. interior
580. interruption    a. persistence   b. decay   c. a breaking in   d. a bursting forth
581. intoothed       a. having inturned teeth   b. twisted   c. toothless   d. tenacious
582. intuitive       a. encroaching   b. of quick perception   c. useful   d. available
583. investment      a. a substitute   b. money laid out   c. a track   d. privacy
584. iodomercurate   a. a rosette   b. a lunatic   c. a yoke   d. a compound
585. Iridomalacia    a. a part of Turkey   b. lichens   c. softening of the iris   d. a Greek town
586. irradiated      a. peaceful   b. salty   c. adorned with rays   d. angry
587. Irvingite       a. a genus of trees   b. a town   c. a Jew   d. one of a sect
588. isodictyal      a. of great heat   b. having equal meshes   c. easy   d. condensed
589. issue           a. rival   b. salvage   c. send forth   d. return
590. itzli           a. a bulb   b. a Mexican peasant   c. goats   d. volcanic rock
591. Jacanidae       a. jack-trees   b. birds   c. monkeys   d. mosses
592. Jacoba          a. a novice   b. a name   c. a lake   d. a district
593. janizary        a. a body-guard   b. a native state   c. a janitress   d. a cake
594. Jathniel        a. a legend   b. a city   c. a desert   d. a name
595. jeopardy        a. an oversight   b. danger   c. an instrument   d. jealousy
596. Jetheth         a. a banker   b. a duke   c. an island   d. a Jesuit
597. Jimmy Low       a. a native state   b. mahogany   c. a town   d. a patriarch
598. John            a. an isthmus   b. a play   c. a god   d. a boy's name
599. jointworm       a. a junction   b. a larva   c. a screw   d. a beam
600. journal         a. a cape   b. an idol   c. a curtsy   d. a diary
601. judgment        a. a wedge   b. a decision reached   c. a melody   d. a fungus
602. Julian          a. wife of Romeo   b. a title   c. a Spanish town   d. a man's name
603. Juno            a. a French marshal   b. a goddess   c. a Swiss peak   d. a river
604. Justicia        a. youths   b. judges   c. herbs and shrubs   d. reeds
605. kagura          a. a dance   b. a shark   c. a notary   d. a monkey
606. kamacite        a. ebony   b. a salt   c. a form   d. a desire
607. Karasubazar     a. a river   b. a sea   c. a low caste   d. a Tatar town
608. keenagh         a. mildew   b. a poona-tree   c. a cudgel   d. despair
609. kenogenesis     a. a trace   b. a development   c. a game   d. cheese
610. kettle          a. a trumpet   b. a vessel   c. a fish-owl   d. a cap
611. khersal         a. a state   b. a compound   c. a clan   d. a cure hall
612. kill            a. to kindle   b. to slay   c. to color   d. a sandpiper
613. kinetograph     a. a bird   b. a diagram   c. a summary   d. a camera
614. kinsman         a. a body-guard   b. lacquer   c. gold wire   d. a blood-relation
615. kite            a. a whelp   b. a kitten   c. a bird   d. friends
616. knee            a. a nap   b. a monument   c. a moth   d. a joint
617. knock           a. to knead   b. a groucher   c. a cable   d. strike hard
618. Knowltonia      a. a district   b. a town   c. herbs   d. worms
619. Konstanz        a. a dance-hall   b. a seaport   c. a district   d. a peninsula
620. kriyasakti      a. minerals   b. a Hindu god   c. a stork   d. creative power
621. kyke            a. to prosper   b. to peep   c. to plow   d. to prevent
622. laborer         a. a camp   b. a valley   c. a worker   d. a splash
623. Lacistemaceae   a. plants   b. snakes   c. rapids   d. the Fates
624. ladder          a. space   b. a set of rungs   c. a boy   d. freight
625. Lagos           a. a province   b. a king   c. a lake   d. a Jewish feast
626. lambda          a. a blow   b. a fishing-net   c. a Greek letter   d. a scarf
627. lamprey         a. a lament   b. a satire   c. a lamp   d. an eel
628. Lander          a. a mountain   b. an island   c. a surveyor   d. Hero's lover
629. langur          a. a hood   b. a tongue   c. weariness   d. a monkey
630. lapideon        a. a musical instrument   b. a lapel   c. a stone-cutter   d. lava
631. Las Casas       a. a missionary   b. a Greek scholar   c. a poet   d. a town
632. lathe           a. a secretion   b. to repel   c. a thin strip   d. a machine
633. Latto           a. an engineer   b. Samoa   c. a mountain   d. a poet
634. lautarite       a. an avalanche   b. a cell   c. a salt   d. a head-dress
635. lay             a. confess   b. dig   c. put down   d. stand
636. lead            a. guide   b. chase   c. choose   d. imitate

637. leafage         a. pride   b. permission   c. leaking   d. foliage
638. leather         a. lithe   b. ease   c. dressed skins   d. a water-course
639. Leda            a. a market town   b. a mythical woman   c. an Ionic city   d. an island
640. legion          a. a plait   b. an army force   c. a barge   d. a myth
641. lemming         a. an animal   b. a fruit   c. a theme   d. a vacancy
642. leopard         a. a panther   b. a pagan   c. a king   d. a rock
643. Leroy-Beaulieu  a. a district   b. an author   c. a river   d. a French spa
644. letter          a. a privilege   b. a sign   c. a remedy   d. a stupor
645. level           a. a vassal   b. a plain   c. an embankment   d. a quay
646. L'Hospital      a. a Latin poet   b. an institution   c. a borough   d. a French marshal
647. libration       a. even balance   b. restraint   c. a sacrifice   d. a billet
648. lief            a. a song   b. willingly   c. a serf   d. hardly
649. ligan           a. a bandage   b. goods cast adrift   c. inorganic   d. prone
650. light-year      a. a depression   b. a unit   c. a science   d. intellect
651. Limari          a. a river   b. a seaport   c. a city   d. a province
652. limoncillo      a. a compound   b. a newt   c. a timber-tree   d. a limeberry
653. lingthorn       a. a starfish   b. a shrub   c. a heavy cord   d. a metal
654. Lio Porgyul     a. a cape   b. a river   c. a mountain   d. an island
655. Lisieux         a. a cape   b. a volcano   c. a monastery   d. a town
656. lithography     a. a texture   b. printing from stone   c. a study of sponges   d. an index
657. live            a. decrease   b. have life   c. benefit   d. decease
658. load            a. to discharge   b. clay   c. dislike   d. a burden
659. local           a. of a loch   b. of a place   c. of a loach   d. of an army
660. Loco-foco       a. a writer   b. a political party   c. a Roman senator   d. a town
661. lodger          a. a paying guest   b. a boat   c. a cataract   d. a safe
662. logomancy       a. foretelling   b. a wrong name   c. logic   d. military science
663. longanimity     a. shyness   b. endurance   c. finance   d. credence
664. loon            a. a bird   b. money lent   c. a machine   d. a blade
665. Lorenz          a. a poet   b. a surgeon   c. a town   d. a school
666. Louisa Wilhelmina   a. a famous singer   b. a witch   c. a spy   d. a queen
667. low             a. freely   b. near the ground   c. a scowl   d. a scamp
668. lucubration     a. clearness   b. greed   c. deep meditation   d. conflict
669. luna-moth       a. a gadabout   b. a night moth   c. a period   d. an idiot
670. luster          a. the sundew   b. juiciness   c. furze   d. gloss
671. Lycopersicon    a. an emperor   b. nightshade   c. puffball   d. snakes
672. lyre            a. an odor   b. a den   c. a stringed instrument   d. a wild cat
673. macana          a. a game   b. a monkey   c. rice   d. a fish
674. machopolyp      a. a mule   b. a blemish   c. stigma   d. an organism
675. macrotome       a. an apparatus   b. a gypsy   c. a female ant   d. longevity
676. Maffei          a. a town   b. a secret society   c. a poem   d. a cardinal
677. magnet          a. a lodestone   b. a cement   c. a Mahatma   d. two quarts
678. Mah             a. a fish   b. the Mahdi   c. a citadel   d. a swindler
679. mailing         a. mating   b. a shrub   c. an alloy   d. posting
680. malacon         a. a gem   b. a Parsee   c. appetite   d. softness
681. malicious       a. ill-bred   b. shrinking   c. spiteful   d. fortified
682. Malvaceae       a. caterpillars   b. mosses   c. mallows   d. molecules
683. Manassas        a. a son of Joseph   b. an inventor   c. a musician   d. a town
684. mani            a. a prayer   b. emperors   c. insanity   d. fruits
685. Mantisia        a. oracles   b. a girl's name   c. plants   d. insects
686. maple           a. a dancer   b. a passage   c. a tree   d. a raccoon
687. Marcy           a. a festival   b. a general   c. a legend   d. a chemist
688. Marinism        a. of a sailor   b. of a school   c. a disease   d. a sprain
689. marksmanship    a. a mural   b. an art   c. a unit   d. a yarn
690. Mars            a. god of war   b. a month   c. an Indian   d. a river
691. marvelous       a. polished   b. wonderful   c. rolling   d. stony
692. mass            a. a surf-boat   b. a church service   c. master   d. a collar
693. mastiff         a. sticky   b. enormous   c. a dog   d. a bat
694. matin           a. a rug   b. marriage   c. a canonical hour   d. a herring
695. maul            a. a hammer   b. a sack   c. a fist   d. a sage
696. May-apple       a. an acorn   b. an herb   c. an oak-apple   d. a fig
697. mean            a. a title   b. intermediate   c. a manner   d. a grain
698. mechanics       a. dimensions   b. health   c. a branch of physics   d. clays
699. medicind        a. aware   b. animate   c. treated   d. intruded
700. meet            a. abound   b. come together   c. eat   d. heat
701. melancholy      a. a plant   b. charcoal   c. an epidemic   d. mournfulness
702. mellow          a. dried   b. soft and ripe   c. gray   d. moldy
703. memory          a. remembrance   b. grievance   c. distance   d. nuisance
704. mensural        a. of conduct   b. of a mouth   c. of a month   d. of measure
705. mercury         a. a sloth   b. forbearance   c. greedy   d. a metallic element
706. Merrimac        a. a river   b. a giant   c. a county   d. a famous singer
707. mesobar         a. a temple   b. a pressure area   c. an extreme   d. a plateau

708. metacenter    a. a chord   b. a fixed center   c. a radius   d. a balance point
709. metamylene    a. a replacement   b. an advocate   c. a compound   d. a trophy
710. meteorological    a. of meteors   b. of records   c. of dates   d. of weather changes
711. Methodist    a. a Catholic   b. a Jew   c. a Wesleyan   d. an atheist
712. metronome    a. an instrument   b. a colonial   c. a cavity   d. a whisper
713. microbe    a. a monkey   b. bacterium   c. a mineral   d. a sneak
714. microsection    a. a thin piece   b. a feature   c. a planter   d. to dissolve
715. mignonette    a. a tiny book   b. a plant   c. a midget   d. a thimble
716. milk    a. a shrub   b. an oyster   c. a needle   d. a liquid
717. Millom    a. a castle   b. a title   c. a town   d. a tree
718. mindful    a. clever   b. heedful   c. curious   d. unconscious
719. minium    a. a compound   b. an office   c. the least   d. a servant
720. miraculous    a. desirous   b. supernatural   c. lucid   d. latent
721. misidentification    a. nearness   b. erroneous sameness   c. modesty   d. inequality
722. miter    a. smaller   b. slavery   c. a head-dress   d. stronger
723. Moabite    a. French   b. one of the tribe   c. Irish   d. of Indo-China
724. moderation    a. heaviness   b. style   c. temperance   d. motion
725. moire    a. a gold coin   b. a fabric   c. a daub   d. a half
726. Mollisiaceae    a. feathers   b. soaps   c. grasses   d. fungi
727. monarchical    a. of an apse   b. of a bridge   c. of one value   d. of a ruler
728. monitor    a. a mongoose   b. a variety   c. a senior pupil   d. a cur
729. monopathic    a. crazy   b. solitary   c. of equal weight   d. having one diseased organ
730. monstrosity    a. a monster   b. uniformity   c. gravity   d. civility
731. moon    a. a satellite   b. a planet   c. a meteor   d. star-dust
732. moral    a. ethical   b. human   c. vicious   d. sleek
733. morphine    a. gloom   b. maroon   c. a narcotic   d. idiocy
734. mosquito    a. a gnat   b. a church   c. an edible bean   d. moss
735. motivate    a. to incite   b. to twist   c. to stem   d. to mortify
736. mountain    a. a boundary   b. a funeral   c. a symbol   d. a high hill
737. movable    a. unchangeable   b. transportable property   c. a toll   d. an insult
738. mugwet    a. to blindfold   b. a wharf   c. lily-of-the-valley   d. mute
739. multifurcate    a. multiple   b. dusty   c. of many forks   d. complex
740. murder    a. gloom   b. killing   c. silence   d. grumbling
741. muscovado    a. of musk   b. a moss   c. impure sugar   d. a crane-fly
742. mussal    a. a torch   b. a float   c. a water-animal   d. wood
743. mutualize    a. to apply   b. to borrow   c. to interchange   d. to rebel
744. myope    a. a title   b. teething   c. a near-sighted person   d. a rupture
745. mysticism    a. contact   b. obscurity   c. repetition   d. culture
746. naevolipoma    a. a tumor   b. a resin   c. a bug   d. a camelopard
747. name    a. an impulse   b. title   c. a knob   d. an impression
748. napping    a. absorbing   b. raising fibers   c. clearing   d. decoying
749. nasturtium    a. a plant   b. a monkey   c. a passage   d. a dislike
750. naturalization    a. gluttony   b. death   c. admission to citizenship   d. haunch
751. navigation    a. nature   b. emptiness   c. seamanship   d. excavation
752. necessity    a. an accident   b. indispensability   c. a spray   d. a nebula
753. needlefish    a. a glow-worm   b. a sea-fish   c. a tailor   d. a trap
754. Nelson    a. a general   b. an admiral   c. a statesman   d. a traitor
755. Neozoic    a. of a period   b. of terns   c. of terms   d. of trees
756. nerve    a. a tendon   b. a salmon   c. a shell   d. a snout
757. Netherlands Indies    a. West Indies   b. Guiana   c. South India   d. Dutch East Indies
758. New England    a. a musician   b. six States   c. a language   d. a town
759. nicety    a. crudity   b. exactness   c. knotty   d. injury
760. niggard    a. nestled   b. negroid   c. ugly   d. stingy
761. nimbus    a. a dark cloud   b. a root   c. a thief   d. speed
762. nitrification    a. a cleft   b. luster   c. darkness   d. formation of nitrates
763. Nocturnae    a. bowstrings   b. prawns   c. owls   d. army-worms
764. nominative    a. naming   b. ruling   c. belonging   d. dealing
765. non obstante    a. instead of   b. in spite of   c. not bright   d. not true
766. Norman    a. a standard   b. a Saxon   c. a duchy   d. a surname
767. noselite    a. a compound   b. a templet   c. a chemist   d. a nostril
768. notional    a. of a text   b. of concepts   c. of notes   d. of fame
769. nucleus    a. a kernel   b. a film   c. a scarf   d. a knob
770. nummulite    a. a coin   b. a count   c. an organism   d. a makeshift
771. nuttallite    a. a mineral   b. a meteor   c. a marsh   d. a minor
772. obcuneate    a. notched   b. heart-shaped   c. flattened   d. wedge-shaped
773. oblique    a. slanting   b. forgetful   c. compel   d. swear
774. obstruct    a. succeed   b. wear out   c. haunt   d. block
775. occupation    a. concealment   b. employment   c. attachment   d. lament
776. octene    a. a policy   b. a hydrocarbon   c. a grant   d. an arc
777. Oeneus    a. a town   b. a king   c. a promontory   d. a lake
778. officialism    a. shyness   b. salutation   c. an authoritative state   d. a sacrifice

779. oil    a. a neutral liquid   b. a spur   c. a locality   d. a legume
780. old    a. recent   b. aged   c. scanty   d. frequent
781. olive    a. a drain   b. an evergreen   c. a misdeal   d. gimp
782. omnipotent    a. all-powerful   b. all-knowing   c. everything   d. total
783. Onias    a. a novel   b. a headland   c. an opera   d. a name
784. oorali    a. arrow-poison   b. destiny   c. stings   d. liver-worts
785. operation    a. obscurity   b. penitence   c. action   d. aperture
786. optical    a. suitable   b. contrary   c. elective   d. visual
787. orange    a. a throat   b. a veil   c. a diadem   d. a fruit
788. orchid    a. a crane   b. Hades   c. a degree   d. a plant
789. ordnance    a. a deacon   b. a camp   c. artillery   d. a decree
790. organic    a. vital   b. visual   c. venial   d. vestal
791. ornithomancy    a. an aviary   b. anatomy   c. analysis   d. divination
792. orthography    a. culture   b. geography   c. correct spelling   d. a creed
793. Ossa    a. a mountain   b. a Greek   c. an island   d. the East
794. Oswichee    a. a cleric   b. a language   c. a town   d. a Goth
795. oundy    a. wavy   b. fairy   c. glassy   d. softly
796. outly    a. badly   b. to escape   c. to outlast   d. outwardly
797. oven    a. an oval   b. a receptacle for baking   c. to iron   d. to violate
798. overhang    a. a potion   b. a projection   c. a search   d. a defect
799. overthrow    a. watch   b. upset   c. reflect   d. broadcast
800. ox    a. a gas   b. an animal   c. an introduction   d. a prickle
801. pacific    a. huddling   b. contentious   c. peacable   d. pathetic
802. padlock    a. a fleece   b. a robber   c. a dungeon   d. a detachable lock
803. painter    a. a chemist   b. a communist   c. a columnist   d. a colorist
804. pale    a. easy   b. wan   c. aching   d. florid
805. pallah    a. an antelope   b. hop-scotch   c. a jaw   d. a hammock
806. palmistry    a. divination   b. pulse-beats   c. infirmity   d. a white metal
807. panada    a. a remedy   b. a dagger   c. bread-pulp   d. a plume
808. panegyris    a. a scorpion   b. a treatise   c. an assembly   d. mastery
809. pant    a. to frame   b. to grasp   c. to complete   d. to gasp
810. paposite    a. a salt   b. a papoose   c. an orang-utan   d. a priest
811. Paradiseidae    a. birds   b. tortoises   c. embryos   d. cobras
812. paramitom    a. false memory   b. a starfish   c. a superior   d. a mistress
813. paratragoedia    a. conductor   b. vestibules   c. organisms   d. a mock tragedy
814. park    a. a garment   b. to enclose for safety   c. to parley   d. gingerbread
815. paroptesis    a. similarity   b. a treatment   c. a vestige   d. a pledge
816. partake    a. share   b. function   c. accomplish   d. favor
817. partner    a. a debate   b. a suite   c. an alloy   d. a sharer
818. pass    a. go beyond   b. hurry   c. overhear   d. patronize
819. paste    a. a sport   b. a procession   c. honor   d. an adhesive compound
820. patent    a. a sufferer   b. a disease   c. a sole right   d. a monk
821. patriotism    a. a mold   b. love of country   c. patriarchy   d. industry
822. pause    a. a rest   b. a beggar   c. feet of animals   d. a shell
823. pea    a. a Hebrew letter   b. a magpie   c. a soothsayer   d. an edible seed
824. pearl    a. a growth used as a gem   b. discretion   c. pure carbon   d. exhaustion
825. pedestal    a. a base   b. a teacher   c. a vine   d. a scholar
826. peewee    a. a lapwing   b. a lake-trout   c. a shovel   d. a crevice
827. pellitory    a. the red-shank   b. an herb   c. a thin crust   d. a pill
828. pendant    a. a criminal   b. a pillory   c. a conduit   d. a hanging ornament
829. penn'orth    a. a bargain   b. a penny's worth   c. a basket   d. an oath
830. pentosan    a. a compound   b. a traitor   c. a trough   d. a roof
831. perceive    a. to appease   b. to apply   c. to appertain   d. to apprehend
832. Perennibranchiata    a. falcons   b. salamanders   c. trout   d. tissues
833. periderm    a. an extract   b. a coil   c. a risk   d. tough skin
834. peripheral    a. of a movement   b. of a circumference   c. dialed   d. heard
835. Permian    a. of a family   b. a dialect   c. a Chinaman   d. a Swede
836. person    a. a pole   b. an individual   c. a minister   d. a gale
837. perturbation    a. purity   b. modesty   c. relation   d. confusion
838. Peter    a. a satyr   b. a town   c. a boy's name   d. a county
839. petticoat    a. a cabbage   b. a petition   c. an underskirt   d. a bone
840. pharmacopoeia    a. a book of drugs   b. a mania   c. a chemist   d. a theory
841. phenol    a. a coast-land   b. a prodigy   c. a compound   d. a bird
842. Philoctetes    a. a warrior   b. a county   c. an organization   d. a prelate
843. phobophobia    a. dislike of dirt   b. dread of fear   c. a small plant   d. a fluid
844. phosphaturia    a. prisms   b. tubes   c. loss of phosphates   d. excess of phosphates
845. phrase    a. an expression   b. an aspect   c. a clan   d. a frenzy
846. phyllotaxis    a. a charm   b. leaf-arrangement   c. a protein   d. a moth
847. piazin    a. a woodpecker   b. a pokeweed   c. a compound   d. a lance
848. picotté    a. a water-wheel   b. made with loops   c. coal-tar   d. a tern
849. pigment    a. a joist   b. a dwarf   c. a pigeon   d. coloring-matter

850. pill             a. a vagrant  b. a shaft  c. a tiny ball  d. a spear
851. pin              a. a bag  b. a badge  c. a plant  d. a plow
852. piner            a. a lumberman  b. an oil  c. an herb  d. a cone
853. Pinus            a. a man's name  b. a tree  c. a town  d. a river
854. piquancy         a. slackness  b. scarcity  c. heresy  d. tart taste
855. pitch            a. sorcery  b. a bequest  c. resinous sap  d. a fiber
856. plaint           a. flatterer  b. a lament  c. a twist  d. a board
857. plangorous       a. wailing  b. waiting  c. wending  d. witty
858. plashy           a. gay  b. plastery  c. swampy  d. a tune
859. platform         a. a dais  b. an orb  c. a plaque  d. a planet
860. playable         a. quick  b. in play  c. peaceful  d. idle
861. plenary          a. punishable  b. poverty  c. swinging  d. entire
862. plicatulate      a. warranted  b. filed  c. easily won  d. minutely pleated
863. plucker          a. a picker  b. a hero  c. a fortune  d. a proof
864. plumosite        a. red-clay  b. a salt  c. eager  d. rare
865. pluvial          a. roomy  b. rainy  c. muddy  d. sooty
866. pocket           a. to appropriate  b. to deliberate  c. to mark  d. to pursue
867. pogonotrophy     a. poesy  b. beard-growing  c. severity  d. polarity
868. pointleted       a. winged  b. tapering  c. belated  d. double
869. polecat          a. a weasel  b. a tadpole  c. a bulrush  d. a wildcat
870. political        a. of exhibits  b. a farcical  c. daily  d. of public affairs
871. polychord        a. excess bile  b. many cells  c. having many chords  d. craven
872. Polynesian       a. of worms  b. of a race  c. of forms  d. of a fable
873. Polyzoa          a. hair growth  b. marine animals  c. mosses  d. gums
874. Pontano          a. a town  b. a poet  c. a bridge-tax  d. an Italian canal
875. pope             a. game-birds  b. bishop of Rome  c. the stern  d. a lake
876. porch            a. a veranda  b. a shark  c. a furrow  d. a shoot
877. port             a. a wart  b. to cram  c. a buoy  d. a hole in a ship's side
878. Port Richmond    a. an arsenal  b. a village  c. a camp  d. a county
879. possible         a. that was proved  b. that can be  c. that is  d. that must occur
880. postmaster       a. a stamp  b. a carrier  c. a newsman  d. a public official
881. potation         a. an onion  b. a servant  c. a drink  d. a river-plant
882. pottery          a. a worry  b. a broth  c. a lottery  d. a workshop
883. pourprite        a. a conference  b. a present  c. a sediment  d. a quilt
884. practics         a. barges  b. aims  c. a science
885. Praxillean verse a. ballads  b. an epic  c. prose-poetry  d. sonnets
886. precontract      a. speed  b. a herald  c. prior agreement  d. a plight
887. prefix           a. insert between  b. place before  c. add after  d. cancel
888. prender          a. the right to seize  b. a barrister  c. a bar sinister  d. a thief
889. present          a. near by  b. on top  c. underneath  d. far away
890. pressman         a. a nerve  b. one who prints  c. a whirlwind  d. a speed
891. prettiness       a. assurance  b. dainty beauty  c. omission  d. neglect
892. primaveral       a. of violets  b. of the first of spring  c. of a primrose  d. primary
893. principal        a. a sensation  b. a head man  c. a rule of conduct  d. a council
894. printing-press   a. a flurry  b. a katydid  c. a mechanism  d. a nautilus
895. privilege        a. an advantage  b. a punch  c. a secret pact  d. an opposite
896. Procellariidae   a. whales  b. petrels  c. snouts  d. antennae
897. proctorrhagia    a. bleeding  b. mucus  c. fever  d. fat
898. profilometer     a. an instrument  b. a burrow  c. a defense  d. a pollution
899. projection       a. a deputy  b. a throwing  c. a restraint  d. a goad
900. prompt           a. puny  b. prolonged  c. prone  d. punctual
901. prop             a. a portico  b. a vehicle  c. a support  d. a fork
902. propolis         a. bee-glue  b. to forestall  c. to set forth  d. fibers
903. prosecution      a. a theater  b. a viceroy  c. oppression  d. pursuit by law
904. protected        a. guarded  b. goaded  c. gauged  d. garbled
905. protoconch       a. a shell  b. a sketch  c. a segment  d. a service
906. provide          a. assist  b. resent  c. discourse  d. prepare
907. Prunus           a. a beetle  b. a fruit tree  c. a Prussian  d. a duke
908. psychology       a. mental science  b. snake-charming  c. provision  d. plague
909. pterygoid        a. fern-like  b. winged  c. a plant base  d. muscular
910. pudency          a. modesty  b. mischief  c. distemper  d. virginity
911. pulley           a. a drink  b. a cuttlefish  c. a chicken  d. an apparatus
912. pump             a. a coot  b. a perfume  c. a device  d. a cushion
913. punishment       a. sawdust  b. decision  c. a forecast  d. a penalty
914. purificator      a. a linen cloth  b. a purge  c. a screen  d. a wrinkle
915. push             a. haul  b. press hard  c. supply  d. fatten
916. pyraconitin      a. a section  b. a steward  c. a shay  d. an organic base
917. pyromorphite     a. a blowpipe  b. a phosphate  c. a corpuscle  d. a pome
918. Quadi            a. rats  b. a people  c. type-metals  d. a prison
919. quality          a. to make fit  b. characteristic  c. to value  d. an amount
920. quartet          a. an altar  b. a prey  c. a jonquil  d. a composition

921. quest    a. to subdue   d. droll   c. a dewdrop   d. to give tongue
922. quill    a. a coil   b. to silence   c. a feather   d. a wedge
923. quintuple    a. an extract   b. queer   c. fifteen lines   d. fivefold
924. rabbit    a. an animal   b. a machine   c. a priest   d. a mob
925. radiation    a. an arc   b. a root   c. sending out rays   d. receiving
926. raft    a. to reduce a sail   b. a float   c. a fissure   d. idle
927. rain    a. a glacier   b. rule   c. a curb   d. condensed vapor
928. Ramath    a. son of Moses   b. a town   c. an epic poem   d. a tribe
929. randy    a. a beggar   b. a rigmarole   c. a Hindu queen   d. aimless
930. rape    a. a twig   b. grape juice   c. a rib   d. a seam
931. rat    a. a myrtle   b. a cordial   c. a guitar   d. an animal
932. rat-tailed    a. rough   b. spiny   c. having hairless tail   d. untidy
933. ray    a. a beam of light   b. a gully   c. a fort   d. a curl
934. readjustment    a. remission   b. reorganization   c. relation   d. reflection
935. rebate    a. deduct from   b. an instrument   c. a water-weed   d. a ream
936. recipe    a. a formula   b. exchangeable   c. acceptance   d. revoke
937. reconstruction    a. a survey   b. submission   c. notoriety   d. building again
938. recurrent    a. excessive   b. occuring again   c. reclining   d. relaxing
939. reed    a. to guess   b. to peruse   c. a hollow stem   d. a grunt
940. reflex    a. reformation   b. refreshment   c. regiment   d. reflection
941. regality    a. royalty   b. an emblem   c. diversion   d. a delicacy
942. regular    a. symmetrical   b. surging   c. a metallic mass   d. an entertainer
943. relapse    a. to liberate   b. to backslide   b. to slacken   d. to narrate
944. religion    a. disregard   b. a system of faith   c. a purple flower   d. connection
945. renunciation    a. reversing   b. giving up   c. earning   d. renewing
946. reposal    a. pacing   b. placing   c. tracing   d. lacing
947. Republican    a. of a river   b. of a political party   c. of a mountain   d. of a race
948. reserve    a. to store up   b. to identify   c. to recur   d. to dislike
949. resolutive    a. relaxing   b. irritable   c. heinous   d. despotic
950. responsory    a. a psalm   b. an absorbent   c. a balm   d. a sound
951. resuscitate    a. to quiet   b. to consent   c. to revive   d. to strive
952. retouching    a. returning   b. bending   c. arriving   d. improving
953. reune    a. eagerly   b. silent   c. to meet again   d. a sign
954. revet    a. to wager   b. to clothe   c. to reverse   d. to face with stone
955. Reyer    a. a convent   b. an Indian State   c. a town   d. a composer
956. rhinalgia    a. layers   b. a pain   c. a plant   d. spleen
957. rhombohedral    a. of a form   b. of a farm   c. of a metal   d. of a flower
958. ribose    a. a recess   b. sugar   c. a shutter   d. indecent
959. ridicule    a. mockery   b. decency   c. frippery   d. flattery
960. righteously    a. rudely   b. rightly   c. restlessly   d. ruefully
961. ring    a. brushwood   b. a ladder   c. a circle   d. a chink
962. rise    a. a cornice   b. an ascent   c. a flax   d. a fog-horn
963. road    a. used an oar   b. a highway   c. a scent   d. mounted a horse
964. rock-cod    a. a cradle   b. a fish   c. a defense   d. road-ballast
965. roller    a. a group   b. a ground-dove   c. a cylinder   d. a kinsman
966. rondeau    a. a poem   b. a shield   c. a script   d. a fort
967. ropable    a. unruly   b. stable   c. docile   d. radical
968. rose    a. a lap-dog   b. powdered   c. a flower   d. a bale
969. rot    a. to register   b. a pulpit   c. to decompose   d. a list
970. roulette    a. a game   b. a quail   c. a degenerate   d. a scoop
971. rover    a. a wanderer   b. a period   c. a rabble   d. an auction
972. rubefacient    a. rough   b. sarcastic   c. envious   d. causing redness
973. ruffie    a. a fish   b. a hatchet   c. a boxer   d. a frill
974. rumination    a. native-shrewdness   b. numeration   c. chewing the cud   d. defiance
975. runner    a. a pity   b. a racer   c. curd   d. forage
976. rust    a. a biscuit   b. a compound   c. an apple   d. a trick
977. Rzhev    a. a mountain   b. a sea   c. a town   d. a village
978. Saccomyidae    a. compounds   b. pouches   c. animals   d. Levantine ships
979. saddle    a. a bagpipe   b. a haircloth   c. a seat   d. a moth
980. sage    a. an oil   b. a myth   c. a plant   d. an officer
981. Saint-Brieuc    a. a mountain pass   b. a spa   c. a town   d. an island
982. Salamiel    a. a hero   b. a Douai Bible name   c. a river   d. a Vedic text
983. salmon    a. a protein   b. a savory dish   c. a nymph   d. a fish
984. saltpeter    a. niter   b. a fish   c. clayey ground   d. a penny
985. Samosatenian    a. a residency   b. a disciple   c. of Samos   d. an ancient capital
986. sand    a. river-boats   b. millet   c. grains of rock   d. posts
987. sanguine    a. a leech   b. dissimilar   c. sprinkled   d. confident
988. sap    a. a taste   b. plant-juice   c. grape jelly   d. soap
989. satchel    a. a rock-pigeon   b. a frame   c. a small bag   d. a cloth
990. Sault Sainte Marie    a. a church   b. two towns   c. a mountain   d. a cape
991. saw    a. a terrace   b. painful   c. six   d. an instrument

992. Scala, La    a. an opera-house   b. a canal   c. a mountain peak   d. an actress
993. scaly    a. flaky   b. circular   c. hollow   d. granular
994. scarificator    a. a parrot-fish   b. a buffoon   c. an alarmist   d. an instrument
995. Scheldt    a. a river   b. a magistrate   c. a scientist   d. a seminary
996. schooner    a. a gem   b. an officer   c. a ship   d. a group
997. scissors    a. a shoot   b. a brick   c. a cutting-implement   d. a compiler
998. scorpion    a. a meteor   b. a chisel   c. a salt   d. a small animal
999. scrap    a. ragged   b. a fragment   c. a socket   d. to scrape
1000. screw    a. an harangue   b. a grooved cylinder   c. a rake   d. a stamp-mill
1001. scrubber    a. a wrangle   b. an animal   c. a squeeze   d. a roll
1002. sea    a. a blade   b. a part   c. the ocean   d. to observe
1003. seaming    a. inspecting   b. pleasing   c. sewing   d. appearing
1004. Secamone    a. daisies   b. scorpions   c. shrubs   d. grass
1005. security    a. savory   b. safety   c. a sally   d. signify
1006. seigniorage    a. beverage   b. a percentage   c. courage   d. postage
1007. self    a. an individual   b. a shrine   c. dross   d. a company
1008. selichoth    a. poems   b. sultans   c. consistency   d. pride
1009. semidome    a. nearly dry   b. a short note   c. a half-mute   d. a roof-structure
1010. send    a. to help   b. to dispatch   c. to begin   d. to receive
1011. sensorium    a. a fabric   b. a reproof   c. the nervous system   d. a marshal
1012. septendecimal    a. of seven   b. of seventeen   c. of seventy   d. of seven years
1013. serpentine    a. winding   b. of a meteor   c. a Rhine wine   d. a bale
1014. servitude    a. penury   b. slavery   c. bravery   d. knavery
1015. setting    a. a bristle   b. a surrounding   c. a sediment   d. a colonist
1016. sewellel    a. an animal   b. a compound   c. a trout   d. a vault
1017. shad    a. a wild sheep   b. to scratch   c. a food-fish   d. a fetter
1018. shaken    a. agitated   b. a sect   c. oakum   d. steady
1019. shard    a. a broken piece   b. a cabin   c. a halter   d. a sun-worshiper
1020. shears    a. sheep   b. an instrument   c. shad   d. shells
1021. Sheffield    a. a volcano   b. a pope   c. a surname   d. a mosque
1022. shepherd    a. a stable   b. wages   c. to disgrace   d. a sheep-herdsman
1023. Shiloh    a. a pool   b. a place   c. a sacred tree   d. a festival
1024. shirkt    a. orderly   b. evaded   c. submerged   d. rounded
1025. shooter    a. a shovel   b. rice-husks   c. a sliding door   d. a gunner
1026. shot    a. a shelf   b. a cataract   c. a lead pellet   d. a rock
1027. shred    a. a sherbet   b. to benumb   c. a snare   d. a scrap
1028. shut    a. to shift   b. to liberate   c. to neglect   d. to close
1029. sickness    a. greatness   b. primness   c. illness   d. rawness
1030. sierra    a. a short nap   b. a province   c. a yellow color   d. a mountain chain
1031. signal    a. a Greek letter   b. a signet-ring   c. a lord   d. a sign
1032. silk    a. a Roman weight   b. a glossy substance   c. sullen   d. a pod
1033. Silvestre    a. science of trees   b. coinage   c. a poet   d. a S. A. forest
1034. single    a. to overlap   b. an overture   c. an endowment   d. to select one
1035. sinus    a. a cavity   b. fusion   c. a sinew   d. of China
1036. sister    a. to sizzle   b. daughter of same parents   c. a finch   d. a fellow
1037. skeptical    a. incredulous   b. unusual   c. irregular   d. scary
1038. skinless    a. flaxen   b. without skin   c. frivolous   d. fleecy
1039. slab    a. coal-dirt   b. a sheep-run   c. saliva   d. an outer cut
1040. slaughter    a. to massacre   b. to flap   c. to dabble   d. to salute
1041. slicken    a. to warm   b. glossy   c. rock-dust   d. to ravel
1042. slippery    a. separate   b. smooth   c. spoony   d. spoken
1043. slug    a. to load   b. to slide   c. to murmur   d. to propel
1044. Smith    a. a volcano   b. a surname   c. a gunboat   d. Adam's third son
1045. snagger    a. a bill-hook   b. to bridle   c. to knot   d. to nibble
1046. sneak    a. to malign   b. to rebound   c. to object   d. to steal
1047. snow    a. dew   b. ice crystals   c. sleet   d. hail
1048. soap-plant    a. soap-wort   b. a lily-wort   c. a grass   d. a tree
1049. soda    a. a compound   b. a vase   c. a bird   d. an oil
1050. solar    a. of the sky.   b. alone   c. of the sun   d. of the soil
1051. solidarity    a. volcanic action   b. celebration   c. union   d. anxiety
1052. sondeli    a. the muskrat   b. trials   c. messengers   d. sounds
1053. sordidin    a. a metal   b. a reed-stop   c. a violin   d. a chemical substance
1054. soul    a. a flat-fish   b. the immaterial part of man   c. part of a shoe   d. alone
1055. Southcott    a. a sculptor   b. a religious prophet   c. a swindler   d. a thief
1056. spacing    a. shaving   b. placing at intervals   c. clawing   d. bracing
1057. spare    a. be careful of   b. a cock-fight   c. a plaster   d. be late with
1058. spawn    a. the shoulder   b. saliva   c. a joint   d. eggs of fish
1059. speckless    a. spiritless   b. tasteless   c. graceless   d. spotless
1060. speech    a. reason   b. rascal   c. dumbness   d. utterance
1061. spermatozoon    a. a living element   b. a poison   c. a cave-temple   d. a splint
1062. spider    a. corruption   b. a bucket   c. a small animal   d. a pike

1063. spine — a. primrose   b. crown   c. back-bone   d. keyboard
1064. spiritual — a. stubborn   b. of the soul   c. voiceless   d. impartial
1065. spodogenous — a. of pottery   b. of refuse   c. of tobacco   d. of a genus
1066. spoond — a. married   b. wound   c. sailed   d. ladled
1067. sprayer — a. a trough   b. a seed   c. an atomizer   d. an axle
1068. sprocket — a. a medieval engine   b. a tooth on a wheel   c. a faucet   d. an anchor
1069. squadron — a. to bubble   b. to pelt   c. to squat   d. to set in array
1070. squeeze — a. to compress   b. to defeat   c. to comply   d. to delegate
1071. stack — a. a novice   b. a pile   c. a bandage   d. a state
1072. stain — a. dislocation   b. destination   c. duplication   d. discoloration
1073. stampede — a. a panicful flight   b. a blunder   c. vigor   d. a stockade
1074. stannous — a. of copper   b. of tin   c. of silver   d. of glass
1075. star — a. a mocassin   b. a heavenly body   c. a faction   d. an opinion
1076. state — a. to surprise   b. to tell in detail   c. to bolt   d. to radiate
1077. staxis — a. bleeding   b. sabotage   c. a surfeit   d. a relief
1078. Stellerida — a. worms   b. starfish   c. sea-cows   d. meteors
1079. stercoral — a. of beliefs   b. of a liter   c. of coral   d. of excrement
1080. stethoscope — a. a muscle   b. an apparatus   c. a spasm   d. an atom
1081. stigmatic — a. pliant   b. trivial   c. branded   d. stifling
1082. stipular — a. of a salary   b. to specify   c. crowded   d. like an appendage
1083. stockworks — a. ducks   b. breakwaters   c. ore deposits   d. heifers
1084. stone — a. a thrust   b. a piece of rock   c. a fringed band   d. a tunic
1085. store — a. to gaze   b. to lay up   c. to impend   d. to offend
1086. stradiot — a. a light-horseman   b. a violin   c. a composer   d. a waif
1087. strategetic — a. of generalship   b. of strata   c. of a valley   d. of clouds
1088. street — a. narrow   b. a highway   c. an arrow   d. straight
1089. strike — a. to inquire   b. to hit   c. to manicure   d. to sup
1090. strive — a. to endeavor   b. to vibrate   c. to lament   d. to inject
1091. Struthio — a. an ostrich   b. a hero   c. a town   d. a gulf
1092. stumpage — a. a puzzle   b. a short post   c. standing timber   d. a boaster
1093. suasion — a. smoothness   b. stealth   c. persuasion   d. ease
1094. subgyre — a. an auction   b. a fold   c. a clan   d. crafty
1095. submit — a. yield   b. ruffle   c. plunge   d. interrupt
1096. substantialism — a. a doctrine   b. a practice   c. a duty   d. a subsidy
1097. succession — a. an adaptation   b. a series   c. a deputy   d. a compass
1098. suffer — a. to feel pain   b. to attach   c. a smother   d. to require
1099. suing — a. a wooing   b. wool-grease   c. oleomargarin   d. a hog
1100. sunflower — a. an aperture   b. a crate   c. a stout herb   d. a ray
1101. superintendent — a. a surface   b. an overseer   c. an eyebrow   d. an excess
1102. supplement — a. an addition   b. a petitioner   c. constant   d. an event
1103. surcharge — a. a cessation   b. an excessive burden   c. a cloth   d. a baseboard
1104. surprise — a. a vestment   b. a remainder   c. to astonish   d. to exceed
1105. sustain — a. to mistrust   b. to dilute   c. to hold up   d. to infatuate
1106. swamp — a. a mallet   b. a marsh   c. a mortar   d. a desert
1107. sweat-house — a. the tropics   b. a place to remove hair   c. an oven   d. a stove
1108. swift — a. a seal   b. to tighten   c. to bulge   d. a bird
1109. swinging — a. banishing   b. securing   c. swaying   d. originating
1110. sycophant — a. to derive   b. to cringe   c. to multiply   d. to swoon
1111. symmetrophobia — a. a creed   b. a dread   c. an odor   d. a stomach
1112. synchronization — a. wasting time   b. keeping time   c. uneven time   d. quick time
1113. syrigmus — a. a Syrian idiom   b. a ringing sound   c. a shrub   d. a spray
1114. Tabard Inn — a. a cloister   b. a tavern   c. a pharmacy   d. a church
1115. tac-au-tac — a. a resin   b. a warding off   c. a tree   d. a language
1116. tag — a. to labor   b. to be liable   c. to libel   d. to label
1117. take — a. decorate   b. lay hold of   c. spoil   d. to hang on
1118. talkee-talkee — a. broken English   b. talkative   c. a charm   d. a conference
1119. tamise — a. a young cod   b. a strainer   c. a fabric   d. a hillock
1120. Tannhäuser — a. a river   b. a crusader   c. a poem   d. a castle
1121. tapster — a. an overseer   b. a machine   c. a bartender   d. a carpet
1122. tarsier — a. an animal   b. a mosaic   c. gout   d. a silk fabric
1123. taw — a. a coiffure   b. a Greek letter   c. to become tight   d. to dress skins
1124. teachable — a. dignified   b. apt to learn   c. excitable   d. credulous
1125. telescope — a. a picture   b. a record   c. an instrument   d. a force
1126. temporal — a. of time   b. of calmness   c. of minerals   d. of passion
1127. Teniers — a. a musician   b. a painter   c. a deputy   d. a tapestry
1128. tergiversant — a. leaning   b. obscure   c. evasive   d. dorsal
1129. Terre Haute — a. a mountain peak   b. a county   c. a city   d. a desert
1130. testamentary — a. variegated   b. bequeathed by   c. outside   d. of a loan
1131. tetrahedroid — a. a square   b. the envelope of a surface   c. a quartet   d. a drum
1132. Thaumaste — a. a magician   b. crabs   c. compounds   d. a scholar
1133. theocracy — a. a psalm   b. a religious mania   c. government by God   d. a mystic union

1134. thermoanesthesia    a. apoplexy   b. an antidote   c. a device   d. a weakening
1135. they    a. a plural pronoun   b. possessive of "thee"   c. than   d. an article
1136. third    a. an ordinal number   b. a hole   c. a thrall   d. a purpose
1137. thorax    a. a mineral   b. an essayist   c. a grass   d. a part of the body
1138. thread    a. a folk-tale   b. superstition   c. a slender cord   d. to writhe
1139. Throscidae    a. thrushes   b. beetles   c. windpipes   d. toads
1140. Thunbergia    a. a queen   b. climbing plants   c. sea fish   d. a State
1141. Tiarella    a. a Spanish town   b. coronets   c. a dance   d. herbs
1142. tie    a. to wrangle   b. a coquet   c. to bind   d. a farm
1143. tillage    a. roofing   b. cultivation   c. nonsense   d. a password
1144. time    a. a solid   b. a prong   c. a period   d. a low shrub
1145. tinkershire    a. a slum   b. fever-root   c. a hamlet   d. a sea-bird
1146. Tisri    a. one of the Furies   b. a Hebrew month   c. a poet   d. herbs
1147. to    a. above   b. in the direction of   c. from   d. outside
1148. toe    a. a hurricane   b. a digit of the foot   c. to drag   d. a hemp fiber
1149. Tom    a. an island   b. a volcano   c. a god   d. Thomas
1150. tongue    a. a secret society   b. a fleshy organ   c. a junk   d. a light coat
1151. toot-poison    a. fern leaves   b. berry-seeds   c. a tare   d. a seaweed
1152. tore    a. a high hill   b. rent   c. a marble   d. a journey
1153. torulose    a. boisterous   b. yeast-like   c. a turtle   d. roundabout
1154. tour de force    a. a journey   b. an appeal   c. a wig   d. a feat
1155. toxin    a. a thorn   b. a wager   c. an alarm-bell   d. a poisonous compound
1156. tractable    a. veritable   b. manageable   c. rough   d. inferable
1157. train    a. to stagger   b. to plot   c. to instruct   d. to pelt
1158. transcendental    a. pierced   b. skeptical   c. prolific   d. surpassing others
1159. translate    a. to infringe   b. to express on another language   c. to countermand   d. to percolate
1160. trappoid    a. of a rock   b. of a harness   c. of a trail   d. of a snare
1161. treasure    a. a disease   b. a squall   c. to store up   d. a burlesque
1162. Trema    a. a town   b. a shrub   c. worms   d. a composer
1163. trial    a. a sea-slug   b. a testing   c. treacle   d. a knife
1164. trigger    a. an artifice   b. a bullet   c. a finger-piece   d. a ship
1165. Trinitarian    a. an island   b. a cape   c. a peninsula   d. one of a sect
1166. tripudium    a. a dance   b. a syllable   c. a panel   d. a root
1167. Trombidiidae    a. mites   b. beetles   c. lizards   d. birds
1168. trout    a. a channel   b. a satire   c. a fish   d. an elf
1169. truncate    a. to roll along   b. to crackle   c. to value   d. to cut the top from
1170. tryst    a. a commotion   b. a meeting-place   c. a sail   d. a pore
1171. tubular    a. of palms   b. wealthy   c. of tubers   d. tube-shaped
1172. tumbling    a. inflating   b. beating   c. somersaulting   d. a box-cart
1173. turban    a. bony   b. foul   c. a head-dress   d. a motor
1174. turn    a. confuse   b. skimp   c. classify   d. cause to rotate
1175. turreted    a. smooth   b. notched   c. having towers   d. having tools
1176. twentyfourmo    a. a chisel   b. a soldier   c. a book.   d. a battle-ax
1177. Two Foscari    a. towns   b. Venetians   c. famous twins   d. duels
1178. typical    a. fatal   b. deprived   c. emblematic   d. of typhus
1179. Ugrian    a. Slavonic   b. Celtic   c. Teutonic   d. Finnic
1180. umbilical    a. central   b. yellow   c. clustered   d. shadowy
1181. uncle    a. a hook   b. a relative   c. a tooth   c. a claw
1182. underground    a. to shore up   b. beneath the surface   c. a demigod   d. to subject
1183. undulous    a. improper   b. perilous   c. wavy   d. private
1184. unicorneal    a. one-sided   b. of one cornea   c. one-horned   d. a bivalve
1185. unit    a. a mussel   b. unison   c. of a faith   d. a single person or thing
1186. unjust    a. not equitable   b. uncouth   c. unfavorable   d. rare
1187. up    a. below   b. within   c. something high   d. a Javanese tree
1188. urachus    a. a structure   b. a compound   c. an asp emblem   d. a hurricane
1189. urinate    a. to pass fluid   b. to chew   c. a mineral   d. a loon
1190. Ustilaginales    a. mosses   b. acids   c. hawks   d. fungi
1191. uzzile    a. a bird   b. an angel   c. a measure   d. a vest
1192. Valerian    a. a Moorish kingdom   b. a caste   c. a fortified seaport   d. of Valerius
1193. valve    a. prowess   b. a controlling device   c. a parapet   d. worth
1194. vantage    a. attraction   b. a gangway   c. superiority   d. boasting
1195. varriated    a. shortened   b. fur-like   c. troublesome   d. rocky
1196. Vaux, Comte de    a. a citadel   b. a pleasure resort   c. a romance   d. a marshal
1197. vend    a. a whitefish   b. to measure   c. to sell   d. a vein
1198. ventre    a. a dance   b. a fin   c. an inn   d. an opening
1199. verdict    a. orally   b. a decision   c. a white grape   d. green
1200. ver sacrum    a. a dedication   b. free verse   c. a lobe   d. a contraction
1201. vesicle    a. a pauper   b. a bat   c. a tiny bladder   d. a wind
1202. vexillum    a. a ravine   b. a cannon   c. a vestment   d. a square flag
1203. Victoria    a. an opera   b. a canal   c. a girl's name   d. a monastery

1204. Villanueva
    de la Serena    a. a town  b. a noble  c. a slave  d. a mountain
1205. violence    a. harvest  b. force  c. a color  d. levity
1206. virtu    a. a rare quality  b. mature  c. a twig  d. a crossbow
1207. visitation    a. perception  b. a visit  c. a garment  d. a doctrine
1208. voice    a. a liquor  b. a fashion  c. human utterance  d. a vacuum
1209. volvelle    a. a nightcap  b. a tome  c. a rotating piece  d. a scroll
1210. vulgar    a. solemn  b. chaste  c. coarse  d. injurious
1211. wain    a. to squander  b. to diminish  c. a lament  d. a wagon
1212. Walker    a. a surname  b. a desert  c. a volcano  d. a play
1213. Wamego    a. a giant  b. a tribe  c. a pigmy  d. a city
1214. warble    a. to review  b. a lizard  c. to trill  d. a hyena
1215. warrant    a. an assault  b. to be wary  c. to guarantee  d. a signal
1216. wasp    a. a spruce  b. an insect  c. a crystal  d. a pledge
1217. water    a. to recoup  b. to whirl  c. to irrigate  d. to split
1218. water-wheel    a. the trumpetleaf  b. a device  c. a water-sprite  d. a leakage
1219. waxweed    a. a hairy herb  b. a Java sparrow  c. a wild yam  d. bayberry
1220. weave    a. to entwince  b. to shirk  c. to measure  d. to clothe
1221. weight    a. a fish-trap  b. a sound  c. a selvage  d. heaviness
1222. Welsh    a. of Wells  b. of Wales  c. Roman  d. Iberian
1223. wet    a. moistened  b. to weigh  c. to sharpen  d. pathetic
1224. wheel    a. a sting  b. a rotatable disk  c. prosperity  d. to swell
1225. whidah    a. a chest  b. to whizz  c. a bird  d. a quarrel
1226. whish    a. a warbler  b. a whorl  c. to swish  d. to desire
1227. white    a. a rod  b. the color of snow  c. a sprite  d. a weight
1228. whoever    a. anyone  b. no one  c. anything  d. nothing
1229. wife    a. a capsule  b. a wanderer  c. a spouse  d. a ghost
1230. will    a. a device  b. stupidity  c. a ruse  d. self-determination
1231. win    a. furze  b. a windlass  c. to gain  d. to crank
1232. window    a. a branch  b. a ridge  c. a reel  d. a glazed opening
1233. wing    a. a fore limb  b. a camel  c. a vestige  d. a canoe
1234. wire    a. a curse  b. a shaft  c. a leech  d. a metal thread
1235. wit    a. ingenuity  b. privacy  c. negation  d. stupidity
1236. wolf    a. a cross-thread  b. a mammal  c. an upland  d. dense
1237. wood    a. a forest  b. past tense of "will"  c. courted  d. a blue dye
1238. woolly    a. wool-like  b. feathery  c. salty  d. finger-like
1239. world    a. the close  b. fire  c. spiral  d. the earth
1240. Wrangel    a. a phantom  b. an explorer  c. a county  d. a college
1241. writ    a. a wart  b. a gown  c. an artificer  d. a sealed mandate
1242. xiphihumeralis    a. a muscle  b. a constellation  c. iris  d. a shrub
1243. yam    a. a serf  b. a god  c. a llama  d. an edible root
1244. yea    a. always  b. to steer  c. yes  d. perhaps
1245. yeoman    a. a freeholder  b. a feast day  c. a Chinese boat  d. a fiber
1246. young    a. far away  b. a giant  c. a sea-cow  d. not full-grown
1247. Zalacca    a. a Chilean dance    b. a genus of palms    c. a Greek legislator
    d. Indians
1248. Zendicism    a. Zoroastrianism  b. a Japanese doctrine  c. atheism  d. a Hindu cult
1249. Ziphiidae    a. rootstocks  b. whales  c. Gipsy songs  d. grass
1250. zooid    a. a polecat  b. an organism  c. a carving  d. a frieze
1251. zygoma    a. a rower  b. a bone  c. a coin  d. a Serbian village

# How To Compute Your Vocabulary Score

Follow the same procedure that you used in the 15-Minute Test on page 8, checking your underlined words against the correct answers which follow. Multiply the total by the key number 123. The result will give you your total English Vocabulary rating. Compare these results with those of the 15-Minute Test. If there is any variation, the longer test, of course, will be more nearly accurate.

## Answers to the Master English Vocabulary Test

| | | | | | | | | |
|---|---|---|---|---|---|---|---|---|
| 1 — c | 57 — c | 113 — b | 169 — a | 225 — b | 281 — a | 337 — b | 393 — a | 449 — b |
| 2 — b | 58 — c | 114 — d | 170 — c | 226 — b | 282 — c | 338 — b | 394 — b | 450 — b |
| 3 — c | 59 — a | 115 — c | 171 — b | 227 — b | 283 — b | 339 — b | 395 — d | 451 — b |
| 4 — c | 60 — b | 116 — c | 172 — a | 228 — c | 284 — a | 340 — b | 396 — a | 452 — c |
| 5 — d | 61 — c | 117 — b | 173 — b | 229 — b | 285 — c | 341 — b | 397 — d | 453 — c |
| 6 — b | 62 — c | 118 — b | 174 — d | 230 — a | 286 — c | 342 — c | 398 — c | 454 — a |
| 7 — b | 63 — a | 119 — a | 175 — a | 231 — b | 287 — c | 343 — c | 399 — c | 455 — c |
| 8 — b | 64 — d | 120 — b | 176 — d | 232 — c | 288 — c | 344 — b | 400 — d | 456 — b |
| 9 — b | 65 — a | 121 — d | 177 — c | 233 — c | 289 — a | 345 — c | 401 — a | 457 — c |
| 10 — c | 66 — a | 122 — c | 178 — d | 234 — b | 290 — c | 346 — b | 402 — c | 458 — b |
| 11 — b | 67 — b | 123 — d | 179 — c | 235 — a | 291 — c | 347 — b | 403 — b | 459 — b |
| 12 — d | 68 — d | 124 — b | 180 — d | 236 — c | 292 — c | 348 — c | 404 — b | 460 — d |
| 13 — c | 69 — b | 125 — b | 181 — a | 237 — a | 293 — d | 349 — d | 405 — d | 461 — b |
| 14 — a | 70 — a | 126 — b | 182 — b | 238 — c | 294 — c | 350 — c | 406 — c | 462 — a |
| 15 — c | 71 — d | 127 — b | 183 — a | 239 — b | 295 — d | 351 — b | 407 — b | 463 — d |
| 16 — b | 72 — c | 128 — a | 184 — b | 240 — c | 296 — a | 352 — b | 408 — d | 464 — c |
| 17 — b | 73 — d | 129 — a | 185 — b | 241 — b | 297 — b | 353 — b | 409 — d | 465 — a |
| 18 — c | 74 — b | 130 — d | 186 — b | 242 — a | 298 — b | 354 — c | 410 — c | 466 — b |
| 19 — d | 75 — c | 131 — d | 187 — b | 243 — b | 299 — a | 355 — c | 411 — c | 467 — c |
| 20 — a | 76 — a | 132 — b | 188 — c | 244 — b | 300 — b | 356 — c | 412 — d | 468 — c |
| 21 — c | 77 — b | 133 — b | 189 — c | 245 — b | 301 — b | 357 — b | 413 — d | 469 — d |
| 22 — b | 78 — b | 134 — b | 190 — b | 246 — c | 302 — a | 358 — a | 414 — b | 470 — c |
| 23 — c | 79 — d | 135 — d | 191 — d | 247 — a | 303 — c | 359 — b | 415 — b | 471 — c |
| 24 — c | 80 — a | 136 — a | 192 — d | 248 — c | 304 — a | 360 — a | 416 — a | 472 — d |
| 25 — c | 81 — c | 137 — d | 193 — c | 249 — c | 305 — b | 361 — d | 417 — c | 473 — c |
| 26 — b | 82 — b | 138 — c | 194 — c | 250 — d | 306 — c | 362 — b | 418 — a | 474 — d |
| 27 — c | 83 — b | 139 — b | 195 — d | 251 — a | 307 — b | 363 — b | 419 — b | 475 — b |
| 28 — d | 84 — d | 140 — b | 196 — d | 252 — b | 308 — c | 364 — b | 420 — c | 476 — a |
| 29 — d | 85 — c | 141 — d | 197 — b | 253 — d | 309 — a | 365 — b | 421 — d | 477 — d |
| 30 — a | 86 — a | 142 — d | 198 — a | 254 — d | 310 — d | 366 — c | 422 — b | 478 — b |
| 31 — b | 87 — b | 143 — b | 199 — b | 255 — a | 311 — c | 367 — b | 423 — b | 479 — d |
| 32 — c | 88 — b | 144 — b | 200 — c | 256 — d | 312 — a | 368 — d | 424 — d | 480 — c |
| 33 — d | 89 — d | 145 — a | 201 — b | 257 — c | 313 — c | 369 — c | 425 — c | 481 — c |
| 34 — b | 90 — c | 146 — b | 202 — d | 258 — b | 314 — b | 370 — d | 426 — b | 482 — a |
| 35 — c | 91 — a | 147 — d | 203 — a | 259 — c | 315 — c | 371 — a | 427 — d | 483 — c |
| 36 — d | 92 — d | 148 — b | 204 — c | 260 — b | 316 — c | 372 — a | 428 — a | 484 — c |
| 37 — c | 93 — b | 149 — b | 205 — d | 261 — c | 317 — b | 373 — c | 429 — d | 485 — b |
| 38 — b | 94 — c | 150 — d | 206 — a | 262 — c | 318 — b | 374 — b | 430 — b | 486 — d |
| 39 — d | 95 — d | 151 — a | 207 — d | 263 — d | 319 — a | 375 — a | 431 — c | 487 — c |
| 40 — c | 96 — c | 152 — b | 208 — b | 264 — c | 320 — c | 376 — b | 432 — b | 488 — c |
| 41 — c | 97 — d | 153 — a | 209 — a | 265 — b | 321 — a | 377 — b | 433 — a | 489 — a |
| 42 — d | 98 — a | 154 — b | 210 — c | 266 — b | 322 — b | 378 — d | 434 — b | 490 — b |
| 43 — a | 99 — c | 155 — b | 211 — c | 267 — c | 323 — b | 379 — c | 435 — b | 491 — a |
| 44 — d | 100 — b | 156 — b | 212 — a | 268 — c | 324 — b | 380 — b | 436 — c | 492 — c |
| 45 — c | 101 — d | 157 — b | 213 — b | 269 — c | 325 — c | 381 — a | 437 — c | 493 — c |
| 46 — c | 102 — a | 158 — d | 214 — c | 270 — a | 326 — d | 382 — d | 438 — c | 494 — d |
| 47 — a | 103 — d | 159 — d | 215 — c | 271 — d | 327 — c | 383 — c | 439 — b | 495 — a |
| 48 — c | 104 — d | 160 — b | 216 — b | 272 — b | 328 — b | 384 — b | 440 — b | 496 — c |
| 49 — a | 105 — a | 161 — b | 217 — c | 273 — b | 329 — b | 385 — a | 441 — d | 497 — d |
| 50 — c | 106 — b | 162 — c | 218 — c | 274 — d | 330 — b | 386 — b | 442 — b | 498 — b |
| 51 — c | 107 — d | 163 — c | 219 — a | 275 — c | 331 — d | 387 — c | 443 — b | 499 — b |
| 52 — b | 108 — a | 164 — c | 220 — a | 276 — c | 332 — c | 388 — c | 444 — c | 500 — d |
| 53 — d | 109 — a | 165 — b | 221 — b | 277 — b | 333 — c | 389 — b | 445 — a | 501 — c |
| 54 — d | 110 — b | 166 — b | 222 — a | 278 — d | 334 — b | 390 — b | 446 — b | 502 — b |
| 55 — b | 111 — c | 167 — d | 223 — a | 279 — c | 335 — c | 391 — b | 447 — a | 503 — c |
| 56 — d | 112 — b | 168 — a | 224 — c | 280 — b | 336 — c | 392 — d | 448 — d | 504 — d |

| | | | | | | | | |
|---|---|---|---|---|---|---|---|---|
| 505 — a | 576 — a | 647 — a | 718 — b | 789 — c | 860 — b | 931 — d | 1002 — c | 1073 — a |
| 506 — d | 577 — c | 648 — b | 719 — a | 790 — a | 861 — d | 932 — c | 1003 — c | 1074 — b |
| 507 — c | 578 — c | 649 — b | 720 — b | 791 — d | 862 — d | 933 — a | 1004 — c | 1075 — b |
| 508 — b | 579 — d | 650 — b | 721 — b | 792 — c | 863 — a | 934 — b | 1005 — b | 1076 — b |
| 509 — b | 580 — c | 651 — a | 722 — c | 793 — a | 864 — b | 935 — a | 1006 — b | 1077 — a |
| 510 — c | 581 — a | 652 — c | 723 — b | 794 — c | 865 — b | 936 — a | 1007 — a | 1078 — b |
| 511 — d | 582 — b | 653 — a | 724 — c | 795 — a | 866 — a | 937 — d | 1008 — a | 1079 — d |
| 512 — c | 583 — b | 654 — c | 725 — b | 796 — d | 867 — b | 938 — b | 1009 — d | 1080 — b |
| 513 — a | 584 — d | 655 — d | 726 — d | 797 — b | 868 — b | 939 — c | 1010 — b | 1081 — c |
| 514 — d | 585 — c | 656 — b | 727 — d | 798 — b | 869 — a | 940 — d | 1011 — c | 1082 — d |
| 515 — b | 586 — c | 657 — b | 728 — c | 799 — c | 870 — d | 941 — a | 1012 — b | 1083 — c |
| 516 — b | 587 — d | 658 — d | 729 — d | 800 — b | 871 — c | 942 — a | 1013 — a | 1084 — b |
| 517 — a | 588 — b | 659 — b | 730 — a | 801 — c | 872 — b | 943 — b | 1014 — b | 1085 — b |
| 518 — a | 589 — c | 660 — a | 731 — a | 802 — d | 873 — b | 944 — b | 1015 — b | 1086 — a |
| 519 — d | 590 — d | 661 — a | 732 — a | 803 — b | 874 — d | 945 — b | 1016 — a | 1087 — b |
| 520 — b | 591 — b | 662 — a | 733 — c | 804 — b | 875 — b | 946 — b | 1017 — c | 1088 — b |
| 521 — b | 592 — b | 663 — b | 734 — a | 805 — a | 876 — a | 947 — b | 1018 — a | 1089 — b |
| 522 — b | 593 — a | 664 — a | 735 — a | 806 — a | 877 — d | 948 — a | 1019 — a | 1090 — a |
| 523 — c | 594 — b | 665 — b | 736 — d | 807 — c | 878 — b | 949 — a | 1020 — b | 1091 — a |
| 524 — b | 595 — b | 666 — d | 737 — b | 808 — c | 879 — b | 950 — a | 1021 — c | 1092 — c |
| 525 — c | 596 — b | 667 — b | 738 — c | 809 — d | 880 — d | 951 — c | 1022 — d | 1093 — c |
| 526 — b | 597 — b | 668 — c | 739 — c | 810 — a | 881 — c | 952 — d | 1023 — b | 1094 — b |
| 527 — d | 598 — d | 669 — d | 740 — b | 811 — a | 882 — d | 953 — c | 1024 — b | 1095 — a |
| 528 — c | 599 — b | 670 — d | 741 — c | 812 — d | 883 — c | 954 — a | 1025 — d | 1096 — a |
| 529 — d | 600 — d | 671 — b | 742 — a | 813 — d | 884 — d | 955 — b | 1026 — c | 1097 — b |
| 530 — b | 601 — b | 672 — c | 743 — c | 814 — b | 885 — c | 956 — b | 1027 — d | 1098 — a |
| 531 — b | 602 — d | 673 — d | 744 — c | 815 — b | 886 — c | 957 — a | 1028 — d | 1099 — a |
| 532 — b | 603 — b | 674 — d | 745 — b | 816 — a | 887 — b | 958 — b | 1029 — c | 1100 — c |
| 533 — b | 604 — c | 675 — a | 746 — a | 817 — d | 888 — a | 959 — a | 1030 — d | 1101 — b |
| 534 — c | 605 — a | 676 — a | 747 — b | 818 — a | 889 — a | 960 — b | 1031 — b | 1102 — b |
| 535 — c | 606 — c | 677 — a | 748 — b | 819 — d | 890 — b | 961 — c | 1032 — b | 1103 — b |
| 536 — b | 607 — d | 678 — a | 749 — c | 820 — c | 891 — b | 962 — b | 1033 — c | 1104 — c |
| 537 — c | 608 — a | 679 — d | 750 — c | 821 — b | 892 — d | 963 — b | 1034 — b | 1105 — c |
| 538 — c | 609 — b | 680 — c | 751 — c | 822 — a | 893 — b | 964 — b | 1035 — a | 1106 — b |
| 539 — b | 610 — b | 681 — c | 752 — b | 823 — d | 894 — c | 965 — c | 1036 — b | 1107 — b |
| 540 — a | 611 — b | 682 — c | 753 — b | 824 — a | 895 — a | 966 — a | 1037 — b | 1108 — d |
| 541 — b | 612 — b | 683 — b | 754 — b | 825 — a | 896 — b | 967 — a | 1038 — b | 1109 — c |
| 542 — d | 613 — d | 684 — a | 755 — a | 826 — a | 897 — a | 968 — c | 1039 — d | 1110 — b |
| 543 — c | 614 — d | 685 — c | 756 — a | 827 — b | 898 — a | 969 — c | 1040 — a | 1111 — b |
| 544 — d | 615 — c | 686 — c | 757 — d | 828 — d | 899 — b | 970 — a | 1041 — b | 1112 — b |
| 545 — b | 616 — d | 687 — b | 758 — b | 829 — b | 900 — d | 971 — a | 1042 — b | 1113 — b |
| 546 — b | 617 — d | 688 — b | 759 — b | 830 — b | 901 — c | 972 — d | 1043 — a | 1114 — b |
| 547 — c | 618 — c | 689 — b | 760 — d | 831 — d | 902 — a | 973 — a | 1044 — b | 1115 — b |
| 548 — b | 619 — c | 690 — a | 761 — a | 832 — b | 903 — d | 974 — c | 1045 — a | 1116 — d |
| 549 — a | 620 — d | 691 — b | 762 — d | 833 — d | 904 — a | 975 — b | 1046 — d | 1117 — b |
| 550 — c | 621 — b | 692 — b | 763 — c | 834 — b | 905 — a | 976 — b | 1047 — b | 1118 — a |
| 551 — c | 622 — c | 693 — c | 764 — a | 835 — b | 906 — d | 977 — c | 1048 — b | 1119 — c |
| 552 — d | 623 — a | 694 — c | 765 — b | 836 — b | 907 — c | 978 — c | 1049 — a | 1120 — b |
| 553 — b | 624 — b | 695 — a | 766 — d | 837 — d | 908 — a | 979 — c | 1050 — c | 1121 — c |
| 554 — c | 625 — a | 696 — b | 767 — a | 838 — c | 909 — b | 980 — c | 1051 — c | 1122 — a |
| 555 — a | 626 — c | 697 — b | 768 — b | 839 — c | 910 — a | 981 — c | 1052 — a | 1123 — d |
| 556 — b | 627 — d | 698 — c | 769 — a | 840 — a | 911 — d | 982 — b | 1053 — d | 1124 — b |
| 557 — a | 628 — c | 699 — b | 770 — c | 841 — c | 912 — c | 983 — d | 1054 — b | 1125 — c |
| 558 — b | 629 — d | 700 — b | 771 — a | 842 — a | 913 — d | 984 — a | 1055 — b | 1126 — a |
| 559 — c | 630 — a | 701 — d | 772 — d | 843 — b | 914 — a | 985 — b | 1056 — b | 1127 — b |
| 560 — a | 631 — a | 702 — b | 773 — a | 844 — c | 915 — b | 986 — c | 1057 — a | 1128 — c |
| 561 — c | 632 — d | 703 — a | 774 — d | 845 — a | 916 — b | 987 — d | 1058 — d | 1129 — c |
| 562 — d | 633 — d | 704 — d | 775 — b | 846 — c | 917 — b | 988 — b | 1059 — d | 1130 — b |
| 563 — c | 634 — c | 705 — a | 776 — b | 847 — c | 918 — b | 989 — c | 1060 — d | 1131 — b |
| 564 — d | 635 — c | 706 — a | 777 — b | 848 — b | 919 — b | 990 — b | 1061 — a | 1132 — d |
| 565 — d | 636 — a | 707 — b | 778 — c | 849 — d | 920 — d | 991 — d | 1062 — c | 1133 — c |
| 566 — b | 637 — d | 708 — d | 779 — a | 850 — c | 921 — d | 992 — a | 1063 — c | 1134 — d |
| 567 — b | 638 — c | 709 — c | 780 — b | 851 — b | 922 — c | 993 — a | 1064 — b | 1135 — a |
| 568 — d | 639 — b | 710 — d | 781 — b | 852 — a | 923 — d | 994 — d | 1065 — b | 1136 — a |
| 569 — b | 640 — b | 711 — c | 782 — c | 853 — b | 924 — a | 995 — a | 1066 — d | 1137 — d |
| 570 — a | 641 — a | 712 — a | 783 — d | 854 — d | 925 — c | 996 — c | 1067 — c | 1138 — c |
| 571 — c | 642 — a | 713 — b | 784 — a | 855 — c | 926 — b | 997 — c | 1068 — b | 1139 — b |
| 572 — d | 643 — b | 714 — a | 785 — c | 856 — b | 927 — d | 998 — d | 1069 — a | 1140 — b |
| 573 — c | 644 — b | 715 — b | 786 — d | 857 — d | 928 — b | 999 — b | 1070 — a | 1141 — d |
| 574 — a | 645 — b | 716 — d | 787 — d | 858 — c | 929 — a | 1000 — b | 1071 — b | 1142 — c |
| 575 — b | 646 — a | 717 — c | 788 — d | 859 — a | 930 — c | 1001 — b | 1072 — d | 1143 — b |

| | | | | | | | | |
|---|---|---|---|---|---|---|---|---|
| 1144 — c | 1156 — b | 1168 — c | 1180 — a | 1192 — d | 1204 — a | 1216 — b | 1228 — a | 1240 — b |
| 1145 — d | 1157 — c | 1169 — d | 1181 — b | 1193 — b | 1205 — b | 1217 — c | 1229 — c | 1241 — d |
| 1146 — b | 1158 — d | 1170 — b | 1182 — b | 1194 — c | 1206 — a | 1218 — b | 1230 — d | 1242 — a |
| 1147 — b | 1159 — b | 1171 — d | 1183 — c | 1195 — b | 1207 — b | 1219 — a | 1231 — c | 1243 — d |
| 1148 — b | 1160 — a | 1172 — c | 1184 — b | 1196 — d | 1208 — c | 1220 — a | 1232 — d | 1244 — c |
| 1149 — d | 1161 — c | 1173 — c | 1185 — d | 1197 — c | 1209 — c | 1221 — d | 1233 — a | 1245 — a |
| 1150 — b | 1162 — b | 1174 — d | 1186 — a | 1198 — a | 1210 — c | 1222 — b | 1234 — d | 1246 — d |
| 1151 — b | 1163 — b | 1175 — c | 1187 — c | 1199 — b | 1211 — d | 1223 — a | 1235 — a | 1247 — b |
| 1152 — b | 1164 — c | 1176 — c | 1188 — a | 1200 — a | 1212 — a | 1224 — b | 1236 — b | 1248 — a |
| 1153 — b | 1165 — d | 1177 — b | 1189 — a | 1201 — c | 1213 — d | 1225 — c | 1237 — a | 1249 — b |
| 1154 — d | 1166 — a | 1178 — c | 1190 — d | 1202 — d | 1214 — c | 1226 — c | 1238 — a | 1250 — b |
| 1155 — d | 1167 — a | 1179 — d | 1191 — a | 1203 — c | 1215 — c | 1227 — b | 1239 — d | 1251 — b |

INDEX

# INDEX

abandon, 60
abandoned, 143
abased, 222
abating, 92
abattoirs, 125
abbreviated, 143
abdicate, 182
abdominal, 245
aberrations, 245
abetted, 143
abeyance, 112
abide, 377
abject, 207
abjures, 19
ablution, 222
abnegations, 299
abnormal, 143
abode, 377
abolition, 182
abomination, 160
aborigines, 323
abortion, 338
abortive, 338
abracadabra, 338
abrasive, 245
abridge, 222
abrogated, 182
abruptly, 211
absconds, 245
absolute, 78
absolution, 360
absolutism, 182
absolving, 360
absorbing, 222
abstain, 377
abstemious, 144
abstinence, 144
abstract, 299, 406
abstracted, 36
abstruse, 406
abundance, 144
abusive, 274
abutted, 323
abysmally, 274
academic, 245
acceded, 203
accelerate, 323
accentuate, 19
acceptations, 406
access, 204
accessible, 204
accession, 299
accessory, 112
acclaim, 19
acclimatized, 222
acclivity, 299
accolade, 338
accommodate, 222
accompaniment, 73
accomplices, 245
accomplished, v., 222
accomplished, adj., 245
accordance, 144
accords, 299
accosted, 377
accountable, 377
accoutered, 299
accredited, 112
accretion, 112
accruing, 112
accumulation, 222
accusatory, 377

acerbated, 19
achieved, 377
Achilles, 338
acidulous, 274
acknowledged, 222
acme, 377
acoustics, 245
acquainted, 223
acquiescence, 36
acquisition, 160
acquisitive, 377
acquittal, 245
acrid, 274
acrimony, 160
activated, 19
actuality, 245
actuated, 19
acuity, 299
acumen, 299
acute, 223
adage, 76
adagio, 406
adamant, 274
adamantine, 274
adaptability, 36
adaptation, 36
addendum, 73
addicted, 246
addled, 377
address, n., 36
address, v., 377
adepts, 245
adequate, 377
adherents, 182
adheres, 377
ad hominem, 125
ad infinitum, 125
ad interim, 125
adipose, 246
adjacent, 323
adjudged, 246
adjudication, 246
adjunct, 73
adjured, 19
ad libitum, 125
administer, 246
admirable, 223
admissible, 209
admixtures, 223
admonishment, 360
admonitions, 360
ad nauseam, 125
adolescent, 246
Adonis, 339
adornment, 377
adroit, 274
adulation, 160
adulterated, 246
adumbrate, 299
advantageous, 223
advent, 215
adventitious, 299
adversary, 92
adversity, 160
advocate, 377
aegis, 339
aeons, 323
aerie, 339
aerodynamic, 246
aeronautical, 246
Aesculapian, 339
aesthete, 406

aesthetic, 406
affable, 144
affectation, 36
affected, 300
affiliated, 112
affinity, 144
affirmation, 144
affixes, 223
afflatus, 360
affliction, 160
affluence, 144
affray, 377
affront, 19
aftermath, 145
agenda, 112
agglomerate, 274
aggrandizement, 145
aggravate, 145
aggregate, 207
aggressive, 206
aggrieved, 36
aghast, 275
agility, 36
agitation, 160
agnostic, 360
agony, 161
agoraphobia, 246
agrarian, 112
aides, 182
akimbo, 92
akin, 223
alabaster, 406
alacrity, 145
Aladdin, 339
à la mode, 125
alchemists, 246
alembic, 339
al fresco, 125
aliases, 246
alibi, 92
alienated, 378
alienist, 246
alignments, 182
allayed, 145
alleged, 223
allegiance, 182
allergic, 246
allegorical, 406
allegro, 406
alleviate, 60
alliteration, 406
allocate, 378
allocutions, 208
allopathic, 246
allotment, 112
allure, 60
alluring, 145
allusions, 223
alluvial, 323
almoner, 360
aloof, 36
altercation, 61
alter ego, 125
alternatives, 92
altruism, 3oo
amalgam, 339
amanuensis, 300
amaranthine, 300
amare, word family, 203
amassed, 92
amatory, 203
amazon, 339

ambidextrousness, 36
ambient, 300
ambiguity, 145
ambit, 323
ambivalence, 300
ambling, 378
ambulatory, 246
ambuscade, 182
ameliorated, 182
amenable, 36
amendment, 182
amenities, 36
amiability, 36
amicable, 145
amiss, 223
amity, 36
amnesia, 246
amnesty, 182
amoeba, 246
amoral, 36
amorous, 203
amorphous, 247
amortization, 112
amour, 125
amphibious, 182
amphitheater, 406
ample, 145
amplification, 378
amplitude, 323
amuck, 92
amulets, 360
anabasis, 182
anachronism, 216
anagram, 406
analagous, 223
analysis, 406
analytically, 406
Ananias, 339
anarchy, 182
anathema, 300
anatomy, 247
ancestral, 323
anchorite, 360
ancillary, 300
andante, 406
anent, 300
anesthesia, 247
anfractuous, 300
Anglophiles, 182
Anglophobia, 182
anguishing, 275
animadversion, 300
animalcules, 247
animate, 37
animated, 223
animosity, 161
animus, 125
annals, 323
annex, 182
annihilated, 20
anno Domini, 125
annotation, 406
annulled, 112
annunciated, 20
anodyne, 247
anointed, 360
anomalies, 407
anomalous, 378
anonymous, 217
antagonisms, 75
antagonistic, 37
antecedent, 323

455